ing narratives of modern history.

IMAGINING THE MIDDLE CLASS

IMAGINING THE MIDDLE CLASS

The political representation of class in Britain,
c. 1780–1840

DROR WAHRMAN

Michigan Society of Fellows

CAMBRIDGE
UNIVERSITY PRESS

Published by the Press Syndicate of the University of Cambridge
The Pitt Building, Trumpington Street, Cambridge CB2 IRP
40 West 20th Street, New York, NY 10011-4211, USA
10 Stamford Road, Oakleigh, Melbourne 3166, Australia

First published 1995

Printed in Great Britain at the University Press, Cambridge

A catalogue record for this book is available from the British Library

Library of Congress cataloguing in publication data
Wahrman, Dror.
Imagining the middle class: the political representation of class in Britain,
c. 1780–1840 / Dror Wahrman.
p. cm.
Includes bibliographical references and index.
ISBN 0 521 47127 3. – ISBN 0 521 47710 7 (pbk)
1. Middle class–Great Britain–History–18th century. 2. Middle class–Great Britain–
History–19th century. 3. Great Britain–Politics and government–18th century. 4. Great
Britain–Politics and government–19th century. I. Title.
HT690.G7W34 1995 94–30858
305.5'5–dc20 CIP

ISBN 0 521 47127 3 hardback
ISBN 0 521 47710 7 paperback

For Noa and Shani, whose willingness to move across half the globe made this book imaginable

Contents

ix

Figures

Acknowledgments

Behind my own voice in the following pages lies a thick palimpsest of the voices of others. At the bottom is the echo of Ruth Kalderon's unsparing and eye-opening reproach, without which the world would have had one more frustrated physicist and one less historian (though I always remember fondly those years spent in physics and mathematics). My teachers in the Tel Aviv University history department convinced me what an exciting step this shift would be. I am especially indebted to Shulamit Volkov, who first introduced me to British social history; this book might be seen as a belated response to her stimulating comparative seminar on the bourgeoisies of Western Europe.

My peers at Princeton proved to be an exceptionally exciting intellectual environment for developing ideas and trying them out: Vincent DiGirolamo, Jonathan Elukin, Philip Harling, Nimrod Hurvitz, Walter Johnson, April Masten, Eve Niedergang, David Nirenberg, Brian Owensby, Andy Weiss and most frequently Marcus Daniel. Many other friends and scholars commented on drafts of various sections of this book: Donna Andrew, David Armitage, David Bien, Peter Brown, Sue Brown, Laura Downs, Elizabeth Elbourne, Andrea Henderson, Joanna Innes, Doron Lamm, Gyan Prakash, Theodore Rabb, David Scobey, Greg Shaya, Gareth Stedman Jones and Carolyn Steedman. Linda Colley, Natalie Davis, Laura Engelstein and Philip Nord read the complete thesis on which this book is based, and made invaluable suggestions towards its subsequent revisions. Gregory Claeys, James Epstein and Don Herzog read the entire final version. David Bell heroically tackled both thesis and book; Ted Steinberg questioned the meaning of almost every paragraph. Finally, no one can wish for a more engaged reader and acute critic than Peter Mandler. Special gratitude I owe to the late

Edward Thompson, who in spite of failing health and innumerable demands on his time developed interest in the project and gave me the benefit of his criticism and hospitality both in the US and in England. At Cambridge University Press, I would like to thank Pauline Leng for her meticulous copyediting, and especially William Davies for treating this book from the start as if it were his own.

How much I owe to my thesis adviser, Lawrence Stone, only his other students can fully appreciate. I hope to be able to emulate his enthusiasm for engaging in an argument, his generosity for opinions different from his own, and his deep sense of responsibility for his students. Most of all, he has provided me with a model of the ideal adviser.

Over the years I have received generous funds from numerous institutions: Tel Aviv University, the Rothschild Foundation, the Fulbright-Hays/Institute of International Education, the Avi Foundation, the Social Science Research Council, Princeton University and the Michigan Society of Fellows. For their help I am most grateful.

I have obviously been fortunate in having these favourable conditions in which to develop my own thinking. My good fortune had already begun many years before, in a mother and a father who combine enthusiasm for both the sciences and the humanities, for both the grand picture and the minute detail, with deep thirst for never-ending learning; and in growing up in a household bursting with that never-ending resource, books, which have been my weakness ever since. Today, my good fortune continues with Noa, Shani and Maya, who embrace my lesser and my greater whims with never-ending love.

CHAPTER I

Imagining the 'middle class': an introduction

When historian R. H. Tawney was pressed to admit middle class people to his Workers Educational Association tutorials in the early 1900s, someone said, 'Of course we should have them, just like any other class; God made the middle classes'; to which Tawney responded wryly, 'Are you sure?'[1]

There is always a *stake* in where things are placed: *tell me how you classify and I'll tell you who you are.*

(Roland Barthes)[2]

This book is not an attempt to write 'The Making of the English Middle Class'. If anything, it explains why such a book cannot be written. It does not answer the question, was the English middle class made by 1832, or by 1846, or by any other date. Instead it wishes to expose the assumptions underlying these questions. It seeks to uncover and historicize the origins of a persistent image haunting the historiography of modern Britain, that of an emergent 'middle class', which like the rising sun, once nature has decreed its gradual emergence above the horizon, becomes inexorably ever more conspicuous and transforms our vision of the world. The question this book sets out to answer, then, is this: how, why and when did the British come to *believe* that they lived in a society centred around a 'middle class'?

We used to have a remarkably straightforward answer to this question, which in broad outline went something like this. Sometime during the late eighteenth and early nineteenth centuries, we have been told, an industrial revolution transformed Britain. This new and unprecedented process was accompanied by the

[1] Recounted in R. Terrill, *R. H. Tawney and His Times: Socialism as Fellowship*, Cambridge, Mass., 1973, p. 44. See also J. P. Kenyon, *The History Men: The Historical Profession in England Since the Renaissance*, London, 1983, p. 242.
[2] R. Barthes, *The Semiotic Challenge*, New York, 1988, p. 47.

formation of a novel social group, the 'middle class'. The 'middle class' was the major engine and beneficiary of these upheavals, and consequently emerged as the new focus of social and economic power. This new social reality was naturally mirrored in social consciousness and language. Ultimately the political system bowed to the widely recognized power of this new 'middle class': hence came the inevitable Reform Bill of 1832, which admitted the 'middle class' into the (parliamentary) political nation, no longer the exclusive preserve of the landed elite.

Lately, however, this seductively coherent account has been recognized by many historians as unsatisfactory. Research has shown, first, that the heuristic notion of an 'industrial revolution' is quite problematic. Some sectors of the economy – notably the cotton industry – certainly underwent swift revolutionary change. But viewed within the broader national context, processes of social change were gradual and protracted, and – importantly – experienced unevenly. In some places social change had commenced long before the alleged industrial 'take-off' of the late eighteenth century, in others it was hardly noticeable well into the nineteenth.[3] Moreover, no clear correlation can be shown between those sectors that spearheaded the process of change and a putative late Georgian 'middle class'. Whether measured against the yardstick of national economic growth or of technological advancement, the outcome of a generation of historical revision has been that the industrialization of this period could not by itself bear the responsibility for an overall restructuring

---

[3] The literature on these issues is vast. A convenient starting point and overview of the gradualist interpretation is N. F. R. Crafts, *British Economic Growth during the Industrial Revolution*, Oxford, 1985. See also the exchange between M. Fores, 'The Myth of a British Industrial Revolution', *History* 66 (1981), pp. 181–98; and A. E. Musson, 'The British Industrial Revolution', *History* 67 (1982), pp. 252–8. Also see Musson's earlier *The Growth of British Industry*, London, 1978. C. K. Harley, 'British Industrialization before 1841: Evidence of Slower Growth During the Industrial Revolution', *Journal of Economic History* 42 (1982), pp. 267–89. The survival of pre-industrial forms of production well into the nineteenth century has been emphasized by R. Samuel, 'The Workshop of the World', *History Workshop Journal* 3 (1977), pp. 6–72. P. H. Lindert and J. G. Williamson, 'Revising England's Social Tables', *Explorations in Economic History* 19 (1982), pp. 385–408, have underscored the significance of the industrial sector before the 'industrial revolution'. Finally, this literature is excellently reviewed in D. Cannadine, 'The Present and the Past in the English Industrial Revolution 1880–1980', *Past and Present* 103 (1984), pp. 159–67. Another overview is P. Mathias, 'The Industrial Revolution: Concept and Reality', in P. Mathias and J. A. Davis (eds.), *The First Industrial Revolutions*, Oxford, 1990, pp. 1–24 (and see also Crafts's contribution to this volume).

of British society. In a national perspective, insofar as social and economic structural transformations are concerned, these particular decades, while certainly witnessing considerable changes, were nevertheless not all that exceptional and distinctive.[4]

These observations, however, have not shaken the confidence of historians – from Whiggish social historians like Asa Briggs, through radical labour historians like E. P. Thompson, to feminist cultural historians like Leonore Davidoff and Catherine Hall – in the belief that in some fundamental way the half-century before the Reform Bill of 1832 *did* witness the rather sudden emergence of a 'middle class'. Nor has this confidence been shaken by a second trend in recent research, establishing the existence of large and vibrant 'middling' social groups already by the *early* eighteenth century, if not before.[5] The transformation of English (and in some cases British) social structure was in fact a remarkably long-term process, well under way many decades before that period in which historians tend to locate the palpable emergence of a distinct 'middle class'. Accordingly, some

---

[4] There are of course dissenting voices: recently, see Maxine Berg and Pat Hudson, 'Rehabilitating the Industrial Revolution', *Economic History Review* 45 (1992), pp. 24–50. Berg and Hudson attempt to reintroduce an emphasis on discontinuity, in part by broadening the scope of inquiry (for instance to transformations in the organization and use of labour), though at the price of stretching the industrial revolution over a whole century (1750–1850). See similarly P. K. O'Brien, 'Modern Conceptions of the Industrial Revolution', in P. K. O'Brien and R. Quinault (eds.), *The Industrial Revolution and British Society*, Cambridge, 1993, pp. 1–30.

[5] L. Stone, 'Social Mobility in England, 1500–1700', *Past and Present* 33 (1966), pp. 16–55. G. Holmes, *Augustan England: Professions, State and Society, 1680–1730*, London, 1982. W. Prest (ed.), *The Professions in Early Modern England*, London, 1987. The significance of a social 'middle' between 1660 and 1800 is variously emphasized, among others, by L. Stone and J. C. F. Stone, *An Open Elite? England 1540–1880*, Oxford, 1984, p. 290 ('perhaps the most important social feature of the age'). P. Earle, *The Making of the English Middle Class: Business, Society and Family Life in London, 1660–1730*, London, 1989. P. Borsay, *The English Urban Renaissance: Culture and Society in the Provincial Town 1660–1770*, Oxford, 1989. P. Langford, *A Polite and Commercial People: England 1727–1783*, Oxford, 1989. L. Davison et al., *Stilling the Grumbling Hive: The Response to Social and Economic Problems in England, 1689–1750*, Stroud, 1992, introduction. J. Smail, 'The Stansfields of Halifax: A Case Study of the Making of the Middle Class', *Albion* 24 (1992), pp. 27–47. And see J. Barry, 'Consumers' Passions: The Middle Class in Eighteenth-Century England', *Historical Journal* 34 (1991), pp. 207–16; and 'Identité urbaine et classes moyennes dans l'Angleterre moderne', *Annales ESC* 48 (1993), pp. 853–83. Our understanding of the eighteenth-century social 'middle' will be further enhanced by Margaret Hunt's *The Middling Sort: Commerce, Gender, and the Family in England 1660–1750*, Berkeley, 1995, and John Smail's *The Origins of Middle-Class Culture: Halifax, Yorkshire, 1660–1780*, Ithaca, 1994.

attempts have been made to relocate the cultural and political emergence of the 'middle class' to an earlier stage; though it remains doubtful whether they have in fact been successful in demonstrating the coherent presence of a 'middle class' as a distinctive cultural or political agent at such a stage.[6] Throughout most of this long period of underlying social change, whose beginnings extend far back into the seventeenth century, the expanding social 'middle' had not yet come to play its own role on the historical stage. Thus E. P. Thompson appears closer to the mark than many of his critics in pointing out that before the late eighteenth century, in terms of *structures of power*, the 'middle class' was all but invisible as a distinctive presence: hence his depiction of the eighteenth-century power structure as a bipolar field of force, set between a patrician elite on the one hand and the plebs on the other.[7] These points are particularly damaging for the implicit assumptions that inform the traditional interpretation: a sociological 'middle' stratum, it seems, could develop for a long period of time without inevitably emerging as a well-delineated focus of social and political power.

The received historical wisdom has not fared much better when considered from the other end of this time span. Where was that formidable 'middle class' in Victorian Britain? How did its alleged new power accord with the obvious continuity of landed predominance? Aside from several 'Cottonopolis' towns, historians have found it difficult to point to a distinctive nation-wide industrial

---

[6] This literature is reviewed in D. Wahrman, 'National Society, Communal Culture: An Argument about the Recent Historiography of Eighteenth-Century Britain', *Social History* 17 (1992), pp. 43–72. This essay suggests that rather than being a distinct unity, the eighteenth-century social 'middle' can perhaps more plausibly be seen as divided by a deep cultural rift, between those oriented towards an aristocratic London-centred culture and those resisting it with assertive localism; and that such a divide might enable us to explain patterns of behaviour – in particular political behaviour – more satisfactorily than explanations based on socio-economic or 'class' categories.

[7] E. P. Thompson, 'Patrician Society, Plebeian Culture', *Journal of Social History* 7 (1974), pp. 382–405; followed by his 'Eighteenth-Century English Society: Class Struggle without Class?', *Social History* 3 (1978), pp. 133–65. Various critics (for instance, Stone and Stone, *An Open Elite?*; Barry, 'Consumers' Passions') have mistakenly taken this to be a statement about *social structure*, which – they have claimed – ignores the obvious presence of 'middle' strata at this period. For Thompson's reply, see his *Customs in Common*, London, 1991, pp. 87–90. His argument has recently received perhaps unintended support from Paul Langford's *Public Life and the Propertied Englishman 1689–1798*, Oxford, 1991, which, although not mentioning Thompson's framework, in fact documents in detail the 'upper half' of Thompson's vision, namely the closing ranks and increasing unity of the propertied Englishmen during the eighteenth century.

'middle class' that would fit even remotely Marxist stereotypes.[8] This has led some historians to present mid Victorian society as 'bourgeoisified' and dominated by 'middle-class' ideals, ideals which constituted the basis for the expansive consensus of the mid Victorian 'age of equipoise'. Such a vision is broad and vague enough to countenance the lack of any demonstrable class specificity.[9] Other historians have been led to precisely the opposite conclusion, pointing to the failure of this new 'middle class', epitomized in its ultimate gentrification.[10] For advocates

---

[8] Studies of the nineteenth-century industrial bourgeoisie – the entrepreneurs and employers of the new industrial towns – are valuable, but confined; their subjects cannot be made to stand vicariously for a putative nation-wide 'middle class'. See most recently T. Koditschek, *Class Formation and Urban-Industrial Society: Bradford, 1750–1850*, Cambridge, 1990, where the problem is acknowledged, but the 'entrepreneurial bourgeoisie' is nevertheless hailed as 'the ideal citizen[s] of the middle class' (pp. 18–19, following Harold Perkin). Also see A. Howe, *The Cotton Masters 1830–1860*, Oxford, 1984, which examines the cotton masters 'develop[ing] a separate identity' which was 'recognizably "middle class"' (p. [v]). J. Wolff and J. Seed (eds.), *The Culture of Capital: Art, Power and the Nineteenth-Century Middle Class*, Manchester, 1988.

[9] As Theodore Koditschek has observed: 'It is as though, under the weight of a bourgeois society, the bourgeoisie, as a class, has disappeared' (*Class Formation*, p. 11; and see his further references). A notable proponent of such a view is H. Perkin, *The Origins of Modern English Society 1780–1880*, London, 1969 (though Perkin seems to have later gravitated more towards the 'failure of the middle class' view: see idem, 'Land Reform and Class Conflict in Victorian Britain', in his *The Structured Crowd: Essays in English Social History*, Brighton, 1981, pp. 100–35). W. L. Burn, *The Age of Equipoise*, New York, 1965. A similar interpretation is also held by those Marxists who insist on the mid Victorian 'bourgeois hegemony': see N. Poulantzas, 'Marxist Political Theory in Great Britain', *New Left Review* 43 (1967), pp. 57–74. R. Gray, 'Bourgeois Hegemony in Victorian Britain', in J. Bloomfield (ed.), *Papers on Class, Hegemony and Party*, London, 1977, pp. 73–93.

[10] The most influential statements of this viewpoint are M. J. Wiener, *English Culture and the Decline of the Industrial Spirit, 1850–1980*, Cambridge, 1981; and P. Anderson, 'The Figures of Descent', in his *English Questions*, London, 1992, pp. 121–92 (originally *New Left Review*, 1987). See also D. C. Coleman, 'Gentlemen and Players', *Economic History Review* 2nd ser., 26 (1973), pp. 92–116. W. L. Arnstein, 'The Myth of the Triumphant Victorian Middle Class', *The Historian* 37 (1975), pp. 205–21. G. Ingham, *Capitalism Divided? The City and Industry in British Social Development*, New York, 1984. P. J. Cain and A. G. Hopkins, 'Gentlemanly Capitalism and British Expansion Overseas I: The Old Colonial System, 1688–1850' and 'II: New Imperialism, 1850–1945', *Economic History Review* 2nd ser., 39 (1986), pp. 501–25, and 40 (1987), pp. 1–26. The best critique of these arguments is P. Thane, 'Aristocracy and Middle Class in Victorian England: The Problem of "Gentrification"', in A. M. Birke and L. Kettenacker (eds.), *Middle Classes, Aristocracy and Monarchy: Patterns of Change and Adaptation in the Age of Modern Nationalism*, Munich, 1989, pp. 93–107. See also Howe, *The Cotton Masters*. S. Gunn, 'The "Failure" of the Victorian Middle Class: A Critique', in J. Wolff and J. Seed (eds.), *The Culture of Capital: Art, Power and the Nineteenth-Century Middle Class*, Manchester, 1988, pp. 17–43. M. J. Daunton, '"Gentlemanly Capitalism" and British Industry 1820–1914', *Past and Present* 122 (1989), pp. 119–58. H. L. Malchow, *Gentlemen Capitalists: The Social and Political World of the Victorian Businessman*, Stanford, 1992.

of the former view, 'the triumph of the middle class' lay in the very fact that it succeeded in effacing its distinctiveness as a social group; for advocates of the latter, a distinct 'middle class' – let alone triumphant – in fact never made it at all.

But why do all these observations seem to constitute a problem? The answer lies in certain assumptions about the correspondence between social being and social consciousness, assumptions which the upholders of the conventional wisdom actually have *in common* with those who would regard such observations as decisive arguments against it. If the late eighteenth century witnessed no radical social transformation, then (by this reasoning), the gut feeling of so many historians notwithstanding, it could not have witnessed the rise of a new form of social consciousness; if the early eighteenth century did witness the emergence of middling social groups, then it was at that point that a corresponding change in social consciousness (invisible though it may be) must have taken place; and if by mid nineteenth century a transformed social consciousness remains elusive, then this necessarily disproves the claims for a corresponding social transformation. But what all these arguments (as well as those against which they are levelled) tend to ignore is *the degree of freedom which in fact exists in the space between social reality and its representation.* The social process certainly imposes certain bearings and certain constraints on the possible and plausible ways in which it can be understood. But within these constraints there still remains a considerable space for different representations and interpretations of this social reality. A priori, moreover, such different representations are all within the bounds of plausibility: none of them is 'objectively' more true to life or more sensible than any other.

Consider the social process that transformed Britain between, say, the mid seventeenth and the mid nineteenth centuries. One can readily acknowledge (and the present argument has no intention to the contrary) those long-term aspects of the transformation often associated with 'bourgeois' society that social historians have chronicled in detail: the emergence of the anonymous-exchange market, the development of the 'bourgeois public sphere' with its concomitant explosion of printed communication, the effects of agricultural improvement, spreading commercialization, accelerating urbanization and gradual industrialization.[11] It can also be readily conceded that these developments prescribed certain limits on the credible ways of describing society. It would have been quite difficult, for example, for a utopian nostalgic speaker in 1820 to mobilize a broad political audience by characterizing England as a landed commonwealth, consisting only of landowners, farmers and agricultural labourers; no more than it could be presented as an industrial nation composed only of a proletariat and its bourgeois employers. And yet, between these limits of plausibility there was still considerable space for manoeuvre, considerable leeway for contemporaries to choose between divergent – even incompatible – representations of their society.[12] During the period discussed in this book, the choice between a 'middle-class'-based or a 'middle-class'-less conceptualization of society fell precisely into this space.[13] We shall

[11] In addition to the aforementioned work of Earle, Borsay, Langford and Hunt, see also N. McKendrick, J. Brewer and J. H. Plumb, *The Birth of a Consumer Society*, Bloomington, 1982. It may be noted that in the voluminous recent literature inspired by Habermas's concept of the bourgeois public sphere, to date predominantly among historians of France, it is often overlooked that Habermas's was basically a suggestive historical – rather than theoretical – essay, for which the evidence was for the most part adduced from eighteenth-century England: J. Habermas, *The Structural Transformation of the Public Sphere: An Inquiry into a Category of Bourgeois Society*, Cambridge, Mass., 1989 (originally 1962).

[12] I am of course much indebted here to Gareth Stedman Jones's pioneering *Languages of Class: Studies in English Working Class History 1832–1982*, Cambridge, 1983. Compare especially p. 101: 'Consciousness cannot be related to experience except through the interposition of a particular language which organizes the understanding of experience, and it is important to stress that more than one language is capable of articulating the same set of experiences.' My thinking about these questions has also been stimulated by William Sewell's powerful *Work and Revolution in France: The Language of Labor from the Old Regime to 1848*, Cambridge, 1980; and by William Reddy's critique of the uses of class as an explanatory principle in history in his *Money and Liberty in Modern Europe: A Critique of Historical Understanding*, Cambridge, 1987. More recently, a similar approach has been put forward in Patrick Joyce's *Visions of the People: Industrial England and the Question of Class, 1848–1914*, Cambridge, 1991; the potentially interesting claims of this book, however, are weakened by a rigid and narrow definition of 'class', as well as by the scarcity of detailed textual analysis of its sources. Instead, the reader is offered an appendix of unanalysed sources, that supposedly should 'speak for themselves'; an odd strategy for a book that purports to present a 'postmodern' theoretical position.

[13] In other contexts, of course, it could be the 'working class' – rather than the 'middle class' – whose presence was similarly conditional and contested, as one possible conceptualization of society among several. For a stimulating example see Z. Lockman, 'Imagining the Working Class: Culture, Nationalism, and Class Formation in Egypt, 1899–1914', *Poetics Today* 15 (1994), pp. 157–90. And for a political reconceptualization of society that contested the very existence of a nobility, see the discussion of Abbé Sieyès in W. Sewell, *A Rhetoric of Bourgeois Revolution: The Abbé Sieyès and What is the*

encounter scores of observers of British society eagerly hailing the 'middle class', just as others were denying its existence or relevance. *Prima facie*, there was nothing inevitable or particularly compelling about a static view of society centred around a 'middle class', or about a dynamic view of society moving along some preordained axis from 'no middle class' to 'strong middle class'. Moreover, with no obvious precedents to draw upon, such views did not even have a particular ring of familiarity to them; the popularization and theorization that were to make them such an essential way of thinking about modern society still lay many years ahead.

Perhaps the most important characteristic of this space of possibilities between social reality and its representation is that what happens in it – in particular, why one possible understanding wins ground over another – has *a logic and a dynamic of its own*. On the one hand, it is not determined or dictated by the social process; on the other hand, it is also not prescribed by some property inherent in language. The latter point addresses an arguable weakness of recent historical arguments focused on language, in leaning toward linguistic determinism, endowing language with the ultimate power to determine the outcome of historical developments.[14] The former point addresses an oft-noted weakness of social history: its difficulties in integrating its *longue durée* narratives, often protracted for centuries, with the *court durée*, the *événementiel*, in anything but an over-determined and teleological fashion. By focusing on the dynamics of choices

Third Estate?, Durham, N.C., 1994, chapter 2. (I am grateful to Zachary Lockman and William Sewell for the opportunity to read their work in manuscript.) However, the argument can also be made that the category of 'middle class' does have an inherent vagueness in relation to social structures and social relations, which renders it perhaps more dependent upon linguistic choices and rhetorical construction than the categories of 'working class' or 'nobility' – a difference in degree, though not in kind. See P. Anderson, 'The Notion of Bourgeois Revolution', in his *English Questions*, p. 112.

14 For a suggestive critique of Stedman Jones along those lines, see D. Mayfield and S. Thorne, 'Social History and Its Discontents: Gareth Stedman Jones and the Politics of Language', *Social History* 17 (1992), pp. 165–88. Also J. E. Cronin, 'Language, Politics and the Critique of Social History', *Journal of Social History* 20 (1986), pp. 177–83. Stedman Jones's projected *Visions of Prometheus* promises however to address many of these issues (I am grateful to Gareth Stedman Jones for permission to cite his work in progress). For caution against linguistic determinism, see also K. M. Baker, *Inventing the French Revolution: Essays on French Political Culture in the Eighteenth Century*, Cambridge, 1990, esp. pp. 6–7; and Sewell, *A Rhetoric of Bourgeois Revolution*.

between different possible representations of social reality, we can recover both agency and contingency in the process of translation from one tier of historical change to the other.

Thus, given generations of underlying social change, *some* transformation of social consciousness in Britain was bound to happen. But in and of itself, the social process did *not* determine – could not determine – the particular form of the transformation of social understanding that did eventually take place. Neither did it determine the specific (and seemingly much delayed) timing of this transformation, its abruptness, its highly specific – and changing – political guises, the particular implications which became associated with its different incarnations, its see-saw progress *vis à vis* other representations of society, and its apparent ultimate triumph over them. Yet it is not suggested that the specific form, content, timing and evolution of this 'middle-class'-based social understanding were somehow spontaneously generated in an internal development wholly contained within this autonomous space of possible representations. If neither the social process nor a discursive process determined by themselves the logic and the dynamic of this development (though both could still influence it), other influences which need to be identified were surely at play. Of those, one stands out as particularly significant: the effects of politics.

In part, the key role of politics is readily understandable: after all, it is an arena where stakes are high and where collective identities count most. This was particularly true for a period of turmoil and mobilization such as the one discussed here: whether the decades following the French Revolution were singular or not in terms of social change, they were surely characterized by distinct and dramatic political strains. Under such circumstances, politics invested choices between particular conceptualizations of society with poignant meaning and force, implicating them in the struggle over the social and political order; politics made such choices *matter*. But there is more to the role of politics than simply its high and charged stakes: it is also where both agency and contingency notably come into play. On the one hand, the dynamics of political events (especially events as climactic as the French Revolution or the massacre of Peterloo) are always undetermined by the intentions of the actors, always complicated by unpredictable developments and unintended consequences.

On the other hand, while the political process itself is thus characterized by *indeterminacy*, at the same time it demands *determinacy* from those involved in it – determinacy of objectives, of alignment, of identity, of loyalty. So the political process opens up new spaces and new configurations, often rapidly and unexpectedly; and then confronts its participants with the pressing need to renegotiate their positions *vis à vis* these new configurations. The autonomy and indeterminacy of politics, therefore, feed into the autonomy and indeterminacy of that space of possible representations of society; while the demands of politics create the driving force for choices to be made between these possible representations. Indeed, the key role of politics is revealed time and again in the following chapters: it will be seen that the political process provides us with a powerful chronological and causal framework for understanding the evolution of the divergent representations of British society between the 1790s and the 1830s, and for making sense of the charged contestations that were precipitated by their competing uses.[15]

The answers to the questions which set the present study in motion have been sought, therefore, primarily in the vast expanses of political language, broadly conceived; that is to say, in the language of writers and speakers as found in those means of public communication geared towards interventions in the political process and towards audiences interested in such interventions, even when a particular enunciation was not directly concerned with politics. Such sources for political language, on which the following is based, include newspapers, quarterly, monthly and weekly periodicals, reports of parliamentary debates,

---

[15] I am not arguing however that politics were the *only* possible driving force affecting choices between different conceptualizations of society, an argument which of course is impossible to demonstrate from within the confines of political sources. In other arenas, in other linguistic contexts, quite different developments may well have been taking place at the same time, with their own dynamics and their own tempo. Indeed one test case, that of the separate genre of writing that might be called domestic literature, is considered in chapter 11. It is suggested that whereas one can apparently trace within this different body of writing an independent evolution of the uses of 'middle-class' language, distinct from that found in the political sources, these uses were overshadowed and ultimately overtaken by the effects of the political developments; and that it was the latter that in the final count proved to have been the most decisive in inscribing upon British society the familiar social scheme centred around a 'middle class'.

extra-parliamentary speeches, sermons (which often trespassed into politics), historical works, and over 1,600 treatises, tracts and pamphlets on an extensive range of political subjects.[16]

'Political language' has become of late a popular formulation among historians of political thought – most visibly J. G. A. Pocock – in defining their own subject matter. What Pocock means by 'political language' becomes evident from the examples prevailing in his work: the languages of classical republicanism, of medieval scholasticism, of natural jurisprudence, of political economy and so on – basically, that is, complex sets of linked political notions (Pocock often calls them 'paradigms') that can infiltrate a text without dominating it entirely.[17] The text can therefore be analysed as a palimpsest of different and not necessarily compatible 'political languages', each with its own history and conceptual baggage, without ascribing to it a unity and a coherence which it did not actually possess; a subtle and seductive approach that has proven immensely fruitful in the practice of the history of political thought. Predominantly, however, the object of such inquiries has not been the public debate *per se*, but rather the logic and evolution of such 'political languages', and the light which they shed in their turn on particular texts. Pocock has revealingly characterized 'a text in the historian's class' as one which has achieved the level of 'a literary artifact of a certain authority and *durée*', and was furthermore produced by 'a single powerful mind concerned to argue at a high level of abstraction and organization'. And even for Quentin Skinner, who most explicitly insists on expanding the investigation of political thought to the wider political debate and its setting, the ultimate goal remains 'to return to the classic texts themselves

---

[16] Given the nature of this inquiry, the research focused primarily on *public* political language. Nevertheless I ventured occasionally into private papers and correspondence, mostly as a kind of 'control-experiment'. With some exceptions, for the most part I could not detect significant divergences between private and public expressions of political language, though it is likely that a certain divergence will be revealed in a closer analysis.

[17] A similar list of 'typical' examples is given in J. G. A. Pocock, 'The Concept of a Language and the *métier d'historien*: Some Considerations on Practice', in A. Pagden (ed.), *The Languages of Political Theory in Early-Modern Europe*, Cambridge, 1987 (p. 23), an essay (and indeed a book) which can serve as a good introduction to this approach. See also Pocock's *Virtue, Commerce, and History*, Cambridge, 1985; and his earlier *Politics, Language and Time: Essays on Political Thought and History*, Chicago, 1989 (originally 1960).

with a clearer prospect of understanding them'. So Skinner, Pocock and their many followers have powerfully placed the study of political texts and concepts in their proper multi-layered and historicized political and linguistic contexts.[18] They have thus prepared the ground for the next logical step, that of reintegrating such political texts and concepts back into their political setting; that is to say, into their place within the broader public debate of which they were part, and which then becomes the focus of inquiry in its own right.[19] It is only thus that 'political language' – now, in the broader and looser sense that it is employed in the present book – can be given its due as a key site for the shaping of the social consciousness of large groups of people.

Taking this next step has important consequences for the sources one uses, for the questions they are supposed to help answer, and therefore for the ways in which they are read. Thus the present study gives as much consideration to 'minor' and ephemeral sources – sources that disappeared together with the

---

[18] Pocock, *Virtue, Commerce, and History*, pp. 22–3. Q. Skinner, *The Foundations of Modern Political Thought, Volume One: The Renaissance*, Cambridge, 1978, preface (quoted, p. xiii); and see also J. Tully (ed.), *Meaning and Context: Quentin Skinner and His Critics*, Oxford, 1988, esp. p. 12. For emphases on the evolution of concepts (in the – unacknowledged – tracks of the German *Begriffsgeschichte* founded by Reinhart Koselleck), see the essays of Skinner and others in T. Ball et al., *Political Innovation and Conceptual Change*, Cambridge, 1989. The distinction drawn here is not so much a critique of such studies of political thought as a reminder of their limitations. In the claims made by some authors, however, these limitations may sometimes be overlooked; as pointed out for example in E. P. Thompson's poignant comments (in his *Customs in Common*, pp. 274–5) on the irrelevance of arguments drawn (in the best manner of the history of political thought) from the debate between eighteenth-century theorists about political economy to the understanding of the actual political behaviour of the crowd during that period.

[19] Attempts to make this next step, from the contextualized study of political thought to its integrated study within the context of the broader political debate, are evident (in different ways) in the work of several scholars associated with the practice of the history of political thought, such as Mark Goldie, Gregory Claeys, David Armitage and (in the French context) Keith Baker. It should also be noted that 'the public debate' as used in this book is mostly taken to mean the *national* debate, a limitation which has rendered the following for the most part insensitive to regional and local variations. By the late eighteenth century, to be sure, the national context of politics had already developed to a point that justifies a discussion of a distinctive national political culture and of nation-wide patterns in political language that were highly relevant to people's political experiences and largely self-contained. Indeed, when I could occasionally check this assumption, as will be seen, it held well. Nevertheless it is plausible – indeed inevitable – that a more careful study of the details of regional variation within their specific contexts of local politics would suggest certain refinements to the following arguments.

changing political circumstances – as to 'major' texts. And when it looks at 'classic' reflective texts, it does not privilege their explication through their contextualized reading; rather it integrates them back into the broader debate in which they were produced, a debate constituted through the collective interactions of numerous utterances (mostly far less articulate than such reflective treatises) which together infused particular notions with a forceful charge in an actual political situation. Indeed, it is such forceful charges, which became affixed to particular notions in circumstance-specific configurations of the political debate, that are the key to the understanding of the dynamics of political language. The focus is therefore on the particular uses for which a given notion was enlisted, on the overtones and connotations which it therefore incurred, and on the resulting stakes in its enunciation, stakes that made people struggle over it. Thus, in the case of a vision of society centred around a 'middle class', my concern is not its intellectual genealogy (which, to be sure, goes back a long way) nor some isolated precedents in which it had been articulated, but rather how and when it came to be used repeatedly in political arguments in particularly freighted, resonant and contested ways.

Furthermore, such a focus shapes the way in which sources are read: for the most part, the more fertile grounds for this kind of inquiry tend to be not expositions that cover in a coherent and interconnected manner as much ground as possible, but rather fragmentary, disconnected utterances that are often confined to one sentence or one paragraph.[20] When these were spoken or written, the purpose of the speaker or writer was only rarely to expound a particular concept, but rather to use his or her preferred vocabulary to carry an often highly contested point across. Such utterances therefore frequently surface almost inadvertently, *en passant*; indeed in many cases the most revealing are semi-conscious or even altogether unwitting utterances that disclose habits of formulation shared in a particular milieu at a particular moment. In order to demonstrate such habits, moreover, the historian's key is *repetition*. The importance of repetition cannot be stressed enough: patterns of use of political language

---

[20] Compare the points made by William Sewell in his *Work and Revolution in France*, pp. 8–9.

(as it is understood here) can be deemed significant only if they can be shown to have been repeated by many people again and again. No single enunciation can by itself constitute evidence for an argument about political language: it is only persistent repetition which turns a disembodied utterance about politics into a resonant utterance which in itself forms a meaningful part of the political process.[21]

This book, then, looks at the dynamics of what has been characterized as the space of possibilities between social reality and its representation by exploring the changing stakes in 'middle-class'-centred visions of society and the contestations over them during the particularly volatile period between the French Revolution and the 1830s. Not that these chronological boundaries represent the beginning and end of a complete historical story; but while they cut a slice from a wider continuum, it will nevertheless be suggested that they signalled decisive turning points in the uses of the language of 'middle class'.

To clarify at the outset one simple point: in referring to the language of 'middle class' (as a shorthand for representations of society centred around a 'middle class'), the emphasis here is on 'middle' rather than on 'class'. Historians have persistently argued (or rather assumed teleologically) that a fundamental transformation in the articulation of social structure occurred sometime between the eighteenth and the nineteenth centuries, in the shift from non-class terminologies, such as 'middle ranks', 'middle station' or 'middling orders', to the more 'modern' term 'middle class'.[22] The latter, we have been told, was already part of a puta-

---

[21] This realization also shaped the practice of my research, which obviously could encompass but a fraction of the totality of the means of political communication during this half century. My reading within any particular context continued until a pattern was repeated often enough to become not only familiar but quite predictable; until additional sources imparted a sense of *déjà lu*, as it were, contributing to already swelling footnotes but not modifying the argument. I therefore do not find the following arguments particularly vulnerable to the consequences of an odd discrepant quote that has been overlooked (which in such vast acres of prose is bound to exist somewhere): rejecting these arguments, like constructing them, would require somewhat more persistent counter-evidence than that possibly found in a single utterance.

[22] See for example G. Crossick, 'From Gentlemen to the Residuum: Languages of Social Description in Victorian Britain', in P. J. Corfield (ed.), *Language, History and Class*, Oxford, 1991, pp. 150–78. Note Crossick's puzzlement at examples of writers like John Wade and J. D. Milne, who in the early and mid Victorian period were still using rank, degree and class indiscriminately; a finding which defies Crossick's teleological ordering of his (disturbingly sporadic) quotes, and which he consequently characterizes

tive vision of a modern class society characterized by class struggle and social flux rather than by deference and immutability. In fact, however, even a rather superficial immersion in the sources makes it readily apparent that throughout the period covered by this book these different formulations of a social 'middle' were by and large interchangeable, and that 'class' had none of the loaded meanings and implications which came to be associated with it later. What constituted the bone of contention was the existence, the relevance and the consequences of a social *middle*, rather than the distinctions between 'class' or 'rank' or 'order' (in singular or in plural form). Indeed, if anything, a closer look may turn the common wisdom on its head: since 'class' could refer to any group from Catholics to tax-gatherers to French *émigrés*, whereas 'rank' was more narrowly associated with positions within the social and political order, we may find some inclination to prefer 'middle rank' to 'middle class' in statements which had an overt and aggressive political agenda.[23]

as 'striking' and 'contradictory' (p. 154). A. Briggs, 'The Language of "Class" in Early Nineteenth-Century England', in M. W. Flinn and T. C. Smout (eds.), *Essays in Social History*, Oxford, 1974, pp. 154–77. See also P. J. Corfield, 'Class by Name and Number in Eighteenth-Century Britain', in Corfield (ed.), *Language, History and Class*, pp. 101–30. Perkin, *The Origins of Modern English Society*, pp. 26 and passim. S. Wallech, '"Class versus Rank": The Transformation of Eighteenth-Century English Social Terms and Theories of Production', *Journal of the History of Ideas* 47 (1986), pp. 409–31. J. Seed, 'From "Middling Sort" to Middle Class in Late Eighteenth- and Early Nineteenth-Century England', in M. L. Bush (ed.), *Social Orders and Social Classes in Europe since 1500: Studies in Social Stratification*, London, 1992, pp. 114–35. E. Hobsbawm, 'The Example of the English Middle Class', in J. Kocka and A. Mitchell (eds.), *Bourgeois Society in Nineteenth-Century Europe*, Oxford, 1993, p. 127. There is likewise an inevitable teleology built into the diachronic lexical account of the evolution of the word 'class' in R. Williams, *Keywords: A Vocabulary of Culture and Society*, revised edn, London, 1983. For criticism of such arguments along lines similar to those presented here, see Stedman Jones's projected *Visions of Prometheus*. And see also the nuanced discussion in Willibald Steinmetz's essay on the uses of 'middle-class' language in Germany, France and England, which has appeared after the present book went to press: W. Steinmetz, 'Gemeineuropäische Tradition und nationale Besonderheiten im Begriff der "Mittelklasse": Ein Vergleich zwischen Deutschland, Frankreich und England', in R. Koselleck and K. Schreiner (eds.), *Bürgerschaften: Alteuropäische und moderne Bürgerschaft*, Stuttgart, 1994.

[23] A famous case in point is James Mill's *Essay on Government*; see below, pp. 257–8. Nonetheless, unless stated otherwise, I refer below to all such formulations uniformly as the language of 'middle class'. It should also be pointed out that these comments are not meant to deny *any* changes in the wording of social terminology: for instance, the obvious fact that the term 'working class(es)' became by the end of this period immensely more prevalent than any other formulation (such as 'labouring classes', etc.), or the apparent disappearance of the formulation 'middling sorts'. But it yet remains to be demonstrated (rather than simply asserted) what was the precise significance of each such development, if any, for people's views of the social and political order.

Moreover, it will also be seen that the precise social referent of the notion of 'middle class' was far from being well defined, and indeed that this vagueness often served the purpose of its users. Many speakers did not seem to have a clear social group in mind at all. Others presented remarkably different conceptions of the identity of this social group, an identity which they often expressed in moral or educational rather than in social, occupational or economic terms. And when conceived in 'sociological' terms, the language of 'middle class' could refer to a surprisingly wide range of social groups, high and low, rural and urban (though certain patterns did develop during this period, as we shall see). The key point here, however, is that we should not allow our own reverence for social categories as analytical tools to mislead us into assuming that a well-defined sociological referent of a social terminology is a prerequisite for its meaningful deployment or for its argumentative impact.

The book is divided into three parts, corresponding to three distinct political configurations that created different stakes in the language of 'middle class', and that resulted in different implications and outcomes of its uses. The first part, focusing on the decade of polarization and war following the French Revolution, shows how the singular political circumstances of this decade underlay the persistent introduction of the language of 'middle class' into the political debate as a pointed rhetorical weapon serving a particular political agenda. As a consequence, adversarial politics were manifest not only in the battle of conflicting arguments but also – more importantly for our purposes here – in the remarkable differentiation of representations of society along partisan lines. It was this political configuration that also determined the outcome of this phase in the uses of 'middle-class' language, as well as its legacy for the future.

The second part begins with the second French war and culminates in the traumatic massacre of Peterloo in 1819. At first, the new alignments and new issues of this period, so unlike those of the 1790s, defused the language of 'middle class' of much of its potency. Later, the changed political configuration prompted renewed invocations of the 'middle class'; only now the stakes in it were quite different from the earlier phase, and this led to crucial transformations in its uses. The third part demonstrates how in the (again) changed political climate of the

1820s, when the winds of reform that were about to carry the
next decade had begun to gather power, the representation of
society based on a 'middle class' became deeply implicated in
these powerful political trends; how these developments were
further enhanced by the conjunction with a new (albeit tardy)
awareness of social change; and why this social scheme came to
be increasingly reinforced with the particular historical narrative
which depicts the 'middle class' as triumphantly rising on the
crest of the tide of social transformation, a narrative which since
then has become so familiar.

Given the chronological progression of the following story and
its culmination in 1832, some will surely feel an irresistible
temptation to explain it teleologically as a simple epiphenomenon
riding on the coat-tails of the deeper underlying social process.
But this will not do. First, the story is not linear: between the
peaks in the uses of the language of 'middle class' were long
protracted lulls, in which it carried little purchase and gave way
to other representations of society.[24] Second, the setback during
the Victorian period, which has been alluded to, should in itself
place grave doubts on a simple linear reading of the story. And,
most important, throughout the story it will be seen that its
explanation, its logic, its dynamic, were all derived from political
circumstances, often contingent and messy, rather than from
pressures arising from the inexorable progression of the social
process.

Thus, in this account the Reform Bill of 1832 plays a key role,
yet a different one from that assigned to it in current historical
understanding. The Reform Bill was not an endpoint of a long
social transformation, the inevitable reality of which was finally

---

[24] Of course, rejecting linearity does not imply a denial of an evolution in the story.
Such an evolution is hardly surprising, since every surge of 'middle-class' language
was influenced in turn not only by different circumstances but also by where the
preceding one had left it, in terms of its associations, connotations and implications.
In short, one need not equate the lack of teleological or linear progression with the
lack of any change, as some revisionist historians – J. C. D. Clark for one – have
done. Indeed, Clark (in his *English Society 1688–1832: Ideology, Social Structure and Political
Practice during the Ancien Regime*, Cambridge, 1985, pp. 90–3) has made some suggestive
comments about the freedom of social language – in particular, the notion of 'middle
class' – from dependence on underlying social 'facts'. But these comments are undermined when he himself endows these social 'facts' with determining power, in his
adamant insistence on the crucial role that the *lack* of any social change plays in
proving his argument.

acknowledged by the political system, but rather in itself an important catalyst in the decisive transformation of people's conceptualizations of their society. In its aftermath, the category of 'middle class' came to play a central role in organizing and understanding social and political experience: it was the specific political circumstances of that historical moment which pushed forward this particular vision of society with such force that it came to be seen so widely as real objective truth. Its contingent, conditional and contested status as merely one possible way of representing society was forgotten. The 'middle class', to invoke Roland Barthes, became a *myth*:

Myth does not deny things [Barthes writes], on the contrary, its function is to talk about them . . . it gives them a natural and eternal justification, it gives them a clarity which is not that of an explanation but that of a statement of fact . . . In passing from history to nature, myth acts economically: it abolishes the complexity of human acts, it gives them the simplicity of essences.[25]

This is exactly what became of the category of 'middle class': it was rendered a natural and self-evidently visible part of social reality; it was seen as an uncontested and unproblematic statement of fact; it was provided with a cogent storyline that explained its origins and justified its existence; it was given the simplicity and the power of an essence (and, one may add, it was then bequeathed as such to future generations of historians). In sum, it was not so much the rising 'middle class' that was the crucial factor in bringing about the Reform Bill of 1832; rather, it was more the Reform Bill of 1832 that was the crucial factor in cementing the invention of the ever-rising 'middle class'.

[25] R. Barthes, *Mythologies*, trans. A. Lavers, New York, 1972, p. 143. It is important to note that 'myth' in this sense, and as it will be used below, does *not* denote – as is often assumed – inherent falsity and spuriousness that are attributed not to the mode of representation but to its subject itself.

PART I

Against the tide

Prelude to the 1790s: was the French Revolution a 'bourgeois revolution'?

The starting point for the present account, then, is the French Revolution. The events in France were the catalysts for the reconfiguration of the British political debate of the 1790s, a reconfiguration in which the language of 'middle class' will be shown to have been suddenly infused with powerful and contested political meanings. It may therefore be apt to preface the discussion of this decade with a few suggestive comments made by contemporaries about the French Revolution itself.

As historians of France often point out, an understanding of the French Revolution based on the 'middle class' did not come out of the Revolution itself, but took hold among French commentators only some decades after the fact.[1] But the French Revolution drew interpretative energy from many others besides the French. Throughout Europe (and beyond) it was keenly observed, analysed and scrutinized for its possible meanings for people's own social and political experiences. In Britain, recalled Lord Cockburn, people talked 'of nothing but the French Revolution and its supposed consequences'. 'Everything, not this or that thing, but literally everything, was soaked in this one event.'[2] So how did the British make sense of the French Revolution? What was the social vocabulary that they invoked in their own reconstructions of the events in France?

An obvious place to start, one that set the terms for much of the

---

[1] For the emphasis on the role of the 'middle class' (*classe moyenne*) in the French Revolution among French writers of the subsequent generation, see below, pp. 281–4. Their choice of words should be noted: although this section follows common practice in employing 'bourgeois revolution' as roughly equivalent to 'middle-class revolution', it was the latter formulation that was in fact the significant one in both France and Britain throughout the period discussed in this book.

[2] Henry Cockburn, *Memorials of His Time*, ed. K. F. C. Miller, Chicago, 1974 (originally published posthumously, 1856), pp. 40–1, 73.

subsequent debate, is Edmund Burke's *Reflections on the Revolution in France*. To Burke the events in France represented an unparalleled break with the past; yet, oddly, his explanation for these events was still framed within a rather traditional social vision, one that by the 1790s had already become well worn with use. Burke blamed the Revolution on the French 'monied interest', which had remained separate and distant from its nemesis, the landed interest. 'In this state of real . . . warfare between the noble ancient landed interest, and the new monied interest', not only did the latter have at its disposal more immediate power, it was also politically irresponsible. 'The monied interest is in its nature more ready for any adventure', went the crux of his argument. 'Being of recent acquisition, it falls in more naturally with any novelties.'[3] Burke was thus invoking one of the most common bogies of early-eighteenth-century 'country ideology' – the rising monied interest – to come to grips with those unprecedented 'novelties' that had just convulsed the French social and political order. It was the same familiar understanding of society which also informed Burke's derision of the French National Assembly. The Assembly, he wrote, was dominated by inferior lawyers and medical practitioners, a few 'country clowns', even more 'traders, who . . . had never known any thing beyond their counting-house'; not to mention (again drawing upon the stock formulations of country ideologues) 'dealers in stocks and funds, who must be eager, at any expence, to change their ideal paper wealth for the more solid substance of land'. With all these lustreless figures, Burke concluded gloomily, one could scarcely find 'the slightest traces of what we call the natural landed interest of the country'.[4]

Among the many enraged voices that came to the defence of the National Assembly was that of James Mackintosh, a Scotsman trained in medicine and law who combined Scottish Enlightenment views with a fairly radical though constitutional position. Replying to Burke's dismissal of the Assembly as the work of the monied interest and the Philosophes, Mackintosh wrote:

The commercial, or monied interest, has in all nations of Europe (taken as a body) been less prejudiced, more liberal, and more intelligent,

---

[3] Edmund Burke, *Reflections on the Revolution in France* (originally November 1790), ed. C. Cruise O'Brien, Harmondsworth, 1984, pp. 210–11.
[4] *Reflections*, pp. 129–32. On country ideology see below, pp. 61ff.

Figure 1. The alleged lowly social origins of the French National Assembly. James Gillray, whose initial favourable response to the French Revolution was reversed immediately after the publication of Burke's *Reflections*, took Burke's derision of the National Assembly further, representing its members (on the occasion of the flight of the royal family, June 1791) as grotesque ragamuffins and tradesmen. The latter include a barber (with comb in hair and scissors in pocket); a tailor (with shears, a tricolour cockade, and a measuring tape around his shoulders); a cook (with spoon, fork and a string of frogs on his belt); and a shoe-black (with shoe in one hand and brush in the other).
Source: BMC 7883.

than the landed gentry. Their views are enlarged by a wider intercourse with mankind, and hence the important influence of commerce in liberalizing the modern world. We cannot wonder then that this enlightened class of men ever prove the most ardent in the cause of freedom, the most zealous for political reform. It is not wonderful that philosophy should find in them more docile pupils and liberty more active friends, than in a haughty and prejudiced aristocracy.

Thus, in response to Burke's image of the malignant monied interest, Mackintosh restated the well-rehearsed eighteenth-century justifications of commercial society, familiar in Scottish writing at least since David Hume. So at this early stage, both Burke and Mackintosh placed the debate on the Revolution within the century-old dialogue between country ideologues and defenders of commerce; a framework in which both were equally conversant, and which both found more congenial than the radical language of natural rights which the French Revolution had done so much to promote.

But Mackintosh also wrote something else. Accepting Burke's observations that the French National Assembly was 'composed of Lawyers, Physicians, Merchants, Men of Letters, Tradesmen and Farmers', Mackintosh then asserted: 'These professions . . . form *the majority of that middle rank among whom almost all the sense and virtue of society reside.*'[5] Was this 'middle rank' simply equivalent to his 'commercial, or monied interest'? Perhaps not. Arguably this characterization of the carriers of the Revolution was based on a rather different (albeit overlapping) conceptualization of society, one which (as we shall see) could lend itself to different uses. Indeed, this was a characterization which – unlike the 'monied interest' – Burke had *failed* to notice: hence Burke's misjudgment (in Mackintosh's eyes) of their consequent sense and virtue. Moreover, the divergence of these two social visions can be seen in the fate of the farmers, who were encompassed explicitly within Mackintosh's virtuous 'middle rank' but were more difficult to fit into his liberal commercial or monied interest.

Mackintosh, then, fused together – somewhat uneasily – two distinct social vocabularies in defending the new regime in France. Others invoked more boldly a revolutionary 'middle

---

[5] James Mackintosh, *Vindiciae Gallicae: Defence of the French Revolution and Its English Admirers against the Accusations of the Right Hon. Edmund Burke . . .*, London, 1791 (published on 7 May), pp. 128–9, 136–7 (my emphasis).

class'. Benjamin Bousfield, for example, was one who had read Burke (rather inaccurately) as imposing upon the events in France a dual social scheme of higher orders versus the people, and who – like Mackintosh – found this understanding deficient precisely in that key social factor, the 'middle class': 'Not in France, not even in Great Britain or Ireland should we look up for public virtue among the higher ranks. It is true, there are some great exceptions, but in general, the public spirit of the country resides among the middle class of men.'[6] The implications of Burke's omission were spelled out even more confidently by Benjamin Vaughan, a Unitarian merchant associated with the reforming circle of the Francophile Marquess of Lansdowne, who characterized opinions such as his own as 'a medium between those of Mr Burke and Mr Paine'. Vaughan reflected cheerfully:

It is a happy circumstance that the success of the [French] revolution is lodged as a deposit in the hands of the *middle* ranks of people, who in all ages have been stedfast to their trust. Liberty, and the elevated views of society peculiar to modern times, have taken possession of their minds; and it would be as easy to exterminate the race of plants from the earth, or to chase the birds and insects from the air, as to extinguish the notions which they have acquired.[7]

Note the tension in Vaughan's faith in the revolutionary 'middle ranks of people' between, on the one hand, the sense of novelty and freshness of this social group, which has recently acquired enlightened views 'peculiar to modern times'; and on the other, the ancient pedigree of its political virtue, attested to 'in all ages'. In a self-avowed 'medium' position between the appeal to antiquity made by Burke and the claim for a radical break with the past made by Paine, it was not easy for a political moderate to determine how the 'middle' should handle history.

Such sanguine assessments of the developments in France were cut short in autumn 1792, with the notorious September Massacres in which crowds in Paris killed prisoners *en masse* for several

[6] Benjamin Bousfield, *Observations on the Right Hon. Edmund Burke's Pamphlet, on the Subject of the French Revolution*, Dublin, 1791, p. 25. Bousfield was as far from Paine as he was from Burke; he approved of the present English Constitution for its consideration of the rights of man and for its continual improvement.

[7] [Benjamin Vaughan], *Two Papers by the Calm Observer, not Printed in the Collection of His Letters Extracted from the Morning Chronicle*, [London], 1795, p. 30 (written in summer 1791). [Idem], *The Essence of the Calm Observer, on the Subjects of the Concert of Princes, the Dismemberment of Poland, and the War with France . . .*, London, 1793, p. 42.

days. Together with these hundreds of hapless prisoners, this event – compounded soon thereafter by the execution of Louis XVI on 21 January 1793 – also killed the optimism which the events in France had initially evoked in relatively moderate political figures like Vaughan or Mackintosh. The political winds changed radically, and so did the social interpretations of the Revolution offered by such moderates.

Consider the following examples. In 1795 Thomas Erskine, a major figure in the respectable moderate opposition, told Members of Parliament:

In the whole of the late proceedings and events, one of the most fatal things had been, that the higher orders of the people separated themselves too much from the lower. This had been one of the causes of the revolution in France. Under their arbitrary monarchs there were literally but two classes of the people: a pampered, profligate proud nobility, and a low, miserable, and abject rabble; *no intermediate class, no knowledge, no virtue.* It was to this that all the horrors that followed the French revolution were to be attributed.[8]

The previous year, a 'British Merchant', who described himself as 'neither a Jacobin nor a leveller', stated that the 'enthusiasm rising almost to phrenzy' among French republicans was a consequence of the oppressive regime to which they had been formerly subjected. 'Under the arbitrary government of France', he explained, 'there was no yeomanry, *no middle class of people*, all were either Princes or beggars, Lords or Vassals'; and this inevitably led to the revolutionary 'phrenzy'.[9] And in 1800 the same interpretation of the French scene was again advanced in parliament by the independent gentleman Thomas Jones. Condemning ministerial policies for depleting 'the fortunes of the middle ranks of men', Jones resorted to the late ordeals of the French as proof of the unspeakable dangers of such a development: 'Let me stop to observe on the destruction of the middle order of men. Old France, before the revolution, had but two descriptions of people, the very highest and the very lowest. God forbid that only two orders of men should ever be found in old England!'[10]

---

[8] *Parliamentary History of England* 32, cols. 313–14 (my emphasis).

[9] *Considerations on the French War, in Which the Circumstances Leading to It, Its Object, and the Resources of Britain for Carrying It on, Are Examined, in a Letter to the Rt Honble William Pitt, by a British Merchant*, London, 1794, pp. 42, 64 (my emphasis).

[10] *Parliamentary History* 35, cols. 697–8. Compare also the portrayal of pre-revolutionary France as consisting of only two classes, 'the very rich and the very poor', while 'the middling class was almost obliterated', in a letter by 'Viator', of 8 August 1796, in

What a different French Revolution. Gone was the glorious 'middle class' which the elated Vaughan, Mackintosh and Bousfield had confidently postulated at its helm. The story as told by these post-Terror moderates was completely reversed. The French Revolution, and especially its horrors, occurred not because a worthy 'middle class' carried it through, but because French society *lacked* a 'middle class', and was hence separated into two distant and alienated classes at the extremes of the social scale. A proper 'middle class' would have provided the valuable thread needed to knit this society together and save it from unfortunate excesses. For these later commentators, then, whereas the 'middle class' (as social agents) played no role in their version of the Revolution, the notion of 'middle class' nevertheless continued to be central to its construction. And either way, in the hands of political moderates the 'middle class' – whether absent or present – always came out looking good.

In the hands of others, however, the 'middle class' fared worse. For a final twist to the story, let us return to Burke. We recall that in 1790 his social interpretation of the Revolution was still confined to the conceptual tools of eighteenth-century country ideologues. A year later Burke modified somewhat the identity of the villains, making it more inclusive. 'Formerly', he argued, 'few, except the ambitious great, or the desperate and indigent, were to be feared as instruments in revolutions'; yet the events in France now revealed new sources of subversion. 'The monied men, merchants, principal tradesmen, and men of letters (hitherto generally thought the peaceable and even timid part of society) are the chief actors in the French Revolution.'[11] Previously, that

---

Moral and Political Magazine of the London Corresponding Society 1, 1796, p. 115. The interpretation of the French Revolution based on a dual scheme of polarized and alienated social extremes was often repeated: examples among political moderates, like Jones contrasting this situation with that in Britain, include Brooke Boothby, *A Letter to the Right Honourable Edmund Burke*, 2nd edn, with additions, London, 1791, pp. 33, 36–7, 51–2. David Hartley, *Argument on the French Revolution*, Bath, 1794, pp. 36, 41. William Frend, *Patriotism: Or, the Love of Our Country*, London, 1804, pp. 133–5.

[11] E. Burke, *Thoughts on French Affairs, &c. &c. Written in December 1791*, in *The Writings and Speeches of Edmund Burke*, vol. VIII, ed. L. G. Mitchell, Oxford, 1989, p. 346. See very similarly another avowedly Burkean analysis of the French Revolution: *An Historical Sketch of the French Revolution from Its Commencement to the Year 1792*, London, 1792, p. 4. (This book is erroneously attributed in the British Library – and hence elsewhere – to James Mackintosh.)

is, social instability could only be caused by the social extremes. But now things were different: the carriers of revolution were a variety of persons between the 'great' and the 'indigent', encompassing more than just the 'monied interest'. And yet, while Burke did admit at the end of 1791 the novelty of the present social alignments, he did not volunteer a novel way to describe them: his social 'middle' as yet remained unnamed.

But listen to Burke's obloquy against the French republicans in 1796, just before his death. At this juncture, this was how he chose to represent the social causes of the French Revolution: 'The chain of subordination, even in cabal and sedition, was broken in its most important links. It was no longer the great and the populace. Other interests were formed, other dependencies, other connexions, other communications. *The middle classes had swelled far beyond their former proportion.*'[12] By 1796 Burke's verdict was explicit and unambiguous: the guilty party was the French 'middle classes'. Nothing could be further from the opinions of the moderates; as one of them had reminded Burke earlier that year, social relations in France were 'irregular, broken and unconnected' because its society 'had been for ages in the situation of all despotic states, *composed of only two classes of men, the rich and the poor*'.[13] Burke, by contrast, underscored further why it was the 'middle classes' who had been responsible for the disruption of French political stability:

Like whatever is most effectively rich and great in society, these classes became the seat of all the active politicks; and the preponderating weight to decide on them. There were all the energies by which fortune is acquired; there the consequence of their success. There were all the talents which assert their pretensions, and are impatient of the place which settled society prescribes to them. These descriptions had got between the great and the populace; and the influence on the lower classes was with them. The spirit of ambition had taken possession of this class as violently as ever it had done of any other.

A dual social structure, which had been inherently stable 'even

---

[12] Edmund Burke, *Two Letters Addressed to a Member of the Present Parliament, on the Proposals for Peace with the Regicide Directory of France*, 10th edn, London, 1796, p. 189 (my emphasis).

[13] William Williams, *Rights of the People: Or, Reasons for a Regicide Peace ... with a Few Anticipating Strictures upon Mr Burke's Long Promised Letters Against a Regicide Peace*, London, 1796, p. 22 (my emphasis).

in sedition', was broken by the expansion of the 'middle classes' in numbers, wealth and power. Between 1790 and 1796, while Burke's basic views seemed obdurate and immutable, the social vocabulary which informed his formulation of the social causes of the French Revolution had actually shifted significantly. In his ultimate analysis, what overturned the political order and shattered the very fabric of society was the unbridled ambition of the 'middle classes', elbowing their way into prominence while pushing France down the whirlpool of radicalization.

So did the French have a 'middle-class' revolution? What were the political inclinations of the French 'middle class' to begin with? And even more fundamentally, did the French have a 'middle class' at all? The answers that one obtained from the British political debate of the 1790s were contradictory: the Revolution occurred either because the 'middle class' swelled beyond its proper proportions, or because it was too negligible to prevent it; the 'middle class' was either the best guarantee of a happy social and political order, or most likely to overthrow it; the events in France were explainable either by the presence of a 'middle class', or by its absence. So much for our progress on the notorious question of a putative 'bourgeois revolution'.

But of course this is not the real question that might be raised by these few selected quotes, assuming that their twists and turns were more than merely a multi-textual fluke. The meaningful context for trying to make sense of them is not the social alignments in France but rather the political alignments in Britain, alignments that were being anxiously formed and re-formed under the shadow of the dramatic events across the Channel. Given the conditionality of 'middle-class'-based conceptualizations of society, as has been suggested above, the fact that these representations of the Revolution could incorporate such divergent visions of French society is in itself not very surprising. But what really needs explaining is not simply how a society could be represented so differently, but why each of these rhetorically conscious speakers chose one particular conceptualization of society over another, and used it in a very specific way. It is in the loaded political alignments and loyalties of the 1790s that such an explanation might be found.

Thus, what the following chapters propose to demonstrate is

how the notion of 'middle class' came to be infused with very specific political resonances in the British political debate following the French Revolution, even though this debate was overtly concerned not with the existence or nature of a 'middle class' but with the momentous issues of rights and wrongs, repression and liberation, war and peace, life and death. Through the recovery of the particular meanings and significance of 'middle-class' language at this juncture we will then be able to understand why the moderate commentators on the one hand, and the immoderate Burke on the other, found need to formulate and modify their interpretations of the Revolution around this social scheme. The question, in short, is this: when the British chose to invoke the 'middle class' in the electrified politics of the 1790s, or not to invoke it, what was really at stake?

CHAPTER 2

The uses of 'middle-class' language in the 1790s

POLITICAL MIDDLE AND SOCIAL MIDDLE IN OPPOSITION TO WAR: THE 'MIDDLE-CLASS IDIOM'

> The late events in France ... have made one party here desperate and the other drunk. Many are become wild Republicans who a few months back were moderate Reformers, and numbers who six weeks ago were contented with plain, old-fashioned Toryism, have now worked themselves up into such apprehensions for the fate of Royalty as to be incapable of distinguishing between Reform and treason.
>
> (George Tierney, October 1792)[1]

> We live in times of violence and extremes.
>
> (Charles James Fox, December 1793)[2]

The 1790s was indeed an extraordinary decade in British history, a decade in which almost everything became political, and politics became almost everything. It saw the unprecedented broadening of the range of possibilities believed to be attainable through political change; it saw the unprecedented broadening of the political public, eager to capture some of these possibilities. Whether enthusiastic or apprehensive, contemporaries were keenly aware of the novel nature of politics.

To say that the 1790s were ushered in by the French Revolution is of course not to imply that all or even most elements of the conflict in Britain were imported from across the Channel. But even if all the components of the contending political visions of

---

[1] Tierney to Grey, 29 October 1792; quoted in G. M. Trevelyan, *Lord Grey of the Reform Bill*, 2nd edn, London, 1952, p. 60.
[2] Fox to Lord Holland, 28 December 1793; quoted in L. G. Mitchell, *Charles James Fox*, Oxford, 1992, p. 130.

this decade were British-made, the possibility of their concrete transformation from vision into reality – or the urgency of the need to prevent their imminent realization – owed their immediacy and potency to the French example. The revolution in France demonstrated that a fundamental change in the social and political order could be within reach: it converted fanciful fantasies into potentially workable blueprints. 'I do not believe', Tom Paine told the hundreds of thousands who imbibed the phenomenally popular second part of his *Rights of Man*, 'that monarchy and aristocracy will continue seven years longer in any of the enlightened countries in Europe.'[3] Unlike the Godwinian utopian confidence in the perfectibility of man, Paine's wishful thinking had a deadline, and a very immediate one at that; it was the age of 'the mania of man-mending', as a sobered Robert Southey said of his more rash youth.[4] In such an atmosphere, obviously, political conflict acquired a new flavour, quite unlike that of previous decades: it was not only about the division of power between elite factions, or about obtaining concessions from a political elite, or about negotiating an improved bargaining position within a given power structure. Political conflict was more overtly than ever about the very identity and legitimacy of the elite, about the immediate prioritization of different components of society, about the foundations of the power structure itself. It was about the *British* revolution.

And, for the most part, contemporaries knew it. Historians have intensely debated the unresolvable question of whether there was a real threat or potential for revolution in Britain during the 1790s. E. P. Thompson and many followers have pointed to what they see as a substantial insurrectionary movement, which was close to eruption more than once; they also point to governmental repression ('Pitt's reign of terror') as indispensable for explaining its abortive fate.[5] The opposite position, recently restated by Ian

---

[3] Thomas Paine, *Rights of Man*, ed. E. Foner, Harmondsworth, 1985, preface to pt. II, p. 156. For the phenomenal sales of the *Rights of Man* see E. P. Thompson, *The Making of the English Working Class*, London, 1963, p. 108 n. 1.

[4] Quoted in A. Cobban (ed.), *The Debate on the French Revolution 1789–1800*, 2nd edn, London, 1960, p. 376.

[5] Thompson, *The Making of the English Working Class*. This view has since been restated, among others, by J. L. Baxter and F. K. Donnelly, 'The Revolutionary "Underground" in the West Riding: Myth or Reality?', *Past and Present* 64 (1974), pp. 124–32.

Christie, stresses the underlying stability of British society in this period, and argues that both the revolutionary potential and the repression from above have been grossly exaggerated.[6] Yet regardless of who may get the upper hand in the argument between twentieth-century historians, it is beyond doubt that late eighteenth-century observers of all political camps *believed* in the potency of the revolutionary threat; perhaps more so than ever before or after. An April Fools' Day placard announcing 'A new and entertaining Farce, called LA GUILLOTINE; or, GEORGE'S HEAD IN THE BASKET!', fifteen months after the execution of Louis XVI, was perhaps farcical, but certainly no joke.[7]

Consequently, and crucially, politics became exceptionally charged, electrified, momentous: the stakes were deemed to be particularly high, and so were the ensuing tensions. It was no coincidence that political debate during this period assumed an extraordinary histrionic tone, manifested perhaps most famously in Burke's dramatic dagger scene in December 1792 (see figure 2). Establishing one's political identity and allegiance was therefore of vital importance: 'Language the most outrageous', recalled the radical Thomas Holcroft, 'was employed to make those who were in the least suspected declare their creed.'[8] Under such circumstances, political classification turned stark and schematic, painted in black and white. Greyness seemed indefensible; this

M. Elliott, 'The "Despard Conspiracy" Reconsidered', *Past and Present* 75 (1977), pp. 46–61. J. Anne Hone, *For the Cause of Truth: Radicalism in London 1796–1821*, Oxford, 1982. R. Wells, *Insurrection: The British Experience 1795–1803*, Gloucester, 1983; and idem, 'English Society and Revolutionary Politics in the 1790s: The Case for Insurrection', in M. Philp (ed.), *The French Revolution and British Popular Politics*, Cambridge, 1991, pp. 188–226.

[6] I. R. Christie, *Stress and Stability in Late Eighteenth-Century Britain: Reflections on the British Avoidance of Revolution*, Oxford, 1984; and idem, 'Conservatism and Stability in British Society', in M. Philp (ed.), *The French Revolution and British Popular Politics*, Cambridge, 1991, pp. 169–87. For similar evaluations, see among others G. A. Williams, *Artisans and Sans-Culottes: Popular Movements in France and Britain during the French Revolution*, London, 1968. C. B. Cone, *The English Jacobins: Reformers in Late 18th Century England*, New York, 1968. M. I. Thomis and P. Holt, *Threats of Revolution in Britain 1789–1848*, London, 1977. For 'Pitt's reign of terror' as an exaggeration, see C. Emsley, 'Repression, "Terror" and the Rule of Law in England during the Decade of the French Revolution', *English Historical Review* 100 (1985), pp. 801–25, and his previous articles cited there.

[7] Quoted in Cobban, *The Debate on the French Revolution*, pp. 285–6. The placard was introduced as evidence of sedition in the treason trial of Thomas Hardy, and was declared by the defence to have been a ministerial fabrication.

[8] *Memoirs of the Late Thomas Holcroft, Written by Himself . . .*, London, 1816, vol. II, p. 151.

Figure 2. Parliamentary histrionics of the 1790s. A caricature of Burke's famous dagger scene in the House of Commons on 28 December 1792, in which he flung a dagger to the floor in order to draw attention (in his words) to the dangers of 'the French infection'. Fox, fleeing, accuses him on his part of 'the French disorder'. Behind, the Speaker (Addington) raises his arms in dismay. The dagger had been manufactured for one Dr William Maxwell, a committed radical who was involved in attempts to supply arms to the French.
Source: BMC 8285.

was not a time for ambivalence and complexity. 'The nation is reduced to the desperate necessity of chusing one of two extremes', complained one pamphlet; 'no mild medium will be allowed by ministerial influence.' Not that one extreme was more responsible for this polarization than the other: the effects of the French Revolution on British politics, Samuel Romilly recollected, were that 'among the higher orders it has produced a horror of every kind of innovation; among the lower, a desire to try the boldest political experiments, and a distrust and contempt of all moderate reforms'.[9]

Indeed, the French Revolution did more: it also provided a model for a total attack on society's power structure. Half a generation earlier another revolution had already been attempted, with which the British were painfully familiar. But the American Revolution, at least overtly, was more of a defence of political principles than a head-on attack on the social order.[10] The meaning of the French Revolution was articulated differently: *Egalité* was from the outset an inseparable counterpart to *Liberté*.[11] Regardless of whether it was in truth a social revolution (which, the majority of its historians now claim, it was not), the French Revolution explicitly politicized social class. As a consequence, the identity of the contenders in the political struggle was perceived differently. Earlier in the eighteenth century it had mostly been sufficient to posit the 'People' versus the 'Aristocracy', in terms that were more political than social. 'People' was non-differentiated and all inclusive, while 'Aristocracy' signified more the opprobrious form of government of the classical lexicon than

---

[9] *The British Tocsin: Or, Proofs of National Ruin*, London, 1795, pp. 36–7. *Memoirs of the Life of Sir Samuel Romilly, Written by Himself; with a Selection from His Correspondence. Edited by His Sons*, 2nd edn, 3 vols., London, 1840, vol. III, 399.

[10] A different argument is made by Gordon Wood in his recent reassessment of the American Revolution as a social revolution (*The Radicalism of the American Revolution*, New York, 1992). It seems to me that Wood is more convincing in discussing the radical (and often unintended) social *consequences* of the revolution than in demonstrating the centrality of social revolution to the *intentions* of its perpetrators, an argument that in large part rests on the debatable interpretation of their quest for 'independence' as a self-consciously social (rather than primarily political) agenda.

[11] Not that this was necessarily a self-explanatory or readily workable combination: one need only think of the continuous shifting of the meaning of *Egalité* in the hands of the revolutionaries in France, especially between equality of rights and equality of property. See M. Ozouf, 'Equality', in F. Furet and M. Ozouf (eds.), *A Critical Dictionary of the French Revolution*, Cambridge, Mass., 1989, pp. 669–83.

a particular group of people.[12] At the end of the century, however, it became a much more pressing issue to recognize the social bases of political groupings, even if only in schematic or stereotypical form.

A key turning point in this explosive fusion of social and political programmatical language was the publication of the second part of Paine's *Rights of Man* in February 1792, a pamphlet which linked political with economic demands and – as has often been noted – anticipated key concepts of the modern welfare state. Paine's themes were then quickly picked up by others, such as John Thelwall – the influential orator who 'took Jacobinism to the borders of Socialism'[13] – or the more extreme 'proto-communist' Thomas Spence. Indeed, as Gregory Claeys has suggested, anti-radical writers were probably more apprehensive about the egalitarian social implications of their opponents' positions than about their directly political critique; 'Jacobinism', Burke threatened his readers, 'is the Revolt of the enterprising talents of a country against its Property.' In the radicalization of the 1790s, in other words, the second part of the *Rights of Man* played a more important role than the first.[14] Political categories as a result were now becoming inseparable from social categories. The political division between radicals and the establishment (as discussed further in chapter 3) thus became closely and explicitly equated with a basic social division, of rich and poor, or higher and lower classes; a phenomenon unfamiliar, for instance, to the radicalism of the 1760s. In between, the scene was set for the identity of political moderates to be projected onto a social middle, a 'middle class'.

For political moderates, the initial sentiments roused by the

---

[12] According to P. Langford, *Public Life and the Propertied Englishman 1689–1798*, Oxford, 1991, p. 535, the meaning of 'Aristocracy' began to change during the American war.

[13] These are the words of Thompson, *The Making of the English Working Class*, p. 160.

[14] Edmund Burke, *Two Letters Addressed to a Member of the Present Parliament, on the Proposals for Peace with the Regicide Directory of France*, 10th edn, London, 1796, p. 98. G. Claeys, *Thomas Paine: Social and Political Thought*, London, 1989, pp. 156–7. Also idem, 'The French Revolution Debate and British Political Thought', *History of Political Thought* 11 (1990), pp. 59–80. J. Dinwiddy, 'Interpretations of Anti-Jacobinism', in M. Philp (ed.), *The French Revolution and British Popular Politics*, Cambridge, 1991, pp. 39–41. For a contemporary observation that Paine's popularity was due to the economic rather than the political aspects of his writing, see [Benjamin Vaughan], *Comments on the Proposed War with France, on the State of Parties, and on the New Act Respecting Aliens . . . By a Lover of Peace*, London, 1793, p. 60.

French Revolution were for the most part coloured by expectant enthusiasm. They could still entertain sanguine hopes, evoked by 'these great events ... [that] make a totally new, a most wonderful, and important, æra in the history of mankind ... a change from darkness to light'. These optimistic words had been written by Dr Joseph Priestley at the beginning of 1791, some six months before a 'Church and King' mob in Birmingham ravaged his books and laboratory in four days of rioting, driving him to exile.[15] His unfortunate lesson was soon to become that of other moderates, as the whirlwinds of extremism gathered power. The autumn of 1792, it has already been noted, was the key moment in the radicalization of the political scene and in the transformation of the political mood. Nowhere, perhaps, did the September Massacres leave a more striking imprint than in the letters of Sir Samuel Romilly. Only in May Romilly had assured a French correspondent that 'my opinion ... is not in the least altered with respect to your revolution ... it is the most glorious event, and the happiest for mankind, that has ever taken place'; but on 10 September, a week after the atrocities in Paris, Romilly exclaimed in frustration, 'how could we ever be so deceived in the character of the French nation as to think them capable of liberty! wretches, who ... employ whole days in murdering women, and priests, and prisoners!' (see figure 3).[16]

At home, the radical movement was gathering momentum – 1792, one historian has written, was 'the *annus mirabilis* of the English popular movement'[17] – beginning with the establishment of the London Corresponding Society (January) and the publication of the second part of *Rights of Man* (February). This increasing momentum coincided with the demotic turn of events in France, and the connection between these seemingly parallel developments could not fail to make their adversaries ever more anxious; an anxiety manifested, notably, in the wide-spread rumours about an insurrection in London that was supposedly

---

[15] Joseph Priestley, *Letters to the Right Honourable Edmund Burke, Occasioned by His Reflections on the Revolution in France*, 2nd edn, Birmingham, 1791, pp. 143–4. The letters were signed on 1 January 1791; the riots took place in mid-July, following a meeting to celebrate the second anniversary of the falling of the Bastille.

[16] Romilly, *Memoirs*, vol. II, pp. 1–2, 4.

[17] A. Goodwin, *The Friends of Liberty: The English Democratic Movement in the Age of the French Revolution*, Cambridge, Mass., 1979, p. 171; and see chapter 6 for a detailed account of the events of this year.

Figure 3. Horrified reaction to the September Massacres. Gillray's particularly appalling engraving of 20 September 1792, exemplifying the powerful impact of the Paris massacres earlier that month. The *sans culottes* (wilfully misrepresented as lacking breeches) eagerly join in a bloody cannibalistic feast, depicted in ghastly detail. *Source*: BMC 8122.

prepared for the first weekend of December.[18] Organized reaction and repression thus set in as well, beginning with the royal proclamation against seditious publications (that is, Paine) in May, and the foundation of John Reeves's Association for the Preservation of Liberty and Property against Republicans and Levellers in November. And then, whatever hopes moderates may still have harboured for keeping these centrifugal tendencies

[18] On this episode see C. Emsley, 'The London "Insurrection" of December 1792: Fact, Fiction, or Fantasy?', *Journal of British Studies* 17:2 (1978), pp. 66–86.

under control, were finally shattered on 1 February 1793, when Britain went to war.

Britain's war against republican and then Napoleonic France was more extensive and more expensive than any of its previous military engagements, involving a sixfold expansion of its army and an expenditure almost three times as great as all its other major wars since 1688 combined. In terms of mobilization of human and financial resources, this war effort was not matched again until the first world war; indeed, considering that the fighting involved major world powers, lasted for more than two decades and spread over four continents, this war itself arguably deserves to be called the first world war. Linda Colley has recently emphasized the role of the French war in forging patriotic unity in Britain.[19] But the enthusiastic rallying for the nation's defence was in itself no small factor in further deepening political polarization, now reconfigured as a binary clash between 'patriots' and 'traitors', and demanding unambiguous proof of well-defined loyalties. And again, caught between vehemently enraged radicals on the one hand and vehemently exhortative loyalists on the other, were those who still preached political moderation. At this juncture, moderation for them meant, first of all, peace.

John Cookson has painted the collective portrait of the much dispersed yet influential body of moderate opinion among the propertied classes which was galvanized against the war, the 'Friends of Peace'. Their active core was a 'voluntary fellowship' of 'liberals' linked through ties of family, religion (primarily, according to Cookson, Rational Christianity), intellect, profession and business.[20] Cookson somewhat too neatly categorizes them alternatively as the emerging industrial interest, the Dissenters, the provincial interest or the middle class, as if all these categories

[19] In fact it was France who declared the war against Britain; but the French merely pre-empted an expected British move. See C. Emsley, *British Society and the French Wars 1793–1815*, London, 1979, esp. the introduction. L. Colley, *Britons: Forging the Nation 1707–1837*, New Haven, 1992, pp. 150, 286–7. Also Emsley, 'The Impact of War and Military Participation on Britain and France 1792–1815', in C. Emsley and J. Walvin (eds.), *Artisans, Peasants and Proletarians 1760–1860*, London, 1985, pp. 57–80 (where it is pointed out that Britain's human losses in the French wars, relatively, were actually heavier than during the first world war).

[20] J. E. Cookson, *The Friends of Peace: Anti-War Liberalism in England, 1793–1815*, Cambridge, 1982. I follow here Cookson's terminology, which was also used by contemporaries: see for example Capel Lofft's use of the term 'Friends of Peace' in Christopher Wyvill, *Political Papers*, vol. v, York, [1804], p. 186, letter of 12 April 1794.

were one and the same, and as if all or most of the members
of each such category had a common political mind.[21] Yet his
account, albeit too schematic, does establish their importance as
a focus of political opposition, all the more so because they were
quite respectable and inordinately articulate. Many of the Friends
of Peace had been active in politics before, whether in opposition
to the American war, in agitations for reform, or in the recently
thwarted campaign for the repeal of the Test and Corporation
Acts. But, as Cookson points out, the intensity and commitment
of their political involvement increased in the 1790s, when confronted with loyalism and 'Pittism' – the former's noxious effects
perceived to penetrate every part of the structure of power, the
latter perceived as a ubiquitous system of misrule.[22]

The Friends of Peace were continually reminded that they
were skating on thin ice: on the one hand eliciting opprobrium
for opposing the government in times of national mobilization
and purported national danger, on the other striving to dissociate
themselves from the popular radicals and to vindicate themselves
from recurrent accusations of Jacobinism.[23] Standing uneasily on
this shrinking middle ground between ever more antagonistic
extremes (note the mood of the epigraphs at the beginning of
this section, as well as figure 4), the propertied opposition was
compelled to defend incessantly the legitimacy and merits of its
position. It wanted Pitt to adopt a 'Sound Policy', which in its
view 'required him to hold a middle course between the two
dangerous extremes of Paine and Burke'.[24] These were the words

---

[21] Dissenters could of course be loyalists (see John Young below, p. 106), and Anglicans
could be fervent opposers of the war (see Vicesimus Knox below, pp. 46ff). More
importantly for my purposes here, members of the 'middle' strata of society in large
numbers were ardent loyalists (see chapter 3, p. 97). And see my 'National Society,
Communal Culture: An Argument about the Recent Historiography of Eighteenth-
Century Britain', *Social History* 17 (1992), pp. 63–4.

[22] Cookson, *The Friends of Peace*, pp. 14–15.

[23] As one of the organs of the Friends of Peace put it: 'The present ministry considered
themselves ... to be opposed by two parties – Reformers and Republicans; – and
after endeavouring in vain to confute the arguments of the reformers, they at last had
recourse to calumny, and endeavoured to confound all their opponents in one odium,
by branding them all with the same name of republicans.' *The Oeconomist* (Newcastle),
6, June 1798, p. 158.

[24] C. Wyvill, *Political Papers*, vols. I–IV, York, 1802, vol. IV, p. 77 (written in 1796).
Claeys (in his *Thomas Paine*, p. 155; and 'The French Revolution Debate') has argued
that in fact the writings of Burke and Paine did *not* embody the two opposite extremes
between which the political debate of the 1790s was polarized. While this appears
convincing in retrospect, there is little doubt that contemporaries did indeed invoke

of the Reverend Christopher Wyvill, that experienced and influential North Riding gentleman who had been the erstwhile founder of the Yorkshire Association for parliamentary reform. Now Wyvill held a key position in the loose network of the Friends of Peace, or as they often called themselves, the 'moderates'. To prevent 'a dreadful collision of opposite parties', Wyvill stated in 1794, 'a moderate party there yet is, who deprecate the extremes of Government and of the Republican Faction, and who, I trust, are strong enough to prevent the impending mischiefs on either hand. With this middle party I wish to act.'[25] While maintaining their faith in 'the middle course of temperate Reformation . . . which benevolence and a just patriotic zeal will most approve', Wyvill and his political friends were all too aware of the truculent political climate. Such days presented 'a melancholy prospect to moderate men', who had 'to be ready to encounter the violence of either side'. After all, never before had the opposition in parliament been driven by its sense of impotence to quit the House altogether, as the frustrated Foxites did in 1797. 'In no period of our History', summarized the anti-war activist Thomas Bigge of Newcastle, 'were moderate men ever placed in a situation more embarrassing than at present.'[26]

It was this need to vindicate the legitimacy and merits of an increasingly unfashionable *political* middle, perched between extremes which in themselves were characterized by a conflation of political and social categories, which led the Friends of Peace to an encomiastic emphasis on the *social* middle. In 1792 Wyvill had already been moved by the Scylla of 'a powerful Aristocracy' and the Charybdis of 'the violence of a furious Populace' to inquire about the possible mediating support from 'persons of

---

the two repeatedly as signifying the two ends of the political spectrum, the 'antipodes in politics' (Professor Dunbar to Wyvill, 5 May 1792; in Wyvill, *Political Papers*, vol. v, p. 59). Compare also Benjamin Vaughan's characterization of the opinions of the Friends of Peace as 'a medium between those of Mr Burke and Mr Paine': above, p. 25.

[25] Wyvill to John Courtney, 18 June 1794: *Political Papers*, vol. v, p. 207. On Wyvill's moderate position in the 1790s and his difficulties in maintaining it, see J. R. Dinwiddy, *Christopher Wyvill and Reform 1790–1820* (Borthwick Papers no. 39), York, 1971, pp. 3–7.

[26] Christopher Wyvill, *A State of the Representation of the People of England, on the Principles of Mr Pitt in 1785*, 1793; rep. in his *Political Papers*, vol. II, p. 622; vol. v, p. 160 (J. R. Fenwick to Wyvill, 4 January 1794), 172 (T. Bigge to Wyvill, 11 March 1794), and 281 (P. Francis to Wyvill, 20 January 1795). Also see Henry Cockburn, *Memorials of His Time*, ed. K. F. C. Miller, Chicago, 1974 (originally 1856), p. 76, on the pressures of 'the intemperance of the wild' on moderates at that juncture.

Figure 4. Politics polarized. An anti-Jacobin representation (by Isaac
Cruikshank?) of politics at the end of 1793, as a duel between the forces of
good and evil, converging on the British constitution. Fox and Sheridan (centre
right) are branded as revolutionaries, preparing to blow up Britannia and the
temple of the constitution; their supporters are of the lower classes. Against
them are arrayed the forces of order, manifestly of higher social standing,
headed by Pitt (using 'truth' to extinguish Fox's torch) and (presumably) John
Reeves. The antithetical symmetry of the composition highlights the void in
its centre, between the opposing camps: in this configuration there was no
political middle. *Source*: BMC 8424.

middling property' (in London).[27] By 1795 Wyvill's blending of the social and political middle became much clearer: the cause of non-radical reform, he stated, needed the support 'not of that class at the lower end of society, many of whom wish for Universal Suffrage only to abuse it, but of those middle classes, who have had some education, who have some property and some character to preserve'. Politically, these men, mellowed by their education, property and social standing, were 'men of mild and patient characters'. Given this interweaving of meanings, it is hardly surprising – and rather telling – that Wyvill's correspondent, Philip Francis, did not quite comprehend the social component of the message, interpreting Wyvill's words in a more limited way simply as another emphasis on the desirable political 'middle path' that 'is the surest proof of political courage'.[28]

The conflation of the political and social middle was even more marked in Thomas Bigge's self-explanatory *Considerations on the State of Parties, and the Means of Effecting a Reconciliation between Them*. His 'considerations' resulted in a predictable picture of three parties: aristocratic, democratic and moderate, the latter being 'derided on both sides'. Bigge then explained the 'means of effecting a reconciliation':

Hostilities between the two opposite parties cannot possibly, in the present distracted state of public opinion . . . lead to any conclusion which the friends to order and liberty united will not deeply deprecate: And it seems highly expedient that their bitter and encreasing animosities should be suspended by patriotic and constitutional means, by the respectable intervention of the middle ranks of men co-operating with the declared and active advocates of moderate reform.[29]

So here it was – the 'middle ranks', that is the social middle, implored to join with the 'advocates of moderate reform', that is the political middle, in order to prevent disastrous disintegration on both fronts. The flip-side of the same coin, in the

---

[27] Wyvill, *Political Papers*, vol. v, pp. 22–4: Wyvill to James Martin, 28 April 1792. This is the first appearance of 'middle-class' language in any form in Wyvill's published papers.

[28] Wyvill to P. Francis, 7 January 1795. Francis to Wyvill, 20 January 1795; ibid., vol. v, pp. 262–3, 281.

[29] Thomas Bigge, *Considerations on the State of Parties, and the Means of Effecting a Reconciliation between Them*, 2nd edn, London, 1793 or 1794, pp. 7, 31. The *Cambridge Intelligencer* 56, 9 August 1794, reprinted this plea for moderation in unusual length, obviously considering it to be significant.

words of one exasperated anti-war Whig in 1795, was that the disappearance of people like himself who were 'hardy enough to persevere in a [political] middle course' led people 'to see only two classes in the state, and those the rich, and the poor'; a situation that had been proven by experience as tending 'to destroy the influence of the middle ranks'. Once again, the fortunes of the political middle and the social middle (the latter, confusingly, both as a political presence and as a conceptual entity) appeared to be inextricably intertwined.[30]

Sad are these days, lamented another writer in 1796, in which country gentlemen lost 'that old and noble character, the jealous guardian of British freedom', which was the concomitant of 'true Whig principles'. Britain's only hope to counteract the harmful consequences of the 'contention from the opposing factions', he continued, 'is in the returning sense and reason of the country gentleman, and middle classes of society, which may influence the legislature to adopt the safe and enlightened policy, of removing the weight of the objections to our constitution by diminishing the truth of them'. The author of these words of moderation, who for reasons known only to himself chose not to publish them, was a then obscure country curate by the name of Thomas Malthus. They were salvaged from oblivion many years later by William Empson, Malthus's future friend and colleague. Empson understood well the political setting of Malthus's appeal to the social middle: 'His first object was, as a friend of freedom, to protest against Mr Pitt's administration. His second, as the friend of order and moderation, [was] to arbitrate between extreme parties.'[31]

Thus emphases on the social middle were directly coupled with non-radical opposition to the war. Sometimes this was stated explicitly: 'Many belonging to the higher ranks are inclined to involve the nation in a War; the middle and more numerous

---

[30] [Sir Robert Adair], *A Whig's Apology for His Consistency: In a Letter from a Member of Parliament to His Friend in the Borough of *****, London, 1795, pp. 21, 192, 194; and see his declaration of moderation in pp. 2–3.

[31] Malthus's unpublished pamphlet was titled 'The Crisis, a View of the Present Interesting State of Great Britain, by a Friend to the Constitution'. Empson published excerpts in the *Edinburgh Review* 64, January 1837 (quoted, p. 479). Compare this explicitly political use of 'middle class' language by Malthus in 1796 with his later works – see below, pp. 241ff.

classes appear as much disposed to Peace.'[32] At other times the 'middle class' was presented simply as an aggrieved victim of the unprecedented war effort. 'If we be forced to persist in this war,' contended the Cambridge scholar John Symonds in 1795 with the pro-war Arthur Young, 'the middle class of the people, of which you and I form a part, must be driven down to the lower.' In the words of the *Monthly Magazine*, when a momentous – and expensive – course of action such as the war was embarked upon, not only the lower classes bore the burden: 'By the middle classes, too, the load has been severely felt; and many conveniences, and many enjoyments, which formerly repaid their industry, and cheered their hours of leisure, are now beyond their reach.'[33] Indeed, it was probably in such contexts, of the financial burden and the economic distress caused by the war, that the language of 'middle class' was more prevalent in the 1790s than in any other. The crest of this wave was the unprecedented effusion of 'middle-class' language in the debate on the Triple Assessment Bill in 1797–8, which will preoccupy us in chapter 4.

The uses of notions of 'middle class' by the Friends of Peace, however, evolved into a much more powerful rhetoric. Their efforts to vindicate and assert their praiseworthy position as the political – and correspondingly the social – middle, pushed their language beyond the immediate exigencies of the anti-war argument to a broader and stronger eulogy of the moral and political virtues of the 'middle class'. Consequently, their prolific writings against the war were strewn with strong evaluative statements, carrying obvious prescriptive implications for the social and politi-

---

[32] *Short Hints to the People of England, upon the Duty of Petitioning against the Present War*, London, 1793, p. 6.

[33] Symonds to Young, 27 March 1795; in *The Autobiography of Arthur Young with Selections from His Correspondence*, ed. M. Betham-Edwards, London, 1898, p. 255. The *Monthly Magazine, and British Register, for 1796* 2, August 1796, p. 536. Similar examples, before their ubiquitous eruption in the winter of 1797, include: Thomas Beddoes, *Where Would Be the Harm of a Speedy Peace?*, London, [1795], p. 4. *Cambridge Intelligencer* 89, 28 March 1795, p. [2]; 186, 4 February 1797, p. [4]. *The Curses and Causes of War, Pointed Out: And the Approaching Cessation of Both Determined*, Spitalfields, 1795, p. [2]. *Analytical Review* 25, May 1797, p. 545. Also see *A Letter from a Member of Parliament to One of the People, upon the Fatal Consequences of the Present War*, 2nd edn, London, 1793, where the readers were urged to petition parliament for an end to 'this cruel and inglorious war', which is necessary 'if we wish to see the middle ranks of our fellow-citizens enjoying the full fruits of honest industry, [and] the lower ranks better fed and better taught' (pp. 17–18).

cal order. The resulting rhetoric, which I call here the 'middle-class idiom', emphasized the singular role of the 'middle class' as the repository of all virtues, the hinge which holds society and the social order together, the major prophylactic mechanism required for a healthy body social and body politic. It bears repeating that in the aftermath of the French Revolution, when the possibility of reconstructing the social order was perceived to be within reach, and when egalitarian impulses politicized social class, rhetoric such as the 'middle-class idiom', based on the evaluation and ranking of social classes, resonated with extraordinary power. This resonance, moreover, was qualitatively and quantitatively new: while praises for 'middle-class' virtues had of course been heard before, throughout most of the eighteenth century – before they became invested with a powerful charge by the specific political circumstances of the 1790s – their occasional utterance (as we shall see later in more detail) did not really move people, mobilize or enrage them, or otherwise significantly resonate with their political convictions.

The full potential of the 'middle-class idiom' in the 1790s can best be introduced through a detailed reading of two anti-war texts, from suitably representative moderate sources, in which it was particularly elaborate. One is the writings of Vicesimus Knox, an Anglican clergyman, once a fellow of St John's College in Oxford and later headmaster of Tonbridge School, who was a strong and vocal opponent of the war. In August 1793 he was already preaching in Brighton a highly politicized sermon on 'The Prospect of Perpetual and Universal Peace'. In the next couple of years he published translations of Erasmus's writings on peace, to which he added overtly political prefaces.[34] His major political work was *The Spirit of Despotism*, written in early 1795, which expanded the critique of the war into a broader condemnation of the aristocratic system of corruption and tyranny.[35] Some three years later, as the war dragged on, several

---

[34] *The Works of Vicesimus Knox, DD with a Biographical Preface*, 7 vols., London, 1824, vol. I, pp. i–xiv. For the Brighton sermon, see vol. VI, pp. 351–70.

[35] Knox later that year suppressed the publication of the book, since he believed that the French had turned from wronged victims to threatening aggressors, but the book reached the United States and was immediately reprinted in Philadelphia. The edition used here was published in Trenton in 1802, claiming on the title page: 'London: Printed in the Year 1795'. See R. Hole, *Pulpits, Politics and Public Order in England 1760–1832*, Cambridge, 1989, pp. 222–3.

Friends of Peace in Newcastle led by Thomas Bigge published a periodical devoted to ending the war, titled *The Oeconomist, or, Englishman's Magazine*. Needless to say, both sources, while strongly opposing the war and Pitt's administration, were also firmly opposed to what they saw as revolutionary principles; both exemplified, as Wyvill once said of Knox, 'the true spirit of moderation'.[36]

In both *The Oeconomist* and *The Spirit of Despotism* the 'middle-class idiom' played a central role. Knox entitled one of his chapters 'The Spirit of Truth, Liberty, and Virtue, public as well as private, chiefly to be found in the middle ranks of the people'. *The Oeconomist's* first issue, published during the furore provoked by Pitt's attempt to enrich the war finances through the controversial Triple Assessment Bill of December 1797, devoted much space to an essay 'On the Importance of the Middle Ranks of Society', a topic which at first glance might strike us as irrelevant to the periodical's political goals.[37] Both began by stating generally the virtues of the social middle (for whom both used the terms 'middle class', 'middle rank', 'middle order', 'middle station' interchangeably, but which neither ever chose to define):

It is certainly true, [affirmed Knox,] that the greatest instances of virtue and excellence of every kind have originated in the middle order. 'Give me neither poverty nor riches' was a prayer founded on a knowledge of human nature, and fully justified by experience. The middle station affords the best opportunities for improvement of mind, is the least exposed to temptation, and the most capable of happiness and virtue . . .

The education of the middle classes is infinitely better than the education of those who are called *great people*.[38]

And *The Oeconomist*:

in a community divided into RICH and POOR there can be no bold and enterprizing efforts, the fruits of free enquiry and generous competition

---

[36] Wyvill, *Political Papers*, vol. VI, p. 265: Wyvill to Knox, 20 November 1804, referring to a previous letter from Knox, sent in 1799. On *The Oeconomist* see Cookson, *The Friends of Peace*, pp. 93–5.

[37] *The Oeconomist* 1, January 1798, pp. 5–8 (all subsequent quotes are from this essay, unless stated otherwise).

[38] *The Spirit of Despotism*, pp. 152–3, 158–9. The verse quoted is from Agur's prayer, Proverbs xxx 8, which was often invoked to support the 'middle-class idiom'.

... a languor and impotence of mind prevail; the powers of thought are palsied. In the higher order, all is jealousy, insolence, and injustice; in the lower, all is ignorance, servility and dread ...

But where there is a MIDDLE ORDER of men, numerous, wealthy, and well-informed, society wears a different aspect.[39]

These were not only ruminations about the innocuous philosophical merits of the Golden Mean (which, of course, already had a long pedigree). They were the preamble to increasingly biting social and political criticisms:

Society in civilized countries [argued *The Oeconomist*] is usually divided into the rich, the middle class, and the lower order of the community. There have indeed been countries, where rich and poor were the only distinction. And in such countries it is unnecessary to observe, that the former were an oppressive aristocracy of lazy, luxurious, and effeminate tyrants, and the latter a mere herd of stupid and miserable slaves.

The middle ranks are the true barriers for defending the liberty and property of the common people, against the weight of the higher powers in every state.

Similarly, Knox found in them 'the best bulwark of liberty': 'They are a natural and most efficacious check on the strides of power ... The middle ranks have their native *freedom* to preserve; their birthright to protect from the dangerous attacks of enormous and overbearing affluence.'[40]

In following Knox's profuse writing, which had begun in the late 1770s, it becomes clear that the timing of these statements was also far from innocuous, but was directly linked to the political developments. Although Knox invoked here biblical and historical experience to prove the enduring truth of 'middle-class' virtues, this truth in fact had not impressed itself upon his writing before 1793, the very year of the commencement of the war. That year Knox published a manual of advice to young noblemen, which – despite predictable criticisms of prevalent aristocratic mores – could nevertheless be read as a rather conventional attempt to buttress and reinvigorate the social position of the aristocracy. Yet this intention was subverted by the only overtly political section of the book, the dedication to Charles James

---

[39] Compare also *The Oeconomist* 11, November 1798, p. 285, commending the 'golden *mediocrity* between wealth and poverty, in which we find the most exalted virtues ... between the vices of extreme poverty, and those of extreme riches'.

[40] *The Spirit of Despotism*, pp. 100–1.

Fox: there Knox commended Fox for his late behaviour in parliament, which manifested his personal nobility, proving his name to be 'higher than it ever yet stood, among independent Englishmen, IN THE MIDDLE RANKS, who neither enjoy nor expect the favours of ministerial influence.'[41] The irony of an emphasis on the political virtue of the 'middle ranks' as a consequence of their distance from the founts of power, placed on the introductory page to a manual for correcting the political virtue of aristocrats, could hardly have been lost on Knox's readers. They also could not have failed to notice that whereas noblemen in Knox's scheme of things could strive to attain high personal virtue (with the aid of such advice), the judgment of their merit was now placed in the hands of this innately virtuous 'middle class'; a power, moreover, that allowed them to elevate to the pinnacle of 'personal nobility' a man like Fox, despite his notoriety as a gambler and a rake. The message here, however, had still been subdued, intimated rather than stated; two years later, with no sign of an end to the war, Knox was spelling out what the 'middle class' meant for him in far more explicit terms.

The flip side of the linkage between the 'middle class' and liberty was the assertion that a dual social structure – consisting merely of rich and poor – tends to turn into oppressive tyranny. For *The Oeconomist* it was important to assert that such differing social structures were 'not a political invention, but the effect of the principles of human nature'. Knox – in a vein closer to the present argument – emphasized precisely the opposite, laying out the possibility of conceptualizing the same society within different social schemes, with correspondingly different political implications. He therefore contrasted his own deliberate focus on the merit of the 'middle class' with the current tendency of those alarmed by the French Revolution to focus only on the Manichean division between 'the great' and 'their inferiors' or the 'plebeians'. Knox insisted that such a dual perception of society, that characterized aristocrats and Tories, was a political factor in its own right, one favourable to despotism.[42] Paternalism,

---

[41] [Vicesimus Knox], *Personal Nobility: Or, Letters to a Young Nobleman, on the Conduct of His Studies, and the Dignity of the Peerage*, London, 1793, p. vi. See further the reference to 'the powerful and very numerous men of property and personal merit in the middle ranks' (p. 314; also 244).

[42] *The Spirit of Despotism*, pp. 115, 154.

therefore, benevolent as it might be, was in Knox's view inevitably a tyrannical expression of 'affected condescension' by the 'great man' towards his social inferiors, which allows him to deny any space to a 'middle class':

The middle rank of people, who reside in his vicinity, he takes no more notice of, than if they lived in the arctic or antarctic pole. He keeps them at a distance, because, though not so rich as himself, yet claiming and supporting the rank of *gentlemen*, they would be likely to approach too near.[43]

(Note in passing the appropriation of gentility by Knox's 'middle class', a point to which we shall return.)

This denial of the 'middle class' was not a mere issue of politeness, but one of power. Not only were aristocratically behaving persons in Knox's view 'insolent and neglectful to the middle ranks', they more ominously 'would not permit, if they could help it, the middle ranks to breathe the common air, or feel the genial sun'. Under such a despotic system,

such is the effect of political artifice, under the management of court sycophants, that the middle ranks of people are taught to believe, that they ought not to trouble themselves with affairs of state. They are taught to think that a certain set of men come into the world like demigods, possessed of right, power, and intellectual abilities, to rule the earth, as God rules the universe, without control . . . They are taught to believe, that they are to labor by the sweat of their brow to get money for the taxes; and when they have paid them, to go to work again for more, to pay the next demand without a murmur . . . The middle ranks are terrified into a tame and silent acquiescence.[44]

Knox repeated the warning against the dangers of despotism in his translation of Erasmus's writings on peace. Had despots triumphed, he wrote, 'the middle ranks, among whom chiefly resides learning, virtue, principle, truth, every thing estimable in society, would have been extinct'. Despotism can be thwarted only by 'the progress of knowledge in the middle ranks, and the prevalence of Christianity in the lowest'.[45] This was hardly a practical political programme. But in *The Spirit of Despotism* Knox

---

[43] Ibid., pp. 219–21.
[44] Ibid., pp. 97–8, 221–2.
[45] Knox, *Antipolemus: Or, the Plea of Reason, Religion, and Humanity against War* (translation of Erasmus's *Dulce bellum inexpertis*), 1795, preface; in *Works*, vol. v, p. 423.

was inching closer to making his 'middle-class idiom' into an agenda for political action: the 'middle ranks', he now suggested, 'possessing, in the aggregate, a vast property, and consequently, if they could act in concert, a vast power also', were therefore capable of filling 'a proud aristocracy' with 'uneasiness'.[46] The political potential or even threat underlying such an exhortation was only thinly veiled.

In *The Oeconomist*, three years deeper into the war, the veil was completely lifted. Echoing Knox's argument that governments inimical to liberty were also inimical to the 'middle class', striving 'to annihilate their importance, and to prevent their uniting', *The Oeconomist* now came back to the question of the war, its most immediate concern. Wars, it claimed, were a key measure in the hands of those intent on curbing liberty: they served this purpose by 'annihilating, by their vexatious expence, the middle orders of society, who are the natural supporters of national freedom'. War taxation – the issue which inflamed public debate at this very moment – was a burden placed almost exclusively on the 'middle class', 'devised to check their growing prosperity'. Through taxation, wars encroached upon 'those who had no voice in their commencement, no interest in their success, and no share in the administration of public affairs'. This indictment led *The Oeconomist* to conclude with an unusually forthright political programme for the 'middle class':

if the middle classes are not well informed, united, and full of public spirit, the design will generally succeed: they will be impoverished and oppressed; their importance will be gone; their union dissolved . . . To counteract effectually the dangerous designs of any particular order or faction in a state, it seems necessary that the middle classes should strive to procure for themselves (what is most justly their due) a decided weight in one branch of the legislature.

As a first practical measure the essay suggested the establishment of a body of 'middle-class' agents or trustees, to take care of their interests. So *The Oeconomist* linked the 'middle-class idiom' to an immediate agenda for reforming the political system; and in view of this fact, it is moreover significant that advertisements for this new periodical specified that it was 'particularly

---

[46] *The Spirit of Despotism*, p. 112.

addressed to the middle and inferior Classes of the Community'.[47]

The Oeconomist's final leap, to specific suggestions for amending the political system in favour of the 'middle class', was in fact quite extraordinary in the rhetoric of the Friends of Peace. And yet the spelling out of an explicit programme was not really necessary for the political potency of the 'middle-class idiom' to be evident. This potency was produced through an expansive web of similar enunciations: though only rarely as extensively detailed as in the writing of Vicesimus Knox or in *The Oeconomist*, such enunciations were repeated often enough to create the linguistic backdrop without which even these articulate examples could not have carried much resonance. That the charged political meanings of the language of 'middle class' were indeed reinforced persistently and frequently by other participants in the same political–linguistic milieu is easily demonstrable. Most common were the invocations of the plight of the 'middle class' during the war; not only as part of a more general concern for the effect of the war on commerce and manufacture, but as a specific concern for its detrimental effects on this especially valuable component of society. 'The enormous increase of taxes', deplored a letter to the anti-war *Argus*, has 'almost annihilated the middle classes, and set the poor at such a distance from the rich, that the real influence of this order of the state is very materially impaired.'[48] 'The enormous weight of taxes . . . has reduced the middling classes to a state of the most pitiable distress', warned a critic of Burke's bellicosity, and the consequences of this war policy for the future of British social relations would inevitably be disastrous.[49]

Several illustrations of how the 'middle-class idiom' became a leitmotif of anti-war literature will suffice. James Bicheno, for instance, was a well-to-do pro-peace Dissenting minister and schoolmaster who declared that 'the middle ranks of life, [were]

[47] For example in the *Newcastle Chronicle* 1746, 16 December 1797, p. [4].

[48] *The Argus: Or, General Observer: a Political Miscellany*, by Sampson Perry, London, 1796, p. 245 (i.e. 244): letter from 'Jean Jacques', 29 December 1795. See also the excerpt from a recent pamphlet in pp. 390–2, which stresses emphatically this predicament of the 'middling ranks' or 'middling class'. As for *The Argus*'s political position, see the 'Ode to Moderation' in p. 44.

[49] William Williams, *Rights of the People: Or, Reasons for a Regicide Peace ... with a Few Anticipating Strictures upon Mr Burke's Long Promised Letters Against a Regicide Peace*, London, 1796, p. 48; the disastrous consequences became evident through Williams's discussion of the example of France (p. 22).

where the greatest share of virtue and piety has ever been to be found', as long as they were not 'infected with the follies and vices of the two extremes'. William Burdon, an erstwhile fellow of Emmanuel College (Cambridge) and a wealthy coalmine owner, contrasted the rich and the poor, both deficient in education and proper principles, with 'the middle ranks of life' in which 'we find greater rectitude of conduct'; while warning elsewhere that the war might continue 'till the middle ranks are nearly annihilated' by its burdens. Or listen to *The Cabinet*, a periodical published by 'a Society of Gentlemen' in Norwich, that declared the war to be 'fatal to the social virtues and hostile to the liberties of man'. *The Cabinet* emphasized that 'the greatest quantity of happiness exists in a state of mediocrity', acknowledging the roots of this 'middle-class idiom' in philosophical thinking: 'The concurring voice of all nations and of all ages, of the philosopher, the poet, and the moralist, has pointed out these men as the happiest of the human race.' But it too turned this eternal philosophical dictum into a statement about the present: 'our only resource is to turn our eyes to those who form the middle rank of civil society', those who are 'not vitiated by luxury on the one hand, and not depressed by poverty on the other'.[50] Finally, this perfunctory survey can take us to the *Monthly Magazine*, another periodical committed to peace and moderate reform, which interpreted its own success as proof that

the cause of liberty is not in so deserted a state as some of its desponding friends have imagined; and that whatever may be the change in the sentiments of the higher classes, and the ignorant apathy of the lowest, the middle ranks, in whom the great mass of information, and of public and private virtue resides, are, by no means, disposed to resign the advantages of liberal discussion, and extensive enquiry.[51]

---

[50] J[ames] Bicheno, *A Word in Season: Or, a Call to the Inhabitants of Great Britain, to Stand Prepared for the Consequences of the Present War. Written on the Fast Day, Feb. 25, 1795,* London, 1795, p. 25. William Burdon, *A Few Words of Plain Truth, on the Subject of the Present Negotiation for Peace,* Cambridge, 1797, pp. 15–16. Idem, *Various Thoughts on Politics, Morality, and Literature,* Newcastle, 1800, pp. 76, 173, 177; and see pp. 157–8 for Burdon's celebration of the political middle. Also idem, *Materials for Thinking,* Newcastle, 1806 (but written 1801), p. 424. *The Cabinet. By a Society of Gentlemen,* Norwich, 1795, vol. I, p. iv; vol. III, pp. 285–6. This essay is signed 'Y', identified through a marked copy in the University of Michigan Library as John Pitchford; see Walter Graham, 'The Authorship of the Norwich *Cabinet,* 1794–5', *Notes and Queries* 162 (1932), pp. 294–5.

[51] *The Monthly Magazine, and British Register* 5, 1798, preface, p. [i]; signed 11 July 1798. See also the apolitical 'middle-class idiom' in pp. 410–11, in the issue of June 1798. The previous volume (4, p. 397; issue of November 1797) expressed the periodical's

The editor of the *Monthly Magazine* at this stage was John
Aikin, MD, an active Dissenting Friend of Peace, who already
in 1790 had addressed his coreligionists (upon the failure to
repeal the Test and Corporation Acts) as 'the most virtuous, the
most enlightened, the most independent part of the community,
the *middle class*', to whom the nation must be indebted for its
freedom and improvement. Indeed, the Dissenters among the
respectable opposition had an additional incentive to embrace
the 'middle-class idiom': after all, it was especially appealing as
a conceptualization of society that placed them at its centre
rather than on its margins. Consequently, some (though by no
means all) of the earlier political uses of the language of 'middle
class' were in the hand of Dissenters. As Aikin's sister, Anna
Barbauld, put it (also in 1790), such an understanding of society
would have made it possible for Dissenters to find themselves
'in that middle rank of life where industry and virtue most
abound', that is to say, 'among that class of the community
which has ever been the source of manners, of population and
of wealth'.[52]

So the anti-war rhetoric of the respectable opposition repeatedly
highlighted the existence of the 'middle class', its virtues, its
wisdom and its moderation, as well as its umbilical link to liberty.
But while such persistent statements obviously carried poignant
political ramifications, during the 1790s these were only rarely
drawn out and given the form of a specific 'middle-class' platform.
The oppression of the 'middle class' through wrongful policies
was a constant concern; restructuring the political system to give

concern for the burden of the war taxation 'upon the middle industrious classes of
citizens'. For other reiterations of the 'middle-class' grievance in the *Monthly Magazine*,
see above, p. 45; 6, p. 408, issue of December 1798; 7, pp. 5, 12, issue of January
1799.

[52] John Aikin, *An Address to the Dissidents of England on Their Late Defeat*, London, 1790,
p. 18. [Anna Laetitia Barbauld], *An Address to the Opposers of the Repeal of the Corporation
and Test Acts*, 2nd edn, London, 1790, p. 23. Barbauld too became an active opposer
of the war: see her *Sins of Government, Sins of the Nation: Or, a Discourse for the Fast,
Appointed on April 19, 1793. By a Volunteer*, 2nd edn, London, 1793. Some of these
Dissenting emphases on the 'middle class', notably in the early 1790s, have been
collected in Isaac Kramnick's *Republicanism and Bourgeois Radicalism: Political Ideology in
Late Eighteenth-Century England and America*, Ithaca, 1990; note in particular Joseph
Priestley's 'middle-class idiom', as cited in pp. 53 (dated 1791) and 61 (from his
memoirs to 1795, published in 1806). Kramnick also puts forward a few earlier
examples, but they are mostly quite distinct from those of the 1790s, in ways that
are discussed below.

the 'middle class' stronger influence over the making of policy was hardly ever so. This fact was all the more significant, first, in view of the reputation of many of the Friends of Peace as champions of parliamentary reform; second, in view of their continuing emphasis on the unjust burdens of taxation, an issue whose link to the nature of representation had only recently – during the American crisis – been at the very heart of the political debate;[53] and, finally, in view of what was to become later an almost automatic association, between the 'middle class' and parliamentary reform. In fact, there was nothing natural or inevitable about the move from a political awareness of 'middle-class' presence to demands for 'middle-class' representation: the logic for this particular coupling was to emerge within specific historical circumstances, which in the 1790s still lay far in the future.

Indeed, in a significant manner the specific circumstances of the 1790s constituted an *impediment* to such a move from the 'middle-class idiom' to proposals for parliamentary reform. In order to understand this we need to realize another, more specific sense in which the language of 'middle class' constituted a medium between two political extremes. The radicals after the French Revolution based their anti-aristocratic critique on the Painite language of natural rights, whose all-inclusive basis guaranteed that no social group was privileged over any other. The conservative reaction, on the other hand, emphasized exclusivity, that is the privileged position of the ruling class, those whom Burke famously described as the Corinthian capital of British society. Between these poles of undivided inclusiveness and sharp exclusiveness stood the 'middle-class idiom'. The ability of its proponents to walk this fine line, allowing for social preference but one which was nevertheless flexible and open-ended, was predicated on the fact that in terms of social signification the language of 'middle class' was *inherently vague*. Few of its proponents ever chose to define it or to specify its

---

[53] As Major Cartwright wrote to Wyvill on 10 December 1797, during the debate on the Triple Assessment Bill: 'The constitutional connexion of Representation and Taxation has never had so good an opportunity as the present, of taking hold of men's minds.' And yet, Cartwright's hopes notwithstanding, this was not the dominant framework in which the debates of the 1790s were formulated (Wyvill, *Political Papers*, vol. v, p. 377).

referents; and those that did turned out to have had quite different social groups in mind, from well-to-do merchants to lowly shop-keepers, from rural yeomen and gentry to urban tradesmen and even artisans. This vagueness was what allowed such speakers to talk about the merits of one component of society without sounding arrogantly restrictive. They managed to present an anti-aristocratic critique which did not embrace democracy as an alternative, but also did not replicate aristocratic elitism by substituting another clearly identifiable social group as the nation's natural leaders. Thus the vagueness of the language of 'middle class' was not merely some unthinking oversight or a consequence of incomplete development: the elasticity which it permitted was integral to the political function and efficacy of this language at this particular juncture. This inherent vagueness greatly increased the potential appeal of the language of 'middle class' as a basis for broad political mobilization, though it also restricted its potential uses in support of well-defined sectarian demands of certain well-defined constituencies.

Thus, even in the few exceptional cases where a specific politi-cal reform in favour of the 'middle class' had been suggested, such practical suggestions failed to resonate and elicit further discussion, in spite of the ceaseless enlisting of the 'middle-class idiom' for other oppositional goals. We have encountered one such exception in the practical political suggestions of *The Oecono-mist*. Another was the plea for 'Peace and Reform' by a self-proclaimed 'moderate', the Scotsman Daniel Stuart, secretary to the Friends of the People and printer (later owner) of the *Morning Post*. Going one step further than his political allies (he was also Mackintosh's brother-in-law), Stuart argued that 'as wisdom and independence prevail more certainly in the middling ranks, than in the whole mass of the people, the elective franchise, should, in my opinion, be confined to them'; an arrangement which would not fail to benefit also 'the poor, as well as the rich'.[54] On this point Stuart claimed the concurrence of a previous authority on reform, John Horne Tooke: 'I agree in opinion with Mr Tooke, that the middling class of society, should elect the

---

[54] [Daniel Stuart], *Peace and Reform, against War and Corruption. In Answer to a Pamphlet, Written by Arthur Young, Esq. Entitled, 'The Example of France, a Warning to Britain'*, London, 1794, pp. 96–7.

Members of Parliament.' Stuart cited Tooke's *Letter to Lord Ashburton* of 1782; but an examination of this earlier reform pamphlet is quite revealing. Tooke had indeed expounded in it quite similar arguments to Stuart's, but in fact he had *not* used the language of 'middle class' in formulating them at all, but only that of aristocracy versus the people.[55] For Tooke in 1782, the language of 'middle class' had not been germane to the issue of reform. But by Stuart's writing in 1794 the language of 'middle class' had assumed new political overtones, on which he was trying to capitalize; and he recast Tooke's language accordingly.

Parallel to the shift from Tooke to Stuart was the evolution of the political language of the person perhaps most famously associated with their respective causes, Christopher Wyvill himself. Wyvill's political reputation was established in the agitation for parliamentary reform in the 1780s: throughout that campaign Wyvill formulated its goals in the same terms as Tooke's – of aristocracy versus people – with occasional references to the venerable country gentlemen (as leading the people) thrown in for good measure. It was only in the early 1790s that notions of 'middle class' began to infiltrate Wyvill's writing, coupled with the emphasis on political moderation; for instance, when he assured Pitt in a public letter in 1793 that to the radical party 'not many of the middle station of life appear to belong'.[56] The same year also saw his first explicitly political use of 'middle-class idiom', in an argument against universal suffrage (one should not forget that these 'moderates' were avowedly *not* radicals): since the lower orders were 'submissive and venal', Wyvill wrote, universal suffrage 'would increase the preponderance of the Great', and thus 'destroy the salutary influence of those disinterested and independent Men, who are chiefly to be found in the middle classes of Mankind'. Limited parliamentary reform, on the other hand, would check 'the habits of corruption now

---

[55] Ibid., p. 98. [John] Horne [Tooke], *A Letter to Lord Ashburton, from Mr Horne, Occasioned by Last Tuesday's Debate in the House of Commons, on Mr Pitt's Motion*, London, 1782; esp. pp. 10–11, 36–7.

[56] Christopher Wyvill, *A Letter to the Right Hon. William Pitt*, 2nd edn, York, [1793], p. 8. On p. 9 the connection to the political middle was made more explicit, when Wyvill advocated 'that middle course by which the dangerous extremes of the rash Leveller and the unprincipled Supporter of every abuse may best be avoided'. And see above, n. 23, for the first occurrence of 'middle-class' language in his published writings.

prevalent alike in the highest and the lowest classes of Men'.[57] Subsequently 'middle-class' language became an integral part of Wyvill's rhetoric. Joining the chorus of the respectable opposition in 1797–8, he too lamented 'the general impoverishment of the middle classes'.[58] By the early 1800s, when – much to Wyvill's dismay – the peace of Amiens had collapsed and the war was renewed, he too – like Stuart – came to make the (yet unusual) step towards linking the 'middle class' with parliamentary reform: the electors choosing the Members of Parliament, he wrote, should be 'of the middle class ... which is at present least exposed to temptation, and least tainted with corruption'. At present, he added, the patriot's best grounds for hope were 'that by the superior integrity of the middle class the Nation may yet be saved from bondage'.[59]

But perhaps no evidence for the gradual transformation of Wyvill's language surpasses the following. In 1801 Wyvill wrote a letter discussing the relative distress of different parts of the community, formulating it within a language of 'interests' – the landed, trading and manufacturing interests. Four years later, however, when he edited his correspondence for publication, he added to this letter a note: 'It is an observation which has been often repeated, and as often admitted without a question, that wisdom and virtue are to be found in a greater proportion in the middle than in any other class of our People.' The triumph of the category of 'middle class' was completed – his later note recasting the pertinent social framework, overriding the division of interests as he had discussed it earlier. And there was more:

And it is almost as generally admitted that in the extensive and diversified range of that class, there is no body of men who from the advantages of education, their habits of life, and the usual independence

---

[57] Idem, *A State of the Representation of the People of England*, in *Political Papers*, vol. II, pp. 628–9.

[58] Idem, *The Secession from Parliament Vindicated*, 1798?; appended to *Political Papers*, vol. VI, p. 27. See also Wyvill to the Earl of Buchan, 27 June 1797 (vol. VI, p. 293); Wyvill to C. J. Fox, 29 January 1798 (vol. VI pt II, p. 20).

[59] Idem, 'Considerations on the Twofold Mode of Election Adopted by the French'; in appendix to his *Political Papers*, vol. V, pp. 442–3 (and see also pp. 438–9). Wyvill's concern here was that a two-stage election system might corrupt the hitherto virtuous 'middle class'.

of their situation, possess so strong a claim to the confidence of the Community in those respects as the Gentry of England.[60]

Quite a transformation. By this stage, not only did the category of 'middle class' displace the language of interests, it moreover subsumed the country gentry, for whom Wyvill had been a spokesman for so long. Without really changing his basic opinions, Wyvill's older social scheme (in which these opinions had been formulated before) was now superseded by a new one. And this new 'middle-class'-centred social scheme, of which Wyvill had been innocent merely fifteen years previously, was now presented as common knowledge, 'often repeated' and 'admitted without a question', to be taken for granted; indeed, as firm enough to allow for internal subdivisions (its 'diversified range') without in itself being endangered.

So how are we to understand these developments in the political language of the 1790s? Social historian Asa Briggs, who remarked upon them some twenty-five years ago in his pathbreaking attempt to trace the emergence of class language in England, provided a simple answer: 'beneath the flattery' which dominated such expressions of 'middle-class' language, he argued, 'was a keen awareness of social trends'. This was the venerable and familiar story: underlying social processes had produced changes in the social structure, changes which were then inevitably reflected in new patterns of language. But Briggs's findings did not quite accord with his presuppositions: expressing puzzlement, he noted that the invocations of 'middle-class' language before 1815 did not draw attention to 'common economic interests', as might have been expected from the central role which he had assigned to the social process in their generation. Instead, they focused first and foremost on 'the special role of the middle classes in society as a strategic and "progressive" group'.[61]

---

[60] Note (dated 28 April 1805) to a letter from Wyvill to William Strickland, 29 January 1801; in *Political Papers*, vol. VI, pp. 142–3. The note praised the mercantile and manufacturing classes for opposing the first war, and castigated the gentry for having failed to do so, since they had been duped by Pitt. Compare this proclamation of 'middle-class idiom' as universal common knowledge with a similar one made by Malthus in 1803: see below, p. 241. For a discussion of the language of 'interests' and its relationship with the language of 'middle class', see below, pp. 90ff.

[61] A. Briggs, 'The Language of "Class" in Early Nineteenth-Century England', in M. W. Flinn and T. C. Smout (eds.), *Essays in Social History*, Oxford, 1974, p. 160 (originally 1967).

Briggs, however, has failed to recognize the reason for this particularly benign representation of the 'middle class' in his sources of this period. Political historian John Cookson was the first to take notice of the very revealing fact that virtually all of Briggs's sources praising the 'middle class' at this period originated in the partisan – and biased – political circles of the Friends of Peace.[62] And yet Cookson modified only the purview of the argument, but not its logic: whereas for Briggs 'middle-class' language in the 1790s was a straightforward reflection of social reality, for Cookson it was a straightforward reflection of political reality – namely the strongly anti-war sentiments common to the 'middle class'. Neither historian has been concerned with the power of representation itself, with the use of language not to describe but to drive home a charged and contested point of view.[63] Neither approach allows for the range of possibilities in conceptualizing society, and for the choices involved in advancing one particular option over another. And yet it is precisely the logic and implications of such choices which can explain the potency of the 'middle-class' language at this particular juncture, its specific political guise, its limits, its abrupt appearance, and, indeed – as we shall see shortly – its no less abrupt subsequent disappearance. Moreover, it is the very fact that such a pattern of linguistic use was *not* the natural and inevitable outcome of some pre-formed social or political map, but instead the cumulative aggregate of charged choices made repeatedly by persons sharing certain views and beliefs, which makes it so meaningful for the historian.

VIRTUE, COMMERCE AND HISTORY: THE LEGACIES OF THE EIGHTEENTH CENTURY

The incorporation of the virtuous gentry into the 'middle class', it has been suggested, was a new and even surprising departure in Wyvill's social vocabulary. But surely this was not the whole

---

[62] Ibid., pp. 160–1. An earlier version of Briggs's argument, using similar examples, was his 'Middle-Class Consciousness in English Politics, 1780–1846', *Past and Present* 9 (1956), esp. pp. 68–9; Cookson (*Friends of Peace*, pp. 271–2, n. 54) has pointed to the anti-war bias in the sources used by Briggs in this essay.

[63] Cookson has since discovered that many – perhaps most – of the middle strata of society in fact supported the war, though he has not followed up on the implications of this finding for his earlier argument: see below, pp. 97–8.

story: after all, his representation of the gentry of England as peculiarly prepared for leadership by their education, their leisured life and – crucially – their independence, was hardly a new breakthrough in English political rhetoric. Neither did Malthus's appeal to country gentlemen, to redeem their 'old and noble character' by reverting to 'true Whig principles', impart a real sense of freshness. And insofar as the 'middle-class idiom' is concerned, had not Robinson Crusoe's father already told his son that he should strive to attain 'the middle state', which was 'the best state in the world, the most suited to human happiness'?[64] The discussion of the uses of 'middle-class' language in the 1790s, then, begs the question, what was in fact new and different about it? There are two distinct issues here: the broader relationship between this language of the 1790s and previous oppositional rhetorics; and its more specific relationship to previous occurrences of the notion of the virtuous 'middle class'.

In appealing to the virtues of landed gentlemen, both Wyvill and Malthus were invoking images which resonated with that powerful oppositional rhetoric of the eighteenth century familiar to historians either simply as 'country ideology' or as a 'neo-Harringtonian' derivative of classical republicanism.[65] Central to this rhetoric was the ancient agrarian ideal of the small independent landed proprietor as the bearer of civic virtue. This gentleman's land, so went this image, guaranteed his manly independence, his possibility of unspecialized leisure and hence his potential for virtue. The pristine versions of country ideology contrasted this landed gentleman with those people involved in networks of dependence and patronage that had been created through exchange relationships (that is, the market) and fuelled by the fortunes of the 'monied interest', and that were the main support of the system of corruption upholding the Whig establishment and the Court.[66] To be sure, later adaptations of

---

[64] Daniel Defoe, *Robinson Crusoe* (originally 1719), ed. A. Ross, Harmondsworth, 1985, p. 28.

[65] The latter of course refers to the work of J. G. A. Pocock: see his *The Machiavellian Moment: Florentine Political Thought and the Atlantic Republican Tradition*, Princeton, 1975. For an account of 'country ideology', similar to Pocock's in its actual contents, see H. T. Dickinson, *Liberty and Property*, London, 1977, chapter 5.

[66] J. G. A. Pocock, *Virtue, Commerce, and History*, Cambridge, 1985, pp. 48–9, 109–10. Idem, 'Cambridge Paradigms and Scotch Philosophers: A Study of the Relations between the Civic Humanist and the Civil Jurisprudential Interpretation of Eighteenth-

this cluster of ideas – to which the epithet 'ideology' imputes the coherence of a comprehensive system of thought which it did not necessarily have – did not always remain as steeped in agrarian nostalgia.[67] In the hands of some speakers, different elements of this rhetoric were reconciled with commercial society and with non-landed forms of property. But it was nevertheless a landed logic that remained at the core of this country rhetoric; its representations of virtue and independence were therefore potentially in tension with the celebrations of commercial society that proliferated throughout the century. As a consequence, ever since the financial and political revolutions of the 1690s, this land-based 'neo-Harringtonian' ideal had informed the critique of the commerce-based oligarchic power of the Whigs. The most recent revival of such rhetoric was in the agitation for reform in the early 1780s instigated by the landed gentlemen of the Yorkshire Association, led by none other than Christopher Wyvill himself.[68]

Now it is indubitable that elements of this familiar and influential oppositional idiom reappeared, somewhat haphazardly, in the 'middle-class' language of the 1790s: notions of courtly influence, seeping corruption, polluting luxury, aristocratic encroachments on liberty, effeminate tyranny and the importance of independence. Certain statements resembled well rehearsed eighteenth-century formulations, with the 'middle class' simply replacing or incorporating the landed gentlemen.[69] And yet the 'middle-class

Century Social Thought', in I. Hont and M. Ignatieff (eds.), *Wealth and Virtue*, Cambridge, 1983, pp. 236–7.

[67] This formulation is that of Isaac Kramnick in his *Bolingbroke and His Circle: The Politics of Nostalgia in the Age of Walpole*, Cambridge, Mass., 1968.

[68] Pocock, *Machiavellian Moment*, p. 547. Dickinson, *Liberty and Property*, p. 225. I. R. Christie, *Wilkes, Wyvill and Reform: The Parliamentary Reform Movement in British Politics 1760–1785*, London, 1962. E. C. Black, *The Association: British Extraparliamentary Political Organization 1769–1793*, Cambridge, Mass., 1963. The Association was predominantly concerned with increasing the representation of lesser county landowners.

[69] In addition to those already cited, see the political hopes which George Edwards, a prolific and eccentric anti-war reformer of moderate views, placed 'in the middle stations of life', by which he meant in particular those who lived in the country and were least affected by the pernicious metropolis: George Edwards, *No. 3: Or Compendium of a Design for Rectifying Public Affairs, Consummating Our Civil and Political Interests, and Introducing Parliamentary Reform at the Present Awful Period*, [London], 1803?, p. 5. Also compare the 1793 address of the Friend of Peace Colonel Norman McLeod to his constituents as 'the middle order of Landholders in Scotland': *Two Letters from Norman M'Leod, Esq. MP to the Chairman of the Friends of the People at Edinburgh*, Edinburgh, 1793, p. 12.

idiom' was at the same time also different in crucial ways. Most obviously, it was not based on the primacy of land and the landed classes. But no less importantly, as has already been noted, it also did not merely replace this emphasis on land with the primacy of any other social group, defined through either property or occupation. Instead, the 'middle-class idiom' was inherently vague, loose and inclusive. Its attribution of a beneficial role to the social middle was justified by general political and philosophical truisms rather than by peculiar traits resulting from their particular professions or forms of property. So whereas landowners could still be included in the valuable 'middle class', this very possibility was in itself also an indication of the fact that the principles on which its group identity was founded had been fundamentally altered.

This new departure merits further attention in view of the road *not* taken by the proponents of the 'middle class'. One move which they did not make – historians' retrospective constructions notwithstanding – was to simply substitute commerce for land as the fount of all virtues, and the commercial classes for the landed classes as their repository. Indeed, throughout the 1790s there was nothing inherently commercial – or urban – in the conceptualization of a 'middle class'. Most significantly, the 'middle-class idiom' owed precious little to the elaborate justifications of commercial society which had been developed during the eighteenth century in dialogue with the 'country' critique. The extolled virtues of the 'middle class' were only rarely presented as emanating from Montesquieu's *doux commerce*, or from the Addisonian confidence in the power of commerce to refine manners and to cultivate sociability, or from the Scottish four-stage model of history which presented commercial society as the most advanced social form. They were not even justified with the aid of Hume's much earlier association of the 'middle class' with 'progress in the arts': 'where luxury nourishes commerce and industry', Hume had written in 1752, it brings 'authority and consideration to that middling rank of men, who are the best and firmest basis of public liberty'.[70] Hume – though himself not

---

[70] David Hume, 'On Refinement in the Arts', in *Essays: Moral, Political, and Literary*, ed. E. F. Miller, Indianapolis, 1987, p. 277 (originally published in 1752 under the title 'Of Luxury'). On eighteenth-century justifications of commerce, see A. O. Hirschman, *The Passions and the Interests: Political Arguments for Capitalism before Its Triumph*, Princeton,

the first to have said so[71] – had thus pointed to the vision of
the 'middle class' which a century later was to become the
predominant one, linking it with the recent and powerful social
transformations involved in the making of a commercial society.
But his cue was not followed by the proponents of the 'middle
class' in the 1790s: in the debate between 'ancients' and 'mod-
erns', these speakers – invoking as they did the timeless authority
of ancient philosophy to prove their point – seem to have fallen
more comfortably with the former camp than with the latter.
With regard to the nostalgic postulation of a golden age in the
distant past, the language of 'middle class' exhibited more continuity with the country ideologues of the eighteenth century than
an affinity with the more familiar nineteenth-century image of
the 'middle class', centred on social change.

Indeed, it was not only the Friends of Peace at the end of the
century who failed to take much notice of Hume's 'middle-class
idiom'. To take one other obvious example, neither did Adam
Smith, whose sparse and vague references to the 'middling rank'
notoriously lacked any political message and significance.[72] View-
ing the eighteenth century as a whole, the more surprising fact
is not that such an opinion as Hume's or Bishop Butler's was
expressed – after all, the idea of the virtuous social middle had
hardly been unfamiliar, going back as far as Aristotle's *Politics* –

1977 (as Hirschman points out, the phrase *le doux commerce* in fact preceded
Montesquieu). Also Pocock, *Virtue, Commerce, and History*, pp. 48–50, 114–15. The
justifications of commerce which are relevant here are not its vindications à la Mande-
ville, applauding its beneficial effects on society as a whole in spite of its baneful ones
on individuals; but those which claimed beneficial effects of commerce on the individual
directly. For a transitional example of the early 1790s, which did combine 'middle-class
idiom' with the virtues of commerce, see Mackintosh above, pp. 22–4.

[71] Compare for example the sermon which Bishop Butler preached in 1740 before the
Lord Mayor and Aldermen of London: 'The improvement of Trade and Commerce
has made another Change ... and I think a very happy one, in the State of the
World, as it has enlarged the middle Rank of People: many of which are, in good
Measure, free from the Vices of the highest and the lowest Part of Mankind.' Joseph
Butler, *Fifteen Sermons Preached at the Rolls Chapel upon the Following Subjects ... To Which
Are Added, Six Sermons Preached on Publick Occasions*, 4th edn, London, 1749, pp. 349–
50; see also p. 472. For yet much earlier uses of 'middle-class idiom', see below, p. 68.

[72] See D. Winch, *Adam Smith's Politics: An Essay in Historiographic Revision*, Cambridge,
1978, pp. 99–102. For the retrospective rewriting of Adam Smith as celebrating the
rising middle classes and their political power, which Winch shows to be unsubstan-
tiated by Smith's writings, see for example D. A. Reisman, *Adam Smith's Sociological
Economics*, London, 1976, pp. 93, 100, 194. Another case in point was John Millar, in
whose writing – contrary to some later readings of it – the 'middle class' did not play
a significant role: see below, p. 238, note 23.

but how feeble and transient were its echoes. Indeed, even for Hume himself we may doubt the centrality of this statement or the sustained conviction behind it: as Duncan Forbes has pointed out, this was one issue on which Hume's thinking was notably inconsistent, having only a decade earlier characterized 'the middling Rank' as consisting of those most susceptible to adhere to mistaken political principles.[73]

But more importantly, the very availability in the eighteenth century of scattered statements prefiguring the 'middle-class idiom' underscores the fact that they were *not* effectively followed upon by contemporaries and incorporated into their considerations of politics. In their most common eighteenth-century form, such statements surfaced in the writings of moralists and essayists, extrapolating the ancient philosophical principle of the Golden Mean to the importance of the 'middle station' for the happiness and virtue of the individual. Even before Defoe's Crusoe, Addison's *Spectator* had already asserted (in 1712) that 'the middle Condition seems to be the most advantageously situated for the gaining of Wisdom' and for a man's improved virtue. Hume too wrote an essay 'Of the Middle Station in Life' in a similar vein, as non-sociological philosophical truth.[74] As Richard Price put it in 1784, the 'happiest state of man is in the middle state between the *savage* and the *refined*, or between the wild and the luxurious state'.[75] Such appreciations of the 'middle station', focusing on its consequences for the individual rather than for a collective

---

[73] Hume was explaining in 1741 the disappearance of Jacobitism from Scotland by the relative deficiency of its 'middling rank': unlike the poor who lack political principles, and the gentlemen who have the time and experience to form correct ones, 'The Middling Rank of Men have Curiosity and Knowledge enough to form Principles, but not enough to form true ones, or correct any Prejudices ... And 'tis among the middling Rank, that TORY Principles do at present prevail most in ENGLAND.' This passage was naturally withdrawn from post-1745 editions. See 'Of the Parties of Great Britain'; in *Essays*, p. 616. D. Forbes, *Hume's Philosophical Politics*, Cambridge, 1985, pp. 94, 176–9; also pp. 276, 300.

[74] *The Spectator*, ed. Donald F. Bond, Oxford, 1965, vol. v, p. 139: 464, 22 August 1712. Hume, *Essays*, pp. 545–51 (originally written in 1742, and withdrawn from later editions).

[75] Richard Price, *Observations on the Importance of the American Revolution, and the Means of Making It a Benefit to the World*, Boston, 1784 (printed in London, same year), p. 57; Price saw this as the general state of American society, of which one example was Connecticut's 'independent and hardy YEOMANRY'. See also Benjamin Franklin's reference to the 'general happy Mediocrity' between rich and poor in his *Information to Those Who Would Remove to America* (1782); in B. Franklin, *The Autobiography and Other Writings*, ed. K. Silverman, New York, 1986, p. 239.

group, had in themselves little political potential, without being carried one step further. And indeed occasionally we can find speakers who had taken this additional step, like Oliver Gold-smith's Vicar of Wakefield who referred to the 'middle order of mankind' not only as the locus of 'all the arts, wisdom, and virtues of society', but also as 'the true preserver of freedom, [that] may be called the People.' It is hardly surprising that in more than a century of vigorous political writing, such uses of directly political 'middle-class' language were tried out. Thus the *Protester* of 9 June 1753 argued that in times of crisis 'the most solid resource ... would be in a Gentry, the liberal professions, the whole mercantile interest and, in short, all who had any Pretense to be comprehended in the middle rank of the people'.[76] A few years later William Beckford delivered an oft-quoted speech in the House of Commons: by 'the sense of the people', he declared, 'I mean the middling people of England, the manufac-turer, the yeoman, the merchant, the country gentleman.'[77]

Yet the crucial point here is the isolation and the ephemeral presence of these utterances. Prior to the French Revolution, there seems to have been no political moment in which their potential was seized upon in a persistent and effective manner: they remained sporadic and evanescent, not charged repeatedly with potent implications serving contested agendas. This remained true even at key moments of political confrontation such as the Wilkes agitation, which is often presented as an important 'middle-class' intervention in eighteenth-century politics. It thus seems a particu-larly significant fact that when John Brewer has wished to demon-strate the 'middle class' (or 'bourgeois') nature of the Wilkites, he had to resort to ingenious anthropological and circumstantial methods of proof for this point on which his sources were virtually silent. Indeed Brewer was directly confronted with what he per-ceived as a puzzle, namely the continuity of a political language

---

[76] Oliver Goldsmith, *The Vicar of Wakefield* (originally 1766); in *Collected Works of Oliver Goldsmith*, ed. A. Friedman, Oxford, 1960, vol. IV, pp. 101–2. The *Protester* is quoted in N. Rogers, *Whigs and Cities: Popular Politics in the Age of Walpole and Pitt*, Oxford, 1989, pp. 129 and again 251 n. 72; Rogers's repetition of this same quote twice may indicate that he has found it not only uncommonly interesting, but also interestingly uncommon.

[77] Speech of 13 November 1761; quoted in L. Sutherland, 'The City of London in Eighteenth-Century Politics', in R. Pares and A. J. P. Taylor (eds.), *Essays Presented to Sir Lewis Namier*, London, 1956, p. 66.

of landed wealth in what he took to be a political movement of the 'middling ranks of society'.[78] Now it is hard to imagine that historians have collectively missed crucial moments of powerful uses of 'middle-class' language: if anything, they are much more likely to err on the side of overemphasizing such utterances rather than on that of ignoring them. Paul Langford, for one, has searched widely for eighteenth-century sources discussing the 'middle class'. Judging from the examples he has found, he has concluded that during the eighteenth century the 'faith in middle-class merit was an almost unchallengeable platitude'.[79] We may turn to Langford's own argument, a more placid restatement of E. P. Thompson's familiar vision of the eighteenth-century patricians, in order to explain this observation: in a period when propertied Englishmen were closing ranks and becoming indistinguishable from one another, the occasional 'middle-class idiom' did not arouse passionate dispute because it lacked political charge and did not involve high stakes. Without a web of similar enunciations against which to resonate, such disparate utterances simply fell flat. The circumstances of the 1790s dramatically changed all that. As the following will make abundantly clear, one thing which without doubt cannot be said of the 'middle-class idiom' during the 1790s is that it was 'an almost unchallengeable platitude'. It was the persistence in enlisting the language of 'middle class' repeatedly to support a highly loaded political position that was the crucial new departure of that decade: a new departure not in the conception of a new idea, but in its unprecedented *use*.[80]

---

[78] J. Brewer, 'English Radicalism in the Age of George III', in J. G. A. Pocock (ed.), *Three British Revolutions: 1641, 1688, 1776*, Princeton, 1980, pp. 323–67 (quoted, p. 332). The anthropological approach is most evident in his 'The Number 45: A Wilkite Political Symbol', in S. B. Baxter (ed.), *England's Rise to Greatness, 1660–1763*, Berkeley, 1983, pp. 349–80, where Wilkite symbolism is interpreted as signs of 'a bourgeois mentality' (p. 374). See also idem, 'Commercialization and Politics', in N. McKendrick, J. Brewer and J. H. Plumb, *The Birth of a Consumer Society*, Bloomington, 1982, pp. 197–262.

[79] Langford, *Public Life and the Propertied Englishman*, pp. 477–9; also pp. 365–6.

[80] A modification in the chronology of this account may be required by further study of the debate on the American war. In the 1770s, in circumstances somewhat comparable to those of the debate on the French wars, a similar logic may have generated a certain surge in political uses of 'middle-class' language prefiguring that of the 1790s, manifested in utterances such as those in note 75 above. Such a finding would not affect the basic argument made here, but would simply add another proto-peak to its uneven unfolding over time. Other such possible indications include [William Johnston Temple], *Moral and Historical Memoirs*, London, 1779, p. 36 (written in 1775–6, and referring to the American crisis). *London Magazine* 1774, pp. 412, 568; 1775, p. 272. *Morning Post* 1 March 1775 (I owe this reference to Donna Andrew). William Keate,

To push the argument further, consider briefly the following statements:

The King's cause and party were favored by the two extreames in the city; the one the wealthy and powerful men, the other of the basest and lowest sort, but [it was] disgusted by the middle ranke, the true and best citizens.

The middle sort of people of England ... will especially oppose [political] change as whereby they from being in the happiest condition of any of their rank perhaps in Europe, nay in the world ... might well be reduced to the terms of the peasants of France.

As the wording and the spelling of these passages reveal, they belong to a former era of political language. In fact, they were both written as early as the 1640s: during the English civil war, it turns out, such utterances were far from unusual. One can find at that juncture the familiar complaints against 'a disproportion' in taxation, which discriminated against 'the middle sort [who] must and shall pay'; as well as the formulations of the 'middle-class idiom', asserting for example that one of the 'most mischievous principles of tyranny ... that ever were invented ... is to disarm the middle sort of people, who are the body of the kingdom'.[81] Rather than evidence of a 'bourgeois revolution' (which historians have found to be as inadequate a depiction of the English revolution of the seventeenth century as it is of the French Revolution of the eighteenth), these utterances may be taken as further indications for the political underpinnings of the uses of such language. The basic notions of the 'middle-class idiom' were already there, a century and a half before the period discussed here: and it was a specific radicalized political situation, rather than some critical mass of social change, which compelled a number of speakers to make use of them. Moreover, the many decades of 'platitude' in the uses of this language between the

---

A Sermon Preached upon the Occasion of the General Thanksgiving, for the Late Peace, July 29th, 1784, Bath, 1784, p. 24.

[81] John Corbet, *An Historicall Relation of the Military Government of Gloucester*, [1645]; *A Soveraigne Salve to Cure the Blind*, 1643; *Considerations Touching Trade*, 1641; Edward Husbands, *An Exact Collection*, 1642. Cited in B. Manning, *The English People and the English Revolution*, Harmondsworth, 1978, pp. 173, 256, 262; and see his numerous additional examples, esp. in pp. 170–80, 254–65. Corbet is quoted in R. Howell, 'The Structure of Urban Politics in the English Civil War', *Albion* 11 (1979), p. 115 n. 14; and note additional sources there. See also the discussion in K. Wrightson, 'Estates, Degrees, and Sorts: Changing Perceptions of Society in Tudor and Stuart England', in P. J. Corfield (ed.), *Language, History and Class*, Oxford, 1991, pp. 49–50.

English civil war and the late eighteenth century should warn us once again against a simple picture of linear progression.

The Friends of Peace of the 1790s may well have been unaware of the uses to which the language of 'middle class' had been put a hundred and fifty years earlier; but it is likely that a certain familiarity with some more recent eighteenth-century precedents indeed rendered this particular rhetorical strategy more appealing to them in vindicating their besieged politics. And they were able to appropriate it as they did precisely because these precedents were platitudinous, so that the notion of 'middle class' arrived at the last decade of the century unencumbered by any specific political overtones. Moreover, the former uses of this language were also of little aid – or little hindrance – in endowing it with any clear *social* signification. Its scattered uses during the eighteenth century had been no more specific in social terms than those of the 1790s: it had stood for rural as much as for urban people – as in William Guthrie's depiction of the 'middling rank of the English' as the keepers of pastoral non-urban England, no less, 'liv[ing] at a distance from the vices and hurry of great cities'; and for gentry as much as for mercantile people, as in the country rhetoric of Thomas Blackwell, who capped his expression of admiration for a 'middle Order', untainted with the vices of both upper and lower, with the proud declaration: 'Such are the Gentry in *Great Britain*.'[82]

So, to the extent that the new uses of the 'middle-class' language after the French Revolution bore some relationship to these scattered earlier utterances, they inherited their social as well as their political vagueness – which, it bears repeating, was crucial for the mediating yet oppositional political message with which

[82] William Guthrie, *History of England*, 1744; quoted in Forbes, *Hume's Philosophical Politics*, p. 176, n. 1; p. 257. Thomas Blackwell, *Memoirs of the Court of Augustus*, Edinburgh, 1753, vol. I, p. 73. Interestingly, Blackwell saw the equestrian order of the Romans as another such example of this obviously perennial truth. Compare also John Brown's vision of society, composed of nobility, people and populace. By 'the People' he meant the county electors (which, he specified, included not only gentry, country clergy and yeomen, but also notable merchants), who 'possess a *middle* State of Life'. Less susceptible to 'those Temptations that surround the *higher* and the *lower* Ranks', their role as 'the firmest *Bulwark* of BRITAIN's *Freedom*' was guaranteed by their situation; an important element in which, he added, was 'their *Dispersion*, and rural Life'. John Brown, *Thoughts on Civil Liberty, on Licentiousness, and Faction*, Newcastle upon Tyne, 1765, pp. 87, 111–15. For the referential vagueness of the language of 'middle class' in Hume's writings, see Forbes, *Hume's Philosophical Politics*, pp. 176–9.

it was infused in the 1790s. Moreover, this vagueness was also important in allowing for the piecemeal appropriation of the legacy of country ideology, which has been pointed out above. It was one thing for the proponents of the 'middle class' to choose not to make use of prevalent defences of commerce. It was rather another thing to actively employ formulations derived from a rhetoric which was manifestly in deep – even if not insurmountable – tension with commerce. Take for example James Bicheno, who in the same anti-war exhortation in which he applauded the virtuous and pious 'middle class' also railed against 'this passion for commerce, this avidity after wealth, as a mean for the gratification of our pride and luxury', which unfortunately may have become 'the all-inspiring spirit which pervades and animates this nation'.[83] Considering the role which commerce and trade must have played in the lives of many of the Friends of Peace (Bicheno's most likely audience), it was only the fact that their specific vocational and professional identities were *not* immediately implicated in the uses of the language of 'middle class' that allowed for such borrowing from country ideology to persist and remain effective. Once again the vagueness of the 'middle-class' language proved to have been intrinsic to its political use.

And yet the tension with the landed elements of the country ideology was not always easily smoothed out; at times it emerged closer to the surface, undermining the rhetoric focused on the 'middle class'. Let us take for example a second look at Vicesimus Knox's *Spirit of Despotism*. One could probably still reconcile Knox's confident 'middle-class idiom' with his no less confident statement that 'the independent country gentleman, seconded by the people, is the character, on whom liberty must rely'. But such accommodation became more difficult when Knox pushed this 'country' strand further: 'In nations enriched by commerce', he also wrote, 'and among families loaded with opulence by the avarice of their forefathers, the mere wantonness of unbound plenty will occasion a corruption of manners, dangerous to all that renders society happy.' From this antithesis of commerce and virtue Knox then drew conclusions regarding the distribution of corruption in society: 'Corruption does not operate, in the

---

[83] Bicheno, *A Word in Season*, p. 36.

increase of the despotic spirit, on the highest orders only, and the aspirants at political distinction and consequence, but also on the crowded ranks of commercial life.'[84] Now juxtapose these passages, obviously akin to eighteenth-century oppositional language, with another, in which Knox evaluated the effectiveness of 'the sun of tory favor'. While it shone radiantly on men who acquire princely fortunes such as nabobs, he asserted here, it did *not* reach 'the millions of humbler adventurers in commerce and manufacture, who are enriching their country, and accommodating human life, in ten thousand modes', and who are 'viewed by the promoters of arbitrary power with sovereign contempt'. This passage continued: 'The truth is, that most of these ... are some of the most independent members of the community. They constitute a very large portion of the middle rank. They are a firm phalanx, and commonly enlisted on the side of liberty.'[85] No easy manoeuvring can square this 'middle-class idiom', praising the 'crowded ranks of commercial [and manufacturing] life' as the bulwarks of liberty, with their former representation as the prey of corruption. In such moments the uneasy alliance between country ideology and the 'middle-class idiom' was certainly wearing thin.

It was not only the critical sensibilities *vis à vis* commerce which could be problematic for the proponents of the 'middle class' in the heritage of the eighteenth-century opposition. Another obviously problematic element was the often exclusive nature of the virtues associated with land, which collided with the inherently looser and more inclusive rhetoric of the 'middle class'. Thus, *The Oeconomist*'s panegyrics to the 'middle class' could be readily reconciled – indeed reinforced – with its recommendation to men of 'moderate fortunes' to choose farming as 'the most liberal, useful, and independent' occupation, and thus, by 'preserving a middle station between the highest and the lowest ranks of society', to become 'an insuperable barrier against every attempt of despotism on one hand, or of anarchy on the other'. But it is difficult to see how its 'middle-class idiom' was commensurate with the following:

---

[84] Knox, *Spirit of Despotism*, pp. 27, 37–8, 40. See also the praise for the yeomanry as key to the preservation of liberty on p. 118. And see above, p. 50, for another use of gentility in his writing.
[85] Ibid., pp. 111–12.

How infinitely superior is the profession of a farmer to that of men who, with much larger capitals, condemn themselves to the drudgery and degradation of retail trade! . . . his emoluments are derived from supplying the universal and necessary wants of the community; not ministering to the caprice or luxury of pampered individuals . . . and on all occasions, where public or private spirit prompts him to act, he feels the manly dignity of Independence.[86]

The difficulty was not in the praise for the proprietor-farmer in itself, but in the grounding of his usefulness, dignity and independence in the quintessential and exclusive traits of his particular occupation. Indeed, it was no coincidence that similar formulations, placing exclusive primacy and emphasis on the virtues derived from land, often found their way into the rhetoric marshalled by the opponents of the Friends of Peace to *counter* the implications of the 'middle-class idiom', as we shall see in the following chapter.

In sum, the relationship between the 'middle-class' language of the 1790s and the political rhetorics of the eighteenth century was a complex one. Some elements its proponents appropriated and reproduced; others they invested with potent political meaning where previously it had been lacking; while yet others they similarly divested of previously crucial implications. None of this of course was deliberate or coordinated: it was rather a haphazard accumulation of trials and errors, judged by the yardstick of rhetorical efficacy in a time of unprecedented political circumstances, and inevitably breeding tensions and contradictions in the process. Overall, then, it would seem that John Pocock has confused matters, or at least oversimplified them, when he has presented the anti-war proponents of the 'middle class' in the 1790s simply as the descendants of the 'neo-Harringtonians'. According to Pocock, they inherited 'precisely the same language' of the earlier country ideologues and used it 'for precisely the same independence and virtue as opposed to corruption'.[87] In

---

[86] *The Oeconomist* 6, June 1798, pp. 148–50 (and see also pp. 31, 62); 9, September 1798, p. 238.

[87] Pocock, 'Varieties of Whiggism', in his *Virtue, Commerce, and History*, p. 287. Pocock repeatedly resists the possible new implications of the language of 'middle class' – not only because of his disposition to establish long-term 'neo-Harringtonian' continuities, but also because of his consistent denial of any development which might give credence to a Marxist notion of a 'rising bourgeoisie': see similarly below, pp. 149 note 10 and 375.

fact, the political uses and implications of the language of 'middle class' in the 1790s, while exhibiting certain continuities with past political rhetoric, were in essence something quite new. New, however, does not necessarily imply 'modern', as the relationship of the 'middle-class idiom' of the 1790s to commerce and to historical progress (or rather the absence of such a relationship) makes very clear. However new these uses of 'middle-class' language were, they surely were *not* a first step in some inevitable and inexorable progression towards that image of the rising 'middle class' so favoured by historians, an image of a novel social group conjured up from pre-industrial society by the magical power of unprecedented social transformations.

CHAPTER 3

Friends and foes of the 'middle class': the dialogic imagination

THE TWO NATIONS: THE VIEW FROM BELOW

[The French National Assembly represented] the majority of that middle rank among whom almost all the sense and virtue of society reside.

There never was, or will be, in civilized society, but two grand interests, that of the RICH and that of the POOR. The differences of interest among the several classes of the rich will be ever too slender to preclude their conspiracy against mankind.

(James Mackintosh, *Vindiciae Gallicae*, 1791)[1]

So which was it to be? Was society according to James Mackintosh structured around a distinct and virtuous 'middle class', or was it fundamentally composed only of rich and poor – eternally torn between the two, the whole two, and nothing but the two? In our sociologically trained ears, this apparent contradiction rankles; but Mackintosh's writing was not hampered by such considerations. At this early moment in our story, the political implications of such different portrayals of society had not yet been as rigidly circumscribed as they were to become later in the decade; and thus Mackintosh could resort to both in the same text, if they could be of service. And indeed, in mid-1791, vacillating between enchantment with the French Revolution and wariness lest the whole thing would be carried too far, Mackintosh's uncertain political views could indeed be served by both.

The potential political alignment of a 'middle-class'-based vision of society has been laid out in the previous chapter.

[1] James Mackintosh, *Vindiciae Gallicae: Defence of the French Revolution and Its English Admirers against the Accusations of the Right Hon. Edmund Burke ...*, London, 1791, pp. 129, 269.

74

Mackintosh's alternative social scheme, a binary one which allowed no room or effective role for a 'middle class', also carried in it the seeds of its own political message. As Mackintosh explained further:

The higher class in society, whatever be their names, of Nobles, Bishops, Judges, or possessors of landed and commercial wealth, have ever been united by a common view, far more powerful than those petty repugnancies of interest . . . they have one common interest to preserve the elevated place to which the social order has raised them.[2]

Gone were the distinctions between good and bad possessors of power and wealth; or, rather, they were not completely gone, but rendered irrelevant, 'petty'. In truth, it turned out, the upper orders were all united by one basic interest, namely to defend and distance themselves from their social inferiors. This was a starkly dichotomized picture of society, divided between upper and lower orders, rulers and ruled, oppressors and oppressed. The sensibilities it embodied, even if Mackintosh was unwilling to commit himself to their consequences, were those of radical Jacobinism.

This is hardly surprising. Most obviously, a Manichean vision of society, composed of the good and the bad, was the most effective for articulating the radical protest against oppression. 'There are two distinct classes of men in the nation', declared Tom Paine; 'those who pay taxes, and those who receive and live upon the taxes.'[3] But in the context of the 1790s, the logic of the radical recourse to such language went deeper than that: the dual conceptualization of society – popularized, notably, by the translation of Comte Volney's *Ruins*[4] – was a necessary

---

[2] Ibid., pp. 268–9.

[3] Thomas Paine, *Letter Addressed to the Addressers of the Late Proclamation*, London, 1792; in *Thomas Paine Reader*, eds. M. Foot and I. Kramnick, Harmondsworth, 1987, pp. 367–8.

[4] [Comte Constantin François de] Volney, *The Ruins, or a Survey of the Revolutions of Empires*, 2nd edn, London, [1795?] (1st edn, 1792). Especially influential was the vision in the fifteenth chapter, frequently reprinted by radicals as a separate tract, a vision in which the 'People' and the 'Priviledged Class' separate from each other and question each other's credentials (and note also chapters 8, 11). As E. P. Thompson has suggested (in his *Witness against the Beast: William Blake and the Moral Law*, New York, 1993, p. 208), this vision might have influenced William Blake's plate 16 in *The Marriage of Heaven and Hell* (1790–93): 'These two classes of men [the 'Prolific' and the 'Devourer'] are always upon earth, & they should be enemies; whoever tries to reconcile them seeks to destroy existence.' For Volney's influence see pp. 199–208; also E. P. Thompson, *The Making of the English Working Class*, London, 1963, pp. 98–9.

corollary to the language of natural rights in which the radical agenda was now formulated. The 'people' deserved their rights; and they were facing an 'aristocracy', which in this framework meant any smaller and more exclusive group that prevented the people from realizing those rights. And then came the additional move characteristic of this decade, of turning this primarily political formulation of 'aristocracy' versus 'people', a formulation which often carried the eighteenth-century sense of 'government' or 'the system' versus 'people', into the more explicitly social formulation of 'rich' versus 'poor'. These schemes – though far from equivalent – could of course easily be conflated, as when Mary Wollstonecraft declared war against 'the whole system of British politics . . . consisting in multiplying dependents and contriving taxes which grind the poor to pamper the rich'.[5] But as the decade moved along, it was the social contents of this dual scheme which often came to occupy centre stage. When Thomas Holcroft, member of the Society for Constitutional Information, complained in 1795 (soon after his release from imprisonment for treason) about the burdens of the war on the poor, he added this for emphasis:

Who are the tillers? Who are the manufacturers? The poor. Without their labour, the earth itself would be barren . . . For this labour, what do the rich give them in return? Oppression, insult, contempt . . . Who make the laws? The rich. – Who alone can with probable impunity break the laws? – The rich. – Who are impelled by want and misery to break them, and afterward are imprisoned, transported, and hanged? – The poor. – Who do the work? – The poor. – Who reap the fruits? – The rich. – Who pay the taxes? – The poor . . . Who impose the taxes? – The rich . . .[6]

Form was reinforcing content: the outcome of the present political system was simply a reiteration of oppressive antitheses.

---

[5] Mary Wollstonecraft, *A Vindication of the Rights of Woman*; in *The Works of Mary Wollstonecraft*, eds. J. Todd and M. Butler, London, 1989, vol. v, p. 214; and compare her *An Historical and Moral View of the Origin and Progress of the French Revolution; and the Effect It Has Produced in Europe* (originally 1794), in *Works*, vol. vi, p. 46. Like Mackintosh, Wollstonecraft too at the beginning of the decade was combining – uneasily – such strong dual language with gestures towards a tripartite social scheme.

[6] Thomas Holcroft, *A Letter to the Right Honourable William Windham, on the Intemperance and Dangerous Tendency of His Public Conduct*, London, 1795, pp. 46–7. See also the dialogue on the rich and the poor in Mrs Inchbald's *Nature and Art*, as quoted in the *Moral and Political Magazine of the London Corresponding Society* 1, June 1796, p. 24.

When protest against the war (and its tax burdens) was expressed within such a binary framework, then – in contrast with the language of the Friends of Peace – there was obviously no place or use whatsoever for a 'middle class'. But the incompatibility of radical rhetoric with the language of 'middle class' was more fundamental than simply the disruption of a neatly polarized duality. The language of natural rights was in its essence universal: whatever social category was employed in formulating its demands had to be all-inclusive, as Mackintosh illustrated nicely (in the second epigraph opening this section) when he slipped from arguing the case of 'the poor' to arguing the case of 'mankind'. When the London Corresponding Society published one of its first public addresses, declaring the opposition of an oppressed people to 'a much alarmed aristocracy', it opened with the following preamble: 'FELLOW CITIZENS, Of every rank and every situation in life, Rich, Poor, High or Low, we address you all as our Brethren.'[7] Within the dichotomies of rich and poor, or high and low, it was obvious where the sympathies – and the fortunes – of the members of the London Corresponding Society lay; but in principle they had to appeal inclusively to every person who would choose not to be complicit in the system of oppression. It was this universal appeal that rendered the language of rights fundamentally irreconcilable with the thrust of the 'middle-class idiom', which, vague though it was in its social signification, nevertheless substituted one social group, singled out through some intrinsic qualities, for another. Consequently it became increasingly difficult to find people who combined these oppositional rhetorics, as Mackintosh and Wollstonecraft had done at the beginning of the decade. In spite of much shared ground, especially with regard to the critique of the war, these languages of opposition remained separate.

Even so, however, the speakers of these distinct oppositional idioms inhabited what may be described as a shared rhetorical environment. That is to say, even when political adversaries did

---

[7] *Address from the London Corresponding Society to the Inhabitants of Great Britain, on the Subject of a Parliamentary Reform*, London, 1792 (signed 6 August), p. [1]; reprinted in part in M. Thale (ed.), *Selections from the Papers of the London Corresponding Society 1792–1799*, Cambridge, 1983, pp. 18–19. Compare, among innumerable examples of inclusive radical language, *Some Account of a Very Seditious Book, Lately Found upon Wimbledon Common . . .*, London, 1794, p. 17: 'The people, therefore, is the uncorrupt and virtuous part of the nation.'

not interact directly in dialogue, their enunciations still need to be understood in reference to each other: how they resorted to a common stock of linguistic practices; how they reacted to one another's metaphors and formulations, whether through appropriation and usurpation, or through denial and inversion; and how each of their statements, in turn, reinforced the effectiveness of the linguistic choices made by their rivals.

Consider for example the rhetorical ground which the proponents of the 'middle class' shared with a more radical tract, George Dyer's *The Complaints of the Poor People of England*. Dyer, a Unitarian who like Holcroft was a member of the Society for Constitutional Information, admitted that 'the orders of rich and poor, within certain limits, are beneficial [to each other]; mutual wants produce mutual obligations and mutual advantages'. But this was hardly the whole story:

At the same time [Dyer continued], were I to say, that the rich are the most valuable part of the community, I should not be true to my convictions. The prosperity and the wealth of nations depend on the poor ... they are the support of the English government, and, on a fair estimate, would be found to be the most valuable part of the community.

The question was once again the relative worth of social classes: and the parallel with the 'middle-class idiom' was manifest, in the emphasis on the poor as the 'most valuable' and as the key element in supporting both the body social (prosperity and wealth) and the body politic (the government). Dyer was drawing upon this common stock of formulations, however, to elucidate a basically dual social scheme, which was entirely adequate for his agenda as advertised in his title. Making the familiar elision of the rich and the government, he complained that far from acknowledging the contribution of the poor, 'the English government is formed by the rich and great, and to them it is favourable, but it has been said to be highly injurious to the poor'. Dyer further reinforced this binary scheme with an oft-repeated historical analogy, reminding his readers of the misfortune brought on Rome, the archetypal dual society, by the spiteful relationships of patricians and plebeians.[8] Like Rome, like Britain: for both

---

[8] G[eorge] Dyer, *The Complaints of the Poor People of England*, 2nd edn, London, 1793, pp. 2–3, 9. The use of the 'Roman' terminology, of patricians and plebeians, to emphasize the dual configuration of society, was very common. Other examples of

cases these terms encompassed the whole of Dyer's social vision.

Nevertheless, with regard to one issue Dyer did engage in direct dialogue with the language of 'middle class'. This issue was the burden of taxation: 'It has been suggested, too, that the taxes principally affect the middling classes of people. But taxes, which directly affect the middling classes of people, will always in the end fall upon the poor, through the increased price of provisions.' The truth of the matter, he therefore concluded, was that the rich were those who always imposed the taxes, whereas the poor were those who always bore their burden.[9] Thus, Dyer – while joining in an uncompromising opposition to the war – dismissed the 'middle-class' grievance that was being foregrounded by the Friends of Peace on two levels. First, its claim was explicitly denied: taxation fell upon the poor, and no one else. And second, in Dyer's own conception of the way taxation worked, purportedly more true to life, the 'middle class' disappeared altogether. The pertinent social scheme for this issue, as for any other, was wholly within dual terms.

Similarly, we can find in the writing of the Nonconformist Painite reformer Thomas Cooper another such multi-layered counterpart to the language of 'middle class'. In 1792, Cooper came into close contact with the French revolutionaries in Paris, for which he was assailed in the House of Commons by Edmund Burke. In his vehement reply, Cooper advocated radical parliamentary reform. If reform were limited only to a partial extension of the franchise to taxable householders, he argued, 'the most important part of the Community, the most oppressed, the most industrious', those to whom Burke had infamously attached the sobriquet 'Swinish Multitude', would be 'placed in perpetual Subjection to a Corporation, an Aristocracy of Property, more or less extended'. In these strong words, the yet unenfranchised taxable householders – those whom latter-day historians will identify as the 'middle class' – were denied a distinct existence. Instead they were unhesitatingly subsumed within a dual polarity

radical voices which emphasized the indispensable value of the lower orders, in terms reminiscent of the 'middle-class idiom', include *The Address of the British Convention, Assembled at Edinburgh, November 19, 1793, to the People of Great Britain*, London, 1793, p. 21. *The Sheffield Register* 317, 28 June 1793, p. [4], letter from 'Aratus'. [John Fenwick], *Letters to the People of Great Britain, Respecting the Present State of Their Public Affairs*, London, [1795?], p. 22.

[9] Dyer, *The Complaints of the Poor People of England*, pp. 12, 34.

under the category of 'Aristocracy', whose boundaries were accordingly redrawn on the basis of property. Cooper went on to argue that public spirit and independence resided not wholly amongst the rich, but first and foremost amongst the poor.[10] 'It is the People,' Cooper finally asserted while gesturing towards the more inclusive formulation, 'the lower Classes of Society, that constitute the Bulk of Mankind, that form the great Mass of Capability, and present to the Politician the most important Object of national Improvement.' Finally, like Dyer, Cooper also resorted only in one instance to explicit 'middle-class' language, again in the context of taxation. The poor, he wrote empathetically, those who end up paying the taxes, are also those who spend their time in honest toil, 'during those hours which the middling classes devote to relaxation from business, and the great to the Zenith of their pleasurable Career – the small beer'.[11] Overall, then, Cooper's tract too shared the same rhetorical ground with the language of 'middle class', while refuting the arguments for which it was used: in locating political virtue, independence, industriousness and social importance in the lower classes; in objecting to any political solution that privileged a partial segment of society as perpetuating the oppression of the people by an aristocracy; in linking the lower classes with national improvement; and in rejecting the familiar 'middle-class' grievance with regard to their particular burden of taxation.

But perhaps the most telling example of the dialogue between the radical language and the language of 'middle class' was that found in the rhetoric of the masterful popular orator John Thelwall. Thelwall, a leading figure in the London Corresponding Society, emerged after his acquittal from a charge of treason in 1794 as the leading plebeian political lecturer, commonly seen

[10] Thomas Cooper, *A Reply to Mr Burke's Invective against Mr Cooper, and Mr Watt, in the House of Commons, on the 30th of April, 1792*, Manchester, 1792, pp. 70, 74. See also the *Newcastle Chronicle* 1712, 22 April 1797, p. [4], where corruption was described as devouring both the upper and the middle classes together, depriving them of independence, which was associated with the poor. Thus, again, the 'middle class' became complicit in the aristocratic system, lacking political distinctiveness; while the virtue of 'independence' was appropriated for the one other distinct component of society, the lower classes. And compare the simultaneous denial of both the possibility of a *political* middle between two extremes and of the relevance of a *social* middle (by acknowledging only a social division of rich and poor) in *The British Tocsin: Or, Proofs of National Ruin*, London, 1795.

[11] Cooper, *A Reply to Mr Burke's Invective*, p. 72.

as a principal target of Pitt's infamous 'Gagging Acts' of December 1795.[12] In 1796, in a response to Burke, Thelwall deviated momentarily from his characteristic social paradigm of aristocracy and people. Are the English people happy, demanded Thelwall, as Burke had declared them to be? Indeed, he persisted, even if we speak only of those 400,000 persons whom Burke had defined as the political public, 'can even these be called happy? Are those middle classes (which we middling people are apt, so selfishly, and so wickedly, to consider as the whole!) – are even they happy? Alas! alas! how dismal the reverse?'[13] This was a response not only to Burke, who – we might add – did not himself employ the language of 'middle class' in this context. Thelwall (whose lectures were not textbook recitations, but *ad hoc* observations on the current state of affairs) was also responding to something else – to the intensifying use of 'middle-class idiom' in the political debate at that juncture, precisely in the self-centred tone on which he was commenting. Counter to the claims of their proponents, Thelwall declared, the 'middle classes' were not happy; and while such speakers were trumpeting their own importance and worth, they were in fact doing no more than confirming their wicked selfishness. This the orator of the people found to be especially troubling: the particularism embodied in the 'middle-class idiom' was no less obnoxious than that manifested in aristocratic corruption.

Indeed Thelwall made precisely this analogy. Even as he located his own identity – as a personal matter – within this 'middle class', he at the same time also denied its collective political relevance as a distinct category by describing Burke's very same political public (the 400,000) as a *'new aristocracy of thinkers and discoursers'*. This new aristocracy included 'a mixed herd of nobles and gentles, placemen, pensioners and court-expectants, of bankers and merchants, manufacturers, lawyers, parsons and physicians, warehousemen and shop-keepers, pimps and king's messengers, fiddlers and auctioneers' – that is, an

---

[12] The two acts were perhaps the most widely protested actions on the part of Pitt's administration to counter what they perceived as the rising tide of sedition. The second one, the Seditious Meetings Act, empowering magistrates to disperse crowds of over fifty persons, was used against Thelwall's audiences.

[13] John Thelwall, *The Rights of Nature, against the Usurpations of Establishments*, London, 1796 (signed 5 November 1796), p. 42. The tract began, predictably enough, by proclaiming the clash between aristocracy and people.

'aristocracy' comprising for the most part those whom we would tend to classify as the 'middle' strata of society.[14] Echoing Cooper, for Thelwall too these expanding 'middle' social groups were not a manifestation of an emerging 'middle class', but rather of the broadening of a national aristocracy, whose boundaries were redefined accordingly; while other members of this social 'middle' – like himself – could choose instead to join the ranks of the people.

On another occasion, however, Thelwall's awareness of the mounting appeal of the 'middle-class' language led him to attempt to harness it for his own purposes. 'Those who seek to *oppress the lower*', Thelwall warned then, 'seek to *annihilate the intermediate orders*. It is their interest to have but two classes, the very high and the very low.' So far, perhaps not too consistently with the criticism of 'middle-class' speakers in his response to Burke, Thelwall himself sounded as if he were propounding the 'middle-class idiom'. But not for long: he quickly qualified this appropriation, assuring his audience that 'it is not to one class of the people [that] I wish to confine myself'; rather, his goal was 'the rights and happiness of the universe, not the amelioration and benefit of a particular class'. Thus he concluded, unsurprisingly, that the danger facing 'the middling orders of society' must persuade them to abandon any sectarian tendencies – that is to say, any distinct political identity – and to join the lower classes in a common front against their oppressors.[15] As Thelwall said explicitly to another audience:

this is not the time for little prejudices of pride and imagined distinction. Do not suppose, that because most of you are of the middling order, and a large majority of the London Corresponding Society are of the industrious poor, that it is any indignity for you to associate with them.[16]

---

[14] Ibid., pp. 19, 33–4.

[15] *The Tribune, a Periodical Publication, Consisting Chiefly of the Political Lectures of J. Thelwall,* 1796, vol. II, pp. 232–5: the lecture was delivered on 9 September 1795.

[16] This lecture was published in the *Moral and Political Magazine of the London Corresponding Society* 1, December 1796; quoted, p. 290. See also Thelwall's efforts to gloss over the alleged differences between shopkeepers and traders on the one hand, and labourers and mechanics on the other, pointing to their shared interests and experience of oppression *vis à vis* the corrupted government and constitution, in his *Peaceful Discussion, and not Tumultuary Violence the Means of Redressing National Grievance,* 2nd edn, London, 1795, p. 9; again Thelwall was moulding a complex social map into a simple dual scheme.

In sum, whether criticizing the 'middle-class' speakers for their self-centred rhetoric, or denying altogether the relevance of the category of 'middle class' in a system of oppression, or appropriating the 'middle-class' rhetoric in pursuit of his own goals, Thelwall was genuflecting to the political efficacy of the language of 'middle class' at this juncture. Yet he was not committed to using the notion of 'middle class' in any particular way; and this allowed him, within a single month, to make use of it both to approve of propertied persons who joined the *people*, as here, and to denounce propertied persons who joined the *aristocracy*, as we have seen in the previous paragraphs. From a radical perspective this made perfect sense: these were the only two ways in which members of a social 'middle' could become politically relevant.

THE TWO NATIONS: THE VIEW FROM ABOVE

The most obvious division of society is into rich and poor ... The whole business of the poor, is to administer to the idleness, folly, and luxury of the rich, and that of the rich in return is to find the best method of confirming the slavery and increasing the burthens of the poor. (Anti-Burkean pamphlet, 1793?)[17]

Under this beneficial order of things the rich furnish the means of industrious livelihood to the poor, by various employments, all advantageous to the public, and the individuals concerned; the poor, in their turn, by their labour, are the instruments that increase the opulence of the rich, which necessarily flows back upon them, by furnishing again the means of honest and advantageous employment to a greater number of poor than before. (Anti-Painite pamphlet, 1793)[18]

The juxtaposition of these two near-simultaneous passages is more than a trifle ironic. When radical 'Old Hubert' portrayed society as composed of rich and poor, the latter working for the former, John Somers Cocks – a highly conservative MP – could not agree more. These two speakers, from the opposite ends of the political spectrum, shared much ground in terms of their mental visions of the society whose future they were hoping to wrest from each other's grip. The same shared ground – to give

[17] Old Hubert (i.e. James Parkinson), *Pearls Cast before Swine, by Edmund Burke, Scraped Together by Old Hubert*, London, 1793?, p. 7.
[18] John Somers Cocks, MP, *A Short Treatise on the Dreadful Tendency of Levelling Principles*, London, 1793, pp. 14–15.

another example – was evident in the contrived dialogue which John Bowles, a place-holding magistrate and one of the most prominent anti-Painite pamphleteers, used as a literary device to expose radical mistakes. To the 'Painite' speaker's complaint 'that the poor are obliged to sustain so many hardships and burthens, while the rich revel in luxury at their expence', the conservative rejoinder was set in precisely the same scheme of rich and poor: 'So far from its being true that burthens are imposed on the poor to supply the luxuries of the wealthy and great', argued the Burkean speaker, the truth of the matter was that 'while the condition of the poor is alleviated as much as possible, the luxuries of the rich are converted into sources of revenue.'[19] Bowles's interlocutors differed not in their understanding of the composition of society or of the basic functions of its constituents, but only in their diametrically opposed evaluations of the quality of the relationship which existed between them. Where radicals saw stark oppression, establishment speakers saw the happy signs of benevolent paternalism. British society, they claimed, was blessed with a paternalist relationship between rich and poor, in which responsibility and care from above were greeted with cheerful and industrious subordination from below.

Thus listen to the Tory preacher James Scott, rector of Simonburn, intent on repudiating those 'turbulent advocates for Equality', who used the pulpit to justify with the aid of Providence the existence of riches and inequality:

the *artificial* wants of the rich are a constant supply to the *real* wants of the poor ... It is in the order of God's Providence that the poor should derive their support from the rich; and, if you cut off the rich, the poor must necessarily wither and decay. The poor can no more

---

[19] [John Bowles], *Dialogues on the Rights of Britons, between a Farmer, a Sailor, and a Manufacturer. Dialogue the First*, London, 1792, pp. 19–21. See also [idem], *Dialogues on the Rights of Britons ... Dialogue the Second*, London, 1792, where the conservative voice further conceded that the labouring class was the 'strength and riches' of the state; 'Their situation is therefore a respectable one as it is both useful and independent' (p. 8). Evidently, such statements had much in common with popular radical language, like that of Charles Pigott, *A Political Dictionary: Explaining the True Meaning of Words...*, London, 1795. Pigott provided sarcastic comments on the uses of key political terms, such as 'vulgar' (p. 164): '*Vulgar*: The aristocratic epithet given to the most useful, the most industrious, and the most valuable part of the community.' On John Bowles as a 'crusading' pro-war writer, see E. Vincent, '"The Real Grounds of the Present War": John Bowles and the French Revolutionary Wars, 1792–1802', *History* 78 (1993), pp. 393–420.

live without the rich, than the rich without the poor; they are mutually dependent upon, and mutually useful to, each other.[20]

There was an implied symmetry in this picture of amicable symbiosis, a symmetry which obscured the inequalities of power; this was precisely why Vicesimus Knox was at pains to expose the purportedly benign language of paternalism as tantamount to despotism.[21] 'The lower [orders] depend on the higher, and the higher upon the lower', stated another admirer of Burke; 'Whilst the lower minister to the comfort and convenience of the higher, the higher contribute to the maintenance and the protection of the lower.' Thus, as he explained further, 'peace and harmony' are achieved through the combined effects of 'a gentle and liberal authority' from above and 'a due but dignified reverence and submission' from below.[22] 'The rich are but the stewards of the poor', echoed the anti-Jacobin William Playfair; fortunately, 'one rich man cannot enjoy his wealth, without giving bread to numbers.' As before, the issue of taxation elicited some of the most outspoken statements of this kind: taxes 'are chiefly paid by the rich', asserted a Tory professor of ecclesiastical history in 1793; 'The heavier taxes are laid immediately on the rich, and they relieve the poor of their whole share of the others, as they are the employers of the poor.'[23]

---

[20] James Scott, *A Sermon, Preached at Park-Street Chapel, on the 19th of April, 1793: Being the Day Appointed for a General Fast*, London, 1793, p. 9. Idem, *Equality Considered and Recommended, in a Sermon ... April the 6th, 1794*, London, 1794, pp. 10–11. See also H. T. Dickinson, 'Popular Conservatism and Militant Loyalism 1789–1815', in H. T. Dickinson (ed.), *Britain and the French Revolution, 1789–1815*, New York, 1989, p. 107, and the sources cited there.

[21] See chapter 2, pp. 49–50.

[22] Edward Tatham, *Letters to the Right Honourable Edmund Burke on Politics*, Oxford, 1791, p. 77. Tatham was a fellow of Lincoln College, Oxford, soon to become its rector; Burke expressed high approbation of his main work, suggesting a new system of logic. Interestingly, Tatham relied heavily on Aristotle's *Politics* in order to support his dual vision of society. Aristotle, however, could also readily be invoked to emphasize the importance of a 'middle class'. A case in point is John Gillies's long introduction to his edition of *Aristotle's Ethics and Politics*, 2 vols., London, 1797, vol. I, pp. 276, 319; and see the review in the *Analytical Review* 28, July-December 1798, pp. 638ff. The uses of Aristotle, too, ultimately depended on one's preferred conceptualization of one's society. See further the discussion in Willibald Steinmetz's essay, as in p. 15 note 22.

[23] William Playfair, *For the Use of the Enemies of England: A Real Statement of the Finances and Resources of Great Britain*, London, 1796, pp. 25–6. See his dialogue with the 'middle-class idiom' below, pp. 165–6. [Thomas Hardy], *The Patriot. Addressed to the People, on the Present State of Affairs in Britain and in France*, Edinburgh, 1793, p. 72; see also p. 32.

Both extremes of the political spectrum, therefore, were committed to a basic dual social scheme; but at the same time their stakes in it were somewhat different. For radicals, it was the abyss between these two social ends which was key, an embodiment of oppression and alienation. Speakers on the right, by contrast, wished to see the gap bridged, to prove the harmonious coexistence of these two social ends. As a consequence, the dual social vision of Pittites was not uncommonly complemented by a scheme of numerous social gradations at small intervals, superimposed as it were on the basic dual paradigm. Indeed, a careful reading of the dialogue between radicals and Pittites might reveal a systematic contestation over this issue. As one radical pamphleteer put it:

Whatever beauties some may see, and others pretend to see, in that order and gradual subordination, so highly extolled, by those who are in the uppermost class; I am of opinion that the distinctions are too great, the gradation is too sudden, and by no means regular. It is either too high or too low.[24]

In addition to mitigating the distance between rich and poor, the multi-graded picture also provided a sense of a more complex social structure. In particular, a somewhat confusing practice was to employ 'middle and lower classes' instead of 'lower classes', or 'higher and middle classes' instead of 'higher classes', thus apparently admitting social complexity while in fact retaining a basic unaltered dual paradigm. In such cases it was not uncommon to find the very same text referring both to the 'higher and middle ranks' and to the 'lower and middle ranks': to such writers these were not really incompatible, since the 'middle' in such combinations did not actually signify any distinct entity, but was more of a rhetorical embellishment.[25]

---

[24] *An Enquiry into the Present Alarming State of the Nation ... By a Friend to Liberty, to the Community, and a Sound Constitution*, London, 1793, p. 49.

[25] See for example [Benjamin Bell], *Three Essays on Taxation of Income*, London, 1799, pp. 57, 70, 79. Another example is John Smith, *An Affectionate Address to the Middling and Lower Classes of British Subjects, on the Present Alarming Crisis*, Edinburgh, 1798, which was a Pittite pro-war exhortation, written clearly within a dual social paradigm of higher/lower orders; the title did not challenge this dual paradigm but simply allowed for more people to be included in it. A very similar case is *Moral Annals of the Poor, and Middle Ranks of Society, in Various Situations of Good and Bad Conduct*, Durham, 1795: again a Pittite tract written in an evident dual social framework of rich and poor, in spite of its title. For a nice example of 'middling and higher ranks' used in an obvious dual social scheme, see British Library, Add. Mss 16920 (Reeves Mss), f. 18: W. Howlett to J. Moore, 1 December 1792.

Notwithstanding these possible secondary differences between the social schemes of radicals and Pittites, it is the accordance of the basic social visions underlying their respective arguments which demands particular emphasis, in view of the intense contestation over the basic conceptualization of society which was provoked by the language of 'middle class'. We should keep in mind that interactions between the participants in the political dialogue could occur simultaneously on different levels. Thus, on one level, radical and conservative speakers could rebut each other's claims while sharing the same conceptual social map. The interaction of both with the political moderates, however, was on a different level altogether: here the disagreement was not only about political opinion, but also about the representation of society chosen for its formulation. And then there was yet another level: even as both radicals and conservatives were presenting a different social scheme from the Friends of Peace, one which allowed no space for a 'middle class', they still inhabited the same rhetorical and metaphorical environment as their opponents. As we have already seen for radicals, this level of shared rhetorical environment was manifest in common formulations and argumentative structures which the specific political circumstances infused with particular force, and in which all sides to the political debate mutually reinforced each other.

What was true of radicals was also true of establishment speakers. 'Our nobles', sermonized the Scottish curate James Hall in 1793, 'are not useless, as the vipers of democracy, and the pests of society, would have us believe'; rather, they are 'highly useful, and of the utmost importance ... as a balance and safeguard to our constitution and form of government.'[26] Other writers depicted the landed classes as 'the most virtuous of our citizens, and the most necessary to, and the best deserving of their country'; or as 'the sober, the affluent, the discreet, the wise, and the honest', whose interests – rooted in the soil – were interwoven with those of the people; or, again, as 'the most loyal support of the crown' as well as 'the most strenuous and weighty

---

[26] James Hall, *The Blessings of Liberty and Peace: Or, the Excellence of the British Constitution. A Sermon Preached ... 18th of April, 1793 ...*, London, 1793, p. 7.

protection of the people' when their liberty is endangered.[27] In these and many similar utterances, the landed classes played an analogous role to that of the 'middle class' in the rhetoric of the Friends of Peace. For such speakers it was the landed classes that were the repository of all virtues, the singular safeguard of the constitution, the defenders of the people. In effect, this was a 'landed-class idiom', whose mutually reinforcing affinity with the 'middle-class idiom' is readily evident. This affinity was even more immediately manifest in a tract that presented the able and worthy aristocracy not only as the protector of the consti-tution and 'the saviour of the state', to whom 'the people of England [are] indebted for that liberty which they fondly cherish', but also as 'the happy medium between despotism and anarchy', a political middle commended by 'the arguments of philosophers and divines in all ages in favour of the golden mean'.[28] Just like his political opponents who praised the 'middle class', this admirer of the landed classes also invoked ancient wisdom to support a vision of his favourite social group as the bulwark of liberty, the happy Golden Mean situated between despotism and anarchy.

Of course, this is not a simple one-way argument about cause and effect: it was not necessarily a challenge from the 'middle-class idiom' which in itself prompted such assertions of the value of the landed classes. Rather, those assertions were first induced by the deep and pervasive crisis in which the British landed elite found itself at this juncture. On the one hand, the French Revol-ution induced unprecedented attacks on its legitimacy and leader-ship: it is not unlikely, for instance, that James Hall was responding in this sermon to Paine's famous characterization of the aristocracy as 'the drones' who 'exist only for lazy enjoy-ment'.[29] On the other hand, the landed elite was entrusted with

---

[27] Sir William Young, *The British Constitution of Government, Compared with that of a Democratic Republic*, 2nd edn, London, 1793, p. 39. *The Voice of Truth to the People of England, of All Ranks and Descriptions, on Occasion of Lord Malmesbury's Return from Lisle*, London, 1797, p. 40. *An Exposure of the Domestic and Foreign Attempts to Destroy the British Constitution, upon the New Doc-trines Recommended. By a Member of Parliament, and of His Majesty's Privy Council*, London, 1793, p. 37; and see pp. 35–9. See also the review of *The Essential Principles of the Wealth of Nations*, 1797, in *Analytical Review* 26, September 1797, pp. 299–300.

[28] *Remarks on the Proceedings of the Society, Who Style Themselves 'The Friends of the People': And Observations on the Principles of Government, as Applicable to the British Constitution. In Two Letters to a Friend*, London, 1792, pp. 55, 63.

[29] Thomas Paine, *Rights of Man*, ed. E. Foner, Harmondsworth, 1985, pt II, p. 227.

the war, a situation which should have underscored its role as the natural leaders of the nation; but this potentially glorious effect on its public standing was offset by the all too dubious record of the last time it had actually led Britain into war, an unfortunate venture which resulted in the loss of the American colonies. Consequently, as Linda Colley has richly demonstrated, the British elite was making spirited efforts along broad and varied fronts to fend off accusations of hedonistic parasitism and to reshape its image as a patriotic leading elite, deserving of the admiration and pride of the nation.[30] It was against this background that the 'middle-class idiom', offering a potential alternative to aristocratic leadership, was so threatening; and at the same time the aristocratic self-justification in rebuttal, in its turn, contributed further to that shared rhetorical environment in which the rival 'middle-class idiom', too, could resonate.

By 1796, if not before, the resonance of the persistent 'middle-class idiom' was quite strong; strong enough, for example, to have elicited those unusually explicit reactions from John Thelwall. At the other political extreme, it was probably during the same year that an anonymous writer, strongly anti-Jacobin, anti-reform, and opposed – using Burke's terms – to 'a regicide peace', was likewise induced to an unusually direct dialogue with the proponents of the 'middle class'. Addressing the Duke of Bedford, this author identified his own social position: 'I hold myself some-where about the middling rank of society.' This however constituted no handicap for sharp criticism to follow: 'Man is not contented in a middling state', he lamented, since such a position places within his reach a higher state, 'in which he vainly imagines contentment to reside.' This led our author to declare resolutely: 'Thus I divide into *two* classes only the people of this country. The middling ranks, who are not rich, will toil industriously to become so; and, therefore, merit the consummation of their wishes.'[31] Thus, in a rather startling statement, the 'middle class' ceased to exist. This self-proclaimed member of the 'middle class' announced its irrelevance as a distinct social category and its eradication from future portrayals of society. In

---

[30] L. Colley, *Britons: Forging the Nation 1707–1837*, New Haven, 1992, esp. chapter 4. Also P. Langford, *Public Life and the Propertied Englishman 1689–1798*, Oxford, 1991, chapter 8.
[31] *Two Letters, Addressed to His Grace the Duke of Bedford, and the People of England*, London, [1796?], pp. 11, 36.

his view this was a well-deserved consequence of its greed; misusing its acclaimed industriousness, it had corrupted the potential happiness of the middle station. His political rivals were repeatedly claiming that the present despotic government was likely to cause the annihilation of the valuable 'middle class'; this writer turned their argument on its head and placed the blame squarely on the shoulders of the 'middle class' itself, which was about to become extinct because of its own undue ambitions. Neither the dual nor the tripartite social scheme were here taken for granted, as a given of social structure: depicting society was rather a matter of conscious choice, a deliberate preference that was determined by one's assessment of people's behaviour. The existence of a 'middle class' depended crucially on the eye of the beholder, and this beholder knew it.

Admittedly, such a keen awareness of the choices involved in envisioning society was unusually rare. It bears repeating that I am not arguing that political debate was manifestly *about* social schemes or vocabularies, or about the existence or non-existence of a 'middle class'. The subjects of debate were overwhelmingly more tangible and pressing – the merits or demerits of the constitution, the legitimacy of resistance or of repression, the fairness of taxation, the reality of dearth, the justification for and effects of an unparalleled war. The differing conceptualizations of society were implicated in this dialogue in a more subtle way, revealed for the most part only in fragmented bits and pieces that formed part of arguments overtly about other things. These were contestations on a less articulate level of dialogue, which are therefore also more difficult for us to recover. Yet they were no less meaningful for it.

THE LANGUAGE OF 'INTERESTS'

A dual vision of society was one possible way to respond to the 'middle-class idiom', one which could serve the political agendas of both left and right. But there was also another possibility, another social scheme that was similarly employed to counter the language of 'middle class'. After all, there was nothing a priori essential or logical about conceptualizing society as a sequence of horizontal layers, be they two or three. In analogy to a cake, society could be described not only in terms of the layers of which it was comprised but also in terms of the slices in which it was apportioned.[32] Such was the logic of the language in 'interests', in which society was represented as composed of distinct interests – landed interest, commercial interest, moneyed interest, manufacturing interest, but also more limited groupings such as the shipping or the East India interests. And again, this was more than simply a descriptive strategy, let alone one dictated and determined by the exigencies of social and economic structure. As Keith Baker has put it, 'the notion of "interest" is itself very much a political one . . . "Interest" is a symbolic and political construction, not simply a preexisting social reality.'[33] The language of 'interests' too embodied a set of particular assumptions and entailed specific political implications. Overall, during the period discussed in this book, these implications fell on the side of those intent on preserving the prevailing social and political order. Discussion of society in terms of 'interests' enabled one to acknowledge multiple interests at variance with each other within a complex society and economy, and to allow for the possibility of conflict; and yet at the same time to represent such conflicts as entirely – and adequately – contained within the given social order, whose stability they could not threaten. In the particular context of the 1790s, therefore, the language of 'interests' could be used effectively to counteract the rhetorical effects of the language of 'middle class'.

Of course the language of 'interests' had not always carried the same meanings; after all, the political uses of this social scheme, as of any other, were not inherent in the scheme itself. Indeed, in important ways the previous implications of the lan-

---

[32] Even thus the geometrical configurations were not exhausted: for traces of yet another possibility, in which society was visualized as a series of concentric circles, see p. 393 note 30.

[33] K. M. Baker, *Inventing the French Revolution: Essays on French Political Culture in the Eighteenth Century*, Cambridge, 1990, pp. 5–6. Baker argues that even if a social division – such as that between the privileged orders and the Third Estate – became at some historical point (in this case, 1788) the foremost issue in people's consciousness, this outcome was not preordained by social structure, but rather it is still necessary to show how 'the logic of political debate' made it so crucial. The affinity of my argument to his is obvious. Also compare John Styles's assertion, that 'politically significant interests do not somehow arise automatically out of the sectoral structure of the economy . . . Economic and other interests do not simply exist. They have to be conceptualised and constructed.' J. Styles, 'An Eighteenth Century Landed Ruling Class? Interest Groups, Lobbying and Parliament in Eighteenth Century England', unpublished paper.

guage of 'interests' were reversed. Very much like the language of 'middle class', the language of 'interests' had assumed political significance as a consequence of war and of conflicts over the apportioning of its burdens; in this case, the Nine Years War and the War of the Spanish Succession, following the Revolution of 1688. In what evolved into 'country ideology', the principal social division was then perceived to be that between the landed and the moneyed interests, irreconcilably inimical to each other.[34] Yet sometime during the second half of the eighteenth century the connotations of the language of 'interests' were transformed, in a process crucial to the Georgian legitimation of commercial society. From a condemnation of commercial society (and the political order under whose auspices it flourished) as the progenitor of the great battle of interests, the language of 'interests' now came to incorporate visions of harmony and benevolent mutual interdependence, and thus, in effect, to vindicate the very same commercial society. (This transformation, it might be added, also produced a shift in the critiques of commerce, focusing now less on the centrifugal pull of vying interests tearing commercial society apart, and more on the invidious moral consequences of commerce.) John Brewer has seen this change in the use of 'interests' as one from a political to an economic category; but in fact the later, 'economic', understanding of 'interests' was hardly less political.[35]

How was this change effected? To begin with, the more benign understanding of 'interests' was predicated on the assumption (obviously influenced by the expanding literature on political economy) that in a complex social structure and a diverse econ-

---

[34] See J. Brewer, *The Sinews of Power: War, Money and the English State, 1688–1783*, New York, 1989, pp. 199–210. A. O. Hirschman, *The Passions and the Interests: Political Arguments for Capitalism before Its Triumph*, Princeton, 1977, pp. 32–7, discusses the early uses of the term 'interest', until it assumed a specific economic meaning in the later seventeenth century. The perceptions of the conflict at this period as one between the two interests, as well as their material justifications, are discussed in W. A. Speck, 'Conflict in Society', in G. Holmes (ed.), *Britain after the Glorious Revolution 1689–1714*, 1969, pp. 135–54. Also G. Holmes, *British Politics in the Age of Anne*, New York, 1967, chapter 5.

[35] Brewer, *The Sinews of Power*, p. 273 n. 50; and see p. 203 for an example of the latter vision which goes back to the mid eighteenth century, in Josiah Tucker's remarks against the supposed distinctions of interests in *A Brief Essay on the Advantages and Disadvantages which Respectively Attend France and Great Britain, with Regard to Trade*, 2nd edn, 1750. For Tucker's opinion later, see J. G. A. Pocock, 'Josiah Tucker on Burke, Locke, and Price', in his *Virtue, Commerce, and History*, Cambridge, 1985, pp. 182–3.

omy, conflicts of interests between different agents or sectors were inevitable and natural. 'A contest between the moneyed and the landed interests', stated one anti-revolutionary account of the French Revolution, 'exist[s] more or less in every society [that] emerged from a state of nature.'[36] At the same time, however, such conflicts, confined to particular economic questions, were dependent on the specific issues that engendered them, and flourished or subsided together with those issues. Such conflicts were represented as relatively minor squabbles, focused and localized disagreements, disturbed ripples under which lay a deeper unifying common interest. Hence, and this was politically the most consequential point, conflicts of interests were explainable, containable and legitimate, even if bothersome. Their occurrence being no one's fault, and being by definition evanescent, they could not pose a real challenge to the social and political order.[37] Conflicts of interests, explained one writer, were evils 'which amongst a free, enlightened and industrious people, the unrestrained operation of individual interest is apt to produce'; by the same token, however, 'the same natural laws which have caused, will tend in a much greater degree to remedy these evils'.[38]

Politically, then, the language of 'interests' – in this particular form – had a basic soothing effect; and it is therefore hardly surprising to find supporters of the prevailing order (like the hostile account of the French Revolution just quoted) enlisting it repeatedly in contestations over representations of society such as those that concern us here. Thomas Somerville, a pro-war critic of the French Revolution, is another convenient case in point. In one tract of 1793 Somerville wrote in the familiar binary manner about 'the families of the lowest fortune' who in Britain were not prevented 'from ascending and mixing with the higher orders of society'. 'The familiarity of such examples', he added, 'has a happy tendency ... to promote a more kindly

---

[36] *An Historical Sketch of the French Revolution from Its Commencement to the Year 1792*, London, 1792, p. 427.

[37] For a later recognition of this distinction between interests, localized in their demands and temporary in their existence, and other political groupings whose permanence and broad demands provoke much deeper and everlasting animosity between parties, see Frederic Calvert, *Letter to the Members of the Bucks Agricultural Association, upon Their Assuming a Political Character*, London, 1833, pp. 7–10.

[38] Cambriensis, *Observations on the Present Difficulties of the Country*, London, 1816, p. 16.

correspondence among all classes of men.' But in another tract
of the same year Somerville chose to supplement this benign
dual vision of society with a different scheme, in commenting on
the partiality of various persons to the advancement of their own
interests:

The landed, commercial, ecclesiastical, manufacturing interests, have
been sometimes considered as repugnant to each other. Now, though
it should be granted, that transient interferences may occur, and that
care ought to be taken not to suffer the balance of power or wealth to
incline too much to any of them; yet it may be demonstrated, that
they have one common, indivisible interest in maintaining the public
order, and the stability and energy of Government.[39]

Similarly, another Burkean author (also in 1793) stated that
although the division into different interests is 'the growth of
nature', in fact, ultimately, 'the furtherance of partial interests
may form its means, but universal welfare is its *end*'. Properly
considered, 'opposite interests converge and coalesce', and (as
he added elsewhere) 'the consequence may be general harmony
and peace'.[40] The authority of natural law was invoked often in
such statements: the landed and trading interests, asserted
another supporter of ministerial policies, are 'so intimately connected . . . and dependent, as they naturally are, upon each
other'.[41] The 'joint support of the State' is the agricultural and
commercial interests, echoed a merchant intent on curbing
popular discontent; 'in these two I dispose of the whole
society'. (Note the sense of agency in his choice of this particular way to represent 'the whole society'.) He continued: 'These
two interests neither are or ought naturally to be the support
and encouragement of each other, although in their nature
[they are] not apparently connected, but are just as different,

---

[39] Thomas Somerville, *Observations on the Constitution and Present State of Britain*, Edinburgh,
  1793, pp. 6–7. Idem, *The Effects of the French Revolution, with Respect to the Interests of
  Humanity, Liberty, Religion, and Morality*, Edinburgh, 1793, pp. 72–3.
[40] William Cusack Smith, *The Patriot: Or, Political Essays*, 2nd edn, Dublin, 1793, pp. 25,
  50, 59. Smith combined these views with deep suspicion of the 'middle class': see
  below, p. 149.
[41] [William Combe], *The Letters of Valerius, on the State of Parties, the War, the Volunteer
  System, and Most of the Political Topics which Have Lately Been Under Public Discussion*,
  London, 1804, p. 51. With regard to taxation, some of Combe's statements can be
  read as direct refutations of the typical 'middle-class' grievance, and of the 'middle-class
  idiom' with which it was combined, though without resorting to this particular language
  (see p. 54).

in my mind, as the *inside* is to the *outside* of any given thing.'[42]

A common indivisible interest, a general harmony, the inside and the outside of the same thing: the political implications of this particular representation of society need hardly have been spelled out more clearly. Consequently, when arguments set in the language of 'middle class' were met with responses set in the language of 'interests', as was often the case, what was at stake – again – was much more than a mere haggling over words.[43] In contrast with the sector-specific atomizing tendency of the language of 'interests', the inclusive vagueness inherent in the language of 'middle class' worked to forge broad supra-occupational alliances. In contrast with the issue-specific containment of conflicts of 'interests', and consequently their transitory and confined nature, the language of 'middle class' could stand on its own, supporting wider demands independent of specific issues, and claiming a permanent stake in politics. In contrast with the restricted applicability of 'interests' to the economic sphere, the category 'middle class' implied broader objectives, not necessarily derived from economic interests and not confined to them. And, most importantly, in contrast with the legitimation of conflicts of 'interests' that at the same time neutralized them as a fundamental social and political threat, the language of 'middle class' – as it was used in the 1790s – could entail

---

[42] John Broadley, *Pandora's Box, and the Evils of Britain: With Effectual, Just and Equitable Means for Their Annihilation; and for the Preservation of the Peace, Happiness and Prosperity of the Country*, London, 1801, p. 4. For later powerful reiterations of the same points about the nature of interests, see Lieutenant-General Craufurd, *Observations on the State of the Country since the Peace: With a Supplementary Section on the Poor Laws*, London, 1817, p. 24. [John Campbell Colquhoun], *The Constitutional Principles of Parliamentary Reform. By a Freeholder and Landholder of Scotland*, Edinburgh, 1831, p. 29. *The Corn Laws: An Authentic Report of the Late Important Discussions in the Manchester Chamber of Commerce, on the Destructive Effects of the Corn Laws upon the Trade and Manufactures of the Country . . .*, London, 1839, pp. 7–8, speech of Samuel Fletcher.

[43] The emphasis here – as throughout this book – is on the *language* of 'interests', involving a whole social map, rather than on the mere word 'interests'. Confusingly, at times the language of 'interests' could be formulated using different words. In particular, 'class' – a term used for a variety of classificatory purposes – was on occasion used interchangeably with 'interest', as in an 1816 tract which discussed '*two* important classes of the community, the *commercial*, and *agricultural*, interests': *A Plain and Popular Apology, for Supporting the Existing Administration of the Country. By an Independent Country Gentleman*, London, 1816, p. 112. See likewise J. Wyatt, *Observations on the Question of the Corn Laws and Free Trade*, London, 1826, pp. 10–11. Such complications inevitably muddy the water in this kind of inquiry, and cannot be disposed of: these texts should not be mechanically read, just as they were not mechanically written.

immediate prescriptive implications that directly challenged the social and political order.[44]

LOYALIST 'MIDDLE-CLASS IDIOM': THE ROAD NOT TAKEN

Our rudimentary mapping of the competing representations of society which were invested with particular significance in the political debate of the 1790s is drawing to a close. We have seen the Friends of Peace as they reinforced political moderation with the 'middle-class idiom'. We have seen the uncompromising stark duality of the radicals. We have seen the supporters of the government, either reiterating the dual scheme but in a more benevolent garb, or preferring the comforting language of 'interests'. But one possibility still remains unexplored. Whereas for radicals a song of praise for the 'middle class' was both incommensurate with their political beliefs and of no strategic use, for the loyalists, given their political convictions and their rhetorical strategy, as well as their social origins, such an emphasis on the 'middle class', *prima facie*, could in fact have proven very attractive.

Loyalism, a term used broadly to describe post-revolutionary support for the constitution and the monarchy, for Pitt's government and for the war, has recently attracted much attention. In the 1960s and 1970s, most historians whose empathies and interests lay in broad-base movements focused on the impact and development of radicalism as the true site of 'history from below'. Yet more recent work suggests that the extent and the organization of popular loyalism was significantly underestimated.[45] One

---

[44] It is therefore obvious that I disagree with the argument made, among others, by S. Wallech, '"Class versus Rank": The Transformation of Eighteenth-Century English Social Terms and Theories of Production', *Journal of the History of Ideas* 47 (1986), pp. 409–31, whereby there was a natural affinity, if not equivalence, and straightforward progression between a tripartite social scheme of landed, commercial and manufacturing interests, and a tripartite scheme of upper, middle and working classes.

[45] It would hardly do, however, to remedy the situation by unreasonably overestimating loyalism, as is the case with R. R. Dozier, *For King, Constitution and Country: The English Loyalists and the French Revolution*, Lexington, 1983; Dozier goes as far as to suggest – without adequate proof – that 'practically every person active in the political community of England was joining the ranks of the loyalists' (p. 76). For more balanced evaluations, see H. T. Dickinson's articles: 'Popular Conservatism and Militant Loyalism 1789–1815', pp. 103–25; 'Popular Loyalism in Britain in the 1790s', in E. Hellmuth (ed.), *The Transformation of Political Culture: England and Germany in the Late Eighteenth Century*, Oxford, 1990, pp. 503–33; 'Britain and the Ideological Crusade against the French Revolution', in L. Domergue and G. Lamoine (eds.), *Après 1789: la révolution*

finding especially significant for the present inquiry is the pervasive hold which loyalism achieved among middle social strata. Investigating the loyalist impulse as seen through the volunteer movement, John Cookson has concluded that 'its social base was urban and middle class to a degree that has never been appreciated'. It is revealing to compare Cookson's conclusion here, that loyalism was a key factor in 'a developing middle-class identity', with his earlier argument in the *Friends of Peace*, that the *opposition* to the war was central to 'the development of [middle-] class attitudes and [middle-] class solidarity'.[46] These conflicting conclusions, derived from two projects anchored in a wide-ranging familiarity with the sources, demonstrate first of all that the political behaviour of the middle social strata in fact defied any socio-economic generalization. Insofar as actual war-time commitments were concerned, persons of the social middle, of common income, status and occupational backgrounds, aligned themselves enthusiastically on both sides.

But, significantly, the language of 'middle class' did not. On the contrary, during the whole of the first war against France, loyalist 'middle-class' language, let alone loyalist 'middle-class idiom', could hardly ever be found. This perhaps surprising fact highlights the second lesson which we can draw from Cookson's conflicting conclusions, a lesson which by now should sound

---

modèle ou repoussoir, Toulouse, 1991, pp. 153–74. D. Eastwood, 'Patriotism and the English State in the 1790s', in M. Philp (ed.), *The French Revolution and British Popular Politics*, Cambridge, 1991, pp. 146–68. Colley, *Britons*, chapter 7 (though note the corrective in E. P. Thompson's review, 'The Making of a Ruling Class', *Dissent*, Summer 1993, esp. pp. 378–9). Also see E. C. Black, *The Association: British Extraparliamentary Political Organization 1769–1793*, Cambridge, Mass., 1963, chapter 7. R. Hole, 'British Counter-Revolutionary Popular Propaganda in the 1790s', in C. Jones (ed.), *Britain and Revolutionary France: Conflict, Subversion and Propaganda*, Exeter, 1983, pp. 53–69. And the exchange between A. Mitchell, 'The Association Movement of 1792–3', *Historical Journal* 4 (1961), pp. 56–77; and D. E. Ginter, 'The Loyalist Association Movement of 1792–3 and British Public Opinion', *Historical Journal* 9 (1966), pp. 179–90.

[46] J. E. Cookson, 'The English Volunteer Movement of the French Wars, 1793–1815: Some Contexts', *Historical Journal* 32 (1989), pp. 867–891 (quoted, p. 868). Idem, *The Friends of Peace: Anti-War Liberalism in England, 1793–1815*, Cambridge, 1982, p. 26 and passim. See also the overwhelmingly loyalist role assigned to the 'middle classes' in idem, 'British Society and the French Wars', *Australian Journal of Politics and History* 31 (1985), pp. 192–203. Cookson however has not explained (or indeed, acknowledged) the apparent incompatibility of these different statements. Clive Emsley has reproduced both conclusions side by side as straightforwardly complementary in his 'The Social Impact of the French Wars', in H. T. Dickinson (ed.), *Britain and the French Revolution, 1789–1815*, New York, 1989, pp. 221–3.

rather familiar: that the recognition of a 'middle class' as it surfaced in the 1790s was not a straightforward reflection of either social or political configurations. Instead it was a very specific representation of these configurations, a representation that was the collective outcome of numerous choices impelled by the political goals of those who made them. As a consequence, in spite of the broad overlap of the social base of loyalism with that of the Friends of Peace, the opposite politics of loyalists prevented them from effectively using notions of 'middle class'. The appropriation of 'middle-class' language by those opposed to the war, which tainted it with particular political colours, was – at least for a while – quite successful.

A priori, there was nothing inherent in the language of 'middle class' that guaranteed this outcome. In fact, before the war was declared it had not necessarily always been the case. Formerly one could find (albeit not very often) occasional loyalist utterances in which 'middle-class' language did play a role. In 1792, for example, one writer of rather humble origins, who opposed the harmful Painite ideas about liberty and equality, argued: 'I find none have at present so much at stake as we middling people, who are in the greatest danger of being deceived into our ruin ... in asserting our liberty, (as they call it) by subverting the present order of things, and making every one *Equal*.'[47] Here, the 'middle class' were those singled out as the greatest potential losers from the possible spread of republican ideas. Also in 1792, another writer of similar political convictions began a letter to Pitt with 'the opinion of Lycurgus, that "the two extremes of great wealth and great indigence are the source of infinite mischiefs in a free State."' By contrast, 'it is a well-known fact, that the middling or trading class of people constitute the riches of a State'. This 'middle-class idiom' was followed with the recommendation, also familiar from later antiwar writings, to avoid the destructive policy of imposing further fiscal burdens on the 'middling class of people', who were

---

[47] *Liberty and Equality: Treated of in a Short History Addressed from a Poor Man to His Equals*, London, 1792, p. [5]. The author, interestingly 'a poor man' but also of the 'middling people', has been 'labouring for my subsistance at a business I have diligently followed for fifteen years' (p. [3]). Purportedly he himself was a follower of Paine before realizing his dangerous mistakes. Notably, in contrast with his own 'middle-class' language, a radical Painite with whom he conversed continually spoke in dual social terms, 'about the hardships of the Poor; [and] the Cruelty of the Rich' (p. 15).

already struggling with severe difficulties. In order to prevent a Painite turbulent democracy of total equality, this Pittite author explained in early 1793, measures which would help the people should be adopted, since '"The middle way is the safest" ... Now, when the *rights* of man are so loudly insisted on. This attention, by gaining the affections of the middling class of the people, would be a greater security to the kingdom than hosts of soldiers in arms.'[48] The conflation in this passage of the political middle and the social middle is highly reminiscent of the rhetoric of the Friends of Peace. Indeed, in 1792, and even in early 1793, such an appeal, which turned the middle position (and with it the 'middle-class idiom') around so that its thrust was aimed at the radicals rather than at the administration, made no less sense.

An unusually direct glimpse of loyalist voices before the war can be found in the letters sent to John Reeves's Association for the Preservation of Liberty and Property against Republicans and Levellers, mostly upon the occasion of its foundation in late 1792.[49] The very successful Association was a catalyst for vigorous local efforts of loyalist organization throughout the country, mostly of propertied and often locally prominent activists. It also triggered a barrage of declarations and letters, of which a considerable number originated in middle social strata. And here again, at this early stage before the beginning of the war, 'middle-class' language did appear with occasional argumentative significance, though it was clearly far from central to these patriotic manifestos. In several hundreds of letters, a handful of 'middle-class' proclamations of loyalty can be found. 'I conceive we shall do splendid service by bringing forward the middle rank of people', wrote one loyalist from Suffolk, thus countering 'whatever disaffection there is in this country [that] has been fomented ... among the lowest of the Farmers and Common

---

[48] [Andrew Becket], *Public Prosperity: Or, Arguments, in Support of a Lately-projected Plan for Raising Six Million Sterling, and for Employing that Sum in Loans to Necessitous and Industrious Persons*, London, 1793, pp. 5–6 (from letter to Pitt, 1 January 1792), and p. 33, written *c.* January 1793 (see p. 16).

[49] These letters are preserved in the British Library, Add. Mss vols. 16919–28. For the Association, see the studies in note 45, as well as C. Brooks, 'John Reeves and His Correspondents: A Contribution to the Study of British Loyalism 1792–1793', in *Après 1789: la révolution modèle ou repoussoir*, pp. 49–76.

People.'⁵⁰ Another objected to the word 'Gentlemen' in the title
of the first resolutions of the Association, since he was 'convinced
that a multitude of Persons in the middle Class of Society,
particularly in the Metropolis, who wish well to the cause and
would be eager to add their Names to the Association, may be
now deterred', through either modesty or jealousy.⁵¹

On the whole, then, early loyalist arguments did occasionally
resort to the language of 'middle class', though it does not appear
to have played a particularly important role nor to have carried
a particularly conspicuous appeal for pre-war supporters of the
administration. Nevertheless, such notions could potentially have
developed into an increasingly effective way of mobilizing propertied folk against plebeian radicalism. But those pivotal months
of 1792 and 1793 – the same months that witnessed the intensifi-
cation of the radical movement, of ministerial repression and of
political polarization, as well as the beginning of the war
– proved to be also a turning point in the loyalist uses of
'middle-class' language: rather than becoming more frequent,
such pronouncements all but disappeared. Whatever potential
'middle-class' language had had for the loyalist cause, sometime
in 1793 it seems to have been completely lost.

Again, it cannot be overemphasized that this turn of events
was far from self-evident. After all, it is easy to imagine what
'middle-class idiom' proclamations in support for the war *could*
have sounded like: stressing the ultimate value and contribution

---

⁵⁰ British Library, Add. Mss 16922, f. 81: W. to J. Reeves, 13 December 1792. See also
16920, f. 98, the letter of G. J. Huntingford to Reeves, 4 December 1792, asserting
that 'persons, who like myself move in the Middle Rank of Life', understood the
people better than 'persons of Quality'.

⁵¹ Add. Mss 16919, f. 162: J. Barnes to J. Moore (secretary of the Association), 30
November 1792. For two rather dubious cases, see also 16926, f. 33, 'Well Wisher to
my Country . . .' to J. Moore, n.d.; and 16923, f. 48, J. Trimmer (to Reeves), 22
December 1792. Likewise, in a tract published by the Association, a writer who
addressed 'the Mistaken Part of the Community' presented his credentials as 'one
who is neither in a superior or inferior situation in life, who is totally disinterested':
Liberty and Property Preserved Against Republicans and Levellers. A Collection of Tracts, London,
[1792?], 7, p. 3 (see also the non-loaded 'middle-class' language in no. 1, p. 12). By
contrast, some letters to Reeves's Association sought to counteract *Jacobinical* tendencies
among the disaffected 'middle and lower ranks', though only one went as far as
declaring the goal of the Association to be 'the Information and Tranquillisation of
all the Middle Ranks of People' (which it then identified with 'the Mercantile and
Trading interests'): British Library, Add. Mss 16919, f. 37, to J. Moore, 26 November
1792. And see 16919, f. 158, W. Tancourt to J. Moore, 30 November 1792; 16924,
f. 53, to Reeves, 8 January 1793; f. 72, Henry Luson to J. Moore, 10 January 1793.

of the loyal, responsible and dependable 'middle class' for the protection of the constitution and the monarchy, when facing the unprecedented threats of the French menace from without and of the Jacobin fermentation of the irresponsible and fickle lower classes from within. Rather than challenging the supremacy of the ruling elite, such statements could have highlighted the interdependence of the 'middle class', the broad-based pillar of society, and its aristocratic Corinthian capital: the former supporting the latter, the latter crowning and adorning the former. In fact, one need not resort to such counterfactuals: as we shall see later, similar statements, loud and clear, were to become an important leitmotif of the propertied reaction to the resurgent radicalism of the immediate post-war period. Their effective reiteration at that future juncture underscores their glaring absence some twenty years earlier. It also illustrates again that the political alignment of the language of 'middle class' in the 1790s was not somehow inherent in its nature, but rather contingent upon the peculiar circumstances of that decade.

It is of course difficult to put forward evidence for such an argument woven from silences, that is to say for an argument about words and formulations *not* used by certain parties. One indication may be taken from the evolution of the social language of a Pittite gentleman such as Arthur Young. In the 1780s and early 1790s, Young wrote appreciatively of the landed 'middle classes' and pointed to their interest in investments as well as to the beneficial effects of their middle-size estates. In his travels in France, published in May 1792, Young noted in passing that 'knowledge, intelligence, information, learning, and wisdom ... are all found to reside most in the middle classes of mankind'. The conclusion was spelled out in the first edition of his *The Example of France, a Warning to Britain*, written in summer 1792 and published in February 1793: 'I am myself in the number of those who wish a reform ... I wish the middle classes of landed property better represented' (though this moderate reform should not be sought after at this dangerous moment). But Young was rapidly turning against any notion of reform; two months later, in a second edition of this tract, enlarged to include a justification of the war against France which had since erupted, he qualified this statement in the list of errata: 'for I am – read I was, for wish – read wished'. And as Young distanced himself further from the camp of moderate reform, he also distanced himself from the language of 'middle class'. Indeed he actually changed his mind about the advantages of medium landed estates, now arguing that in fact it was the larger ones that were more productive and efficient, and the big landowners who were more capable of improvements in the long term. By 1797, when Young appealed at length to the patriotic sense of the yeomanry, by which he undoubtedly meant his very same landed 'middle class' of the previous years, he refrained throughout from using this by-now loaded term.[52] The contrast with Christopher Wyvill's writing, which changed during the same period in precisely the opposite direction as it came increasingly to incorporate a distinct sense of 'middle-class' presence and importance, is especially instructive. Both Wyvill and Young were middling gentlemen who saw themselves as spokesmen for the landed classes; where they differed, increasingly so in the 1790s, was in their politics.

Other loyalist writings also present silences which we may take as suggestive. Particularly revealing are loyalists who were singing the patriotic praises of social groups that could readily have been encompassed under the category of 'middle class', and yet, conspicuously, failed to do so. Take John Bowles: in one of his fervent exhortations for contributions to support the war, addressed to 'a British Merchant', Bowles stated that in the present patriotic effort, 'it cannot be denied that the Commercial Interest would, with peculiar propriety, take the lead'; the 'wealthy and respectable' merchants of London should 'set the example' for loyalist mobilization.[53] One can easily see how such a statement could have benefited from explicit 'middle-class idiom', but that was not the case. Nor was it the case in another enthusiastic pro-war tract which expressed in 1793 confidence in the ability of the nation to withstand the present challenge, since it could depend on the rallying of 'a respectable yeomanry; a

---

[52] Arthur Young, *Travels, during the Years 1787, 1788, and 1789 . . . [in] the Kingdom of France*, Bury St Edmunds, 1792, p. 549n. (and see 552n.). Idem, *The Example of France, a Warning to Britain*, London, 1793, p. 42 (based on articles dated 20 August–12 October 1792); 2nd edn, London, 1793, corrections for pp. 398–9. Idem, *National Danger and the Means of Safety*, London, 1797. Note also the *critical* perspective on the 'middle class' which Young adopted in another context in 1798: see pp. 398–9. I owe the observations on Young's opinions about landowners to Peter Mandler.

[53] [John Bowles], *Two Letters Addressed to a British Merchant, a Short Time Before the Expected Meeting of the New Parliament in 1796*, 3rd edn, London, 1796, pp. 82–3.

hardy, vigorous peasantry; an infinite multitude of artisans and manufacturers, and people of all descriptions' – all descriptions, that is, but a 'middle class'. Additional such examples from numerous loyalist sources can readily be adduced.[54]

Obviously I do not claim complete familiarity with the whole body of loyalist literature. But having confronted pro-war sources roughly to the same extent as their anti-war counterparts, the enormous disparity between the marked prevalence of the 'middle-class idiom' in the latter and the precious few examples which could be found in the former is ultimately my strongest evidence in support of the argument made here. In fact, from the beginning of the war until the debate on the Triple Assessment Bill at the end of 1797, I have found only two instances where 'middle-class idiom' was incorporated into pro-government rhetoric. Only two, from sources representing almost five years of war.

The first such exception, in an early tract of 1794 whose intention was not to exhort to war but to prevent a revolution in England, is an excellent illustration of the rhetorical potential that the loyalists lost. The 'middle ranks', went the argument of the (anonymous) author Thomas Atkinson, 'are aware of the dreadful consequences of civil commotions', and have much to lose in terms of the property which they have been able to accumulate 'under an indulgent government'. Moreover, 'they are too virtuous in principle to sanction sedition, rapine, and murder; men of too great sense to be duped by the *cant* of

---

[54] [Rev. J. Hampson], *Observations on the Present War, the Projected Invasion, and a Decree of the National Convention, for the Emancipation of the Slaves in the French Colonies*, Sunderland, [1793], p. 50. Some further instances include William Brooke, *The True Causes of Our Present Distress for Provisions*, London, 1800, pp. 7–8, where an appreciation of the aristocracy as the most valuable branch of the constitution was combined with remarks about the meritorious small farmer and peasant, and about 'moderate farmers', but without any 'middle-class' language; C. W. B. Rouse (later Sir C. W. R. Boughton), *Substance of an Address to a Parochial Meeting Held at Chiswick ... on ... the 20th Feb. 1798, to Consider the Propriety of a Voluntary Contribution for the Defence of the Country ...*, London, 1798, which referred to loyalist merchants, traders and bankers, 'whose occupations [are] of meritorious and useful industry' (p. 14), but mentioned no 'middle class'; or George Brewer, *The Rights of the Poor Considered*, London, 1800, in which the anti-radical author presented a detailed classification of society by ranks, compounded with a dual vision of rich and poor (pp. 20–1, 27–30). Again, in both of Brewer's social visions the 'middle class' was conspicuously absent; as it was also in William Ogilvie's letter of 1794 (as quoted in Dickinson, 'Popular Loyalism', p. 523) enumerating in detail the loyalist propertied classes.

Philosophy, and value their religion too much to exchange it for the barren reveries of re-animated paganism'. Therefore, concluded Atkinson, 'I declare myself perfectly convinced, that this is the class in society, which in concurrence with a government so excellent as ours, is always capable of stemming the torrent of sedition.'[55] A confident and promising statement indeed, but virtually a unique one. The one other case I came across was a sermon occasioned by a national fast day in February 1795, wherein Henry Reginald Courtenay, Bishop of Bristol, expressed satisfaction with the efforts on behalf of the establishment made by 'that useful and respectable class of men, unknown to other States, who, by the peculiar happiness of the British Constitution, form the intermediate links of that chain which unites the higher to the lower orders of society'.[56] All in all, this couple of isolated seedlings (to which perhaps a handful more can be added), in the absence of a fertile rhetorical soil for them to fall on, apparently withered away.[57] Certainly they did not amount to much of a counter-trend to the rich thicket of 'middle-class idiom' in which the anti-war rhetoric became entwined.

The divergence in the language used to discuss the composition of society between the anti-war and the pro-war voices can best be recovered by examining their interactions in direct dialogue. One can demonstrate most convincingly the extent and signifi-

---

[55] [Thomas Atkinson], *A Concise Sketch of the Intended Revolution, in England: With a Few Hints on the Obvious Methods to Avert It*, London, 1794, pp. 15–16. (I owe this attribution to Gregory Claeys.)

[56] Henry Reginald Courtenay, *A Sermon, Preached before the Lords Spiritual and Temporal . . . on Wednesday, February 25, 1795, Being the Day Appointed by His Majesty's Proclamation for a General Fast*, London, 1795, p. 12. It is perhaps significant that the direct audience of this unusual (albeit somewhat vague) 'middle-class idiom' was not the loyalists of the social 'middle' strata, but rather the aristocratic members of the House of Lords. Fast days were annual days of 'national humiliation and prayer' observed throughout the war, and thus were key moments of loyalist expressions. Proclaimed by the Privy Council, they were the only formally appointed days of national observance outside the ecclesiastical calendar.

[57] In one other possible exception, another clergyman who seems to have favoured the war described in 1796 the plight of the 'middle ranks', as part of the distress which has become prevalent in almost all ranks of society: *Three Sermons inscribed to the Friends of Peace, Reason and Revelation. By a Clergyman of the Church of England*, 1796, p. 23; as quoted in *Analytical Review* 25, January 1797, p. 58. I have been unable to locate a copy of this pamphlet, and thus to determine its contents and political inclinations. And see below, pp. 123–5, for the no less sparse exceptions to this persistent pattern of political differentiation of social language in the extensive debates on the Triple Assessment Bill.

cance of silences when they are juxtaposed with the utterances which they deny; that is to say, when one side's insistent reiteration of 'middle-class' language was met with a correspondingly insistent failure to respond in the same terms. Of course, such a situation tended to camouflage the very existence of dialogue: employing different vocabularies, it was not immediately evident that the interlocutors were in fact talking to each other.

Thus, when that prolific pro-war writer, John Bowles, responded angrily to 'the ever-lively apprehensions of the Merchant and the Manufacturer' about the burdens of the war, what he did *not* say was as telling as what he did. 'Of all classes of persons', he remarked, 'the Commercial has the least reason to indulge restlessness and impatience under the War', since they, 'the Trading Interest', would also derive the most extensive advantages from its successful conclusion. 'The Merchant, the Manufacturer, the Peasant, and the Peer' – all were endangered by the present crisis, and hence all should support the war.[58] Between the common topoi for the ends of the social scale, the peasant and the peer, what Bowles noticed were the particular complaints of merchants and manufacturers, of a commercial class, of a trading interest: anything but a 'middle class', whose complaint was in fact conspicuously central to the rhetoric of his opponents to which he was responding.[59] To take another example, the readers of the moderately radical *Analytical Review* could get a sense of this differentiation of social language from two adjacent articles in their issue of May 1797: one expressed the editors' opinion, that because of the war 'the *rich* [are] monopolizing commerce and trade, [and] the middle classes [are]

---

[58] John Bowles, *Objections to the Continuance of the War Examined and Refuted*, 2nd edn, London, 1794, pp. 27–32, 37–8. Similarly, another pro-war tract of the same year accepted the 'middle-class' grievance against the war in its own terms, admitting that it may indeed be harmful to manufacturers and merchants, and seeing the problem as one between the two interests of trade and land: *War with France, the Only Security of Britain, at the Present Momentous Crisis Set Forth in an Earnest Address to His Fellow-Subjects, by an Old Englishman*, London, 1794, pp. 33–4.

[59] Bowles repeated the same refutation three years later, again avoiding 'middle-class' language (which by now had become ubiquitous in oppositional anti-war arguments revolving around taxation): 'of all classes of men, the mercantile interest is most subject to those sudden alarms and apprehensions, which induce a blind and inconsiderate impatience to get rid of War, almost on any terms' – a mistake which is due to their selfish and short-sighted understanding of their own interests. (Idem, *A Third Letter to a British Merchant* ..., London, 1797, p. 74.)

ruined and undone'; the other quoted a Pittite author advising the minister not to heed the complaints about war taxation coming from 'the whole body of merchants [who] would, perhaps, unitedly, exclaim, that their commerce was ruined'.[60] So here the readers had the two alternatives side by side – the typical 'middle-class' grievance against the war, and the no less typical response in support of the war which recast the issue in a different social vocabulary.

Or take the observations on taxation in the ardent pro-war tract published by John Young in Glasgow in 1794. Young, as he proudly emphasized, was a Dissenting minister of rather humble origins – an interesting corrective to frequent wholesale depictions of all Dissenters as anti-Pittites.[61] The burdens of taxation, Young argued, were in reality not as severe as they seemed. Yet, unfortunately, among some classes who felt particularly hurt by duties or excise laws, such as West-India merchants, distillers or tallow-chandlers, 'a person of a turbulent spirit' might arise, who would 'raise a fermentation in the minds of well-meaning labourers and mechanics'. Having thus blamed political instability on middle social groups, who incited the well-meaning lower classes, Young also imputed to the former the responsibility for financial instability: it was not the war that was the main cause of recent commercial and manufacturing misfortunes and failures, he claimed, but rather their having 'stretched themselves beyond their capital, in hopes of growing suddenly rich' – that is, their uncontrolled ambitions. By contrast, Young asserted, 'land is the most fixed kind of property, and the radical source of national wealth'; from which he concluded that legislators ought to be of the landed classes. 'I have never

---

[60] Reviews of J. Brand, *Considerations on the Depression of the Funds, and the Present Embarrassments of Circulation, with Propositions for Some Remedies to Each*, and of *A General Address to the Representatives of Great Britain, on Important National Subjects, Agitating at the Present Period. By an Elector*, Stockdale, 1797; in the *Analytical Review* 25, May 1797, pp. 535, 547. On this periodical and its moderate radicalism see B. Rigby, 'Radical Spectators of the Revolution: The Case of the *Analytical Review*', in C. Crossley and I. Small (eds.), *The French Revolution and British Culture*, Oxford, 1989, pp. 63–83.

[61] Other self-proclaimed loyalist Dissenters can be found, for instance, in the correspondence of John Reeves, head of the Association for the Preservation of Liberty and Property against Republicans and Levellers: see British Library, Add. Mss 16922, f. 121; 16927, f. 41. See also the various examples in Langford, *Public Life and the Propertied Englishman*, pp. 90–3. For the opposite viewpoint, using 'anti-war liberals' and 'Dissenters' interchangeably, see Cookson, *The Friends of Peace*, passim.

yet observed', concluded Young, 'that there was a greater proportion of morally honest men, in the lowest ranks of life, than
among their superiors.'[62] Overall, Young was obviously in dialogue with the proponents of the 'middle class', countering their
claims across the board: the members of the social middle were
potentially revolutionary, selfishly ambitious and not as burdened
by taxation as they ceaselessly complained to be; their contribution to national wealth was doubtful, and their moral claims
were just as questionable; whereas in truth it was the landed
classes who were the reliable support of the nation. Again, however, in all of these rebuttals of his opponents' claims, not even
once did Young acknowledge that he was refuting arguments
made about a 'middle class'.

As these examples suggest, the issue which most often brought
the political adversaries of these years into direct dialogue with
each other was the burden of the war taxes. At no point was
this issue more vehemently argued over than in the debate over
Pitt's triple assessment proposals in the winter of 1797. This
debate was a peak moment in the appropriation of 'middle-class'
language by the respectable opposition on the one hand, and in
the attempts of the pro-Pittites to resist it on the other. The
differentiation of social vocabularies along partisan lines in this
debate forms the subject of the next chapter. But as we look into
it more closely, one word of caution bears repeating. Although the
present discussion at times appears to convey an image of languages combating each other in the battlefield of lexical warfare,
in fact it is important to keep constantly in mind that words by
themselves carried no power and had no agency. The contestation
over language was one manifestation of adversarial politics, whose
agents were human actors vying for power in a particularly
turbulent political scene, striving in their own conflicting ways
to shape or to save the world around them, and for whom the
use of language was but a means towards those ends.

[62] John Young, *Essays on the Following Interesting Subjects* . . ., 2nd edn, corrected, Glasgow,
1794, quoted, pp. 31, 86, 89, 150. For his social origin see p. 35.

CHAPTER 4

The political differentiation of social language: the debate on the triple assessment, 1797–1798

The greater part of the weight [is] upon the middle classes.
(John Nicholls in parliament on 14 December 1797 against the Triple Assessment Bill, as reported in the oppositional *Morning Chronicle*)

It went to destroy the comforts of the lower classes . . . The measure went to destroy the lowest orders.
(John Nicholls in parliament on 14 December 1797 against the Triple Assessment Bill, as reported in the pro-ministerial *True Briton*)[1]

In spring 1797, the young Tory wit George Canning addressed William Windham, Pitt's Secretary at War, with the following lines:

Come, Windham! celebrate with me
This day of joy and jubilee.
This day of *no* disaster!
Our Government is *not* o'erturned –
Huzza! – Our Fleet has *not* been burned;
Our Army's *not* our master.[2]

Canning's sarcasm hit home hard. The year 1797 was, indeed, disastrous for the nation at war. February witnessed a thousand French troops actually landing on British soil at Fishguard in Pembrokeshire (following a larger attempt which did not materialize in December), exacerbating anxieties about an imminent French invasion. April saw one naval mutiny at Spithead, and May another at the Nore. In May the remaining illusions of business as usual were shattered when the Foxite opposition, in

---

[1] Speech on 14 December 1797: *Morning Chronicle* 8911, 15 December 1797; *True Briton* 1553, 15 December 1797.
[2] Quoted in A. Bryant, *The Years of Endurance 1793–1802*, New York, 1942, p. 193.

a most extraordinary step, withdrew from the House of Commons. In October Austria, Britain's last powerful ally, backed out of the conflict in the peace treaty of Campo Formio, while in Ireland unrest was increasing.

Perhaps even more ominous was the precarious state of British finances, encumbered by a rapidly swelling debt. The increasing doubts about the government's ability to redeem its debts were dramatically revealed in the rush on the Bank of England in late February, following the dangerous dwindling of its specie reserves; the Bank was saved only by the Privy Council's emergency measure of suspending cash payments (that is, allowing banks to refuse payment of bullion in exchange for notes, thus creating a controversial system of 'paper credit'). The urgency of the crisis was further revealed in the preliminary steps taken that year towards arming the nation by raising a militia. And when the mounting pressures of this predicament pushed Pitt to make some overtures towards negotiating peace, the peace efforts proved no more successful than the war efforts. By December, the situation seemed grave enough for General Cornwallis, a war veteran who had experienced many a tight spot, to lose heart: 'Torn as we are by faction', he wrote, 'without an army, without money, trusting entirely to a navy whom we may not be able to pay, and on whose loyalty, even if we can, no firm reliance is to be placed, how are we to get out of this cursed war without a Revolution?'[3]

The answer, of course, was more money. At the very moment that Cornwallis was writing these gloomy words, parliament was busy debating Pitt's new financial plan for obtaining supplies requisite for the war effort in the following year. Whereas previously Pitt had attempted to meet the unprecedented expenditure of this war by adding to the national debt rather than by imposing additional taxes, the doubts about the solvency of the government and other economic circumstances now persuaded

---

[3] Cornwallis (then Master-General of the Ordnance) to Ross, 15 December 1797, quoted in J. Holland Rose, *William Pitt and the Great War*, London, 1911, p. 299; and chapter 14 for the crisis of 1797. See also C. Emsley, *British Society and the French Wars 1793–1815*, London, 1979, pp. 56–64. J. E. Cookson, *The Friends of Peace: Anti-War Liberalism in England, 1793–1815*, Cambridge, 1982, pp. 157–8. The 'emotional atmosphere' of 1797, that 'crucial year in British moral history', resulting in 'the fear of England's decline and fall', is noted in E. Trudgill, *Madonnas and Magdalens: The Origins and Development of Victorian Sexual Attitudes*, New York, 1976, pp. 31–2, 166.

him to shift more of the war burden to taxation raised within
the year.[4] This was the logic behind the proposals which Pitt
placed before the House at the end of November: the most
important innovation was the Triple Assessment Bill, actually
consisting of a scaled increase (ranging from 25 per cent to 500
per cent) in the assessed taxes, which were taxes on purported
luxuries (such as house windows, male servants, horses and
carriages, dogs, etc.).[5] Given the burden of these proposed taxes
(see figure 5), the ignominious record of the previous year, and
the general fatigue with a war protracted beyond the hope of a
quick resolution, it was inevitable that the debate about Pitt's
proposals would turn into an especially fierce argument about
the war itself; an argument deemed important enough for the
Foxites to return momentarily from their self-imposed political
exile. The debate indoors, in turn, aroused keen interest out of
doors, and dominated the various means of political communication throughout the country from the end of November to early
January. As one Sophia Briscoe of Leyton wrote in a letter to
Pitt (one of many of its kind) in mid December: 'The War has
been said to have made us a nation of Politicians, and now from
the severity of the proposed extra assessments, many will become
Financiers.'[6]

In the noisy protests against Pitt's plan, reiterated daily in
parliament, in newspapers, in pamphlets, in public meetings and
in petitions, the 'middle-class' grievance played a central role.

---

[4] P. K. O'Brien, 'Public Finance in the Wars with France 1793–1815', in H. T. Dickinson
(ed.), *Britain and the French Revolution, 1789–1815*, New York, 1989, pp. 165–87; and
idem, 'The Political Economy of British Taxation, 1660–1815', *Economic History Review*
2nd ser., 41 (1988), pp. 20–2. Also R. Cooper, 'William Pitt, Taxation, and the Needs
of War', *Journal of British Studies* 22:1 (1982), pp. 94–103. On the pessimism about
Britain's ability to shoulder the unprecedented war burdens (which for the most part
was assuaged only after 1798), see also J. E. Cookson, 'Political Arithmetic and War
in Britain, 1793–1815', *War and Society* 1:2 (1983), pp. 37–60.

[5] For details of the Triple Assessment Bill, see S. Dowell, *A History of Taxation and Taxes
in England from the Earliest Times to the Present Day*, 4 vols., London, 1884; rep. New
York, 1965, vol. II, pp. 220–2. Also Emsley, *British Society and the French Wars*, pp. 70–1.

[6] Sophia Briscoe to W. Pitt, 14 December 1797: PRO, Chatham Papers, vol. 264, f.
168. Apparently publicly encouraged by Pitt, hundreds of citizens sent letters to him
(and later to his successors at the Treasury) making sundry suggestions about adequate
taxation measures. These letters present an interesting array of common people's
perceptions of what constituted luxuries, demonstrating their repeated conviction that,
as it were, one's neighbour's grass was always taxable. These letters yet await systematic
analysis, which may provide interesting insights into lay reactions to the scaled
expansion of a consumer culture.

Figure 5. The burden of taxation at the end of 1797. John Bull as a shackled Atlas, kneeling under the burden of 'A World of Taxes'. A prominent place is given to the triple assessed taxes that preoccupied parliament and the nation at that moment (note the dates of drawing and publication, both by Richard Newton). *Source*: BMC 9159.

Since the lower classes were exempt, the critics warned, and since
the higher classes would remain in practice largely unaffected by
this rise of the assessment, the brunt of the increase would fall
with particular severity on the 'middle class': either directly by
curtailing its consumption, which would be reduced from 'comforts' to bare 'necessities'; or indirectly by limiting its employment
in producing articles of consumption for its social superiors (an
argument not necessarily consistent with the claim that the latter
would not be affected). It was often added that the poor would
also suffer indirectly, since the 'middle class' would be unable
to afford to employ them as much as they had done before. The
partisan connotations of the language of 'middle class' both
enhanced the force of these arguments and were reinforced again
by them. The opposition speakers frequently supported their
claims with statements of the evaluative 'middle-class idiom':
they stressed the importance of this valuable social group which
was now oppressed by Pitt's schemes, an inescapable consequence
of a ruinous war. The centrality of the language of 'middle class'
to the case of the opposition makes this moment particularly
valuable in examining in detail the contestation over competing
social languages and over their political implications. The present
chapter focuses on the ensuing differentiation of social vocabularies during this debate, which aligned them with striking consistency along marked partisan lines. The divergence in the two
versions of John Nicholls's utterance in parliament, in the epigraphs above, will be seen to have been far from a coincidence,
but rather part of an extraordinary pattern: during this electrified
debate, the 'middle class' was quite literally dependent on the
eye (or ear, rather) of the beholder.

   The *Morning Chronicle*, the most important and outspoken opposition newspaper, repeatedly emphasized the 'middle-class' grievance: 'It is truly insulting to the feelings of the middling classes
of the community to be told that the triple assessment will bear
hardest on the higher ranks'; 'it is not the Nobility and Gentry,
but the Middle Classes of Society whom this new-fangled Tax
will grind!'; and so on. The issue produced a flurry among
Morning Chronicle readers, who within the first week of the discussion inundated the editors with 'no fewer than 200 letters of
remonstrance against the new plan of a forced Assessment, and
from every part of the country. It has struck a panic to the heart

of the nation.'[7] One anxious correspondent, 'Junius', claimed that the tax

> in truth is principally operative on the middle classes, whilst it will be hardly felt by the higher classes at all . . . The effect of this plan then is to destroy the present structure of society, and to leave only two orders – the highest and the lowest . . . [Savings] will be devoured by the greedy rapacity of an unfeeling Minister, who having never moved in any but the higher circles of life, has no idea of the situation of the middle classes, and is therefore regardless of their interests.[8]

Overall, between the editorials and letters published in the *Morning Chronicle*, in addition to – as we shall see – parish resolutions and reports of parliamentary debates, there was scarcely a day during these weeks in which the readers of this insistent newspaper did not receive some reinforcement of the specific 'middle-class' case against the pending Bill, mostly set in broader anti-war arguments.[9]

Similar 'middle-class' grievances abounded in other opposition newspapers and periodicals. Like 'Junius', the *Newcastle Chronicle* also saw the proposals as proof of the direct animosity of Pitt towards the 'middle class': 'Mr Pitt in all his measures seems to level the great force of his artillery against the middle ranks of the people, apparently wishing to have only two classes in the state, the *overgrown rich*, and the *miserably poor!*'[10] 'The most oppressive part of this unparalleled plan falls on the middle class', echoed the *Cambridge Intelligencer*.[11] The *Monthly Magazine* protested that the triple assessment

[7] *Morning Chronicle*, editorials in 8900, 8905, 8909; 2, 8, 13 December 1797.

[8] Letter by 'Junius' to Pitt, *Morning Chronicle* 8899, 1 December 1797. For similar letters, see 8900, 2 December 1797; 8916, 21 December 1797.

[9] For similar statements in other editorials of the *Morning Chronicle*, amounting to about once every other issue during the month of December, see 8898, 8900, 8904, 8908, 8913, 8914, 8917 (twice), 8920, 8921; on 30 November, 2, 7, 12, 18, 19, 22, 26 and 27 December 1797.

[10] Editorial in *Newcastle Chronicle* 1744, 2 December 1797. We may also recall the elaborate essay 'On the Importance of the Middle Ranks of Society' published in the January 1798 issue of *The Oeconomist*.

[11] Editorial in *Cambridge Intelligencer* 230, 9 December 1797. It continued: 'We might shew its more mischievous consequences to the various descriptions of people in the middle class of life – The hitherto independent country gentleman – The inferior, though more respectable part of the clergy – The farmer – The tradesman: but the perusal of the plan itself will, to the attentive reader, most effectually discover its horrors.' See also the editorial in the following issue (231, 16 December 1797).

will not bear upon the great and opulent, who will not be taxed either according to their property or expenditure; but it will bear upon the middle industrious classes of citizens, who will by this means, be robbed of all their little savings; and in many instances be reduced to beggary.[12]

Or listen to the numerous resolutions of parish committees – mostly representing persons of middle social strata – against the proposed increase in the assessment. The *Morning Chronicle* alone published in about a fortnight more than twenty such resolutions, mostly from the metropolitan area, voicing the plight of the 'middle class'; and other newspapers followed suit. Usually the references to the 'middle class', at times joined with the 'lower class', were rather short: the taxes, proclaimed the united parishes of St Margaret and St John the Evangelist at Westminster, would 'totally ruin the Middle Class of Householders'. More elaborate was the resolution taken in Hammersmith against the plan, as 'tending to destroy the middle orders of society, who in former times were considered as the strength of the country'.[13] One letter to the *Morning Herald* perhaps epitomized best this wave of protest: the letter was titled 'Ruined! Ruined! Ruined!', and was signed 'ONE OF THE MIDDLE CLASS OF PEOPLE'.[14]

These examples are only a small fraction of the myriad of such protestations which were voiced against Pitt's proposals in the winter of 1797. Within this widespread explosion of 'middle-class' language one can notice different levels of argumentative potency: some focused on the 'middle class' as the principal

---

[12] *Monthly Magazine* 4, November 1797, p. 397. For 'middle-class idiom' in this periodical see above, p. 53. Compare also Capel Lofft's letter to Wyvill (20 December 1797): 'I have been making what individual effort I could against Mr Pitt's delusive and baneful project of aggravated taxation, when the middle class, and consequently those connected with this class for employment and support, are sinking under their present burthens.' (C. Wyvill, *Political Papers*, York, [1804], vol. v, p. 386.) Lofft, a Dissenting reformist barrister, believed that the shock which Pitt's proposals would have induced among his supporters could cause his downfall.

[13] Both resolutions were printed in the *Morning Chronicle* 8914, 19 December 1797. Compare the resolutions sent by the parish of Christ Church, Spitalfields, to the *Star* (2916, 21 December 1797): 'this Parish in particular being situate in the centre of the Silk Manufactory, and many of the middle classes of People, consisting of Tradesmen and Shopkeepers, being in a great degree dependant on the said Manufactory . . . the burthen will fall [on them] with peculiar weight'. See also the statement of the Ward of the Castle Precincts in the same issue.

[14] *Morning Herald* 5386, 25 December 1797; see also editorials in 5825, 5826, 5828, 5379 (there is some irregularity in issue numbering): 2, 4, 6, 16 December 1797. For the 'middle-class' complaint in the oppositional *Star*, see editorial in 2907, 11 December 1797; letter to editor in 2920, 26 December 1797.

victim, others saw it as one of several social groups oppressed by Pitt's policies; some compounded this language with strong assertions of 'middle-class idiom', others were less committal. Yet in one form or another the language of 'middle class' unquestionably became a quintessential component of oppositional rhetoric in the debate on the Triple Assessment Bill, as it had never been before. Consequently the partisan political implications of this language, which had been building up since the commencement of the war, became now more conspicuous than ever.

Pro-ministerial speakers were quick to respond. On one level, they straightforwardly denied what their opponents were saying. The increase of the assessed taxes was scaled in such a way, reassured the *True Briton*, that it would not burden anyone who cannot pay; 'So much for the peculiar oppression upon the lower and middle classes', misleadingly denounced by the opposition.[15] A different response, not necessarily compatible, granted that the 'middle' of society would indeed bear a large part of the burden, but found this to be just and proper, because recent years and current government policies had proven particularly favourable to the well-being and prosperity of these members of society. Once again, the proponents of these arguments were not altogether clear or consistent about the social identity of the people they were talking about: some preferred to present the clamour as that of wealthy merchants, while others sought to assuage the concerns of 'manufacturers and labourers, in the possession of incomes below sixty pounds a year', whose situation in recent years 'has been greatly meliorated'.[16] On the other hand, Pittites also pointed to the particularly heavy burdens shouldered by the landed classes:

while merchants and manufacturers, are, very universally all over the kingdom, living in ease, luxury, and affluence, a great proportion of those whose property consists entirely in land, find it impossible to live upon their income, and are therefore deeply in debt. So that while the situation of one part of the community has been daily improving better, that of landed proprietors has become considerably worse.

---

[15] *True Briton* 1551, 13 December 1797.

[16] [Benjamin Bell], *Three Essays on Taxation of Income*, London, 1799, p. 55. The role of wealthy merchants in the outcry against the taxes (which was therefore unjustified) was central to *A New Enquiry into the Principles and Policy of Taxation, in the Political System of Great Britain*, Brentford and London, 1798, passim.

Or in the words of another writer, 'the burden of assessed taxes' was 'bearing far more heavily on the inhabitants of the country than those of towns, and consequently on land-owners than on other men of property'. Traders, it was moreover pointed out, could always raise prices and thus remove any burden from themselves onto the rest of the community.[17]

On one level, then, Pittites rejected straightforwardly the reasoning of their opponents. But their responses countered the opposition arguments on another level as well. With striking persistence, they were also denying the very social language in which the opposition arguments were couched, and replacing it with alternative formulations. Overall, while responding to a rhetoric thick with explicit 'middle-class' grievances, the supporters of the Triple Assessment Bill themselves only rarely used the language of 'middle class'.

Take for example the *Anti-Jacobin: Or, Weekly Examiner*, headed by George Canning and edited by William Gifford, which was a precursor of the better-known monthly *Anti-Jacobin Review*. The *Anti-Jacobin* appeared weekly during the eight months of the 1797–8 parliamentary session, beginning in late November 1797, when the main item on the agenda of the House was the triple assessment plan. Its several discussions of the plan, and responses to the objections raised against it, were all consistently put within a dual social framework of higher and lower classes. For 'the Highest Classes', the *Anti-Jacobin* argued, it would not be too difficult to bear, while for 'the Lower it will be in a much lighter proportion'. Furthermore, it was added elsewhere, any alternative was surely worse, 'if (under the pretence of relieving the Poor) the burden is disproportionably and unreasonably accumulated on the Rich'.[18] At other moments the *Anti-Jacobin* paraphrased

---

[17] [Bell], *Three Essays on Taxation of Income*, pp. 100–1. See also p. 110, pointing to the difficulties of the landed classes in meeting tax demands. H[enry] Beeke, *Observations on the Produce of the Income Tax, and on Its Proportion to the Whole Income of Great Britain ... (Part the First)*, London, 1799, pp. 59–61. *A New Enquiry into the Principles and Policy of Taxation*, pp. 20–2. *Thoughts on Taxation: In the Course of Which the Policy of a Tax on Income is Impartially Investigated*, London, 1798, pp. 6, 43–4.

[18] *The Anti-Jacobin, or Weekly Examiner*, 2 vols., 4th edn, London, 1799, vol. 1, pp. 46 (27 November 1797), 156 (11 December 1797). For information about this short-lived periodical and its connections with the *Anti-Jacobin Review* which superseded it, see E. Lorrain de Montluzin, *The Anti-Jacobins, 1798–1800*, New York, 1988, pp. 21–5. Similar examples, of pro-ministerial discussions of the taxation scheme using only dual social terms, include the editorial in *True Briton* 1546, 7 December 1797; or the staunch

the charges of its opponents in a social language that was fragmented and particularized into occupational categories: the opposition, it remarked, mistakenly feared 'the ruin of the Tradesman, the Mechanic, the Shopkeeper, and various other descriptions'; that is, all other descriptions but that 'middle class' which in fact figured so prominently in the fears of the opposition.[19] In the whole of the first volume of the *Anti-Jacobin* (covering the period of the triple assessment debates) no 'middle-class' language can be found, save two exceptions, which are by themselves amusingly telling. In both cases, 'middle-class' grievances against Pitt's proposals were introduced briefly through direct citation of oppositional sources, inserted merely in order to refute them: one case was introduced under the heading of 'LIES', the other under the heading of 'MISAPPREHENSION'.[20]

So far, the two levels of the debate were congruent with each other; the Pittites' resistance to the opposition's 'middle-class' language went hand in hand with their rejection of the objections formulated with it. But perhaps even more telling are those instances where these two levels were detached from each other; that is to say, when certain pro-war Pittites, in spite of their general partisan loyalties, acknowledged that in this particular case the opposition's complaints had some truth in them. Such Pittites, however, still refrained from using 'middle-class' language, and recast the argument – with which they now tended to agree – in different terms. The divergence over language proved stronger than the divergence over taxes. A case in point is Joseph Cawthorne, himself of the 'middle' of society (most probably a trader), a government pension-holder who supported the war and the administration, but who at this juncture strongly opposed Pitt's taxation proposals on grounds very similar to those of the opposition. Yet, while concurring with their concerns regarding the effects of the assessed taxes, he at the same time contested their representation of the 'middle class'. Without

---

Pittite tract, F. Adams, *A Plan for Raising the Taxes Impartially and Almost Free of Expense in War*, London, 1798, p. 7.

[19] *The Anti-Jacobin*, vol. 1, p. 247 (1 January 1798).

[20] Ibid., p. 178 (18 December 1797), quoting the *Morning Post*; and 194, quoting resolutions of a parochial meeting in St Anne, Westminster. In one case the 'middle-class' terminology was repeated in the *Anti-Jacobin*'s refutation. In the other, the response was again recast in particularized social categories, rather high up on the social scale (West India proprietors, bankers, brewers, wealthy manufacturers).

resorting himself to the language of 'middle class', Cawthorne
attempted to sever the association of middle social groups with
anti-war rhetoric by emphasizing 'the conviction of the trading
community, who are ready to give the most energetic and effectual
support to their country, by ample contributions'. Manufactures
and commerce, he asserted, were the sources of national wealth;
the British are 'a trading people'. Cawthorne suggested alternative taxation on the 'landed interest', since it was proper 'to lay
the burden upon those who have acquired great property which
is inactive', while maintaining 'as much indulgence as possible
to the industrious part of a manufacturing and trading people'.
All this – in many points echoing the opposition – was stated
without any 'middle-class' language. Its absence was further
underscored when Cawthorne quoted a speech that Lord
Chatham had made thirty years earlier, and which had included
a 'middle-class idiom'-type statement. While Chatham's language
was not uncongenial to Cawthorne, in 1798 he could not write
in the same terms, as this language had since become charged
and politically tainted.[21]

A similar case was that of N. Cooke. Cooke did not declare
his political allegiance as overtly as Cawthorne, but still made
it clear that his taxation suggestions (obviously meant to replace
the triple assessment) should not be read as hostile to the administration or to the constitution. Like Cawthorne, he too opposed
the proposed taxes since he considered 'the trading part' of the
country as the source of its prosperity, which should be protected
above all. Like Cawthorne, he too had praise for those in trade,
who were 'so respectable, and of such consequence collectively
to the nation'. But like Cawthorne, in spite of repeated references
to such people, Cooke too refrained from the 'middle-class' language used so frequently by the anti-war camp to convey very
similar points. Furthermore, in his social analysis Cooke managed
to incorporate the 'trading part' of the nation into a social scheme
which was explicitly dual: the key division in society, he argued,

---

[21] [Joseph Cawthorne], *The Injustice and Impolicy of the Bill to Increase the Assessed Taxes,
&c. With a Commutation*, London, 1798, pp. 5–6, 27, 57, 74–5. Regarding Cawthorne's
pension see L. Werkmeister, *A Newspaper History of England 1792–1793*, Lincoln, 1967,
p. 27 (though her index assigns him a premature death). The same quote from
Chatham could be incorporated more easily into the rhetoric of the opposition; as it
was, for example, shortly after the triple assessment debate, in the *Cambridge Intelligencer*
179, 24 February 1798.

was determined by the question, whether a man depends on his labour; 'and from this circumstance the peasant, the farmer, the tradesman, the shop-keeper, the merchant, &c. come under the same description'. On the other hand, there was no real difference between men of acquired property, whether in land or in funds, whether of £10 or £100,000 per annum. Society, Cooke summarized, was therefore composed basically of two categories, the 'peer-type' and the 'peasant-type'. In this dual structure any distinct space for a 'middle class' was explicitly denied: 'the intermediate degrees of each class must be of the nature and quality of the extremes'.[22]

Or consider the changing positions of the *Evening Mail*, an anti-Jacobin newspaper whose favourable disposition towards the administration and its war efforts was widely recognized. At first, the *Evening Mail* dismissed the 'middle-class' grievance:

We are told that the measure proposed is unjust, and that the middle classes, the industrious tradesmen, will pay more than the men of large fortune. We confess we see no ground for such assertions . . . it should be remembered that this measure does not affect the poorer classes at all; and those one step higher, who pay house and windows only, in a very small degree.[23]

Note that the 'middle class' (as equivalent to tradesmen) was introduced in this case in paraphrasing the opposition, but was not repeated in the newspaper's refutation of the argument. But more interestingly, the *Evening Mail* also did not repeat the language of 'middle class' some two weeks later, when it came around to admitting that the opposition may have been right: 'we must yield to the general opinion, that it [the Bill] needs revision, so as not to fall so heavy on the Tradesman and Shopkeeper'. As the newspaper explained later, Pitt ought to have consulted with men of business and trade, and thus could have avoided a measure which was 'particularly burthensome on Shopkeepers'. Again, however, this change of position did not

[22] [N. Cooke], *The Test of Taxation: Or Assessment on Income Alone Equal to the Exigencies of the State*, London, 1798, pp. 21, 24; published again that year with the author's name and under a different title, *The Just Proportion which Each Class of the People, from the Peasant to the Peer, Have in the Support and Prosperity of the State: Or, Test of Taxation . . .*, 2nd edn.

[23] 'On the Proposed Encreased Assessments': *Evening Mail*, 29 November–1 December 1797.

entail a change in the uses of social vocabulary: the 'general opinion' to which the newspaper claimed to succumb was in fact supported by strong 'middle-class' language, whose inclusive effect was undercut by replacing it with the particularized categories of 'tradesmen' and 'shopkeepers'.[24]

Moreover, just as the opposition bolstered its 'middle-class'-based objections with 'middle-class idiom', so the Pittite responses often went beyond clarifications of the Bill to broader counter-statements about relative social worth. One Pittite treatise, for example, began with the familiar assertion that 'the merchant or trader uniformly makes the *consumer* pay . . . in fact it is not the merchant who feels the *burthen* of the duties'. What followed, however, turned into a more general moral invective:

let not the tradesman pretend to exclaim against the duties of *Public Taxation* . . . He *feels none* of the disadvantages of such imposts, and yet has all the advantages of political protection, under the auspices whereof he flourishes in luxuriant wealth, alike gratifying the lust of avarice and the lust of ambition.

Furthermore, the treatise added, the benefits from trade to public revenue and to the state 'bear no sort of proportion to the benefits enjoyed by the tradesmen or individuals engaged in commerce', which allows them 'to bask in the sunshine of unabatable prosperity, and even to *wallow* in the *luxury* of wealth!'[25] This was a direct rejoinder to the 'middle-class' rhetoric on all possible fronts: the social group who complained of the heaviest burden proved to be least affected by taxation, indeed basking in luxury; their declared moral virtue (the moral aspect of the 'middle-class idiom') was refuted, as they turned out to be creatures of avarice and ambition; their singular contribution to the polity (the political aspect of the 'middle-class idiom') was

---

[24] Editorials in the *Evening Mail*, 11–13 December 1797, and 15–18 December 1797. Likewise, the pro-ministerial *Whitehall Evening Post* also refrained from notions of 'middle class' while admitting in its own preferred language the substance of the 'middle-class' grievances. Thus it acknowledged the need for 'a due anxiety to spare the numerous and important class above manual labour, but below easy and independent circumstances', and commended Pitt for amendments which it believed would relieve the plight of 'shopkeepers' (7969, 9–12 December 1797; 7970, 12–14 December 1797).

[25] *A New Enquiry into the Principles and Policy of Taxation*, pp. 19, 22, 40. For similar arguments about the debt of commercial men to the state, combined with certain doubts about their morality, see *Thoughts on Taxation*, pp. 64–7; *An Appeal to the People of England, Occasioned by the Late Declaration of the French Directory*, London, 1798, pp. 62–6.

reversed, presented instead as sheer parasitism; and, finally, their social terminology was rejected – they were not 'middle class' but merely 'tradesmen' or 'merchants'.

The point was made in even stronger terms by a rather pessimistic 'Nottinghamshire magistrate' at 'the commencement of the year M,DCC,XCVIII' – that is, precisely in the midst of the debate on the triple assessment. 'The Mercantile part of the nation', wrote the magistrate, had formerly been 'frugal, temperate and unassuming: Preserving the situation of mediocrity, which nature and education intended for the sphere of their exertions'. Alas, at present this was no longer the case: 'ranks are blended; orders confounded'; country gentlemen are in decline, replaced by 'Adventurers without property [i.e. landed property], by Strangers without interest, and by Shop-men without manners, dignity or independence'. The landed interest is 'depressed and humbled', while 'the mercantile interest is ridiculously and ruinously aggrandized . . . superficial pertness and mercantile dulness have usurped those places in Society which, in better times, were filled by manly firmness, and the honorable pride of family distinction.' Moreover, political understanding is attainable only among classes of 'high birth, superior talents and cultivated education'; but cannot inhabit the less cultivated minds of 'the Merchant, the Manufacturer, the Farmer, or the Laborer', who can therefore become no more than a discontented mob.[26] The rebuttal to the 'middle-class idiom' was loud and clear. These people, rather than enjoying the advantages of a state of mediocrity, were selfishly transgressing its limits; they lacked culture, manners, refinement and independence; and they were unfit for proper political involvement. Finally, while mostly using terms other than 'middle class', at one point the Nottinghamshire magistrate deviated from this pattern to drive home his unequivocal conclusion: 'the middle ranks', he asserted, are 'selfish, extravagant, and vain'.[27]

---

[26] *Thoughts on the Commencement of the Year* M,DCC,XCVIII. *By a Nottinghamshire Magistrate,* London, 1798, pp. 16–20, 32.

[27] Ibid., p. 9. It is true that the author's criticism did not spare the other components of society: 'The upper ranks, to a great degree, [are] ignorant, servile, and voluptuous . . . the lowest orders [are] frantic enthusiasts.' Yet, while the moral decline of the landed classes was primarily explained by the effects of unfortunate circumstances beyond their control, the 'middle ranks' were depicted as motivated by their own desires and ambitions.

Such examples could continue for many more pages. But we can suffice here with one more telling denial of 'middle-class' language, in the pamphlet which Geoffrey Mowbray, a staunch anti-Foxite, published in response to a treatise on finances by the Earl of Lauderdale. Lauderdale, a high Whig who was usually not too interested in the 'middle class', wrote against the triple assessment primarily in other social terminologies. Nevertheless, he did incorporate peripherally some 'middle-class' grievances as well, arguing that the deterioration of their situation since the beginning of the war had decreased their income and forced them to live beyond their means.[28] Interestingly, Mowbray found Lauderdale's 'middle-class' language more loaded with meaning than the latter had originally intended and amplified its significance in his response, attempting to refute it on several levels. First, turning his rival's argument on its head, he stated that Lauderdale's assertions in fact castigated the 'middle class' as immoral and irresponsible, since for such people 'notoriously to exceed their income, is such scandalous and disgraceful conduct'. At the same time, he also tried to prove that '99 out of 100 of the mercantile and manufacturing classes' were in fact not included in Lauderdale's 'middle class'; that is, that the category 'middle class' as used in this oppositional context was inappropriate and did not correspond at all to the 'middle' of society. Accordingly, Mowbray used 'middle class' language only when quoting and requoting Lauderdale; but insofar as his own arguments were concerned, they were adequately served by a dual social scheme of rich and poor.[29]

From such refutations of the 'middle-class' rhetoric it was but a small step for government supporters to slide into a renewed counter-emphasis on the importance of the landed classes. One supporter of the Bill, who was quoted above for contrasting the luxuries of merchants and manufacturers with the hardships of

---

[28] James Maitland, eighth Earl of Lauderdale, *A Letter on the Present Measures of Finance; in Which the Bill Now Depending in Parliament Is Particularly Considered*, London, 1798, p. 35. The following year, in the context of the income tax debate, Lauderdale repeated similar arguments without any 'middle-class' terminology: idem, *Plan for Altering the Manner of Collecting a Large Part of the Public Revenue . . .*, n.p., 1799?, esp. pp. 12–13. And see below, p. 152 n. 16, for his remarks on the 'middle class' in the context of the French Revolution.

[29] Geoffrey Mowbray, *Remarks on the Conduct of Opposition during the Present Parliament*, London, 1798, pp. 80–1, 92.

landed proprietors, added several pages later that the only object of real importance for Britain was the improvement of agriculture, the only guarantee of British spirit and independence, whose relationship to commerce and manufacture was like that of substance to shadow.[30] Another followed the dismissal of the 'middle-class' argument against the triple assessment with a more general address to 'the richer and higher ranks of society', who are 'English gentlemen':

I am not ashamed to own my opinion that Aristocracy ought to be the principal ingredient amidst the powers of a well-regulated State. But not a Gothic and feudal Aristocracy: I mean an Aristocracy where power is chiefly lodged in the hands of property, where commercial property is respected, and where, amongst landed proprietors, they whose families have been longest (as it were) rooted into the very soil of their country, are *caeteris paribus*, held most worthy to obtain the rank of legislators.[31]

Significantly, although the social hierarchy advocated here was evidently incompatible with the 'middle-class idiom', this writer did not reject commercial society but rather attempted to incorporate it into the existing social and political order. This is a point worth repeating: one could be an advocate of commercial society, as indeed many were, and at the same time be opposed to the politically charged 'middle-class idiom'.[32] By contrast, the previous writer, as well as others, combined their counter-'middle-class' rhetoric with reiterations of the familiar eighteenth-century critiques of commerce, associating it with luxury and moral corruption.

I have managed to find but one significant exception in the debates on Pitt's fiscal proposals to this overall remarkably unfailing pattern of differentiation of social language along political lines, in the pages of the *Morning Herald*. The political position

---

[30] [Bell], *Three Essays on Taxation of Income*, pp. 116, 119; and pp. 7–8, where agriculture (as opposed to the pursuit of extensive fortunes) is associated with patriotism and public virtue.

[31] *An Appeal to the People of England, Occasioned by the Late Declaration of the French Directory*, London, 1798, pp. 67, 70. Compare the Pittite *Evening Mail* (25–27 December 1797, editorial): 'But surely no class is more conspicuously interested [in the welfare of the country] than the nobility; nor is there any one, whose example and vigorous exertions are more capable of being productive of public benefit.'

[32] Examples encountered above include Cawthorne and Cooke, as well as *A New Enquiry into the Principles and Policy of Taxation*.

of the *Morning Herald* was an idiosyncratic intermediate one, critical of both the ministry and the opposition. It was ambivalent about the war; as one editorial put it, Britain faced a 'lamentable dilemma' between 'a ruinous War' and 'an ignominious Peace'.[33] This ambiguous political stance of the *Morning Herald* may have been a factor in the dithering uses of 'middle-class' language found in it during this debate. While concurring in opposition to the Bill, editorials and readers' letters were divided between pro-Pitt and anti-Pitt statements. And here, surprisingly, notions of 'middle class' were incorporated not only into the latter, but – in a sharp divergence from pro-ministerial rhetoric elsewhere – also into the former. In the most pronounced example, an anti-Jacobin letter opposing the Bill warned against the imminent threat of revolution:

Our grand palladium against it lies in the *content* and *comforts* enjoyed by the middle class; in which class I include from the substantial Tradesman up to the Country Gentleman of 1,500l. a year. That this class, which forms the majority of the effective part of the nation, can continue in the former, when deprived of the latter, I deny to be possible ... Thus far our grand safeguard is removed.

Elsewhere, an editorial complained that the taxation plan would deprive 'the middling range of people' of their comforts, thus 'annihilat[ing] ... every resource in reserve for the national salvation'; i.e. harming the source of the nation's strength at this dangerous moment. The following year, in the debate on the income tax, the newspaper again warned against crushing the useful 'middle class', 'of whose loyalty he [Pitt] has no doubt, and in whose patriotism he knows he can confide'.[34]

Repeatedly, then, the *Morning Herald* presented beside the famil-

[33] *Morning Herald* 5383, 21 December 1797. The newspaper welcomed the war as anti-Jacobin, yet criticized it for representing only the interests of the higher orders: see editorials in 5836, 14 December 1797; 5826, 4 December 1797; and letter to editor the following year, 5685, 8 December 1798. The confusion which this equivocal position could create was acknowledged in the newspaper's need to clarify that its criticism of Fox did not imply 'partiality to the Minister': 5833, 12 December 1797.

[34] Ibid., 5823, 30 November 1797 (letter to editor by 'Voice of Truth'); 5825, 2 December 1797; 5683, 5 December 1798. See also letters to Pitt in 5821, 28 November 1797, and 5387, 26 December 1797, which came close to expressing loyalist 'middle-class idiom', although without explicit 'middle-class' terms. The former hastened to add (in contrast to the antithesis between Pitt and the 'middle class' drawn by the opposition) that 'it is accident, and not design', which brought Pitt to suggest measures so harmful to this valuable class.

iar anti-Pittite 'middle-class' language also another type of 'middle-class' rhetoric, strikingly unlike that put forward by any other source. In part, this idiosyncratic finding may be explained by the ambiguous political stance of the *Morning Herald*; in part, perhaps, by the combined effect of the contributions of individuals of different political convictions working for the newspaper.[35] Be that as it may, what should be noted is, first, the constancy of this finding within the *Morning Herald* and its exclusive confinement to it: even when consisting of an exception which muddles the neatly schematized pattern that I have been trying to delineate, still the political use of 'middle-class' language was evidently far from random. Second, these few examples underscore again the powerful potential which the language of 'middle class' might have carried for the loyalist camp, if only such attempts to counteract the oppositional appropriation of this particular social scheme had not been confined to a handful of voices in one single newspaper.

THE LANGUAGE OF 'MIDDLE CLASS' IN DIVERGING PARLIAMENTARY HEARINGS

It may be objected that in the preceding pages the purported 'dialogue' between friends and foes of the administration is to a certain extent an artificial construction, which juxtaposes independent pronouncements as if they were addressing each other directly, when in fact their purported interaction is only a matter of conjecture. Of course, as has already been noted, the differentiation of language had precisely this effect of obscuring the existence of a direct dialogue: using differing formulations, the interlocutors in such an exchange were in a literal sense talking past each other. Now, even by itself, the consistent recurrence of this strongly demarcated differentiation between opposing social languages, according closely with opposing political inclinations, is a considerable argument against such an objection. However, the case can be further reinforced by shifting our attention to another manifestation of the same differentiation, perhaps at a somewhat less conscious level of linguistic choices, but where the connection between its two sides is immediately and indisputably evident.

---

[35] For possible evidence for this supposition, see below, note 55.

Let us return to the *Anti-Jacobin: Or, Weekly Examiner*. In one of its habitual allusions to the opposition press, under the category 'Mistakes', the periodical presented quotations from the *Morning Chronicle*, organized under the categories 'THE RICH' and 'THE POOR': 'The Rich will not be affected by the Assessed Taxes – even should they be more than trebled, they will not be scratched by them.' Conversely, continued the next quote, 'it exempts the absolutely Poor, and those who are so in the next degree.'[36] But should we take the *Anti-Jacobin*'s word for the arguments of its rival? Perhaps not. Going back to the *Morning Chronicle* and tracking down the original passage quoted – taken from a letter by 'Drusus' – we find it to have been formulated rather differently: 'As the Assessed Taxes at present . . . fall lightly on the rich: this will also [be the case], even if raised beyond triple as to them . . . It will hardly graze the rich, but the middle orders it will grind.'[37] Rather different indeed. Aside of other inaccuracies, the selective quoting in the *Anti-Jacobin* focused precisely on the contested language of 'middle class'. Whereas the opposition *Morning Chronicle* emphasized the predicament of the 'middle orders' as against the rich, when the Pittite periodical reproduced its complaint, supposedly literally, it in fact recast it in terms of rich and poor, omitting all references to the 'middle class'.

Or consider the press reporting of the protest voiced by the tax-collectors of London and Westminster, whose expressed professional opinion was that raising the assessed taxes as proposed was unrealistic. The pro-ministerial *True Briton* presented it to its readers as follows: 'It has been said . . . that some of the Collectors have declared, that they have great difficulty in obtaining, from the poorer class, the present Assessed Taxes.' The *Morning Chronicle*, however, reported: 'The Collectors of London and Westminster have shewn him [Pitt] fatal proof that the persons in the great and middle class are at this moment so far behind with the existing taxes, that any addition must be fatal to their industry.' It may be difficult to find out what the collectors had actually said. However, rather than trying to

---

[36] *Anti-Jacobin*, vol. I, p. 221 (25 December 1797).
[37] *Morning Chronicle* 8900, 2 December 1797. The letter continued: 'The rich, however, will do well to consider whether they can stand, when the middle classes are crushed.'

reconcile these different renditions of the same statement in the two leading newspapers (renditions which in fact gave their respective readers quite different ideas of what the collectors really thought), we may wish to highlight precisely their divergence. It is through such a divergence that the stakes in differing represen- tations of society were revealed; and again, the 'middle-class' grievance, which featured prominently in the opposition version, was conspicuously absent from the pro-ministerial one.[38]

It should be stressed that I am not arguing here for the existence of a deliberate process of manipulation of social lan- guage. Some writers or speakers perhaps did consciously avoid 'middle-class' language, being more or less aware of its political connotations; just as the Friends of Peace could deliberately enlist this language to buttress their own agenda. But surely it was often the case that political rhetoric underwent a less conscious process of filtering, in which the meaning and conse- quences of linguistic or conceptual choices were not fully acknowledged. Such a process of linguistic differentiation was propelled by the cumulative exposure to the rhetorical practices of others who shared one's political views; as it was of course also enhanced by repeated encounters with the opposite rhetori- cal practices, that came to be shared by one's rivals. It is here that the explosion of 'middle-class' language in the debate over the Triple Assessment Bill was important in itself in further reinforcing these linguistic patterns by its sheer aggre- gate effect.

Thus, there was probably no intentional manipulation respon- sible for the divergence of the reports of the meeting held in the borough of Southwark to discuss objections to Pitt's taxation proposals on 11 December 1797. The resolutions of the meeting, as published in the oppositional *Morning Chronicle*, stated that the measure 'will (if carried into law) be highly oppressive on the middle orders of the people, particularly on those engaged in trade and manufactories ... the measure proposed will leave

---

[38] *True Briton* 1548, 9 December 1797. *Morning Chronicle* 8900, 2 December 1797. Compare also the more general paraphrasing of oppositional rhetoric by the *True Briton* (1562, 26 December 1797): 'The only assertion we recollect to have been made in the shape of argument against its policy, is ... that people must retrench; that the use of Luxuries will be discontinued; and that upon the Luxuries of the Rich the Poor thrive.' Yet again, the recollection of the *True Briton* failed to register any of the 'middle-class' language which in fact was so marked in the objections to the Bill.

untaxed a very numerous class of persons who enjoy great wealth'.[39] The *Morning Chronicle* added its own report of the meeting, reiterating that protest was expressed 'against a measure so big with destruction to the comforts and happiness of the middle and lower ranks of society as this was'. However, compare this opposition version with that of the pro-ministerial *Times*, also reprinted (as was often the case) in the Pittite *Evening Mail*. In the immediate reports of the Southwark meeting in both newspapers the 'middle-class' arguments or language were absent. A week later both returned to the subject, quoting parts of the Southwark resolutions against the taxes, including the statement that it 'will leave untaxed a very numerous class of persons, who enjoy great wealth';[40] again, the 'middle-class' portion of the resolutions was not mentioned.

Such cases offer a valuable way for further exploring the political differentiation of social language, through a comparison of different versions of the same pronouncements as they were communicated in the opposing political camps. Nowhere can this comparative strategy be employed more strikingly to demonstrate the charge and power of the language of 'middle class', as it (and the resistance to it) became ingrained in political rhetorical habits at this juncture, than in a comparison of newspapers' reports of parliamentary debates.

The influential political and cultural role of parliamentary reporting in the press in the late eighteenth century cannot easily be overestimated (though, especially from a viewpoint formed in the political culture of the late twentieth century, it can easily be overlooked). Virtually every newspaper and many periodicals, both in London and in the provinces, wishing to have some political relevance, put a high priority on purportedly accurate detailed reports of parliamentary proceedings, and devoted to them much space in every issue during parliamentary sessions. (Key sessions could actually take over the whole newspaper, to the exclusion of everything else.) Since the newspapers were

---

[39] *Morning Chronicle* 8908, 12 December 1797; also printed in the *Morning Herald* 5833, 12 December 1797.

[40] *The Times* 4064, 12 December 1797; 4072, 21 December 1797. *Evening Mail*, 11–13 December 1797, 20–22 December 1797. Compare also the language of 'middle class' in the anti-assessment resolutions of the Common Council with its rather subtle dilution in the report of these resolutions by the Pittite *Whitehall Evening Post* (7970, 12–14 December 1797, following the original notice by the Council).

commercial enterprises that needed to be marketed, their proprietors and editors must have had good reasons to believe
that their readers devoted as much attention to reading the
parliamentary reports as they did to publishing them.

One might have assumed that the debates in parliament would
provide some of the best examples of dialogue between political
rivals, a dialogue which was both institutionalized and well
recorded; and that therefore the exchanges between MPs could
provide rich material for the analysis of differing political languages. However, despite the fact that historians have mostly
taken the existence of an 'objective' record for granted, in fact
we do *not* have an adequate protocol of the parliamentary proceedings of this period. Later compilations were based on the
reports in the press, and as it turns out, the reports in different
newspapers diverged considerably from each other. The practice
of parliamentary reporters, working under conditions which in
any case did not allow for a full recording of the proceedings,
was to take short and partial notes in the House, and then
reconstruct the debates later for publication.[41] Consequently, the
newspapers' representations of parliamentary debates that were
put forward as allegedly accurate reports, often purporting to be
verbatim quotations, were in fact distinct *reconstructions*, mediated
through rhetorical practices specific to every newspaper and
dependent on its political convictions. The divergences became
particularly significant around notions which were politically
charged and contested at a given moment, such as the 'middle

---

[41] A visitor to parliament in 1810 noted: 'Far from setting down all that is said, they
only take notes, to appearance very carelessly, one word in a hundred, to mark the
leading points. It is difficult to understand how they can afterwards give the connected
speeches we see in the papers, out of such slender materials, and with so little time
to prepare them.' ([Louis Simond], *Journal of a Tour and Residence in Great Britain, during
the Years 1810 and 1811, by a French Traveller . . .*, 2 vols., New York, 1815, vol. I, pp.
57–8.) Short-hand apparently did not come to be used by parliamentary reporters
before about 1812; as one parliamentary reporter at the turn of the century put it, 'I
knew nothing, and did not desire to know anything, of *short-hand*. Short-hand writers
are very useful in taking down evidence as given in a court of justice, but they are
wholly incompetent to report a good speech. They attend to words without entering
into the thoughts of the speaker.' (*Life of John, Lord Campbell, Lord High Chancellor of
Great Britain*, ed. Mary Scarlet Hardcastle, 2 vols., London, 1881, vol. I, pp. 105–6.)
For a more detailed discussion, and remarks regarding the limitations of compilations
such as William Cobbett's *Parliamentary History*, see D. Wahrman, 'Virtual Representation: Parliamentary Reporting and Languages of Class in the 1790s', *Past and Present*
136 (1992), section 1.

class' in the debates on the Triple Assessment Bill. It is through highlighting these points of incongruence and divergence, the contexts in which they occurred and the vocabularies in which they were expressed, rather than through striving to eliminate them in order to salvage a single narrative, that we can gain valuable insights into the political uses of social language.[42]

One of the most vocal and persistent opponents of the war was the Foxite ex-barrister John Nicholls. What did he have to say against the trebling of the assessed taxes? As presented in the epigraphs to this chapter, according to the opposition newspapers, the *Morning Chronicle* and the *Star*, in one speech he denounced the Bill because 'the greater part of the weight [is] upon the middle classes'. However, according to the *True Briton*, a pro-government newspaper (and similarly in the pro-government *Times* and *Evening Mail*), in a likewise purportedly verbatim report of the same speech, he objected to the Bill since 'it went to destroy the comforts of the lower classes . . . The measure went to destroy the lowest orders.'[43] In the former version there was no mention of 'the lower classes', while the latter one lacked any reference to 'the middle classes'. On another occasion Nicholls said, as reported in the *Morning Chronicle*, that 'by compelling the higher orders of the middle class to economize, it would destroy the employment of the artizans'. The same sentence was reported differently in the *True Briton*: 'the next objection [in Nicholls's speech] was, that it would throw the Artizan out of employ, by obliging the Rich to economize'; and the same statement again, as it appeared several days later in the pro-ministerial *E. Johnson's British Gazette*: the Bill 'affected the lower orders indirectly, though it affected to throw the whole burden upon the rich'.[44] Similarly, the *Morning Chronicle* and the *Star* reported yet another speech as if Nicholls had warned against the effects of the Bill on the 'middle orders', declaring further that he would never 'give his assent to a mode of taxation that must so cruelly crush the middle classes of society, who in all countries must

---

[42] For a more detailed analysis than what follows of the differentiation of social language in the reports of the debates on Pitt's proposals in 1797/8, see my 'Virtual Representation'.

[43] Speech of 14 December 1797: *Morning Chronicle* 8911, 15 December 1797; *Star* 2911, 15 December 1797; *True Briton* 1553, 15 December 1797; *The Times* 4067, 15 December 1797; *Evening Mail*, 13–15 December 1797.

[44] Speech of 3 January 1798: *Morning Chronicle* 8928, 4 January 1798; *True Briton* 1570, 4 January 1798; *E. Johnson's British Gazette, and Sunday Monitor* 949, 7 January 1798.

form the chief strength and support of society at large'. The rendition of Nicholls's very same sentence in the pro-ministerial *Whitehall Evening Post* was merely that the Bill 'had directly taxed the Rich, and indirectly the Poor'.[45]

So, what *did* Nicholls say? Was he repeatedly voicing the plight of the 'middle classes', or was he talking about the 'rich' and the 'poor'? Who were at the heart of his concerns, the 'middle orders' or the 'lower orders'? For my purposes here, this is not the significant question.[46] What Nicholls had purportedly said depended on which newspaper was one's habitual source of political information. Thus, for the readers of the oppositional newspapers, the *Morning Chronicle* and the *Star*, Nicholls persistently reiterated the effects of the proposed taxation scheme on the 'middle orders'; while for the readers of the pro-ministerial press, the *True Briton*, *The Times*, the *Evening Mail*, the *E. Johnson's British Gazette* and the *Whitehall Evening Post*, his objections to it were based on a social framework comprising only of higher and lower orders, rich and poor. Similar differentiations occurred in the representations of other opposition MPs as well.[47]

These divergences become more significant in cases where 'middle-class idiom' was used in (some versions of) statements against the Bill, implying more directly the prescriptive connotations of the 'middle-class' language. A case in point is that of William Lushington, associated with banking and the West Indian interest and representing the City of London, who nor-

---

[45] Speech of 4 December 1797: *Morning Chronicle* 8902, 5 December 1797; *Whitehall Evening Post* 7966, 2–4 December 1797.

[46] Given the common features in Nicholls's speeches, though, there is little doubt that he was indeed committed to repeating the grievance of the 'middle class'. In one case this is corroborated by the printed version of his speech, published presumably with his consent or support, which was very similar to the immediate oppositional newspapers' version, dominated by 'middle-class' vocabulary (*The Speech of John Nicholls, Esq. in the House of Commons, Wednesday, January 3, 1798, on the Bill for Augmenting the Assessed Taxes*, London, 1798, p. 6). However, establishing this point is not crucial to my argument.

[47] See for example the speeches of William Plumer and Edmund Wigley, on 4 and 5 December 1797, respectively. As reported in most newspapers, both referred to the particular 'middle-class' grievance against the Bill; for both, however, we find pro-ministerial versions in which they were modified – to 'some classes of men' (Plumer in the *True Briton* 1544, 5 December 1797), or to 'many classes of society' (Wigley in the *E. Johnson's British Gazette* 945, 10 December 1797). Furthermore, only in the *Morning Herald* (5827, 5 December 1797), which opposed the Bill, was Plumer found to enhance his 'middle-class' language by declaring this class to be 'the pride of England'.

mally supported Pitt and the war, but on this occasion opposed the proposed Bill (though in the end he voted for it). The *Morning Chronicle*'s version of his objection was that 'the extensive distribution of property in this country had been one of the principal causes of the stability of the Government', which checked 'the frenzy of revolutionary principles'. 'This stability was owing in a very important degree to the middling classes, and it was owing to their possessing a certain share of property, and being encouraged in its acquisition.' Their 'existence was so important to the State', and to do away with them would mean to 'divide the State into the two descriptions of the poor and the rich', without 'that middling class of men on whom the stability of the state so essentially depended'. So, according to this (oppositional) version, Lushington hailed the 'middling classes' as a crucial pillar of stable government.

This celebratory association of the 'middle classes' with political stability, however, was not part of Lushington's speech in the pro-ministerial *St James's Chronicle*, which reported him saying merely that 'he must think the present measure likely to break down the middle classes, and he advised them to be cautious of persisting in it'. Rather, the social fulcrum of political stability was relocated: according to this version, it was the 'lower classes' and the 'humbler classes' which Lushington praised as 'these classes in which the strength of the country so much consisted'. Thus, in this pro-ministerial representation of his speech, Lushington's emphasis on the singular contribution of the 'middle classes' to the political order, which resonated so strongly in the oppositional *Morning Chronicle*, was absent, and indeed reversed. In another pro-ministerial newspaper, *The Times*, Lushington's 'middle-class' language was gone altogether.[48]

And again, when the Whig oppositionist George Tierney railed against the Bill, his speech, according to its reports in the *True Briton* and the *St James's Chronicle*, did not include any mention of the 'middle class'. The reports in *The Times* and the *Evening Mail* had one short statement: 'The present tax would fall almost exclusively on the middle classes.' But in the version of the speech published in the *Morning Chronicle* (followed as usual by

---

[48] Speech of 7 December 1797: *Morning Chronicle* 8905, 8 December 1797; *St James's Chronicle* 6236, 7–9 December 1797; *The Times* 4061, 8 December 1797.

the *Star*), the grievance of the 'middle class' appeared much more pronounced, stressing its national importance:

> But let us consider the effect which is likely to follow this measure upon the middle class of society. I apprehend much danger in that view of the subject. If you prevent the middle orders from keeping up that appearance to which they have been accustomed you will destroy that noble pride which has been so much the guardian of their morals, and drive them to a state which leads directly to a desperate contempt of prudence. This consideration is very important in a national view.[49]

As the debates on the triple assessment were coming to a close, the oppositionist lawyer Joseph Jekyll directed an unusually pointed attack at Pitt, accusing him of total ignorance of the social conditions of those affected by the Bill. In the *Morning Chronicle* his words were formulated as a specific and personal antithesis between Pitt and the 'middle class', reminiscent of other strong statements we have seen:

> in the mass of his other inability and incapacity, was to be included his utter ignorance of the condition of the different classes of which our society was composed, especially that of the middling class. Whether it was to be ascribed to his very sudden rise himself, or to some other cause, he knew not, but certain it was, the Minister was very ignorant of the condition of the middling class of society.[50]

The *Morning Post*'s version was similar, though somewhat less poignant. These were much stronger 'middle-class' statements than those found in any of the pro-ministerial papers. In the *True Briton* these two instances of 'middle-class' terminology appeared in a far more diluted form, as 'middling and poorer ranks' and 'Gentlemen of small fortunes', while the reference to Pitt's background was missing altogether. In the *St James's Chronicle* (and similarly in the *Evening Mail*), Jekyll's subjects of concern completely lost their 'middle-class' characterization, but gained a different identity together with a compliment: 'He considered

---

[49] Speech of 4 December 1797: *True Briton* 1544, 5 December 1797; *St James's Chronicle* 6234, 2–5 December 1797; *The Times* 4058, 5 December 1797; *Evening Mail*, 4–6 December 1797; *Morning Chronicle* 8902, 5 December 1797; *Star* 2902, 5 December 1797. Another speech of Tierney's was reported in the *Morning Chronicle* (8929, 5 January 1798) as incorporating strong (landed) 'middle-class idiom', which was subverted in the pro-ministerial press (for instance, *The Times* 4085, 5 January 1798): see my 'Virtual Representation', p. 100.

[50] Speech of 3 January 1798: *Morning Chronicle* 8928, 4 January 1798. Compare the antithetical juxtapositions of Pitt and the 'middle class' above, p. 113.

the Minister as really ignorant of the true character of the People of England; he meant particularly Gentlemen of 400l. 500l. and 600l. a year, who were certainly the most intelligent and useful class in the community.'[51] Taken together, the differing versions of Jekyll's speech present us with the whole spectrum of uses of 'middle-class' language, corresponding to the political spectrum of the different newspapers.

Overall, in the variations of the reports from parliament, as in the whole debate on the triple assessment, the language of 'middle class' was overwhelmingly the terrain of the opposition. Only rarely can we find signs of resistance on the part of Pittite voices, trying to reappropriate 'middle-class' language and avail themselves of its potential. Pro-ministerial newspapers could achieve this by *emphasizing* 'middle-class' language in reporting *pro-ministerial* pronouncements. Not that they did so often: in fact, such cases can be found in one newspaper only, and even then they were few and far between. By far, the prevalent pattern on the part of the ministerial speakers defending the Bill was to shift the discussion to other social vocabularies.

Consider the reports of the speech of Thomas Tyrwhitt, owner of Bank and South Sea stock, one of the Whigs who seceded with Windham and later supported Pitt's war policy. Tyrwhitt was opposed to the trebling of the assessed taxes, although he did support the income tax the following year. In his speech Tyrwhitt combined acclaim for the administration and the war with concern for the social effects of the proposals. According to the *Morning Chronicle*, he said simply that 'instead of one-tenth, the Tax would amount to one-sixth of the property of the rich, and that could not fail to lessen consumption, to fall ultimately upon the poor, and in that way to alienate their affections'. *The Times*'s version (and similarly in the *True Briton*, as well as the

---

[51] *Morning Post* 9045, 4 January 1798; *True Briton* 1570, 4 January 1798; *St James's Chronicle* 6247, 2–4 January 1798; *Evening Mail*, 3–5 January 1798. John Debrett's *Parliamentary Register* (vol. IV, p. 547) provides yet another version of this speech, whose immediate source (perhaps Jekyll's own notes?) I was unable to find, but which seems very close to that of the *Morning Chronicle* (including the remark on Pitt's upstart origins), only more detailed and embellished. Here we find what was almost certainly the flip-side of the praise which in the Pittite newspapers was attached to the 'gentlemen' of £400–600 per annum – only now as explicit 'middle-class idiom': Pitt was accused of 'total ignorance of the middling class of society, perhaps the most useful and efficient, as to the interior welfare of a great empire'.

Morning Post) was in more general terms: 'To be called upon for a sixth part of their income would, he feared, alienate the affections of the people when most wanted.' However, compare these with the account in *St James's Chronicle*: Tyrwhitt 'asserted, that ... all the middle class of people will be obliged to contribute a sixth, instead of a tenth, of their income; it would tend to alienate their affections, at a time when they were most wanting'. Contrary to the pattern seen before, here, in the context of a speech *favourable* to the administration, it is only in the pro-ministerial *St James's Chronicle*, rather than in the oppositional *Morning Chronicle*, that we find the 'middle-class' terminology, replacing either the 'poor' or the 'people'.[52]

Perhaps a stronger flicker of pro-ministerial resistance to the opposition's appropriation of 'middle-class' language can be seen in the representations of the speech made by Lord Hawkesbury (later Lord Liverpool) in defence of the taxes and of the war. Several sources concur in the contents of his speech, in which Hawkesbury explained the difficulties that the 'middle classes' must inevitably face. Thus it was reported in the *True Briton*: 'The orders of men were, the Poor consuming the necessaries – the Rich consuming also the luxuries – and the middle ranks, or poorer Gentry, who used the articles of the middle class'; since the poor were naturally exempt, and the rich did not consume sufficient luxuries to finance the needs of the state, the burden of the tax 'must therefore fall upon the middle classes of life – the poorer Gentry must feel it'. Similar reports appeared in *The Times* and the *Evening Mail*. The *Morning Chronicle* omitted any reference to the 'middle classes' or 'middle ranks' in its own version of this pro-ministerial speech. On the other side, in the version provided by the *St James's Chronicle*, Hawkesbury allegedly elaborated further:

The middle classes of society were certainly of the greatest importance to the State; and he should be extremely sorry to see any measure press with undue severity on them; yet in the natural order of things, they must feel the operation of most of the Taxes which are imposed.[53]

---

[52] Speech of 3 January 1798: *Morning Chronicle* 8928, 4 January 1798; *The Times* 4084, 4 January 1798; *True Briton* 1570, 4 January 1798; *Morning Post* 9045, 4 January 1798; *St James's Chronicle* 6247, 2–4 January 1798. Note in passing that the actual content of Tyrwhitt's argument, with regard to the social location of these potentially alienated affections and to their origins, came out differently in the different newspapers.

[53] Speech of 14 December 1797: *True Briton* 1553, 15 December 1797; *The Times* 4067, 15 December 1797; *Evening Mail*, 13–15 December 1797; *Morning Chronicle* 8911, 15

Similarly to the case of Thomas Tyrwhitt, the same newspaper – the *St James's Chronicle* – was again resisting the appropriation of 'middle-class' notions by the opposition, and trying to re-appropriate this language by emphasizing it within a pro-ministerial context.[54]

The further transformations of Hawkesbury's speech in that debate are even more revealing. Fox, speaking later in the same evening, quoted or paraphrased Hawkesbury's words, in order to respond to them as part of his long invective against the administration. In the *True Briton*, Fox's rendition of Hawkesbury did indeed sound like Hawkesbury (as reported in the same newspaper): 'It had been said by the Noble Lord,' said Fox, 'that this Tax would, it was true, fall heavy on the middling classes of people; but that this was a misfortune incident to most Taxes.' The Pittite *St James's Chronicle* (as well as *The Times* and the *Evening Mail*), however, reported Fox's words differently: 'A Noble Lord had said, that if the assessments were made upon the great alone, the lower classes would experience their effects by a retrenchment of articles in use.' But the *Morning Chronicle* read: 'It is stated by a Noble Lord, that this Tax will necessarily fall heavy upon the middling class, because, generally speaking, they consume articles which partake of the double quality of luxuries of life and necessaries.'

What a telling flip. In this *oppositional* context (that is Fox's speech), Hawkesbury's argument in the *St James's Chronicle* (and in the other two pro-ministerial newspapers) lost its previously emphasized 'middle-class' language, which then – lo and behold – re-emerged in the *Morning Chronicle*, that had ignored them in

---

December 1797; *St James's Chronicle* 6239, 14–16 December 1797. It seems likely that this strong 'middle-class idiom', which cannot be found in other accounts (including favourable ones), was an embellishment added by the latter newspaper to the argument; though we cannot rule out the possibility that these were in fact Hawkesbury's words in the House, which resonated more strongly with the reporters or editors of this newspaper than with others. Hawkesbury's position, we might add, was remarkably similar to that of the *St James's Chronicle* itself, as stated in the editorial of the previous issue (6238, 12–14 December 1797).

[54] For one additional minor example, see also the report in *St James's Chronicle* (6236, 7–9 December 1797) of Pitt's speech (7 December), which added some flavour of 'middle-class' terminology to his language, differing in this from all other accounts of Pitt's rhetoric during these debates. It should be noted that since the *St James's Chronicle* was a semi-weekly publication, its editors often had more of an opportunity to pause and consult other reports in the daily press before constructing their own, with its particular embellishments and emphases.

the pro-ministerial context! Reversing the political context of these pronouncements brought about a complete reversal of the uses of notions of 'middle class' in their representations.

As this movement back and forth between speakers and newspapers on both sides of the political divide may be confusing (not least so, in the twists and turns of the various guises of Lord Hawkesbury's speech), it may be useful to recapitulate the pattern which has emerged so far. When speakers belonged to the opposition, the use of notions of 'middle class' in their rhetoric in parliament was reproduced or enhanced by opposition newspapers, and was often played down or replaced altogether in pro-ministerial ones. The reverse occurred, though much less often, with pro-ministerial speakers: in the very few cases where they appear associated in any version of the debates with 'middle-class' language, it was a pro-ministerial newspaper which underscored it, while in the opposition press it was absent or diluted. Moreover, this pattern of differentiation predominated both in 'weak' uses of 'middle-class' terminology as part of a tripartite descriptive social scheme, and in 'strong' evaluative statements of 'middle-class idiom'. At times, again, the alterations appear to be fairly minor, perhaps not amounting to much if one were looking for the operation of a policy of deliberate suppression or rewriting. But as evidence of a persistent subterranean process, in which a newspaper's ingrained political rhetorical practices acted as a semi-permeable membrane, filtering out incongruent formulations while reconstructing the parliamentary proceedings, they add up to a significant picture. It was also a remarkably consistent picture.[55] To be sure, 'middle-class' utterances were

---

[55] This strong consistency becomes even more significant in view of the simplifying – albeit inevitable – tendency of this analysis to treat single newspapers as unified homogeneous entities. Such a presupposition does not allow for the consequences of differentiations within a given newspaper, between the rhetorical practices of distinct individuals involved in reconstructing a debate – reporters, editors, etc. Although they probably shared overall political sympathies, divergences could be considerable. Thus the final result, as it appeared on paper, should ideally be read and explained as a palimpsest of their separate individual linguistic predilections. It is almost impossible to uncover in practice such interactions behind the scene; but glimpses of them may come through. For example, in a day by day analysis of the reports in the *Morning Herald*, too detailed to be included here, there is evidence of certain patterns (strong enhancements of 'middle-class idiom', or – conversely – their dilution) which occurred consistently only on certain days, but not in others; which may suggest the stamp of different individuals, working on different occasions.

not necessarily differentiated in each and every case: this process of semi-permeable filtering could at times leave them unchanged. Yet when modifications did occur, then in virtually every case they followed the pattern described here.[56]

It is probably no coincidence that most of the speakers in parliament who apparently made use of 'middle-class' language (Nicholls, Lushington, Tyrwhitt, Hobhouse, Wilberforce Bird[57]) were not simply landed gentlemen, but were directly connected in some way with commercial or professional interests; one can also add Lord Hawkesbury, a landed aristocrat but with commercial interests and expertise. Similarly, it is no coincidence that this language was hardly mentioned at all in the debate in the House of Lords. The use of 'middle-class' language in parliament was a reactive response to external impulses initiated in broader arenas of public discussion, impulses which had invested this particular representation of society with stakes high enough to induce such a consistent pattern as we have seen here. Nowhere, perhaps, were these extraparliamentary impulses more evident than in the changing language of Charles James Fox's speech on the triple assessment on 4 January 1798. In his long peroration in parliament, addressed to an audience dominated by landed gentlemen, Fox – himself a high Whig aristocrat – apparently found no use for any mention of the 'middle class'. However, when he later prepared the speech for publication as a pamphlet to be widely circulated among the broader public, Fox did not fail to insert two strong 'middle-class' grievances into his argument.[58] By doing so, Fox was clearly (even if unwittingly)

---

[56] One marginal exception, with regard to 'weak' uses of 'middle-class' language as reported in a single newspaper, was a short anti-war speech of Benjamin Hobhouse. Most newspapers concurred that Hobhouse referred to the proposed Bill's effects on persons of varying degrees of property; but only according to the detailed version in the *True Briton* (1544, 5 December 1797) – a Pittite paper – did he include among them 'the middling classes' and 'housekeepers in the middling ranks of life'.

[57] Wilberforce Bird, a Foxite of a prominent silk-masters' family, spoke on 7 December 1797 about the plight of 'the middle classes of merchants and manufacturers'; basically all reports of his speech concur, except for the *St James's Chronicle* (6236, 7–9 December 1797), where typically only 'the class of traders and manufacturers' was mentioned.

[58] The 'middle-class' statements ('It will fall with tremendous weight upon the middle class'; 'Why are the middle class of society to be reduced to poverty?') are absent from *all* newspaper reports of this speech. They are included in: C. J. Fox, *Speech of the Right Honourable Charles-James Fox, in the House of Commons, on Friday, the 4th of January, 1798, on the Assessed Taxes Bill . . .*, London, 1798, pp. 25, 29. They were also included in Cobbett's *Parliamentary History of England* (33, cols. 1223, 1253–4) as well as in Debrett's *Parliamentary Register*, based undoubtedly on the published version.

acknowledging the power and resonance which the language of 'middle class' had come to carry by this point in the national political debate.

WHAT WAS SO SPECIAL ABOUT THE TRIPLE ASSESSMENT?

The principle of the scaled increase in the assessed taxes was not really all that innovative. Rather, it continued a long trend of fiscal policy throughout most of the eighteenth century, in which the government refrained from direct taxes on land and other types of wealth, or from customs, in favour of taxation on domestically produced goods and services. In the estimation of the best-informed student of British taxation during this period, Patrick O'Brien, this trend of fiscal policy 'probably implies that the "middling ranks" in British society paid for foreign and strategic policies from which they derived a disproportionately small share of the benefits'.[59]

In other words, the opposition speakers of the 1790s who relentlessly insisted on the 'middle-class' grievance were probably right. But more importantly, the same grievance could have been voiced on just as sound grounds throughout the eighteenth century: O'Brien's judgment refers not specifically to the 1790s, but to the whole of British taxation since the end of King William's wars of the 1690s. Indeed, another historian has claimed that in fact the only point to commend Pitt's plan for increasing the assessments was that it was more *progressive* than any previous scheme.[60] That is to say, while the 'middle-class' grievance was not unfounded, it cannot by itself account for the role of 'middle-class' language in the debate on Pitt's proposals. Since the novel rhetorical framework of discussion was not due to any novelty in the oppressive nature of the tax on the 'middle' strata of society, its origins must have lain outside the realm of taxation – arguably, in the particular power which had been conferred upon the language of 'middle class' during this decade. Whatever

---

[59] O'Brien, 'The Political Economy of British Taxation', p. 17.

[60] Cookson, *The Friends of Peace*, p. 78. Indeed, as Cooper ('William Pitt, Taxation, and the Needs of War') points out, the graduated scale of the increase in the assessment was the more innovative element in Pitt's proposals, preparing the grounds for the income tax of the following year.

explanation one puts forward to account for the ubiquitous presence of this language in the debate on the triple assessment in
1797–8, should also account for its virtual absence in previous
discussions of similar fiscal measures.

As an example, compare the debate on the assessed taxes in
1797–8 with that on the window tax of 1784. Pitt, then a new
Chancellor of the Exchequer, proposed the so-called Commutation Bill, which bound together the lowering of duties on tea
with a new tax on house windows. The proposed window tax
was widely unpopular, often because of objections similar to
those raised in 1797–8 against the triple assessment: it was
perceived to be a regressive tax that spared the rich and fell
most severely on the 'middle' of society. The debate of 1784,
however, was carried out in very different terms from that of
1797–8. In parliament, to be sure, the opposition asserted the
oppressive nature of the tax: but this was phrased either in terms
of oppression of the poor by the rich, as oppressive to the whole
country or to 'the public', or as particularly burdensome to a
variety of specific groups – Scots, minors, farmers, and in one
single case 'the poor and middling rank of people.'[61] Clearly the
language of 'middle class' was not enlisted in any significant
way to oppose the Bill. Furthermore, there was no contestation
regarding social language: this can be seen, for example, in Pitt's
reply to Fox, which reproduced accurately his criticism in terms
of rich and poor, without any skewed dialogue of the kind we
have seen for the 1790s.[62] Consequently, one also cannot find a
differentiation of social vocabularies in the representations of the
parliamentary proceedings of 1784 in the press, similar to that
strongly evident during the later debates on Pitt's proposals for
financing the war.

This difference between the debates in 1784 and 1797–8 is epitomized in a long oppositional letter sent to Pitt by one M. Beden
of the town of Irvine.[63] The letter, objecting in strong terms to the

---

[61] *Parliamentary History of England* 24, cols. 1334, 1339, 1341, 1342 ('poor and middling'),
1343 ('the public'), 1344, 1379. In fact it was clear from Pitt's proposal that the actual
poor, who had fewer than seven windows in their house, were to be exempt.
[62] Ibid., col. 1351.
[63] PRO, Chatham Papers, vol. 264, fs. 93–9.

window tax, presented specifically the grievance of the 'middle' of society against the tax, prefiguring in essence the 'middle-class' arguments of the 1790s. Beden wrote alternatively about the plight of 'many Thousands of small Household property', of 'Industrous [sic] Traders and Merchants', and – in a manner reminiscent of the future 'middle-class idiom' – of 'the very Industrious & active sett of people in any State ... the Industrius [sic] & Frugal Merchant & Mechanick'. Nevertheless, he still perceived the clash basically as one between trading and landed interests, or between town and country, or between rich and poor. What Beden was struggling against was political despotism, in which the administration oppressed the people, and the remedy for which was a political reform that would give those injured (clearly, in actuality, the same 'middle' of society) a representation in parliament. Not only did this letter lack any 'middle class', or a tripartite social scheme in which to place a 'middle class' grievance, but the framework for explaining its plight was the familiar political (rather than social) dichotomy of the administration versus the people, one central to opposition rhetoric in the eighteenth century but quite distinct from the 'middle-class' argument of the 1790s.

So whatever was novel about the debate on the triple assessment, it was not the nature of the fiscal policy involved, nor the actual apportioning of its burdens. The following year, however, did see a major fiscal innovation – the much better known introduction of the income tax. In comparison with this first shot at raising direct taxation in a century or more, states O'Brien, Pitt's plans for increasing the assessed taxes were mere 'tinkering'.[64] A few words of explanation are therefore needed to account for the absence in the preceding pages of the debate over this radical fiscal measure; all the more so, since in Asa Briggs's influential narrative of the rise of 'middle-class' consciousness, the imposition of Pitt's income tax consists of the first of his four successive factors contributing to this process.[65] In fact, however, none of the few sources which

[64] O'Brien, 'The Political Economy of British Taxation', pp. 21–2. Note however O'Brien's admission that his interest lies in policies, not in their perception or reception by the public, which was often captivated by what O'Brien perceives as 'trivial causes' (p. 18). On the war income tax, see also O'Brien, 'Public Finance in the Wars with France', pp. 183–4.

[65] A. Briggs, 'Middle-Class Consciousness in English Politics, 1780–1846', *Past and Present* 9 (1956), p. 67. Cookson, 'Political Arithmetic', p. 54, also stresses the particularly oppressive effects of the income tax on the 'middle class'.

Briggs quotes on the issue of taxation deal specifically with the income tax. While Briggs does not appear to have differentiated here between the income tax and other types of impositions, this distinction was important to the uses of social language in the debates that these measures provoked.

For the most part, the uses of social language in the debate on the income tax were a rather faint echo of those in the debate on the triple assessment. Take for example the *Morning Chronicle*. Its first reaction to the announcement of the income tax plan was along familiar lines: 'It is the middling classes, however, that will be ground to atoms by this tax. It is the most honest, the most independent, the most virtuous class of the community that will be annihilated.' Unlike the previous year, however, rather than becoming a major issue, during the ensuing weeks the 'middle-class' argument disappeared from the pages of the *Morning Chronicle* almost completely, even when it could be expected. In fact, the most significant feature of the debate on the income tax, as it was reflected in the London press (including major pro-ministerial papers, like the *True Briton*), was the *lack* of interest in it; as the *Morning Chronicle* itself put it, 'No Tax Bill, in the memory of man, has had so singular a fate as the Income Bill. The turning of a path-way, or the building of a bridge, has often excited more debate.'[66]

In part, it may have been the threat of invasion, perceived as imminent in 1798 to a degree which made the opposition to the war suspend its objections momentarily, that allowed the income tax to sail through so easily. Another important reason for this popular indifference, however, lies in the different nature of these taxes: unlike the triple assessment, which was imposed on consumption, and thus was perceived to burden especially 'middle' social strata, the income tax looked very much like an improved land tax. It was easier to assess and raise from landed income than from commercial income (which could be manipulated in various ways); moreover the manner of choosing the commissioners seemed to privilege commercial people over landed ones. Thus, with regard to the income tax, it was the landed classes that rose to articulate

---

[66] *Morning Chronicle* 9216, 6 December 1798, editorial; 9238, 1 January 1799, editorial. Examples of conspicuous absences of the 'middle-class' argument include 9219, 10 December 1798, in the editorial; 9217, 7 December 1798, letter by 'Mercator'.

their own distinct – and felt to be severe – grievance; and this argument came to overshadow the expressions of the plight of the 'middle class'.

This is not to say that the language of 'middle class' disappeared altogether. The Unitarian mathematician William Frend, an ardent opponent of the war, could still single out the 'middle class' – in the manner typical of the Friends of Peace – as a political middle caught in between radical and pro-ministerial views (though with more emphasis on the familiar antithesis between Pitt and the 'middle class'):

Tom Paine and Mr Pitt are more nearly united to each other in their financial schemes, than either would be willing to acknowledge. The one is unjust to the higher, the other to the middle classes, and both affect an equal regard to the poor. The one would bring the poor and the rich together by levelling the rich; the other would increase the distance between the poor and the rich by demolishing the middle class.[67]

Yet such statements were far less conspicuous than during the previous year. In parliament, only a couple of 'middle-class' proponents (John Nicholls and Benjamin Hobhouse) could be heard, dwarfed by the overwhelming discussion of the effects of the proposed income tax on the landed classes. Consequently, the disagreements in this debate were not accompanied by a significant contestation over social language: outside parliament the broad public was less directly interested, while indoors virtually all speakers shared a similar (landed) social vocabulary.[68] This was revealingly reflected in the parliamentary reporting in the press: while the language of the few 'middle-class' arguments was again differentiated between newspapers according to the

---

[67] William Frend, *Principles of Taxation*, London, 1799, pp. iv–v.
[68] The Earl of Lauderdale, for example, could write to Arthur Young, his erstwhile political opponent, about their shared concern for 'the mischiefs that the intended Tax upon Income must produce if it is laid on Farmers' (Lauderdale to Young, n.d.; British Library, Add. Mss 35128, fs. 28–30). Also compare the anti-tax 'landed-classes idiom' in the *Morning Herald* 5701, 26 December 1798 (letter from 'The Farmer's Friend') with the pro-tax 'landed-classes idiom' in [Bell], *Three Essays on Taxation of Income*, and in Henry Merttins Bird, *Proposals for Paying off the Whole of the Present National Debt, and for Reducing Taxes Immediately . . .*, 2nd edn, London, 1799. In parliament too, 'landed-classes idiom' could be found in the rhetoric of both sides of the House. In a couple of cases (William Pulteney's speech in the Commons on 27 December 1798, Lord Holland's in the Lords on 8 January 1799) seemingly 'middle-class idiom' was used, but a careful reading shows that it in fact referred emphatically to *landed* classes.

same partisan lines as before,[69] the reports of 'landed-idiom' speeches were not differentiated at all in any meaningful way.

Not that these findings should really surprise us. Behind the expectation that it took a radical departure in fiscal policy (the income tax) in order to bring out a 'middle-class' consciousness lies a weighty presupposition. Such an expectation assumes that this 'middle-class' consciousness arose as a direct consequence of pressures of a given situation (here, taxation policy), which threatened the socio-economic interests of a pre-existing social group (here, the 'middle class'), and thus led to the mobilization of this social group in order to protect its interests. But, on the contrary, what these chapters have shown is that the invocation of a 'middle class' in the 1790s was not the consequence of any particular fiscal or other policy affecting socio-economic interests, but rather of a particular political situation (and therefore that the involvement of this language in this particular taxation debate was in large part incidental to the actual tax proposed); that the people who were mobilized around the language of 'middle class' were not a group unified primarily by social position (that is, not the middle social strata), but rather a group unified primarily by a circumstance-specific political outlook; and that the very existence of the 'middle class', rather than essentially preceding these developments in language, was in itself embodied in and dependent upon that very language of the heated battle of politics.

[69] Thus Nicholls's speech of 31 December 1798 referred only to 'the lower and higher orders of People' according to the *True Briton* (1877, 1 January 1799) and *The Times* (4371, 1 January 1799), but to the 'middle classes [who] would chiefly be affected' in the *Morning Chronicle* (9238, 1 January 1799). Hobhouse's speech of 4 December 1798, referring to the destruction of the 'middle classes' in most newspapers, was similarly enhanced and prolonged in the *Morning Chronicle* (9215, 5 December 1798); subverted in *The Times* (4349, 5 December 1798), where he was quoted to have said only that 'the professional man, the manufacturer, and the merchant, each in his class, would considerably suffer by it'; and omitted altogether in the *St James's Chronicle* (6391, 4–6 December 1798).

Postlude to the 1790s: the uses of 'bourgeois revolution'

Having arrived at the end of the 1790s with a deeply politicized and contested representation of society centred around a 'middle class', we can turn our attention once more to the divergent commentaries on the social origins of the French Revolution which opened our discussion of this turbulent decade. By now, the task of explaining their twists and turns dissolves almost effortlessly. To be sure, their explication has to do only obliquely with the events in France. That the relevant context for the language of these commentaries was the volatile political situation in Britain is underscored by a comparison with a different genre of writing on the French Revolution, namely those detailed historical works which purported to be primarily descriptive (though not without opinions), and which by tenor and by form (often running more than a thousand pages) were not intended as passionate polemical interventions in the political debate. Whereas in the more explicitly political commentaries the English terms 'middle class' or 'middle rank' were almost always substituted for the French term *bourgeoisie* (with little concern for possible shifts in meaning), this was hardly ever the case in the more explicitly historical ones, wherein the French terminology was invariably retained.[1]

---

[1] The neutral implications of the French terminology are suggested, for example, by the incarnations of one interpretation of the Revolution, whereby it was a consequence of the haughty superiority exhibited by the *Noblesse* towards the strengthening *Bourgeoisie*. This interpretation, in those words, was introduced by a strong opposer of the French Revolution, John Moore, in his popular *A View of the Causes and Progress of the French Revolution*, 2 vols., London, 1795, vol. I, pp. 25–6. Later, however, it was lifted almost word for word by another similarly obese account, but one which was in fact favourable to the Revolution: *An Historical View of the French Revolution . . .*, 2 vols., Newcastle upon Tyne, 1796, vol. I, pp. 19–20. In this genre of writing, and while expressed in an alien and unloaded French vocabulary (rather than in the loaded English one), the disparity of their politics did not impede the two authors from sharing this interpretation and its wording.

During the initial wave of optimism unleashed by the French Revolution, it made perfect sense for moderates (and future Friends of Peace) such as Mackintosh and Vaughan, repulsed by Burke but also not too keen on Paine, to portray the Revolution as a deed of the 'middle class'. In one gratifying move they could thus both advance their sanguine version of the events in France and confirm the soundness of their own middle position back home. In their hands the language of 'middle class' was one of social promise and reconstruction. On the other hand, when Burke wished in his *Reflections* to put forward a bleak and ominous interpretation of the same events, the social language which he found most useful was that of contending interests; not in its late-eighteenth-century guise, which presupposed underlying harmony and thus could not serve to portray deep social conflict, but by reviving the earlier image of hopelessly inimical interests pulling society apart.[2]

With the radicalization of the events in France from autumn 1792 onwards, however, the British moderates had lost the French Revolution: now they had to justify their position in spite of it, not with it. With the Terror and the war, the implications of representing the 'middle class' as involved in the revolutionary process became far more radical than these speakers were prepared to go. So their social interpretation of the Revolution was now reversed: the Revolution was blown off course and flung into the maelstrom of radicalization and terror because French society – unlike the British, of course – *lacked* that bastion of moderation and temperance, the 'middle class'. It is therefore not surprising to discover that those whom we have heard blaming the excesses of the Revolution on the deficiency of a proper 'middle class' – Thomas Erskine, Thomas Jones and the anonymous 'British Merchant' – were all avowed Friends of Peace; Erskine, in fact, having been the author of the most widely circulated attack on the war ever published.[3] With an increasing stake in the particular 'middle-class'-based portrayal of their own

---

[2] The relevance of Burke's picture of inimical interests to the British context was highlighted, for example, by a writer who immediately transposed it to politics at home: *Temperate Comments upon Intemperate Reflections: Or, a Review of Mr Burke's Letter*, London, 1791, pp. 43–4.

[3] This was his *A View of the Causes and Consequences of the Present War with France*, London, 1797, which went through at least thirty-five (!) editions by the end of the year.

society, these Friends of Peace reinterpreted the French Revolution as well in the way most suitable for their domestic politics.

Confronting them, again, was Burke, increasingly more irascible (not to say hysterical). Immediately following the Revolution, whereas Burke's image of the 'monied interest' tapped into strong antipathies that long predated these events, the language of 'middle class' did not carry for him a particular political significance. Indeed, in an altogether different context, Burke in 1791 in fact presented *himself* – when attempting to exonerate himself in the eyes of his erstwhile fellow Whigs – as fulfilling the role of a political middle. His position, he explained, 'between the principal leaders in parliament, and the lowest followers out of doors', placed him among those 'middle sort of men . . . who, by the spirit of that middle situation, are the fittest for preventing things from running to excess'.[4] In 1791, then, Burke too could still avail himself of the political-cum-social-middle rhetorical strategy.

In the subsequent reconfiguration of politics over the next few years, however, this statement – at least insofar as it was part of the public debate, Burke's personal feelings notwithstanding – became less credible. The claims for the political middle ground were usurped by Burke's respectable opponents, who increasingly invested the language of 'middle class' with the specific implications and overtones of their own politics; and the more meaning they packed into this vocabulary, the less it could be used in a neutral, non-committed way. John Thelwall, that forceful radical orator, was one who acknowledged in 1796 the resonance of this new social scheme. At the other extreme, when Burke – a man no less aware of the power of language˙ – was employing the notion of 'middle class' at precisely the same time (in the letters to which Thelwall was responding), he too was adapting his own social vocabulary to these developments. So now that the moderate opposition were attempting to absolve their cherished 'middle class' from any implication in the derailed French Revolution, it was left to Burke to bring the 'middle-class' interpretation of the Revolution back with a vengeance: hence his placing the onus

---

[4] Edmund Burke, *An Appeal from the New to the Old Whigs*, 1791; in *The Works of Edmund Burke*, Boston, 1839, vol. III, p. 437. But, he added further, 'the irresolution and timidity of those who compose this middle order, often prevents the effect of their controlling situation'.

of responsibility for the Revolution squarely on the shoulders of
the 'middle class'. Intrinsically a potentially malignant growth
in an otherwise stable and healthy body social and body politic,
driven by energetic impatience and violent ambition, it was a
far cry from a political middle, which the Burke of 1791 had
characterized as erring, in anything, on the side of irresolution,
passivity and timidity.[5] These assertions of Burke in 1796 of
course flatly contradicted the claims made for the 'middle class'
by those who were in favour of the said 'regicide' peace. Interestingly, they were also a long way from Burke's own proud depiction of himself some fifteen years earlier, when the language of
'middle class' had still been unloaded and unproblematic: 'I am
no peer, nor like to be; but am in middle life, in the mass of
citizens.'[6]

So when Burke and Thelwall were exchanging rhetorical blows
in 1796, the influence of the 'middle-class idiom' (whose political
origins were uncongenial to both) was powerful enough to per-
meate and shape parts of their heated exchange.[7] Indeed, this
influence was revealed even further in Burke's posthumous sequel
to his letters of 1796, the *Third Letter on a Regicide Peace*. Standing
again on the shoulders of previous generations of country ideologues, Burke persisted in emphasizing the singular contribution
of the landed classes to political stability. Nevertheless, in reiterating the song of praise for the landed classes, Burke was now not
only counteracting the 'middle-class idiom' but also simultaneously modelling his own formulations after it:

The present war is, above all others . . . a war against landed property.
That description of property is in its nature the firm base of every stable
government; and has been so considered, by all the wisest writers of the
old philosophy . . . if in our own history, there is any one circumstance to
which, under God, are to be attributed the steady resistance, the fortunate issue, and sober settlement, of all our struggles for liberty, it is,
that while the landed interest, instead of forming a separate body, as
in other countries, has, at all times, been in close connexion and union

---

[5] See previous note.
[6] Speech against the repeal of the Marriage Act: *Works*, vol. v, p. 434. Burke is often
described as typically 'bourgeois': see I. Kramnick, *The Rage of Edmund Burke: Portrait
of an Ambivalent Conservative*, New York, 1977.
[7] And compare its influence on another anti-Jacobin tract of 1796: above, p. 89.

with the other great interests of the country, it has been spontaneously allowed to lead and direct, and moderate all the rest.[8]

All this sounds strikingly familiar. While justifying the war in terms of a 'landed-class idiom', and thus directly refuting both the political and the social arguments of the proponents of the 'middle class', Burke's language at the same time closely replicated their own: in interpreting the war as a specific threat to a valuable component of society; in presenting the landed classes as those who 'moderate' between the other constituents of society, thus reappropriating for them the role of the political middle; in characterizing them with adjectives such as 'steady' and 'sober'; in claiming to identify the social group who by its nature is the keystone of stable government and of the preservation of liberty; and in invoking 'the wisest writers of the old philosophy' as the authority for this identification.[9]

On the whole, then, in berating the 'middle class', in offering an alternative social locus for the virtues claimed by the 'middle-class idiom', and in replicating its formulations, Burke's last statements appear to have been in direct dialogue – in direct conflict – with this increasingly conspicuous oppositional rhetoric.[10] Nor was Burke alone. Already in 1793 William Cusack Smith, a writer whose political reasoning had been commended by Burke himself, asserted that political tumult was hardly to be expected from the rich or the poor; no, he explained in somewhat vague terms, 'the seditious orders of modern patriotism' would be found among those 'who hold a middle place between the industrious and the rabble; and vibrate betwixt the opposites of restlessness and

---

[8] The full title of Burke's pamphlet was *A Third Letter to a Member of the Present Parliament, on the Proposals for Peace with the Regicide Directory of France*; here quoted from 2nd edn, London, 1797, pp. 144–5.

[9] Compare the latter, for example, with *The Cabinet*'s similar invocation of 'the concurring voice of all nations and of all ages, of the philosopher, the poet, and the moralist' at precisely the same time, to buttress 'middle-class idiom': see above, p. 53.

[10] John Pocock (*Virtue, Commerce, and History*, Cambridge, 1985, pp. 207–9) has noticed the change in the social vocabulary of Burke's analyses of the French Revolution. But Pocock, apprehensive again lest the Marxist notion of a bourgeois revolution might find contemporary endorsement, does not provide an explanation or context for these observations, preferring to work his way around them. See also his comments in E. Burke, *Reflections on the Revolution in France*, ed. J. G. A. Pocock, Indianapolis, 1987, introduction, pp. xxxvii–xxxix.

sloth; – they are a politer sort of mob'.[11] And in 1798 – Burke already being dead – the same dialogue was recreated by an Irish 'gentleman', who was induced by the uprising in Ireland to reconsider the French Revolution as an analogy to these latter disturbances at home. Both the middle and the lower classes in France, he complained, were suddenly and dangerously exalted to supreme power. But whereas the conduct of the lower classes was not surprising,

the too general disaffection of the better sort, who had neither ignorance nor poverty to plead in extenuation of trespass, deserves more severe reprehension. The persons to whom I now allude belong to the middle class, being composed of substantial landholders, professional men and merchants, whose defection is the more inexcusable.

Echoing Burke, this writer further pointed to the inherent tendency of the 'middle class' to 'preposterous ambition', arising from 'the vanity of the *upstart*': its dissatisfaction with the 'enjoyments of middle life' resulted in 'sedition and conspiracy'. The 'gentleman' then offered an alternative for the social repository of political stability, a 'landed-class idiom', which – again like Burke's – replicated the formulations of the 'middle-class idiom' at the same time that it was refuting its content: in contrast with the 'middle class', he stated, the 'flourishing and industrious Yeomanry constitute the strength of a Country . . . Ambition disturbs not the happy mediocrity of their situation.'[12] Note in particular the 'happy mediocrity' which he associated with the yeomanry, in an attempt to wrest the Golden Mean from the grip of the opposition; an attempt, one might add, which was

---

[11] William Cusack Smith, *The Patriot: Or, Political Essays*, 2nd edn, Dublin, 1793, p. 3. And see Burke's approving letter to Smith, 22 July 1791, in *The Correspondence of Edmund Burke*, vol. VI, eds. A. Cobban and R. A. Smith, Cambridge, 1967, pp. 302–5. Smith's preferred vision of society was one based on the harmonious coexistence of interests: see above, p. 94. And compare also an earlier Burkean writer, to whom the French Revolution came as no surprise, since already ten years previously he had 'found the middle class of people almost universally of one sentiment, namely, alienated from the established government': J. E. Hamilton, *Reflections on the Revolution in France, by the Right Honourable Edmund Burke, Considered: Also, Observations on Mr Paine's Pamphlet, Intituled the Rights of Men [sic]* . . ., London, 1791, p. 3.

[12] *Letters from a Gentleman in Ireland, to His Friend at Bath*, Cork, 1798, pp. 11, 23–4, 27, 39–40. Similar echoes of Burke's remarks on the pernicious effects of 'middle-class' ambition can be clearly seen in *A New Enquiry into the Principles and Policy of Taxation* and *Thoughts on the Commencement of the Year* M,DCC,XCVIII as quoted above, pp. 120–1.

not in complete consistency with his previous critical appraisal of the 'substantial landholders' of the 'middle class'.

Such associations of the 'middle class' with revolution could not but make political moderates squirm uncomfortably. Perhaps even worse for the moderates' reputation were instances in which radical speakers implicated the notion of 'middle class' in articulating their own agenda. We have seen that radicals were employing stark dual social schemes to great effect, and therefore found the notion of 'middle class' on the whole irrelevant to their political objectives. But while the language of 'middle class' remained marginal to their rhetoric, they could still at times taint it with Jacobin politics, as was the case for instance when Thelwall suddenly switched tack and tried to use the language of 'middle class' to win further support. Likewise, some uneasiness may have been caused by the hairdresser John Lovett of the London Corresponding Society when he implicated the notion of 'middle class' in levelling politics: the rich, Lovett declared, 'must . . . give up part of their wealth, before they can enjoy that tranquillity and happiness that is reserved for those in a middling sphere of life'.[13] By 1798, the damaging consequences of the image of a 'middle class' prone to political instability were laid bare much more clearly in a Jacobin appeal to the inhabitants of Scotland. This tract, calling to denounce the corrupt and bellicose ministry and to hope for a French invasion, was divided into separate addresses – to men, to women, to clergy, and finally to one social group that was singled out: 'YE MIDDLE RANKS OF SOCIETY . . . you must no longer devote your substance or services to the support of an iniquitous system, and a profligate ministry . . . what have the middle ranks of society to expect from supporting the present system? Their own degradation and final ruin.'[14] Such a call for the conversion of the 'middle class' surely played straight into the hands of those who believed that the 'middle class' was indeed potentially revolutionary; as must have also been the effect of a letter in the *Morning Chronicle* during the debates on the triple assessment which threatened Pitt that if he did not alter his oppressive policies, 'you may, perhaps, live to see the middle classes make a common cause with the lowest,

---

[13] John Lovett, *The Citizen of the World*, London, 1793, p. 15.
[14] *Unite, or Be Ruined, Alias the Weaver's Budget. No. IV.*, Edinburgh, 1798, p. 7.

and by your own impolicy realize in this country those enormities which we deplore in another'.[15]

Thus, a significant legacy of the debates of the 1790s was the representation of the 'middle class' as prone to political innovation and agitation.[16] Such an image could serve the goals of speakers from the two political extremes, but it was highly embarrassing to the political moderates – those who had the most invested in the language of 'middle class'. As we shall see, the association with a revolutionary disposition came back time and again to haunt the proponents of the responsible and respectable 'middle class', who were continually at pains to try to dodge it or explain it away. By the time, then, that Marx and Engels famously wrote that 'the bourgeoisie, historically, has played a most revolutionary part', the notion of a revolutionary 'middle class', historically, had in fact already played a tortuous variety of competing and often contradictory parts.[17]

For Marx and Engels, the revolutionary role of the bourgeoisie was its redeeming feature, since the part it played facilitated the next stages of the ultimate revolutionary process. Marx and Engels's representation of this revolutionary role was part of an attempt to wrest power from what by the mid nineteenth century will come to be broadly seen as a triumphant 'middle class'. But

---

[15] *Morning Chronicle* 8899, 1 December 1797, letter by 'Junius'.
[16] Indeed this representation of the 'middle class' found its way into diverse quarters. See for example the Earl of Lauderdale's address to his fellow peers, in which he too subscribed to the view that 'the middling orders whom the scene [of the Revolution] had brought forward', and who lacked proper aristocratic guidance, were to be blamed for the attempt to establish a republic. 'In the middling orders of society', Lauderdale wrote, a class corrupted by commerce, 'we also found the disciples of Voltaire, Rousseau, Mably, Turgot, and the economists'. By contrast, his favoured state of affairs was one of 'friendly intercourse and relation . . . between the wealthy and the indigent', a benevolent social situation reassuringly containable within dual terms, which was 'the best cement to the stability of our constitution': James Maitland, eighth Earl of Lauderdale, *Letters to the Peers of Scotland*, London, 1794, pp. 59–60, 316 (also p. 67). For another glimpse of this image of the revolutionary 'middle class', see Henry Meister, *Letters Written during a Residence in England. Translated from the French . . .*, London, 1799, pp. 154–5.
[17] *Manifesto of the Communist Party*, 1848; in *The Marx–Engels Reader*, ed. R. C. Tucker, 2nd edn., New York, 1978, p. 475. In fact this phrase itself has had a somewhat tortuous history: whereas today it is commonly taken to refer specifically to (political) 'bourgeois revolutions', originally it referred more broadly to the bourgeoisie's role in revolutionizing economic relations. (See P. Anderson, 'The Notion of Bourgeois Revolution', in his *English Questions*, London, 1992, p. 107.) And for subsequent changes in the representations of the French Revolution and the role of the 'middle class' in it, on both sides of the Channel, see below, pp. 281–4, 291–2, 367–9.

all this lay a long way ahead. In the 1790s, those who believed in a 'middle class' could see it as anything but triumphant, and a revolutionary role was for them anything but a redeeming feature. Rather, in the particular political configuration of this decade, the language of 'middle class' was wedded to a losing political trend. It was inextricably linked with a political camp whose naïve optimism turned into embarrassment, whose confidence was displaced by uncomfortable defensiveness and whose political aspirations proved frustratingly futile. The proponents of the 'middle class' faced the resistance of the more formidable contenders of this period, be they potential revolutionaries or actual counter-revolutionaries, flanking them on either side. The champions of the language of 'middle class' in the 1790s were swimming hopelessly against the tide; and therefore it will not be very surprising to discover that its heyday was short-lived, and that with the change of the political configuration which had encouraged its use in the first place, the language of 'middle class', in its specific guise of this decade, quickly faded away.

PART II

The tug of war

CHAPTER 5

Taming the 'middle class'

[The] middle rank [consists of those] among whom almost all the sense and virtue of society reside. Their pretended incapacity for political affairs is an arrogant fiction of Statesmen which the history of Revolutions has ever belied.

(James Mackintosh, 1791)[1]

[The middle classes] are inert and timid, and almost as little qualified to defend a throne as they are disposed to overthrow it.

(James Mackintosh, 1815)[2]

During the later years of the Napoleonic war, the two leading literary and political periodicals in Britain, the Whig *Edinburgh Review* and its Tory rival the *Quarterly Review*, published articles about the social and political state of affairs in Sicily. The *Edinburgh*, in a review of a travel book by the future novelist John Galt, expressed approval both of Galt's 'very unfavourable' discussion of the Sicilian nobility and of observations on 'the formation, in Palermo, of that comfortable middle class which is the best proof of a prosperous and free community'.[3] The readers of the *Quarterly*, however, in its own review of another book about Sicily by G. Francis Leckie, learned about the island's social and political structure exclusively in the dual terms of nobles and commoners, or of higher and lower orders, between which – so the readers were assured – existed a benevolent paternalistic

---

[1] James Mackintosh, *Vindiciae Gallicae. Defence of the French Revolution and Its English Admirers against the Accusations of the Right Hon. Edmund Burke ...*, London, 1791, p. 129.

[2] *Edinburgh Review* 24, February 1815, p. 525.

[3] *Edinburgh Review* 23, April 1814, p. 47 (by Henry Brougham); reviewing John Galt, *Voyages and Travels, in the Years 1809, 1810, and 1811: Containing Statistical, Commercial and Miscellaneous Observations on Gibraltar, Sardinia, Sicily, Malta, Serigo, and Turkey*, London, 1812 (pp. 29–30 quoted about Palermo).

relationship.[4] Since Leckie himself denied the existence of such
a benevolent relationship, the Tory periodical denounced his
book as dangerously Jacobinical, seditiously inciting the Sicilian
lower classes to revolution.

The plot thickens when one reads Leckie's book, only to
discover that in fact, not only did Leckie acknowledge the existence of a 'middle class' in Sicily, he even gave one section the
title 'Character of the middling Ranks'.[5] So the *Quarterly Review*,
at the same time that it rejected Leckie's political views, also
rejected his social vocabulary, recasting his vision of Sicilian
society in a way that obliterated these 'middling ranks' and left
only higher and lower orders. Furthermore, elsewhere the *Quarterly* reviewers actually did the same to our other author, John
Galt, as well: in *their* paraphrased rendition of the very same
passage on Palermo that was highlighted by the *Edinburgh Review*,
they recapitulated it as purportedly including only 'a number of
common-place observations on nobility, government, and the
clergy': again, the 'middle class' – together with Galt's 'middle-
class idiom' – was gone.[6]

This scene seems by now quite familiar: another war, another
pair of political opponents from the right and the moderate left,
and another divergence of social descriptions, whereby 'middle-
class' presence was emphasized by the latter but downplayed by
the former. And yet the first decade and a half of the nineteenth
century were not simply a continuation of the story that we have
been following for the 1790s. It should be stressed at the outset
that after the charge and the resonance with which the language
of 'middle class' was invested in the decade following the French
Revolution, the next fifteen years were surprisingly quiescent.
Overall, this period represents one long lull in the uses and
power of the language of 'middle class', a lull which ended only
in a renewed peak in the late 1810s. A closer look, however,
allows some more refined patterns to become visible. Thus a
limited surge of political 'middle-class' language can be noted
around 1806–9, following the rather meek reforming tide of the

---

[4] *Quarterly Review* 1, May 1809, pp. 409–15.
[5] Gould Francis Leckie, *An Historical Survey of the Foreign Affairs of Great Britain, with a
View to Explain the Causes of the Disasters of the Late and Present Wars*, London, 1808,
p. 80; see also p. 50.
[6] *Quarterly Review* 7, June 1812, p. 301.

mid-decade. More significantly, these years begin to reveal a perhaps unexpected range of new uses of this language, not all of which will sound as familiar as the differentiation between the *Edinburgh* and the *Quarterly*. The explanation for both the overall subdued role of the language of 'middle class' during this period, and for the new ways in which it was beginning to be used, lies in the new political configuration brought about by the second French war.

The war against Napoleon, commenced after the collapse of the short-lived peace of Amiens in the spring of 1803, was widely viewed as distinctly different from the first French war. 'The peace,' commented one observer, 'short as its duration has been, has been highly beneficial. The English are no longer a divided people. They are ready and almost eager for the commencement of hostilities, because they are persuaded that war is unavoidable.'[7] Few had doubts regarding either Napoleon's aggressive intentions or – at least initially – the measures required to stop him. The rampant invasion fears of 1803–5 (in village streets, lines of wagons were waiting to evacuate women and children upon the arrival of the French[8]) went far to secure this consensus, instigating a wave of patriotic exhortations. Instead of sticking out as a major bone of contention, as had been the case in the 1790s, the French issue now provided any ministry with a powerful cement for maintaining domestic unity (Ireland apart) and feeling of common purpose. As John Cookson points out, the early years of this war found the Friends of Peace on the whole supporting the ministry's military effort, which they too perceived now to be a defensive and necessary measure. As the *Sheffield Iris*, an erstwhile 'liberal' newspaper, observed, 'a spirit of unanimity and patriotism, unexampled even in the annals of this favoured country, displays itself among all ranks of people'.[9]

[7] [Robert Southey], *Letters from England: By Don Manuel Alvarez Espriella: Translated from the Spanish*, London, 1807; rep. edn, ed. J. Simmons, London, 1951, p. 374. The next passage reiterated: 'Never was there a time when the English were so decidedly Anti-Gallican, those very persons being the most so who formerly regarded France with the warmest hopes.'

[8] L. Colley, *Britons: Forging the Nation 1707–1837*, New Haven, 1992, p. 306. C. Emsley, *British Society and the French Wars 1793–1815*, London, 1979, chapter 6.

[9] *Sheffield Iris*, 28 July 1803, quoted in Emsley, *British Society and the French Wars*, p. 113; and see to p. 119. F. Knight, *University Rebel: The Life of William Frend (1757–1841)*, London, 1971, pp. 233–6. J. E. Cookson, *The Friends of Peace*, Cambridge, 1982, chapter 7.

Domestically, too, the political situation in the 1800s was quite different from that of the previous decade. Popular radicalism was largely defeated and demoralized. 'It simply lost coherence', writes E. P. Thompson; 'For years it was made inarticulate by censorship and intimidation . . . it lost its own sense of direction.' The Corresponding Societies were closed down. Some radicals turned to more desperate means, which could result in (inevitably ineffective) revolutionary schemes; like that for which the hapless Irishman Colonel Despard was blamed (and executed) in 1803, bringing to an end the 'last flaring-up of the old Jacobinism of the 1790s'.[10] Many who had previously held radical or reforming views became disillusioned, disappointed or disaffected, and were found to speak in increasingly conservative voices. Furthermore, when Pitt resigned in 1801, the stage was set for a new administration less crippled by the partisanship and the bitterness of the 1790s; resentment of Pitt's policies was often replaced by tolerance for his successor, Henry Addington, and his lacklustre administration. The trigger for Pitt's resignation, namely the opposition of George III to his proposals for Catholic emancipation in Ireland, was in itself an indication of the liberation of politics from its monoaxial polarization of the previous decade. And then, once the war had recommenced and Pitt was brought back, it was on account of his war leadership skills, which overshadowed the more questionable legacy of his internal policies. The new unity and consensus were publicly demonstrated by Pitt's 1804 suggestion to incorporate the Foxites in his administration, a suggestion which was foiled only by the resistance of the King.

One consequence was that the former political middle lost its particular distinctiveness. On a reconfigured political map whose fissure lines were not as deep or clear-cut as previously, 'moderates' now had less of a pressing need to dissociate themselves from a dynamic radical camp on the one hand, and less of an inclination to dissociate themselves from the pro-ministerial party on the other. The language of 'middle class', therefore, lost much of its former charge. Moreover, together with the blurring of political lines came a blurring of rhetorical ones. Now that the

---

[10] E. P. Thompson, *The Making of the English Working Class*, London, 1963, pp. 451, 483. On Despard see M. Elliott, 'The "Despard Conspiracy" Reconsidered', *Past and Present* 75 (1977), pp. 46–61; idem, *Partners in Revolution: The United Irishmen and France*, New Haven, 1982, pp. 282–97.

language of 'middle class' was no longer associated as unambiguously with a clear political position (an association which was, to repeat once more, conjunctural rather than somehow organic to this particular representation of society), it could be picked up and enlisted in support of other agendas; a transformation strikingly evident in the contrast between James Mackintosh's two pronouncements a quarter of a century apart, quoted in the epigraphs above. Indeed, by the time the language of 'middle class' again became charged and its uses manifestly politicized, in the increasingly radicalized circumstances of the late 1810s, the meanings which were infused into this language turned out to be very different from those of the 1790s.

Not that the language of 'middle class' disappeared from anti-war rhetoric overnight, of course. When the widespread consensus of the early years of the second French war was replaced by increasing scepticism and renewed agitation for peace, some familiar 'middle-class' formulations (and familiar responses to them) reappeared. This happened mostly in 1806–7, which like 1797 was a moment of particular despondency. In Europe, Napoleon was relentlessly successful in diplomatic as well as in military encounters; Britain's last allies were either alienated or conquered. At home, the deaths within less than one year of the two great political leaders of the age, Pitt and Fox, brought many to take a gloomy view of future prospects; as Francis Horner put it, 'the giant race is extinct; and we are left in the hands of little ones'.[11] The 'Ministry of All Talents' that succeeded Pitt hardly lived up to its epithet: it increased taxation, had only limited military success and failed to negotiate peace. The subsequent administration, led by the Duke of Portland, was responsible for the Orders in Council of late 1807, which imposed restrictions on neutral trade with France and eventually resulted in dragging the United States into the war, to the dismay of many. The blockade also exacerbated the economic depression, which affected most severely the industrial north and became increasingly burdensome, reaching its nadir in 1808.

The prime cause of the Friends of Peace at this stage was the

---

[11] F. Horner to F. Jeffrey, 15 September 1806; in L. Horner (ed.), *Memoirs and Correspondence of Francis Horner, MP*, 2 vols., London, 1843, vol. 1, p. 373. Pitt died in January of 1806; Fox in October.

campaign against the Orders in Council. Significantly, however, during these renewed endeavours of the Friends of Peace – their most successful ever, leading to the repeal of the Orders in Council in 1812 – the notion of 'middle class' did *not* play a central role; this campaign relied heavily on representations of distinct interests – especially the provincial merchants and manufacturers – rather than on the language of 'middle class'.[12] Indeed, this fact is probably more significant than those instances in which the language of 'middle class' did reappear, replicating the anti-war language of the 1790s. The issue that elicited the bulk of such cases (an issue, we may note, which subsided before the debate over the Orders in Council) was the financial proposals of Lord Henry Petty, the Talents' Chancellor of the Exchequer.

A few examples will suffice here. Excessive taxation, warned the veteran Friend of Peace John Aikin in 1807, corrupts those who have always been recognized as 'the most valuable . . . members of society, the middle ranks of people', and may result dangerously in their disaffection.[13] War taxes, warned others, 'deprived, that by far most virtuous and most industrious part of Society, – the MIDDLE CLASS, of a very large portion of their comforts and common necessaries of life'; by these taxes, 'the middling classes of society are despoiled of their *independence*'.[14] These words were echoed in an early 1809 fast-day sermon against 'the longest, most expensive, and most destructive war':

---

[12] See Cookson, *The Friends of Peace*, pp. 82, 216–19; and more generally chapter 9.

[13] *Athenaeum, a Magazine of Literary and Miscellaneous Information*, ed. J. Aikin, 1:2, February 1807, p. 124. (That month Petty presented a new plan for raising loans, which was abandoned when the ministry fell.) Like Vicesimus Knox the previous decade, Aikin too realized that his conceptualization of society was an act of choice, and indeed one which was politically loaded; as he remarked elsewhere, whenever 'patricians or noblesse' attempted to separate themselves from 'plebeians', and 'endeavoured to inculcate the idea of two classes in society' and two classes only, the respectables and the ignorants, the political consequence was inevitably tyranny and alienation. (John Aikin, *Essays Literary and Miscellaneous*, London, 1811, pp. 385–6.)

[14] Charles Rivers (solicitor), *The Appeal of an Injured Individual to the British Nation, on the Arbitrary and Inquisitorial Consequences of the Tax on Income. . .*, London, 1808, p. 3 (also 5). Richard Warner [curate of Bath], *A Letter to the People of England: On Petitioning the Throne for the Restoration of Peace*, Bath, 1808, p. 11. See similarly Capel Lofft, *On the Revival of the Cause of Reform in the Representation of the Commons in Parliament*, London, 1809, p. 33; and the *Monthly Repository* of 1809, as quoted in A. Briggs, 'Middle-Class Consciousness in English Politics, 1780–1846', *Past and Present* 9 (1956), p. 68.

the middle order must be supported, or the whole fabric will tumble in; if the higher ranks have been oratorically termed 'the corinthian capital of polished society', the middle class is the strong pillar that supports, and lifts it from the dust. It forms that arch in our constitution, which springing from the foundation, supports the superstructure.[15]

Leigh Hunt's newly established *Examiner*, about to become a key voice of 'liberal' opinions, concurred that war taxation 'invaded the comforts of the middling, while the upper class is scarcely affected in its luxuries'; consequently, 'the middling class assimilated with the lower; that golden mean, in which the best strength and truest felicity of a nation resides, is annihilated', leading inevitably to despotism.[16]

Or take what is perhaps the best-known 'liberal' voice of these years, the exceptionally successful *Edinburgh Review*. It is a common assertion that the *Edinburgh Review*, propagating Whig and Scottish views since its beginning in 1802, was a major vehicle for representing and catering for the 'middle class'.[17] Yet if it is read not as a coherent and unified body of thought (as is usually the case), but instead as a dynamic expressive organ changing over time, it becomes evident that the awareness of the 'middle class' in its pages was anything but even. In fact, its first few years were relatively barren in this respect. It was only

[15] Rev. C[harles Caleb] Colton, *A Sermon, Preached at St Peter's Church, in Tiverton, on Wednesday, 9th of February 1809. Being the Day Appointed, for a General Fast*, Tiverton, [1809], pp. 12, 29 (note again the interchangeability of 'middle order' and 'middle class'). Like other Friends of Peace, Colton admitted his initial support for this war as a defensive measure, but was now advocating peace – though not unconditionally. He still continued to view Napoleon as the ultimate arch-villain, as was clear in his vigorous *Napoleon: A Poem; in which that Apostate from the Cause of Liberty is Held up to the Just Indignation of an Injured People ...*, London, [1812].

[16] *Examiner* 18, 1 May 1808, p. 273, leading article: 'On the Inequality of Our Taxation, and the Importance of Sustaining the Middling Class of the Community'. Tellingly, the *Examiner* – like many others – revealed a need to explain its use of 'middle class' even as it was emphasizing its significance: 'By the middling, I mean generally that respectable class which fills up the space between the larger portion of the people who are manually employed, and the smaller who possess independent or other wealth.' See also the 'middle-class idiom' two weeks earlier in another context (16, 17 April 1808, p. 241), as well as the references to the peculiar burden of taxation on the 'middle orders' or 'middle ranks' in 71, 7 May 1809, p. 290; 95, 22 October 1809, p. 678; and again 262, 3 January 1813, pp. 9–10.

[17] J. Clive, *Scotch Reviewers: The Edinburgh Review, 1802–1815*, London, 1957, chapter 5, esp. pp. 142–8. B. Fontana, *Rethinking the Politics of Commercial Society: The Edinburgh Review 1802–1832*, Cambridge, 1985, passim.

in the context of the broader anti-war rhetoric of early 1807 that
we find the first significant appearance of 'middle-class' language
in the *Edinburgh*, when Henry Brougham acidly observed how
the vicissitudes of war, 'happening many whole leagues from this
country, or affecting only the middling orders of the people, are
a great way distant from, or far beneath the consideration of our
lovers of war'. In the following issue David Buchanan stressed
again 'the extreme severity with which the property-tax already
presses on the middling classes of society'.[18] The next couple of
years saw a sharp increase in the uses of 'middle-class' language
in the *Edinburgh Review*, a surge which subsided by 1809.[19]

Given such replications of anti-war patterns of the previous
decade, it is not surprising to find some pro-war voices similarly
reproducing their own rhetoric of the 1790s, denying both the
claims of the 'middle-class idiom' and its language at the same
time. Such a differentiation of social language can be clearly shown
for the *Quarterly Review* (established 1809) versus the *Edinburgh
Review*, for instance, as the opening of this chapter has suggested.
The *Quarterly* preferred to celebrate the manners and honour of
the higher orders, as well as the natural feelings of the peasantry;
apparently it could find some measure of virtue anywhere but
in the middle – a middle that remained unnamed.[20] The same
differentiation also characterized the writings of William Burdon,
a former Friend of Peace who in 1803 dramatically announced a
bellicose change of heart: together with his politics, his manner of

---

[18] *Edinburgh Review* 9, January 1807, p. 433 (Brougham had previously made two brief
references to the burden of taxation on the 'middle class': 3, January 1804, p. 473;
and 5, October 1804, p. 117); 10, April 1807, p. 76. Identification of authorship of
reviews in the *Edinburgh Review* follows *The Wellesley Index to Victorian Periodicals 1824–
1900*, ed. W. E. Houghton, vol. I, Toronto, 1966.

[19] See among others *Edinburgh Review* 9, January 1807, p. 490; 10, April 1807, p. 3, and
July 1807, p. 386; 11, October 1807, p. 111; 12, July 1808, p. 277; 13, January 1809,
p. 408. Francis Horner's unusually detailed letter to Jeffrey (both among the founders
of the *Edinburgh Review*) in late 1806, singling out 'the middling order of the people'
as the only political hope in the new lacklustre age ushered in by the death of Fox,
also fit nicely into this trend: Horner to Jeffrey, 15 September 1806, in his *Memoirs
and Correspondence*, vol. I, pp. 374–5.

[20] Before 1815, a 'middle class' in Britain was mentioned only twice in the *Quarterly*, in
both cases in apolitical and, if anything, critical contexts (3, February 1810, p. 57; 7,
June 1812, p. 376); compared with about twenty meaningful instances in the *Edinburgh*
during the same years. For examples of emphases in the *Quarterly Review* on the
'manners, and a sense of honour' of the higher orders, and on the 'simple and natural
feeling which characterizes an uncorrupted peasantry', see 4, November 1810, p. 487;
7, December 1812, pp. 336–8.

discussing society changed as well, replacing his earlier emphasis on the 'middle class' with a consistent dual framework.[21]

Among such pro-ministerial voices that re-enacted the debate patterns of the previous decade, the most interesting were those who responded with vigorous vindications of the aristocracy. Aristocratic claims for natural leadership were being challenged during these years on numerous fronts. The paucity of successes in a war against a conscript army led by professional officers of fairly broad social origins was casting doubts upon the fundamental justification for the existence of the aristocracy, namely its role in leading the British army. This, as well as the deaths of Pitt and Fox, which for some portended the natural death of the old order, probably had much to do with the urgent need to reassert that the landed elite was alive and kicking. Consequently, the surge of pro-aristocratic rhetoric centred around 1807–9 seemed more defensive and more directly confrontational than before.[22]

A particularly spirited example, which was directly pitted against 'middle-class' rhetoric, was that of the inventor-cum-publicist William Playfair, whose *British Family Antiquity* was candidly designed 'to prove the merit and utility of a hereditary race of nobles'.[23] Replicating at length the formulations of the 'middle-class idiom',

---

[21] This remained true even when a tripartite structure of Burdon's argument seemed to invite 'middle-class' language: 'Some ranks must give up their luxuries, and others their comforts: the poor give their *all*, when they give their labour'; again, the 'others' in the middle remained unnamed (W[illiam] Burdon, *Unanimity Recommended*, Newcastle upon Tyne, 1803, p. 18). Burdon's dual social framework (which also entailed appropriating 'independence' to characterize the labouring classes) was reiterated in his *Advice Addressed to the Lower Ranks of Society: Useful at All Times, More Especially in the Present*, Newcastle upon Tyne, 1803.

[22] Indeed it encompassed a broad political spectrum: compare the praises for the responsible country gentry as the source of the people's happiness in the *Quarterly Review* (5, February 1811, pp. 111–12) with the linking of the country's happiness to the power of a proper natural aristocracy in the *Edinburgh Review* – which was, after all, a Whig organ (10, July 1807, pp. 408, 417; also 13, October 1808, p. 233).

[23] William Playfair, *A Fair and Candid Address to the British Nobility: Accompanied with Illustrations and Proofs of the Advantage of Hereditary Rank and Title in a Free Country*, London, 1809, p. [3]. See also his *Second Address to the British Nobility* ..., London, 1810. These addresses accompanied his nine-volume compilation, *British Family Antiquity*, published in 1809–11. Compare also the quest for a new image of a praiseworthy aristocracy in the almost simultaneous reissue of *Collins's Peerage of England* in nine volumes, enlarged and edited by Sir Egerton Brydges. Brydges promised to replace Collins's reverence and indiscriminate flattery with a more critical yet appreciative stance; a change, he assured, which reflected a transformation in the nature of the aristocracy itself, open to new talents, and who at present 'instead of separate rights and views ... possess mingled interests with the commonalty' (vol. 1, London, 1812, p. x).

Playfair stressed the aristocracy's 'individual merit and general utility', its key role in defending the liberties and the rights of the people, its unique midway political independence (being independent of both king and people), its innocence of any particularistic self-interest, its reliance on the support of public opinion and the virtues of its members 'as private men'. All in all, he wished to refute the altogether mistaken claim that noble families 'were inferior to the other classes of society', in particular to the 'middle class'. 'It is, however, amongst those two dissimilar and opposite classes of society', Playfair asserted, the nobility and the industrious lower orders, 'that we find the greatest talents and genius; and [by contrast] we find the least where there are wealth and affluence without rank.' Not to leave any doubts, Playfair supplemented the latter comment with a note that specified who precisely were those least likely to display talent:

I do not mean the lower order of labourers, or mechanics, but that rank of men who have been properly bred to business, got some education, and at the same time are compelled to labour for existence. Such men are very frequently employed on works for which they have no genius, or works where genius has no means of shewing itself.[24]

Without ever using the term 'middle class', a more definite denunciation of the social 'middle' in a tripartite social scheme – and thus a more direct rebuttal of the 'middle-class idiom' – is hard to imagine.[25]

---

[24] Playfair, *A Fair and Candid Address to the British Nobility*, pp. 45–6, 52–3, 56–9, 68; and see his rendering of the (unmentionable) social middle responsible for imminent political instability in pp. 61–3. Compare his *Political Portraits, in This New Aera: With Explanatory Notes – Historical and Biographical*, 2 vols., London, 1813, vol. i, pp. 24–5, and 30n., where Playfair described men of business as varying so much from each other as to defy any categorization into one social group; that is, denying the social middle a distinctive group identity. And his *France as It Is, not Lady Morgan's France*, 2 vols., London, 1819, where the 'middling class of people' in France were juxtaposed with the 'people in trade' in England (using 'middle-class' language, it may be noted, only for the alien context), finding the latter more 'the slaves of mammon' (vol. i, p. 60).

[25] Other cases of the familiar Tory denial of the 'middle-class idiom' while refraining from 'middle-class' language include [William Combe], *The Letters of Valerius, on the State of Parties, the War, the Volunteer System* . . ., London, 1804. Patrioticus [i.e. William P. Russel], *Solid Reasons for Continuance of War: With Means Suggested to Carry It on Without Additional Taxes* . . ., [London], 1807. For a later conservative statement by a person of 'middle' social standing, who evidently had a functional tripartite understanding of society but who nevertheless insisted on forcing it into dual social terms, see *A Letter from a Manufacturer to His Son, upon Radical Reform*, [London], [1815?], esp. p. 12.

Like Playfair, Francis Randolph, chaplain to the Duke of York and prebendary of Bristol, was another Tory who combined at this juncture praise for both the lower orders and the landed interest ('upon which every other national benefit must ultimately depend') with a more critical view of the social middle. Randolph too mostly refrained from the language of 'middle class', preferring to speak of the vices spread by 'the mercantile spirit' and the 'inordinate desire of wealth' that corrupted mercantile people and 'tend[ed] to raise the mercantile on the ruins of the landed capital'. The dialogue with the 'middle-class' rhetoric became most obvious when Randolph commented on the longing for a medium state, as represented by Agur's prayer (which, as we have seen, often accompanied the 'middle-class idiom'): 'The medium state of Agur's prayer might possibly be the best for nations as well as individuals,' Randolph wrote; 'but we know of none that ever were placed, or at least continued, in this happy mediocrity' – a state that was no more than a misleading illusion. In truth, those in the medium state, never satisfied with their lot, were more corrupted and less useful than those either above or below them on the social scale.[26]

Several years later, in the hands of the anti-reformist 'Criticus', the defensive praise for the aristocracy as well as for the peasantry – in contradistinction to the 'middle class' – became even more poignant. Criticus wished to disprove what he took to be a common assertion, that the aristocracy embodied frenchified cosmopolitanism whereas the 'middle class' was the true repository of 'Englishness'.[27] Arguably, Criticus's concern reveals the effects of the long war and the national mobilization against Napoleon (noticeable for others as well), in the shift from seeking the social repository of moral and political virtue (as had been the case in the 1790s) to seeking the social repository of *national character*. But be that as it may, Criticus surely emphasized his

---

[26] F[rancis] Randolph, *A Few Observations on the Present State of the Nation: In a Letter to His Grace the Duke of Bedford*, Bath, 1808, pp. 56, 61, 64, 66, 73–5. For another comparison of the landed classes with the 'mercantile portion of the community', in which the former is declared more deserving of the affections and confidence of the people, see the speech of John Curwen on 4 May 1809 in *Hansard's Parliamentary Debates* 14, cols. 361–2.

[27] The critique of the aristocracy since the mid eighteenth century as cosmopolitan and frenchified, mostly in literary sources, is discussed in G. Newman, *The Rise of English Nationalism: A Cultural History 1740–1830*, New York, 1987.

'pride as an Englishman' in an aristocracy more moral and less degraded than that of any other country, who 'bear about them more of the genuine English character than is to be found in any other class except the peasantry'. Having said that, Criticus was ready for the final blow: in contrast with these two extremes of society, he asserted, it was the 'middle classes' who

> have all become so modified by reading, by thinking (I am loth to call it philosophy) and by intercourse with foreigners in various ways, that though they possess almost all the talent, and a great part of the virtue to be found, yet I think they have lost much of that peculiar manner and style by which their countrymen were distinguishable two centuries, or even one century ago.[28]

The 'middle class', it turned out, was not all that English. True, Criticus grudgingly admitted bits of the 'middle-class idiom'; but he nevertheless reversed it on the point which now seemed particularly damaging, by anchoring the irreplaceable value of the aristocracy in its essence as the embodiment of national character. To drive the point further, Criticus went on to enumerate the traits of Englishness in which the aristocracy excelled most, and the 'middle class' least: pride, obstinacy, spirit, independence and sturdy honesty. Turning the image of the frenchified fashionable world on its head, he portrayed the aristocracy as lacking in social graces, yet overwhelmingly patriotic – merely, as it were, a titled version of John Bull:

> The manners indeed of our highest Nobility are in general very clumsy and unpolished . . . They possess however what is better – a simplicity and straitforwardness of thinking, an abhorrence of meanness, an enthusiastic generosity, a fearlessness of danger, and a strong uncalculating admiration and love of their country, which compensate all their faults.[29]

With such an aristocracy, who needed a 'middle class'?

In sum, then, some Tory pro-war speakers of the 1800s, just like their adversaries, did follow the familiar paths which had

---

[28] *Examiner* 317, 23 January 1814, p. 57, 'Parliamentary Criticism'. Like many others, Criticus felt the need to define what he meant by this social terminology: 'The middle classes, including the merchants, the professions, and those cadets of rank who must make their way in the world.' Criticus, though a correspondent of the *Examiner*, did not share its political views, in particular regarding reform: see ibid., 360, 20 November 1814, p. 749 (note).

[29] Ibid., 317, 23 January 1814, p. 58.

been established in the 1790s, a decade in which the political consciousness of many of them had been formed. But not all of them did. For others, the transformation of the political playing field also suggested recasting the rhetorical game rules. In so doing they were breaking new ground.

THE PILLAR OF THE SOCIAL AND POLITICAL ORDER

In 1807 the publication of the *Letters from England* by Don Manuel Alvarez Espriella created somewhat of a stir. The intriguing topic of speculation among literati was the true identity of the purportedly Spanish author, whom most reviewers rightly recognized as English. As the Lichfield poet Anna Seward observed in a letter to Robert Southey, the *Letters*, which gave her 'infinite amusement and interest . . . are not what they seem'; their 'purity and ease of language', she insisted, ascertained that they could not be a translation. Little did she know that their author, as was soon to be discovered, was none other than her correspondent, Robert Southey himself.[30] Southey, the son of a Bristol linendraper, had been in the 1790s a young and vehement republican. By the early 1800s, however, his political views – like those of many others – had changed considerably, leaning further and further towards Toryism; small wonder therefore that Espriella was so confident in proclaiming the striking political shift which had taken place in England since the renewal of the war.[31]

One question raised by Espriella, provoked by the recently exposed insurrectionary conspiracy of Colonel Despard, was the possibility of a revolution in England. Espriella singled out vital factors that militated against such an eventuality. In addition to the spread of Methodism and the reliability of the army, he noted in particular the fact that

the English people, by which denomination I mean, as distinguishing them from the populace, that middle class from whom an estimate of the national character is to be formed, have that wonderful activity and courage, that unless the superiority of numbers against them were

---

[30] [Southey], *Letters from England*, editor's introduction, p. xxii. The book went through two further English editions, in 1808 and 1814. It was written between 1803 and 1807, representing Espriella's purported impressions in 1802–3.

[31] As quoted above, p. 159.

more than tenfold, they would put out an insurrection, as they put out a fire.[32]

A refreshing thought indeed. The 'middle class', the reader was now told, was the key guarantee against a revolution, the saviour of the constitution and of the present political order. Casting the 'middle class' in this role was in sharp contrast with the political language of the 1790s. It also differed materially from contemporaneous statements in support of the political order like that of William Playfair or Criticus, which were predicated on bolstering the reputation of the landed elite while refuting the 'middle-class idiom'. Southey, on the other hand, while not having a very different political goal in mind, chose to glorify the 'middle class', which was the essence of the 'people'. For him it was the 'middle class' that was the repository of national character. Consequently it was in its active and courageous hands to prevent a revolution in England.

Still, like that of the Friends of Peace, Southey's vision did not bode well for the 'middle class'. It was endangered, he warned, since 'the tendency of the present system is to lessen the middle class and to increase the lower ones'. But while this statement indeed sounded like the 'middle-class' arguments against the war taxation of the 1790s, here the villain was quite different. As Southey explained in detail, by 'the present system' he did *not* mean the political system, but rather the 'commercial system', which had long been undermining the social structure; and the 'manufacturing system' inseparable from it, which would render a revolution inevitable, given its pernicious consequences in swelling the numbers of the miserable poor. The primary cause of the difficulties of the 'middle class', then, was not the war or the direct consequences of ministerial policies, but first and foremost the processes of social change, accompanied by a malevolent commercial spirit that 'poisons every thing' (a formulation reminiscent of the anti-commercial rhetoric of the eighteenth century). In particular, the effect of the commercial system was to destroy 'the peasants, and little landholders, the yeomanry as they were called, who were once the strength of England'. Recent improvements had materially benefited agriculture, but their evil consequence was the disappearance of such men, pre-

[32] Ibid., pp. 375–6.

viously renowned for their independence, so that 'there is one gradation the less in society; that the second step in the ladder is taken away'.[33] The 'middle class', here primarily in its rural form, was in the process of being destroyed by social change, by 'improvement'.

As the modern editor of Espriella's letters notes, they represented a transitional stage between Southey's republicanism of the 1790s and his Toryism of the early nineteenth century. True, they can still be characterized to a certain degree as a political middle position: after all, Espriella also remarked that a House of Commons is less valuable and effective when it consists only of the rich, thereby excluding talent and knowledge.[34] But for our purposes the crucial point to note is that the 'middle class' appeared here *in defence of the present social and political order,* conservatively resisting abrupt changes in both politics (revolution) and society (improvement). The political 'taming' of the language of 'middle class' – that is, its harnessing to buttress the prevailing system – was in part achieved through a reshuffling of emphases. Thus, even while remaining in a middle political position, an important change in the implications of this language was achieved by shifting the target of its effective edge. Whereas previously this edge had been directed upwards, against the ruling elite and the government, it was now redirected downwards; hence Southey's effort to clearly distinguish the 'middle class' not from those above it but from those below it, 'the populace'.

Southey was not alone in the early 1800s in reneging on the enthusiasm of the 1790s. Another romantic poet who was experiencing a similar drift from youthful radicalism to increasing establishmentarian conformism was Southey's brother-in-law and erstwhile close friend, Samuel Taylor Coleridge. Tellingly, as Coleridge's politics shifted, so did the uses of 'middle-class' language in his voluminous writings, mostly in the press (whether in his own short-lived periodicals, or as contributions to other newspapers).

[33] Ibid., pp. 367–9, 375–6 (quoted in more detail below, p. 227); see also p. 146. Southey too invoked Agur's prayer to support his appeal on behalf of a 'middle class' (p. 371).
[34] Ibid., pp. xx–xxi, 286. For Southey's social and political thought see also D. Eastwood, 'Robert Southey and the Intellectual Origins of Romantic Conservatism', *English Historical Review* 104 (1989), pp. 308–31.

In the mid-1790s, the radical Coleridge – then thought by many to be one of the most dangerous Jacobins in the West Country – had as yet no use for the language of 'middle class'; his position was encompassed in enmity towards the rich and empathy towards the poor. 'Society as at present constituted does not resemble a chain that ascends in a continuity of Links', he observed in 1795. Instead, it was polarized in a stark division of higher and lower classes, whereby 'between the Parlour and the Kitchen, the Tap and the Coffee-Room – there is a gulph that may not be passed'. At a public meeting in Bristol that year Coleridge railed against the injustice of the imbalanced war burdens in similar dual terms, comparing the light burdens on the rich with the much heavier ones on the poor. The pages of his short-lived *Watchman*, established in March 1796 in reaction to Pitt's 'Gagging Acts', were suffused with this underlying conceptualization of the present oppressive system as an oppression of 'the poor and labouring classes' by 'the rich and powerful'. At one point in 1796 Coleridge came very close to formulations of 'middle-class' rhetoric which by then were quite common among the moderate opposition, warning that 'the rapid and sure consequence [of the war burdens] must be the extinction of all the active class of society, and that we shall soon have but two orders', the rich and the poor. Yet for Coleridge this middle active class in danger of extinction was not a 'middle class', but the industrious labourers; the role of the 'middle class' in his own rhetoric was yet to come.[35]

In the following years, towards the end of the first war, Coleridge increasingly expressed a more critical view of Jacobins and sympathizers with the French Revolution. And as his politics became less clearly polarized, so did his conceptualization of society. In one plea for peace at the turn of the century Coleridge warned that the war turned 'the high, and the low, and the middle classes' into politicians, and thus was inextricably linked with the spread of Jacobinism. A few days earlier he criticized the 'Friends of Freedom' for their indiscriminate apologies for

---

[35] *The Collected Works of Samuel Taylor Coleridge: Lectures 1795 on Politics and Religion*, ed. L. Patton and P. Mann, Princeton, 1971, p. 43: 'Conciones ad Populum or Addresses to the People'. *The Collected Works . . .: The Watchman*, ed. L. Patton, Princeton, 1970, vol. I, introduction, pp. xxviii–xxix, quoting the *Star*, 23 November 1795; p. 54, no. 2, 9 March 1796 (and see also pp. 102, 135); p. 110, no. 3, 17 March 1796.

the conduct of French revolutionaries. In the process, Coleridge acknowledged precisely the role of 'middle-class' language in their rhetoric that we have seen in the earlier chapters: some of the 'Friends of Freedom', he rightly noted, looked upon the ministry 'as prosecuting a direct system of hostility against the hopes and comforts of the middle-ranks', as well as against the lower classes. Coleridge's own affinity to the 'middle-class idiom' at this particular juncture became evident in another essay, which objected to Fox's comparison of the present war with the crusades, giving it – according to Coleridge – a compliment it certainly did not deserve. The crusades, he claimed, increased commerce by liberating it from Venetian and Genoese monopolists; consequently 'there began to arise in all countries, but more especially in England, that greatest blessing and ornament of human nature, an important and respectable middle class'. But in contrast with this beneficial outcome of the crusades, surely it cannot be said that the present war, 'spite of the Assessed and Income Taxes, is peculiarly favourable to the increase and permanence of a middle class'.[36] So here, in mid-1800, we find Coleridge – like other anti-war moderates – combining a clear statement of 'middle-class idiom' with the antithesis between the war and the welfare of the 'middle class', linked particularly – again, a familiar theme – to the burdens of taxation; the same war taxation which several years earlier, during his more radical phase, he had characterized simply as an oppression of the poor by the rich. At this moment, Coleridge's personal political path from left to right intersected with the middle position of the Friends of Peace, and his social language accordingly coincided with theirs.

Coleridge's politics, however, like Southey's, continued to shift ground. The second French war aroused in Coleridge strongly anti-Napoleonic sentiments, and as he moved further across the political map, he took the language of 'middle class' with him. Writing in 1809 to explain his now belligerent views, Coleridge

---

[36] *The Collected Works . . ..: Essays on His Times in The Morning Post and The Courier*, ed. D. V. Erdman, Princeton, 1978, vol. I, pp. 38–9, 'Advice to the Friends of Freedom', *Morning Post*, 12 December 1799; pp. 241–2, 'The War not a Crusade', *Morning Post*, 6 August 1800. Note the interchangeability of 'middle classes' and 'middle ranks' for Coleridge. On Coleridge's political metamorphosis (together with that of other romantic writers) see E. P. Thompson, 'Disenchantment or Default? A Lay Sermon', in C. C. O'Brien and W. D. Vanech (eds.), *Power and Consciousness*, London, 1969, pp. 149–81.

claimed that Napoleon intended not merely to attack England, but to 'reduce the Continent of Europe to a state of barbarism'. He explained: by the destruction of commerce, Napoleon would 'destroy the principal source of civilization, and abolish a *middle class* throughout Christendom; for this, Sir, I declared him the common enemy of mankind!' The concern for the 'middle class', so long an argument for peace, now became a justification for war. And now that Coleridge had figured it out, it was a point worth repeating: in uprooting European commerce and trade, he stated on another occasion, Napoleon destroyed 'a principal source of civilization, the origin of a *middle class* throughout Christendom, and with it the true balance of society, the parent of international law, the foster-nurse of general humanity', as well as the major force drawing different nations together into one system. In terms reminiscent of Scottish celebrations of commercial society, Coleridge here presented commerce as the major vehicle for the transformation from barbarism and war to a civilized, interconnected, peaceful world; the epitome and embodiment of which was a 'middle class', the key to social balance. Shortly thereafter he asserted even more emphatically that Napoleon was conducting 'the most cruel and systematic war against the source of the virtue, comforts, and increasing amity of mankind, the commercial and middle classes'.[37]

So, as the Friends of Peace had maintained, the 'middle class' was indeed invaluable, and was indeed endangered. But whereas in the first war it was represented – by Coleridge himself, among others – as endangered by ministerial bellicose policies, now Coleridge asserted that it was precisely such policies that were going to save it. Furthermore, Coleridge went beyond his support for the war to incorporate the 'middle class' more broadly into a

---

[37] *Essays on His Times*, vol. II, p. 76, *The Courier*, 21 December 1809; p. 348, *The Courier*, 14 May 1812. *The Collected Works . . .: The Friend*, ed. B. E. Rooke, Princeton, 1969, vol. I, p. 231: 'On The Vulgar Errors Respecting Taxes and Taxation', originally in no. 12, 9 November 1809. (This essay, in fact, was intended to refute arguments that necessarily linked taxation to war; which, of course, had been Coleridge's own view earlier.) See also the lecture in Bristol, 11 November 1813, in *The Collected Works . . .: Lectures 1808–1819 on Literature*, ed. R. A. Foakes, Princeton, 1987, vol. I, p. 546. It is curious to contrast Coleridge's assessment of Napoleon with that put forward many years later by Ralph Waldo Emerson: 'I call Napoleon the agent or attorney of the middle class of modern society'; 'He had their virtues and their vices; above all, he had their spirit or aim.' R. W. Emerson, *Representative Men* (originally 1850); in his *Essays and Lectures*, New York, 1983, pp. 727, 742.

more conservative vision of the social and political order. He continued to represent the 'middle class' as a key component of society, yet one which was organically integrated with the whole. In one celebratory essay on England as 'the happiest, most prosperous and rapidly progressive' society (in contrast with Ireland), he asserted that this propitious social state was manifested 'in the number, respectability, and influence of its middle class, and in the interdependence of all classes'. The influence of the 'middle class' (equated with progress) was inseparable from its enmeshing in an interdependent network encompassing the whole of society. This is what Coleridge referred to elsewhere as 'the ordained and beneficient interdependence of the higher, middle and lower ranks', engendering benevolent moral feelings and principles. This providential order, he warned, was endangered on the one hand by the abdication of paternalistic duties by the higher classes, and on the other hand by the pernicious operation of Jacobinical associations among the 'Working Classes', in particular 'the mechanics and lower craftsmen of every description'.[38]

It was the dangers from these lower classes, however, that were now Coleridge's primary concern. As was also the case for Southey's Espriella, the political edge of the social middle was reversed. In Coleridge's hands, too, the 'middle class' was becoming more exclusive, stressing its distinct separation from those below rather than its implications for those above. Clearly, in the image of paternalistic relationships between higher and lower classes that Coleridge often conjoined with a tripartite social scheme, the 'middle class' formed part of the higher, distinctly separate from the lower classes from which the threats to the social order might emerge.[39] The new political edge of the language of

---

[38] *Essays on His Times*, vol. II, pp. 280–1, *The Courier*, 13 September 1811; pp. 392–4, *The Courier*, 2 November 1814, Letter to Mr Justice Fletcher. Elsewhere Coleridge resorted to the language of interests and its underlying presupposition of harmony in order to express his belief in the 'indissoluble union' between 'all the interests of the state, the landed with the commercial, and the man of independent fortune with the stirring tradesman and reposing annuitant'. (*The Friend*, vol. I, p. 233, originally no. 12, 9 November 1809).

[39] In Coleridge's lectures on education in the 1810s the 'middle class' was consistently joined with the higher classes, admittedly different but only in degree: *Lectures 1808–1819 on Literature*, vol. I, pp. 578, 589; vol. II, pp. 27, 39. Later, this became even clearer in his 'A Lay Sermon Addressed to the Higher and Middle Classes on the Existing Distresses and Discontents' of 1817: *The Collected Works . . . : Lay Sermons*, ed. R. J. White, Princeton, 1972.

'middle class', now directed against popular threats, was clearly revealed in an essay against parliamentary reform which Coleridge published in late 1809, when interest in the issue seemed to be awakening. 'Our ancestors', Coleridge asserted, 'established the right of voting in a particular class of men, forming at that time the middle rank of society, and known to be all of them, or almost all, legal proprietors – and these were then called the Freemen of England.' And since the 'middle class' had already been accommodated in the present constitution, it had a stake in defending it against any change; especially such change as desired by present-day reformers, who mistakenly designated as 'freemen' the lower classes that possessed no property and therefore wished to extend the vote to them as well.[40] Thus, logically following its increasing exclusivity (though perhaps unexpectedly for the historian), Coleridge was enlisting the language of 'middle class' in opposition to parliamentary reform. His conservative guise of this representation of society was complete.

One final point needs to be underscored, in view of other uses of 'middle-class' language that still lie ahead. For Southey the 'middle class' was in direct conflict with recent waves of social change and 'improvement' that threatened to eradicate it. Coleridge did not present things as starkly; yet it is clear from his association of the 'middle class' with the crusades, and from his stress on the 'middle-class' vote as incorporated in the constitution by 'our ancestors', that the 'middle class' for him was anything but a modern novelty. Rather, it was a formidable presence, indeed linked to long-term progress (through the rise of commerce) and thus not altogether timeless, but surely with a very long pedigree. Coleridge's 'middle class' was not part of a novel social order, generated in recent times by unprecedented social forces and abrupt transformations. If anything, it was a social force whose duty it was to counteract the undue effects of such upheavals.[41]

Although hardly a torrent yet, more examples of loyalist, pro-ministerial and anti-radical 'middle-class' language, indeed 'middle-class idiom', can readily be found at this juncture. Thus, one publication which aroused much interest in 1807 was the

---

[40] *The Friend*, vol. 1, p. 247: originally no. 15, 30 November 1809.
[41] See further below, chapter 7.

anonymous *The Dangers of the Country*. Its author was James Stephen, a lawyer with West Indian connections of fairly humble social background, who had moved from rather liberal views in his youth to ardent Evangelical Toryism; the following year he was to become an MP under the patronage of the Tory Spencer Perceval, a major figure in the Duke of Portland's administration. Stephen was the most renowned advocate of the Orders in Council (many, including Henry Brougham, erroneously regarded him as the 'father' of this system), which attracted the brunt of Friends of Peace criticism from 1807 onwards. Stephen favoured a 'perpetual' war with France until Napoleon was overthrown. His purpose in *The Dangers of the Country* was to depict in painstaking detail the horrendous consequences of a possible invasion of Britain, and thus to exhort the country to a more vigorous and united war effort.

It was into such a bellicose context that Stephen integrated the 'middle-class idiom': should an invasion occur, he warned,

that probity of character also, which has distinguished the middle ranks of Englishmen, in commercial and private life, that abhorrence of falsehood and fraud ... that disdain of servility ... would soon be found no more. The next generation, if not the present, would all be *frenchified*, and debased ... Yes, Englishmen! your children would become in morals, as well as in allegiance, *Frenchmen!* I can say to you nothing worse.

Nothing worse, indeed, than succumbing to French influence, a disaster epitomized in the loss of 'middle-class' character. This endangered 'middle class', whose sphere of action as portrayed by Stephen was not politics but 'commercial and private life', embodied sincerity and independence, which rendered it emphatically *English*.[42] During the Napoleonic war, as we have seen in

---

[42] [James Stephen], *The Dangers of the Country*, London, 1807, p. 68; see also the 'middle-class' language in pp. 31 (joined with upper classes), 48 (joined with lower classes), 129. Note that Stephen's 'middle class' was also not distinctively novel but rather part of some pre-existing golden age, once again unconnected to recent social transformations. And compare Montagu Burgoyne, *A Letter from Montagu Burgoyne, Esquire, of Mark Hall, on the Present State of Public Affairs ...*, London, 1808, in which (qualified) support for the war effort was again joined with 'middle-class idiom' formulations, here focusing on one (perennial) social group, the yeomanry: 'Placed in a kind of middle situation, between the rich and the poor, they seem to form a sort of barrier against the unreasonable demands of either; and promote the harmony, and good understanding, which gives more strength and security to our constitution than all our fleets and armies' (p. 65).

Southey's 'middle-class idiom' as well as in Criticus's song of
praise for the aristocracy, the social locus of Englishness became
an important – and contested – measure of social worth, over-
shadowing (for some) the political virtues that had been so
esteemed in the 1790s. This emphasis on the 'middle class' as a
national asset, rather than on traits pitting it against other classes,
of course not only better suited the national war effort (which
was Stephen's main goal) but also rendered this representation
of society less threatening in the context of domestic politics. In
passing, note how different was Stephen's expression of support
for the war from that of Criticus's, which was predicated on the
assertion that the 'middle class' was in its nature *unEnglish*:
another demonstration of the variegated guises in which the
language of 'middle class' could be found at this juncture.

Stephen's *The Dangers of the Country* was reviewed in the *Edinburgh Review* by its editor, Francis Jeffrey: it is interesting to
contrast both writers' uses of the language of 'middle class'.
Jeffrey basically approved of Stephen's ominous portrayal of what
Britain stood to lose if its commercial greatness was undermined.
He recommended Stephen's book, in particular, 'to the consideration of all those who think that industry is secure of its reward
in every civilized society, and that it is mere romance for people
in the middling conditions of life to fight for political privileges,
or for the choice of their rulers'.[43] Thus, while ostensibly concurring with Stephen, Jeffrey in effect subverted the political meaning
of his 'middle-class idiom'. In what was really an unwarranted
deviation from the topic of discussion, Jeffrey turned the 'middle
class' from the embodiment of Englishness, which in Stephen's
hands had served to induce unity in face of an external enemy,
into a combative contender in internal political struggles. Both
Stephen and Jeffrey agreed that under the present circumstances
the 'middle class' was threatened. But whereas the former's
conclusion was to stress that the 'middle class' had a stake in
supporting the national war effort, the latter transformed it into
a demonstration that the 'middle class' had a stake in challenging
the national political system. Unlike the 1790s, we find here not

---

[43] *Edinburgh Review* 10, April 1807, p. 3. Of course, this assertion was also an argument
against familiar Scottish views which downplayed the effects of a particular political
regime on the progress of commercial society.

a contestation between competing social vocabularies leading to the differentiation of social language along political lines, but rather a social language whose connotations and implications were becoming versatile enough to be appropriated differently by competing political camps.

The expanding political versatility of the language of 'middle class' was also evident in the debates on taxation induced by Petty's fiscal proposals in 1806–7. True, these proposals elicited some 'middle-class' grievances and responses to them that reproduced a watered down version of the pattern which had been so prevalent a decade earlier. Yet by now this was no longer the only possible deployment of 'middle-class' language in this context. Take for example a public letter to Petty published in 1806 by 'a middling man', who reasoned that under foreign conquest the 'middle class' would not suffer more than the higher classes. 'Why, therefore,' he wondered, 'should the middling classes contribute to the expence of opposing that enemy in a greater proportion than the higher orders?' In the 1790s such a complaint, strewn throughout with 'middle-class' language, would have been readily recognizable as a product of anti-ministerial sentiments. But for the present author this was not a foregone conclusion. Loyalty cannot be measured in shillings, he proclaimed, since for the same contribution 'the wealthy man suffers no privation, the middling man suffers much'. Displaying a certain anxiety about being 'suspected of disloyalty', the author left no doubt that such a suspicion was completely unwarranted:

Though the man of the middling order in these dominions may be out of humour with the tax-gatherer compelling an exposure of his shivering penury, he is ill prepared, so naked, and so bereft, to dance whilst Buonaparte fiddles, and Talleyrand holds the chain. We have not been so taught, and we desire not so to learn.

The message was clear: 'middle-class' grievances could be expressed without implying disloyal or oppositional stances, without doubting their ultimate support for the war. By now, even grumbling complaints in the name of the 'middle class' were beginning to lose their oppositional edge. Furthermore, the political shift of this language was again accompanied by an increased emphasis on its exclusiveness, directed at those lower on the social scale: with regard to 'the low or labouring orders of the community', declared this 'middling man', 'as I wish them to keep their distance, I shall keep mine'.[44]

Now that certain speakers began to use the 'middle-class idiom' in novel political guises, it could be found together with some unexpected bedfellows. The most unexpected of all, perhaps, was the wave of reassertions of aristocratic worth around 1808. In the hands of writers such as William Playfair and Francis Randolph, such a pro-aristocratic emphasis was essentially antithetical to the 'middle-class' rhetoric; yet this antithesis, too, was no longer inevitable. One similar appeal to an invigorated aristocracy, prompted by a sense of deep crisis in 1808, was made by an 'Englishman of no party': 'To its nobles, the English Nation ... looks up with just confidence, as to its principal directors', whose duty as well as interest was 'to stem the torrent of iniquity that now threatens our destruction.' The emphasis on aristocratic predominance, however, was in this case accompanied by a properly 'tamed' version of the 'middle-class idiom'. 'To the middling classes', continued this writer, 'that independent part of the constitution, which contributes to preserve its wonderful equilibrium', religion is highly necessary, so that 'they may jealously resist every attempted abridgement of their known rights; and yet, at the same time, forbear to intrude on the monarchial and aristocratical systems.'[45] This author's 'middling classes' were surely no political threat. The famous independent stance of the 'middle class' as a bulwark of its rights (significantly, its 'known' rights, as opposed to some previously unnoticed 'natural' rights) was now qualified by its expected collusion with the political system: both behaviours were now comprised in its proclaimed political virtues. Whatever it did, it could be counted upon (especially when buttressed by an invigorated religion) to refrain from any encroachment upon the established social and political hierarchies, governed by the monarchy and the aristocracy.

Of course, once the stark polarization of the 1790s gave way to a more diverse set of possibilities, the political implications of

---

[44] *A Letter, Addressed to the Right Honourable Lord Henry Petty, wherein the General Tendency of the Principles of His Great Predecessor's Financial Administration, Are Freely and Plainly Examined ...*, London, 1806, pp. 14, 24–7, 41; see also pp. 9, 34–5. For this 'middling man' too, 'middling classes' and 'middling order' were interchangeable.

[45] *The State of Britain, Abroad and at Home, in the Eventful Year, 1808: By an Englishman, of No Party*, London, 1808, pp. 33–4, 39–40.

the 'middle-class idiom' were no longer always reducible to simple dichotomies. The following example, an exhortation induced by a perceived crisis in 1812, is a case of such multivalence. This anonymous tract was deeply conservative, supporting the Church, the king and the constitution, and fiercely anti-revolutionary and anti-French. It harked back to a golden age of social harmony, paternalistic benevolence and mutual interdependence of all components of society; a golden age in which a place of honour was reserved for the 'middle class'. 'When I look back to the distance of less than forty years', the author reflected, 'I discover that the higher orders were respected and respectable, the middling class happy and prosperous, and the poor comfortable and obedient.' Rural society at that time included 'happy cottagers' who had formed 'an intermediate and invaluable class between the yeomanry and labourers', but who were now brought to the verge of annihilation by processes of social change. Echoing Southey's Espriella, this writer too warned that as a consequence of social change 'the middling class [was] fast amalgamating with that above or beneath them'. The resulting programme of this tract, therefore, was a startling combination of conservative political principles with a fundamental reordering of the social hierarchy:

if ever this country is brought to the brink of ruin, it will be by the LANDED INTEREST. I say to the brink of ruin, for I am well convinced that it will never be actually ruined, unless the middle class of society is annihilated; and while that is not the case, I feel assured that *this class will*, on any great emergency which really calls forth the energies of the people, *furnish virtue and ability sufficient to rescue the country* from every impending danger.[46]

The saviours of the country, it turned out, were not the landed elite but rather the 'middle class'. This author – who went on to accuse the landed interest of a self-interested manipulation of the House of Commons – was using a politically 'tame' 'middle-class' language within a self-proclaimed conservative perspective, while at the same time underscoring its socially revolutionary ramifications. Between the unsettling implications of the language of 'middle class' of the previous decade, and the more benign

---

[46] *Hints to All Classes on the State of the Country in This Momentous Crisis. By One of the People*, London, 1812, pp. 6–7, 10, 13–14.

ones which were now being tried out, the final outcome could be rather confusing.

Finally, nowhere was the political 'taming' of the language of 'middle class' better exemplified than in the writings of James Mackintosh, whose fairly radical position in the years following the French Revolution gravitated towards a more haughty conservative emphasis combined with limited reformism later on.[47] In his *Vindiciae Gallicae* of 1791, we may recall, Mackintosh had praised the French National Assembly for its composition predominantly of persons of the 'middle rank': being the repository of virtue and sense, they were more prone to liberal politics free of prejudice, and thus to political reform, innovation and change. Moreover, in 1791 Mackintosh directly associated the steadfast political virtues of the 'middle class' with political revolutions (as quoted in the first epigraph to this chapter).

By 1815, however, the transformation of the role which Mackintosh assigned the 'middle class' – concomitant with the broader shift in his political disposition – could hardly have been greater. Again in the context of France (brought into the spotlight by Napoleon's return to Paris), Mackintosh affirmed once more that the 'middle classes' were implicated in the Revolution of 1789 (though not in its subsequent excesses, a consequence of 'plebeian passions'), after having been oppressed by 'constant disdain' under the nobility of the *ancien régime*. But his tone became markedly more sceptical and less appreciative than in 1791: he now described how the 'middle classes', driven by their 'vanity', 'rushed into the stations which the gentry . . . could no longer fill. The whole government fell into their hands.' Subsequently, however, despite their role in the Revolution, 'it is certain that, among the class called "*La bonne bourgeoisie*," are to be found the greatest number of those who approved the restoration of the

---

[47] Mackintosh himself declared this as a radical change. It did not go unnoticed by contemporaries; see among others the angry vituperation on Mackintosh's betrayal of the people's cause in *The Gorgon* 46, 3 April 1819, pp. 363–4. Historians have played down the extent to which Mackintosh really underwent a radical break with his earlier views; but the question of the consistency of his thinking notwithstanding, neither contemporaries nor historians have denied the marked transformation of his tone and emphasis. See W. A. Christian, 'James Mackintosh, Burke, and the Cause of Reform', *Eighteenth Century Studies* 7 (1973/4), pp. 193–206. L. A. McKenzie, 'The French Revolution and English Parliamentary Reform: James Mackintosh and the *Vindiciae Gallicae*', *Eighteenth Century Studies* 14 (1981), pp. 264–82.

Bourbons as the means of security and quiet. They were weary of revolution, and they dreaded confusion'. Mackintosh's conclusion from the role of the 'middle class' in the drive to political stability in the Restoration (as quoted in the second epigraph to this chapter) was that politically the 'middle class' was a force of inertia and complicity, not of principled activism and stubborn stance-taking. 'Unfortunately', he continued, 'their voice, of great weight in the administration of regular governments, is scarcely heard in convulsions. They are destined to stoop to the bold; – too often, though with vain sorrow and indignation, to crouch under the yoke of the guilty and the desperate.'[48] Gone was the virtuous, liberal and intelligent 'middle class' of 1791, that 'enlightened class of men [that] ever prove the most ardent in the cause of freedom, the most zealous for political reform', whose political disposition had been proven by 'the history of Revolutions'.[49] A quarter of a century later, Mackintosh perceived the 'middle class' as politically 'tame', as a social group whose weight and influence joined the conservative forces in politics. A far cry from the intransigent bulwark of liberty, he now presented the French 'middle class' as resigned, acquiescent, even submissive.

Not that in Mackintosh's later writing the bulwark of liberty disappeared altogether; it was simply relocated. British society, he added, had an edge over the French in that the latter, unfortunately, lacked a 'landed gentry'. As a consequence French society lacked leadership, influence, animating spirit, and powers of restraint; such a situation 'is destructive of liberty, because it annihilates the strongest bulwarks against the power of the crown'.[50] The gentry, it therefore turned out, were those responsible for the political defence of liberty, a responsibility previously attributed (mistakenly, one assumes) to the 'middle class'. At this stage, however, the practical consequences of this reshuffling of political roles and virtues remained implicit. But before long, the changing political configuration following the end of the war, with its peculiar concerns and dynamics that rapidly intensified into an extraordinary crescendo, was about to bring Mackintosh and others to draw the implications of these changing uses of 'middle-class' language in a much more explicit fashion.

---

[48] *Edinburgh Review* 24, February 1815, pp. 524–5: review of several tracts on France.
[49] Mackintosh, *Vindiciae Gallicae*; quoted above, pp. 24, 157.
[50] *Edinburgh Review* 24, February 1815, p. 523.

CHAPTER 6

The tug of war and its resolution

Any attempt . . . to push the great question of *Radical Reform*, while the middling classes continued in such a state of apathy, would have been abortive . . .

Something is necessary to rouse the middling classes to a sense of their perilous situation. For a long time, they have been neither willing to *follow* nor *lead* the People.

(Radical appeal to the 'middle class', 1819)[1]

Thus, the gathering snow-ball of rebellion rolls on, making its vast collections. If it be not impeded and dispersed by the rising of the great middle class of the community, who, from some unaccountable infatuation, have hitherto been the passive spectators of its progress, the links of society are dissolved. (Conservative appeal to the 'middle class', 1819)[2]

Mackintosh's 1815 essay in the *Edinburgh Review* notwithstanding, from about 1809 the language of 'middle class' went into considerable hibernation for the better part of a decade. To be sure, this is not to say that these years simply saw no major debates in which it *could* be invoked. One needs only remind oneself again of the anti-war campaign against the Orders in Council, or of the debates around the corn laws in 1815, rendered acute by the distress following the end of the war: in both cases, despite what current historiographical wisdom might lead us to expect, 'middle-class' language played no significant role.

We may wish here to experiment momentarily with a more distant perspective on the broader pattern over time. As a con-

[1] *The Gorgon* 36, 23 January 1819, pp. 282–3.
[2] Rev. Lionel Thomas Berguer, *A Warning Letter to His Royal Highness the Prince Regent, Intended Principally as a Call upon the Middle Ranks, at This Important Crisis*, 3rd edn., London, 1819, pp. 31–2.

venient shortcut, let us juxtapose the unfolding of the present account with the chronology of the evolution of radicalism as it is related in E. P. Thompson's *The Making of the English Working Class*. Both commence with the politically turbulent 1790s, a decade which saw a major surge of 'middle-class' language. It should be noted, however, that the uses of this language peaked not during the mid-decade spell of dearth and hardship, but in the relatively prosperous years of 1797–8; and that it then subsided prior to the severe subsistence crisis of 1799–1801. Subsequently, a relatively intensive invocation of notions of 'middle class' was evident in 1806–7, years which witnessed some renewed political radicalism focused around parliamentary contests (especially at Westminster), but which preceded the blockade-induced depression of 1808. The next decade opened with the threat of Luddism, following upon the economic crisis of 1811–12: but, again, at this moment of economic difficulties and social unrest (and in spite of the concurrent campaign of the Friends of Peace against the Orders in Council), we can find only few signs of the language of 'middle class'. Indeed, as has been pointed out, it remained in low key throughout the renewed distress engendered by the painful shift to peace-time economy in 1815–16. It was only as part of the strong resurgence of focused constitutional radicalism from late 1816 onwards – coinciding, again, with an uplift in the economy and a better harvest in 1817 – that the language of 'middle class' returned to centre stage.

All in all, the outcome of this exercise – crude and approximated as it evidently is – is not quite what we might expect from a language with putative social and/or economic origins. First, the see-saw chronology of the uses of 'middle-class' language suggests yet again caution in presenting it as a straightforward reflection of linear social transformations. But more interestingly, let us allow for a moment an admittedly over-simplistic distinction between agitations focused more on social and economic issues, corresponding to moments of economic crises, and agitations focused more on constitutional issues. This distinction should not be read as a reductive (and wrong-headed) attempt to separate two allegedly unrelated types of phenomena; yet one can still heuristically distinguish protests (and reactions to them) whose triggers and declared goals were primarily social and

economic, such as food riots or Luddism, from those which were
concerned more narrowly with constitutional politics. So, when
such a distinction is made, one observation immediately stands
out: during political conflicts provoked by the former type of
protests, in moments when the explicit expression of political
contention revolved predominantly around social and economic
issues, the 'middle-class' language fell into relative disuse. Whatever this language stood for, therefore, at least up to this point,
it surely did not constitute part of a social discourse developed
for addressing social and economic problems, for defining interests
affected by them, or for giving meaning to political actions and
reactions which they provoked.

So what was it about the intense political conflict of the late
1810s that invested the language of 'middle class' once again
with political charge, more so than it had carried at any point
since the late 1790s? The period between the end of the Napoleonic war and the Peterloo massacre, writes E. P. Thompson,
was 'the heroic age of popular Radicalism'.[3] Post-war radicalism,
he asserts, appeared at times less as a movement of an organized
minority than as representing broader sections of society, indeed
almost whole communities. Radicalism was unmistakably on the
rise from late 1816 onwards, with the remarkable growth of the
Hampden Clubs (leading to their national convention at the end
of January 1817) and of Union Societies; with the publication
from November 1816 of William Cobbett's cheap *Twopenny Trash*
defying (or rather circumventing) stamp regulations and achiev-
ing enormous sales; and with the multitudes attending the Spa
Fields demonstrations of November and December, providing a
taste of what was yet to come. The issues at the forefront of
radical criticism, self-avowedly constitutional, were those of 'Old
Corruption', such as borough-mongering, place-holding, fiscal
abuses and sinecures: for which the advocated remedy was parliamentary reform. Radical constitutionalism, James Epstein has
recently emphasized, was flexible enough to retain the spectre of
potential revolution together with the respectability of accepted
constitutionalist forms (such as the many hundreds of radical
petitions submitted to parliament).[4] As Thompson points out, it

---

[3] E. P. Thompson, *The Making of the English Working Class*, London, 1963, p. 603.
[4] J. E. Epstein, *Radical Expression: Political Language, Ritual, and Symbol in England,
1790–1850*, New York, 1994.

was this ominous combination that spread panic among the upper classes and in government circles. As a consequence, the mounting wave of radicalism was met by increasing ministerial repression, leading to the final clash in the massacre of Peterloo. This was the popular name given to the events of 16 August 1819, when a meeting encompassing tens of thousands of Lancashire reformers at St Peter's Fields in Manchester was dispersed violently at the order of local magistrates by the yeomanry cavalry, leaving eleven dead and hundreds injured. Subsequently, exacerbated repression, which took substance in the Six Acts of the end of 1819 (and which was further justified in government eyes by the exposure of the so-called Cato Street conspiracy), put out the remaining embers of this conflagration of popular radicalism.

Returning to our question, then, what was it about these political circumstances that once again freighted the language of 'middle class' with particular meaning? After all, as by now should be clear, there was nothing inherent in intense politicking *per se* that induced talk of a 'middle class'; just as there was nothing inherent in the social circumstances in and of themselves to make such a representation of society inevitable (we should only remind ourselves of its relative insignificance in the immediately preceding conflicts, engendered by the post-war social distress). No, again we must probe the specific logic of the political configuration (here, that which prevailed between about 1817 and 1821) to understand why – and how – the language of 'middle class' was reintroduced into the public debate at this juncture.

In part, though far less so than in the 1790s, 'middle-class' language was remobilized to defend the viability of a political middle position. This period too was characterized by strong political polarization, by an increasing difficulty in finding and maintaining a middle position between the two clearly demarcated extremes. As Lord Grey lamented in a letter to that veteran moderate, Christopher Wyvill: 'I have now no hope of seeing a moderate & useful reform effected during my life, & we have to thank Major Cartwright Mr Cobbett & Co. principally for it.'[5]

---

[5] Grey to Wyvill, 10 April 1817; quoted in J. R. Dinwiddy, *Christopher Wyvill and Reform 1790–1820* (Borthwick Papers no. 39), York, 1971, p. 29. And see Thompson, *The Making of the English Working Class*, p. 689.

The quest for a moderate position (combining support for qualified parliamentary reform with a denunciation of popular
radicalism) was induced by the resurgent threat of democracy:
in this these years closely resembled those following the French
Revolution. Yet in the political climate of the late 1810s, thick
with apprehension about a remarkably powerful popular movement, the implications of this midway positioning turned out to
be quite different. Building on the beginnings of a 'tame' 'middle-
class' language in the previous decade, the edge of this rhetoric
was now thrust more against the popular radicals than against
the government and the political elite.

Thus James Mackintosh, for example, apprehensive in 1818
lest the popular agitation would create 'so wide a schism in
society, such an impassable gulph ... between its different
classes, [that it] would lead to a violent subversion of government', advocated a 'middle' course of action – namely, limited
and qualified reform, which he indeed joined with 'middle-class
idiom'. Yet Mackintosh made no secret of his respective sympathies towards the two political camps between which his own
position was supposed to mediate. On the one hand, he asserted
that universal suffrage (the radical platform) would increase the
two opposite evils of preponderant influence of wealth (through
its influence on its enfranchised dependants) and of 'subjecting
property to the multitude'; inevitably, the pernicious consequence
would be that 'the power of the middle classes would be annihilated'. On the other hand, he hastened to admit the justice of the
anti-radical reliance on the talents, virtues and impartiality of
the English landed elite, which rendered it particularly suited
for preserving democracy: 'An ascendancy, therefore, of landed
proprieters must be considered, on the whole, as a beneficial
circumstance in a representative body.' Small wonder then that
Mackintosh's 'middle-class idiom', as in 1815 (and again directly
contradicting the judgments he had made in 1791), reaffirmed
once more the indisposition of the 'middle class' to political
change: 'the virtues of that excellent class are generally of a
circumspect nature, and apt to degenerate into timidity. They
have little of that political boldness which sometimes belongs to
commanding fortune, and often, in too great a degree, to thoughtless poverty'. In this representation of the political-cum-social
middle, 'middle-class' political intransigence, let alone revolution,

became unthinkable. Instead it turned out to be the most 'tame', the most acquiescent component of society – more so than those above or below it.[6]

In short, if the political circumstances were now urging a sharply delineated dual division, then Mackintosh made it all too clear which side his 'middle class' was on. It was clear, for example, to the anonymous radical critic of Mackintosh, who retorted to the latter's *Edinburgh Review* essay with a call for universal suffrage and the ballot. This author accused Mackintosh of concealing behind his alleged concern for social distinctions what in truth was a basic polarized scheme of a ruling minority and an oppressed majority. Setting Mackintosh's rhetorical stratagems aside, this was the only valid understanding of the present situation: 'Now we have two classes existing in the country – the many and the few.' It was with this understanding that he paraphrased Mackintosh, transposing – or, in his view, exposing – his language into dual terms. Hence, when this radical author referred explicitly to Mackintosh's claim that universal suffrage would bring about the annihilation of the 'middle class', he recast it in different terms: 'Universal suffrage, it is said [by Mackintosh], will impair the dominion and influence of the great proprietors', those who are in a position to enslave the rest of the community.[7] This selective representation of Mackintosh's argument lost its 'middle-class' language altogether, and presented it as this writer understood it, as part of a dual scheme of oppression.

So we find again a differentiation and subversion of social language between political rivals. Only that whereas in the 1790s the ministerialists had been struggling against an oppositional use of 'middle-class' language, now it was in the more establishmentarian text that an emphasis on the role of the 'middle class' was found useful; and this, in turn, was seen as a veneer for oppression by the more radical voice, who recast it in dual social terms. For Mackintosh's critic, the language of 'middle class' had indeed completed the transition into the conservative camp, and thus needed to be counteracted with other social vocabularies not as complicit in the prevailing political order.

---

[6] *Edinburgh Review* 31, December 1818, pp. 172, 176, 189, 192.
[7] *Statement of the Question of Parliamentary Reform: With a Reply to the Objections of the Edinburgh Review, No. LXI*, London, 1821, pp. 63, 72.

To a certain extent, then, the uses of 'middle-class' language accompanied political moderation, albeit a moderation primarily intended to check the popular tide rather than to curb the power of the established elite. And yet this political-cum-social middle explanation for the sudden pervasiveness of this language is not really sufficient. In particular, given that the political middle turned out to be equipped with an anti-radical edge, it can hardly explain the frequent recurrence of 'middle-class' language in radical rhetoric. It would also hardly do to suggest that the radicals' emphasis on the language of 'middle class' was simply a response to its revitalized use by their opponents; as had been true in the 1790s, and as was to be largely true again in 1830–1, there was no a priori reason for radicals to accept the social vocabulary of their opponents rather than replace it with formulations more suitable for their own purposes. In fact, the recourse to the language of 'middle class' by both political camps in the late 1810s had its own distinct logic, a logic anchored in a specific feature of the public debate at this point: the prominent role assigned to the notion of *public opinion*.

THE HEYDAY OF 'PUBLIC OPINION'

We hear from all quarters appeals to the shelter and countenance of public opinion: Every one recognises its jurisdiction, and courts it as a tribunal before which roguery and imposture are disarmed and unmasked, and from whence a righteous verdict is sure to emanate. (Anonymous, 1821)[8]

Although 'public opinion' had been part of British political language since way back in the eighteenth century, the intensity both of the appeals to 'public opinion' and of the confrontation over its role in the late 1810s and early 1820s was probably unprecedented.[9] As the anonymous writer of this epigraph noted, the power attributed during these years to 'public opinion' was all-pervasive. Pamphleteers began their writing by justifying it as

---

[8] Ibid., p. 125.

[9] For a political history of the concept of 'public opinion' in England, see J. A. W. Gunn, 'Public Spirit to Public Opinion', in his *Beyond Liberty and Property: The Process of Self-Recognition in Eighteenth-Century Political Thought*, Kingston, 1983, pp. 260–315; idem, 'Public Opinion', in T. Ball et al. (eds.), *Political Innovation and Conceptual Change*, Cambridge, 1989, pp. 247–65. So far, this topic has attracted far less attention among historians of Britain than among those of France at this period.

an appeal to 'public opinion'. Political periodicals were suffused with panegyrics to its omnipotence. Everywhere one could find statements invoking its quasi-magical power in tireless repetition: 'The great security of the Constitution, then, [is] the vigilance of public opinion'; 'a new Leviathan has grown up, called Public Opinion'; 'The crown is dependant upon the public opinion' (see figure 6); 'the *Borough-mongers* [will] vanish in the unanimous, aweful, and omnipotent voice of public opinion'; 'the power of public opinion is become so great, that every other must finally bend to its decrees'; 'Public opinion, [is] that great ultimate arbiter of all human merit.'[10] Not only was the political present perceived through this seductive prism, but the past as well; 'public opinion' proved to be indispensable to the understanding of past political events, from the English civil war through the Glorious Revolution to Robert Walpole's ministry.[11] (An analogous extrapolation from the political debate to the rewriting of history will be seen later to

[10] Henry Brougham in the *Edinburgh Review* 27, September 1816, p. 250 (and see also pp. 245, 249); *Examiner* 472, 12 January 1817, p. 17 (and see similarly, among virtually innumerable examples, 480, 9 March 1817, pp. 146–7; 535, 29 March 1818, p. 193; 654, 9 July 1820, pp. 433–4); [Thomas Attwood], *Prosperity Restored: Or, Reflections on the Cause of the Public Distresses, and on the Only Means of Relieving Them*, London, 1817, p. 133 (echoed in *The King's Treatment of the Queen Shortly Stated to the People of England*, 2nd edn, London, 1820, p. 17); *The Gorgon* 7, 4 July 1818, p. 50 (and see more below, note 20); J. Nightingale (ed.), *The Spirit of the Addresses Presented to the Queen, with Her Majesty's Answers*, n.p., [1820?], p. 29 (and see also p. 30); Charles Maclean, *The Triumph of Public Opinion; Being a Standing Lesson to the Throne, the Parliament, and the People: ... in the Case of Her Majesty Caroline, Queen of England*, London, 1820, p. [1]. 'Public opinion' was invoked with especial force on the issue of Queen Caroline in 1820 (see below, pp. 384–5). Deference to it was not restricted to the anti-ministerial camp; see the popular defence of the king's actions: [John Wilson Croker?], *A Letter from the King to his People*, 12th edn, London, [1820], pp. 2–3; or the *Anti-Jacobin Review and Magazine* 59, September 1820, p. 34. Compare also William Benbow (whose command of geography perhaps did not match that of politics): 'The march of public opinion ... is more stronger than the waters that sweep from the *Nile* to the oceans and fertilize the countries over which they pass': *The Whigs Exposed: Or, Truth by Day-Light. Addressed to the Reformers of Britain*, London, 1820, p. 12.

[11] Among many examples, see Jeffrey in the *Edinburgh Review* 30, September 1818, p. 285. Carolus Candidus (pseud.), *A Short Reply to a Short Defence of the Whigs ...*, London, 1819. Lord John Russell, *An Essay on the History of the English Government and Constitution, from the Reign of Henry VII. to the Present Time*, 2nd edn, greatly enlarged, London, 1823 (1st edn, 1821), p. 431. Or listen to the Manchester radical remonstrance which according to John Belchem set the tone for the radical campaign of 1819: 'Had Charles the first, and James the Second shewn a becoming deference for public opinion ... the one would not have lost his head on a scaffold, nor the other have been driven from the throne by an insulted and justly enraged People.' Quoted in D. Read, *Peterloo: The 'Massacre' and Its Background*, Manchester, 1958, appendix A, p. 215. See J. Belchem, *'Orator' Hunt: Henry Hunt and English Working-Class Radicalism*, Oxford, 1985, p. 87.

Figure 6. The power of 'public opinion', 1820. 'Public opinion' (triumphing over 'persecution and malice') blows the crown off the head of George IV (left profile) and breaks it in half. 'Half a crown' was a popular symbol for Queen Caroline (right profile), whose thwarting of her husband's attempt to divorce her was widely attributed to the power of 'public opinion'. (Published by S. Vowles) *Source*: BMC 13993.

have similarly accompanied the heyday of the language of 'middle class' in the 1830s.)

In the eyes of a reputable series of writers, commencing – not accidentally, as we shall see – during the 1820s and 1830s, and culminating perhaps in Jürgen Habermas, 'public opinion' has been repeatedly presented as somehow inherently 'bourgeois', and thus intuitively linked to the notion of 'middle class'.[12] One key underpinning of this purportedly organic association has been the representation of the 'middle class' as the repository of education and intelligence, that is as possessing the faculties of reason seemingly prerequisite for the formation of an informed 'public opinion'. Yet we should be wary of taking on trust such purposeful representations: either that the 'middle class' – however it may be defined – indeed had a monopoly over or a privileged access to political reasoning, or that assigning 'public opinion' a political role – however 'public opinion' may be gauged – was indeed the outcome of the pure operation of reason.[13] Moreover, in the actual use of these notions in contemporary political debate there was no demonstrable affinity between 'public opinion' and 'middle class'. Indeed, the reverse

---

[12] J. Habermas, *The Structural Transformation of the Public Sphere: An Inquiry into a Category of Bourgeois Society*, trans. T. Burger, Cambridge, Mass., 1989; originally 1962. Of course, 'bourgeois' here refers not only to a social group, but also – unobjectionably – to the general nature of post-aristocratic society, in which structural transformations made a public sphere as Habermas conceives it possible. However, for post-Habermas understandings of 'bourgeois' in this context as referring more specifically to a particular social group (which is then associated with the public sphere and with public opinion), see J. B. Landes, *Women and the Public Sphere in the Age of the French Revolution*, Ithaca, 1988; S. Maza, 'Women, the Bourgeoisie, and the Public Sphere', *French Historical Studies* 17 (1992), pp. 935–50. See also F. K. Wilson, 'Public Opinion and the Middle Class', *Review of Politics* 17 (1955), pp. 486–510, which commences thus: 'Two ancient symbols – public opinion and the middle class – have nearly always been associated in some degree.'

[13] The arguably uncritical presupposition of the connection between public opinion and reason is strongly evident in R. Chartier, *The Cultural Origins of the French Revolution*, Durham, 1991. Following Habermas, Chartier argues that public opinion emanated from the new critical application of reason in the Enlightenment: yet he never pauses to discover whence came the powerful belief in the existence of a unified univocal public opinion, in its absolute infallibility, or in the possibility of recovering its verdicts. Such beliefs were surely in defiance of people's political common sense: they were absolute, uncritical and hardly based on pure reason, placing public opinion itself beyond the bounds of critical reasoning. For a stimulating discussion of the unattainability of an accepted standard of reason, see W. M. Motooka, 'The Age of Reasons: Quixotism and Sentiment in Eighteenth-Century Britain', unpublished Ph.D, University of Michigan, 1992. See further my 'Violence, Public Opinion, and the Limits of Constitutional Politics', in J. Vernon (ed.), *Rereading the Constitution*, Cambridge, 1996.

Figure 7. 'Public opinion' and political polarization. Isaac Cruikshank's elaborate representation of the political scene in June 1820, in the form of a clock
whose hands are the arms of Queen Caroline. The symmetrical design emphasizes the polarization of politics, repeated in the antithetical positioning of the
two boxers below the dial (Castlereagh and Brougham), the cornucopia and
the cap of liberty supporting the dial, and the two supports of the clock's
beam – one representing the ministerial camp, the other the radicals. Note the
central rod of the pendulum, significantly labelled 'unhappy medium'. (In the
pendulum stands Canning, the butt of the print, dithering between a crown
and a cap of liberty.) Presiding over this polarized political scene is John Bull,
here (as often) a metaphor for 'public opinion': wearing a huge judge's wig,
he is a tribunal labelled 'Chief Justice Bull – Jurisdiction – ad Infinitum'.
Source: BMC 13738.

was often the case, when 'public opinion' – representing the universalistic good of the people – was put forward to *counteract* the particularistic tendencies of 'middle-class' rhetoric.[14]

So it was not simply the natural order of things that assigned the 'middle class' an important role in the discussion of 'public opinion' in the late 1810s: this connection too was a product of particular circumstances. As the selection of quotes above exemplifies, speakers across the board were continually appealing to (their own understandings of) 'public opinion', while attempting to represent their own positions as its particular embodiment and thus as the opinion of 'the people'. The resonance of 'public opinion' at this point was crucially related to the constitutionalist form of popular radicalism. As John Belchem and James Epstein have pointed out, mainstream radicals in the post-war years were formulating their claims more in the Cartwrightian language of popular constitutionalism than in the Painite language of natural rights (though the latter did not altogether fade away).[15] In arguing from within a shared constitutionalist idiom rather than against it, these popular radicals could find important rhetorical support in 'public opinion', as a notion that was sanctioned by their adversaries but was at the same time vague and pliable enough to be used for legitimizing their own demands. Thus, underlying the shared reverence for 'public opinion' was a struggle between its competing appropriations by the contending political camps.

In the ensuing contestation, moreover, it was crucial for the self-declared advocates of 'public opinion' to be able to show

---

[14] A number of speakers who opposed the 'middle-class idiom' relied at the same time on the notion of 'public opinion', including (among those we have already encountered) the radical John Thelwall and the loyalist William Playfair. It can also be shown that the prevalence of 'middle-class' language and of appeals to 'public opinion' in periodicals such as the *Edinburgh Review* and the *Examiner*, when gauged crudely over time, was inversely correlated.

[15] J. Belchem, 'Republicanism, Popular Constitutionalism and the Radical Platform in Early Nineteenth-Century England', *Social History* 6 (1981), pp. 1–32. Idem, *'Orator' Hunt*, pp. 3–5, 107–9, and passim. Idem, 'Radical Language and Ideology in Early Nineteenth-Century England: The Challenge of the Platform', *Albion* 20 (1988), pp. 247–59. J. Epstein, 'Understanding the Cap of Liberty: Symbolic Practice and Social Conflict in Early Nineteenth Century England', *Past and Present* 122 (1989), pp. 83–6. Idem, *Radical Expression*. Epstein also reminds us of the resilience of the language of natural rights in periodicals such as *Sherwin's Political Register* and Thomas Davidson's *Medusa* at the side of the more prevalent constitutionalism characterizing organs like the *Black Dwarf* and *Cobbett's Political Register*.

that they were not representing merely a narrow interested group but rather an inclusive social range, indeed a universalistic alignment from which only self-serving sectionalists (that is, their opponents) excluded themselves. This changed the way in which social and political schemas were correlated. Previously (think again of the 1790s), it had seemed sensible and effective to correlate one's perception of the social map with one's perception of the political map (whether, say, in dual or in tripartite terms). Now, the claim for universality of one's positions made it necessary to prove that one's political camp encompassed manifestly *more* than one's social camp. This feature of the political debate at this juncture, it is suggested, had a lot to do with the sudden prominence of appeals to the 'middle class' and for the ensuing struggle over its alliance. The social middle was now brought up and sought after by those who *denied* a political middle, precisely for this reason: whichever of the opposing political camps could demonstrate that the 'middle class' was joining its ranks, would have thus proved itself to be speaking for 'the people', that is to truly represent 'public opinion'.

In this impulse both political camps were reinforcing each other. On the one hand, those alarmed by popular politics were concerned to distinguish the respectable and intelligent 'public opinion' (which of course included the paragons of these virtues, the 'middle class') from the ill winds among the populace. Furthermore, faced with a mass popular movement, it was crucial for supporters of the establishment to demonstrate that they too could mobilize large numbers, as counterweights to the numbers that were obviously mobilizing on the other side; and again, it was the alliance of the 'middle class' which could supply them with such numbers. On the other hand, the radicals, with their urgent bid to establish their legitimacy and to assert their universal role as speakers for 'public opinion', had on their part a no lesser stake – at least initially – in demonstrating that the 'middle class' was on *their* side. Moreover, a serious obstacle which stood in the way of radical uses of 'middle-class' language in the 1790s, namely its incompatibility with the language of natural rights, was now significantly eliminated with the downplaying of the latter in mainstream radical rhetoric and its submersion in constitutionalism. Ultimately, therefore, the outcome turned out to be a 'tug of war' between the two opposite political camps, each attempting to draw a social middle – which they both perceived to be lacking any corollary political middle – into their own lines. In the process both sides developed a significant stake in a conceptualization of society which acknowledged the distinct existence of a 'middle class'.

Indeed, as is manifest in the epigraphs opening this chapter, the two camps could sound very much alike. On the ministerialist side, nobody broadcast the appeal to the 'middle class' more relentlessly than an obscure clergyman (and fellow extraordinary of the Royal Medical Society of Edinburgh), Reverend Lionel Thomas Berguer, a man whose self-assigned mission in these dangerously tumultous times was that 'my voice might sound like an angel's trumpet through the land, and rouse the middle classes'. Given the 'vast collections' enlisted on the side of anarchy, he believed, only 'the MIDDLE CLASSES' can come forward as 'an universal movement'.[16] Theirs was 'the power of public opinion', inevitably lined up on the side of justice, freedom and tranquillity. In the contestation over who represents the real voice of 'public opinion', Berguer made his point loud and clear: 'the *Middle Ranks*', that is to say as Berguer perceived them, 'are, *in point of efficiency, the* PEOPLE'. Consequently, when Berguer paused to define his 'middle class' (evidently not taking the term to be self-explanatory), it turned out – which by now should come as no surprise – to delineate primarily a political rather than a social category:

It is most important, that the term MIDDLE CLASSES should be well understood; as it is used throughout this appeal, not to designate *the little gentry, and men of moderate fortune merely*, but ALL THOSE, – of whatever rank or station, – who are *intermediately placed* between MINISTERS, and a *disorderly* and *disordered* RABBLE: in short, *the whole respectable and independent population of the country*.[17]

---

[16] Rev. Lionel Thomas Berguer, *A Warning Letter to His Royal Highness the Prince Regent: Intended Principally as a Call upon the Middle Ranks, at This Important Crisis*, 3rd edn, London, 1819, pp. 31, 34. Idem, *A Second Warning Letter to His Royal Highness the Prince Regent: Intended Principally as a Call upon the Middle Ranks, at This Important Crisis*, 2nd edn, London, 1819, pp. 4, 47, and 36: 'I am standing upon a great *arena*, conspicuous to my country, and to the world: and the MIDDLE CLASSES, in whom there is an inherent *power* of salvation equal to your own, *are awakening at my call*.'

[17] [Rev. Lionel Thomas Berguer], *A Letter to the Gentlemen of England, upon the Present Critical Conjuncture of Affairs*, London, 1819, p. 9; idem, *A Second Warning Letter*, p. 51 and pp. 4–5. Berguer, while vehemently anti-radical (a cause to which he put all his

There was much urgency in Berguer's appeal to the 'middle class' to take their leading place in the anti-revolutionary 'public opinion'. Berguer had no doubt as to the commitment of the 'middle class' to 'peace, tranquillity and order', which guaranteed that they 'can never as a body entertain any ambitious or violent intentions'; a confidence which he believed was shared by those in government, who 'would feel it absurd to accuse you of exciting tumult for the purposes of anarchy'. Yet, as highlighted in the passage quoted in the epigraph to this chapter, the 'middle class' at the present crisis still needed to be spurred out of its apathy: 'Things have reached their climax: but a REVOLUTION will either be prevented, or induced, according as the MIDDLE RANKS bestir themselves during the REBELLION.'[18]

Now listen on the other side to *The Gorgon*, a radical periodical that attempted to marry utilitarianism with working-class experience and politics. It was edited by John Wade, a former journeyman wool-sorter whose well-researched writings were to become increasingly influential.[19] With Berguer's assessment of the actual and potential role of the 'middle class' at the present crisis, Wade's *Gorgon* could hardly agree more. It too accused the 'middle class' (see the second epigraph above) of an unfortunate 'state of apathy' and a failure to take a stand. The 'middling classes', it complained further, were like 'the ill-natured dog on the bundle of hay', who

---

rhetorical energy), was also critical of the ministers and favoured their replacement, as well as some measures of reform; as in this passage, his 'middle-class idiom' at times conflated social and political middle. Also note in passing that 'middle class' was again interchangeable with 'middle rank', even for a writer so committed to this language.

[18] *A Letter to the Gentlemen of England*, pp. 8–9. *A Warning Letter*, p. 38; and see also pp. vi ('*the saving power is in the MIDDLE RANKS*'), 50, 52. *A Second Warning Letter*, pp. 3–4, 19, 51. For another clergyman appealing to the 'middle class' in an effort to avert a lower-class revolution, compare Melville Horne, *The Moral and Political Crisis of England: Most Respectfully Inscribed to the Higher and Middle Classes*, London, 1820; and recall Coleridge's 1817 'Lay Sermon Addressed to the Higher and Middle Classes on the Existing Distresses and Discontents': see p. 175 n. 39. Of course, not all Tory writers adopted the language of 'middle class': others preferred to issue strong appeals in dual social terms, exhorting the propertied to unite against the propertyless. Examples include *Observations on the Present State of Affairs, and the Conduct of the Whigs. By a Freeholder*, London, 1819, esp. pp. 20–1. *An Examination of Universal Suffrage, with Reference to the Principles of Government, the British Constitution, and the Present Circumstances of the Country*, London, 1819, pp. 8–9.

[19] Others involved in *The Gorgon* during its publication from May 1818 to April 1819 were Francis Place and John Gast; its first issues were printed by Richard Carlile. See Thompson, *The Making of the English Working Class*, pp. 768–74.

could not feed itself on the hay but nevertheless prevented the ox from eating it until both perished from hunger; 'and this must shortly be the fate of the middling and working classes'. *The Gorgon* acknowledged the 'tug of war' over the heart of the 'middle class' in which it was engaged against ministerial writers, whose tactic was 'to alarm the middling classes'. As a consequence, 'though, of necessity, they hate the system', their undue alarm prompted them to 'wink at measures on the part of Government, which, under other circumstances, they would resolutely oppose'. In a counter-gambit to that of its opponents, *The Gorgon* advanced its own bid for the alliance of the 'middle class': 'We do not wish a Reform to be accomplished by the labouring classes nor the middling classes *singly*, but by the joint efforts of the PRODUCTIVE CLASSES of the community.'[20] Just like Berguer, *The Gorgon* felt the cooperation with the 'middle class' to be important to prove that its own politics, unlike those of its adversaries, represented the broad public good. Indeed, in light of previous divergences of such social language between competing political camps, the symmetry of their rhetoric at this juncture is striking. Not that it was achieved without some tension: on another occasion *The Gorgon*, not very consistently with its arguments elsewhere but more in line with the radical dual social language of the preceding decades, could be found distinguishing clearly between the 'productive classes' and the 'middling classes'; the latter, it stated on that occasion, included 'the active, working, *journeymen* of Corruption', who consequently 'from a principle of self-preservation will resolutely oppose every attempt at Reform'.[21] It was this habitual distrust, underpinned by the incommensurability of the 'middle-class' language with the inclusive radical platform, that radicals at this moment were attempting, conditionally, to suspend; but before long the futility of this step struck back at them with a vengeance.

---

[20] *The Gorgon* 7, 4 July 1818, p. 55; 10, 25 July 1818, p. 74; 36, 23 January 1819, pp. 282–3. Compare the formulation in the *Black Dwarf*, below, p. 211. Together with its appeal to a broad inclusive political alliance, *The Gorgon* too was repeatedly invoking the power and authority of 'public opinion': see among others 7, 4 July 1818, pp. 50, 53; 10, 25 July 1818, p. 73; 17, 12 September 1818, p. 129; 26, 14 November 1818, p. 205 ('that *Tribunal*, to which sensible men alone think of appealing – namely, PUBLIC OPINION').

[21] *The Gorgon* 12, 8 August 1818, p. 90; though note the qualification of this statement to only a 'portion' of the 'middle class' on the next page. See also 1, 23 May 1818, p. 6, where the 'middling classes' were declared to be a privileged class, part of the oppressive system.

PETERLOO'S AFTERMATH: THE CLOSURE OF OPTIONS

Men of moderate incomes . . . should stand in the gap between anarchy and despotism, and endeavour to hold the balance of benefits and friendly intercourse between rich and poor. ('The Folly of the Middle Classes', *Black Dwarf*, 1817)

It is certain that by far the great majority of the middle classes, who can boast of comforts, have derived them from the ruin of their neighbours . . .

That class never did its duty, either to itself, or to society . . . in all countries, the middle class has been the instrument by which tyranny has been consolidated. (*Black Dwarf*, 1821)[22]

Of all the heated political moments in the post-war years, it was the massacre of Peterloo that sent shock waves throughout the nation (see figure 8). As Harriet Martineau recalled, it 'was at once felt on all hands to have made an epoch in the history of the contest with Radicalism'. For Earl Grey, whose political career spanned the whole period discussed in this book, it was 'by far the most important event that had occurred in the course of his political life'.[23] The impact of Peterloo was immediate and strong: in spite of a spontaneous widespread outrage, it soon induced many of the propertied classes to recoil from the radical cause, thus leaving the working-class radicals isolated. For many alarmed observers (such as Reverend Berguer), Peterloo drove home the urgent need to demonstrate the rallying of the 'middle class' on the side of order and stability, parading its cumulative weight – in numbers and importance – against what was feared to be a burgeoning revolutionary mass movement. For others, more sympathetic to the cause of the radical reformers, it was precisely this identifiable affinity between themselves and the popular radicals that made it imperative to re-emphasize the 'middleness' of their position, which meant qualified support for popular demands but not necessarily for popular actions. One way or another, there was a noticeable effort following the events

---

[22] *Black Dwarf* 1:3, 12 February 1817, col. 37; 6:15, 11 April 1821, cols. 503–5.
[23] Harriet Martineau, *A History of the Thirty Years' Peace 1816–1846*, rep. edn, Shannon, 1971 (originally London, 1849–50), vol. I, p. 305. Grey is quoted in R. Quinault, 'The Industrial Revolution and Parliamentary Reform', in P. O'Brien and R. Quinault (eds.), *The Industrial Revolution and British Society*, Cambridge, 1993, pp. 195–6.

Figure 8. Peterloo. A wood-engraving printed on coarse calico, as a handkerchief, commemorating the reform meeting of St Peter's Fields dispersed by the slashing yeomanry. The powerful image emphasizes the magnitude, density, and respectability of the crowd that surrounded the platform (in the middle distance, surrounded by sabres). (Slack, *c.* August 1819) *Source*: BMC 13262.

in St Peter's Fields to demarcate the 'middle class' ever more clearly from the lower classes.

Consider, for example, Francis Jeffrey's numerous contributions to the *Edinburgh Review*. Following his political 'middle-class idiom' in 1807, for more than a decade Jeffrey refrained from political allusions to the 'middle class' (even in contexts where it was likely), while in non-political literary contexts he often coupled together the 'middling and lower classes' as constituting the literary public.[24] But in his immediate reaction to Peterloo in October 1819, deploring the 'unhappy estrangement between the two grand divisions of which the population consists', Jeffrey all of a sudden redrew the lines of social division differently: 'We take the most alarming sign of the times to be, that separation of the upper and middle classes of the community from the lower, which is now daily and visibly increasing.'[25] At this moment, Jeffrey's 'middle class' reappeared in a political context, now safely positioned on the side of the establishment as against the rising numbers of the lower orders; just as it was positioned by the *Newcastle Chronicle* a couple of weeks later, when it called for cooperation of 'the upper and middle classes of society' in order to allay the present discontent.[26]

The sudden effects of Peterloo were also unmistakable in the pages of Leigh Hunt's *Examiner*. As in Jeffrey's writings, the years preceding 1819 saw little political 'middle-class' language in the *Examiner*.[27] This remained true throughout 1817–18, when the

[24] For such non-political examples, see among others *Edinburgh Review* 1, October 1802, p. 67; 4, July 1804, p. 330 (attribution to Jeffrey uncertain); 14, July 1809, p. 376; 20, November 1812, pp. 279–80; 28, August 1817, p. 396. For Jeffrey's political 'middle-class' language in 1807, see above, p. 178, as well as 10, July 1807, p. 386. The following year, still within a political context, he was already coupling 'the lower and middling orders' as a corrective check to ministerial corruption: 12, July 1808, p. 277 (and see also 13, October 1808, pp. 220, 223 [written jointly with Brougham]; 14, July 1809, pp. 292, 296). Subsequent instances where his writing seemed to avoid 'middle-class' language even when it could have been expected include his discussion of a political middle in 15, January 1810, p. 504; his repeated discussions of public opinion and 'the people', in 16, April 1810, pp. 1ff.; 17, February 1811, pp. 253ff. (with Brougham); 20, July 1812, p. 247 (with James Loch); 20, November 1812, pp. 315ff.; 21, February 1813, pp. 1ff.; 23, April 1814, pp. 1ff.; 30, September 1818, pp. 283–4; his discussion of the opposition to the war and its taxes by 'the sound and disinterested part of the community' in 24, November 1814, p. 264; and his analysis of French affairs which seemed to make a real effort to avoid 'middle-class' language in 25, October 1815, esp. p. 506. And see below, pp. 237–8.

[25] *Edinburgh Review* 32, October 1819, p. 294. Compare Brougham's concerned letter to Earl Grey, 19 September 1819: 'the tendency of things at present – [is] to end in a total separation of the upper and middling from the lower classes' (*The Life and Times of Henry Lord Brougham, Written by Himself*, New York, 1871, vol. II, p. 264). Brougham had already expressed a similarly bifurcated concern in *Edinburgh Review* 28, August 1817, p. 543.

[26] *Newcastle Chronicle*, 13 November 1819. As for Jeffrey, several years later, once the political scene had calmed down, he no longer emphasized this dividing line between the lower and the 'middle class': contrast his 1819 writing with his 1825 portrayal of the 'middle rank/class' as a social class 'approaching more nearly, and connected more intimately, with the lower than the higher orders' (*Edinburgh Review* 41, January 1825, pp. 309–11).

[27] The *Examiner* too had an earlier moment of anti-war 'middle-class' language, around its foundation in 1808: see above, p. 163. Indeed at one point the periodical, praising

periodical retained predominantly a dual view of the political struggle: 'The question now depending between the rich and poor, the maintainers of parliamentary corruption and the insisters upon its abolition', it declared only a day before the events of Peterloo, 'is simply this – Whether the most monstrous inequality is to be suffered to exist.'[28] But the next few weeks saw a significant change, as the *Examiner* hastened to distinguish between the 'middle class' and the lower orders. While strongly condemning the recent confrontation, the periodical at the same time asserted that the real voices for reform were not those heard in St Peter's Fields: 'A number of reflecting persons, chiefly among the middling classes, have long been engaged in pointing out the abuses in the State, and have often foretold the effects of the extravagance and oppression to which they gave rise.' These rational and proper efforts on behalf of reform, the *Examiner* insisted, that had been carried out for some time by 'Moderates', should not be distracted by the 'present disturbances' nor by the lower orders who 'do not much attend to nice distinctions, and . . . are more impressed by broad and simple propositions'.[29] Given the emphasis on this distinction, it was certainly no coincidence that these very weeks saw a conspicuous surge of 'middle-class' language in virtually every issue of the *Examiner*; not only in discussions of the recent political tragedy, but also in a variety of other contexts, including the effects of profuse government expenditure, the mistaken social identification of reformers by Tory newspapers, and even a comparative look at social injustice in Lisbon, Portugal.[30]

itself for its 'English sincerity', identified its target audience as those 'multitudes of persons, particularly in the middle classes, who care not an atom for any party strictly so called, and who only desire to see a question treated upon those simple and obvious principles of right and wrong'. (*Examiner* 271, 7 March 1813, p. 145; and also 285, 13 June 1813, p. 369).

[28] *Examiner* 607, 15 August 1819, p. 513: leading article, 'Increasing Dispute between the Reformers and Their Opponents'. Recent articles manifesting clearly this dual perspective, both in political and in social terms, included 453, 1 September 1816, pp. 545–6; 482, 23 March 1817, pp. 180–1; 560, 20 September 1818, p. 600; 605, 1 August 1819, p. 481.

[29] *Examiner* 610, 5 September 1819, pp. 562–3. Compare also 683, 4 February 1821, p. 67, as quoted in part below, p. 261.

[30] *Examiner* 612, 19 September 1819, p. 604; 613, 26 September 1819, p. 618; 614, 3 October 1819, pp. 625–6; 616, 17 October 1819, p. 664. The sudden effect of Peterloo on the use of 'middle-class' language in the *Examiner* can be crudely demonstrated by simple enumeration: whereas in the three years preceding Peterloo one can find only seven or eight significant instances of 'middle-class' language in the pages of the *Examiner*, the three years following this event saw over twenty-five such instances (an abundance, one may add, not matched again until the debates on the Reform Bill in

The partial retreat of the *Examiner* from its previous advocacy of the struggle of 'the people' against their oppressors in undifferentiated dual terms was suggestively manifest several months later in an exchange with the Tory *Courier*. The *Courier* criticized a speech of Sir Francis Burdett for being too populist, 'of the true tavern strain', inappropriately invoking 'the people' and 'the public'. Flattery of the people, maintained the Tory newspaper, was no less sycophantic than flattery of a king: 'He who tells a Monarch that he is the wisest, bravest, and best of men, is scoffed at for his servility. What then should be his reward who tells shoemakers, tallow chandlers, and tailors, that they are paragons of wisdom, patriotism, virtue, and knowledge?'[31] The *Examiner* responded: 'is there no difference between playing the sycophant to a king ... and telling a mixed assembly composed of the boasted middle classes of the metropolis of England, that they are the most "enlightened" and "patriotic" electors in the kingdom?'[32] This exchange is very interesting. On the one hand, it is reminiscent of that between Burke and Mackintosh with regard to the composition of the French National Assembly in 1790–1, in which the more 'progressive' interlocutor had counteracted social derision against the newly politicized social groups with an emphasis on their political worth as 'middle class'. On the other hand, however, this very similarity also demonstrates the limits of the *Examiner*'s position at this juncture: rather than defend Burdett's 'flattery of the people' by reasserting the political value of the *people* (which was the periodical's unequivocal tone a year or two earlier), it preferred now to vindicate him by recasting the alleged language of his praise, limiting its subjects to 'the boasted middle classes'. In 1791, Mackintosh had introduced an oppositionally charged language of 'middle class' in order to raise the image of the people; by 1820, the *Examiner* introduced a recently 'tamed' language of 'middle class' in order to erase it.

As for the radicals, they were hardly unaware of this erasure. These developments could only confirm their sense of betrayal and isolation after Peterloo: and indeed the sharp impact of this

[31] *The Courier* 8880, 24 May 1820 (editorial). Burdett's speech took place at a Westminster elections anniversary meeting.
[32] *Examiner* 649, 4 June 1820, p. 365.

event immediately registered in radical rhetoric, displacing the appeal to the 'middle class' with a backlash of anger.

Signs of the change were apparent, for example, in the first edition of John Wade's important critique of Old Corruption, *The Black Book* of 1820, separated from his edited *Gorgon* by the events of 1819. Acknowledging again the tug of war against Tory attempts 'to alarm the middling classes' and thus to make them 'the dupes of their selfish fears and misrepresentations', Wade was as yet unwilling to give up hope that 'the middling classes [would] have sufficient virtue, sense, and courage, to come forward to frustrate the diabolical machinations of the Executive Government'. After all, unlike the 'privileged orders', 'they have not been wallowing in the plunder of the people; nor have they usurped the rights of their fellow-citizens'. But at the same time, in spite of himself, Wade admitted defeat. The 'state of apathy' of the 'middling classes', which he had noted in *The Gorgon*, he now denounced more emphatically as 'a state of criminal apathy', confirmed by 'their present conduct [which] is culpable in the highest degree'. The behaviour of these 'middling classes' no longer constituted merely sitting on the fence, but was in itself a political choice: 'how can they reconcile to their consciences', he pleaded, 'that criminal neutrality, which neither supports any measures to alleviate the sufferings [of the people], nor to guard them against the diabolical machinations of their enemies'. It was clearly Peterloo that was most urgently on Wade's mind: 'Nay, the conduct of some is still more deplorably wicked and fatuous. They have taken arms to defend a plundering Oligarchy, and, with tiger ferocity, lent their aid to stifle the complaints of misery and famine, by the sabre, the bayonet, and the dungeon!'[33]

---

[33] [John Wade], *The Black Book; Or, Corruption Unmasked* ..., London, 1820, pp. 143–4, 189, 202, and passim. The *Black Book* played an important role in the radicalism of the next two decades, going through several subsequent editions with cumulative sales of more than 50,000 copies; see below, pp. 354–6. The same combination of sobered disillusionment and lingering hope also characterized the post-Peterloo writing of John Edward Taylor of Manchester. Taylor explained the recent clash between the 'middle class' and the lower orders in that the 'middle class', having been 'busily occupied with their own private affairs', avoided politics 'by a general determination to "*support the government*,*"* meaning thereby the ministry of the day'; but he too believed that their sentiments might be changed. [John Edward Taylor], *Notes and Observations, Critical and Explanatory, on the Papers Relative to the Internal State of the Country ... By a Member of the Manchester Committee For Relieving the Sufferers of the 16th of August, 1819*, London, 1820, pp. 201–2 (also pp. 163–4).

Despite his disappointment, Wade still tried to give the 'middle class' another chance. The judgment of others was more conclusive. In Newcastle, a disenchanted speaker in a popular meeting protesting the massacre of Peterloo, one Mr Mackenzie, left no doubt as to his own opinion:

The insensate selfishness and torpid indifference of the middle ranks of society is much to be regretted at this trying crisis. But these men who used to boast of being the descendants of Hampden and Sidney, of Shakespeare and of Milton – the bulwarks of public liberty – the repositories of national intelligence – these men are now seen sacrificing every honest emotion, every ennobling sentiment, at the altar of Mammon.

Whatever claims 'the middle ranks' had had to constituting the bulwark of liberty or the repository of intelligence, they were now exposed as lost to self-serving selfishness; otherwise, Mackenzie continued bitterly, 'they could never be silent when blood calls aloud from the earth for vengeance'. The lower orders, by contrast, who were 'prepared to act and to suffer in support of their rights', were those proclaimed by Mackenzie to be 'the salt of the land' and 'the most valuable part of the community'. In the struggle over representing 'public opinion' or 'the bulk of the people' (the framework in which the report of this Newcastle meeting was set), the labouring classes were now on their own: the verdict on the defection of the 'middle class' was beyond appeal.[34]

The vituperative transformation of the radical tone regarding the 'middle class' was perhaps nowhere more striking than in the pages of the *Black Dwarf*. This weekly newspaper, edited by the printer turned political writer Thomas J. Wooler (who was closely associated with Major Cartwright, the doyen of constitutionalist radicals), was one of the most important popular organs, and probably commanded the widest radical audience once William Cobbett had suddenly left for America in early 1817. The changes in the representation of the 'middle class' in the *Black Dwarf* between 1817 and 1821 (encapsulated in the contrast between the two epigraphs at the beginning of this

---

[34] *A Full Account of the General Meeting of the Inhabitants of Newcastle upon Tyne and the Vicinity ... for the Purpose of Taking into Consideration the Late Proceedings in Manchester*, Newcastle upon Tyne, 1819, pp. [2], 9.

section), shifting from hopeful expectancy to frustrated disillusionment, merit a more detailed examination.

Almost immediately after its launching in early 1817, the *Black
Dwarf* devoted prime space to an elaborate appeal to the 'middle
class', titled 'The Folly of the Middle Classes, in Supporting the
Present System'. Anticipating John Wade's *Gorgon*, the *Black
Dwarf* too acknowledged the tug of war over the hearts of the
'middle class', who had been blinded to its real interests as well
as to its true beneficial role in society. Like *The Gorgon*, this
language was in tension with the *Black Dwarf*'s more fundamental
perception of politics as a battle between the privileged classes
and the government, on the one hand, and the people on the
other; a tension which the periodical glossed over in a masterful
rhetorical manoeuvre:

> The *rabble* in high life, and the *rabble* in low life differ only in dress.
> Their intellects are quite on a par, and they are equally mischievous
> when they take the lead. The *people* are distinct from both; that title
> should unite the thinking and honest portion of all classes: and they
> form a body too numerous to be conquered, too wise to be deceived.
> In this body should be found all the middling classes, as in their
> natural sphere.[35]

If the people were *all* a political middle, then it became possible
for the *Black Dwarf* to single out for particular notice the 'natural'
position of a virtuous 'middle class'. Yet this 'middle-class idiom',
like Wade's, was conditional. The 'middling classes' were faced
with a choice: '*Against* the people . . . they can only succeed by
ruining themselves. *With* the people, they can at any time arrest
the progress of those evils' that were already subverting the
constitution. Turning the tables on the 'middle-class idiom', as
it were, the *Black Dwarf* was now holding it to the 'middle
class' as a bill to redeem. The prescriptive implications of the
'middle-class idiom' were no longer directed at other components
of society, but instead at the 'middle class' itself.

The significance of the *Black Dwarf*'s appeal to the respectable
'middle class', and the potential tension between such an appeal
and its radical stance, were not lost on Wooler's rivals. In the
following months two conservative political caricatures were quick
to turn it to their own advantage. In a political cartoon recently

---

[35] *Black Dwarf* 1:3, 12 February 1817, col. 37.

Figure 9. George Cruikshank's 'A Patriot Luminary Extinguishing Noxious
Gas!!!', 26 February 1817. *Source*: BMC 12867A.

described as 'one of the most damaging of the anti-radical prints'
(see figure 9), George Cruikshank ably argued for the non-
viability of a political middle at that moment. The print depicted
Brougham employing a fire extinguisher in order to put out the
radical gas container, headed by Cobbett, Hunt and others;
suggesting that the moderates would ultimately be forced to
confront the radical monster which they themselves had helped
create. At the centre of the image Cruikshank conspicuously
placed the *Black Dwarf*'s 'Folly of the Middling Classes Supporting Their Government' (not quite the original title, but close); by
thus exposing the implications of the radical bid for 'middle-class'
support, he evidently hoped to alienate the latter from the radical
cause and pull them to the other side. The following year the
same address could be found at the centre of yet another of

Figure 10. Cruikshank's 'One More Parody!!! on the Frontispiece to 1ˢᵗ Vol. of Black Dwarf' (detail). A satyr (derived, presumably, from the ancient confusion between satyr and satire) holds a rope around the neck of the Black Dwarf (with the features of T. J. Wooler). A fool's cap is pulled over the latter's eyes, as if in preparation for a hanging. The satyr holds a conspicuous scroll: 'Folly of Loyalty in the Middling Classes'. (Knahskiurcegroeg, i.e. George Cruikshank, April 1818) *Source*: BMC 12988.

Cruikshank's prints, again attempting to wrest the 'middle class' from the radical pull (see figure 10).[36]

While editing the *Black Dwarf*, Wooler ran as a candidate for parliament in Coventry and Hull in the general elections of 1818. Interestingly, a speech made during the Coventry campaign in support of Wooler, by one Peter Walker, revealed the same tension in fitting the 'middle class' into a basically dual political

---

[36] M. D. George, *Catalogue of Political and Personal Satires Preserved in the Department of Prints and Drawings in the British Museum*, vol. IX, London, 1949, nos. 12867A, 12988. Cruikshank's print is reproduced and thus described in H. T. Dickinson, *Caricatures and the Constitution 1760–1832*, Cambridge, 1986, p. 238.

struggle. On the one hand, Walker asserted that Wooler would
be 'a rock of support to the people', 'the greatest assistant and
protector of that body against which the aristocracy would direct
their greatest exertion'. But while the political contenders were
thus clearly presented as 'people' versus 'aristocracy', the speaker
went on to describe Wooler himself as 'a man of sterling merit
and independence, coming from the middle rank of society, in
which there was more honest worth than in any other'.[37] Just as
in the pages of the *Black Dwarf*, this assertion of Wooler's merits
was an attempt to enlist the 'middle-class idiom' on the side of
the people in a binary struggle. The 'middle class' was relevant
to personal political virtues, but not to the overall political
agenda.

Then, by mid-1819, came the ultimate closure and the angry
disillusionment. Two and a half years after its bid for the support
of the 'middle class', the *Black Dwarf* too admitted defeat. Already
several weeks before Peterloo, an essay revealingly titled 'The
Superior Virtue of the "LOWER ORDERS"' signalled the forthcoming onslaught on the pretensions of the 'middle class'. The
author did not mince words: 'There is nothing', he summarily
declared, which 'disgusts me so much as the meanness of what
are called the middle classes.'[38] The essay went on to sketch
their character in some detail, as selfish, penny-conscious and
materialistic, having 'no other ideas than what are comprised in
eating, drinking, sleeping, and putting on their clothes'. For the
'middle class', it asserted in a vein very similar to that of
Mackenzie of Newcastle a few months later, 'money is the universal cry', as if they believe 'that it was freedom, and virtue, and
energy, and courage – the great one thing needful'. Having
forsaken all political virtues by their 'culpable negligence' (a
term also used by Wade), and having turned alarmists and
anti-reformists, the 'middle class' betrayed the lower classes. Yet
the latter were hardly weakened by it: the ministers, boasted the
Black Dwarf, trembled from the resolution of the lower classes,

---

[37] Speech of Peter Walker, in a meeting chaired by Major Cartwright: quoted in *Examiner*
547, 21 June 1818, p. 392.
[38] *Black Dwarf* 3:25, 23 June 1819, cols. 415–16. Note in passing the tenacious clause
'what are called' appended yet again to the category of 'middle class', ever betraying
its uncertainty.

but – being aware of the political nature of the 'middle class' – 'cared nothing for the *respectful* petitions of the middling slaves'.[39]

The events at St Peter's Fields initially gave the *Black Dwarf* new hope that the 'middle class' would awaken to the iniquities of the system. It was given (in terms closely echoing *The Gorgon* of the previous year) the benefit of the doubt for being cowardly yet honest: 'The middle orders . . . are disposed to be quiet, not out of affection to the system, which they detest most sincerely, since it has been unmasked at Manchester, but out of fear for themselves. But although they will not attack, they will never defend the system.'[40] At the same time, these events also reinforced the basic representation of the social and political fissure as one between two – and only two – clearly delineated camps: 'The operation of the present system, has been to *divide* the interests of the *higher* and *lower orders*. We use the common terms, to be understood without circumlocution.' Put differently, 'the people begin to divide themselves from their oppressors and deluders'; and as they failed to find other allies, 'it is essential that the people should depend only and solely upon THEMSELVES'. It became clear that 'PUBLIC OPINION! THE TYRANT'S GREATEST FOE, EXCEPT HIMSELF', which the *Black Dwarf* repeatedly hailed at this juncture, was explicitly and exclusively nothing else but the voice of 'the working classes'.[41]

The backlash against the seemingly perfidious 'middle class' was especially fierce. 'There is not a more destructive characteristic of the system, under which we groan', asserted one article, than the degeneration of the 'middle class'; it sank 'into the slough of ignorant venality, in which they have been struggling with each other through the filth for what they might chance to grope up from the bottom'. Elsewhere the *Black Dwarf* declared:

Unfortunately, the *middle classes* of society have been subjected to the operation of such a grinding system of oppression for so many years,

---

[39] Compare the even stronger statement two years later: 'The ministers know what the middling classes are. They know their timidity, and the unmeaning ineffectual dilatoriness of their movements.' (Ibid., 6:15, 11 April 1821, col. 509.)

[40] Ibid., 3:41, 13 October 1819, col. 668.

[41] Ibid., 3:52, 29 December 1819, col. 842 (see also the letter from the Black Dwarf in col. 846); 5:15, 11 October 1820, cols. 521–2; 4:1, 12 January 1820, col. 3; 6:12, 21 March 1821, cols. 417ff.

that those who ought to swell the *middle ranks* are reduced to a scale of degradation, of which the lowest were wont to be ashamed.[42]

Their wealth, it continued, was predicated on the misfortunes of others, yet 'all their sympathies for the sufferers are lost in the appropriation of the spoil'. They lacked courage, political conviction and principles, and were inextricably implicated in the prevailing system; consequently, 'if the *middle classes* were to be considered as the *nation*' – that is, if they were ever given the power to endanger 'public liberty' – they would guarantee the perpetuity of Tory misrule.

There was no further doubt: once again, as in the 1790s, the 'middle class' was associated exclusively with one political camp. With regard to its possible inclusion in 'the People', it had made its choice. The same verdict was reached by one of the *Black Dwarf*'s correspondents, 'True Blue' of Newcastle. His denunciation of the 'middle class' replicated the others so closely, as to almost appear as a new political topos. 'Moral and political principles are eagerly sacrificed to the dagon of lucre', he declared; 'Talk not of the worth and independence of the *middle ranks*. It does not exist.'

Lost to every sentiment of liberal humanity, they naturally look upon all pursuits as vain and foolish which do not terminate in some pecuniary advantage. It is not virtue – it is not courage – it is not public spirit, they admire; it is the gorgeous unsubstantial edifice of public credit.[43]

They knew nothing of freedom, of true honour, of real talents, of integrity, of sympathy with the suffering, of patriotism; instead, they supported repression and oppression, including – interestingly, in view of the image of 'middle-class' politics perpetuated later by historians – 'Laws restricting the freedom of trade'. Their vacuous charade as 'the natural defenders of the labouring classes', 'True Blue' asserted contemptuously, was exposed at the Manchester massacre: 'Was it the middle classes; the pretended elect, the independent – the enlightened men of England, that rushed for-

---

[42] Ibid., 6:15, 11 April 1821, col. 503 (and see to 505): from here was also taken the second epigraph on p. 200; 7:11, 12 September 1821, cols. 366–7. Note that the *Black Dwarf* too was using 'middle classes' (or 'middling classes'), 'middle ranks', and 'middle orders' interchangeably.

[43] Ibid., 7:6, 8 August 1821, cols. 206ff.: 'Where Does the Old English Spirit Exist?', signed by 'True Blue', Newcastle, 9 July 1821. Here, too, 'middle classes' and 'middle ranks' were interchangeable.

ward, and boldly vindicated the rights of outraged humanity, regardless of the frowns and threats of power?' Of course not. 'In short,' 'True Blue' concluded, 'taking the middle ranks in England as a body, what do they present but a disgusting mass of meanness, hypocrisy, and cowardice?' Strong words indeed.

Finally, the abrupt closure brought about by Peterloo was intriguingly evident in the writing of that inimitable master of popular journalism, William Cobbett, the man who has been credited with having '*created* this Radical intellectual culture . . . [he] provided a common means of exchange between the experiences of men of widely differing attainments'.[44] At the end of the decade Cobbett addressed two public letters to the 'middle class' in his *Political Register*: the first he had written from his self-imposed exile in America in September 1819, a few days before receiving the news of Peterloo, and the second in August 1820 (having returned to England), after the popular movement had in effect ground to a halt. The difference between them was striking.

In the earlier letter Cobbett – no different from other radicals in the late 1810s – was trying to stir the 'middle classes', who 'stand aloof', to support the Reform sought by '*the people*'. In underscoring the benefits which they too would derive from reform, Cobbett was avowedly trying to counteract the pull of his opponents' rhetoric, whose effect was to '*make the Middle Class keep aloof from the Labouring Class*'.[45] By Cobbett's second letter, however, this tug of war had been resolved. 'That the system has been upheld', he joined the chorus of indignant radicals, 'has been owing to the apathy of the middle classes of the community'. Not only did the 'middle class' do nothing to change the system, it was 'actively instrumental' in its spiteful repression of its critics. His accusing finger was relentless:

You have all along been crying out against the danger of reform . . . you applauded Sidmouth who applauded the Magistrates and Yeomanry of Manchester . . . You have quietly and even complaisantly seen your countrymen sent off to jail . . . You preferred being slaves to others;

---

[44] Thompson, *The Making of the English Working Class*, p. 746.
[45] *Cobbett's Political Register* 35:12, 13 November 1819, cols. 353–58, 373. The letter was dated 24 September 1819, and was followed by another to Henry Hunt, dated 26 September 1819, in which Cobbett announced having 'just got a short account of the "*Manchester Murders*"' (col. 375).

you cared not for this, so long as it gave you the power of domineering over another class.[46]

A hopeful vision of mutual cooperation as the productive forces of 'the people' gave way to one of explicit class war. As far as Cobbett's working class was concerned, the 'middle class' had become an enemy beyond redemption.

But more than anywhere, the transformed understanding of the political character of the 'middle class' was betrayed in the respective titles of Cobbett's two public letters. His first letter, as yet full with hope and optimism, Cobbett addressed 'To THE MIDDLE CLASSES OF ENGLAND. On the benefits which Reform would produce to them'. How telling was the change which took place by Cobbett's second letter, less than a year later, now addressed resignedly 'To THE MIDDLE CLASS of PEOPLE, (Who are enemies of Reform)'.

THE TRANSFORMATION OF 'MIDDLE-CLASS' VIRTUES

Neither will plain people, in the *Middle ranks* of life, withdraw their valuable and bounden allegiance [to the King]. They have large reasons for forbearance with the occasional excesses, for admiration at the arduous cares, for gratitude to the general texture and tendency of established governments . . . In this class of Your Majesty's subjects the virtue and the strength of the Empire mainly rest. From this class, therefore, may support be expected with confidence. Slow to evil, but never hesitating in a righteous cause, they are less likely to be seduced from it by those whom a righteous cause has ceased to influence. (Conservative declaration of loyalty to the new King, 1821)[47]

We have arrived once again at a point of closure, when the notion of 'middle class' – endowed with specific meaning and relevance by the political configuration of this particular moment – became associated once more with certain political options but barred from others. Only that a quarter of a century

---

[46] Ibid., 37:5, 19 August 1820, cols. 289–90, 301–3; the letter was prompted by the trial of Queen Caroline. Viscount Sidmouth was Liverpool's Home Secretary from 1812 to 1822.

[47] *The Declaration of the People of England to Their Sovereign Lord the King*, London, 1821, pp. 38–9. This pamphlet (dated 10 January 1821) was strongly conservative: anti-radical, anti-Whig, warning against the prevalent spirit of insubordination and recommending more stringent repression.

earlier, when the language of 'middle class' had been circumscribed to anti-ministerial opposition, its proponents anchored
the 'middle class's' claim to fame in its notorious independence
and stubborn defence of liberty against elite corruption and
creeping despotism; virtues which for the later proponents of the
'middle class', advancing its 'tame' political image, could hardly
have carried the same appeal.

Indeed they did not. With sometimes striking rapidity, the
vaunted 'middle-class' virtues of yesteryear were discarded in
favour of new and different ones. The most notable casualty of
this metamorphosis was the notion of 'independence'. For James
Mackintosh in 1818, it was certainly true that the 'middle class'
possessed 'the largest share of sense and virtue'; but it was at
the same time also true (and hardly incompatible) that

this sound and pure body have more to hope from the favour of
Government, than any other part of the nation. The higher classes
may, if they please, be independent of its influence. The lower are
almost below its direct action. On the middling classes, it acts with
concentrated and unbroken force.[48]

A far cry from the proudly independent 'middle class' of the
former Friends of Peace, Mackintosh's 'middle class' turned out
to be precisely the opposite – the most dependent of all.

In Mackintosh's eyes this state of affairs still appeared somewhat 'unfortunate'; just as its peculiar political timidity – a far
cry from its alleged stance as courageous defenders of liberty –
appeared to him somewhat circumspect.[49] Others, however, were
happy to abandon 'independence' more wholeheartedly. 'It is
the middle class', a London tradesman proclaimed in 1819, 'that
is useful', and therefore singularly happy; whereas, by contrast,
'raise a man to independence and he is useless, and a curse to
society; sink him below work, and he is wretched and useless'.
Or hear Henry Brougham contrast the 'middle classes', among
whom 'the most respectable opinions, both as to honesty and
sound sense, are to be found', with the 'inferior ranks', who
were 'daily becoming more . . . independent in their views'; views
which surely did not appear to Brougham quite as praise-

---

[48] *Edinburgh Review* 31, December 1818, p. 192.
[49] See above, p. 183.

worthy.[50] The *Examiner* concurred: the 'unsocial disposition' of the people in America, it reported, was found by one astute observer to be 'owing to the complete independence of each other, felt even by the lowest class'. The consequences were inevitably detrimental for the social and political order: 'This spirit of independence is often carried to a pernicious extreme, and destroys a proper social subordination.'[51]

Elsewhere the *Examiner* made another move, perhaps more significant in the long run for the political devaluation of 'independence'. In asserting in 1817 that 'independence is the goal of the professional and trading parts of the community', what the *Examiner* had in mind (as it further explained) was not a political characteristic, but rather economic self-sufficiency, aspiring to which gave meaning to 'their enterprise and perseverance'.[52] This dissociation of political from economic independence divested this vaunted virtue from its political edge. The same move was therefore also latched upon by disappointed radicals, intent on repudiating the old proud image of the 'middle class'. Why is it, puzzled the *Black Dwarf* sarcastically in one discussion of the 'middle class', 'that the more independent a man is said to be in point of fortune, the more servile he becomes to any system under which he lives'? Economic independence, it insisted, in fact 'operate[s] in so singular a method to promote slavery' – a carefully calculated choice of words. In fact radicals echoed Mackintosh's appraisal of the position of the 'middle class', though in much more critical terms. Since they 'have acquired their wealth and importance under what is denominated the Pitt System', wrote John Wade, the 'middling classes' 'look to that system with a sort of filial gratitude as the author of their being'.[53]

---

[50] [William Andrew], *Letter from a Tradesman in London, to His Uncle, a Farmer in Yorkshire*, [London], [1819], p. 13. *Edinburgh Review* 37, November 1822, p. 404: Brougham used this distinction to argue for limited 'middle-class' enfranchisement.

[51] *Examiner* 568, 15 November 1818, p. 722. Compare the remark of a county magistrate many years later, in asserting the mutual interdependence of the agricultural and the trading interests: 'He disliked the term *independence*, whether applied to individuals, countries, or nations; for it had pleased God to make us all dependent upon each other.' (*The Corn Laws: An Authentic Report of the Late Important Discussions in the Manchester Chamber of Commerce, on the Destructive Effects of the Corn Laws* ..., London, 1839, p. 8, speech of Samuel Fletcher.)

[52] *Examiner* 487, 27 April 1817, p. 261.

[53] [Wade], *The Black Book*, pp. 340–1. *Black Dwarf* 3:25, 23 June 1819, col. 415; and compare 6:15, 11 April 1821, col. 504: 'the enormous expenditure and patronage of

Wealthy perhaps they were, but politically hardly an independent lot.

Now that the 'middle class' was declared innocent of 'independence' in its more political sense, that which posed a potential threat to the prevailing social and political order, other 'middle-class' virtues were brought to the fore in its stead: usefulness, respectability and intelligence. The latter two in particular, which conveyed a sense of responsibility, sound judgment and commitment to stability and order (a sense which strongly permeated the passage in the epigraph to this section), will be seen to have become crucial in the image of the 'middle class' in the following decade, leading to the Reform Bill of 1832.

Likewise, the perception of the role of the 'middle class' in society, positioned as it was at its centre, was transformed as well. In the 1790s, conservatives bent on proving the organic symbiosis of the different components of society highlighted the benevolent paternalistic relationship between patricians and plebeians, between rich and poor; while the champions of the 'middle class' underscored its importance as the protector of the lower orders against the encroachment of the higher ones. Now, once the 'middle class' was enlisted by the anti-radical speakers, they integrated it into their organic view of social relations, and reversed its responsibility from a role of political protection to one of moral correction. As one author put it in 1817, it was up to the '*middle* classes', who were 'more intimately connected with those immediately below them, [and] have felt the strongest sympathies' with them, to 'persever[e] in their benevolent exertions' in order to counteract the malevolent influences to which the lower orders had been exposed.[54] The same substitution of 'middle-class' benevolence for the paternalistic benevolence which had previously characterized dual visions of society proved key to another writer intent upon 'correct[ing] those disorders which exist principally among the lower orders of society'. It was the 'middle class', he wrote in 1821, to which 'the poor are accus-

the government, swells the list of the middling classes with the mere minions of the local authorities, who are the minions of the system'.

[54] Thomas Williams, *Constitutional Politics: Or the British Constitution Vindicated* . . ., London, 1817, pp. 14–15. Like many others, this author too found it necessary to explicate what he meant by the 'middle classes' – those who 'form the second portion of the pyramid of society, (namely, tradesmen, master-mechanics, &c.)'

tomed to look for instruction and employment', that bore most directly the 'moral responsibility' in society. Therefore, 'as they are the strongest links in the chain of society, which connect the rich and the poor together, their influence and example are of the first consequence to the order, health, and well-being of the social body'. Rather than joining forces with the lower orders in order to guard them against oppression from without, the 'middle class' was now expected to apply its own moral force in order to guard the lower orders against their depravity from within.[55]

As always, much of the change was a matter of emphasis. Consider for example the case of James Bicheno, the only son of James Bicheno Sr whom we have encountered as a Dissenting Friend of Peace in the 1790s. On the one hand, there was a marked continuity between the statement made by Bicheno Jr in 1817, that whereas the 'middle class' constituted 'the vital core of society', 'there is at the two extremes a want of competition of moral qualities', and his father's hope for 'the greatest share of virtue and piety' to be found in the 'middle class' when not infected with the 'follies and vices of the two extremes'. On the other hand, there was a distinct shift in the implications of these statements in their respective texts. Bicheno Sr, writing in 1795, incorporated his own 'middle-class idiom' into an anti-government sermon intended to force a policy change upon the ministry; whereas for Bicheno Jr, twenty-two years later, the 'moral worth in the middle classes' (guaranteed, to be sure, by their peculiar amenability to the 'tribunal of public opinion') was not contrasted primarily with the lax morals of the upper class, but rather with the 'accumulating mass of dissoluteness and delinquency' among the lower classes.[56] As the language of

[55] William Davis, *Hints to Philanthropists: Or, a Collective View of Practical Means for Improving the Condition of the Poor and Labouring Classes of Society*, Bath, 1821, pp. vi–vii, 155. Moreover, even the older notion of the protection of the lower orders against oppression could be turned around: 'The poor are so protected by the middle classes', asserted one vehement anti-reform writer, that they simply 'could not be in danger of what is properly called oppression', and therefore their recent actions could in no way be justified. (*The Oppositionist: Or, Reflections on the Present State of Parties* . . ., London, 1820, p. 54.) This claim was in fact grafted at the end of a long pamphlet in which only stark dual social language predominated; indicating again the advantage to which the anti-radical camp could put the language of 'middle class' in the aftermath of Peterloo, even for a writer whose habitual social vision had no use for it whatsoever.

[56] J[ames] Bicheno, *A Word in Season: Or, a Call to the Inhabitants of Great Britain, to Stand Prepared for the Consequences of the Present War* . . ., London, 1795, p. 25 (see above,

'middle class' descended from father to son, its effective political sting and pedagogic consequence, as it were, descended from the higher to the lower classes.

Finally, the 'middle-class idiom' was also divested of its political poignancy more generally by reverting back to its philosophical eighteenth-century form, in which the middle state was commended as conducive to the utmost happiness of the individual. Not that this idea was altogether alien to those pronouncements of the 'middle-class idiom' that had previously posed serious political challenges. Yet making it central to the celebration of a 'middle class' could have strong establishmentarian implications: not only by substituting an individual private benefit of belonging to a 'middle class' for a broader social agenda, but also by investing the 'middle class' with a strong stake in the present system. Let us return to the strongly conservative declaration of loyalty that opened this section, in which the virtues of the 'middle class' – first and foremost its sound judgment – were inseparable from 'forbearance', 'admiration' and 'gratitude' to established government. It was certainly no coincidence that this passage was accompanied by the following evaluation of its position:

They [the middle ranks] are in that enviable state where man, if he knew his own interest, would desire to be; where his cares are brought into the smallest compass, and his comforts stretch to their widest extent; where he is in the enjoyment of as much of the good as this world affords, with as little of its evil; and where, if his ambitions run in a narrow channel, his temptations suffer a proportional confinement.[57]

Nobody, therefore, was less likely to rock the boat. It was this enviable middle state, focused on the interests and pleasure of the individual, that guaranteed the loyalty of the 'middle class'. Far from flaunting virtues which might lead the 'middle class' to endorse political action and political change, such a representation of the merits of its current situation readily led to assertions of its strong vested interest in upholding the social and political order.

On the one hand, the perception of the 'middle class' as

---

pp. 52–3). J[ames] E[benezer] Bicheno, *An Inquiry into the Nature of Benevolence . . .*, London, 1817, pp. 3–5.

[57] *The Declaration of the People of England to Their Sovereign Lord the King*, pp. 38–9.

displayed in this loyalist declaration of 1821 was the culmination of the 'taming' process which has been the subject of the last two chapters; a process induced by changing political circumstances that led to a gradual digression from the rigid patterns of the late 1790s, and ultimately (following a period of considerable fluidity) resulted in a different but no less rigid pattern by the aftermath of Peterloo. On the other hand, however, by 1821 this perception of the 'middle class' was also crucially implicated in another political trend, one that was about to gain much momentum over the subsequent fifteen years, and that invested the language of 'middle class' with even higher political stakes. This important new development, that was key to the triumphant phase in the power of the particular conceptualization of society centred around a 'middle class', is where the next part of our story begins.

PART III

With the tide

CHAPTER 7

The social construction of the 'middle class'

A crucial if elusive change in British constitutional politics occurred at the beginning of the 1820s. It was that kind of moment, notes John Cannon, when a movement – here, for parliamentary reform – 'changes from a crusade to become an accepted creed'; a moment when 'suddenly, often within a surprisingly short period, resistance crumbled'; a moment when the opposition, while still formidable, assumed the air of 'fighting for a lost cause' (see figure 11).[1] The popular agitations of the previous several years, whether culminating in the events of Peterloo which went out of control or in the support for Queen Caroline which – no less significantly – did not, were unmistakable writing on the wall. They served as catalysts for a fast-spreading realization that some form of reform must be undertaken, if for no other reason than to prevent worse upheavals due to extraparliamentary pressures. 'Do not you think', wrote Robert Peel to John Croker in March 1820, 'that there is a feeling, becoming daily more general and more confirmed . . . in favor of some undefined change in the mode of governing of this country?'[2] Croker himself, later a notorious opposer of the Reform Bill, could hardly fail to notice this recent change of mood: 'at tables where ten years ago you would have no more heard reform advocated than treason', he wrote in 1822, 'you will now find half the company reformers'. Reform had 'got into the people's

---

[1] J. Cannon, *Parliamentary Reform 1640–1832*, Cambridge, 1973, pp. 182–3.
[2] Peel to Croker, 23 March 1820; in L. J. Jennings (ed.), *The Croker Papers: The Correspondence and Diaries of the Late Right Honourable John Wilson Croker . . .*, New York, 1884, vol. 1, p. 156. Peel continued: 'Can we resist – I mean, not next session or the session after that – but can we resist for seven years Reform in Parliament? . . . And if reform cannot be resisted, is it not more probable that Whigs and Tories will unite, and carry through moderate reform, than remain opposed to each other?'

Figure 11. 'Symptoms of Reform', March 1822. The Tory ministry's anti-reform position has become precariously unstable: the ground under their feet, supported by the heads of Liverpool and Londonderry (Castlereagh), is ominously shrinking. (The occasion for this print was a vote on retrenchment in the navy, 1 March 1822, lost by the administration 182 to 128 – as denoted on the rope pulling the ministers to the edge.) *Source*: BMC 14358.

marrow', observed John Russell in a similar though less troubled vein, 'and nothing will now take it out'.[3]

It was during these years that many political figures, in particular Whigs, who previously had been either opposed to reform or lukewarm in their support, came now – like 'that tiny shift of pebbles that anticipates the avalanche' – to stand actively behind it.[4] The harbinger of the new political wave was the reform of the rotten borough of Grampound in 1821, in the eyes of John Russell 'the beginning of the end of the old representative system': for the first time in generations a borough lost its representation through delinquency, and its seats in parliament were redistributed (transferred to the county of York). Tellingly, what appeared to dismay the Tory Prime Minister Lord Liverpool in the Grampound proceedings was the changed attitude of his own backbenchers, 'the idle conceit of the Country Gentlemen that a temperate Reform would put an end to grievances and distress'.[5] The fast-spreading malady seemed to know no bounds.

And yet, the new converts to reform were on the whole far from radical. The 'liberal' interpretations of reform that were to carry the day for the next decade were basically conservative (using the word loosely): conservative in their objectives, which

---

[3] Lord John Russell to Lord Normanby, 30 December 1821: quoted in P. Mandler, *Aristocratic Government in the Age of Reform: Whigs and Liberals, 1830–1852*, Oxford, 1990, p. 61. Croker is quoted in Cannon, *Parliamentary Reform*, p. 183. Compare also *Manchester Guardian* 3:92, 1 February 1823, approving of 'the rapid manner in which the principles of reform are spreading amongst us, but especially amongst the upper classes of the community ... we daily see so many men of rank and consequence in the country, recanting their former opinions, and avowing themselves converts to reform'. Also see very similarly *Leeds Mercury* 54:2908, 3 March 1821. D. Fraser, 'The Agitation for Parliamentary Reform', in J. T. Ward (ed.), *Popular Movements c. 1830–1850*, London, 1970, pp. 32–4. And for the parallel realization among radicals, of 'the march of progress of those principles of Reform' (as formulated in a radical dinner in May 1823), see J. Ann Hone, *For the Cause of Truth: Radicalism in London 1796–1821*, Oxford, 1982, pp. 358–60.

[4] Cannon, *Parliamentary Reform*, p. 183. See A. Mitchell, 'The Whigs and Parliamentary Reform Before 1830', *Historical Studies* 12 (1965), pp. 22–42. Idem, *The Whigs in Opposition 1815–1830*, Oxford, 1967, p. 167; and generally chapter 7. E. A. Wasson, 'The Great Whigs and Parliamentary Reform, 1809–1830', *Journal of British Studies* 24 (1985) pp. 434–64. Mandler, *Aristocratic Government in the Age of Reform*, p. 22. And see examples below, pp. 253–5.

[5] This was the assessment of Liverpool's indignation by William Huskisson in a letter to George Canning, 20 February 1821; quoted in J. E. Cookson, *Lord Liverpool's Administration: The Crucial Years 1815–1822*, Hamden, 1975, p. 306. Russell is quoted in A. Briggs, 'The Background of the Parliamentary Reform Movement in Three English Cities, 1830–1832', in *The Collected Essays of Asa Briggs*, Urbana, 1985, vol. I, pp. 181–2. The Grampound Act came into effect in 1826.

were to secure political stability and prevent more drastic political upheavals; and conservative in their underlying understanding of representation, which disavowed any claims based on natural rights. Representation, in this view, was not founded on the rights of individuals to participate in the electoral process. It was based on a conception of society as consisting of different interests or sectors, each of which needed to have a voice in parliament. Reform could therefore be presented as anything but a radical break in the basis of representation. Quite the contrary, it could be justified as a necessary adjustment of the electoral map to a new composition of society, always in accordance with the perennial principles of the constitution.

It was for this political move, intended to counteract popular pressures without conceding to popular demands, that the 'middle class' became singularly valuable. The 'middle class' – by now confirmed as 'tame', anti-popular and committed to political stability – could readily be made to fulfil the part of that social sector for which such an adjustment of the electoral map was required. This use of the notion of 'middle class' had important consequences: it was no longer grounded in the ancient and perhaps diminished role of the 'middle class' in the balance of the constitution, nor in the venerable virtues of the middle station. Instead, it was crucially predicated upon the representation of the 'middle class' as *a new and rising social constituency*, that is, upon its identification as an expanding component of society that had not been there previously and therefore was not accommodated by the present electoral system. Only thus could limited reform be justified as 'updating' the constitutional system without fundamentally tampering with the constitution. The political logic of this particular moment, therefore, produced a crucial stake in portraying the 'middle class' – whoever they were – as *the outcome of unprecedented and discontinuous social transformations*. Like the 1790s, a very specific understanding of a 'middle class' (one which was at the same time very different from that of the 1790s) proved to be peculiarly suitable for the specifics of a particular political agenda; but unlike that of the 1790s, this agenda of the 1820s was about to become a powerful winner – which made all the difference in the final outcome.

From 1820 onwards, therefore, two key – linked – developments suddenly became conspicuous: the coupling of 'middle class' with social change and the coupling of 'middle class' with demands for parliamentary representation. Importantly, neither of these associations had previously appeared natural or self-evident. But before we proceed to demonstrate these new developments in more detail, one further point of clarification is in order. The present argument should not be construed too simplistically. In the case of both developments, it is not suggested that this particular understanding of the 'middle class' was an altogether opportunistic invention, sprung *ex nihilo* and imposed arbitrarily upon people's perceptions of society and politics. On the contrary, in both cases this particular understanding dovetailed nicely with people's growing realization of new features of the world around them. It suited their increasing awareness of the transforming consequences of social change, as well as their increasing awareness of the transformation of the political map, especially due to the growing political weight of the manufacturing districts. But here again lies the crucial point which distinguishes the present argument from the familiar historical account of these changes and their consequences. In both cases, that of a more dynamic understanding of society and that of a more dynamic understanding of the political playing field, there was no a priori reason – let alone an inevitable logic – for understanding and articulating these new features in terms of a rising 'middle class'; so we still have to account for the fact that they were. Once again, my emphasis is on the degree of freedom which existed in the space between the (changing) social and political reality and its representation; and it is here that the logic of the political configuration of this moment becomes important, in order to explain the decisive appeal of one very specific choice made within this space of plausible representations.

THE 'MIDDLE CLASS' AND SOCIAL CHANGE: FROM MUTUAL ESTRANGEMENT TO HAPPY UNION

The commercial system has long been undermining the distinction of ranks in society . . .

If the manufacturing system continues to be extended, increasing as it necessarily does increase the number, the misery, and the depravity

of the poor ... the tendency of the present system is to lessen the
middle class and to increase the lower ones.

(Robert Southey, 1807)

The middle class, increases in greater ratio than the lower class. . .

The middle class arises ... from the creation of capital made by
commerce or manufactures. In no country in Europe have these been
so flourishing as in England; in no country in Europe has more capital
been created, or does a more extensive middle-class exist. (William
Mackinnon, 1828)[6]

Social change was hardly a novelty in Britain of the 1820s. It
had already been an important feature of social and economic
life for at least a century, manifested in those (interrelated)
developments which historians have dubbed the 'agricultural
revolution', the 'market revolution', the 'consumer revolution',
the 'communications revolution' and of course the 'industrial
revolution'. As Paul Langford has recently reminded us, 'no
student of eighteenth-century life can safely ignore the immense
changes which affected it, or contemporary awareness of those
changes'.[7] This contemporary awareness could take the form of
an optimistic emphasis on 'improvement' – intertwined with
Scottish views of progress, or with Arthur Young's enthusiasm
for agricultural entrepreneurship, or with Whig apologias for
commercial society, or with the new provincial urban culture; or
it could take a more pessimistic form, whether in apprehensions
about the corrupting effects of commercialization, in a preoccupation with the causes of the decline of empires, in concerns
about the disruptive consequences of mechanization, or in a
Malthusian pessimism about demographic growth.

So the British by the 1810s and 1820s had already been well
accustomed to social change. Nevertheless, the period after the
wars saw what was probably an unprecedented qualitative leap in
people's awareness of the processes of social change unravelling
around them, and in their articulation and comprehension of these
transformations. Even if we accept historians' current gradualist
perspective on industrialization, we can still concede together with

---

[6] [Robert Southey], *Letters from England: By Don Manuel Alvarez Espriella. Translated from
the Spanish*, London, 1807; rep. edn, ed. J. Simmons, London, 1951, pp. 367, 375–6.
[William A. Mackinnon], *On the Rise, Progress, and Present State of Public Opinion, in
Great Britain, and Other Parts of the World*, London, 1828 (rep. Shannon, 1971), pp. 1, 5.
[7] P. Langford, *Public Life and the Propertied Englishman 1689–1798*, Oxford, 1991, p. [v].

Maxine Berg that 'even so, it must be admitted that the shocks of a rapid process of mechanisation were there'. To contemporaries, Berg observes, it seemed evident that economic and technological transformations of the 1820s and 1830s were more rapid and discontinuous than those of any previous period. Berg argues further that this awareness of economic change was encapsulated in the debate on 'the machinery question', bringing it to the consciousness of broad social classes; it was no less than 'a national debate'. The importance of the machine at this juncture, it may be added, was not primarily due to its role as the primary mover of particular changes in the economy; in some sectors machines had already been introduced a generation earlier, while in numerous others – as Raphael Samuel has documented in detail – the era of the machine was yet as distant as ever.[8] Rather, the importance of the machine lay in its emergence as the symbol of the abruptness of current social processes entailed by industrialization and of their potential disruptive consequences. It thus came to stand for an overall uneasiness about the irreversible disjunctures effected by social change, which were brought to the nation's attention once the war had ended, and which could no longer be disregarded. The point was made most clearly in Thomas Carlyle's powerful expression of this uneasiness, the 'Signs of the Times' of 1829. 'Were we required to characterise this age of ours by any single epithet,' he wrote, 'we should be tempted to call it, not an Heroical, Devotional, Philosophical, or Moral Age, but, above all others, the Mechanical Age' (see figure 12).[9]

The increasing awareness of the drama of social change was carried and propagated by new or newly adapted intellectual and institutional vehicles. As E. P. Thompson has written, this

---

[8] M. Berg, *The Machinery Question and the Making of Political Economy 1815–1848*, Cambridge, 1980, pp. 15, 21; see also the contemporary voices in M. Berg and P. Hudson, 'Rehabilitating the Industrial Revolution', *Economic History Review* 45 (1992), p. 26. R. Samuel, 'The Workshop of the World', *History Workshop Journal* 3 (1977), pp. 6–72. The emphasis here is on the breadth and pervasiveness of the machinery debate throughout the nation rather than on its origins. In fact, by the time that the issue of machinery achieved such broad resonance, certain sectors of production had already been struggling with it for quite a while: see A. Randall, *Before the Luddites: Custom, Community and Machinery in the English Woollen Industry, 1776–1809*, Cambridge, 1991.

[9] *Edinburgh Review* 49, June 1829, pp. 441–2. See R. Williams, *Culture and Society 1780–1950*, Harmondsworth, 1984, chapter 5; it was a few years later that Carlyle introduced into English (in his *Sartor Resartus*, 1833–4) the term 'industrialism' to describe the social system resulting from mechanization.

HEAVEN & EARTH.

"Oh! it's very well to Live on the Taxes-but the devil to pay them."

Figure 12. Industrial awareness, 1830. One of the earliest prints pointing to industrialization as a key source of social and political oppression. The regaling tax-eaters (Cobbett's phrase), arching over the image and to the left, are supported by clouds of smoke (marked 'taxes') from the chimneys of factories, whose names emphasize the ubiquity of steam and machinery. The machines have driven the protesting operatives out of work (and to 'Cheap Gin'), as the supplicating woman displaying her starving children (forefront) is being told. This is also one of the earliest prints to highlight the contrast between the rich manufacturer (note the stables and the steam-coach next to 'Engine Hall') and the workers. (Robert Seymour) *Source*: BMC 16189 (detail).

was the decade in which contemporaries were attempting to render the experience of industrialization into theory. 'We hear nothing on all sides,' remarked one observer in 1826, 'at dinners, parties, in church and at the theatre, but discussions on political economy and the distresses of the times.'[10] Political economy, of

[10] Henry Addington to Charles Vaughan, 2 March 1826; quoted in B. Hilton, *The Age of Atonement: The Influence of Evangelicalism on Social and Economic Thought, 1795–1865*,

course, was by now a well-established discipline, with a respectable body of writings which had already achieved the status of 'classics'. But it was in the 1820s that the great popularization of political economy took off, closely linked to the debate on the machinery question.

This development was apparent both in high-brow channels and in an unprecedented flurry of interest among popular working-class circles. Manifestations of the former included various settings such as the Political Economy Club (founded in London in 1821), the remarkably well-attended Ricardo Memorial Lectures on political economy commenced in 1824, the anti-Ricardian group that gathered around William Whewell in Cambridge from the mid-1820s with the intention of developing a modern science of society, the sermons of Thomas Chalmers that brought him into the public eye from 1817 as the formulator of the Christian understanding of political economy, the *Westminster Review* (established in 1824) that propounded the utilitarian views on these subjects, the other major periodicals that also became increasingly preoccupied with them, and the chair of political economy at Oxford University, established in 1825 with Nassau Senior as its first incumbent.[11] John Ramsay McCulloch, the major contributor on economic issues for the *Edinburgh Review* from 1818 onwards and the author of the highly popular *Principles of Political Economy* published in 1825, observed in the same year that 'at present the rage is for Political Economy'.[12] Similarly, the literature of the 1820s has been noted by Marilyn Butler for its 'heightened sociological

Oxford, 1988, p. 36. E. P. Thompson, *The Making of the English Working Class*, London, 1963, p. 711.

[11] This was not the first chair of political economy in Britain: this distinction was reserved for the professorship in political economy established in 1805 for Thomas Malthus in the newly founded East India College. Cambridge had lectures on political economy since 1816, and its first professor on the subject since 1828. For these developments see Hilton, *The Age of Atonement*, chapter 2. One vehicle for this propagation of political economy was Ricardo's influential writings (his acclaimed *Principles of Political Economy* was published in 1817), as well as his presence in parliament since 1819. For the 'unusual vogue' of his ideas both in and out of parliament in the early 1820s, see B. Gordon, *Political Economy in Parliament 1819–1823*, London, 1976; and idem, *Economic Doctrine and Tory Liberalism 1824–1830*, London, 1979 (quoted, p. 10).

[12] McCulloch to Napier, 23 April 1825; quoted in D. P. O'Brien, *J. R. McCulloch: A Study in Classical Economics*, London, 1970, p. 53, n. 6. (McCulloch himself became the first incumbent of the Chair of Political Economy at London University in 1828.) Also in 1825, Charles Greville observed similarly that 'so great and absorbing is the interest which the present discussions excite, that all men are become political economists and financiers'; quoted in Gordon, *Economic Doctrine and Tory Liberalism*, p. 13.

awareness'. Indeed it betrayed a mounting concern for the impact of industrial change (a concern that was soon to spawn numerous industrial novels) already in books such as John Galt's *Annals of the Parish* of 1821, or (more obliquely) in the vogue for nostalgic celebrations of a world that had been lost – 'Merry Old England' – signalled by Walter Scott's *Ivanhoe* (1819) and *Kenilworth* (1821). Industrial histories and lives of inventors were also becoming increasingly popular.[13]

This intensified interest was not confined to high-brow intellectuals. This period, writes Noel Thompson, saw 'the emergence of an anti-capitalist and socialist political economy'; both formally – the writings of the so-called Ricardian Socialists, published mostly in 1824–27 – and at a popular level, manifested most obviously in popularized political economy in the working-class press during the late 1820s and the early 1830s. An important contribution to this popularization was Mrs Marcet's enormously successful *Conversations on Political Economy*, which first appeared in 1816 and went through six editions within a decade. The increasing concern for the consequences of industrial society was evident in Owenism – the most conspicuous of dozens of plans, proposals and theories floated in the wake of the post-war distress – and in the experimental attempts to establish alternative communities in an industrial age. Owen himself dated his own recognition of 'the importance of machinery . . . and its rapid annual improvements' to about 1815; Owenite pamphlets and periodicals began to appear soon thereafter.[14] Institutionally, the propagation of political economy

---

[13] M. Butler, *Romantics, Rebels and Reactionaries: English Literature and Its Background 1760–1830*, Oxford, 1982, p. 182. Berg, *The Machinery Question*, pp. 179–80. On Galt's *Annals of the Parish* as an early – albeit idiosyncratic – industrial novel (preceding their swell in the next couple of decades), see I. Melada, *The Captain of Industry in English Fiction 1821–1871*, Albuquerque, 1970, pp. 14–17; A. R. Divine, 'The Changing Village: Loss of Community in John Galt's *Annals of the Parish*', *Studies in Scottish Literature* 25 (1990), pp. 121–33. Note also Alex Potts's comment (in 'Picturing the Modern Metropolis: Images of London in the Nineteenth Century', *History Workshop Journal* 26 (1988), p. 29 and n. 3) on the darker dramatization of London as an exploding metropolis, which also began in the 1820s.

[14] N. W. Thompson, *The People's Science: The Popular Political Economy of Exploitation and Crisis 1816–1834*, Cambridge, 1984; quoted, p. 35, and Owen's autobiography as cited in p. 73, n. 26. As Neville Kirk has put it, Thompson demonstrates the emergence of 'a *new* mode of discourse which gained greatly in popularity during the late 1820's and early 1830's, increasingly at the expense of non-economic explanations': N. Kirk, 'In Defence of Class: A Critique of Recent Revisionist Writing upon the Nineteenth-Century English Working Class', *International Review of Social History* 32 (1987), p. 16.

was advanced by what Maxine Berg has called 'the scientific movement', epitomized by the Mechanics Institutes, whose heyday was, again, the second half of the 1820s. Brougham, for example, launched a series of lectures on political economy at the London Mechanics Institute in 1825. And in a rural rather than an urban setting, it was around the same time that William Cobbett (together with many others in the countryside) discovered the inroads that 'new-fashioned' farmers, the products of emerging agrarian capitalism, had recently made into the static, benevolent rural society of his youth.[15]

An important factor in awakening this new awareness of economic and social change was government policy. British governments in the eighteenth and early nineteenth centuries had not been greatly concerned with the processes of industrialization or economic transformation. After 1815, however, when faced with the severe problems of the post-war economy, this attitude was replaced with an unprecedented involvement of the state in social and economic matters. The period between 1815 and 1832 was dominated by Tory ministries that became as much concerned with the long-term problem of adjusting to an industrializing economy as with the short-term problem of economic crises. As Boyd Hilton has pointed out, the Liverpool administration (1815–27) was 'the first to strive for a coherent theory of economic policy'; it also marked the transition from treating industrialization as a 'malignant aberration', possibly containable or reversible, to conceding that, for better or for worse, it was inevitable. There were those who believed that economic and social issues were in fact completely transforming politics. Take Lord Holland at the end of 1826: 'Political parties are no more. Whig and Tory, Foxite and Pittite, Minister and Opposition have ceased to be distinctions, but the divisions of classes and great interests are arrayed against each other, – grower and consumer, lands

---

For Owenite writings, see G. Claeys, *Machinery, Money and the Millennium: From Moral Economy to Socialism, 1815–1860*, Princeton, 1987.
[15] Berg, *The Machinery Question*, pp. 145, 166. J. F. C. Harrison, *Learning and Living 1790–1960: A Study in the History of the English Adult Education Movement*, London, 1961, pp. 57ff. I. Dyck, *William Cobbett and Rural Popular Culture*, Cambridge, 1992, esp. chapter 3. Idem, 'William Cobbett and the Rural Radical Platform', *Social History* 18 (1993), p. 188.

and funds, Irish and English, Catholick and Protestant.'[16] Lord Holland was perhaps overreacting, in his consternation (not unreasonable in the calm mid-1820s, but unjustified in light of the developments of the next few years) that economic issues (as well as Ireland) were driving out constitutional ones and blurring political parties. But the point itself was well taken, as demonstrated by the rift that such economic matters had produced between liberal Tories and high Tories. So government policies did much to put economic change on the agenda, indeed to make it into a potent political issue. And the suffusion of the political debate with questions of economic change, propagated in pamphlets, in the press and in published parliamentary proceedings, had an immediate effect on the public. Corn, cash and commerce were now in everyone's political vocabulary, more so than ever before.

By the 1820s, therefore, the confrontation with what came to be perceived as an unprecedented and rapidly changing social and economic reality became increasingly inescapable. 'To come to terms with it', writes Noel Thompson, 'required new tools of analysis, new concepts and new theoretical constructs.'[17] The realization of contemporaries that society around them was in irreversible flux, a realization which had been brewing during many preceding decades and now burst into the open, made people more willing to endorse new, dynamic social views; that is to say, conceptualizations of society in which change and motion played an integral role. Some change in people's understanding of their society, therefore, was bound to happen, and to be given concrete shape with the aid of such new concepts and tools of analysis. Moreover, the extension of government involvement in social and economic matters meant that people's political stakes in their social identities (that is, in those identities through which they saw themselves affected by such government policies) increased. But still, the precise form of these new depar-

---

[16] Holland to Grey, 21 December 1826, quoted in K. G. Feiling, *The Second Tory Party 1714–1832*, London, 1959, appendix, pp. 401–2; and compare Holland's very similar statement in an 1826 letter to his son Henry Fox, as quoted in A. D. Kriegel (ed.), *The Holland House Diaries 1831–1840*, London, 1977, introduction, p. xxv. B. Hilton, *Corn, Cash, Commerce: The Economic Policies of the Tory Governments 1815–1830*, Oxford, 1977; quoted, pp. [vii]–viii. Also Berg, *The Machinery Question*, pp. 39–40. I owe much in this paragraph to Peter Mandler.

[17] N. W. Thompson, *The People's Science*, p. 46; and see also p. 52.

tures in people's social thinking was not determined by this heightened awareness of social change in and of itself. It was not a preordained outcome that such change would be articulated in terms of a rising 'middle class'.

Indeed, formerly this had not necessarily been the case: discussions of social change did not automatically invoke the 'middle class', and discussions of the 'middle class' did not instinctively associate it with social change. Moreover, even when such an association was suggested, the 'middle class' was not necessarily identified as the carrier and beneficiary of this social change. As the two epigraphs at the beginning of this section demonstrate, a priori there was considerable leeway for different – indeed contradictory – representations of the relationship between the 'middle class' and social transformation.

For the most part, up to the end of the war the 'middle class' and social change were simply not deemed to bear much relevance to each other. Thus, during the extensive preoccupation with the 'middle class' in the 1790s, it was overwhelmingly represented as timeless and ahistorical, as a largely static component of society. The 'middle class', asserted its proponents repeatedly, '*has ever been* the source of manners, of population and of wealth'; '*in all ages* [they] have been stedfast to their trust'; and it was they 'who *in former times* were considered as the strength of the country'.[18] The 'middle class' was noted time and again as distinguishing England (rarely Britain) from other nations, but virtually never as distinguishing the present generation from previous ones. Overall, the uses of 'middle-class' language at that juncture communicated a strong sense of stasis, permanence and immutability. Of course, such representations had little to do with the actual novelty of the meanings with which the 'middle class' was infused in the 1790s; a novelty which in itself probably contributed to this insistence on its timelessness. In support of the claim for timelessness the advocates of the 'middle-

---

[18] [Anna Laetitia Barbauld], *An Address to the Opposers of the Repeal* . . ., 1790; [Benjamin Vaughan], *Two Papers by the Calm Observer* . . ., 1795; Hammersmith resolution against the triple assessment, 1797 (my emphases). For these quotes, see above, pp. 25, 54, 114. For Vaughan, note the tension with his tendency to associate the 'middle class' with 'modern times', as pointed out above; but also his reference to the anti-aristocratic influence of the 'middle class' already at the time of Henry VIII, in his *Comments on the Proposed War with France, on the State of Parties, and on the New Act Respecting Aliens* . . . *By a Lover of Peace*, London, 1793, p. 53.

class idiom' invoked the authority of ancient philosophers and of commonplace knowledge which stood the test of time. The virtues of the 'middle class', they averred, were attested to by 'the concurring voice of all nations and all ages, the philosopher, the poet and the moralist'. These virtues were 'a well-known fact' affirmed by the ancient wisdom of Lycurgus, or by the eternal prayer of Agur which was then 'fully justified by experience . . . [and] has long been received and acknowledged'. The 'middle ranks of people' 'have always [been] accounted the most valuable . . . members of society' by 'the wisest politicians (I speak not here [added this writer] of the present times)'. After all, as a timely annotated edition of Aristotle's *Politics* reminded its readers, it was the ancient sage who had already pointed out the connection between 'the preponderancy of the middle ranks' and political moderation, due to 'their ability to defy the pride and oppression of the great, as well as to resist the rapacity and malignity of the vulgar'.[19] The 'middle class' of the 1790s, in sum, was a characteristic – perhaps a vestige – of a distant golden past, rather than the harbinger of a new golden future.

Therefore, if change over time was considered at all, it was not likely to be 'the rise of the middle class' but rather the danger of its decline, the pending doom which now came to threaten this perennial pillar of the social edifice. The word that was uttered perhaps more than any other in the same breath with 'middle class' was 'annihilation': quickly becoming a trope, this phrase expressed the concern of the advocates of the 'middle class' for its imminent demise, which would leave behind only the rich and the poor – thus 'destroy[ing] the present structure of society'.[20] The 'middle class' was presented as hampered, not pampered, by processes of change. And even then, such processes of change as were associated

---

[19] *The Cabinet*, 1795; [Andrew Becket], *Public Prosperity*, 1793; Vicesimus Knox, *The Spirit of Despotism*, 1795; John Aikin's *Athenaeum* 1:2, February 1807, p. 124; see above, pp. 47, 53, 98. For yet another example of the virtues of the 'intermediate classes' over the two social extremes, which 'Philosophers have long considered', see *Edinburgh Review* 20, November 1812, p. 255 (review by Jeffrey). *Aristotle's Ethics and Politics*, trans. and ed. John Gillies, London, 1797, vol. II, pp. 319–20 (editor's introduction to book VII); see also p. 276.

[20] Letter by 'Junius', *Morning Chronicle*, 1797; quoted above, p. 113. See also Raymond Williams's interesting observations on the tendency of 'intermediate [social] groups' to combine nostalgic views of a past golden age with antagonism towards present social change, a tendency which he traces back to the sixteenth century: R. Williams, *The Country and the City*, London, 1985, p. 43.

with the fortunes of the 'middle class' were mostly not *social* processes; it was first and foremost the *political* process which was thought to spell its ruin. It is telling that the single exception to this pattern among the many voices of the 1790s we have encountered came from a very hostile witness, as it were – namely Burke, in his attempt to blame the disruption of French society on the sudden swelling of the 'middle class'.[21]

Accordingly, as we have already noted, 'middle-class' virtues in the 1790s were only rarely grounded in the well-known eighteenth-century vindications of the progress of commercial society. And by the same token, the 'middle class' did not often find its way into discussions of this progress of commercial society. An important test case is the *Edinburgh Review*: given its central role in the 1820s and 1830s in asserting the link between the 'middle class' and the beneficial consequences of social progress, it is significant that the most detailed discussions of social progress during the periodical's earlier years were carried on without any reference to the 'middle class', even in contexts where later such an omission would have been unlikely. These essays were penned by Francis Jeffrey between 1808 and 1812, expounding a view of modern history as a continuous march of progress. The principal actors in Jeffrey's Whiggish storyline were repeatedly 'the common people', those who 'by a great improvement in their education and circumstances, came to acquire a large share of that intelligence, and skill and ambition, which was formerly engrossed by their chieftains'. When society became 'filled from top to bottom with wealth and industry', he repeated elsewhere, the beneficiaries were 'the nation at large'. And when Jeffrey occasionally referred in these essays to the people as the 'lower and middling classes' together, it was still as part of a basic dual framework of 'aristocracy' and 'people' (represented by 'public opinion'): in his narrative at this point the 'middle class' played no meaningful role.[22] This is not to say, of course, that the *Edinburgh* reviewers were surreptitiously *adverse* to the notion

---

[21] Edmund Burke, *Two Letters Addressed to a Member of the Present Parliament, on the Proposals for Peace with the Regicide Directory of France*, 10th edn, London, 1796; quoted above, p. 28.

[22] *Edinburgh Review* 14, July 1809, pp. 291–6; 20, November 1812, p. 327. See similarly 12, July 1808, pp. 275–7 (here actually positing 'the lower and middling orders' as a *counterforce* to the corrupting influences of luxuries emanating from trade); 15, January 1810, pp. 505–6; 17, February 1811, pp. 281–8.

of 'middle class' in discussions of social change.[23] The point, rather, is that they did not automatically or necessarily make any kind of connection between the two.

On the other political side, when Tory writers (like James Stephen and Samuel Taylor Coleridge) began to avail themselves of the language of 'middle class' in the early years of the nineteenth century, they were even more predisposed to presenting it as a timeless component of society which was now under threat. For Coleridge, as we have seen, the 'middle class', 'that greatest blessing and ornament of human nature', was perhaps a product of a progressing civilizing process, but only so in a *longue durée* perspective going back all the way to the middle ages. 'Our ancestors', he also asserted, had already focused their own polity a long time ago on this beneficial social component. And at present, far from partaking in social upheavals, the 'middle class' was in fact endangered by their detrimental consequences.[24] Another Tory in 1812 similarly placed the 'middle class' (rural as well as urban) within a vision of a golden past, one which was now being eroded by social change; and this was also the understanding of the Evan-

---

[23] Thus, when Jeffrey found such a connection suggested in John Millar's *An Historical View of the English Government*, he actually strengthened it further. Millar, despite claims made by some historians on his behalf, did not emphasize the role of the 'middle class' in commercial society, though he occasionally referred to its presence, mostly together with the 'higher ranks' (ibid., 1812 London edn, vol. IV, pp. 205, 212, 305, 314; the 'middle class' also did not figure in Millar's *The Origins of the Distinction of Ranks* . . ., 3rd edn, corrected and enlarged, London, 1781). Whereas Jeffrey (in the *Edinburgh Review* 3, October 1803, pp. 174–5) claimed that Millar had credited 'the rapid improvement in arts and manufactures' with creating the ease, affluence and leisure of 'all the middling classes of the community', Millar in fact had formulated his discussion not with 'middle-class' language but in dual terms, explaining the tendency of commerce and manufactures 'to form two distinct and separate classes of the learned and the ignorant' (Millar, *Historical View*, vol. IV, p. 158; and see essays III–IV, passim). So placing the 'middle class' within the story of social progress was not impossible for Jeffrey; however, as evident in his later essays expounding his own views, neither did he find it particularly compelling. For Millar and the 'middle class', see W. C. Lehmann, *John Millar of Glasgow 1735–1801: His Life and Thought and His Contributions to Sociological Analysis*, Cambridge, 1960, chapter 13. A. O. Hirschman, *The Passions and the Interests: Political Arguments for Capitalism before Its Triumph*, Princeton, 1977, pp. 87–91.

[24] Quoted above, pp. 173, 176. Coleridge's appreciation for the 'middle class' was combined with a critique of 'the moneyed and commercial interests' in familiar country-ideology terms, presented as distinctly separate entities: see *The Collected Works of Samuel Taylor Coleridge: Essays on His Times in The Morning Post and The Courier*, ed. D. V. Erdman, Princeton, 1978, vol. I, p. 139 (*Morning Post*, 30 January 1800) and 143–4 (1 February 1800). For Stephen, see pp. 177–8.

gelical moralist Jane West in 1806. And then of course there was Robert Southey, whose 'middle-class idiom' surpassed any other's in its explicit aversion to social change. The emerging commercial and manufacturing system, Southey warned in the passage quoted at the beginning of this section, will inevitably lead to the destruction of the great 'middle class' (the key element in which was rural); and the disappearance of those 'who were once the strength of England' will make a revolution, heretofore impossible, probable.[25] As Southey saw it in the early years of the nineteenth century, nothing was more antithetical to commercial and industrial progress, and to the advancement of 'improvement', than the 'middle class'. Indeed, for one writer in 1819 it made sense to state that whereas the high prices of provisions were 'very little understood by the middling classes', they made perfect sense 'to the wholesale dealer, to the merchant, to the negotiator of foreign exchanges, to town and country banks' – that is, to the forerunners of commercial society, clearly distinct in this view from the 'middle class'.[26]

The same antithesis surfaced in the late 1810s in Leigh Hunt's *Examiner*. Together with many others, the *Examiner* displayed at that juncture a mounting concern for the effects of social change. What had caused the demise of 'Merry Old England'? It wondered in 1817. 'The causes of this habitual indisposition to enjoyment', was the quick reply, 'we conceive to be, first, the commercial and jobbing spirit, which has infected Government as well as the middle classes, and almost destroyed the middle gentry' (the other culprits were views that equated merriment with vice, and the spirit of utility). An ideal of a pure 'middle class' (in which the rural component was particularly singled out) was incorporated into a nostalgic yearning for some previous happier age, which had since been eroded by commerce and

---

[25] *Hints to All Classes on the State of the Country in This Momentous Crisis. By One of the People*, London, 1812; [Southey], *Letters from England*, p. 375; see above, pp. 170–1, 181. For the similar assertions of Jane West in 1806, see below, pp. 397–8.

[26] Joshua Collier, *Dearness not Scarcity: Its Cause and Remedy*, London, 1819, p. 5. Collier further distinguished the 'middling classes' from professional men and men of letters. Compare also the clear distinction between 'the middle and most valuable' classes on the one hand, and 'capitalists' on the other, in *The Proceedings in Herefordshire, Connected with the Visit of Joseph Hume, Esq., MP . . .*, Hereford, 1822, p. 12 (speech of Joseph Hume).

utilitarianism.[27] In the following months the *Examiner* became
even more insistent:

> It is no news to tell the reader that the race of *middle* country gentlemen,
> who used to form so useful and indeed noble a link between the upper
> class and the peasantry, has long been extinct in this country . . .
> As the money-getters rose, and the taxes pressed, the middle gentry
> disappeared; – they were gradually withered where they grew, or trans-
> planted to the metropolis where they were compelled to change their
> nature.

The familiar 'middle-class idiom' was mobilized to eulogize a
blissful rural world that had been lost. The familiar concern of
the advocates of the 'middle class' for its annihilation (especially
by taxation) evolved here into a resigned post-factum observation.
It was commerce, finance and the city that had colluded to
destroy the 'middle class'. For the *Examiner*'s was an unrestrained
tirade against industrialization and urbanization, transformations
which entailed 'crowding cities and forsaking the fields' as well as
'manufactures and disease'. The antithesis between the *Examiner*'s
declining 'middle class' and this injurious social process was
driven home with a graphic image: 'a considerable addition to
the town smoke is just what the country has gained by the
extinction of this once illustrious body of Englishmen'.[28] The
once illustrious 'middle class' went up in industrial smoke.

Of course, there was nothing inevitable about the image of a
declining 'middle class', any more than about the image of a
rising one. By 1820, the outcry about the imminent annihilation
of the timeless 'middle class', which had suited so well the
political objectives of its advocates in the 1790s as well as those
of the Tories of the early 1800s, was not the only available or
potentially convincing social narrative. For a suggestive illus-

---

[27] *Examiner* 521, 21 December 1817, p. 802. Not surprisingly, the periodical did not see
the 'middle class' as a peculiar characteristic of the modern age: on another occasion
it credited 'a certain [medieval] Caliph of Bagdad' with attempts 'to ascertain the
true condition of the middle class of society' in his realm (421, 21 January 1816,
p. 43).

[28] *Examiner* 530, 22 February 1818, p. 113; 541, 10 May 1818, p. 289. See also the
connection between the erosion of liberty and the 'drain[ing of] the blood and resources
of the middle gentry and the lower orders' in 531, 1 March 1818, p. 129; and the
satirical allusion to the demise of the 'middlegent', who had 'died about twenty years
back, in decayed circumstances, a clerk in the War Office', in 597, 6 June 1819,
p. 353.

tration of the broadening of possibilities in the interim period, let us look at the writings of Thomas Malthus.

In his first (unpublished) work in 1796, as we have seen, Malthus's 'middle-class idiom' shared the features characteristic of that decade. He too portrayed the 'middle class' (with a particular emphasis on its rural component) as belonging to a past golden age that had since been lost, and he too saw the restitution of the former political virtues of the 'middle class' as a prerequisite to forcing the government into an enlightened policy of moderate reform. In his writings over the next three decades, key elements in his early representation of the 'middle class' – its nostalgic grounding in a past ahistorical age, the sense of its present decay (the 'middle classes of society would very soon be blended with the poor', he reiterated in 1800[29]), the emphasis on its rural or gentrified component, and its oppositional edge – were all gradually transformed.

Whereas in the first edition of Malthus's *Essay on the Principle of Population*, published in 1798, the 'middle class' was not mentioned, by his 'very much enlarged' second edition of 1803 the 'middle-class idiom' was incorporated as common knowledge: 'It has been generally found that middle parts of society are most favourable to virtuous and industrious habits, and to the growth of all kinds of talents.' We may recall Christopher Wyvill's realization of this purported common knowledge in the early 1800s; Malthus also discovered now this seemingly timeless truth and altered his writing to acknowledge it. But Malthus's 1803 vision of the 'middle class' was not quite the same as that which he had expressed in his earlier and more radical pamphlet. His previous concern about the consequences of their decline was now replaced with a hope that 'an increase in the happiness of the mass of human society' would follow upon 'the prospect of an *increase* of the relative proportions of the middle parts': increase, not decline.[30] And as the years went by, Malthus's

---

[29] [Thomas Malthus], *An Investigation of the Cause of the Present High Price of Provisions*, London, 1800; rep. in *The Works of Thomas Robert Malthus*, eds. E. A. Wrigley and D. Souden, London, 1986, vol. VII, p. 13. For his 1796 pamphlet see above, p. 44.

[30] Thomas Malthus, *An Essay on the Principle of Population*, 2nd edn, very much enlarged, 1803 (variorum edn, ed. P. James, Cambridge, 1989), vol. II, p. 194 (my emphasis). For the virtuous habits of the 'middle class', see also p. 155. Malthus's increasing notice of the 'middle class' in the successive editions of the *Essay on the Principle of Population* has been noted in S. Collini et al., *That Noble Science of Politics: A Study in*

'middle class' further lost the potential for nostalgia, the rural emphasis and the sense of decay; instead, it acquired a well-defined historical anchoring and direction. Ever since 1740, Malthus wrote in 1814, English society had witnessed 'the great increase of the middle classes'. 'The effects of manufactures and commerce on the general state of society', he explained, had been 'in the highest degree beneficial'; 'above all, [they] give a new and happier structure to society, by increasing the proportion of the middle classes, that body on which the liberty, public spirit, and good government of every country must mainly depend.' So here it was – the rise of the 'middle class' as a distinctly datable historical phenomenon, a crucial (and fortunate) consequence of the recent unmistakable processes of social transformation.[31]

By the end of the decade, Malthus's association of the 'middle class' with social change had become key to his understanding and evaluation of its existence. In the 1817 edition of the *Essay on the Principle of Population*, and again in his *Principles of Political Economy* of 1820, Malthus contrasted former feudal society, which had been divided 'into two classes ... the rich and the poor, one of which is in a state of abject dependence upon the other', with the present. Recently, he wrote, 'the accumulation of capital, and the existence of manufacturers or merchants, wholesale dealers, and retail dealers', had momentous consequences: 'The face of society is thus wholly changed. A middle class of persons, living upon the profits of stock, rises into wealth and consequence.' Moreover, 'the increase in the proportion of the middle classes of society' was a transformation of social structure 'which the growth of manufacturing and mercantile capital cannot fail to create'. And indeed, with regard to Britain's recent history, Malthus stated confidently that 'it is certain, that a very large body of what may be called the

---

Nineteenth-Century Intellectual History, Cambridge, 1983, p. 84; though the characterization of this development simply as becoming 'steadily warmer' may be somewhat incomplete.

[31] Thomas Malthus, *Observations on the Effects of the Corn Laws, and of a Rise or Fall in the Price of Corn on the Agriculture and General Wealth of the Country*, London, 1814; rep. in *Works*, vol. VII, pp. 87–109 (quoted, pp. 101–2, 108). It was no coincidence that this passage, combining social change and the 'middle-class idiom', was selected for quotation (with some additional emphasis) by J. R. McCulloch as an ending for an essay on the recent rise of cotton manufacture in the *Edinburgh Review* 46, June 1827, p. 39, at a period when the periodical was itself strongly committed to the propagation of such views.

middle classes of society has been established in this country'.[32]

Politically, the unfolding of such views accorded well with the gradual blunting of the political edge of the 'middle-class' language at this time. Malthus's 'middle class' was a consequence of social progress, not its meritorious and deserving cause; it owed its existence, and thus its gratitude, to the present social and political order. Indeed Malthus explicitly hastened to defuse the possible political implications of his 'middle-class' language. In 1803 he qualified his 'middle-class idiom' with the statement that not *all* virtue and talent were in the middle, so that the 'superior and inferior parts [of society] are, in the nature of things . . . not only necessary, but strikingly beneficial'. And to his 'middle-class idiom' of 1820 he appended a most unambiguous disclaimer:

It is an historical truth which cannot for a moment be disputed, that the first formation, and subsequent preservation and improvement, of our present constitution, and of the liberties and privileges which have so long distinguished Englishmen, are mainly due to a landed aristocracy.[33]

He therefore concluded reassuringly that it would be ill advised to jeopardize present social relationships, and thus to put the constitution and these liberties at risk. Insofar as Malthus was giving the rise of the 'middle class' an inevitable historical logic, he was surely not prepared to allow it to emerge as a consequence as a challenge to the present political order.

So by 1820 Malthus had developed a dispassionate theoretical framework for relating the 'middle class' to recent social progress, indeed for rendering it the embodiment of commercial and industrial developments.[34] In the process, the 'middle class' had

---

[32] Note how even such an assertion of certitude was undermined by Malthus's own language, when he too prefixed to the purportedly observable and incontrovertible 'middle classes' the more tentative and experimental qualifying clause 'what may be called'. Thomas Malthus, *Principles of Political Economy*, 1820; rep. (2nd edn, 1836, with variant readings of 1st edn) in *Works*, vols. v–vi (quoted, vol. v, p. 35; vol. vi, pp. 298–9, 302). Compare the 1817 edition of his *Essay*, in *Works*, vol. ii, p. 84. Malthus also repeated these observations in his *Definitions in Political Economy*, London, 1827; in *Works*, vol. viii, p. 38.

[33] *An Essay on the Principle of Population*, 2nd edn, 1803, vol. ii, p. 194. *Principles of Political Economy*, vol. vi, p. 303.

[34] It was within this dispassionate descriptive framework, for instance, that David Ricardo debated with Malthus – as nothing more than a detached academic question – the contribution of the national debt to the creation of a 'middle class': David Ricardo, 'Notes on Malthus's Principles of Political Economy' (these notes, written in 1820,

acquired a fairly clear occupational identity – manufacturers, merchants, wholesale and retail traders – that is to say, the carriers and beneficiaries of these social developments; and they were also central to this new order in their role as consumers – 'the demanders in the middle ranks of life'. Most important, the 'middle class' was endowed with a powerful sense of inevitability: its existence and expansion were presented as readily observable and datable social facts, an inseparable and unavoidable consequence of the progress of society. It was this storyline, of the inevitable and beneficial rise of the 'middle class' as characterizing the present age, which was to become so central in subsequent years. And of course, all this was a very far cry from the precariously situated (if not positively decayed) and partially landed 'middle class' about which Malthus had written in 1796, whose heyday had been in some ahistorical golden past, and whose reawakening and support were required in order to force the hands of the government to concede some measures of political reform.[35]

In 1820, when the social transformations of late seemed ever more in need of articulation, Malthus's cogent storyline, which bound together these new social developments with a new social force, could appear quite persuasive. During the 1810s it had surfaced occasionally in the writings of others, such as James Mill, Francis Horner and, in one instance, even Coleridge.[36] Still, it is worth repeating that in and of itself (as the dissociation of

remained unpublished): in *The Works and Correspondence of David Ricardo*, ed. Piero Sraffa, Cambridge, 1951, vol. II, pp. 444–5.

[35] *Principles of Political Economy*, vol. VI, p. 298. It may be argued that in fact Malthus's emphasis on the country gentlemen in 1796 was not very different from his eulogy to the political importance of the aristocracy in 1820. But the issue here is not whether his broad political convictions had changed, but rather how his conception of the 'middle class' and its political role was transformed within the exposition of his political views. The fact, therefore, that the country gentlemen in 1796, characterized by political independence and virtue, were part of Malthus's 'middle class', while the politically praiseworthy aristocrats of 1820 were clearly pitted against it, is a significant metamorphosis.

[36] For Mill, see below, p. 257. For Horner's linking of the 'middle class' and social change see *Memoirs and Correspondence of Francis Horner, MP*, ed. Leonard Horner, 2 vols., London, 1843, vol. I, p. 375 (letter to Jeffrey, 15 September 1806); vol. II, p. 26 (22 January 1810). Coleridge, despite his usually nostalgic view of the 'middle class', was prompted once by a comparison with backward Ireland to associate it with the 'rapidly progressive' state of England in the last century and a half: *The Courier*, 13 September 1811, in *Essays on His Times*, vol. II, p. 280. See also Jeffrey's review of Millar in note 23 above.

the 'middle class' and social change in the previous generation makes clear) this storyline was not an obvious and natural candidate for that new dynamic understanding of society compelled by the heightened awareness of social flux at this juncture. Thus, for example, for the radical popularizers of political economy this post-war awareness of social and economic forces resulted not in breaking away from the dual social scheme underlying radical rhetoric, but in its reformulation in the political economical categories of 'productive' and 'unproductive' labour.[37] But just as the latter scheme suited the political disposition of radicals, so for many others it was the 'middle-class' storyline that came now to hold a strong political appeal. In 1820, the year after Peterloo, when the trickle of limited reform was rapidly turning into a torrent, this storyline suddenly proved to have valuable potential for these accelerating trends; and it was the realization of this potential that invested the 'middle-class' storyline with much power in the following decades.

THE 'MIDDLE CLASS': AN IMAGINED CONSTITUENCY

The last two years have produced a considerable change – a change which is still going on, in the sentiments of the middle classes. They begin to find, that they *must* interfere with domestic politics, because politics *will* interfere with them. (John Edward Taylor, 1820)[38]

To see how the expanding awareness of social change and the swell of interest in limited constitutional reform came together after Peterloo, let us turn one more time to James Mackintosh. The last in his series of political essays in the *Edinburgh Review*, published in November 1820, clearly registered the marks of recent events. The deep social rift which Mackintosh had foreseen in 1818 as a potential danger he now saw as a *fait accompli*: 'the bonds which hold together the various orders of society', he observed, 'have for the last six years been rapidly loosening',

---

[37] See G. Claeys, 'The Reaction to Political Radicalism and the Popularisation of Political Economy in Early Nineteenth-Century Britain: The Case of "Productive" and "Unproductive" Labour', in T. Shinn and R. Whitley (eds.), *Expository Science: Forms and Functions of Popularisation*, Dordrecht, 1985, pp. 119–36.

[38] [John Edward Taylor], *Notes and Observations, Critical and Explanatory, on the Papers Relative to the Internal State of the Country . . . By a Member of the Manchester Committee For Relieving the Sufferers of the 16th of August, 1819*, London, 1820, p. 202.

and the consequence must be 'a mortal combat between extreme and irreconcileable factions'. The only hope yet remaining was to 'unit[e] the more moderate of both parties': it was the duty of those 'called *Moderate Reformers*' to save liberty and peace by mediating between the two polarized extremes pulling society asunder. Reverting to a pattern familiar from the 1790s, Mackintosh's plea for a political middle immediately became a plea to the social middle:

> The great strength of the cause of Moderate Reform, lies in the middle classes, who at the present moment have a strong feeling that there are serious defects and abuses in the Government, and a warm desire of reformation, without any very distinct notion of its particular nature.

Like other speakers after Peterloo, Mackintosh was sure to affirm that whatever the recent political turbulence was about, the 'middle class' was not involved. On the contrary, its own political feelings, though strong, were not yet translated into a 'very distinct' political programme; a hiatus which he feared could be exploited by irresponsible radical extremists. To make a pre-emptive strike, therefore, Mackintosh stepped in himself: his goal now was to provide the 'middle class', which he evidently considered – together with the author of the epigraph at the beginning of this section – to be a nascent political constituency, with a programme that would 'form a point of union between themselves'.[39]

Mackintosh's 'middle-class' programme focused on the issue of representation, and its exposition was predicated on a cogent historical narrative. In previous generations, Mackintosh asserted, a modification of the representation had been unnecessary, 'for few changes then occurred which called for its exercise'. Society was hardly expanding in terms of numbers, wealth, or new industry; and 'the change in the condition and importance of various classes of men was so gradual as scarcely to be remarked by contemporary observers'. In recent times, by contrast, 'the change in the relative importance of different classes of society' was 'greater than during any equal period in the history of the world'. Both the timing and the causes of this conspicuous process were readily apparent:

[39] *Edinburgh Review* 34, November 1820, pp. 463–7.

It was not, however, till the great impulse given to English industry, in the middle of the eighteenth century, that the disparity between the old system of representation, and the new state of society, became very remarkable. This was very soon followed by the sudden and enormous growth of the manufacturing towns.

This development, the greatest change in the whole of human history, turned out in Mackintosh's story to be precisely what had made the 'middle class' into a new political presence:

Villages have since sprung up into immense cities; great manufactures have spread over wastes and mountains; ease, comfort and leisure, have introduced, among the middling classes of society, their natural companions, curiosity, intelligence, boldness, and activity of mind. A much greater proportion of the collective knowledge and wealth of the nation has thus fallen to their lot.

Armed with this historical narrative, Mackintosh was quick to draw the obvious political conclusions. As a consequence of these dramatic social transformations, 'the power of establishing some proportion between political rights and social importance, was no longer exercised' – the 'middle class' was rising in social importance but not in 'constitutional privileges'. 'The Constitution no longer opened her arms to receive rising classes and communities into her bosom'; or to be more specific, 'our representative system . . . did not allot a sufficient share of power to the middle class' – a fact that 'became, in this state of things, more apparent and more humiliating'.[40]

So here it was, in as much detail as one could ever hope for, the entire storyline with which we are all so familiar. The 'middle class', created by the unprecedented modern progress of industrialization and urbanization, now came to maturity on its own as a new political constituency, demanding political rights to suit its rising social position; hence its demand for limited parliamentary reform, or rather adjustment, which would give it proportional political power in accordance with the venerable and time-tested doctrine of sectoral representation.[41] This was the

---

[40] Ibid., pp. 478–9.

[41] It should be noted that Mackintosh's essay was a comment on John Russell's fairly timid reform proposal of December 1819, which was limited to the disfranchisement of Grampound and to an extension of the franchise to a small number of unrepresented opulent communities. While Mackintosh's reasoning justified a broad yet limited extension of the franchise, its conversion into a comprehensive reform plan still remained to be spelled out more fully in the years to come.

storyline that was later to become immortalized by successive generations of historians; and yet their cumulative authority should not obscure the fact that it originated at a given moment as a product of very specific circumstances, serving a very specific political agenda, and not as a detached observation of the impartial social scientist.

Before taking our leave from Mackintosh, it may be interesting to recall his previous discussion of the 'middle class' in the *Edinburgh Review* some two years earlier. Then, too, Mackintosh's emphasis on the 'middle class' had already led him in one passage to the issue of parliamentary representation:

> If we were compelled to confine all elective influence to one order [he had written in 1818], we must indeed vest it in the middling classes; both because they possess the largest share of sense and virtue, and because they have the most numerous connexions of interest with the other parts of society. It is right that they should have a preponderating influence, because they are likely to make the best choice.

The differences between Mackintosh's pronouncements in 1818 and 1820 are worth noting. First, with regard to the justification for such 'middle-class' elective influence: in 1818 it had nothing to do with a changing social map, but rather with the renowned virtues of the 'middle class' praised from time immemorial. These, however, proved to be more shaky ground to stand on: after all, as we have seen often enough, it was not all that clear what exactly these virtues were. In fact Mackintosh himself was at pains in 1818 (as in 1815) to prove the political acquiescence and timidity of the 'middle class' (thus negating his own understanding of its political virtues during his younger and more radical incarnation in the early 1790s). It is therefore hardly surprising that in the 1818 essay he immediately retreated from this ostensible argument for 'middle-class' enfranchisement, hastily ascertaining that the possible benefit to be derived from it 'is not the sole object of representation; and, if it were, there are not wanting circumstances which render it unfit that they should engross the whole influence'.[42] His 1818 stab at 'middle-class' representation turned out to have been merely hypothetical, without practical meaning; in practice, as we have noted, he remained content at that juncture with parliamentary landed ascendancy. More than anything, in 1818

---

[42] *Edinburgh Review* 31, December 1818, pp. 191–2.

Mackintosh's 'middle class' had been the social group least inclined to political change: it lacked, he had asserted then, any 'political boldness'.[43] In 1820, by contrast, Mackintosh himself was suddenly providing the 'middle class' with a programme for political change (though surely not a radical one), grounded in the newly acquired narrative of its recent origins. And to cap this abrupt change, Mackintosh's 'middle class' of 1820 – as quoted two paragraphs ago – also regained the quality of 'boldness' which he had emphatically denied it only two years before.

Mackintosh in 1820 was hardly alone in this sudden emphasis on 'middle-class' representation, anchored in its conceptualization as a new constituency generated by recent social transformations. Another 1820 discussion of 'middle-class' enfranchisement that immediately comes to mind is James Mill's famous *Essay on Government*, to which we shall return shortly. Less famous was the anonymous merchant who noted (also in 1820) the new political awareness of 'the great proportion of the middling ranks, who now think and reflect upon the conduct of the government'. Their now conspicuous presence, he hoped, would spur such reform measures as would turn parliament into 'the *actual*, not the *virtual*, representatives of the middle and independent class of our population'.[44] Or take a social observer in 1822, Joseph Lowe, who like many others was struck by the drama of social change that surrounded him: 'What a different aspect of society', Lowe exclaimed, 'is exhibited after the rise of towns and the general increase of numbers!' Among the effects of this cataclysmic transformation, he noted, one in particular stood out: in comparing regions which had not been thus transformed (such as Russia, Poland, or the Scottish Highlands) with those which had, 'we find a surprising difference in the number and comfort of the middle class'. The 'middle class', then, associated with recent urbanization and demographic growth, was a quintessential component of the modern age, that which gave society 'a

---

[43] See above, p. 188.

[44] *Hints on Our Foreign and Domestic Policy, Addressed to the Members of the New Parliament. By a Merchant*, London, 1820, p. 39; note also the concern for the interests of the 'middling classes' (or 'middling ranks') in pp. 13, 16. The association of social change with parliamentary reform, as a move which distinguished the 1820s from previous decades, has recently been noted by R. Quinault, 'The Industrial Revolution and Parliamentary Reform', in P. O'Brien and R. Quinault (eds.), *The Industrial Revolution and British Society*, Cambridge, 1993, p. 184.

different aspect'. And having tied the 'middle class' to social change, Lowe too made the next step to the corollary changes in parliamentary representation: 'How different is the England of the present age', he proudly observed, 'from the England of feudal times, when our towns were in their infancy, and when the Commons or middle class were too unimportant to hold a share in the representation.'[45]

To illustrate further the new directions that the image of the 'middle class' took in the 1820s, let us look again at Robert Southey. Towards the end of the decade Southey published his most important work of social criticism, in the form of a dialogue with the ghost of Sir Thomas More on the nature of modern society. Southey maintained his basic hostility towards the expanding commercial and manufacturing system that had already been evident in Espriella's letters of 1807; but with regard to the place of the 'middle class' in this process, the change in his writing was striking. Whereas in 1807 he had seen the 'middle class' as an island of stability *resisting* the flood of social change, now he presented the 'middle class' as triumphantly riding on its (ruinous) waves. Hence, whereas in 1807 Southey had been concerned about the consequent *destruction* of the 'middle class', now he noted how this flood of social change was responsible for its 'great increase' and 'progress of education'. And whereas in 1807 Southey had seen in the 'middle class' a key pillar of the social and political order, now he put its members together with the forces challenging it: by their growing numbers and ambitions, he warned, they were contributing to 'the danger, with which our institutions are threatened' (a comment alluding, presumably, to the clamour for parliamentary reform). These sharp reversals of his earlier appraisal of the 'middle class', then, bear eloquent testimony to the compelling force of the developing representation of the 'middle class' in the 1820s.[46]

---

[45] Joseph Lowe, *The Present State of England in Regard to Agriculture, Trade, and Finance: With a Comparison of the Prospects of England and France*, London, 1822, pp. 208–9. Note, however, that Lowe's 'middle class' was vague enough (as was clear from its elision with 'the Commons') not to lead him to an activist political programme, as it did for Mackintosh and others; yet the logic behind its association with parliamentary representation remained the same.

[46] Robert Southey, *Sir Thomas More: Or, Colloquies on the Progress and Prospects of Society*, 2 vols., London, 1829, vol. II, pp. 131, 216, 265. And see Williams, *Culture and Society*, pp. 39–43.

Like the association of the 'middle class' with recent processes of social transformation, this sudden linking of the 'middle class' with parliamentary representation, noticeable from about 1820, was anything but obvious or self-explanatory. Previously, in fact, it had typically been the exception rather than the rule. By the death of George III, British politics had already witnessed a long series of efforts to secure parliamentary reform, extending back into the earlier part of his reign in the eighteenth century. In these repeated reform efforts, the role of a concept of 'middle class' had been minimal, virtually non-existent. This remained true not only for radical reformers, but for moderate ones as well, from whom such language might have been more plausibly expected. On the whole, before the late 1810s, the language of 'middle class' had not played much of a role in discussions of reform, and the issue of parliamentary representation had not figured in the political invocations of the 'middle class'.

Again, of course, the argument is not that there was something intrinsic to the language of 'middle class' that made such a link inherently impossible. During the 1790s (and earlier), one could occasionally find discussions of the 'middle class' that included a sporadic reference to the franchise. In addition to Daniel Stuart's pamphlet of 1794 and one utterance of Christopher Wyvill's which we have encountered above, one can mention the oft-quoted clarification that the controversial Irish MP Henry Flood appended to his reform motion in March 1790 (but which was not included in his original presentation). Flood explained then that his motion was intended to extend the franchise to the 'middle classes [who] alone can be depended upon' in order 'to fortify the constitution, and to render it impregnable'. Significantly, Flood in 1790 argued for the limited enfranchisement of the 'middle class' not (as was later to become the case) on the basis of their emergence as a new social group, but rather – in accordance with the prevalent understanding at that juncture – on the basis of Aristotelian truisms regarding their timeless virtues, which should have been apparent to 'wise statesmen' of 'every state'.[47] More to the point, such cases were at that time

---

[47] Speech of 4 March 1790: *Parliamentary History of England* 28, col. 476. Reprinted in C. Wyvill, *Political Papers*, York, 1802, vol. II, p. 562. The fact that John Cannon's authoritative account of reform (*Parliamentary Reform*, p. 117) cites only this passage from Flood's speech, unusual as it actually was (which is also the case for H. T.

remarkably few and far between, and invariably failed to resonate. Their conspicuous paucity, it has already been noted, is even more significant in view of the extensive use of 'middle-class' language in other oppositional contexts during that decade; of the active reforming interests of many of the Friends of Peace; and of the strong constitutional links between taxation and representation that had been established in the political debates of the 1760s and 1770s.

Henry Flood notwithstanding, the absence of the 'middle class' from discussions of reform before 1820 was most readily observable in parliament. Particularly revealing was its absence from the debate on Grey's motion for reform in May 1797, only several months before the explosion of the language of 'middle class' in the debate on the Triple Assessment Bill; or from the long speech made in December 1800 by John Nicholls – the erstwhile committed proponent of the 'middle class' throughout the taxation debates – when he talked about constitutional matters and issues of representation.[48] The 'middle class' continued to play no role in subsequent parliamentary debates on various motions for reform, in 1804, 1809, 1810, 1812, and finally in early July 1819, a month before the massacre of Peterloo.[49]

The sudden change after Peterloo – paralleling that in Mackintosh's essays – could hardly have been more striking. It was surely no coincidence that what were apparently the first parliamentary deliberations on reform in thirty years in which the merits of the 'middle class' were brought up took place on several separate occasions soon thereafter, in spring 1820. The first was a reform petition from the 'merchants, bankers, and tradesmen' of

Dickinson's concise account in *British Radicalism and the French Revolution 1789–1815*, Oxford, 1985, p. 7), reminds us that given the powerful grip of the rising 'middle-class' narrative on historical understanding, historians have been more likely to err on the side of over-emphasizing such utterances than on that of overlooking them. For Wyvill and Stuart, see pp. 56–8; and also *The Oeconomist*'s vague suggestion of 'middle class' agents or trustees, in order to increase their weight in the legislature (p. 51).

[48] *Parliamentary History* 33, cols. 644ff; 35, cols. 754ff. One can also note the apparent absence of the 'middle class' in the language of the Friends of the People: see for instance their papers in Christopher Wyvill, *Political Papers*, 6 vols., York, 1794–1804.

[49] *Hansard's Parliamentary Debates* 1, cols. 1011–16 and 2, cols. 143–130*, 387–97, 513–18, 681–3 (Aylesbury Election Bill, spring 1804); 14, cols. 353–80, 617–20, 717–84, 837–51, 899–905, 924–8, 1032*–1040* (John Curwen's motion, spring 1809); 17, cols. 123–65 (Thomas Brand's motion, May 1810); 23, cols. 99–161 (Brand again, May 1812); 40, cols. 1440–504 (Burdett's motion, July 1819).

Newcastle, presented to parliament on 12 May. Among its supporters were John Lambton, Grey's son-in-law and later the Earl of Durham, and the committed Whig Matthew White Ridley. Both men spoke distinctly in praise of the respectability of the 'middle class', 'that class of society [in Lambton's words] which had not hitherto taken so great a share in the consideration of public affairs'; an oversight which they both suddenly found disturbing, and which they hoped would now be remedied if 'the middle classes of society . . . would come forward without delay, and distinctly declare their sentiments'. And it was only a week later, in another parliamentary reform debate (regarding the Grampound Disfranchisement Bill), that George Tierney, the veteran Foxite, echoed their respect for 'that great and respectable body who composed the middle classes . . . to whose opinions the House ought to attach the utmost weight'.[50]

Reform debates thereafter became routinely prone to 'middle-class' language, in sharp contrast with the preceding years. Listen for example to Viscount Milton's conversion to the cause. Milton, who had opposed reform a decade earlier on the grounds that 'there could be found no description of persons in the country who were not represented' in parliament, now found that assertion impossible to maintain. As he declared to the House of Commons in 1821, he had changed his mind because 'the great mass of the middle classes of society were in favour of reform'.[51] Exactly a year later the Marquis of Tavistock – together with Milton, a mainstay of the 'Young Whigs' – followed suit: in presenting another reform petition, Tavistock assured the House that reform was universally supported by 'the great body of the Commons of England, the industrious and intelligent and moral middle class of society'.[52]

---

[50] *Hansard* n.s., 1, cols. 332–3, 501.

[51] *Hansard* 23, col. 149, debate of 8 May 1812; n.s., 5, col. 437, debate of 17 April 1821. On 22 October 1822 Milton wrote to Grey that at this time 'almost all the middle classes are in favour of reform' (second Earl Grey Papers, University of Durham). On Milton and his views of reform, see Wasson, 'The Great Whigs'.

[52] *Hansard* n.s., 7, col. 51 (25 April 1822). Mandler, *Aristocratic Government in the Age of Reform*, pp. 85–96, draws a persuasive portrait of the Young Whigs as scions of the Grand Whiggery who through their attraction to the liberal understanding of commercial society became from the 1820s particularly predisposed to heeding what they perceived to be the political aspirations of a 'middle class'. Mandler argues that this concern distinguished them clearly from the high aristocratic Foxite Whigs; but the latter – most notably, as we shall see, John Russell – could of course join in the

Nobody made the point more clearly than Lord John Russell, when he presented his own motion for parliamentary reform on the very same day. 'The people of England have undergone a considerable change during the last forty years', Russell asserted, a social transformation that was characterized by 'a tendency to increase the importance of the middle classes of society'. Removed from poverty and idleness, connected with those above and below, they were 'the best class of the community . . . one of the most solid pillars of the state'. Therefore, Russell concluded, 'I know not that I could select a better sign of the future prosperity of a country, than the wealth, comfort, and intelligence of its middle orders.' No longer remnants of a golden past, the 'middle class' now came to epitomize a better future. But to make this future possible, the parliamentary system needed to be modified 'so as to represent this increased importance of the middling, the manufacturing, and the commercial classes'.[53] It is worth noting that during this decade the 'middle class' was increasingly identified with the forces behind commercial and industrial progress: whereas in the 1790s the inherent vagueness of the category of 'middle class' was valuable for one specific political agenda, in the 1820s a different agenda prompted attempts (that were not always successful) to pinpoint its social identity more precisely.

Prominent Whigs could similarly be heard outside parliament. Lambton surpassed his parliamentary 'middle-class idiom' at a reform dinner in 1821, declaring that 'the *middling classes* of the population, the *very sinews* of the nation, are eager and desirous of Reform' – a statement which prompted angry responses from radicals. In 1818, James Abercromby, another active parliamentary Whig, observed that 'the diffusion of knowledge and wealth among the middle classes' – that is to say their rise – had

sudden attention to this ostensible rising constituency, even without being as committed to its interests.

[53] *Hansard* n.s., 7, cols. 55, 59. By now it may be superfluous to point to the interchangeability in Russell's language of 'middle classes/orders', as well as 'middling classes' and 'middling orders' (see cols. 59–60). Also compare Russell's arguments for limited reform which he published in 1821: relying on a theory of representation in which all sectors of society should find their voice in parliament, he objected to universal suffrage which 'gives the whole power to the highest and the lowest . . . and thus disfranchises the middle class, the most disinterested, the most independent, and the most unprejudiced of all'. Lord John Russell, *An Essay on the History of the English Government and Constitution, from the Reign of Henry VII. to the Present Time*, London, 1821, pp. 247–8. The essay went through a second enlarged edition in 1823.

rendered them 'determined to assert their power and to have some share in the government of the country' – that is to say to demand reform. Henry Brougham, also struck by the diffusion of knowledge 'unexampled in former times', revealed a no less dynamic sense of society and politics: in 1822 he too proclaimed (in what may have been the first statement of this kind in his career, but certainly not the last) that 'the time is approaching, if it is not arrived, when a considerable number of the middle classes must be admitted within the walls of the Legislature'.[54] The sudden unison of all these statements is worth emphasizing: after all, Russell, Lambton (that is, Lord Durham), Brougham, Grey, Althorp, as well as James Graham (whose affinity to such a view is discussed below), now in opposition, were all to hold ministerial offices in the Whig administration responsible for the passing of the Reform Bill of 1832 (and Abercromby was to join them soon thereafter). Even more to the point, Russell, Durham, Grey, Althorp and Graham were five of the six men that were to dominate almost exclusively the drafting of the details of the Reform Bill.[55] It was their common discovery of the 'middle class' as a purportedly rising and increasingly powerful constituency engendered by recent processes of social change, a discovery urged upon them by the particular circumstances of the early 1820s, that was about to carry the day in their political apogee a decade later.

Propelled by the powerful drive for limited reform, and warranted and further propagated (even when the interest in reform subsided temporarily by the mid-decade) by the widespread receptiveness to a dynamic reconceptualization of society, this new vision of a rising 'middle-class' constituency carried from the early 1820s a broad and pervasive appeal. It was moreover a plausible sequel to the repeated entreaties directed ever since the late 1810s at the 'middle class' to join with 'public opinion'. Indeed, the image of this new powerful constituency could now

---

[54] Lambton in *The Times* 11212, 5 April 1821. Abercromby to Tierney, quoted in H. K. Olphin, *George Tierney*, London, 1934, p. 184. Brougham in *Edinburgh Review* 37, November 1822, p. 404; he further referred to this 'middle class' as 'yeomen and . . . tradesmen'. And see further the Whig sources, including Grey and Althorp, cited in E. A. Wasson, *Whig Renaissance: Lord Althorp and the Whig Party 1782–1845*, New York, 1987, pp. 399–400 n. 155.

[55] See J. Parry, *The Rise and Fall of Liberal Government in Victorian Britain*, New Haven, 1993, p. 72 (the sixth was Viscount Duncannon).

come to subsume 'public opinion' altogether. Take Alexander Mundell, another commentator who repeated that ubiquitous observation of the 1820s that 'the frame of society is undergoing imperceptible changes, working results of mighty import', and who saw the key consequence of this process in the diffusion of knowledge. Social change, Mundell wrote, created 'a description of persons in the middling ranks, unknown among any other people', who 'in aggregate wealth and information' surpassed all former elites; and it was among them that 'the knowledge of the times is diffused', leading them to dominate 'public opinion' – that force 'which ultimately bears down all before it'.[56]

This new vision of the 'middle class', however, did not always fit as snugly with one's political positions as it did for the champions of limited reform. For others it created points of tension, as they tried to understand the meaning of this purportedly inescapable political innovation and its consequences for their own views. Mundell, for instance, was no reformer; but as the more radical *Examiner* was quick to point out, his argument about the diffusion of knowledge among the 'middle class' led in spite of itself to the conclusion that parliament was not 'fairly *representing* this advanced state of intellect'.[57] Mundell's political position was unsettled by consequences of the notion of 'middle class' that were more radical than he had intended. On the other political side, a similar tension, but operating in precisely the opposite direction, was manifest in the best-known statement of 'middle-class idiom' in the context of representation, James Mill's *Essay on Government*, a text which was written – again, not coincidentally – in 1820, and bore the clear marks of Peterloo.

Several years earlier Mill had already endowed the 'middle class' with significant social meaning. In 1811, when his colleague in the *Edinburgh Review* Francis Jeffrey was still writing about social change in a framework unencumbered by a 'middle class', Mill presented the periodical with a different view. Building upon

---

[56] Alexander Mundell, *The Influence of Interest and Prejudice upon Proceedings in Parliament Stated . . .*, London, 1825, pp. 1–3, 9, 56. Appropriately, Mundell dedicated his book to the Public (a move anticipated by W. J. Fox in the *Westminster Review* 1, January 1824, p. 2: 'Flattering dedications are defunct; the public is the best patron now for your literary adventure'). For another powerful statement equating the rising 'middle class' and 'public opinion', see William Mackinnon below, pp. 300–1. And see Parry, *The Rise and Fall of Liberal Government*, p. 28.

[57] *Examiner* 937, 22 January 1826, p. 49.

stock Scottish formulations of the progress of society from feudal times to its present 'civilized and refined stage', Mill added that such progress was not as beneficial for the higher and lower classes as it was for 'the increasing numbers and improving character of the middling class of the people'. This class was umbilically linked to social progress: 'A middling class', Mill wrote, 'is itself, in fact, a creature of civilization. It had no existence in the rude state of society; and it increases as the benefits of civilization increase.' The epitome of civilizing social change for Mill was in 'the middling rank of society advancing in strength from age to age'.[58]

Mill's 'middle class' of 1811 also had political meaning: its mission – for which, he asserted, it was singularly suitable – was 'to counterbalance the despotic tendencies engendered in the other classes by the progress of improvement'. In political terms, then, Mill had little to add in 1811 to the abstract antithesis between the 'middle class' and despotism which had been so prevalent in the 1790s. By the *Essay on Government* of 1820, however, Mill's emphasis had shifted, in accordance with the political debate around him: he now attempted to integrate – in more concrete programmatical terms – the significance of the 'middle class' as a powerful new social constituency with his Benthamite views about parliamentary reform. The *Essay* was an elaborate argument in favour of, basically, universal male suffrage; and yet it ended with a long encomium to the political influence of

the class which is universally described as both the most wise and the most virtuous part of the community, the middle rank . . . which gives to science, to art, and to legislation itself, their most distinguished ornaments, the chief source of all that has exalted and refined human nature.

The rationale behind Mill's introduction of this 'middle-class idiom' into his argument was that the opinions of those lower down the social scale 'are formed . . . by that intelligent and virtuous rank, who come the most immediately in contact with them', and on whom they so regularly depend. Consequently, he maintained, their beneficial influence would prevent the lower

---

[58] *Edinburgh Review* 17, February 1811, pp. 416–18.

orders from dangerously abusing universal suffrage.[59] For Mill too, the 'middle class' in 1820 was less emphatically a bulwark against despotism than a guarantee of order and stability amongst its social inferiors.

Ever since Macaulay's incisive attack in 1829 on Mill's *Essay on Government*, 'perhaps the most remarkable of the works to which Mr Mill owes his fame', the question has been repeatedly raised whether Mill's long celebration of the 'middle class' (dubbed sarcastically by Macaulay 'a delicious *bonne bouche* of wisdom') was consistent with the rest of his argument.[60] But regardless of the reconcilability of Mill's arguments, these persistent debates over his intended meaning surely point to an inherent tension in the *Essay*: whether logically consistent or not, the elaborate particularistic emphasis on one component of society, rhetorically (even if not constitutionally) endowing it with a privileged status, did not agree easily with the utilitarian universalistic language prevalent in the work as a whole. This tension has endured persistent attempts to explain it away;[61] a more

---

[59] James Mill, *An Essay on Government*, ed. E. Barker, Cambridge, 1937, pp. 71–3. Mill wrote the *Essay* for the supplement of the fifth edition of the *Encyclopaedia Britannica*; it was reprinted separately three times during the 1820s. On the significance of the *male* identity of Mill's 'middle class', see below, p. 388.

[60] Thomas Babington Macaulay in the *Edinburgh Review* 49, March 1829, pp. 159ff. (quoted, pp. 160, 184). In fact, Mill's alleged inconsistencies have already been pointed out in William Thompson, *Appeal of One Half the Human Race, Women, against the Pretensions of the Other Half, Men, to Retain Them in Political, and Thence in Civil and Domestic Slavery*, [London?], 1825 (rep. edn, London, 1983). Later discussions of the tension between Mill's Benthamite radicalism and his 'middle-class idiom' include A. V. Dicey, *Lectures on the Relation between Law and Public Opinion in England during the Nineteenth Century*, 2nd edn, 1914, pp. 160–1. E. Halévy, *The Growth of Philosophic Radicalism*, London, 1972 (originally 1928), pp. 427–8. J. Hamburger, 'James Mill on Universal Suffrage and the Middle Class', *The Journal of Politics* 24 (1962), pp. 167–90. W. Thomas, 'James Mill's Politics: The "Essay on Government" and the Movement for Reform', *Historical Journal* 12 (1969), pp. 249–84. W. R. Carr, 'James Mill's Politics Reconsidered: Parliamentary Reform and the Triumph of Truth', *Historical Journal* 14 (1971), pp. 553–80 (and Thomas's rejoinder, pp. 735–50). D. C. Moore, *The Politics of Deference*, Hassocks, 1976, pp. 423–8. W. Thomas, *The Philosophic Radicals: Nine Studies in Theory and Practice 1817–1841*, Oxford, 1979, pp. 123, 137. Collini et al., *That Noble Science of Politics*, pp. 101, 122–3.

[61] One means of doing so, most recently highlighted by Terence Ball in his introduction to *James Mill: Political Writings* (Cambridge, 1992, pp. xx–xxi), has been to focus on the tidy distinction between the terms 'middle rank' and 'middle class'. Following many historians, Ball insists that Mill's use of 'middle rank' was a more archaic term, meaning a selected group which can cut across sociological strata, as opposed to the more modern class-bound 'middle class'. This teleological argument should be sufficiently countered by the evidence presented thus far (including, in this chapter alone, the interchangeability of these different formulations for Thomas Malthus, John Russell,

fruitful approach might be to highlight precisely its ineradicable presence. Such tension was the uneasy outcome of a fusion between two contradictory impulses, that of the utilitarian logic on the one hand and that of Mill's growing conviction of the power and relevance of the rising 'middle class' on the other. Like others, Mill was groping for the implications of this appealing social narrative for his understanding of politics: he obviously deemed it now too significant to be ignored, albeit not without paying a price in terms of coherence and consistency.

In the following years, it may be added, Mill's fellow utilitarians in the *Westminster Review* coterie were to grapple with the same difficulty. Theirs was a commitment to the greatest happiness to the greatest number, and to speaking for and to the people (in contradistinction to both the *Edinburgh* and the *Quarterly* reviews, which in their view represented two comparable aristocratic factions). It was therefore not easy for the *Westminster* reviewers to justify their repeated emphasis on 'that portion of our people to whom every thing that is good among us may with certainty be traced', 'the middle class . . . which gives to the nation its character'.[62] As one of them explained apologetically, 'such an exaltation of the character of the middle class' would necessarily benefit the classes above and below them; therefore, despite its particularistic appearance, 'the improvement which would immediately take place would be universal, and without any bound which it is possible to fix'.[63] One is also reminded here of William Cobbett's rather

---

the *Examiner* and the *Manchester Guardian*, as well as for Mill's mentor, Jeremy Bentham – see n. 63). Even more damning is the fact that Mill himself, in his *Edinburgh Review* essay of 1811 as quoted above, had praised 'the middling class' and 'the middling rank' interchangeably; as he was to do again within a single paragraph in the *Westminster Review* 6, October 1826, pp. 269–70.

[62] Thomas Southwood Smith in *Westminster Review* 1, January 1824, pp. 68–9; James Mill in 6, October 1826, p. 269. See also 7, April 1827, p. 270; and G. L. Nesbitt, *Benthamite Reviewing: The First Twelve Years of the Westminster Review 1824–1836*, New York, 1934, p. 84 and passim. The characterization of the *Edinburgh* and the *Quarterly* was Mill's: *Westminster Review* 1, January 1824, pp. 210–11.

[63] These were the concluding comments to Smith's essay on education in the *Westminster Review* 1, January 1824, p. 79. Similar apologetics for an emphasis on 'middle-class' education characterized a letter from Francis Place to William Allen, 7 March 1814; quoted in J. Bentham, *Chrestomathia*, eds. M. J. Smith and W. H. Burston, Oxford, 1983, introduction, p. xiii n. 2. See also pp. 39, 45, for Bentham's own consideration of the educational needs of the 'middle rank/middle classes' in this work, first published in 1815 'for the use of the middling and higher ranks in life' (titlepage). On the utilitarian interest in 'middle-class' education see B. Simon, *Studies in the History of Education 1780–1870*, London, 1960, pp. 74–9.

unexpected realization in 1822 that 'without the middling classes to *take the lead*' parliamentary reform would be impossible – an uncomfortable acknowledgment of the power of a 'middle-class' constituency which Cobbett then hastily redefined, in terms more congenial to his politics, as a need for 'an overpowering call from *the people*'.[64]

No less awkward were occasional attempts from the opposite political corner to graft the now seemingly inevitable 'middle class' constituency onto its own political goals. Thus the Grenvill-ite MP Sir Edward Hyde East was led by a discussion of reform in 1823 to laud 'the increased and increasing knowledge, wealth, and real independence in opinion and action of the great body of gentry and middle classes of the people'; only that for him this constituted an argument *against* reform, since the present electoral system had already achieved the best representation of this social group. Two anti-reform pamphlets of 1818 had made the same point, asserting that 'the present electors of Great Britain, consist[ed] of the most respectable among the middle classes, and the least dependent among the poor'. Reform would therefore devalue their independence and drown them in the votes of the numerous dependants of the rich, with the result that 'the middle class ... would be destroyed, or what is the same thing politically, would be reduced to such a state of comparative insignificance'.[65] Such arguments, facilitated by the referential vagueness of the notion of 'middle class', were perhaps eccentric, and probably left many in their audience unconvinced; but their persistence through the debates on the Reform Bill is another demonstration of the power assumed by the vision of a

---

[64] William Cobbett, *Rural Rides*, ed. Pitt Cobbett, London, 1885, vol. 1, p. 146, entry for 29 September 1822 (second emphasis added); Cobbett explained that by 'the middling classes' he did 'not mean to confine [himself] to yeomen and farmers, but to take in all, tradesmen and men of property'. Only two years earlier, we may recall (see pp. 213–14), Cobbett had portrayed the 'middle class' as the decided enemies of reform.

[65] *Hansard* n.s., 8, col. 1278. Kent (pseud.), *A View of the Great Constitutional Questions, Addressed to the Electors of the United Kingdom. (Part the First)*, Canterbury, 1818, p. 72; *An Investigation of the Policy of Ministers*, London, 1818, p. 70. Interestingly, 'Kent' objected to 'the Advocate for the united interests of the Merchant, the Manufacturer, and the Tradesman' (p. 65), rejecting arguments for their need to organize themselves in order to improve their representation; he obviously saw such an initiative, which historians might associate retrospectively with the political mobilization of a 'middle class', as something quite distinct from his own vision of a valuable 'middle class', and quite deplorable at that.

'middle-class' constituency at this juncture, and of the experimentation in fitting it into people's understandings of the political map.

The attempts to give political meaning to the newly discovered presence of this social constituency were rarely as elaborate and striking as in the pages of the London *Examiner*. Like others, the *Examiner* in the early 1820s recurrently associated the 'middle class' with parliamentary reform: criticizing the present system for preventing the election of 'the most worthy and intellectual [who] are generally to be found in the middle ranks of life'; singling out 'the middling classes in particular' as those who 'abound with sound and steady thinkers' on practical plans of reform; or linking the progress of reform to 'the growing intelligence of the middling ranks of society'.[66] In April 1822 this tendency culminated in a series of leading articles on parties and opinions in the nation. In order 'to estimate the character and objects of the liberals and reformers', the *Examiner* stated, it was necessary to look at those sections of society most convinced of the need to expand the franchise. First and foremost among those, it asserted, was the 'middle class'.

At the outset, the *Examiner* acknowledged the need to delineate precisely what it meant by the 'middle class'. It proposed to do so by employing socio-economic and occupational categories:

And first as to what we are disposed to term the middle classes, from which we exclude the professions legal, military, and naval, as utterly disconnected, in general objects and interests. With these exceptions, we understand all persons of moderate or very small capital; and the still greater number with no capital at all, who, by dint of a decent parentage and respectable bringing up, may hope to succeed in the world by prudence and industry.[67]

Once again, note how an attempt at a clear-cut socio-economic definition of the 'middle class' was confounded by behavioural and moral considerations. But be that as it may, the *Examiner*'s

---

[66] *Examiner* 640, 2 April 1820, p. 212; 683, 4 February 1821, p. 67 (and compare 610, 5 September 1819, pp. 562–3, as quoted above, p. 203); 685, 18 February 1821, pp. 97–8. See also letter to editor in 556, 23 August 1818, p. 530, regarding 'the middle ranks of society [displaying] a great longing for a share of political power'; and 574, 27 December 1818, p. 818, rejecting the argument of the 'corruptionists' that 'an extension of the right of suffrage, even to the middling class, would be attended with danger'.

[67] *Examiner* 742, 14 April 1822, pp. 225–6.

point was that these 'men of small property and active industry' were perhaps nominally represented in parliament, but only by people who had little or no common interest with them. Consequently, the next issue proposed to provide this 'middle class' (here, however, characterized differently as those 'who depend more especially on trade') with a concrete political programme, specific to their own social position and circumstances:

in reference to the middle classes of British society, we will conclude with enumerating one or two national grievances, independent of onerous and expensive government, to which the individuals composing it are more peculiarly exposed, and to the removal of which their exertions are and should be directed.

The *Examiner*, then, was about to lay down an agenda supposedly capable of uniting the 'middle class' for political action (beyond its interest in parliamentary reform which it shared with other components of society). This agenda was based on common grievances which in the periodical's view affected predominantly if not exclusively the 'middle class' throughout the country. First was 'the monstrous cost and uncertainty of law', and in particular the Insolvent Act, which 'operates most directly on the middle classes', as did also the revenue laws. A second encroachment affecting primarily the 'middle class' was 'the incessant attempt to narrow social privileges, which, from the Treasury Bench to the Select Vestry, is the order of the day' – that is to say, an increasing exclusiveness in appointments to government and local administrative positions, which according to this article abetted 'venal influence and close government'. At present, these specifically 'middle-class' grievances could not be effectively addressed because this class had no true representation in parliament. The 'middle class' (or 'middle rank'), the *Examiner* affirmed, certainly could not be represented through the agency of 'the great Capitalists'. The latter were in fact 'their most direct opponents', with interests opposed to their own, 'especially when heavy duties are in question'.[68]

This was indeed a striking document, one that can be put forward as a compelling manifestation of class consciousness. It sought to endow the nebulous perception of a new social constitu-

---

[68] Ibid., 743, 21 April 1822, pp. 241–2. The article was signed 'Q'.

ency with tangible political meaning, by providing the 'middle class' with a precise definition as well as a coherent understanding of its common interests; interests which united its divergent members and set them apart from other classes. It gave the 'middle class' a concrete political agenda for realizing its shared interests and obtaining the power of redress: namely, by transforming the system of representation. On the whole, it made a valiant attempt to proclaim this social group a *class*. (It should also be noted, however, in anticipation of the discussion below, that – perhaps at odds with common historiographical presuppositions – this unusual statement, which originated in London, did *not* single out the new industrial classes within this 'middle class' or the corn laws as its political touchstone.)

No less striking than the content of this proposed 'middle-class' political programme, however, was its uniqueness. It was a singular experiment which had no echoes, no follow-ups, no parallels. The *Examiner* never again referred to this programme or to any of its points; in fact, its 'middle-class' language waned during the next few years, and its few recurrences neither implied distinctive class interests nor went beyond the issue of parliamentary reform.[69] I have not found any comparable statement elsewhere. While this of course does not preclude its possible existence beneath stones that have been left unturned, it does make the pre-1830 evidence for a clear vision of the 'middle class' as a coherent social class with distinctive interests seem very thin; which contrasts sharply with the profusion of analogous statements with regard to the working class. Indeed, the difficulty of translating a conceptualization of society based on the 'middle class' into a concrete socio-political programme was always to remain a fundamental one. It is in this sense that the title of the present section refers to an *imagined* constituency: although the belief in the existence of a 'middle class' where it had not been visible before was rapidly strengthening, inducing people to modify and revise their views of society and politics, this did not mean that its actual existence as a discernible and politically relevant social constituency had in fact been estab-

---

[69] One more instance in the *Examiner* can conceivably be seen as a (feeble) attempt to arouse the 'middle class' to its shared interests, in this case as encroached upon by Church tithes: 765, 22 September 1822, p. 593.

lished, or was any more 'real' now than it had been previously.

It may appear odd, however, that a metropolitan periodical such as the *Examiner* is taken as the bellwether for a meaningful understanding of the new 'middle-class' constituency in the 1820s. Arguably, the cradle of the English 'middle class' as we have come to think of it was Manchester, not London. Now it is certainly true that one can see a growing realization of the political relevance of northern (manufacturing) interests at this juncture. Such a realization – the political corollary to an increasing awareness of social change – could fit nicely into a vision of a rising 'middle-class' constituency. But, again, this was not an inevitable or necessarily plausible way to make sense of the increasing political pull of the northern districts. Various studies of manufacturing towns have actually pointed to the slow and feeble beginnings of any purported 'middle-class' self-awareness (let alone political consciousness) before the 1830s, particularly with regard to parliamentary reform.[70] While the present study is admittedly insensitive to the distinctiveness of local political contexts, at present there does not seem to be much evidence for a claim that the northern towns spearheaded the 1820s trend for proclaiming the importance of a 'middle-class' constituency and for demanding its enfranchisement. Let us look at one example more closely.

The *Manchester Guardian*, edited by the Unitarian ex-cotton merchant John Edward Taylor, is often taken as a quintessential northern 'middle-class' voice, manifesting typical 'middle-class' views – support for moderate but not radical reform, opposition to the corn laws and other landed privileges, and a patronizing condescension towards the lower orders.[71] Indeed, in October

---

[70] Briggs, 'The Background of the Parliamentary Reform Movement', pp. 180–213. D. Read, *The English Provinces c.1760–1960: A Study in Influence*, London, 1964. C. Flick, *The Birmingham Political Union and the Movements for Reform in Britain 1830–1839*, Hamden, 1978. V. A. C. Gatrell, 'Incorporation and the Pursuit of Liberal Hegemony in Manchester 1790–1839', in D. Fraser (ed.), *Municipal Reform and the Industrial City*, Leicester, 1982, pp. 15–60. A. Howe, *The Cotton Masters 1830–1860*, Oxford, 1984. R. J. Morris, *Class, Sect and Party: The Making of the British Middle Class, Leeds 1820–1850*, Manchester, 1990. T. Koditschek, *Class Formation and Urban-Industrial Society: Bradford 1750–1850*, Cambridge, 1990. On another issue, see the corrective regarding the rural rather than the industrial origins of the interest in 'middle-class' education before the 1830s in D. I. Allsobrook, *Schools for the Shires: The Reform of Middle-Class Education in Mid-Victorian England*, Manchester, 1986.

[71] For example Briggs, 'The Background of the Parliamentary Reform Movement', p. 193 and passim. D. Read, *Press and People 1790–1850: Opinion in Three English Cities*, London, 1961, pp. 79–87; and more generally pp. 137–52.

1821 – a few months after its inception – the *Manchester Guardian* brought the association between parliamentary representation and the 'middle class' into its own local setting. Noting the Cheshire Whig Club for its pro-reform stance, the newspaper commended the role of this club in 'bringing the aristocracy into occasional contact with the most important portion of our population, the middle class', who represented 'the opinions, the objects, and the intelligence, of the great body of their countrymen'. But this was a single isolated instance, in the midst of a national chorus of similar formulations at that moment (including Taylor's own proc-lamation of the importance of the new post-Peterloo 'middle class' constituency, as quoted in the epigraph to this section). It was more than six years and three hundred issues later before the matter of 'middle-class' representation was again broached in the pages of the *Manchester Guardian.*[72] Indeed, in the interim the news-paper hardly noticed the 'middle class' at all, in any context, with only one consequential exception – in an onslaught on aristocratic game laws.[73] The contrast with the end of the decade was striking, as the newspaper – like so many other contemporaries – came to see the efforts for reform repeatedly as an attempt to enfranchise the 'middle class'. Indeed it was only then, but not before, that the *Manchester Guardian* (in accordance with the role which historians have later bestowed upon it) came to see its own readers as 'the mass of the middle ranks [who] still look for progressive improvement in the institutions of their country', and itself as voicing the opinions of 'the vast majority of the middle classes'.[74]

This is not to say, of course, that prior to the end of the 1820s the *Manchester Guardian* had not concerned itself with parliamen-tary representation or with other issues in which its Mancunian manufacturing and mercantile readers had a vested interest. Only that until then it apparently had not found it necessary to reconceptualize society in order to do so. Instead, the newspaper's editorials repeatedly expounded the positions and grievances of the commercial, manufacturing or trading interests, using a lan-

---

[72] *Manchester Guardian* 1:24, 13 October 1821, editorial; 7:345, 8 December 1827, and 347, 22 December 1827 (see below, p. 304). These statements are based on a complete run of the *Manchester Guardian*'s editorials from its beginning in May 1821 through to 1832.

[73] Ibid., 6:295, 23 December 1826, editorial. One other reference, to the distress of the 'middle ranks', can be found in 7:257, 1 April 1826.

[74] Ibid., 11:505, 1 January 1831; 549, 5 November 1831.

guage that for many decades had proven suitable for economic pressure groups. The *Manchester Guardian* of the 1820s did not resort to new conceptual tools in order to voice the interests of its readership; wherever the notion of a rising 'middle-class' constituency came from, the *Guardian* was not at its forefront. And when the newspaper did succumb wholeheartedly to this notion at the end of the decade, as we shall see, the triumph of the 'middle class' in its pages was more of an echo of the national political debate than its clarion call.

The *Manchester Guardian* is only one example, albeit a rather significant one. But if one turns to its main rival among the provincial newspapers, the *Leeds Mercury*, a remarkably similar picture emerges. Following the national trend, in 1820 this newspaper too burst into roaring declarations for reform joined with 'middle-class idiom' that had been unprecedented in its pages, only to then lose this language altogether all the way up to the Reform Bill debates a decade later.[75] And in yet another provincial context, a similar pattern is evident in the writings of Thomas Attwood, Birmingham's most prominent public speaker of a 'middle' social position. Attwood wrote extensively from the late 1810s about economic issues, such as the currency and the corn laws, without any reference to 'middle-class' interests; the one exception, as for the *Manchester Guardian* and the *Leeds Mercury*, being in late 1819, in the immediate aftermath of Peterloo, in the context of parliamentary representation.[76] And like his contemporaries, it was in the early 1830s that Attwood too came

---

[75] This statement is based on the *Leeds Mercury* editorials between 1818 and 1832. On 1 January 1820 (53:2847), in discussing the Grampound issue, it stressed the political credentials of 'the genuine *middle class* of society', whose 'stake in the country is immense'; on 30 December 1820 (ibid., 2899) it asserted that 'amongst the middle class, which is inferiour to none in public virtue and in private worth, there is a "vast majority" who are the friends of the liberties of their country, and the enemies of [the present] system of abuse and misrule'. See also, not so strongly, the references to the 'middle class' in 52:2817, 5 June 1819, and 2831, 11 September 1819; 53:2851, 29 January 1820; and 54:2900, 6 January 1821. Thereafter, with a single minor exception (59:3183, 22 July 1826), the *Leeds Mercury* made no more references to a 'middle class' until the end of the decade, and even then it picked it up again rather slowly (see 62:3167, 19 September 1829; 64:3248, 16 April 1831, and 3282, 3 December 1831; 65:3303, 28 April 1832, and 3312, 23 June 1832).

[76] Thomas Attwood, *A Second Letter to the Earl of Liverpool, on the Bank Reports, as Occasioning the National Dangers and Distresses*, Birmingham, 1819, pp. 81, 90. In the same long pamphlet, the 'middle class' was absent from discussions of social and economic issues; as it was also not mentioned in his *The Remedy: Or, Thoughts on the Present Distresses ...*, London, 1816; *A Letter to the Right Honourable Nicholas Vansittart, on the*

to acknowledge more readily the relevance of the 'middle class'; only that rather than seeing himself then as its spokesman, he criticized it as worse than the higher and lower classes, 'as full of vice as the egg is full of meat . . . servile to our superiors, arrogant to our inferiors, jealous towards each other, indignant towards all'.[77] So while our picture of the evolution of differing conceptualizations of society in such varying local contexts remains patchy, it also remains true that there seems to be little evidence for any leading or formative role of the manufacturing districts in propagating a social vision based on a rising 'middle class'.

To recapitulate the basic argument, the 1820s saw a growing belief in the existence of a newly risen 'middle-class' constituency. This belief was driven by the strong impulse for limited parliamentary reform at the beginning of the decade, which required a demonstrable new social constituency that could justify an adjustment of constitutional arrangements without tampering with constitutional principles. At the same time it tallied with

Creation of Money, and on Its Action Upon National Prosperity, Birmingham, 1817; *Prosperity Restored: Or, Reflections on the Cause of the Public Distresses, and on the Only Means of Relieving Them*, London, 1817; *Observations on Currency, Population, and Pauperism, in Two Letters to Arthur Young*, Birmingham, 1818; *A [First] Letter to the Earl of Liverpool . . .*, Birmingham, 1819; *Mr Attwood's Letter and Tables, Shewing the Unjust Payment from the Landed to the Moneyed Interest, by the Present System; with the Ruin of the Landlord and Tenant*, Stamford, 1822; (with Sir John Sinclair), *The Late Prosperity, and the Present Adversity, Explained; . . . in a Correspondence . . .*, London, 1826 (where Sinclair put 'middle-class' language into Attwood's mouth, [p. 101], who himself had not used it [pp. 76–7]); *Causes of the Present Distress: Speech of Thomas Attwood, Esq. at the Public Meeting, Held in Birmingham, on the 8th of May, 1829, for the Purpose of Considering the Distressed State of the Country*, Birmingham, 1829.

[77] *Report of the Proceedings (of the Birmingham Political Union)*, 4 July 1831, quoted in Briggs, 'The Background of the Parliamentary Reform Movement', p. 206 n. 53. And see also *Speech of Thomas Attwood, Esq. MP, on the State of the Country, in the House of Commons, on Thursday, the 21st of March, 1833*, London, 1833, pp. 8, 20. Attwood had already expressed similar derision in 1820, commenting privately on 'Voltaire's favourites, the Middle Classes, [who] are fit for nothing but *dumb sheep* to be shorn at the will of their masters': letter to his wife, August 1820, quoted in D. J. Moss, *Thomas Attwood: The Biography of a Radical*, Montreal, 1990, p. 92. A tentative counter-example to the argument here may be presented from Liverpool, where already in 1813 it had been stated that 'the present irregular and shackled state of the right of voting' engendered 'discontent among the numerous and unrepresented middle class of society', consisting of 'the great body of the town', who were 'generally well informed' and consequently 'always liberal': *Brougham's Speeches: The Speeches Delivered During the Election at Liverpool, in October, 1812, by Henry Brougham, Esq . . . Together with an Impartial Account of the Election . . .*, Liverpool, 1813, pp. 6–7 (observations made by the anonymous author of the pamphlet, not by Brougham).

people's sense of a changing society and a changing political
arena – a fact that made it all the more convincing. Yet its
primary origin and logic remained the political configuration, not
the social one; ultimately, it was not the outcome of a developing
understanding of new social interests, nor of a rising consciousness
of a new social force conjured up by industrialization. There is
perhaps no better place, therefore, to conclude the latter part of
the argument – stressing the *imagined* social corollary to this
purported 'middle-class' constituency – than in the debate that
most famously brought economic interests into the political lime-
light, namely that on the corn laws.

What first stands out most strikingly in reading through the
many dozens of tracts, pamphlets, articles and speeches for and
against the corn laws (pouring not least from the northern manufacturing towns), is the fact that in their overwhelming majority
the 'middle class' played no role whatsoever. Ever since the re-
enactment of the corn law in 1815, virtually all participants in the
ensuing debates consistently formulated their arguments using the
language of 'interests', a language which carried with it (as we
have seen) very specific implications for the understanding of the
nature and limits of social conflicts. This was precisely the observation made by one pamphleteer in 1825, who set out to analyse
and compare the rhetoric of the opposing sides in this debate:

All the writers on the Corn-question [concluded this writer,] coincide
as to the *identity* of interests which subsists in a community between
the agriculturists and the manufacturers, the merchants and consumers
of all classes; but they disagree with respect to the *means* by which
these interests are brought to bear, to amalgamate and to har-
monize . . .
    That the interests of all classes are closely interwoven is, then,
unanimously acknowledged.[78]

The pamphlet demonstrated this shared social language, and
its shared underlying assumptions, with examples from eight
publications, both for and against the corn laws; and little more
can be achieved here than to repeat this exercise with innumer-

---

[78] *A Collection of Conflicting Opinions upon the Corn Question, Extracted from the Writings of the
Most Eminent Economists; and Contrasted in Parallel Columns, with Notes and Observations*,
London, 1825, pp. 10–11. The language of 'interests', it should be noted, was itself
evolving in interesting ways which are beyond my scope here, in particular with regard
to the implied assumptions about the evanescence of social conflicts.

able additional examples. Overall, notwithstanding the retrospective portrayal of the corn laws by historians as a key locus for the emergence of 'middle-class' consciousness,[79] hardly anyone in the 1810s and 1820s (and, for that matter, most of the 1830s) could find the all-too-vague category of 'middle class' helpful in defining and debating the specific social interests involved in this question.

Furthermore, even more telling were those infrequent exceptions in which the 'middle class' *was* invoked by writers on the corn laws – telling because of the very particular way in which they found it to be relevant to their arguments. Take for example one of the better-known anti-corn law tracts, James Graham's *Corn and Currency* of 1826. Throughout this 114-page discussion of corn and currency, the issues raised were all adequately resolved within other social vocabularies, be they the broad categories of productive versus unproductive classes, or the more specific language of 'interests' – the landed, commercial, manufacturing, shipping or monied interests. Only once, however, did the 'middle class' make an appearance – indeed quite a powerful one – in this tract:

Are there then no limits to the power of the Land Proprietors . . .? I freely answer, that I know no bound but public opinion; and this is a barrier which they cannot pass . . .

The seat of public opinion is in the middle ranks of life – in that numerous class, removed alike from the wants of labour and the cravings of ambition, enjoying the advantages of leisure, and possessing intelligence sufficient for the formation of a sound judgment, neither warped by interest nor obscured by passion.[80]

This passage could not easily be squared with the other social vocabularies Graham employed throughout the rest of his argument; it was, as it were, an alien intrusion. A more important point, however, is that the category of 'middle class' surfaced in Graham's tract *not* as a concrete social constituency whose inter-

---

[79] The classic statement here is A. Briggs, 'Middle-Class Consciousness in English Politics, 1780–1846', *Past and Present* 9 (1956): 'During the long battle for Repeal [of the corn laws], middle-class consciousness was forged as it never had been before' (p. 71). Briggs was extrapolating back from Richard Cobden's remarks on the Anti-Corn Law League of the 1840s, though those in fact marked a sharp break with the previous thirty years of corn law discussions: see below, pp. 409–10.

[80] James Graham, *Corn and Currency: In an Address to the Land Owners*, London, 1826, p. 9.

ests were infringed upon by specific social and economic policies.
Rather, it was invoked only in its familiar guise of the 1820s, as
a contender in the political playing field. It was defined not
primarily by its position in relation to consumption, production
and trade, but by its middle social position conducive to those
political virtues that made it the bearer of the much-revered
'public opinion'.

The same year, J. R. McCulloch contributed a long essay on
the corn laws to the *Edinburgh Review*. This issue, McCulloch
explained at the outset, 'affect[ed] the interests of the landlords
and farmers, or those of the manufacturing, mercantile, and
monied classes'; a terminology which he maintained for the
subsequent forty pages. But then, in the final paragraph, which
was separated physically from the rest of the essay by a blank
line, McCulloch turned to parliamentary politics. The present
political moment, he believed, was especially auspicious for a
decisive resolution of this thorny issue. McCulloch concluded his
essay by assuring the ministers that

notwithstanding the outcry and clamour that a small faction, opposed
to every species of improvement, and attached to every thing that is
antiquated and vicious, has raised against them, they may be assured
that their late measures are cordially approved by the vast majority of
the middle classes.[81]

The similarity with the writing of James Graham is striking. Just
like Graham, McCulloch did not integrate the 'middle class' into
the rest of his discussion, either in content or in form. Just like
Graham, McCulloch found the 'middle class' relevant not to the
issue of corn, but to the making of laws. Just like Graham,
McCulloch envisioned the 'middle class' as a political – but not
a social or economic – player.

Or take another important anti-corn law tract, T. Perronet
Thompson's *Catechism on the Corn Laws*, whose publication in 1827
was followed by at least fifteen editions within five years. The

---

[81] *Edinburgh Review* 44, September 1826, pp. 319, 359. See similarly the *Examiner* 646, 14
May 1820, p. 315, where again the 'middle class' was explicitly represented as
victims not of the corn laws but of the political system which favoured ministerial
boroughmongers. As for McCulloch, although the language of 'middle class' became
more common in his post-1832 writings, it was still absent from a sequel to his
discussion of the corn laws in the *Edinburgh Review* 58, January 1834, pp. 271ff., even
as it was incorporated into another discussion in the same essay (p. 306).

pattern was again repeated: after a protracted analysis of the grievances and interests involved in the corn laws, for which Thompson employed conceptual schemes that did not involve a 'middle class', when he came to speak of the political setting required to pass the repeal of these laws, his social language suddenly changed:

The middle classes in this country have an insuperable aversion to unnecessary changes; but if they find out that their distresses, though not coming precisely in the shape of want of bread, but in the shape of the bankruptcy of their sons and of their daughters' husbands, the general stagnation of trade and the impossibility of rising in the world by honourable industry, are traceable to a common cause, – they will join the others, and make a mass of opinion which it will be impossible to resist.[82]

True, Thompson – a military officer, son of a Hull merchant-banker and later Hull's MP – was pointing in this passage to the interests and the particular difficulties of the 'middle class', thus coming closer to positing it as a social constituency. But even so, these purported grievances failed to attract his attention as 'middle-class' problems in the detailed expositions of the consequences of the corn laws throughout his *Catechism*. Once again, the one meaningful invocation of the 'middle class' – and the appeal to its self-interest – was elicited by an effort to mobilize 'a mass of opinion' as political pressure on what Thompson referred to as 'the house of landlords'. The same pattern was evident several years later in another long tract on economic and social issues – John Gray's *The Social System* – in which the 'middle

---

[82] [T. Perronet Thompson], *A Catechism on the Corn Laws* . . ., London, 1827, p. 46; and see p. 20 for one more oblique reference to the 'middle class'. This is the only source cited by Asa Briggs ('Middle-Class Consciousness in English Politics') – in addition to Cobden's retrospection of the 1840s – as proof of the role of the corn laws in forging a 'middle class' consciousness. It is also suggestive that Alexander Mundell, who in 1825 announced (as we have seen) the political advent of the 'middle class', used no 'middle-class' language (but only the language of 'manufacturing' versus 'agricultural' interests) in a subsequent series of tracts on the corn laws: see his *The Necessary Operation of the Corn Laws . . . with a Remedy for Those Evils*, London, 1831; *The Operation of the Corn Laws During the Last Sixty Years . . .*, London, 1833; *Four Letters . . . Showing the Operation of the Corn Laws . . .*, London, 1836. Earlier examples of corn law tracts in which the 'middle class' did appear, but not as part of the discussion of social and economic policies and their consequences, include Thomas Malthus, *Observations on the Effects of the Corn Laws*, 1814; in *Works*, vol. VII (for the 'middle class', pp. 101–2); *Remarks on the Commercial Policy of Great Britain, Principally as It Relates to the Corn Trade*, London, 1815 (the 'middle class', pp. 8, 14, 16).

class' appeared again only in an appeal to 'public opinion'
(and in the self-identification of the author) in the last few
paragraphs.[83]

In sum, these occasional references to the 'middle class' in the
debates on the corn laws all invoked it primarily as a powerful
component in the political playing field, rather than as a specific
social group with shared interests affected by economic policy.
The notion of 'middle class' was not as helpful in conceptualizing
the social problems created by such policy as it was in conceptualizing the political means for its resolution. True, as this
chapter has shown, the 'middle class' was endowed in the 1820s
with a powerful narrative of social change that explained its
origins and power; and true, this social construction of the rising
'middle class' constituency was forcefully coupled with the political move to constitutional reform; and yet it also remained true
that this constituency was no less imaginary for all that.

---

[83] John Gray, *The Social System: A Treatise on the Principle of Exchange*, Edinburgh, 1831
(rep. Clifton, N.J., 1973), pp. 328, 332–3. At a later date, compare *The Late Commercial
Crisis; Being a Retrospect of the Years 1836 to 1838: ... A Safe, Speedy, and Equitable Plan
for the Abolition of the Corn Laws. By a Glasgow Manufacturer*, Glasgow, 1839, in which a
mainstay of the alleged new and assertive 'middle class' discussed the corn laws for
110 pages with a variety of elaborate social schemes but without any 'middle-class'
language; only to change his vocabulary in the final paragraph (pp. 110–11), which
appealed to the 'middling classes' as the new electorate – evidently, that is, relevant
only as a political pressure group.

CHAPTER 8

The parallels across the Channel: a French aside

All the higher ranks [*supériorités*], whatever their age and their nature, must, I repeat, accept this fact, the definitive fact of our era, namely the triumph of the middle classes.

(François Guizot, 1837)[1]

The word *middle classes*, I repeat, is a lie. There are no middle classes.

(Henri Fonfrède, 1839)[2]

By now the reader might have been struck by one peculiar consequence of the present argument. The rise of the 'middle class', familiar *ad nauseam* as one of the most *universal* characterizations of modern society, here turns out to be a notion that emerged from very *particular* circumstances, circumstances that prevailed in a specific society at a specific historical moment. As we shall see further, the leap to a universalized understanding of the 'middle class' had in itself specific historical origins and logic. But even without universalizing presuppositions, we may still want to raise our heads above British waters and ask similar questions of other comparable societies, in their own no less distinct and historically specific conditions. When and how did people elsewhere come to believe that they too lived in societies structured around a 'middle class', and what further light can such comparisons shed on the uses of this particular conceptualization of society?

---

[1] 'Il faut que toutes les supériorités, quelles que soient leur date et leur nature, je le répète, acceptent ce fait, ce fait définitif de notre époque, le triomphe des classes moyennes': François Guizot, *Histoire parlementaire de France: recueil complet des discours prononcés dans les chambres de 1819 à 1848*, Paris, 1863, vol. III, p. 75, debate of 3 May 1837.

[2] 'Le mot *classes moyennes*, nous le répétons, est un mensonge. Il n'y a pas de classes moyennes.' Henri Fonfrède, *De la société, du gouvernement et de l'administration* (originally 1839); see below, note 32.

The case of America, an interesting contrast with that of Britain, is considered later. The present chapter examines, however briefly, the developments in France following the Bourbon Restoration in 1815. Its goal is not to provide an analogous study of the uses of 'middle-class' language in post-Napoleonic France, nor merely to establish ideational pipe-lines, as it were, through which a genealogy of concepts can be traced from London to Paris and back. Rather, it is to gain further insights into the dynamics and logic of the evolving uses of 'middle-class' language in Britain, by highlighting both surprising resemblances and significant differences between them and those in France after 1815. This comparative exercise will suggest, first, that in defiance of conventional wisdom about the expected correlation between a critical mass of social change and certain changes in social consciousness, it was the country that lagged markedly behind in the former – France – that gained the distinctive lead in the latter. Second, the comparison again underscores the key role of the political (rather than the social) process in producing such a dynamic in the uses of social language; that is to say, in infusing (quite abruptly) persuasive force into a particular representation of social experience, experience for which this particular representation was not necessarily an obvious or inevitable one. It is through their respective political configurations that both similarities and differences between the developments of 'middle-class' language in the two countries can be accounted for. These observations will hopefully justify the momentary digression from the main narrative of this book, which is resumed again in chapter 9.

It is an observation more often remarked upon than carefully documented that during the post-1815 Restoration in France the power of the 'middle class' was widely announced and celebrated. The prime harbingers of the sudden advent of the 'middle class' (which does not seem to have particularly struck anyone before the demise of Napoleon) were the political liberals, a vague term in which one particular group stands out, the 'doctrinaires'. The doctrinaires emerged towards the end of 1817 as a remarkably influential circle within the centre-left fragment of Richelieu's splintering constitutional party, whose effectiveness in propagating their 'doctrines' was less a consequence of their numerical weight or voting power than of their political skill and eloquence.

Take for example a key figure in their ranks, perhaps the first to have been called 'doctrinaire': Pierre-Paul Royer-Collard, who at the beginning of the Restoration had left a chair of philosophy in the Sorbonne for a career in politics. Having never published significant political works, Royer-Collard's influential ideas were expressed in political speeches, each of which was an event in itself. One occasion for such a speech, soon after the Restoration, was the important debate about the voting law, whose form depended on different interpretations of the Charter of 1814. Royer-Collard supported a limited franchise (for taxpayers of more than 300 francs per annum), and this is how he put it to the Chamber of Deputies in 1816: the Charter demanded that both electors and the elected would maintain 'une sage indépendence', and that no interest in the nation would remain unrepresented. Therefore, he concluded,

Clearly, it is the middle class that could provide natural representation for all social interests [*intérêts*]; above this level one finds a certain need to dominate, against which we must guard; below lies ignorance, habit, a lack of independence, and consequently a complete inaptitude for the positions in question.[3]

Addressing the Chamber again in March 1819, Royer-Collard explained that these political virtues of the 'middle class' were not a mere theoretical matter. Rejecting criticisms of the voting law as giving an undue preponderance to the 'middle class', he asserted:

The influence of the middle class is not simply an arbitrary, if judicious preference of the law; and doubtless reason and justice also play a role; but it has other causes as well ... The influence of the middle class is a fact, a powerful and formidable fact. It is a living, well-organized theory, one capable of repelling its adversaries' attacks. It was developed

---

[3] 'C'est, en effet, évidemment dans la classe moyenne que tous les intérêts pouvaient trouver leur représentation naturelle; au-dessus est un certain besoin de la domination, contre lequel il faut se tenir en garde; au-dessous, l'ignorance, l'habitude et le besoin de l'indépendence, et par conséquent inaptitude complète aux fonctions dont il s'agit.' Prosper de Barante, *La Vie politique de M. Royer-Collard*, Paris, 1861, vol. I, p. 290. Barante commented on this debate, that Royer-Collard was never again so involved in a discussion in the Chamber. On Royer-Collard and the doctrinaires, see D. Johnson, *Guizot: Aspects of French History 1787–1874*, London, 1963, pp. 32–5.

over many centuries, and was made manifest in the revolution. It is to this class that the new social interests [*intérêts*] belong.[4]

Moreover, he warned, the security of the 'middle class' cannot be impinged upon (as would be the consequence of tampering with the voting law) without posing imminent danger to the established order as a whole.

Royer-Collard's 'middle class', then, characterized by intelligence and independence, was politically more valuable than the power-greedy upper classes and the ignorant and dependent lower classes: what a familiar picture. In passing, note that Royer-Collard was using the term 'classe moyenne', equivalent to the English 'middle class', rather than the term 'bourgeoisie', which is often assumed to be the French counterpart to 'middle class'. During the Restoration and the July Monarchy, in fact, 'classe(s) moyenne(s)' was used with increasing frequency, at times interchangeably with 'bourgeoisie' but more often displacing and incorporating it.[5] For Royer-Collard, the advent of the 'middle class' was the outcome of a prolonged historical process of social change that introduced new and powerful interests; as he explained elsewhere, 'it is true that industry and property [have] long and ceaselessly [been] causing the middle classes to multiply, expand and rise'.[6]

Royer-Collard's voting law speech of March 1819 was quoted at length by Benjamin Constant, a liberal who mostly found himself to the left of the doctrinaires, as proof of the former's 'irresistible eloquence'. Constant then remarked: 'his observations on the necessary and inevitable influence of the middle class are

[4] 'L'influence de la classe moyenne n'est pas une préférence arbitraire, quoique judicieuse, de la loi; sans doute elle est avouée par la raison et par la justice; mais elle a d'autres fondements encore ... L'influence de la classe moyenne est un fait, un fait puissant et redoutable; c'est une théorie vivante, organisée, capable de repousser les coups de ses adversaires. Les siècles l'ont préparée; la révolution l'a déclarée. C'est à cette classe que les intérêts nouveaux appartiennent.' Barante, *La Vie politique de M. Royer-Collard*, vol. I, p. 456.

[5] The significant exception to this pattern was in discussions of the bourgeoisie's long-term historical development. See A. Daumard, *Les Bourgeois et la bourgeoisie en France depuis 1815*, Paris, 1987, pp. 44–51. Also E. J. Hobsbawm, *Echoes of the Marseillaise: Two Centuries Look Back on the French Revolution*, New Brunswick, 1990, p. 22. Considering this pattern in the French sources of this period, I chose to maintain here the same 'middle-class' terminology as throughout the rest of this book. Also see Willibald Steinmetz's discussion of the French sources in his essay cited in p. 15, note 22.

[6] 'Il est vrai que, dès longtemps, l'industrie et la propriété ne cess[ent] de féconder, d'accroître, d'élever les classes moyennes': Barante, *La Vie politique de M. Royer-Collard*, vol. II, p. 134, debate of 2 January 1822.

very sound; they contain the idea on which all our institutions must now be based, the true secret of modern government, the fruit of experience and the wisdom of the century'.[7] In Constant's eyes, Royer-Collard's 'middle-class idiom' was nothing less than the inevitable secret of the future, the foundation of modern society. It was a view which Constant himself reiterated in discussions of the voting law in 1817–19, talking often about 'la classe intermédiaire' created by the changes which industry had recently introduced into society: it embodied education, talent and enlightenment; it was the repository of independence, 'because everyone needs it and it needs no-one'; it represented all interests in society with more impartiality than the upper classes and with less ignorance than the lower classes; it was the repository of patriotism, with interests inseparable from the national interests. And for Constant too it was the 'middle class' that guaranteed political stability and order: 'The poor have too little to lose, but the rich could risk too much. It is in between, in the intermediate class, where the interest of conservation, and thus of order, eminently lies.'[8] Interestingly, ever since his college days at Edinburgh Constant had been a personal friend of James Mackintosh, who was making surprisingly similar observations about the English 'middle class' at precisely the same time.[9]

While Royer-Collard was speaking for the doctrinaires in the

---

[7] 'Ses observations sur l'influence nécessaire, inévitable, de la classe moyenne, sont pleines de justesse; elles contiennent l'idée sur laquelle doivent reposer désormais toutes nos institutions, le véritable secret des gouvernements modernes, le fruit de l'expérience et la sagesse du siècle': Benjamin Constant, *Cours de politique constitutionnelle*, 3rd edn, Brussels, 1837 (originally Paris, 1819), pp. 403–4. Compare Guizot's appreciation for Royer-Collard's 'middle-class idiom' in *Mémoires pour servir à l'histoire de mon temps*, Paris, 1864, vol. VI, pp. 347–8.

[8] 'La pauvreté a trop peu à perdre, mais la richesse peut trop risquer. Dans la médiocrité, dans la classe intermédiaire, est éminemment l'intérêt de la conservation, et, par-là même, de l'ordre.' Constant, *Cours de politique constitutionnelle*, pp. 247–8, 453. Constant commented on these passages: 'Jamais je n'ai rien écrit avec une conviction plus profonde.'

[9] Mackintosh also wrote about the 'middle class' being the repository of sense and virtue, about their connections of interest with the rest of society, as well as about their inclination to political order, when compared both to commanding fortune and to thoughtless poverty. Mackintosh further asserted that the 'middle class' 'should have a preponderating influence, because they are likely to make the best choice' (*Edinburgh Review* 31, December 1818, p. 191); reminiscent of Constant's words, that 'à elle appartient d'affermir par ses choix la liberté constitutionnelle' (ibid., p. 453). Mackintosh indeed referred explicitly to the voting law in France, as we shall see below.

Chamber of Deputies, another of their ranks, who was as yet
too young to be eligible for the Chamber, was busily putting
together the historical framework for the advent of the 'middle
class': this was François Guizot. Guizot's role during the 1820s
and 1830s in providing the French 'middle class' with a collective
memory and history, and his self-proclaimed goal of realizing
their ultimate political preponderance, have been amply documented; only a few signposts, imparting the flavour of his voluminous writings and relentless speeches on this subject, need
be briefly considered here.[10] As Guizot himself put it retrospectively to the Chamber of Deputies in 1837:

I am faithful today to the political idea which has guided me for my
whole life. Yes! today, as in 1817, as in 1820, as in 1830, I desire, I
seek, I devote all my strength to the political supremacy of the middle
classes in France, to the regular and definitive formation of this great
victory which the middle classes gained over privilege and absolute
power between 1789 and 1830. This is the goal towards which I have
consistently striven, towards which I still strive today.[11]

During the 1820s, when he was out of political office, Guizot's
main celebrations of the 'middle class' were incorporated into
his historical works. This was a decade, after all, in which
historical writing played a major political role in France, perhaps
analogous to that played by philosophy in the eighteenth century:
as Stanley Mellon has put it, 'history was the language of politics'.[12] In 1823 Guizot explained the decline of the Roman
empire – which, as we have seen, often provided British commen-

---

[10] The most elaborate discussion of 'the prophet of the rise of the bourgeoisie to political
power' is in P. Rosanvallon, *Le Moment Guizot*, Paris, 1985, esp. pp. 44–54, 177–220
(quoted, p. 185). See also Johnson, *Guizot*, pp. 75–8.

[11] 'Je suis fidèle aujourd'hui à l'idée politique qui m'a dirigé pendant toute ma vie. Oui!
aujourd'hui, comme en 1817, comme en 1820, comme en 1830, je veux, je cherche,
je sers de tous mes efforts la prépondérance politique des classes moyennes en France,
l'organisation définitive et régulière de cette grande victoire que les classes moyennes
ont remportée sur le privilége et sur le pouvoir absolu de 1789 à 1830. Voilà le but
vers lequel j'ai constamment marché, vers lequel je marche encore aujourd'hui.' Guizot,
Histoire parlementaire, vol. III, p. 74, debate of 3 May 1837; this speech was printed and
distributed in 30,000 copies. Compare also idem, *Mémoires pour servir à l'histoire de mon
temps*, Paris, 1870, vol. I, p. 296.

[12] According to Comte Daru, Stendhal's uncle, during 1825 alone were printed almost
forty million pages of history – some ten million more than the next largest category
(*belles-lettres*), and an enormous increase from the three million pages of history published in 1811. See S. Mellon, *The Political Uses of History: A Study of the Historians of
the French Restoration*, Stanford, 1958 (quoted, p. 1).

tators with a framework for *dual* conceptualizations of society –
in the destruction of the Roman 'middle class' by imperial despotism. His university lectures of 1828–30, published as the history
of civilization in Europe and France, were focused around the
formation and the progress of the bourgeoisie from its medieval
achievements of communal freedom through a series of social
transformations leading into the nineteenth century. At first,
Guizot maintained, the medieval bourgeois 'had no public,
common existence as a class'. But as time went by, their shared
situation, interests and habits could not fail to engender certain
ties and a certain unity. Ultimately, 'the formation of a great
social class, the bourgeoisie, necessarily followed from the local
emancipation of the bourgeois'. And yet for a long time its social
formation was not accompanied by political assertion. One cannot
but be astounded by a singular fact in the history of the bourgeoisie, Guizot continued (in words reminiscent, again, of James
Mackintosh's – with whom Guizot too had personal contacts):
'I wish to speak of the prodigious timidity of the bourgeois, of
their humility, of the excessive modesty of their claims relative
to the government of their country.' Guizot's wish was to turn
the present-day 'middle class' into something quite different from
the bourgeoisie of older times, into 'a great and proud power
. . . a true political power'.[13]

For Guizot too, 'bourgeoisie' (a more historical term) and
'classe moyenne' (a more present-oriented one) were largely interchangeable. As for the precise sociological definition of this terminology, Guizot made it clear that it lacked any, in the past
as well as in the present. This vagueness of definition was its

---

[13] '[Ils] n'avaient, comme classe, aucune existence publique et commune.' 'La formation
d'une grande classe sociale, de la bourgeoisie, était le résultat nécessaire de l'affranchis-
sement local des bourgeois.' 'Je veux parler de la prodigieuse timidité d'esprit des
bourgeois, de leur humilité, de l'excessive modestie de leurs prétentions quant au
gouvernement de leur pays.' 'Une grande et fière puissance . . . une puissance vraiment
politique.' Idem, *Histoire générale de la civilisation en Europe*, 3rd edn, Paris, 1840 (originally
1830), pp. 216–21; also p. 201. In 1837 Guizot remarked, 'ne croyez pas . . . que la
classe moyenne actuelle ressemble à la bourgeoisie du moyen âge' (*Histoire parlementaire*,
vol. III, p. 74, debate of 3 May 1837). As Shirley Gruner has pointed out ('Political
Historiography in Restoration France', *History and Theory* 8 (1969), pp. 346–65), the
interest in the medieval struggles for freedom in the communes and in the trajectory
from them to the French Revolution was raised by Comte de Montlosier's *De la
monarchie française* of 1814: yet for him – significantly, writing before the Restoration –
the same story was set entirely within a dual social scheme, without any 'middle
class'.

particular strength: 'Have I set limits to the middle class? Have you heard me say where it begins, or where it ends? I have scrupulously abstained from doing so; I have distinguished it neither from a higher class, nor from the lower ones.' Indeed, in Guizot's hands 'middle class' became equivalent to the 'third estate' (*tiers état*).[14] Needless to say, as Alexis de Tocqueville had already pointed out, this was not an inevitable nor a necessarily plausible way to understand the latter term, as used, for instance, by Abbé Sieyès in his famous *Qu'est-ce que le Tiers Etat?*[15] Instead, such a representation was imposing a very specific gloss on French history, and in particular on the French Revolution.

And it was undoubtedly a gloss that was becoming popular among Restoration historians, writing about distant epochs or about the momentous events of the preceding generation. History was being rewritten with the 'middle class' at its centre stage. Take for example Augustin Thierry, whose 1829 edition of the *Lettres sur l'histoire de France* directed attention to the medieval bourgeois and their struggles for liberty as the unduly neglected precursors of the present 'middle class':

[14] 'Ai-je assigné des limites à la classe moyenne? M'avez-vous entendu dire où elle commençait, où elle finissait? Je m'en suis soigneusement abstenu; je ne l'ai distinguée ni d'une classe supérieure, ni des classes inférieures': Guizot, *Histoire parlementaire*, vol. III, p. 104; and see also his *Histoire générale de la civilisation en Europe*, p. 217. Guizot repeated this, and many of his other observations about the 'middle class' as the most important component in French history, in an article on the 'Tiers-état' in Maurice Block, *Dictionnaire générale de la politique*, Paris, 1864–5; paraphrased in Johnson, *Guizot*, pp. 76–7. Such an inclusive understanding of the bourgeoisie was similarly heard in the Chamber of Deputies in 1830: 'Quiconque dans les classes inférieures a de l'intelligence et de la probité entre avec sa famille dans les rangs de la bourgeoisie . . . Sans cesse la bourgeoisie se recrute dans le peuple, sans cesse il y a de nouvelles familles bourgeoises.' (*Journal des débats*, 13 September 1830; quoted in Daumard, *Les Bourgeois et la bourgeoisie*, p. 129; and p. 45 for a further similar statement by P. Duvergier de Hauranne in 1838.)

[15] Sieyès's understanding of the 'tiers état', which at least at first sight was something quite different from Guizot's 'classe moyenne', is amply evident in the opening passages of the first chapter: see Emmanuel Sieyès, *Qu'est-ce que le Tiers Etat?*, ed. R. Zapperi, Geneva, 1970, pp. 121–2. See also W. H. Sewell, *Work and Revolution in France: The Language of Labor from the Old Regime to 1848*, Cambridge, 1980, pp. 78–84. More recently, Sewell has actually come around to seeing Sieyès as speaking primarily for a 'bourgeoisie', albeit very loosely defined, and has emphasized the resulting tensions with the democratic implications of his argument (idem, *A Rhetoric of Bourgeois Revolution: The Abbé Sieyès and What is the Third Estate?*, Durham, N.C., 1994). For Tocqueville's detailed rejection of the misleading equivalence between the inclusive 'tiers état' and the restrictive category of 'middle class', see his contribution to the *Westminster Review* in 1836 (translated by John Stuart Mill), as reprinted in [Gustave de Beaumont (ed.)], *Memoirs, Letters and Remains of Alexis de Tocqueville*, 2 vols., Boston, 1862, vol. I, p. 218.

these bourgeois of the middle ages . . . We should believe that they were worth something, and that the most numerous and most forgotten portion of the nation deserves to live again in history. We should not imagine that the middle class or the popular classes only acquired patriotism and energy yesterday.[16]

Tellingly, in an earlier version of this essay (published in 1820) Thierry had included much of the same passage, but with a different group singled out as that component of society whose struggles for liberty had been so important: in 1820 it had not yet been the 'middle class' or the bourgeoisie (neither of which were mentioned), but 'those serfs who had escaped from the soil'.[17] At some point during the 1820s, it seems, Thierry had come to appreciate the specific historical importance of the 'middle class' and reconstructed his history accordingly. From the middle ages through to 1789, he now wrote in conclusion to his *Lettres*, 'the word bourgeois was not simply a sign of freedom, but an honourable title, for it expressed both the idea of personal liberties and of participation in municipal sovereignty'.[18]

Only hinted at by Thierry, a key event whose history was being rewritten was of course the French Revolution, now presented (in its unobjectionable aspects) as a revolution of the 'middle class'.

[16] 'Ces bourgeois du moyen âge . . . Croyons qu'ils ont valu quelque chose, et que la partie la plus nombreuse et la plus oubliée de la nation mérite de revivre dans l'histoire. Il ne faut pas s'imaginer que la classe moyenne ou les classes populaires soient nées d'hier pour le patriotisme et l'energie.' Augustin Thierry, *Lettres sur l'histoire de France*, in *Dix ans d'études historiques*, Paris, 1859 (originally in this form, 1827), p. 12. See also Mellon, *The Political Uses of History*, pp. 11–12. Another doctrinaire who was intensely interested in similar historical themes was Prosper de Barante, in his *Des Communes et de l'aristocratie*, Paris, 1821; and *Histoire des ducs des Bourgogne, de la maison de Valois, 1364–1477*, Paris, 1824–6.

[17] Letter to the *Courrier français*, 13 July 1820, reprinted in *Dix ans d'études historiques*, p. 503; by 1829, 'ces serfs échappés de la glèbe' were replaced by the bourgeois in what was identifiably the same sentence. On these variations, and more generally on Thierry's views of the 'middle class', see R. L. Smithson, *Augustin Thierry: Social and Political Consciousness in the Evolution of a Historical Method*, Geneva, 1972, pp. 136–8, 150–2. J. Walch, *Les Maîtres de l'histoire 1815–1850*, Geneva, 1986, pp. 69–71.

[18] 'Le nom de bourgeois n'était pas seulement un signe de liberté, mais un titre d'honneur: car il exprimait à la fois les idées de franchises personnelles et de participation à la souveraineté municipale.' *Dix ans d'études historiques*, p. 289. In 1840 his judgment was even more confident: in the medieval communes and cities were the origins of our present social order, he wrote, 'qui ont donné, sous mille formes, le spectacle de ce gouvernement de la bourgeoisie, qui est aujourd'hui, et sera, pour des siècles, la loi fondamentale du pays'. (*Considérations sur l'histoire de France*; cited in Smithson, *Augustin Thierry*, p. 213.) See also L. Gossman, 'Augustin Thierry and Liberal Historiography', *History and Theory*, supplement 15, 1976.

Before 1815 such an understanding of the French Revolution, while often voiced in Britain, had only rarely been found in France. But during the Restoration it came to be shared by many, including Thierry and Royer-Collard, as well as Guizot, who described thus the purpose of his writing of 1820: 'to prove that our revolution of 1789 was the final, glorious victory of the middle class over privilege and absolute power'.[19] Or listen to Benjamin Constant in 1829: 'The great benefit of the French revolution, the one which compensates for all the harm this revolution caused, was the introduction of the intermediate class into the administration of affairs of state.' Ever since the Revolution, he asserted, 'the men of the intermediate class, the strength of the nation, gained legitimate access to the handling of national interests'. But while the Revolution freed the 'middle class' from aristocratic condescension, this did not imply that the 'middle class' was predisposed to political upheaval; as Constant hastened to reassure his readers, whereas support for such upheavals is readily found among the great landowners, 'it is in the middle class that the enemies of revolutions are to be found'.[20]

Already much earlier, shortly after the return of the Bourbons in 1815, Comte Roederer – who himself had played a role in the Revolution of 1789 – stressed its long-term germination among the 'middle class': 'The revolution took place in people's minds before it did so in law, and it took place in the habits of the middle class before it did so in the nation as a whole.' In the opening paragraphs of his essay on the spirit of the Revolution he explained further: 'The revolution . . . took root in that middle

---

[19] 'De prouver que notre révolution de 1789 était la victoire glorieuse et définitive de la classe moyenne sur le privilége et sur le pouvoir absolu.' *Histoire parlementaire*, vol. III, p. 73, speech of 3 May 1837. In a famous letter to Weydemeyer in 1852, Karl Marx acknowledged his debt to the French 'bourgeois historians' for discovering the existence of classes and of class struggle; of whom Engels many years later mentioned specifically Thierry, Mignet and Guizot. Quoted in G. C. Comninel, *Rethinking the French Revolution: Marxism and the Revisionist Challenge*, London, 1987, pp. 55–6. See also R. Fossaert, 'La Théorie des classes chez Guizot et Thierry', *La Pensée* 59 (1955), pp. 59–69.

[20] 'Le grand bienfait de la révolution française, celui qui compense tous les maux que cette révolution a causés, c'est l'introduction de la classe intermédiaire dans l'administration des affaires de l'Etat.' 'Les hommes de la classe intermédiaire, la force de la nation, entrent de plein droit dans le maniement des intérêts nationaux'; 'c'est dans la classe moyenne que sont les ennemis des révolutions'. Benjamin Constant, *Mélanges de littérature et de politique*, Paris, 1829, pp. 416–19. And see B. Fontana, *Benjamin Constant and the Post-Revolutionary Mind*, New Haven, 1991, p. 72.

class which is attached to the two extremes of society, which feels, thinks, reads, converses, and reflects; in that class where all complaints are heard, and where all the suffering of the lower classes are noticed.' Consequently, Roederer continued, the 'middle class' was the real engine of the Revolution: 'It was the opinion of this middling [*mitoyenne*] class which gave the signal to the lower classes; it was the revolt of opinion which triggered the insurrection of misery.' Remarkably, this formulation which Roederer found useful in explaining the Revolution at the end of 1815 had apparently failed to occur to him previously, ever since his own revolutionary experience.[21]

But of all the history writers of the Restoration, it was François Mignet who provided the most elaborate interpretation of the French Revolution as a revolution of the 'middle class'. In his *Histoire de la révolution française* of 1824 Mignet distinguished between two successive stages in the Revolution. The first, benign and welcome, culminated in the constitution of 1791: 'This constitution was the work of the middle class, which then found itself the strongest.' At that stage the people were the source of all power but exercised none: both elections and public functions were restricted to 'the enlightened nation', expanded daily by the progress of civilization, that is to say the 'middle class' which alone had the intelligence required for government. Indeed, where the absence of social change had failed to produce a 'middle class', the revolution failed to take root: 'In the Vendée, there was neither enlightenment nor civilization, because there was no middle class; and there was no middle class, because there were

---

[21] 'La révolution a été faite dans les esprits avant de l'être par les lois, et dans les mœurs de la classe moyenne avant de l'être dans la nation.' 'La révolution ... était établie dans cette classe moyenne qui tient aux deux extrêmes de la société générale, qui sent, qui pense, qui lit, converse, réfléchit; dans cette classe où s'entendent toutes les plaintes, où se remarquent toutes les souffrances des classes inférieurs.' 'C'est l'opinion de cette classe mitoyenne qui a donné le signal aux classes inférieures; c'est la révolte de l'opinion qui a fait éclater l'insurrection des souffrances.' P. L. Roederer, 'L'esprit de la révolution', originally written at the end of 1815; in *Œuvres du comte P. L. Roederer*, ed. A. M. Roederer, Paris, 1854, vol. III, pp. 7–56 (quoted, pp. 7–8). For his social language in the 1790s, which revealed recognition of the Third Estate, rich and poor, and various interests, but apparently not a 'middle class', see K. Margerison, *P.-L. Roederer: Political Thought and Practice during the French Revolution* (Transactions of the American Philosophical Society 73:1), Philadelphia, 1983, esp. pp. 25–6, 48, and chapter 6.

no cities, or hardly any.'[22] But subsequently, Mignet continued gloomily, the 'middle class' lost control. In this scenario, the party of the Girondins 'in the revolution was only an intermediary party between the middle class and the multitude'. The revolution of the 'middle class' was doomed by its middle position between the attacks of the aristocracy and the usurpation of the multitude; the government needed the help of the latter for the defence of the country and thus sealed its own fate. Ultimately, 'the multitude . . . made its own revolution, just as the middle class had done'.[23] This two-stage conception of the Revolution expounded by Mignet was remarkably similar to that of the other notable French historian of the mid-1820s, Adolphe Thiers: for him, too, while revolutions commenced with 'the most enlightened classes', they quickly lost control under the pressures from below; 'and, in this class struggle . . . the plain bourgeois ended up being called an aristocrat by the manual labourer, and persecuted as one too'.[24]

Royer-Collard, Constant, Guizot, Thierry, Roederer, Mignet, Thiers: together they formed a rather coherent ideological group-

---

[22] 'Cette constitution était l'œuvre de la classe moyenne, qui se trouvait alors la plus forte.' 'Dans la Vendée, il n'y avait pas de lumières ni de civilisation, parce qu'il n'y avait pas de classe moyenne; et il n'y avait pas de classe moyenne, parce qu'il n'y avait pas ou qu'il y avait peu de villes.' F.-A. Mignet, *Histoire de la révolution française*, Brussels, 1839 (originally Paris, 1824), pp. 106, 206 (see also p. 116). On Mignet's interpretation of the French Revolution, see Comninel, *Rethinking the French Revolution*, pp. 58–60.

[23] Les girondins 'ne fut dans la révolution qu'un parti de passage de la classe moyenne à la multitude'. 'La multitude . . . fit sa révolution, comme la classe moyenne avait fait la sienne.' The turning point from one stage to another was the attack on the Tuileries and the suspension of the king on 10 August 1792: 'cette journée . . . fut l'insurrection de la multitude contre la classe moyenne et contre le trône constitutionnel, comme le 14 juillet avait été l'insurrection de la classe moyenne contre les classes privilégiées et le pouvoir absolu de la couronne.' (Ibid., pp. 108, 113, 156, 172; and see the same story in pp. 133 and 158, with 'bourgeoisie' instead of 'classe moyenne'.) Later events in France were in Mignet's narrative attempts of the 'middle class' to regain power. Ever since the end of the Terror and the beginning of the Directory, he wrote, 'la classe moyenne reprit au dehors la conduite de la révolution'; whereas the property voting qualifications set by the Convention 'redonnèrent l'importance politique à la classe moyenne, à laquelle il fallait forcément revenir après le licenciement de la multitude.' (Ibid., pp. 313, 323; see also pp. 308, 319–20, 326, 373.)

[24] 'Et, dans cette lutte des classes . . . le simple bourgeois finit par être appelé aristocrate par le manouvrier, et poursuivi comme tel.' Adolphe Thiers, *Histoire de la révolution française*, Paris, 1823–7; here quoted from 5th edn, Paris, 1836, vol. II, pp. 6–7. Note this early use of 'lutte des classes'.

ing of political players (to whom more can readily be added[25]), players who obviously found the language of 'middle class' from 1815 onwards quite attractive. To what extent was this sudden attraction shared by others on the political playing field? The scope of this particular conceptualization of French society at this period, as well as its limits and possible alternatives, are as yet open questions, answered neither by previous historians of France nor by the present sketchy survey of some select sources. Given the political stakes involved, it would be rather surprising if the social narrative of the Restoration liberals remained uncontested. Indeed, as suggested by the epigraphs to this chapter, indications of such a contestation are not hard to come by, though little more can be done here than to touch upon them briefly.

Let us return for instance to the debates on the voting law, debates which elicited strong 'middle-class idiom' from Royer-Collard and Constant. The contestation in the Chamber of Deputies was quite explicit; as Constant remarked, 'this intermediate class inspires in the enemies of the law a fear they could not disguise'.[26] Constant sarcastically quoted such commentators, for instance those who claimed that among the 'middle class' 'one finds the core of turbulence, of agitation, of ambition and of intrigue'. A key figure among the Ultras on the right (whom Constant paraphrased anonymously) was Comte Jean Baptiste Villèle, who later recounted his speech to his father:

For as long as the world has existed, the lowest class has been under the influence of the highest, to which it owes its life, while the middle class, envied by the lowest and the enemy of the highest, forms the revolutionary portion of society in every State. If you want the highest class to end up in your assemblies, have it nominated by its auxiliaries in the lowest class, go as low as you can, and in this way cancel out the middle class, which is the only one you have to dread.[27]

---

[25] For instance, the idéologues Destutt de Tracy and Pierre Daunou, whose 'middle-class' language during the early years of the Restoration is briefly discussed in C. B. Welch, *Liberty and Utility: The French Idéologues and the Transformation of Liberalism*, New York, 1984, pp. 134, 147.

[26] 'Cette classe intermédiaire inspire aux ennemis du projet de loi un effroi qu'ils ne sauraient déguiser.' Constant, *Cours de politique*, pp. 247–8.

[27] 'Depuis que le monde existe, la dernière classe est sous l'influence de la première qui la fait vivre, et la classe moyenne, enviée de la dernière et ennemie de la première, compose la partie révolutionnaire de la société dans tous les Etats. Si vous voulez que la première classe arrive dans vos assemblées, faites-la nommer par les auxiliaires

For Villèle, then, as for others in his camp, the 'middle class' was – and had always been – the most revolutionary component of society, which could only be annihilated through an alliance of the lower and the higher classes.[28]

Or we can look after the revolution of 1830, when Guizot and the other advocates of the 'middle class' were celebrating the fact that (in the Guizotesque words of Maurice de Guérin) 'the middle class [had] arrived in power'.[29] Even then, however, not everyone necessarily accepted either this statement or the conceptualization of society on which it was predicated. Neither, we may add, do historians, who have at the very least raised considerable doubts about the adequacy of this 'middle-class' vision of 1830 in terms of the actual transferal of power after the revolution.[30] Among French contemporaries on the right, one

qu'elle a dans la dernière classe, descendez aussi bas que vous pourrez, et annulez ainsi la classe moyenne, qui est la seule que vous ayez à redouter.' Letter of 6 March 1816, in *Mémoires et correspondance du comte de Villèle*, 2nd edn, Paris, 1904, vol. i, pp. 489–90. The letter reported another speech against the law, threatening that it would betray society into the hands of the 'middle class' and thus bring about the demise of France. See R. Rémond, *The Right Wing in France from 1815 to de Gaulle*, Philadelphia, 1968, p. 59.

[28] Compare Charles Cottu, legitimist and ardent defender of the government of Charles X, who in 1829 voiced the same fear of the Jacobinical 'middle class', consequently warning against the dangers of the doctrinaires' political aspirations; cited in Mellon, *The Political Uses of History*, p. 85.

[29] 'La classe moyenne est arrivée au pouvoir': Maurice de Guérin, 'Correspondence 1824–1839', in *Œuvres complètes*, ed. B. d'Harcourt (Paris, 1947), p. 165 (quoted in Hobsbawm, *Echoes of the Marseillaise*, p. 124 n. 53). Tocqueville also believed that this was a 'middle-class' revolution: see S. Drescher, *Dilemmas of Democracy: Tocqueville and Modernization*, Pittsburgh, 1968, p. 201n. (and see also Gustave de Beaumont as cited there). Note also Edouard Alletz, *De la démocratie nouvelle, ou de mœurs et de la puissance des classes moyennes en France*, 2nd edn, 2 vols., Paris, 1838 (1st edn, 1837): Alletz's professed goal, now that the ages of autocracy, oligarchy and democracy were replaced by 'cet âge de l'univers marqué par la puissance des classes moyennes', was 'de chercher les lois du governement des classes moyennes' (vol. i, pp. ix, xi). He consequently attempted to provide this new political order with the requisite political theory (and history, from the medieval communes to yet another 'middle-class'-based account of the French Revolution and the subsequent events): see especially vol. ii, pp. 219ff. For further examples see D. W. Lovell, 'Early French Socialism and Class Struggle', *History of Political Thought* 9 (1988), p. 335.

[30] D. H. Pinkney, 'The Myth of the French Revolution of 1830', in D. H. Pinkney and T. Ropp (eds.), *A Festschrift for Frederick B. Artz*, Durham, 1964, pp. 52–71. A. Cobban, 'The "Middle Class" in France, 1815–1848', *French Historical Studies* 5 (1967), pp. 41–52. D. H. Pinkney, *Decisive Years in France 1840–1847*, Princeton, 1986, chapter 1. And also A.-J. Tudesq, *Les grands notables en France (1840–1849): étude historique d'une psychologie sociale*, Paris, 1964, vol. i, p. 8: 'la prépondérance des classes moyennes . . . dont Guizot avait été le plus brillant théoricien, était plus une pétition de principes qu'une traduction de la réalité'.

articulate example of such doubt was Henri Fonfrède, a journalist from Bordeaux who was the main spokesman for Orleanism in the south-west. Speaking of the electorate during the July Monarchy, Fonfrède was particularly keen on exposing what he saw as a fundamental artifice underlying the rhetoric of the doctrinaires:

These electors are chosen from a supposed middle class, which is in no way a class, which has no collective existence at all, which has neither unity, nor direction, nor stability. This supposed middle class [is] actually a confused jumble of twenty, fifty, a hundred different classes, each having moral and industrial interests that are often dissimilar, and sometimes contradictory.[31]

Consequently, he argued, a government founded on their pretended rule could have no homogeneity, system or direction. Elsewhere Fonfrède stormed again against 'the sacramental expression of the triumph of the middle classes': 'the present-day bourgeoisie is in no way a class: it is a strange compound, lacking in cohesion and homogeneity . . . The word middle class is thus a political misnomer.' Fonfrède further denied the political virtues claimed on behalf of this alleged 'middle class', as well as the equivalence between the medieval municipal bourgeoisie, whose action for democracy had been 'excellent and civilizing', and the present parliamentary bourgeoisie, which was 'detestable and anti-social'.[32]

On the left, an example of resistance to the 'middle-class idiom' can be found in the writing on the French Revolution of the

---

[31] 'Ces électeurs sont pris dans une prétendue classe moyenne, qui n'est point une classe, qui n'a point d'être collectif, qui n'a ni unité, ni direction, ni stabilité. Cette prétendue classe moyenne, confusion pêle-mêle de vingt, cinquante, cent classes différentes, ayant chacune des intérêts moraux et industriels, souvent dissemblables, quelquefois opposés.' Henri Fonfrède, *Du Gouvernement du Roi, et des limites constitutionnelles de la prérogative parlementaire* (originally 1839), in *Œuvres de Henri Fonfrède*, ed. C.-A. Campan, Bordeaux, 1844, vol. VI, p. 62. Contrast with Alletz, *De la démocratie nouvelle*, vol. I, p. xiv, who explicitly rejected the arguments alleging that the 'middle class' could not have a unifying 'esprit de corps' because of its numbers and diversity.

[32] 'L'expression sacramentelle de *triomphe des classes moyennes*'; 'la bourgeoisie actuelle n'est point *une classe*: elle est un composé bizarre, sans ensemble, sans homogénéité . . . Le mot classe moyenne est donc une fausse expression politique.' Henri Fonfrède, *De la société, du gouvernement et de l'administration* (originally 1839); in *Œuvres*, vol. I, pp. 139ff., chapter 6: 'Le Gouvernement n'appartient point aux classes moyennes' (quoted, p. 140). For further denials of the existence of a 'middle class' during the July Monarchy, see Daumard, *Les Bourgeois et la bourgeoisie*, pp. 30, 50.

idéologue Auguste Fabre, the author – together with his brother
Victorin – of the most overtly republican journalism of the later
Restoration years. Both, interestingly, acquired political experience in the liberal society Aide-toi et le ciel t'aidera, founded in
1827 under the presidency of Guizot. Fabre contrasted the revolutions of 1789 and 1830. In 1789, Fabre wrote, the 'middle class'
had played an honourable role. But its corruption ever since,
inspired by the detestable doctrinaires, caused it to snatch
the victory of 1830 from the hands of the betrayed republicans
(a feeling that was to be echoed by English radicals after
1832):

> The French people are superior to what they were in 1789 . . . But
> although there are still many truly distinguished men in the middle
> class, the majority of this class is well below what it was then. It was
> generous, it has become corrupt; it was enlightened, it has become
> boorish. Instead of arousing patriotism in the people, it makes patriotism
> in the people a crime, for it would like to see the people as greedy,
> cowardly and servile as itself.[33]

Similarly, Odilon Barrot, of the dynastic left and closer to republicans than other partisans of the July regime, attacked Guizot
for appropriating the victories of the French Revolution, 'which
were won by everyone', for 'the middle class . . . a class apart'.[34]
Other writers, such as Pierre Leroux, Louis Blanc and Flora
Tristan, attempted to define the 'middle class' in economic terms
as a small and exclusive component of society, those who were
exploiting the working class; a new twist in the contestations
over the language of 'middle class' in France which brings us

---

[33] 'Le peuple en France est supérieur à ce qu'il était en 89 . . . Mais quoiqu'on trouve
encore dans la classe moyenne beaucoup d'hommes vraiment distingués, la majorité
de cette classe est bien au-dessous de ce qu'elle était à cette époque. Elle était
généreuse, elle est corrompue; elle était éclairée, elle est ignare. Au lieu d'exciter le
patriotisme du peuple, elle lui en fait un crime; elle le voudrait avide, lâche et servile
comme elle.' Auguste Fabre, *Histoire de la révolution française*, Paris, 1833, vol. II,
pp. 99–100; also vol. I, pp. xxix–xxxi, cii, cxvi–cxvii. On Fabre, see Welch, *Liberty and
Utility*, pp. 162–71.

[34] Quoted in Guizot, *Histoire parlementaire*, vol. III, p. 102, from a debate in May 1837.
See also the criticism of the 'middle class' in the *Revue indépendente* of July 1842, quoted
in Johnson, *Guizot*, p. 79; and Philippe Joseph Buchez's assertion in 1833, that society
is composed of two classes only, namely owners of 'instruments de travail' and those
who worked for them (quoted in Lovell, 'Early French Socialism', p. 331). This view
among Saint-Simonists after 1830 is discussed in S. Gruner, 'The Revolution of July
1830 and the Expression "Bourgeoisie"', *Historical Journal* 11 (1968), pp. 462–71.

closer to the very particular understanding of this language that was soon thereafter to be proclaimed as universal by Karl Marx.[35]

FRANCE AND BRITAIN: THE COMPARATIVE PERSPECTIVE

The influence of the middle class [in France] is a fact, a powerful and formidable fact. (Pierre-Paul Royer-Collard, 1819)[36]

The goal one should strive for in England is to increase the political influence of the middle classes. (Auguste de Staël-Holstein, 1825)[37]

This cursory detour into the French political debate is sufficient to demonstrate the unmistakable affinities between the uses of 'middle-class' language by some speakers in France and in Britain after 1815. The similarities are often striking: the 'middle class' as the repository of intelligence; its association with social change, and in particular with the growth of industry; its inherent vagueness as a social category; its purported empathy with the interests of all social groups, high and low; its commitment to political stability, and the consequent wisdom of granting it decisive electoral powers; the tension between the latter assertions and the representation of the 'middle class' as predisposed to political revolutions; as well as further parallels (in the rewriting of history as revolving around the 'middle class', and in radical disillusionment with an alleged 'middle-class' betrayal) that will become apparent in the following chapters.

On one level, these parallels should be seen against the backdrop of the relationship between the two diffusely delineated camps of liberals on both sides of the Channel, be they direct

---

[35] See Johnson, *Guizot*, p. 77. For Tristan, see Lovell, 'Early French Socialism', p. 344. This restrictive trend was resisted by the proponents of the 'middle class', as we have seen for Guizot. Another example, as Johnson points out, is Adolphe Granier de Cassagnac's *Histoire des classes ouvrières et des classes bourgeoises*, Paris, 1837, which by contrast attempted through an economic definition to make the 'middle class' all-inclusive. And as for Marx, the very specific historical origins of his concept of 'middle class', later camouflaged by the universalizing language of himself and his followers, and the consequences of these specific origins in limiting the applicability of his theory, are suggested by Gareth Stedman Jones in his projected *Visions of Prometheus*.

[36] Barante, *La Vie politique de M. Royer-Collard*, vol. I, p. 456; quoted above, p. 275.

[37] 'Le but vers lequel on doit tendre en Angleterre, est d'augmenter l'influence politique des classes moyennes': Auguste de Staël-Holstein, *Lettres sur l'Angleterre*, Paris, 1825, p. 346.

personal contacts (as between Constant and Mackintosh) or broader intellectual affinities with each other.[38] The French liberals, always keenly interested in British history and politics, consciously presented themselves as the French analogue to the Whigs; as one doctrinaire put it, 'we were the Whigs of our country'. The British liberals, for their part, concurred. Lord John Russell spoke of 'the French Whigs', and the *Edinburgh Review* of the '*Juste milieu* Whigs' in France; numerous essays in the Whig periodical vied with each other in praising the views of the French liberals.[39] In short, these two intellectual and political milieus – milieus that provided the 'middle class' with some of its most committed champions in both countries – were continually aware of each other, reacting to each other, and interacting with each other.

Moreover, not only were the British liberals familiar with and sympathetic to their French counterparts, they – like many others, who continually maintained one finger on the political pulse of their perennially relevant neighbours – also took politics in France as an example for Britain. And whereas the events of the 1790s had turned embarrassing for British moderates in associating the 'middle class' with political instability, the developments in France after 1815 proved much more congenial. Now, the newly heralded French 'middle class' was associated with the restoration of political stability, with the end of despotism, with constitutional monarchy and with a circumscribed definition of the electorate that rejected theories of natural rights; a guise which the proponents of this language in Britain could welcome heartily. This,

---

[38] The imprecise term 'liberals' is employed here advisedly. For an unfortunately disappointing attempt to highlight the correlations between the liberal ideas of the doctrinaires (focused on Royer-Collard and Guizot) and the Whigs (focused on Brougham and Macaulay), see V. E. Starzinger, *Middlingness: Juste Milieu Political Theory in France and England, 1815–48*, Charlottesville, 1965; for their perceptions of the 'middle class', see chapter 3. The relationship between English and French utilitarians (for instance, between Destutt de Tracy and James Mill) is discussed in Welch, *Liberty and Utility*, chapter 5.

[39] Earl Russell, *Recollections and Suggestions, 1813–1873*, London, 1875, p. 448. *Edinburgh Review* 56, January 1833, pp. 490–1. The parallel between the French and the English *juste milieu* was often pointed out (critically) in the *Poor Man's Guardian* (rep. edn, New York, 1968); see 84, 12 January 1833 (vol. II, 14); 145, 15 March 1834 (vol. III, p. 41); and passim. The doctrinaire cited was Duc de Broglie (himself a friend of Henry Brougham), commenting upon Guizot's establishment of the *Revue française*, which was considered the equivalent of the *Edinburgh Review*; quoted in Johnson, *Guizot*, p. 53.

for instance, was the case for James Mackintosh: on one occasion Mackintosh pointed to the French 'middle-class' support for the stabilizing restoration of the Bourbons as proof of the political commitment of their British counterparts to order and stability; on another he put forward the French voting law of 1817 as proof of the overall beneficial influence of the 'middle class' on politics. 'In the system now established in France', Mackintosh wrote, 'the object is evidently to vest the whole power in the hands of the middling classes', an object that should be 'approved as politic' and adopted for the likewise meritorious 'middle class' in England.[40] Or to take a liberal Tory rather than a liberal Whig, consider an 1822 pamphlet by Lewis Goldsmith, a Canningite who had spent considerable time in France. While professing anti-democratic and anti-Whig sentiments, Goldsmith also objected to the 'unEnglish' contempt of the (English) aristocracy towards the bourgeoisie (he always used the French term), which was consequently excluded from politics and culture. The opposite situation Goldsmith found in the exemplary social and political order in contemporary France, where 'every Ministry that has been formed since the restoration has been almost wholly formed of *Bourgeoise*'.[41]

The British advocates of the 'middle class' could likewise find reassurance in the representations of the French Revolution put forward by the Restoration historians (reminiscent, of course, of how some British observers had seen the Revolution already in the 1790s). When the corrupt French nobility fled at the beginning of the Revolution, went the story in one essay in the *Edinburgh Review*, 'their greatest enemies were among the middling classes; for the labouring multitude took no active part in the Revolution'. It was only later that 'the divisions between the great and the small proprietors, the noblesse and the tiers état,

---

[40] *Edinburgh Review* 24, February 1815, pp. 524–5; 31, December 1818, p. 191. Compare also Louis Simond's sympathetic discussion of the views of the doctrinaires on parliamentary representation in 34, August 1820, p. 38; Anthony Panizzi's comments on the 1817 election law as calling forth 'a fair proportion of the intelligence and independence of the nation' (40, July 1824, p. 531); and Brougham's comparison of the virtuous 'middle class' in England and France in 49, March 1829, pp. 49–50.

[41] Lewis Goldsmith, *Observations on the Appointment of the Right Hon. Geo. Canning to the Foreign Department . . .*, London, 1822, p. 19; and see pp. 14–15. The pamphlet presented Canning's appointment as a triumph of merit and intellect over aristocratic arrogance.

had made an opening for them [the multitude] to invade at once property, liberty and life, and lay society prostrate at their feet'.[42] 'The revolution was occasioned by the middle class', echoed the Tory William Mackinnon, but then it was 'taken from the middle class by the leaders of the lower class.' In the subsequent 'sanguinary deeds that cast such a stain on the occurrences of that period', it was 'the middle class of society which became its victims'. Things went astray, Mackinnon asserted, because in France at that stage the 'middle class was not sufficiently powerful'; had another fifty years gone by, 'then, in all probability, a more extensive middle class would have been formed', and such 'outrages' could have been prevented.[43] Small wonder that Mignet's history of the French Revolution, the most elaborate vindication of the role of the 'middle class' in those events, was immediately translated into English and went through a second English edition within a year.[44]

But, as has been proposed at the outset of this comparative exercise, its primary objective is not simply to establish that contemporaries were attentive to the possible parallels between developments in Britain and France; or, in particular, that the uses of 'middle-class' language in one country were reinforced by those in the other. Its purpose, rather, is to underscore once again the problems inherent in common assumptions about the relationship between social representations and social change, and to highlight the effects of politics on choices made in the space of possibilities open between them.

To be sure, it is likely that these intellectual connections criss-crossing the Channel contributed to the ready availability of the language of 'middle class' on one side or the other; and yet they cannot explain its reception at a given moment. The

---

[42] Louis Simond in the *Edinburgh Review* 34, August 1820, pp. 20–1 (note the distinction here between the 'tiers état' and the lower orders). Compare Mackintosh's 1815 assertion that the 'middle class' had been implicated in the Revolution but not in its excesses, which were the result of 'plebeian passions': see above, p. 182.

[43] [William A. Mackinnon], *On the Rise, Progress, and Present State of Public Opinion, in Great Britain, and Other Parts of the World*, London, 1828 (rep. edn, Shannon, 1971), pp. 125, 224–9 (on Mackinnon's views see more below, pp. 298–302).

[44] François Mignet, *History of the French Revolution from 1789 to 1814*, 2 vols., London, 1826; 2nd edn, Paris, 1827. The *Eclectic Review* (25, 1826, pp. 231–42), in reviewing Mignet's third French edition, recounted his breaking down of the revolution into a revolution of the 'middle class' and a subsequent revolution against the 'middle class', and remarked that it was 'if not satisfactory, at least highly ingenious' (p. 238).

decisive question still remains, why did the representation of political experience through the particular lens of a 'middle-class'-based vision of society find such fertile ground at these particular junctures in both countries? To repeat again, it does not follow from the fact that concepts were available, that they were therefore necessarily invested with significance or deployed in a meaningful way. Thus, when George Comninel – rightly, no doubt – points to David Hume as a source for Augustin Thierry's 'middle-class' interpretation of history, he begs the question of why Hume (whose writings, after all, had already been available for the better part of a century) had failed to produce a similar effect on French history writers before the 1820s.[45] And perhaps more to the point, why did the 'middle-class' interpretations of the French Revolution that had been suggested by British writers of the 1790s such as Mackintosh and Burke (both widely read in France) fail to impress themselves upon the French commentators before 1815? And why did such an interpretation suddenly emerge as a major theme afterwards? Indeed one probably does not need to travel abroad in order to pose this question: in France, as in Britain, a survey of eighteenth-century sources would surely unearth occasional instances of indigenous 'middle-class' language, even of 'middle-class idiom'.[46] And yet it would not bring us any closer to understanding the new uses and the unprecedented resonance of this language after 1815.

Once again we arrive at the prevalent (albeit often implicit) explanation for such a change in social language, namely its putative correlation with the 'underlying' social process. Put somewhat crudely, the accepted historical wisdom is that the

---

[45] Comninel, *Rethinking the French Revolution*, pp. 60–2.

[46] Consider for example the *ancien régime* Frenchman who wrote in 1768 that the 'Bourgeois Estate' was 'always the most useful, the most important, and the wealthiest in all kinds of countries. It supports the first [estate] and manipulates the last according to its will'; see R. Darnton, 'A Bourgeois Puts His World in Order: The City as a Text', in his *The Great Cat Massacre and Other Episodes in French Cultural History*, New York, 1985, p. 125. Or take another, who, while apparently not having in mind such a clear tripartite social scheme, still found the true and estimable French national character to reside 'dans le fond des mœurs bourgeoises': Jean-Louis Castilhon, *Considérations sur les causes physiques et morales de la diversité du génie des mœurs, et du gouvernement des nations . . .*, 2 vols., Bouillon, 2nd edn, 1770, vol. I, p. 296 (adapted from a previous work of François-Ignace Espiard de la Borde, 1752). I am grateful to David Bell for this reference.

emergence of a 'middle class' – which in this account is practically equivalent to the appearance of 'middle-class' language – was consequent upon some critical mass of social change, in particular of industrialization. But if any lesson at all can be learned from the comparison between Britain and France, it is the need for caution in such assumptions. After all, whatever critical mass of industrialization, technological innovation and urbanization was attained in France by 1815, it had been surpassed by Britain many years earlier.[47] Likewise, in comparing the extent and the pace of changes in social structure, Britain was surely in the lead by a comfortable margin. And yet in terms of developing a coherent theory of history and society based on a 'middle class', linked to an awareness and theorization of social change, France – at least within certain circles – was very far from lagging behind. Quite the contrary.

Consider the two epigraphs at the beginning of this section: on the one hand, Royer-Collard declaring in 1819 that the influence of the 'middle class' in France had already become by that point a formidable *fait accompli*; and on the other hand, the opinion of a fellow doctrinaire in the mid-1820s, the Anglophile Auguste de Staël-Holstein, that in Britain such an influence of the 'middle class' was as yet largely a thing of the future.[48] Or take another Frenchman, Vicomte de Chateaubriand, who compared his impressions of England in 1822 to his earlier sojourn there in the 1790s:

The English at the end of the last century preserved their customs and their national character . . . only two large classes were known, friends to each other and linked by a common interest: patrons and clients. That jealous class, called the bourgeoisie in France, and which is now

---

[47] For a convenient overview, which questions the condemnation implied in the notion of French 'retardation' but not the basic differences between the developments in both countries, see P. O'Brien and C. Keyder, *Economic Growth in Britain and France 1780–1914: Two Paths to the Twentieth Century*, London, 1978. Also T. Kemp, *Industrialization in Nineteenth-Century Europe*, 2nd edn, London, 1985. Pinkney, *Decisive Years in France*, chapters 1–2.

[48] Like many of his liberal friends in England during this decade, Staël-Holstein too put forward an argument for 'middle-class'-based parliamentary reform, the only measure in his view that could ensure the future against lower class turbulence: Staël-Holstein, *Lettres sur l'Angleterre*, pp. 345–7; and see also pp. 28, 175. As for Royer-Collard, his confidence was revealed again when he reaffirmed in January 1822 that 'Les classes moyennes ont abordé les affaires publiques': Barante, *La Vie politique de M. Royer-Collard*, vol. II, p. 134.

starting to be born in England, did not exist. Nothing was interposed between the rich property-owners and men devoted to their labour. Machines were not yet everything in the manufacturing trades.[49]

An interesting comment indeed. France, in Chateaubriand's eyes, was way ahead of England in terms of changes in social structure. A 'middle class' – or rather 'bourgeoisie' – had not existed in England of the 1790s (a decade when, as Restoration historians were insisting, it had already been a key actor in France); and it was only budding there now, in the early 1820s, following in the footsteps of its well-developed French counterpart. Now this statement, or Royer-Collard's and Staël-Holstein's observations, obviously cannot be read as testimony of differences in social structure; rather, they are testimony to the confidence with which the advent of the French 'middle class' was proclaimed as a concluded matter of fact during the Restoration.[50] Moreover, the power of this particular understanding of society to override social reality, as it were, was evident in Chateaubriand's own language: in relating the progress of a nascent 'middle class' in England to the progress of the machine he was buying into the 'middle-class' storyline, which associated the rise of the 'middle class' with the progress of industrialization, even when his own observations about the headstart of the 'middle class' in France (where mechanization was observably lagging behind) were in fact evidence precisely to the contrary.

But Chateaubriand was probably closer to the mark in his sense – which is what this passage was really about – that an acknowledgment of the power of the British 'middle class' was slower to emerge. Indeed, whether one considers timing, level of articulation or tone, the heralding of the age of the 'middle class' in France appears to have preceded and surpassed that in Britain.

---

[49] 'Les Anglais conservaient, à la fin du dernier siècle, leurs mœurs et leur caractère nationale . . . on ne connaissait que deux grandes classes amies et liées d'un commun intérêt, les patrons et les clients. Cette classe jalouse, appelée bourgeoisie en France, qui commence à naître en Angleterre, n'existait pas: rien ne s'interposait entre les riches propriétaires et les hommes occupés de leur industrie. Tout n'était pas encore machine dans les professions manufacturières': François Réné, Vicomte de Chateaubriand, *Mémoires d'outre-tombe*, ed. Maurice Levaillant, 4 vols., n.p., 1969, vol. I, p. 562. Chateaubriand lived in London between 1793 and 1800.

[50] Compare the comments of J. C. D. Clark, *Revolution and Rebellion: State and Society in England in the Seventeenth and Eighteenth Centuries*, Cambridge, 1986, pp. 31–2 and esp. n. 23, that present Chateaubriand's observations as one alternative way of visualizing society that did not necessarily reflect social reality better than another.

Throughout the 1810s and 1820s the British were still discussing the predominance of the 'middle class' overwhelmingly as a budding novelty, a thing of the future, not as the outcome of past concluded events. Its power was not yet presented as an incontrovertible *fait accompli*, nor its influence as 'necessary and inevitable' – as Benjamin Constant had already asserted for France in 1819. Where the 'middle-class idiom' of the French during those years strikes one as most distinct from that of the British is in its degree of unreserved conviction.

How can we explain, then, the sudden resonance of notions of 'middle class' in post-1815 France, the confident propagation of the French 'middle-class' historical narrative thereafter, and the edge which it gained over the corresponding developments in Britain? The answers, of course, should be sought in politics. If Restoration France was behind in terms of industrialization and changing social structure, it was surely ahead in terms of changing political circumstances and the consequent need to reconceptualize the social and political order. As Larry Siedentop has suggested more generally, the politics of the Restoration were crucial in generating among French liberals – in contradistinction to the English ones – what he describes as 'a sociological approach to political theory', and which he sees as their great innovation.[51] Indeed, pioneering French articulation of social change at this juncture went beyond merely the language of 'middle class': the Restoration also witnessed the launching of a politicized theory of 'industrialism', as well as the earliest uses of the term 'industrial revolution'.[52]

---

[51] L. Siedentop, 'Two Liberal Traditions', in A. Ryan (ed.), *The Idea of Freedom: Essays in Honour of Isaiah Berlin*, Oxford, 1979, pp. 153–74 (quoted, p. 157). For the particular suitability of the language of 'middle class' for the liberal politics of the Restoration, see also G. Stedman Jones, 'The Rise and Fall of "Class Struggle"', in his projected *Visions of Prometheus*.

[52] The theory of industrialism was developed in two journals: *Le Censeur européen*, edited by Charles Comte and Charles Dunoyer, and *L'Industrie* edited by Augustin Thierry and Henri de Saint-Simon. See Gruner, 'Political Historiography in Restoration France', and 'The Revolution of July 1830'. M. James, 'Pierre-Louis Roederer, Jean-Baptiste Say, and the Concept of *industrie*', *History of Political Economy* 9 (1977), esp. pp. 472–5. By comparison, 'industrialism' was apparently introduced in Britain only in the 1830s: see R. Williams, *Keywords*, London, 1985, p. 166. For Charles Comte's own depiction of the 'classe moyenne' as an important component of French society in 1789, see his *Histoire complète de la garde nationale*, Paris, 1831 (originally 1827), esp. pp. 4–5. And for the genealogy of 'industrial revolution', see A. Bezanson, 'The Early Use of the Term Industrial Revolution', *Quarterly Journal of Economics* 36 (1922), pp. 343–9. A. E. Bestor, 'The Evolution of the Socialist Vocabulary', *Journal of the*

In particular, ever since 1815 (and we should note again the abruptness which characterized the appearance of meaningful 'middle-class' rhetoric at that point) recourse to the language of 'middle class' became for many Frenchmen – importantly, including those in power – a singularly suitable framework for making sense of their recent post-aristocratic political experiences and for justifying their own political positions. In Britain, by contrast, it was only in 1832 that the political wave in which the language of 'middle class' had been implicated became triumphant, and that a 'middle class'-based conceptualization of society became similarly indispensable for making sense of recent ostensibly post-aristocratic political experiences. Consequently, as we shall now see, it was only the Reform Bill that prompted among so many Britons such a confident acknowledgment of the historical and political importance of the 'middle class', an acknowledgment which came closer to the self-assured pronouncements of Guizot and his ilk. In sum, what explains the distinctive evolutions in both countries of that particular representation of society which was centred on a rising 'middle class', and the differences between them, is not the differential in social change (in spite of the insistence of the 'middle-class' narrative upon its close correlation with such change), but rather the differential in their respective political circumstances.

History of Ideas 9 (1948), pp. 283–5. G. N. Clark, *The Idea of the Industrial Revolution*, Glasgow, 1953.

CHAPTER 9

The debates on the Reform Bill: bowing to a new representation of the 'middle class'

The elective franchise ought only to be intrusted to those, who would exercise it with the most wisdom and independence; and as wisdom and independence certainly, prevail more in the middling ranks, than in the whole mass of the people, the elective franchise should accordingly be principally enjoyed by them . . . yet the benefits which would flow from a representative body, properly constituted, would be general . . . the poor, as well as the rich, would equally partake of them.

(John Sinclair, advocate of moderate reform, 1831)

The poorer classes in general have an understanding sufficiently just, docile, and unprejudiced to elect and to submit to the same legislators whom the middling classes themselves . . . would single out . . . [Under a radical enfranchisement of a million voters, the elected nevertheless would still be] identified in heart and spirit with the happiness of the middling classes.

(George Grote, advocate of radical reform, 1831)

The qualification they have adopted, will have the effect of introducing, not this intelligent and educated portion of the middle ranks alone, but a vast majority very differently endowed . . . I am sure, that to no portion of the community would this measure be practically more unsatisfactory, than to that valuable part of the middle classes, who would be thus confounded with those so much their inferiors.

(Sir John Walsh, opposer of reform, 1831)[1]

The end of the 1820s saw the publication of what may well have

---

[1] John Sinclair, *Thoughts on Parliamentary Reform* . . ., Edinburgh, 1831, p. 20. George Grote, *Essentials of Parliamentary Reform*, London, 1831, pp. 29–32. John B. Walsh, [Baron Ormathwaite], *Observations on the Ministerial Plan of Reform*, London, 1831, pp. 46–7 (note yet again the interchangeability of 'middle ranks' and 'middle classes').

Figure 13. 'Opinions on Reform', March 1831. (William Heath)
Source: BMC 16604.

been the single book most obsessed with the 'middle class' ever
to appear in English: *On the Rise, Progress, and Present State of
Public Opinion*. It is likely that this obsession bore the imprint
of the personal background of its author, William Mackinnon.
Mackinnon, whose family had acquired considerable wealth in
the West Indies, became in 1809, at the age of twenty-five, the
head of the clan bearing his name in the western islands of
Scotland. As Walter Scott observed upon Mackinnon's first visit
to his newly acquired ancestral property, he was 'a young gentleman born and bred in England but nevertheless a Highland
Chief'.[2] What attracted Walter Scott's attention was the striking
contrast that confronted Mackinnon, between society as he had
experienced it during his English upbringing (which took him
through St John's College, Cambridge and the metropolitan Lincoln's Inn) and the state of society in the Scottish Highlands as
he now came to know it in his capacity as head of Clan Mackin-

[2] Quoted in R. G. Thorne, *The House of Commons 1790–1820*, London, 1986, vol. IV,
   p. 498.

non. It was this contrast, we may conjecture, that helped impress upon Mackinnon the absolutely crucial role which 'civilization' and 'progress', embodied in commercialization and industrialization, must play in any discussion of human affairs; and by the late 1820s, these social developments were all readily envisaged as entwined with the rise of a 'middle class'.

Mackinnon therefore left little doubt as to what should be considered the most momentous development of his day. In comparison to all previous social progress, he asserted, 'the powers of machinery', discovered in late years, unleashed 'a future power of extension and improvement that sets all reasoning by analogy at defiance': indeed, a true industrial revolution. And as Mackinnon never tired of reiterating, 'to allude to the extension of machinery, is to account for the increase of the middle class of society'. It was only very recently, however, that Britain's social map had begun changing along those lines, a change of 'great importance': 'Since the peace with France', went Mackinnon's historical narrative, 'several causes have combined to increase the middle class of society in this country in a very unusual proportion, – in a much greater ratio than could be anticipated.' By the late 1820s, the fact 'that an extensive middle class at present exists in England cannot be denied'; which was in Mackinnon's eyes a peculiarly English phenomenon, unparalleled in any other country or in any previous historical age.[3]

The effects of this new social fact were noticeable everywhere, but nowhere more significantly than in politics. A liberal and constitutional government, Mackinnon believed, was predicated upon a strong 'public opinion' (which was the real subject of his book); but

---

[3] [William A. Mackinnon], *On the Rise, Progress, and Present State of Public Opinion, in Great Britain, and Other Parts of the World*, London, 1828 (rep. edn, Shannon, 1971), pp. 5, 9–10, 147, 173, and passim. The emphasis on the unprecedented modernity of the recently expanding 'middle class' did not prevent Mackinnon from assigning it – not too consistently – an important role in reconstructing more distant historical events: see below, pp. 359–61. Mackinnon's conviction, one might add, was not matched by a confidence of definition. Although he did try early on to designate the 'middle class' with some precision as those 'who have the means of supporting from two to a hundred men fit for labour' (p. 3), he never came back to this definition nor related it to the statements about the 'middle class' so pervasive in the book. Like future historians, Mackinnon displayed a need to provide concrete sociological content for a category which he was using constantly and effectively, though ultimately its effectiveness was altogether irrespective of and unrelated to this purported content.

the extent or power of public opinion . . . resolves itself into the question whether such a community is possessed of an extensive middle class of society, when compared to the lower class; for the advantages called requisites for public opinion, cannot exist without forming a proportionate middle class.

Such a 'public opinion' as existed in England protected a nation from its pernicious opposite, 'popular clamour': 'Where civilization and an extensive middle class are spread through a country, or, in fact, as public opinion is powerful, popular clamour is less so.' Hence, Mackinnon concluded, 'such a class is perhaps the greatest security for the preservation of civil liberty, and against the chance of a revolution, that can be found in any country'.[4]

Few of these assertions seem by now very surprising. But the main novelty in Mackinnon's sizeable book was not in any particular statement: what put it in a qualitatively different category from all other works we have been considering, works in which the language of 'middle class' had usually been patchy and confined to several paragraphs, was the relentless encounter with the 'middle class' on virtually every page.[5] It is therefore an appropriate (though admittedly idiosyncratic) preamble to the last phase of the present story, that of the Reform Bill and its aftermath, in which the uses of 'middle-class' language proliferated to the point that their cumulative effects on public debate were qualitatively different. For more than two years of intense public discussion that aroused keen interest throughout the country (rarely matched by other issues before or since), the question of the 'middle class' was manifestly at the political centre-stage. Key issues in the heated debate were the existence of the 'middle class', its identity, its boundaries, its social and moral characteristics, its political nature, its pretensions, its power – in short, the various implications of endorsing a 'middle-

---

[4] Ibid., pp. 6, 17–18, 173. One particular contrast which preoccupied Mackinnon (p. 112n.) was that with the circumstances and experience of his own ancestors in the Scottish Highlands. Their support for the backward Jacobite cause, he explained, had been the consequence of the feudal power held by the chiefs of clans over the clansmen, in a society that had had 'no middle class of society, and no influence of public opinion'; and that presumably had not developed any since.

[5] At one point, Mackinnon himself acknowledged that 'it may be thought that, in the following observations, too much stress is laid on the middle class of society, and its influence over-rated', but then proceeded to argue why this in fact was not the case (ibid., p. 16).

class'-based conceptualization of society. Ultimately, the most significant feature of this protracted debate – like that of Mackinnon's book – was less the specific arguments that were presented in it than its sheer volume and persistence, which inundated the public with the language of 'middle class' as perhaps the most relevant social conceptual tool of the day. This inundation – together with the Reform Act itself – prepared the ground, as we shall see, for the climactic triumph of the 'middle-class' narrative immediately following the passing of the Act.

But Mackinnon also exemplified a less conspicuous tendency in the uses of 'middle-class' language in the late 1820s and early 1830s, one that was reversed subsequently, once the Reform Bill had become law. Mackinnon, we may recall, was no great reformer, but rather a committed *Tory*, who had been introduced a decade earlier into the conservative side of parliament as a client of the Barne family, and was to re-enter it again in 1831. Mackinnon did not see his Tory politics as contradicting his confidence in the narrative of the rising 'middle class'. Speaking in parliament against reform in 1832, he made sure to distinguish between his unparalleled accolade to the 'middle class' as the bearer of public opinion and the proposed measure, which in his view was supported only by popular clamour and the lower orders.[6] Admittedly, by 1832 this position probably left many in his audience sceptical. But what was accurately registered in Mackinnon's speech was the *openness* of the uses of 'middle-class' language before and up to the Reform Bill, an openness that (as we have seen) had already created tensions in the early 1820s for political speakers from both right and left. The intervening years, it should also be noted, described by one historian as 'strangely quiet', were a period in which social change had been more of an issue than political change, and in which the perceived emergence of a 'middle-class' constituency had been variously promulgated in *prima facie* non-controversial contexts.[7]

---

[6] *Hansard's Parliamentary Debates* 3rd ser., 11, cols. 524–6.

[7] In addition to the examples in chapter 7, one may add for instance the frequent justifications of the opening of London University in 1826 in terms of the rising 'middle class': see among others Brougham's comments in *Edinburgh Review* 42, August 1825, pp. 349, 353–4; James Mill's comments in *Westminster Review* 6, October 1826, p. 269; or *A Christian View of the Present State of the Country, Its Causes and Consequences*, London, 1829, p. 57 ('The increase of numbers, wealth, and power, of the middling class, rendered it necessary to establish another university for their instruction'). Another

So when the winds of reform began to stir again towards the
end of the decade, while the language of 'middle class' was
surely implicated first and foremost in the move for limited
reform, it was not as yet associated *exclusively* with this particular agenda. The rising-'middle-class'-constituency-requiring-
an-adjustment-of-the-franchise narrative had not yet become the
sole possible representation of the 'middle class'. As the divergent
epigraphs above illustrate, the prevalent reformist appropriation
of the language of 'middle class' still left some space for others
to enlist it in support of differing – indeed contradicting – political
positions. In the next few years, however, this space was about
to shrink to a virtual close.

For the late 1820s and early 1830s, the evidence for this space
of possibilities is abundant. Thus, it was perhaps not too surprising to find both sides in the famous exchange between James
Mill and Thomas Macaulay, an exchange which did much to
trigger the reform debate in 1829, agreeing on one thing –
namely, their admiration for the 'middle class'; after all, this was
by now a familiar tenet in both the *Edinburgh* and the *Westminster*
reviews, regardless of their differing views about the extent of
desired reform.[8] But it was perhaps more surprising to find their
Tory counterpart, the *Quarterly Review*, which a decade or two
earlier had tended to refrain from 'middle-class' language or from
celebrations of commercial and social progress, now publishing
a review of Mackinnon's book that reiterated Mackinnon's tribute
to the 'unavoidable' and 'inevitable' effects of progress together
with his appreciation for the 'middle class'. Indeed the *Examiner*,
for one, deemed this change in the *Quarterly Review* remarkable:

example is the equivalence established in a meeting for the abolition of slavery between
the power of 'public opinion' and 'the vast influence which those called the middle
class exercised in this country': *Second Report of the Committee of the Society for the Mitigation
and Gradual Abolition of Slavery Throughout the British Dominions* ..., London, 1825, p. 51
(speech of Lord Calthorpe); reprinted in *Anti-Slavery Monthly Reporter*, vol. 1, London,
1827, p. 2. The historian quoted is E. P. Thompson, *The Making of the English Working
Class*, London, 1963, p. 711.

[8] The shared admiration of Mill and Macaulay for the 'middle class' has often been
remarked upon; see L. Stephen, *The English Utilitarians*, New York, 1950, vol. 11,
p. 97. S. Collini et al., *That Noble Science of Politics: A Study in Nineteenth-Century Intellectual
History*, Cambridge, 1983, p. 122. This admiration was also shared by the *Morning
Chronicle*'s commentary on this debate, in which it expressed doubts about the 'rabble'
following the example of the 'middle class' as Mill had claimed, but not about the
beneficial nature of this example; quoted in the *Examiner* 1128, 13 September 1829,
p. 577.

it expressed approval of the periodical's sudden 'hold[ing] up
the middle classes of the community to respect', hopefully an
indication that the *Quarterly* was giving up on the cause of
despotism.[9] By the same token, when the *Manchester Guardian*
began from the end of 1827 onwards – ending its long years of
silence on the subject – to declare its support for 'extend[ing]
the elective privilege to the mass of the middle ranks', the change
probably did not come as a much of a surprise; but it was an
'infinite surprise' – in the words of the *Guardian* itself – to find
its long-time Tory opponent, the *Manchester Courier*, professing in
response that the most sincere concern for the 'middle class' was
in fact its own.[10] And again, it is telling that when one writer
constructed an imaginary dialogue between several interlocutors
of opposing political dispositions regarding the ballot, the one
thing they all had in common was an appreciation for the 'middle
class'.[11] The following discussion of the debates on the Reform
Bill – inevitably, to be sure, limited only to the very tip of the
iceberg – provides more examples of this openness, resulting in
multiple and contradictory uses of the language of 'middle class'
and therefore in a variety of contestations; a situation that contrasts sharply with the much more exclusive grip of one coherent
'middle-class' storyline immediately after 1832.

But first let us remind ourselves briefly of the major turning
points in the renewed preoccupation with reform and in the
tortuous but ultimately successful route to the Reform Bill of
1832. Catholic Emancipation in 1829 constituted an important
trigger, in undermining the alliance of Church and State (more
so than the repeal of the Test and Corporation Acts the previous
year) and in curtailing the ability of the Tory party as well as
of the crown to resist reform. The role of this step in leading to
the subsequent ones is worth emphasizing, since it defies the
post-1832 narratives of reform as driven by a rising 'middle
class'. Not only was Catholic Emancipation a measure that was
conceived and justified without resorting to any purported 'middle

---

[9] *Quarterly Review* 39, April 1829, p. 495. *Examiner* 1116, 21 June 1829, p. 386.
[10] *Manchester Guardian* 7:345, 8 December 1827 ('the grievance [of the English system of
Suffrage] is – not the exclusion of the "lower orders", but that of the middle classes');
347, 22 December 1827. The periodical's suddenly discovered support for 'middle
class' enfranchisement was repeated at length in 9:423, 6 June 1829; 432, 8 August
1829; 10:493, 9 October 1830; 501, 4 December 1830.
[11] William Henry Ord, *A Dialogue on Election by Ballot*, London, 1831, pp. 6, 7, 9, 14, 26.

class', it was moreover implemented in considerable part *against* what was seen to be the tide of 'public opinion' and of 'middle-class' opinion – which on this occasion did not prove to be as progressive and liberal as their proponents had liked to present them.[12]

The subsequent developments are well known: the effect of the severe economic crisis and social distress of the winter of 1829–30, which rekindled the agitation for reform out-of-doors; the fall of Wellington's Tory administration, succeeded (in November 1830) by Earl Grey's Whig ministry, which was publicly (perhaps more than privately[13]) committed to reform; the dramatic victory of their proposed Bill in the Commons by one vote, only to be overturned later over amendments, leading to a dissolution of parliament; the overwhelming victory of the Whigs in the ensuing elections, preparing the endorsement of a modified Reform Bill by the Commons; its rejection by the House of Lords (September 1831), resulting in a complete deadlock and in riots throughout the country; the threat of a massive creation of new peers, which finally compelled the Lords to approve the Bill; its further vicissitudes in the Committee stage, leading to the resignation of Grey's cabinet; the Whigs' triumphant return after the failure

---

[12] Indeed, following the debate on Catholic Emancipation one can find a wave of sceptical discussions of 'public opinion' and its limits, even where least expected – among the Edinburgh reviewers: see William Empson in the *Edinburgh Review* 49, March 1829, p. 241; Carlyle in 49, June 1829, pp. 439ff.; and Macaulay in 50, January 1830, p. 549 ('Public opinion is not infallible'). In parliament Macaulay deplored more specifically the illiberal anti-Catholic sentiments of 'a large proportion – a majority, I fear – of the middle class of Englishmen': *Hansard* 3rd ser., 7, col. 306. And see the attempt to vindicate 'public opinion' from the imputation of illiberal sentiments on the Catholic issue in the *Manchester Guardian* 9:409, 28 February 1829. The significance of Catholic Emancipation in bringing about the constitutional crisis of 1830–2, and the resulting complications for the Whig narratives of reform, have been emphasized by J. C. D. Clark, *English Society 1688–1832*, Cambridge, 1985.

[13] This is the argument of L. G. Mitchell in his recent 'Foxite Politics and the Great Reform Bill', *English Historical Review* 108 (1993), pp. 338–64: Grey was grudgingly compelled to pass the Reform Bill 'by his earlier career [as a Foxite], much of which, in old age, he would have preferred to forget' (p. 340). Mitchell stresses the long-term continuity of the goals which were achieved in 1832 but had already been formulated in the eighteenth century – curtailing the power of the crown, and giving 'the new property and intelligence of the middle classes or middling sorts ... an absolute right to representation' (p. 352). But while the argument regarding the struggle against the crown appears convincing, with regard to the 'middle class' it seems that Mitchell too has taken the narrative presented by the reformers at face value. In fact, as we have seen, the argument for the right of the propertied and intelligent 'middle class' for representation was quite novel, only rarely predating the 1820s.

of the Tories to form a ministry of their own (during the 'days of May'); and the final passing of the Reform Bill, which was made into law on 7 June 1832. The Reform Act redistributed parliamentary seats by disfranchising some constituencies and creating others; and extended the franchise – in the counties according to several property qualifications, and in the boroughs to £10 householders.[14]

In the hands of the advocates of the Reform Bill, as one might imagine, the uses of the language of 'middle class' that had taken shape during the previous decade now came together with unprecedented force; after all, what many reformers believed they were doing was to confer the franchise singularly upon the deserving 'middle class' – 'the pride and flower of England'.[15] Expressions of 'middle-class idiom' therefore became an almost ritualistic commonplace. The great mission of the Whig administration, in the words of one supporter, was to 'enable that great and influential body of men, the middle class of the populacy of the United Kingdoms, *conscientiously* and *patriotically* . . . to rally around the Government'; and in the words of Macaulay in the *Edinburgh Review*, it was to render the votes in the House of Commons 'the express image of the opinion of the middle orders of Britain'.[16] Parliament was told that the proposed Bill was 'placing the franchise as much as possible in the hands of the middle classes' (Lord Althorp); that

---

[14] For general accounts, see J. Cannon, *Parliamentary Reform 1640–1832*, Cambridge, 1973, chapters 9–10. D. Fraser, 'The Agitation for Parliamentary Reform', in J. T. Ward (ed.), *Popular Movements c. 1830–1850*, London, 1970, pp. 31–53. M. Brock, *The Great Reform Act*, London, 1973. Older works include W. N. Molesworth, *The History of the Reform Bill of 1832*, London, 1865. J. R. M. Butler, *The Passing of the Great Reform Bill*, London, 1914 (rep. edn, 1964). G. M. Trevelyan, *Lord Grey of the Reform Bill*, London, 1920.

[15] The words of Lord Dudley Stuart in parliament: *Hansard* 3rd ser., 3, col. 136.

[16] Thomas Bailey, *A Letter to Earl Grey, on the Necessity of Fixing a Principle of Representation in the Constitution*, London, 1831, p. 13 (also p. 15); Bailey justified his suggestions by his 'extensive intercourse with the middle ranks of agricultural and commercial society' (p. 4). Macaulay in *Edinburgh Review* 50, October 1829, p. 125; see similarly 52, October 1830, p. 224, regarding reform in Scotland which should 'have the effect of admitting the intelligence of the middle rank of society, and of the upper part of the lower rank' (Henry Cockburn). Also compare, among virtually innumerable examples, the *Manchester Guardian* 10:493, 9 October 1830: 'No kind of reform, in fact, would be likely to be beneficial . . . [without] the concurrence and good opinion of the bulk of the intelligent part of society; – of that middle rank, particularly, the extent of which constitutes, both morally and politically, so large a portion of our national security and strength.' Also James Graham's view of the reform needed for 'the middle class, which is the life and marrow of the State'; quoted in J. T. Ward, *Sir James Graham*, London, 1967, pp. 92–3, and again 95.

it would 'give a fair expression of the sense of the middling classes' (the Marquis of Tavistock); and that it would 'include a vast proportion of the more respectable of the middle classes of the country' (Viscount Palmerston).[17]

More importantly, such statements were coupled with repeated justifications of the measure based on the 'middle-class' historical narrative as it had been constructed in the 1820s – the emphasis on recent trends of social change (what James Mackintosh now called 'the social revolution of the last sixty years'), resulting in the rise of the new 'middle-class' constituency that now required an adaptation of the representative system. 'Time', Viscount Falkland proclaimed, 'has entirely changed the face of society. A middle class, differing both from land-holders and from free-burghers, has arisen'; but it was still 'destitute of the elective franchise, though obviously . . . qualified to exercise it'.[18] In the words of Lord Durham, 'a great change has taken place within the last fifty years in the state of society'. He explained: 'it cannot be concealed, that the middle classes have increased, of late, in skill, talent, political intelligence, and wealth, to such an extent, that they are, and feel that they are, competent to the performance of higher duties'.[19] 'A great change has taken place in all parts of Europe since the end of the war in the distribution of property', echoed Earl Grey; 'This change requires a greater influence to be yielded to the middle classes, who have made wonderful advances both in property and intelligence.' The great change occurred within the last twenty-five or thirty years, con-

[17] *Hansard* 3rd ser., 2, cols. 1141, 1318, 1327. Further examples include col. 1176 (Lord Darlington); 1191 (Macaulay); 3, col. 150 (John Wood); 656 (E. W. W. Pendarvis); 7, col. 1359 (Marquis of Lansdowne); 11, col. 442 (Robert Slaney). For the uses of the language of 'middle class' by the supporters of the Bill, see also N. Gash, *Politics in the Age of Peel: A Study in the Technique of Parliamentary Representation 1830–1850*, 2nd edn, Hassocks, 1977, pp. 14–17. Oddly, in the face of such ample evidence, see the denial of the role of 'middle-class' language in the Reform Bill debates in J. Hamburger, *James Mill and the Art of Revolution*, New Haven, 1963, p. 256 and n. 8.

[18] [Viscount Cary (L. B.) Falkland], *A Letter to All the Friends of Parliamentary Reform in the Present Crisis of Affairs, and on the Steps Now Proper to Be Taken* (2nd edn, with postscript), London, 1830, p. 19. Falkland attempted at length to define precisely who were the members of this 'middle class'. Mackintosh's parliamentary speech, which pressed for a 'much needed' adaptation of the elective system to the 'rapid and prodigious' social transformations, primarily urbanization and industrialization, was reprinted in *The Miscellaneous Works of the Right Honourable Sir James Mackintosh*, 3 vols. complete in one, Boston, 1868 (quoted, p. 584).

[19] *Speeches of the Earl of Durham, on Reform of Parliament*, London, 1835, pp. 117–18. Compare also Macaulay's speech in *Hansard* 3rd ser., 2, cols. 1196–201.

curred Francis Jeffrey (now Lord Advocate of Scotland); it produced a 'great number of persons of wealth, respectability, intelligence, and loyalty, belonging to the middle ranks ... who are
now unrepresented'. Or take the clear words of Lord John
Russell:

the middle class, as compared with the corresponding body in the
preceding century, had risen in wealth, and intelligence, and knowledge,
and influence; and as they advanced, the limits of the Constitution
became narrower and narrower, while the basis upon which the middle
classes had established themselves was becoming broader and broader.
Considering the increase of importance in that class, he had come to
the conclusion that they were not sufficiently represented in the House.[20]

Be it twenty-five, fifty, sixty years or a century, the story that
these Whig speakers were all telling was extraordinarily consistent. The move which Russell, Grey, Durham and Jeffrey – among
others – had launched in the early 1820s, was now bearing its
political fruits; and it was this political achievement, as we shall
see, that was to make possible the widespread success of the
particular historical narrative on which this move had been
predicated.

To be sure, pro-reform speakers did not fail to reaffirm yet
again what they took to be the political virtues of this newly
risen 'middle class'. Brougham summed it up in a famous speech:
the 'middle classes'

are solid, right-judging men, and, above all, not given to change. If
they have a fault, it is that error on the right side, a suspicion of State
quacks – a dogged love of existing institutions – a perfect contempt of
all political nostrums ... Grave – intelligent – rational – fond of
thinking for themselves – they consider a subject long before they make
up their minds on it; and the opinions they are thus slow to form,
they are not swift to abandon.[21]

---

[20] Grey in the winter of 1830–1, to Maurice Fitzgerald, the Knight of Kerry; quoted in
Trevelyan, *Lord Grey of the Reform Bill*, p. 237n. [Francis Jeffrey], *Corrected Report of the
Speech of the Right Honourable the Lord Advocate of Scotland, upon the Motion of Lord John
Russell, in the House of Commons, on the First of March, 1831, for Reform of Parliament*,
London, 1831, pp. 7–8. *Hansard* 3rd ser., 3, col. 309. Compare yet another supporter:
'as at present constituted, the House of Commons is not an adequate – is not a fair –
is not a sufficient – is not a faithful representation of the people of this country. The
House of Commons *does not* contain within its walls any *representation* of the middle
classes of society'; *The Question of Reform Considered: With Hints for a Plan*, London, 1831,
pp. 25–6.
[21] *Hansard* 3rd ser., 8, cols. 251–2. Other emphases on 'middle-class' respectability,
intelligence and patriotism included the speeches of Ralph Bernal (2, col. 21); John
Hobhouse (1292); Palmerston (their 'love of order' and 'attachment to the Throne

Unsurprisingly, those 'middle-class' virtues that Brougham and the other reformers emphasized were political responsibility and intelligence, rather than intransigence; loyalty to the crown, rather than to the rights of the people; value as a bulwark against revolution, rather than against encroachments on liberty. The most vital message of the reformers, in the words of the *Manchester Guardian*, was that the 'middle class' wished 'to repair and modify, not to destroy and reconstruct, our political institutions'. 'It will have Reform,' proclaimed Macaulay, 'it will not have revolution.'[22]

And naturally, therefore, moderate reformers did not wish to be confronted with evidence to the contrary. Thus, one curious consequence of the nature of the reform debate in Britain was the uncharacteristically terse reception of the French revolution of 1830. Norman Gash already pointed out many years ago that British liberals and moderates failed to express strong reactions to the July revolution, from which he concluded that they found the events in France largely irrelevant as an analogy for Britain.[23] But in fact, considering the characteristic liberal penchant for such analogies, one might suggest as explanation the exact opposite: that many liberals were reticent about the events in France precisely because these events *could* indeed seem quite relevant to their own situation, only damagingly so, given the emphatically non-revolutionary image that they were at pains to present. Thus, for once, and rather against the force of habit, the British liberals do not seem to have followed the cue of their French counterparts as well as of many other French commen-

---

and the Constitution', cols. 1327–8); Jeffrey (3, cols. 63, 81); Richard Bethell (238); Slaney (674); Wilbraham (1616); Grey (8, col. 323). See also the assertion that the 'middle class' was 'usually slow to engage in political contests', and its opinions were 'likely to be the result of deliberate reflection, or of some practical grievance', in *The Question of Reform Considered*, p. 6. As for Brougham, he also made similar statements in the *Edinburgh Review* 52, January 1831, pp. 536–7, 544; 56, October 1832, p. 250.

[22] *Manchester Guardian* 10:493, 9 October 1830. Macaulay's speech on 16 December 1831, reprinted in *The Miscellaneous Works of Lord Macaulay*, ed. Lady Trevelyan, Philadelphia, n.d., vol. IX, p. 91. Macaulay placed particular emphasis on that occasion on the equivalence of the intelligent 'middle class' with a political middle course; and see similarly Sir John Scott Lillie, *Observations on the Origin and Progress of Parliamentary Corruption and on the Probable Consequences of Parliamentary Reform . . .*, London, 1832, p. 69.

[23] N. Gash, 'English Reform and French Revolution in the General Election of 1830', in R. Pares and A. J. P. Taylor (eds.), *Essays Presented to Sir Lewis Namier*, London, 1956, pp. 258–88.

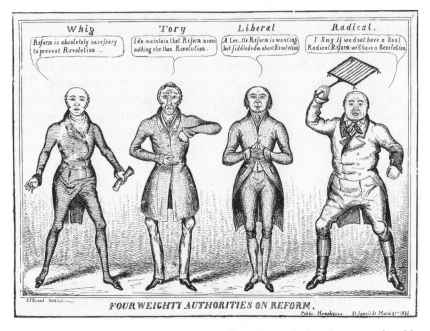

Figure 14. Reform and revolution, 1831. Note in particular the uncomfortable
words of the 'Liberal' (perhaps John Lee Lee, MP). The 'Whig' is Grey, the
'Tory' is Wellington, the 'Radical' is Cobbett. (Charles Jameson Grant) *Source*:
BMC 16618.

tators in asserting that, in the words of Tocqueville in late
August, 'the middle classes made the [July] Revolution'. In
Britain, in the midst of efforts to enfranchise the 'middle class'
which was professed to be 'quite as much alive to the dangers
of violent change, as to the defects of the existing system', such
assertions could prove rather embarrassing (see figure 14). As
one Whig MP put it, 'it was stigmatizing the middle classes to
describe them as revolutionary'.[24]

Liberal discussions of the 1830 revolution were therefore surprisingly few and far between. Moreover, when a key figure
such as Henry Brougham broke this relative silence with a
long sympathetic essay in the *Edinburgh Review*, he described the

---

[24] Tocqueville to Charles Stoffels, 26 August 1830; quoted in S. Drescher, *Dilemmas of
Democracy: Tocqueville and Modernization*, Pittsburgh, 1968, p. 201n. (and see more
examples above, in chapter 8). *Manchester Guardian* 10:493, 9 October 1830. George
Wilbraham's speech, *Hansard* 3rd ser., 3, col. 1616.

revolution wholly within a scheme of despotism versus 'the people' or 'public opinion'. Even when calling on England to emulate France and reform itself, Brougham – who in other contexts at this juncture was second to none in invoking the language of 'middle class' – never mentioned the 'middle class' of either nation as involved in any way.[25] It is also suggestive to consider Lord John Russell's *Causes of the French Revolution*, which he had begun writing in the 1820s but published only in 1832. Although Russell constructed what in some ways resembled the 'middle-class' interpretation of the French Revolution as it had been put forward by various writers in both France and Britain in the 1820s, he refrained from implicating the 'middle class' itself, preferring instead to present the 1789 Revolution as a clash between aristocracy and people. Russell's timidity in introducing the 'middle class' into his political drama was highlighted by his single distinctive use of this language, when he spoke of 'the simple manners of the middle class' in which Rousseau had been educated. The 'middle class' could tamely be associated with Rousseau's family background, but not with the tumultuous political actions that had been undertaken in his name.[26]

On the other hand, it is no less suggestive to see who *did* choose to highlight the role of the 'middle class' in the revolution of 1830. Thus, one ostensibly pro-reform writer who asserted that as a consequence of these events in France 'the Government appears to be fixed exclusively, *for the present*, in the hands of the middle classes of society', turned out to be more radical than most supporters of the Reform Bill, calling in strong anti-aristocratic terms for 'a total change of system [that] must speedily take place'. For such a writer, the direct analogy with France was indeed appealing: what he wanted to see in his own country too, he explained, was the placing of political power 'exclusively in those [hands] alone of the *middle classes of society*'. The other side of the same coin was that when the understanding of the

[25] *Edinburgh Review* 52, October 1830, pp. 1–25. This essay was important enough for Brougham to insist on writing it even though Macaulay had already prepared an article for the *Review* on the same subject: A. Aspinall, *Lord Brougham and the Whig Party*, Manchester, 1927, p. 178.

[26] [Lord John Russell], *The Causes of the French Revolution*, London, 1832, p. 141. On p. 85 Russell mentioned the diffusion of knowledge in 'the middle and lower classes', indistinctly, as an equivalent to the people that was juxtaposed with 'the ruling classes'.

July revolution as 'a combination of the middle classes assisted by the physical forces of the lower classes' was introduced into the parliamentary reform debates, it was not by one of the reformers, but by their Tory adversary, the 'middle-class'-obsessed William Mackinnon. As Gash has also noted, the analogies with the French revolution of 1830 proved more congenial to the *opponents* of moderate reform from both right and left, than to the moderate reformers themselves.[27]

Having the 'middle class' actively implicated in an actual revolution, however, was not the same thing as an occasional reminder of its latent potential to threaten an intransigent political system: the former was a political liability for the reformers, the latter not necessarily so. In 1867, Royden Harrison has argued, the British working class reached a moment in which it displayed increasing respectability but also 'had not wholly lost its revolutionary potentialities'; a carefully cultivated balance that made it seem 'safe to concede its enfranchisement and dangerous to withhold it'.[28] A similar argument can be made for the 'middle class' in 1832: some speakers, at least, combined praises for its political respectability and loyalty with only partially veiled allusions to its notorious revolutionary potentiality. 'It is the permanent interest of that class to preserve the public tranquillity; they are steadily attached to the government of Kings, Lords, and Commons', asserted one pamphlet; but, it intimated more ominously, it was also true that by 'an obstinate adherence to abuses', 'they can be alienated from that attachment'.[29]

But even here one can sense the reluctance of moderate reformers to exploit this stick-and-carrot tactic, which some of

---

[27] *Alarming State of the Nation Considered: The Evil Traced to Its Source, and Remedies Pointed out. By a Country Gentleman*, London, 1830, pp. 64–7, 88. *Hansard* 3rd ser., 11, col. 526. Gash, 'English Reform and French Revolution', p. 263. For the radical uses of the analogies with the July revolution see also H. Weisser, *British Working-Class Movements and Europe 1815–48*, Manchester, 1975, pp. 32–42, and pp. 60–61 n. 27 for the contrast with the liberal press.

[28] R. Harrison, 'The Tenth April of Spencer Walpole: The Problem of Revolution in Relation to Reform, 1865–67', in his *Before the Socialists: Studies in Labour and Politics 1861–1881*, London, 1965, pp. 78–136 (quoted, p. 133).

[29] *The Question of Reform Considered*, p. 115. Compare Robert Grant's and the Duke of Sussex's parliamentary speeches: *Hansard* 3rd ser., 3, col. 172; 8, col. 306. 'If the great mass of the middle class are bent upon that method of enforcing their views,' Holland wrote privately to Grey (5 November 1831), 'there is not in the nature of society any real force that can prevent them.' (Quoted in I. Newbould, *Whiggery and Reform, 1830–41: The Politics of Government*, Basingstoke, 1990, p. 57.)

the more radical reformers found attractive. Compare for instance the words of the Whig Lord Durham and the more radical Benthamite Charles Buller. Durham combined the assertion that in no class 'will the supporters of the Constitution find greater friends henceforward, or more stedfast allies, than among the middle classes', with a warning: were they to be alienated, without their support even Wellington himself 'would have found it no easy matter, by the mere aid of an armed soldiery', to prevent revolutionary disturbances.[30] In other words, Durham warned that without reform a revolution might take place, not because 'the middle classes' themselves would execute it, but because they might not be as motivated to prevent *others* from executing it. Buller, on his part, echoed closely the assessment of the role of the 'middle class' in preventing a 'revolt' by others: 'the fate of the country depended on the tranquillity of the manufacturing districts', he maintained, and it was 'the middling classes alone [who] can restrain these elements of danger'. But Buller did not stop there; he also asserted that

if the great body of the middling classes, the possessors of the wealth and intelligence of the country, the natural leaders of the physical force of the community, are bent on effecting a revolution which shall give them the controul over the management of their own affairs, they must have it.[31]

In Buller's threatening words, the 'middle class' itself commanded the use of force and was capable of executing its own revolution. Now Buller was part of the Benthamite circle, who (as Joseph Hamburger has shown) made the most of the potential revolutionary threat during the Reform Bill debates; indeed he was also one who invoked the analogy with the July revolution in order to amplify his warnings. The more moderate Whigs (with the

---

[30] *Hansard* 3rd ser., 3, cols. 1019, 1029; reprinted in *Speeches of the Earl of Durham*, pp. 84–5, 100; and see the further 'middle-class idiom' throughout his speech. For his 'middle class' language in 1821, see above, pp. 253–4. Compare also Henry Bunbury's warning in the Commons that 'the middle classes . . . had begun to regard revolutions with indifference' (*Hansard* 3rd ser., 7, col. 221).

[31] Charles Buller, *On the Necessity of a Radical Reform*, London, 1831, pp. 19, 24–5; and passim. Compare also the *Examiner* (1237, 16 October 1831, p. 668), edited by another Benthamite radical, Albany Fonblanque: 'At no time within the last century was ever such direct expression given to a determination on the part of the middle classes to obtain their rights by force, should their peaceable demands be rejected' (and note 1208, 27 March 1831, p. 203, where the *Examiner* had urged a 'middle-class' revolution in Spain).

partial exception of Macaulay), for the most part, like Durham, shied away from the possible implications of such explicit formulations, benefiting only obliquely from this ambiguity which for decades had been latent in the political understanding of a 'middle class'.[32]

There was another ambiguity, however, which now became more pronounced than ever before: the tension between the universalistic claims of the 'middle-class' language and its particularism. On the one hand, there was no lack of affirmations on the part of the moderate reformers that 'the mass of the middle classes never can have any interests adverse to the happiness and prosperity of those below them in society'.[33] But on the other hand it also became imperative for many reformers to underscore in the clearest possible terms the distinction (the 'impassable barrier', in Jeffrey's words) between the 'middle class' and its social inferiors: 'It is unjust to confound the sober, steady, middling class of society with the turbulent rabble that sometimes have disturbed the public peace'; 'One of the great hopes that was built upon this measure was, that it would be the means of separating the respectable part of the community from those who thought they could never demand enough.'[34] Whomever the

[32] Hamburger, *James Mill and the Art of Revolution* (for Buller's invocation of the July revolution, p. 223 and n. 17). Hamburger notes the difference in this regard between Whigs and Benthamites (see esp. pp. 66–7), as well as the atypicality of Macaulay's occasional alarmist outbursts. For Macaulay's allusion in parliament to a possible 'middle-class' revolution, see *Hansard* 3rd ser., 2, col. 1196 (and below, p. 357); and compare Macaulay's forceful comments a few years earlier about both the attachment of the 'middling orders' to the institutions of the country and the dangerous limits of this attachment, in *Edinburgh Review* 46, June 1827, pp. 260–3. On the other hand, Macaulay also emphasized the 'middle class's' aversion to revolution, as quoted above.

[33] In the words of the *Manchester Guardian* 10:501, 4 December 1830; and compare 9:432, 8 August 1829: 'the middle classes indubitably do not constitute an absolute majority of the population; but it seems to us quite impossible that they should ever have an interest opposed to that of the mass, and utterly improbable, that representatives, *bona fide* elected by them, should direct their power to their own private advantage, and the injury of the community at large'.

[34] *The Question of Reform Considered*, p. 114. Speech of the Solicitor General William Horne, *Hansard* 3rd ser., 3, col. 681. Jeffrey's full statement (col. 71) was: 'In the present agitated state of the country, when the flood is growing on the land, I would fain draw a firmament, and impassable barrier, between the pure and wholesome waters that are above, and the noisome and polluted contents of the dark abysses below: and this is the first good effect I venture to anticipate from the Bill now proposed.' Further examples include Thomas William Beaumont's speech (cols. 253–4). [John Campbell Colquhoun], *The Constitutional Principles of Parliamentary Reform. By a Freeholder and Landholder of Scotland*, Edinburgh, 1831, pp. 58–60. *A Letter from a Freeholder of Middlesex, to His Brother Freeholders*, London, 1831, p. 18.

category of 'middle class' was intended to bring in, it was becoming more evident than ever before that it was intended to keep many people out.

It was for this reason that popular radicals found this language irksome, and used it at this stage only intermittently. True, the language of 'middle class' was still malleable for differing political uses, a versatility that was to disappear only once the Reform Bill had become fact; but the tensions that had riddled James Mill's *Essay on Government* a decade earlier were becoming more difficult to bear. George Grote, who combined what Halévy has designated 'the minimum programme of the Radical party' with much attention to the 'middle class' (as seen in the epigraph to this chapter), was indeed a prominent disciple of James Mill. Advocating a much broader suffrage than the ministerial proposals as well as the ballot, Grote still asserted that under such a system, 'the interest and well-being of the middling classes would become the predominant object of solicitude'. Similar reassurances were given by the Benthamite *Westminster Review*; but elsewhere they did not enjoy too wide a currency.[35]

Unlike Grote, other radicals during these debates opted not to reinforce the understanding of the 'middle class' as embodied in the Reform Bill. For the most part they simply ignored it, resorting to the time-tested simple schemes of rich and poor, oppressors and oppressed; but on occasion they could be found contesting it, exposing the element of deliberate choice – and consequent closure – in what was being presented by the supporters of the Bill as a straightforward observable social fact. In parliament, the veteran radical Henry Hunt (who opposed the Bill) reproached Macaulay for distinguishing 'the rabble as opposed to *what he was pleased to call the middle classes*', thus emphasizing the wilfulness of the reformers' particular represen-

---

[35] Grote, *Essentials of Parliamentary Reform*, p. 31 and passim. On Grote see E. Halévy, *The Growth of Philosophic Radicalism*, London, 1972 (originally 1928), pp. 424–5; W. Thomas, *The Philosophic Radicals: Nine Studies in Theory and Practice 1817–1841*, Oxford, 1979, chapter 9; and for his concern about a lamentable political separation between the 'middle class' and its social inferiors, G. Wallas, *The Life of Francis Place 1771–1854*, London, 1898, p. 279. In the *Westminster Review*, see Thomas Peronnet Thompson's words in 12, January 1830, pp. 222–32 (esp. p. 231).

tation of society.[36] The exclusion entailed by this representation was resisted more directly by William Carpenter, champion of the unstamped popular press: 'I most confidently state', wrote Carpenter in *An Address to the Working Classes*, 'that the middle classes of 1831 are not only *not* a class of persons having interests different from your own . . . They are the *same* class; they are, generally speaking, *working* or *labouring* men.'[37] It is doubtful whether many in late 1831 were persuaded by this alternative, inclusive understanding of the 'middle class'; indeed elsewhere Carpenter himself appeared resigned to accepting the 'middle class' as an exclusive grouping that left out the working class.[38] But Carpenter's perhaps desperate appeal demonstrates again the lingering leeway in that space of possibilities for the use of 'middle-class' language, a space that was rapidly closing down as the ultimate act of exclusion – the Reform Bill itself – was taking concrete shape. A year later, as we shall see, while radicals were to use the language of 'middle class' much more often, it was always within its hegemonic exclusive understanding.

Similar points were made by the conservative opponents of the Reform Bill. Sounding much like Henry Hunt, the former Tory Secretary at War Sir Henry Hardinge complained that the ministerial proposals 'erected a barrier between the lower classes and those *which by this Bill were considered the middle classes*': he too made it clear that this definition of the 'middle class' was not the only one possible. Or take Sir John Walsh, a recently elected Tory MP who published in 1831 a popular anti-reform tract that went through six editions within the year. The reformers, Walsh wrote perceptively, 'have eagerly adopted a [social] classification so favourable to their views', in which they 'trace[d] at pleasure new and capricious boundaries in the map of social life'. But,

---

[36] *Hansard* 3rd ser., 2, col. 1209 (my emphasis). See also 3, col. 19, for Hunt's appropriation of 'middle-class-idiom' formulations for 'mechanics'. And compare Hunt's condemnation of the Bill in Manchester in April 1831, addressing a huge crowd on the site of Peterloo, as a measure intended 'to give *what they call the middle classes* . . . a share in the representation': quoted in J. Belchem, *'Orator' Hunt: Henry Hunt and English Working-Class Radicalism*, Oxford, 1985, p. 228 (my emphasis).

[37] William Carpenter, *An Address to the Working Classes, on the Reform Bill*, London, [1831; signed 14 October], p. 14. Carpenter oscillated between using the term 'middle class' and doubting its meaning; see pp. 15–16. His opinion was that although the Bill was deficient in many obvious ways, it was better for the interests of the working classes to support it than to reject it.

[38] See for example his *A Political Reflector*, 18 March 1831, p. 15.

he continued, 'in their frequent panegyrics of the independence and intelligence of the middle ranks, and in their fierce attacks upon what they term the oligarchy, they either inadvertently, or designedly, omit all mention of that most important part of the nation, the gentry'. Underlying the reformers' 'middle-class'-based vision of society, Walsh pointed out, was in fact a 'capricious' choice; a choice that obliterated his own preferred view of society which happened to be focused on the gentry. He therefore proposed further to reconceptualize the 'middle class' as a gentry-centred category; and thus, since the gentry were not only superior in property, intelligence, respectability and independence, but were already predominant in the House of Commons, no change of representation – either of society, or of the electorate – was necessary.[39]

As a consequence, John Walsh's opinion (quoted in the epigraph to this chapter) was that the valuable 'middle class' – now, of course, as Walsh himself chose to understand it – was unequivocally opposed to the Reform Bill. In this assertion Walsh was not alone: while the later perceptions of the Reform Bill make it sound rather improbable, during the debates in 1830–2 these perceptions themselves were not yet etched in stone. Not only were the political uses of 'middle-class' language during these debates more versatile than subsequently; so also were the social meanings attached to the category of 'middle class' – another dimension of indeterminacy that the Reform Bill was about to curtail. True, the bottom line separating the 'middle class' from its social inferiors was already becoming more sharply delineated. But in other respects, as long as 'middle classness' was not defined by and equated with the new enfranchisement qualifications of 1832, its precise meaning remained nebulous enough to support such contradicting interpretations.

Consider the following exclamation of 'middle-class idiom':

[The] middle class, should enjoy a predominant influence in the House of Commons, because that class is composed of individuals who are less exposed to the pernicious exhalations of democratic prejudices than the lower classes, and further removed than the higher from the sphere

---

[39] *Hansard* 3rd ser., 3, col. 889 (my emphasis). John B. Walsh, [Baron Ormathwaite], *Popular Opinions on Parliamentary Reform Considered*, 4th edn, London, 1831, pp. 103–5 and passim.

in which the sunshine of royalty exerts its influence; and because the persons of whom it is composed contribute more largely towards the exigencies of the state than the members of any other class.

The proponents of the Reform Bill could hardly have put it better. But this particular writer was not supporting the Bill: he was opposing it, and quite strongly so. In his view, the 'middle class' – which he took to mean very specifically 'persons of the three learned professions, merchants, bankers, gentlemen farmers, opulent tradesmen, and the superior public officers' – was the biggest loser under the ministerial proposals. The Reform Bill, he warned, would place absolute influence in the hands of the higher classes during times of peace, and in the hands of the lower classes during 'public excitement'; whereas the 'middle class', 'which ought to be represented more efficaciously than any of the rest', would become altogether voiceless.[40] As another anti-reform MP put it, nobody could claim 'that the wealth, the intelligence, and the interests of the middle classes' – in his understanding of the term – were not already 'fully and fairly represented' in the unreformed House of Commons. And should reform take place, warned another pamphlet, 'the moderate and middle class' (to which its author claimed to belong), that 'are our real country', would be overwhelmed by 'men of no property'; and when the 'middle class' would 'cease to raise their voice with effect, England will be no more'. Yet another anti-reformer mockingly rejected the claim that 'the ten pound free-holders' – those about to be enfranchised – were 'the virtuous Spartans who are to restore the tone of public morality'; but at the same time also asserted that 'the middling classes, the sound-headed, straightforward members of society', with whom this writer was proud of having 'large intercourse', were becoming aware of the spurious misrepresentations of the reformers and were consequently withdrawing their support from the Bill.[41] The disagree-

---

[40] *A Plain Man's Estimate of the State of Affairs*, London, 1835, from the appendix which reprinted a pamphlet published during the debates on the Reform Bill; quoted, pp. 48–9, 53–5. Virtually the same argument, in just as strong terms of praise for the 'middle class' and of concern for its imminent loss of political importance, was put forward by Archibald Alison in *Blackwood's Edinburgh Magazine* 30, October 1831, p. 608.

[41] Speech of Matthias Attwood, *Hansard* 3rd ser., 3, col. 210. William Roberts, *Letters on Parliamentary and Ecclesiastical Reform*, London, 1831, pp. 38, 40; Roberts speculated that the 'middle class' would therefore oppose the Bill. *On the Draught of a New Constitution*

ment between such speakers and the advocates of reform was not about the importance of 'middle-class' influence, but about who this 'middle class' really was.

We may note in passing that even among the reformers themselves the identity of the 'middle class' was not always clear. A revealing case in point was a 'Country Gentleman' of 1830 who wanted the franchise transferred from the hands of 'the very wealthiest classes of the community, – a set of *Princes*', exclusively to the hands of 'the *middle classes of society*'. The latter, went his familiar tune, 'contain[ed] the greatest portion of intelligence, as well as aptitude for business'; they were 'the best and most competent judges of the situation and wants of a nation, and the properest depositaries of its power'. So far, no surprises. But read further:

It is in the middle classes of society only in England where a body of electors could be found who might be *safely trusted*, as feeling in *themselves* a direct wish for maintaining the ancient institutions of the country, with its existing forms of government, and the preponderance that is justly due to *agriculture* over *manufacturers and commerce*.

Note again the last sentence: the 'Country Gentleman' was enlisting the 'middle class' to counteract the expanding interests of commerce and manufacture – that is, the forces produced by social change – and to guarantee, no less, the continued predominance of agriculture! Defying assumptions often made by historians, for this reformer the 'middle class' was the vehicle for reinstating a landed 'neo-Harringtonian' social order, obviously complementary to the reinstating of a proper constitutional balance. In his eyes the great heroes within this 'middle class' were first and foremost country gentlemen (like himself) and yeomen.[42] Even now, then, the linkage between the 'middle class' and social transformations was not inevitable; indeed a year later, even in a bastion of Whig views such as the *Edinburgh Review*, one could

---

About to be Sent up to the House of Peers. In a Letter to a Noble Lord, London, 1831, pp. 23–4 (signed W. M., 1 August 1831).

[42] *Alarming State of the Nation Considered*, pp. 45, 64–5, and passim. The 'Country Gentleman' also combined his 'middle-class idiom' with opposition to free trade: see appendix. Compare the equivalence of 'middle class' and 'yeomanry' in Colquhoun, *The Constitutional Principles of Parliamentary Reform*, p. 41; and see the comments on the indefinite and not necessarily urban nature of the 'middle class' in the rhetoric of the reform debates in R. W. Davis, 'Deference and Aristocracy in the Time of the Great Reform Act', *American Historical Review* 81 (1976), p. 538.

still read about 'the enmity to machinery [which] is fostered by the middle classes' (surely meaning here anything but an industrial bourgeoisie) because of their ignorance of the subject.[43]

To return to the confrontation between reformers and their opponents, can we also find the form of contestation over the 'middle class' as we have encountered it in the 1790s, resulting in the differentiation of social language between political adversaries? To a certain extent, yes. The language of 'middle class' was manifestly more common in the rhetoric of the reformers than in that of their opponents. One can also find moments reminiscent of the 1790s when the social language of one side was transformed by the other into terms more congenial for its own purposes. Whereas in the 1790s, however, it had been primarily the ministerialist camp that tended to avoid the language of 'middle class', with its then oppositional overtones, in the early 1830s, unsurprisingly, such avoidance (of a language now enrolled on the side of the party of order) was more a characteristic of radical rhetoric. A case in point is the *Examiner*, which under the editorship of Albany Fonblanque displayed a rather radical tone: the *Examiner* not only tended now to prefer dual social vocabulary over 'middle-class' language in discussing reform, but also often paraphrased pro-reform rhetoric in a way that recast it in terms other than 'middle class' – be they 'smaller gentry', 'superior trading men', 'the New Rich', or 'the monied class'.[44] And in reporting on Thomas Attwood's foundation of 'an Union of the middle and the lower classes for attainment of Parliamentary Reform', the *Examiner*'s approval of this initiative at the same time subsumed it under a more stark social division of rich and poor.[45]

---

[43] Walter Coulson in *Edinburgh Review* 52, January 1831, pp. 338–9. On the 'middle class' in the *Edinburgh* during the reform debates, as a category not necessarily well-defined or economy-based, see B. Fontana, *Rethinking the Politics of Commercial Society: The 'Edinburgh Review' 1802–1832*, Cambridge, 1985, pp. 156–7.

[44] See for example Fonblanque's recasting of the *Morning Chronicle*'s language while refuting its arguments about the purported independence of the 'middle class', in the *Examiner* 1134, 25 October 1829, p. 673 (reprinted in Albany Fonblanque, *England under Seven Administrations*, 3 vols., London, 1837, vol. I, pp. 236–40), and again in 1135, 1 November 1829, p. 691. The independence of middle social strata was denied again without any 'middle-class' language in 1192, 5 December 1830, pp. 769–70. And note the preference for 'landed gentry' and 'the monied class', incorporated into a basic dual social scheme, in the discussion of social progress in 1201, 6 February 1831, p. 83.

[45] 'One argument urged by him [Attwood], is an argument we have unceasingly pressed, namely, the unfitness of the rich to legislate for the poor, of whose condition they are careless': *Examiner* 1148, 31 January 1830, p. 68. Many more enunciations reformulated

Unlike the 1790s, however, during the Reform Bill debates such implicit differentiations were not very significant. What was striking, on the contrary, was the unprecedented *explicit* level of the contestation over the uses of 'middle-class' language. Nothing in the 1790s, to give one more example, compared with the explicit argument provoked by Henry Brougham's speech in parliament in October 1831. Brougham said:

if there is the mob, there is the people also. I speak now of the middle classes – of those hundreds of thousands of respectable persons – the most numerous, and by far the most wealthy order in the community ... those middle classes, who are also the genuine depositaries of sober, rational, intelligent, and honest English feeling.[46]

Let us look at one response from each political end to this oft-quoted passage. First, one anti-reformer quoted this passage in order to expose the pretence in its use of 'people', 'here defined to be the middling classes'. Not only were the 'middle classes' far from equivalent to 'the people', they were also not equivalent – as Brougham had implied – to the reform camp: 'I should be glad to know', retorted this writer sarcastically, 'who went through the country asking the middling classes whether such a Bill, or such a Bill would secure their support for the Government? Who took their votes upon schedules A and B?' On the contrary, the majority of the real 'middling classes' were against the Bill and alarmed by its probable consequences: 'The responsibility' for this measure, this writer concluded, 'rests upon ministers, not upon the middling classes.'[47]

in non-'middle-class' vocabularies could be adduced, from radical as well as from conservative sources. The latter include the anti-reform barrister who cautioned (in effect, echoing the *Examiner*) that the franchise would fall into the hands of the most dependent class in the country, 'the small shopkeepers': *Notes on the Reform Bill. By a Barrister*, London, 1831, p. 43. Also see *View of the Representation of Scotland in 1831: A Letter to the Scottish Landed Proprietors*, London, 1831, pp. 11, 14. *Reform: A Letter to Lord John Russell on Reform in Parliament*, London, 1831. *A Practical View of the Question of Parliamentary Reform*, London, 1831 (esp. p. 23, for strong 'interest' language). Y. Z. and F. J. Hext, *Letters on Reform in Parliament, Addressed to Sir R. R. Vyvyan, Bart. MP ... Originally Published in the Royal Cornwall Gazette ...*, Truro, 1831.

[46] *Hansard* 3rd ser., 8, col. 251; and see also 265. Brougham was echoing a previous statement of Lord Althorp, whereby 'by the people he meant the great majority of the respectable middle classes of the country' (2, col. 1143).

[47] *Reply to a Pamphlet, Entitled Speech of the Right Hon. Lord Brougham, Lord High Chancellor of England ... on Friday, Oct. 7, 1831*, 3rd edn, London, 1831, pp. 33–4. (Schedules A and B were lists of boroughs to be disfranchised by the Reform Bill, respectively losing both seats or only one seat.) See also John Wilson's attack on Brougham in a review of this pamphlet, ridiculing the reformers' reverence for the 'middle class': *Blackwood's Edinburgh Magazine* 31, January 1832, p. 131 (quoted below, p. 324).

Second, take a response from the opposite political corner, expressing no less annoyance with Brougham's usurpation of the term 'the people' in confounding it with the 'middle class'. Brougham, the radical *Poor Man's Guardian* angrily exclaimed, 'did *not* mean by PEOPLE the "MOB" or the "POPULACE!" And who are this mob and populace? why, YOU, the mechanics and working classes!' Moreover, 'he does not exactly stick at the truth we see; the "middle-class" the most numerous!' – surely there were greater numbers employed by the 'middle class' than the 'middle class' themselves? The *Poor Man's Guardian*'s indignation, targeted somewhat confusingly both at the 'middle class' as it understood it itself and at Brougham's use of the term, grew stronger:

Brougham goes on, at some length, fulsomely flattering these *middle classes*, and insisting that government must look to '*that people' for support*, as *contradistinguished from the* 'populace' – 'this middle-class who were connected with, and looked upon as *protectors* by, the lower-classes.' – Alas! precious protectors are they, giving the poor working man a mere fraction of the value of his labour, and putting the rest into their own pockets![48]

Was the 'middle class' then honest and disinterested, or self-interested and avaricious? Was it the inclusive representatives of the people, or their exclusive group of exploiters? Should it be flattered or denounced? Who had the authority to determine its identity? Undoubtedly – as we have seen throughout this chapter, from William Mackinnon onwards – such direct discussion of the merits or demerits of the 'middle class', and of the ways in which participants in the political debate chose to employ this category, was different in kind and not only in degree from the uses of 'middle-class' language prior to the debates on the Reform Bill.

Finally, consider once more the debates in parliament. Here, again, some of the anti-reformers certainly refrained from 'middle-

---

[48] *Poor Man's Guardian* 16, 15 October 1831; rep. edn, New York, 1968, vol. i, pp. 123–4 (leading article). Although this was not an exact quotation of Brougham's words, it was in fact quite close. Compare also *The Voice of the West Riding* 1, 1 June 1833: 'We have long seen the hollow-hearted advocacy of the working man's cause even by those styling themselves "liberals". They use the word "people", but it is with the Whigish Broughamic sense.' (Quoted in R. Gray, 'The Deconstructing of the English Working Class', *Social History* 11 (1986), p. 370.)

class' language altogether, reconceptualizing the question under discussion as one about the balance between competing interests, or between the aristocracy and the lower classes, or employing some other social vocabulary that avoided the formulation most strongly proposed by the advocates of the Bill.[49] Others appropriated the rhetoric of the reformers while subverting and suppressing its 'middle-class' elements, like Michael Sadler, who compounded a strong dual paternalistic vision with the following view of social progress: 'Commerce multiplied the wealth of the nation', Sadler began unobjectionably, and thus 'mingled society into a more undistinguishable mass, infusing through the whole a portion of its own spirit of enterprise and independence'.[50] So much for the 'middle-class' narrative favoured by the reformers: while following them in emphasizing commercial progress and its effects on industriousness and independence, in Sadler's own representation of society the outcome was not the rise of a 'middle class' but rather the erasure of social distinctions and the spreading of these virtues throughout the whole of society. Nevertheless, one again has the sense that the stakes in such linguistic differentiation during these debates were not as high as in the 1790s: now, when push came to shove, it was more important for the opponents of the Reform Bill to clarify their opinion about the 'middle class' than to avoid talking about it. Nowhere was this better seen than in the tribulations of the Tory MP Horace Twiss.

The first time that Horace Twiss rose to oppose the Reform Bill, he spoke about representation in terms of 'interests', whether professional, labouring, colonial or those of 'fundholders and money capitalists'. Twiss objected to the proposed expansion of the franchise to 'men of limited information, of strong prejudices, of narrow and contracted views, such as shop-keepers and small attorneys'. The reformers, not unreasonably, heard this statement as a direct response to their 'middle-class idiom'. Consequently,

---

[49] Examples include the speeches of Sir Robert Harry Inglis (*Hansard* 3rd ser., 2, cols. 1108–9), Winthrop Praed (3, col. 241), Thomas Courtenay (296–7), Sir Richard Vyvyan (635–42), Sir John Shelley (728), Sir Robert Bateson (746–7), Lord Wharncliffe (1000–3), Henry Fane (1613–14), Francis Baring (1803–4), Thomas Pemberton (7, cols. 170–1; and again 11, cols. 445–7), Lord Mahon (11, cols. 419–20), Pigott (502–4).

[50] Ibid., 3, col. 1561. Compare also Sir James Scarlett's replication of a 'middle-class idiom' formulation without any 'middle-class' language in col. 778 (and see Scarlett's language of 'interests' in 7, col. 166).

one after another they rose to accuse Twiss of 'ridicul[ing] the whole of the middle classes', in the process putting their own language into his mouth.[51] In the rhetorical climate of these months this was a particularly damaging accusation, a fact which drew a derisive sneer from John Wilson of the *Blackwood's Edinburgh Magazine*:

You may abuse at present any body, or any body of men, you please – except ten-pound shop or householders. Speak of them slightingly as judges of men and manners in all political affairs, and you are, if not sacrificed on the spot, at least snubbed by some sour Whig and sore, for calumniating the 'middle classes.' The middle classes![52]

But Horace Twiss proved to have less of a thick skin than the *Blackwood's* reviewer; and when he came back defensively to explain himself (twice), he adopted his opponents' 'middle-class' language in an effort to fend off their charges.

Twiss's first reaction was to assure the House that 'he did not speak disparagingly of the middle classes, as a class, because he was aware that there were among them some of the most estimable members of society'; but that he was only cautioning against some dangerous political tendencies among them.[53] A week later Twiss denied these accusations again: he now declared (somewhat inconsistently with his first response) that those people mentioned in his first speech, in whose hands a monopoly of the franchise should not be placed, 'were not those who, even in the largest phraseology, could be termed the middle classes of this country'. Once again, the discussion was about who could be represented as 'middle class'. Twiss continued tellingly:

Of the middle classes I never spoke at all – the phrase 'middle classes' never passed my lips. The idea of the middle classes was not even in my mind, for my argument related to a totally different order of persons. It was to the predominance of a body far below the middle class, both in property and intelligence, that I objected.

---

[51] Twiss's speech – ibid., 2, cols. 1132–4; Lord Althorp, col. 1141. Similarly see Hobhouse in col. 1292; Palmerston in col. 1327; and Grant in 3, col. 173, 'expressing his surprise – to use a mild term – at the sneers of the hon. member for Newport, at the middle classes of society in this country'. See also 7, col. 202, where the opposers of the Bill were asked to admit that in truth they had little respect for the political views of the 'middle class'.

[52] *Blackwood's Edinburgh Magazine* 31, January 1832, p. 131.

[53] *Hansard* 3rd ser., 2, col. 1144; and see Lord Gower's further attempts to vindicate Twiss from this charge in col. 1147.

His nervous indignation was betrayed several sentences later by his impassioned repetition:

And as to the middle classes, to whose number I myself belong, – classes which I never once named, nor even alluded to, but which I am daily calumniated as though I had sought to libel – men who . . . are placed by their character and intelligence altogether upon a different level from that of the indiscriminate multitude now proposed to be made absolute in all the towns – in a word, as to all the middle classes, so far from uttering one word of ridicule, I did not even deny their competency for the possession of political power.[54]

One could remain sceptical of this retroactive explanation, recalling that Twiss had originally referred to attorneys, shop-keepers and tradesmen as members of the group which he now labelled as 'the indiscriminate multitude'. More to the point, while it was true – as Twiss himself was anxiously trying to point out – that he had originally refrained from 'middle-class' language altogether, he evidently had now a higher stake in exonerating himself from the accusation of slandering the 'middle class' than in maintaining these linguistic preferences.[55] Thus Twiss ended up scrambling to reconcile his rejection of reform as best as he could with appreciation for the 'middle class', believing that he could accept one without the other. The fact, however, that a few weeks after this clumsy performance Twiss lost his seat in parliament is perhaps an indication of how difficult it was becoming to maintain such a position.

There was one more twist to Twiss's self-defence, namely the trumpeting of his own 'middle-class' identity (as a grandson of an overseas merchant, the son of a compiler and himself a lawyer). In this too Twiss was signalling the things to come, and he was surely not alone. Other opponents of reform, too,

---

[54] Ibid., 3, cols. 496–8. Twiss nevertheless admitted that even for the sake of this 'middle class' he would hesitate to tamper with the constitution.

[55] A similar situation occurred in an exchange between Lord Wharncliffe and Lord Durham in the upper House: the former objected to the Bill wholly within a language of 'interests', but once Durham used 'middle-class' language in his rejoinder, Wharncliffe came back to explain his first speech, now differentiating clearly between 'middle classes' and the 'lower classes' (ibid., 3, cols. 1034–5). See also the speech of Lord Norreys, who presented his objections to the Bill in a language of 'interests' (the Bill would be 'giving a preponderance to the manufacturing interest'), but then went on to refute possible insinuations that he was 'opposing himself to the interests of the middle class' (cols. 675–6).

far from denying or disregarding the alleged presence of a 'middle class', chose on the contrary to underscore their own 'middle-class' affinities. Thus Sir Edward Sugden – a Tory barrister and hairdresser's son – combined his objections to the Bill with an assurance that 'he belonged to the middle classes, he sprung from them, and among them he was destined to remain. He, therefore, had no interests separate from theirs.' Lord Tenterden, another hairdresser's son who made a career in law (in this case culminating as a chief justice and in a peerage), likewise assured the House of Lords that his opposition to reform did not mean any disrespect for 'the middle classes'. Tenterden added parenthetically: 'he ought to tell their Lordships, that he entertained a respect and affection for those classes, since he was sprung from them' – a revelation which was noted appreciatively by the next speaker, the Duke of Sussex. And given his future role in the conservative party, such pronouncements were especially meaningful when they came from the mouth of Robert Peel. Professing his conviction that the intelligent 'middle class' would object to the proposed subversion of the constitution, Peel hastened to add: 'I beg not to be included among those who are charged with making any one observation disparaging to the middle classes of society in this country. I repudiate such sentiment – sprung as I am, from those classes, and proud of my connection with them.'[56] Peel could indeed make a case for himself as a new social type: his maternal grandfather was a partner in a firm of cotton manufacturers in Bury, and his paternal grandfather mortgaged the family estates in 1764 in order to establish a calico-printing firm. Peel was also a new political type, one of a new wave of politicians who were to stamp their mark on the country in the period following the Reform Bill. His self-association with the 'middle class' at this juncture, overriding his particular position in the debate, was equally meaningful on both counts.

Overall, then, for every voice that can be shown to have

---

[56] *Hansard* 3rd ser., 3, col. 686 (and see 11, col. 697, for more of Sugden's 'middle-class idiom'); 8, cols. 301, 306; 2, cols. 1338–9 (Peel's speech of 3 March 1831). Not that Peel was beyond making such disparaging observations, at least in private: see Peel to Croker, 15 April 1831, in L. J. Jennings (ed.), *The Croker Papers: The Correspondence and Diaries of the Late Right Honourable John Wilson Croker . . .* New York, 1884, vol. 1, pp. 506–7.

rendered the reform debate into social categories other than
'middle class', one can point to many others of similar political
convictions who, by contrast, conspicuously incorporated this
language into their own rhetoric. The sheer volume and
explicitness of 'middle-class' language in the public debate – only
a small fraction of which has been sampled in the preceding
pages – made the more implicit resistance to it irrelevant. 'We
hear ample and frequent admission of the superior virtues of the
middle classes', Fonblanque's *Examiner* observed resignedly in
summer 1831; and thus it too gave in, shifting imperceptibly
during that year to formulating its own objections within the
same language used by the reformers. 'Lord JOHN RUSSELL's plan
of the franchise proceeds upon the policy of admitting the middle
classes to the constituency', Fonblanque now wrote; but 'upon
what principle he admits the middle, and stops short of the
respectable classes of mechanics and artizans?'[57] But in fact it
was Fonblanque himself, like Twiss and Peel, who was now
coming around to admitting the middle. In this they were registering an important effect of the debates on the Reform Bill, and
pointing the way to its immediate aftermath.

[57] *Examiner* 1205, 6 March 1831, p. 145 (reprinted in Fonblanque, *England under Seven
Administrations*, vol. II, p. 88); 1227, 7 August 1831, p. 498. Not surprisingly, these
months saw a surge of 'middle-class' language in the *Examiner* in other contexts as
well: see 1205, 6 March 1831, p. 155; 1208, 27 March 1831, p. 203; 1219, 5 June
1831, pp. 356, 358.

CHAPTER 10

Inventing the ever-rising 'middle class': the aftermath of 1832

The following preamble, though not a verbatim copy of the Reform Bill, gives, in my humble opinion, the spirit or true meaning of that bill. – Whereas the People which, according to the idea of our ancestors, means the middle classes, being from the decay of some towns, and the rapid prosperity of new ones that have started up, not sufficiently represented, though from their independence, honesty, and morality, they are one of the most respectable classes of society, a Reform Bill is much wanted, embracing the full and complete representation of the people, alias the middle classes.

(Thomas Lowndes, *A Letter Addressed to the Wide-Spreading John Bull Family*, 1833)[1]

Thomas Lowndes, esq., was no friend of reform. Writing in 1833, he believed that Britain had just taken a serious political turn for the worse. But his sarcastic imaginary preamble to a 'mad-headed' Bill captured one realization that was not in dispute: whether the Reform Act was seen as a cause for celebration or for grief, virtually everyone at this point came to perceive it as a 'middle-class' measure, driven by recent social transformations. 'The great reform bill', rejoiced one pamphlet, 'has transferred the government of these kingdoms from the grasp of a greedy oligarchy, in effect, to the middling classes.' 'The middle classes', echoed Richard Cobden, were those 'in whom the government of this country is now vested.' Robert Peel stated that following the Act, to which he had previously been opposed, 'the middle classes . . . are mainly the depositaries of the elective franchise'; and the Tory *Blackwood's*

---

[1] Thomas Lowndes, *A Letter Addressed to the Wide-Spreading John Bull Family, on the Accomplishments of Our Late Enlightened Monarch George the Fourth* . . ., London, 1833, pp. 54–5. Lowndes however also argued that in fact the Bill contributed to the annihilation of the 'middle class', swamped by the new electorate.

Edinburgh Magazine referred to 'the middle classes, to whom, in so great a proportion, political power has been handed over by the Reform Bill'.[2] Radicals complained that the reformed House of Commons 'was chosen by the middle class, [and hence] it represented, and still continues to represent, the middle class'. And again: 'The middle classes enjoy the right of choosing parliamentary representatives – and the right is enjoyed by them almost exclusively', which meant that following 1832, 'the House of Commons is their creature.' Overall, it was common knowledge – always couched in the same social vocabulary – that, in John Stuart Mill's succinct phrase, the present age saw at least the first step towards 'the *régime* of the middle class'.[3]

Not, of course, that 1832 really witnessed the straightforward transfer of the keys to political power into the hands of a 'middle class', as many contemporaries were soon to discover. Indeed, it is an oft-repeated truism – *pace* Charles Greville's expectation in summer 1832 that the composition of the next parliament would be considerably altered because 'the middle classes are pressing on'[4] – that the reformed parliament was in fact not all that radically different from the unreformed one. Some historians have therefore concluded that, in the words of Frank O'Gorman,

[2] Matthew Bridges, *An Address to the Electors of England: More Especially Those of the Middle and Operative Classes*, London, 1832, p. 10. [Richard Cobden], *England, Ireland, and America. By a Manchester Manufacturer*, London, 1835, p. 100. Robert Peel, *Speech of Sir Robert Peel, Bart. Delivered at Merchant Tailors' Hall, 11th May, 1835*, 8th edn, London, 1835, p. 10. *Blackwood's Edinburgh Magazine*, 46, September 1839, p. 295. Among many others, see also Edward George Bulwer-Lytton, *England and the English*, 2 vols., New York, 1833 (also London), vol. II, p. 11. W. Shepherd, *Speech of the Rev. W. Shepherd, at the Public Dinner to Celebrate the Passing of the Reform Bills in Liverpool, on Tuesday the 4th of Sept. 1832*, Liverpool, [1832], p. [1]. *Westminster Review* 32, April 1839, pp. 484ff. Also compare the ultra-Tory James Bernard, *Appeal to the Conservatives, on the Imminent Danger to which the Nation Is Exposed from the Democratic Propensities of the House of Commons ...*, London, 1835, p. 26.

[3] Henry S. Chapman, 'Preliminary Reforms: Being a Summary of the Principles Advocated in These Pamphlets', in J. A. Roebuck (ed.), *Pamphlets for the People*, [London, 1835], vol. I, [no. 22], p. 11. *Reconciliation between the Middle and Labouring Classes: Re-Printed from the Nonconformist*, Manchester, 1842, pp. 10–11 (introduction by Joseph Sturge, 13 December 1841). J. S. Mill in the *Edinburgh Review* 72, October 1840; reprinted in his *Essays on Politics and Society*, in *Collected Works*, Toronto, 1977, vol. XVIII, p. 167.

[4] *The Greville Memoirs 1814–1860*, eds. L. Strachey and R. Fulford, London, 1938, vol. II, p. 312 (25 July 1832). Greville was not overly enthusiastic about the consequences of the new opening given to these 'middle-class' men, characterized by 'fortune, energy, activity, zeal and ambition', among whom 'no Cannings perhaps or Broughams [can be found], but a host of fellows of the calibre of the actors in the old French Constituent Assembly'.

'one electoral system disappeared and gave way, then, to one remarkably like itself'.[5] Indeed, one strand of 'revisionism', spearheaded by D. C. Moore, has gone beyond denying 'the arrival of the urban middle class to political power' to contend that the Bill in truth was a ruling-class strategy – if not ploy – to capitalize on powerful links of deference that bound their social inferiors to their authority, and thus to retain power and check the influence of the 'middle class'.[6] In the opinion of Perry Anderson, the exclusionary nature of the Reform Act prevented 'an autonomous bourgeois party' from 'enter[ing] the parliamentary arena on its own terms'; thus 'the founding moment of independent bourgeois representation was missed', the result being 'a fundamentally unaltered aristocratic ascendancy in English politics'.[7]

[5] F. O'Gorman, *Voters, Patrons, and Parties: The Unreformed Electoral System of Hanoverian England 1734–1832*, Oxford, 1989, p. 392; also see pp. 11, 178–82. O'Gorman argues that the pre–1832 electoral system was more sophisticated than commonly assumed, and that consequently the changes introduced by the Reform Act were not as drastic as they are often presented. Similar arguments for continuity in personal or institutional terms include S. F. Woolley, 'The Personnel of the Parliament of 1833', *English Historical Review* 53 (1938), pp. 240–62. E. Halévy, *A History of the English People in the Nineteenth Century III: The Triumph of Reform 1830–1841*, London, 1950, pp. 62–4. A. Aspinall (ed.), *Three Early Nineteenth Century Diaries*, London, 1952, introduction, pp. xxx–xxxiv. W. L. Guttsman, *The British Political Elite*, London, 1963, chapter 2. N. Gash, *Politics in the Age of Peel: A Study in the Technique of Parliamentary Representation 1830–1850*, 2nd edn, Hassocks, 1977 (Gash points out, however, the more radical effects of the Reform Bill in Scotland and Ireland (p. 35)). And compare Greville's own admission of the continuity in the nature of parliament despite its 'rather different' composition (*The Greville Memoirs*, vol. II, pp. 412–14, 3 September 1833); also Brougham's opinion in 1835 as discussed below.

[6] For D. C. Moore's thesis, see his 'The Other Face of Reform', *Victorian Studies* 5 (1961), pp. 7–34 (quoted, p. 8); 'Concession or Cure: The Sociological Premises of the First Reform Act', *Historical Journal* 9 (1966), pp. 39–59; 'Social Structure, Political Structure, and Public Opinion in Mid-Victorian England', in R. Robson (ed.), *Ideas and Institutions of Victorian Britain*, London, 1967, pp. 20–57; 'Political Morality in Mid-Nineteenth Century England: Concepts, Norms, Violations', *Victorian Studies* 13 (1969), pp. 5–36; *The Politics of Deference: A Study of the Mid-Nineteenth Century English Political System*, Hassocks, 1976. Many historians have criticized Moore's thesis as rigid and overdrawn, but have retained a sober assessment of the limits of the political transformation in 1832; see E. P. Hennock, 'The Sociological Premises of the First Reform Act: A Critical Note', *Victorian Studies* 14 (1971), pp. 321–7, and Moore's response, pp. 328–37. J. Milton-Smith, 'Earl Grey's Cabinet and the Objects of Parliamentary Reform', *Historical Journal* 15 (1972), pp. 55–74. R. W. Davis, 'The Whigs and the Idea of Electoral Deference: Some Further Thoughts on the Great Reform Act', *Durham University Journal* 67 (1974), pp. 79–91. Idem, 'Deference and Aristocracy in the Time of the Great Reform Act', *American Historical Review* 81 (1976), pp. 532–9.

[7] P. Anderson, 'The Figures of Descent', in his *English Questions*, London, 1992, p. 145. See further W. L. Burn, *The Age of Equipoise: A Study of the Mid-Victorian Generation*, New York, 1965, p. 8. W. L. Arnstein, 'The Survival of the Victorian Aristocracy', in F. C. Jaher (ed.), *The Rich, the Well Born, and the Powerful: Elites and Upper Classes*

Other historians have dissented from the continuity argument, stressing the ways in which 1832 was nevertheless a turning point. Thus John Phillips has argued persuasively that the Reform Act did have important political consequences. Only that these turned out to be not in terms of transferral of power from one group to another, but rather – much like the argument here – in changes produced by the intense reform agitation on the terms of the post-1832 public national debate, rendering it more politicized and its participants more consistently partisan than previously. Peter Mandler has offered a subtly argued view of 1832: not only was it not a triumph of new political actors from a 'middle class', it was also anything but a triumph of a spirit of *embourgeoisement*. Instead, it was the renaissance – or perhaps the swan song – of old high aristocratic ideals of government; thus it was indeed a turning point – one which manifested itself in a resurgence of *aristocratic* power in the 1830s and 1840s.[8] But ultimately, whether historians stress continuity or change, there seems to be an overall agreement with John Cannon (or, for that matter, with Karl Marx), that the Act 'did not hand over power to the middle classes because it was not intended to'.[9]

in History, Urbana, 1973, pp. 203–57. Idem, 'The Myth of the Triumphant Victorian Middle Class', *The Historian* 37 (1975), pp. 205–21. See also the questioning of a 'middle-class' triumph – indeed of the adequacy of the category 'middle class' – in R. S. Neale's work, esp. 'Class and Class Consciousness in Early Nineteenth-Century England: Three Classes or Five?', in his *Class and Ideology in the Nineteenth Century*, London, 1972, pp. 15–40; and 'The Bourgeoisie, Historically, Has Played a Most Revolutionary Part', in his *Writing Marxist History: British Society, Economy and Culture since 1700*, Oxford, 1985, pp. 67–85.

[8] J. A. Phillips, *The Great Reform Bill in the Boroughs: English Electoral Behaviour, 1818–1841*, Oxford, 1992; see esp. pp. 6, 10–11, 298–300. P. Mandler, *Aristocratic Government in the Age of Reform: Whigs and Liberals, 1830–1852*, Oxford, 1990. See also J. Parry, *The Rise and Fall of Liberal Government in Victorian Britain*, New Haven, 1993, chapters 3–4. Curiously, the most adamant argument in recent years for 1829–32 as a radical watershed, no less than 'a dissolution of the social order', comes from J. C. D. Clark, elsewhere the arch-champion of historical continuity and stasis. Clark's categorical denial of any change in England's purported '*ancien régime*' before 1832 forces him to turn this particular moment into a full-scale revolution; only by bolstering one overdrawn argument with another can he account for the different place in which England found itself in the 1830s when compared, say, with a century earlier. See J. C. D. Clark, *English Society 1688–1832*, Cambridge, 1985, pp. 408–13 (quoted, p. 410).

[9] J. Cannon, *Parliamentary Reform 1640–1832*, Cambridge, 1973, p. 257; and see 246ff. Karl Marx wrote: 'The new arrangements were, on the whole, calculated not for increasing middle-class influence, but for the exclusion of Tory and the promotion of Whig patronage.' ('Lord John Russell', 1 August 1855, in *Karl Marx and Frederick Engels on Britain*, Moscow, 1953, p. 432.) See similarly *Westminster Review* 51, April 1849, p. 179.

The pervasive invocation of the 'middle class' during the decade of reform, therefore, did not necessarily reflect a deeper correlation with 'objective' social and political reality than previously.[10] And yet, insofar as contemporary perceptions were concerned, this particular social category was singularly suitable for the present circumstances. The protracted discussions of the nature, character and relevance of the 'middle class' throughout the debates on the Reform Bill had impressed its presence daily upon everyone's consciousness. Now that the Bill had become fact, few contemporaries doubted (at least for a short while) that they had just witnessed an event of momentous historical significance, one that could be dubbed alternately 'the magna charta of the nineteenth century' or (less favourably) a 'revolution' (and in the words of one excitable youth at Eton, 'the worst crime since the Crucifixion'); indeed, from their perspective, the legislative initiatives of the following decade did not prove them wrong.[11] And in assessing the meaning of this event and fitting it into a broader understanding of society, the 'middle class' became indispensable. It was through a 'middle-class'-based conceptualization of society that the new situation could be placed within an ordered and logical framework, one which moreover had roots in a recognizable reconstruction of the recent past. This realization was facilitated by the fact that now, for the first time, the franchise qualifications as established by law

---

[10] Doubts about the 'objective' existence and the relevance of a 'middle class' in 1832 have already been raised by N. McCord, 'Some Difficulties of Parliamentary Reform', *Historical Journal* 10 (1967), pp. 376–90. Idem, 'Some Limitations of the Age of Reform', in H. Hearder and H. R. Loyn (eds.), *British Government and Administration: Studies Presented to S. B. Chrimes*, Cardiff, 1974, esp. p. 192. See also D. J. Rowe, 'Class and Political Radicalism in London, 1831–2', *Historical Journal* 13 (1970), pp. 31–47. A. Tyrrell, 'Class Consciousness in Early Victorian Britain: Samuel Smiles, Leeds Politics, and the Self-Help Creed', *Journal of British Studies* 9:2 (1970), pp. 102–25.

[11] Bridges, *An Address to the Electors of England*, p. 10. Duke of Wellington to Croker, 6 March 1833; in L. J. Jennings (ed.), *The Croker Papers: The Correspondence and Diaries of the Late Right Honourable John Wilson Croker* ... New York, 1884, vol. II, p. 9. R. Ollard, *An English Education: A Perspective of Eton*, London, 1982, p. 56. For a radical perspective, see J. A. Roebuck, *The Crisis! What Ought the Ministers to Do?* (in *Pamphlets for the People*, vol. 1 [no. 12], p. 2), who referred to the Reform Bill as 'A REVOLUTION – a bloodless, peaceable one, it is true, but still a Revolution'. The Bill was likewise the biggest revolution in British history for Wentworth Holworthy, *The Book of Reform ... Humbly Submitted to the Consideration of Honest Men of All Parties*, London, 1833. And see Halévy, *A History of the English People in the Nineteenth Century III*, p. 64, for the distance between contemporary evaluations of 1832 and those of some latter-day historians.

also provided a clear-cut (albeit arbitrary) definition of who belonged to this elusive category, and – more importantly – who did not.

Consequently, as the following pages demonstrate, the years immediately following the Reform Act saw a staggering and concentrated barrage of writings about society and politics that made the category of 'middle class' – together with the particular historical storyline explaining its origins and ascent – crucially central to organizing social and political experience. Not only was the existence and relevance of a 'middle class' now assumed, reasserted, proclaimed daily; and not only was the 'middle class' appealed to repeatedly as a major national constituency; it was also presented as a most important factor in understanding almost everything else, often overriding previous perceptions that had lacked this quasi-magical component. The explanatory power assumed by the category of 'middle class' was unprecedented, and perhaps never matched again; the overall effect was a radically new departure. The triumph of the 'middle class', then, was achieved less in the Reform Act itself than in its immediate aftermath; and it had to do less with people's choices of parliamentary representatives than with people's choices of representations of society within which they framed their mental vision of the world.

THE POLITICAL TRIUMPH OF THE 'MIDDLE CLASS'

The middling class we politically reverence. (Opening Address in first issue of *The Public Communicator*, 14 January 1832)

The middle class, therefore, may be now considered as part of society. (Opening Address in first issue of *The Truth*, 10 February 1833)[12]

In 1835, the world of political hacks was stirred by a pamphlet titled *Thoughts upon the Aristocracy*, which, with thirteen editions by the end of the year, propelled its author, one Isaac Tomkins, from complete anonymity to the head of the political bestseller list. Tomkins challenged the privileged status of the aristocracy and its influence, as felt by 'we of the middle classes'. He

---

[12] *The Public Communicator, and General Advertiser* 1, 14 January 1832, p. [1]. *The Truth, A Weekly Radical Christian, and Family Newspaper* 1:1, 10 February 1833, p. [1]. 'Society' here was an evaluative as well as descriptive category (meaning respectable society, to which 'the mob' could not belong).

juxtaposed his 'sorrowful observation' on the aristocracy with estimation for that class with whom he explicitly identified himself:

The middle, not the upper class, are the part of the nation which is entitled to command respect, and enabled to win esteem or challenge admiration. They read, they reflect, they reason, they think for themselves ... They are the nation – the people – in every rational or correct sense of the word.

Tomkins's matter-of-factual 'middle-class idiom' readily turned into a concrete political agenda, its 'inevitable consequences':

By them, through them, for them, the fabric of the government is reared, continued, designed. How long are they likely to suffer a few persons of overgrown wealth, laughable folly, and considerable profligacy, to usurp, and exclusively to hold, all consideration, all individual importance?

Small wonder that a sympathetic *Edinburgh* reviewer assumed that 'the middle classes, in whose favour [this pamphlet] is very warmly, and indeed most feelingly, conceived, will no doubt exceedingly enjoy it'.[13]

Tomkins's anti-aristocratic invective was soon seconded by another pamphleteer, likewise unfamiliar to the public, by the name of Peter Jenkins. Jenkins complimented Tomkins on his 'able and just remarks', and only wished he had gone further in his denunciation of 'the present Aristocratical Government' in the name of 'we and our fellow-citizens of the middle classes'. Yet another follow-up, by one Matthew Hicks, vied with Jenkins in praise for Tomkins: 'I am much beholden to you,' he began his public letter, 'as many of my rank in life are, for your able exposure of our oppressors the Aristocracy, being a shopkeeper, and therefore of the *middle classes*.' Hicks too agreed that the case could be stated in even stronger terms, since 'the taxes are more of them, by far, paid by us, the middle classes, than by all the rest of the country together'; and consequently, 'we of the

---

[13] Isaac Tomkins, *Thoughts upon the Aristocracy of England*, 5th edn, London, 1835, pp. 12, 17–18 (according to the publisher's note, written in November 1834). *Edinburgh Review* 61, April 1835, p. 64.

middle-class are the losers by the expensive Aristocracy, and only we'.[14]

Isaac Tomkins, Peter Jenkins and Matthew Hicks were all pseudonyms. At least for the first two, whose writings circulated more extensively, contemporaries were quick to discover their real authors. It turned out that both Tomkins and Jenkins stood in fact for one and the same person: Henry Brougham, by now Lord Brougham, Baron Brougham and Vaux.[15] Furthermore, textual similarities may indicate that Hicks was yet another creation of Brougham's.[16] Be that as it may, Brougham, whose falling out with the leading Whigs had left him bitterly disillusioned and out of office since late 1834, wished to expose in his pseudonymous pamphlets what he saw as an unfortunate persistence of 'Aristocratic Government'. But again, at the same time that he was casting doubt on the post-1832 accession to power of the 'middle class' (a doubt that more contemporaries were coming to share now that the real consequences of 1832 could be better assessed), Brougham's pamphlets themselves signalled in a striking way the post-1832 triumph of the 'middle class' as a political category. They were significant not only in placing in front of the public such forceful self-identifications with the 'middle class'. Even more telling was the fact that the erstwhile Lord Chancellor, Baron Brougham and Vaux, a

[14] Peter Jenkins, *A Letter to Isaac Tomkins, Gent. Author of Thoughts upon the Aristocracy. (11th ed., with a Postscript) and a Letter to John Richards, Esq. MP*, London, 1835, pp. [3]–4; this pamphlet went through four editions. Matthew Hicks, *A Letter to Isaac Tomkins, Gent., Author of the 'Thoughts upon the Aristocracy'*, London, 1835, pp. [3], 6 (written on 1 May 1835). These exchanges continued in Isaac Tomkins, *'We Can't Afford It!' Being Thoughts upon the Aristocracy of England. Part the Second*, 3rd edn, London, 1835; and Timothy Winterbottom, *A Letter to Isaac Tomkins and Peter Jenkins on Primogeniture*, 2nd edn, London, 1835.

[15] Historians have not paid much attention to this episode and its implications for Brougham's public image, now that he was out of office. One brief exception is R. Reynolds (ed.), *British Pamphleteers Volume Two: From the French Revolution to the Nineteen-Thirties*, London, 1951, in which the editor suggests that given the veil of anonymity, these pamphlets were more likely to represent Brougham's sincere opinions than his carefully weighed public statements (p. 115).

[16] Beyond the fact that Brougham's identity as Tomkins and Jenkins makes Hicks, another pseudonymous participant in the same exchange, a likely candidate as well, the pamphlets by Jenkins and Hicks manifest obvious similarities in the general structure of their argument (agreeing with Tomkins and strengthening his case), in their similarly worded compliments to his able production in their opening statements, and in their statements in the name of 'we of the middle classes'.

well-known upper-class public figure, now chose to hide his true identity behind this array of invented 'middle-class' personalities. After all, as the *Edinburgh Review* put it, what commanded its 'entire sympathy' with Tomkins was 'his affectionate and even zealous attachment to his *"order"* [the 'middle class'] – the hope, the stay, the comfort, and the true ornament of their country'. (The reader might not be surprised to learn, however – could it be otherwise? – that the anonymous Edinburgh reviewer who was so gratified with Tomkins's 'middle-class' identity was once again none other than Lord Brougham himself . . .) Brougham had already famously sung the praises of the 'middle class' on numerous occasions, but always from the outside. Now, while his panegyrics remained pretty much the same, he evidently found it more attractive to declare the 'middle-class' agenda as an anonymous figure from the inside. Brougham's post-1832 'middle class' was a powerful and relevant political constituency, capable of adopting a particular political programme; it was not wishful thinking, but a power already in existence, belonging to which could increase one's political efficacy.

For one final touch to this episode, let us turn to a hostile reaction to these pamphlets, addressed openly to Lord Brougham as their exposed author. Brougham's critic – this time a real one – was the Whig MP John Richards, on whom the irony of Brougham's masquerade was not lost. Richards was at pains to show how Brougham's assumption of 'middle-class' identity in fact undermined his own cause by revealing his condescending pretensions: 'It is a tolerable specimen of your Lordship's modesty and consistency', Richards wrote sarcastically, 'to suppose that one of the middle class, that class which you, questionless for the best purpose, so much extol, cannot write as well as *Peter Jenkins*.' In other words, if the 'middle class' were as able as 'Tomkins' and 'Jenkins' had made it out to be, why did it need Brougham to intercede on its behalf? And as for the substance of Brougham's claim 'that persons of the middle class of life labour under great disadvantages', Richards contended that in fact 'the middle class of persons, in this country, are most felicitously circumstanced'. So Brougham not only insulted the 'middle class' in his patronizing charades. By his language, which was designed 'to excite the anger and ill-will of one class of society against another', he was also operating in effect 'to destroy the middle class' – a calamity that Richards, it became clear, wished to prevent.[17] Thus concluded another round in a fairly intricate rhetorical contest over the sympathies and the support of what was coming to be perceived as the great political audience in the nation, the 'middle class'.

Politics during these years (and surely also other domains, as we shall see later) reverberated ceaselessly with direct appeals to the 'middle class', with self-conscious proclamations of 'middle-class' identity, and with matter-of-factual assertions of its political existence and relevance. Consider the opening addresses of two ephemeral periodicals, the *Public Communicator* and *The Truth*, quoted as epigraphs to the present section. Founded respectively in 1832 and 1833, both periodicals commenced their first issues with addresses to the readers that justified their enterprise in terms of the new and powerful political advent of the 'middle class', whose needs required to be catered for.[18] And when the more durable *Penny Magazine* was founded in 1832 with a much more popular audience in mind, its editors too set their goals in juxtaposition to the 'middle class' as a clear point of reference. In the *Examiner* one finds towards the end of the Reform Bill debate a marked surge in the incorporation of the 'middle class' as key agents whose public actions and opinions deserved particular notice.[19]

[17] John Richards, *A Letter to Lord Brougham, in Reply to Isaac Tomkins, Gent. and Mr Peter Jenkins . . .*, 2nd edn, London, 1835, pp. 7–8, 21–3, and passim. See also the savagely sarcastic comments on these 'tricks of authorship', especially because of the social station of their purported author, in *A Word of Wisdom for the Witty: Addressed to Isaac Tomkins, Gent.*, London, 1835 (quoted, p. 8). Brougham's authorship had already been suggested in the *Quarterly Review* 53, April 1835, pp. 540–8.

[18] 'The heavy pressure of taxation is alone *felt* by them – they are the vital part of our constitution' (*The Public Communicator* 1, 14 January 1832, p. [1]); 'the middle class . . . are ten times more important than the upper . . . and extremely powerful in the direct mastery which they possess over all the labouring classes' (*The Truth* 1, 10 February 1833, p. [1]). We may also recall the 1831 discovery by the *Manchester Guardian* that its audience was in fact none other than this ascending 'middle class': see p. 265.

[19] *The Penny Magazine of the Society for the Diffusion of Useful Knowledge* 1:1, 31 March 1832, p. [1]: 'What the stage-coach has become to the middle classes, we hope our Penny Magazine will be to *all* classes – an universal convenience and enjoyment.' For the *Examiner*, examples of this surge from October 1831 onwards include 1237, 16 October 1831, pp. 666–8 (four different instances); 1239, 30 October 1831, p. 690; 1240, 6 November 1831, p. 705; 1244, 4 December 1831, p. 769; 1249, 8 January 1832, p. 17; and note the characterization of the *Kent Herald* in 1236, 9 October 1831, p. 652, as well as the *Brighton Guardian* as quoted in 1242, 20 November 1831, p. 738. Compare also the memoirs of Robert Chambers on the beginnings of the *Chambers's Edinburgh*

Or listen to 'ONE OF THE MIDDLING CLASSES', writing in 1835 in a vein reminiscent of Brougham's pamphlets of the same year:

I am, fellow countrymen, one of the Middling Classes, one of your-selves – as distinct from that class called the 'upper' or aristocracy; and it is because I have been made to feel the evils under which we labour, in common with millions of our country, that I have taken up my pen to address you.

What this writer advocated was further reform in order to secure government wholly in the hands of the 'middle class', which now came to stand vicariously for millions of his (as yet unenfranchised) countrymen.[20] It was this kind of move, redefin-ing the 'middle class' with apparently radical implications, that made the liberal-turned-conservative historian William Smyth very anxious. The following year Smyth added a 'supplementary lecture' to his celebrated discourses on the French Revolution (delivered in Cambridge since 1810); in this lecture he expressed his concern about the view which 'has of late become fashionable, not only in France but in this country', seeking 'to place the power of the state . . . in the hands of the middle classes'. Smyth commented dismissively that 'something more may be, and has been, accomplished by our constitution than what can ever arise from the domination of the middle classes'. He continued: 'In politics, every thing . . . is a question of degree. Those who insist upon the government of the middle classes would probably make a very objectionable definition of the middle classes' – that is to say, a definition that would be broad enough to risk republican-ism and democracy.[21] Speaking in 1836, then, Smyth – whose

Journal, founded by himself and his brother William in February 1832: 'it was my design from the first to be the essayist of the middle class, – that in which I was born, and to which I continued to belong'. Quoted in *Memoir of Robert Chambers with Autobiographic Reminiscences of William Chambers*, New York, 1872, p. 217.

[20] *Three Letters to the People. By One of the Middling Classes*, London, [1835], pp. 3, 31, 125–7, 171. The author stressed the superiority of the 'middle class' over the higher orders in virtues, wealth and connections with the people; and note p. 60 for his opposition to the social language of 'interests'. Compare also *A Few Facts: Addressed to the Electors of the United Kingdom*, [London, 1835], whose addressees turned out to be 'the middle classes of the country', sharing a common interest distinct from that of the upper classes in opposing indirect taxation (p. 3).

[21] William Smyth, *Lectures on History: Second and Concluding Series on the French Revolution*, 3 vols., Cambridge, 1840, vol. III, pp. 340, 392–3, 396; also 307, 312. Smyth had already imparted a sense of anxiety about the 'middle class' in a lecture added in 1833. Before 1832, by contrast, the language of 'middle class' appeared only marginally in his lectures: see vol. I, 120, 136; vol. III, 30. This sudden shift in Smyth's social vocabulary has been noted in H. Ben-Israel, *English Historians on the French Revolution*, Cambridge, 1968, chapter 5.

own opinion was that 'the great bulwark and cement of all and of every thing is the aristocracy' – recognized the currently fashionable category of 'middle class' for what it was: a purposeful construction, politically defined, conditional and malleable, and forwarded to bolster a particular agenda – an agenda which he, for one, found objectionable.[22]

Unsurprisingly, some of the most notable rhetorical adaptations to a widespreading recognition of 'middle-class' power took place in the public statements of politicians. As the *Westminster Review* observed, *pace* William Smyth, 'no practical and judicious statesman' could allow himself these days to 'take his stand anywhere but on the middle class', the only ones 'who can give him a majority in Parliament'.[23] Take for example Matthew Bridges, a Midlands parliamentary candidate in 1832, whose election campaign was quick to register the changing circumstances. Bridges joined the national chorus in declaring the great Reform Bill a triumph of the 'middle class'; a reassuring triumph because 'our middling classes are moderate in their demands; religious, and sober, and sound in their principles; growing every day more and more educated and enlightened; and not enamoured of innovation'. Moreover, 'four-fifths of the property of the country are in their possession!' In short, 'the fact is written, in letters as large as life, that the middling and operative classes in this great and glorious country, are, in importance, paramount; in fact all but every thing'. Reminiscent of Royer-Collard's announcement of 1819 in France, for Bridges in 1832 the importance of the 'middle class' (with some gestures towards the lower classes) was a *fait accompli*; a fact that was supposed to make him particularly attractive to the electors, since the 'most important' of his principles was 'my complete identification with the claims, the sympathies, and general welfare' of the 'middle class'.[24] Bridges came to see the 'middle

---

[22] Smyth (*Lectures on History*, p. 394) exposed similarly the constructed and conditional nature of 'public opinion': 'though the opinion of the public is a very popular phrase, and the influence which ought to belong to it is loudly contended for, still it must be allowed that it is a phrase which, in every word of it, admits very different meanings.'

[23] *Westminster Review* 32, April 1839, p. 493.

[24] Bridges, *An Address to the Electors*, pp. [3], 12. While referring occasionally to 'middling and operative classes' together, it was obvious where Bridges placed his true emphasis; as quoted on p. 328 above, he believed that in 1832 government was transferred from an oligarchy to the 'middle class'. See also the *Examiner* 1253, 5 February 1832, p. 84, where it was deemed important to identify a political writer as personally connected with 'the middle classes of London'; and by contrast the *Edinburgh Review* 61, April

class' as his political constituency, and it was to them that his
rhetoric was directed.

From the Midlands we can turn to the northern Scottish
islands of Orkney and Shetland, where the merchant Samuel
Laing, also a contender in the elections following the Reform
Act, wished to establish his credentials 'to appear as a candidate
for the representation of my native county'. During his constant
residence there for many years, Laing explained, he had had
daily contacts with the kelp-makers and the herring-fishers, and
more generally 'with all the middle class of people in the county,
having myself originated from that class, and having many rela-
tives in that class'.[25] Kelp and the herring notwithstanding, it is
worth noting the distinct familiarity with which Laing's 'middle-
class' language strikes us by this point. After all, Laing's county
was one of the most remote corners of the kingdom. Moreover,
the political context in which he operated was that of the *Scottish*
Reform Act, which was very different from the English one,
basically turning Scotland from 'one vast, rotten borough' into
a somewhat broader but still considerably circumscribed landed
oligarchy.[26] But in spite of a distant and different social and
political context, and moreover one in which a 'middle-class'
triumph might have seemed even less likely, Laing's appeal to
the electors was remarkably in tune with those of his counterparts
south of the border. Nor was Laing unusual in this: to give one
more example, the second Earl of Rosslyn, a Scottish Tory, also
saw his political future (in 1834) in 'the returning good sense of
the middle ranks of people who have some property to save'.[27]
Likewise, during the Reform Bill debates, discussions of the

1835, p. 243, where it was deemed effective to sully a politician's reputation by noting
  that he 'proudly disdain[s] the middle ranks'.
[25] Samuel Laing, *Address to the Electors of Scotland*, Edinburgh, 1833, p. 4; signed on 11
  January 1833 in Papdale, Kirkwall, Laing's birthplace and where he had been living
  continuously as a trader since 1818. The pamphlet blamed Laing's failure (as a radical
  candidate) on Francis Jeffrey's undue interference in favour of the Whig contender.
[26] Gash, *Politics in the Age of Peel*, pp. 34–50 (quoted, p. 36). R. Mitchinson, 'Scotland
  1750–1850', in F. M. L. Thompson (ed.), *The Cambridge Social History of Britain
  1750–1950*, Cambridge, 1990, vol. 1, esp. p. 203. For the peculiarities of the Scottish
  Reform Act, see also W. Ferguson, 'The Reform Act (Scotland) of 1832: Intention
  and Effect', *Scottish History Review* 44 (1966), pp. 105–14.
[27] Lord Rosslyn to Sir J. Oswald, 30 October 1834; quoted in I. G. C. Hutchison, *A
  Political History of Scotland 1832–1924: Parties, Elections and Issues*, Edinburgh, 1986, p.
  13. Note also the Stirlingshire baronet quoted there.

merits of the 'middle class' were not noticeably less common in debates on Scottish reform than in debates on English reform.[28] So while a closer study may reveal certain variations in political language in different local settings, the Scottish evidence nevertheless seems to justify the present focus on the overarching national context of political debate.

That Lord Rosslyn was a Tory should not surprise us. The post-1832 appeals to the 'middle class' on the part of the erstwhile critics of its enfranchisement were hardly less keen than those of their opponents. It is a preposterous misrepresentation, the prominent Tory MP William Follett told his Exeter constituents, to say 'that we [the conservatives], who stand forth in defence of the Constitution of England, are the enemies of the middle classes of the kingdom and the supporters of the aristocracy'. On the contrary, he contended, 'the charge is absurd, when we look at what the Conservative party is, when we know that its great strength is in the middle classes' – a statement that was loudly cheered by his audience. Moreover, demanded Follett – himself son of a timber merchant – who were the leader of the conservative ministry (Robert Peel), and the Lord Chancellor of his ministry (Lord Lyndhurst, son of a portrait painter), but men 'sprung from the middle classes of the people'?[29]

Most important, take Peel himself. On 11 May 1835 Peel made a major statement in front of the London merchants, bankers and traders in the Merchant Taylors' Hall, a much reprinted

---

[28] Examples include Alex Dunlop, *Letter to the Freeholders of the County of Dumbarton, on Parliamentary Reform*, Edinburgh, 1830, pp. 40–1. Henry Cockburn, 'Parliamentary Representation of Scotland', *Edinburgh Review* 52, October 1830, p. 224 (quoted above, p. 306 n. 16). [John Campbell Colquhoun], *The Constitutional Principles of Parliamentary Reform. By a Freeholder and Landholder of Scotland*, Edinburgh, 1831, p. 60. Lucius Verus (pseud.), *Letter to the Right Hon. Francis Jeffrey, Lord Advocate of Scotland*, Glasgow, 1831, passim (regarding the opinions of the 'middling classes' of the West of Scotland). Consider also the memorandum on Scottish reform submitted to Lord John Russell in November 1830 by Thomas Kennedy of Dunure, warning against reform which 'fails to give satisfaction to the middle and respectable ranks of society, and drives them to a union founded on dissatisfaction, with the lower orders'. (*Letters Chiefly Connected with the Affairs of Scotland, From Henry Cockburn ... To Thomas Francis Kennedy, MP ...*, London, 1874, p. 259.)

[29] *The Speech of Sir William Follett, Delivered at Exeter, October 21st, 1835*, Beverley, 1835, p. 15; and see too the editor's introduction, p. [2], also affirming the conservative tendencies of the 'middle class'. Follett, a protégé of John Wilson Croker, was appointed Solicitor General in the short Peel administration of 1834–5. Compare also the mock dialogue in the *Examiner* 1249, 8 January 1832, p. 17, in which an alleged voice of a Tory politician asserted that 'my constituency includ[es] the middle class'.

speech which *The Times* found so 'spirit stirring' that it called
for the distribution of 100,000 copies. Peel's speech elucidated
'the appeal we [the conservative party] make to the middle
classes of the community', now admitted as the main component
of the electorate. His rhetoric was no less striking than Follett's,
and it elicited just as enthusiastic responses from his audience:

> Above all, we deny that we are separated by any fancied line of interest,
> or of pride, or of privilege, from the middling classes of this country.
> (Cheers) Why, who are we ... that any one should tell us that we
> have an interest separate, or feelings discordant from those of the
> middling classes of society? (Cheers) ... Speaking in behalf of nine-
> tenths at least of those assembled within these walls, I say we disclaim
> any separation from the middling classes of society in this country. O
> no, – we are bound to them by a thousand ramifications of direct
> personal connexion, and common interests, and common feelings. (Loud
> cheers)

Charles Greville noted that this speech 'made a great deal of
noise', since Peel publicly gave up on his High Tory friends
'very completely', and 'exhibited a determination to adapt his
opinions and conduct to the spirit of the times'.[30] The former
might have been wishful thinking; the latter was undoubtedly
true. In 1831, as we have seen, Peel had claimed 'middle-class'
identity as an individual, while attempting at the same time to
bar the 'middle class' collectively from the political realm – an
uneasy combination whose problematic nature was not lost on
contemporaries.[31] Now, by contrast, he was wooing the 'middle
class' as a collective political force, identified not primarily with
his private person, but with his public party. For Peel, too, the
'middle class' as a pivotal political constituency had unmistakably
arrived. Peel carried immense influence in interpreting and
concretizing the new social and political order for the British

---

[30] *Speech of Sir Robert Peel, Bart. Delivered at Merchant Tailors' Hall*, pp. 9–10; this speech
went through at least thirteen editions within the year. *The Greville Memoirs*, 24 May
1835, vol. III, p. 202. For the speech and its reception, see D. Read, *Peel and the
Victorians*, Oxford, 1987, p. 78. Peel's appeal to the 'middle class' in this speech was
much more explicit than in his famous Tamworth Manifesto of the previous year,
though its seeds had already been noticeable there. Also compare his 'middle-class
idiom' at another speech at Tamworth, as quoted in McCord, 'Some Difficulties of
Parliamentary Reform', p. 378.

[31] Thus Bulwer-Lytton, *England and the English*, vol. II, pp. 181–2, pointed out the
unfortunate incongruity of the fact that Peel, whose moral character 'seems to ally
him naturally to the decorous respectabilities of the great middle class to which his
connexions attach him', was nevertheless 'the defender of the oligarchical party'.

people. His acknowledgment of the advent and importance of the 'middle class', therefore, was possibly more consequential for the propagation of this particular understanding of society and politics than that of any other public figure.[32]

Shortly thereafter, conservative appeals to the 'middle class' became part of the battle against Chartism, the best-organized and most ominous working-class movement of the nineteenth century. Reminiscent of anti-radical 'middle-class' language in the late 1810s, these appeals of the late 1830s were more common and more insistent. Examples included Montague Gore's self-explanatory *A Letter to the Middle Classes on the Present Disturbed State of the Country, Especially with Reference to the Chartist Meetings* (1839), or *An Earnest Appeal to the Aristocracy, Middle, and Operative Classes. By a Conservative* (1840). The latter was not deterred by its expressed regret for the Reform Act from appealing ardently to 'the middle class who are in every country, but more particularly in this commercial one, the sinews of the state, the real and ostensible source of national strength'; a 'most worthy, most intelligent, and most important body' that surely would not be deluded by a 'specious deception'. With nothing to gain and everything to lose by a revolution, argued this writer, it was 'upon their good sense and moral courage [that] the salvation of the empire rests'.[33] Similar conviction characterized Archibald Alison's address to the 'middle class' from the pages of *Blackwood's Edinburgh Magazine*, a notorious bastion of resistance to reform. 'The middle classes of England', Alison assured his readers not unanxiously, 'will neither fly their country, nor desert their property, at the waving of the Chartist torch.'[34]

---

[32] As Greville put it in retrospect upon Peel's death, Peel offended 'the old anti-liberal spirit' of his party colleagues, since it was 'the middle classes (those formidable masses, occupying the vast space between aristocracy and democracy) with whom Peel was evidently anxious to ingratiate himself and whose support he considered his best alliance': *The Greville Memoirs*, 6 July 1850, vol. VI, p. 241; also 16 December 1845, vol. V, p. 262. On Peel's appeal to the 'middle class' in the 1830s and 1840s see Read, *Peel and the Victorians*, pp. 15–16. Mandler, *Aristocratic Government in the Age of Reform*, p. 118.

[33] *An Earnest Appeal to the Aristocracy, Middle, and Operative Classes. By a Conservative*, London, 1840, pp. 12–13.

[34] Alison was rallying emphatic 'middle-class idiom' against the Chartist peril: 'It is in their industry and frugality that the foundation is laid for almost all the wealth and prosperity of society. It is in their multitude and opulence that Great Britain finds both the sources of its greatness, and its proud pre-eminence over every other country of the globe.' *Blackwood's Edinburgh Magazine* 46, September 1839, pp. 289ff. (quoted, pp. 296, 301). Compare also ibid., October 1839, pp. 500–1, where Alison was actually

So much for the conservative appropriation of a 'middle-class' constituency. Among working-class radicals, if anything, the need for a notion of 'middle class' after 1832 was even more pressing. Ever since the 1790s (and, for that matter, throughout the eighteenth century) radicals were well served by dual social frameworks that adequately encompassed their perceptions of social and political reality. Whether it was a schema of patricians and plebeians, rich and poor, employers and employed, or productive and unproductive labour, radical conceptualizations of society always boiled down – with compelling logic – to a Manichean duality. The exceptions that we have encountered so far, when radicals spoke of a 'middle class', were either in the context of appeals to this purported 'middle class' to join their ranks in the true (dual) struggle between oppressors and oppressed, or of angry protestations against assertions of 'middle-class' identity as if it had no share in this dual structure of oppression.

The Reform Act changed all that. In these new political circumstances, something else besides upper and lower orders was required to make sense of the radicals' own recent experience: how could it be that the constitution was finally altered, reform was enacted and yet the working classes came out empty handed? It was the need to provide this sense of disillusionment and betrayal with tangible logic and social location that suddenly made the category of 'middle class' indispensable: the members of the 'middle class' were those who had gained from the Reform Act and who had betrayed the working classes. Furthermore, over the next few years their treachery was recurrently reconfirmed, in what seemed to radical eyes as manifestly oppressive class-based legislation: the new Poor Law of 1834; the Municipal Reform Act of 1835 (which, in the words of the future Chartist Thomas Cooper, made possible 'the relentless and grinding tyrannies of the recreant middle classes'[35]); the Newspaper Tax (imposed in 1830, and reduced in 1836 after a vigorous campaign for its repeal), which unambiguously divided the respectable press from

stressing the commitment of the *Blackwood's* to 'middle-class idiom', in contrast with the attitude of the 'Liberal journals'.

[35] Cooper, writing in 1845, explained further that the 'municipal honours have drawn [the middle classes] off from their hot-blooded radicalism, and converted [them] into cold, unfeeling wielders of magisterial or other local power'. Quoted in D. Thompson (ed.), *The Early Chartists*, Columbia, 1971, p. 8.

the unstamped popular press; the changes in the composition of the magistracy and the introduction of rural police (1839). As one writer proclaimed reproachfully in the early 1840s, ever since the Reform Act 'the middle-class constituency has done any thing but prove its peculiar and exclusive fitness for political power', or its vaunted 'intelligence' or 'incorruptibility'.[36] Society, radicals suddenly discovered, consisted not only of the good and the bad, but rather of the good, the bad and the ugly.

The transformation of the social vision underlying radical rhetoric was nowhere more striking than in the pages of Henry Hetherington's unstamped *Poor Man's Guardian*. Established in early July 1831 and edited predominantly by Bronterre O'Brien, this widely circulated newspaper has been rated by E. P. Thompson as 'undoubtedly the finest working-class weekly which had (until that time) been published in Britain'.[37] In its first few months the *Poor Man's Guardian* did not assign much importance to the concept of 'middle class'; and when it referred to the beneficiaries of the imminent Reform Bill, the £10 householders, the term it used most often was not 'middle class' but 'the *middle men*'. This clever allusion – influenced by Owenite accounts of exchange – condemned them for their non-productive and exploitative role, while evoking not an image of a novel social presence but instead a traditionally obnoxious term whose resonance in popular political language went back a long way.[38] But from the autumn of 1832 onwards the *Poor Man's Guardian*'s social vocabulary changed sharply: it now became difficult to find two

---

[36] *Reconciliation between the Middle and Labouring Classes*, pp. 18–20, 25, and passim. Aside from the Newspaper Tax, this was the list of class legislation that Feargus O'Connor attacked in 1842: quoted in D. Thompson, *The Chartists: Popular Politics in the Industrial Revolution*, New York, 1984, p. 256.

[37] E. P. Thompson, *The Making of the English Working Class*, London, 1963, p. 812. See also J. H. Wiener, *The War of the Unstamped: The Movement to Repeal the British Newspaper Tax, 1830–1836*, Ithaca, 1969, esp. pp. 143–6. P. Hollis, *The Pauper Press: A Study in Working Class Radicalism of the 1830s*, Oxford, 1970, pp. 116–21, 293, and passim.

[38] For some examples, see the *Poor Man's Guardian* 4 (30 July 1831), rep. edn, New York, 1968, vol. 1, pp. 25–6; 6 (13 August 1831), p. 43; 12 (24 September 1831), p. 89; and 23 (26 November 1831), pp. 178–9, where it quoted William Carpenter's attempt to equate the interests of the 'middle classes' and 'the working people' (see above, p. 316), and then rephrased Carpenter's language, substituting 'shopkeepers, or middle men' for Carpenter's 'middle classes'. Carpenter in his turn criticized the *Poor Man's Guardian* precisely for its 'invidious' use of 'middle class' and 'middle men' as 'convertible terms': William Carpenter, *An Address to the Working Classes, on the Reform Bill*, London, 1831, pp. 14–15.

consecutive issues without reference to the 'middle class'. This trend began with the *Poor Man's Guardian* explaining to its readers what had *really* happened in 'the middle-class Bill of Reform':

> The Bill was never intended to do you one particle of good. The object of its promoters was not to change that '*glorious constitution,*' which has entailed upon you so such misery, but to make it immortal. They projected the Bill, not with a view to subvert, or even re-model our aristocratic institutions, but to consolidate them by a reinforcement of sub-aristocracy from the middle classes.[39]

This sobered assessment, one may add, was of course precisely what so many supporters of the Bill had been saying about it all along. Propelled by this realization, the *Poor Man's Guardian* held the 'middle class' from this point on to be the perennial villains of society, the progenitors of all evil, the omnipresent arch-enemies of the working classes whose true face had finally been unmasked.

The periodical's repeated condemnations of the 'middle class' were remarkable feats of vituperation. For the most part they came from the relentless pen of Bronterre O'Brien, who in the early 1840s reflected back on the 'withering denunciations of the middle classes which [had] formerly characterized our writing'.[40] The influence of the 'middle classes', O'Brien insisted, was inevitably conducive to despotism: 'taken as a body they are the basest of society. Occupying an intermediate position between the workman and the aristocrat – employing the one and being employed by the other, they insensibly contract the vices of both tyrant and slave.' His resounding conclusion – diametrically opposed to the claims of the advocates of the 'middle class' – was that 'the middle classes are the destroyers of liberty and

---

[39] *Poor Man's Guardian* 72, 27 October 1832, vol. I, p. 577. The phrase 'middle-class Bill of Reform' was introduced (twice) in the previous issue (71, 20 October 1832, p. 570); it is approximately from this issue onwards that we can date the flood of 'middle-class' language in the *Poor Man's Guardian*. For other such characterizations of the Reform Bill see 115, 17 August 1833, vol. II, p. 261 ('By that Bill the Government of the country is essentially lodged in the hands of the middle classes'); and 228, 17 October 1835, vol. III, p. 706.

[40] In the *British Statesman*, 9 July 1842; quoted in P. Hollis (ed.), *Class and Conflict in Nineteenth-Century England 1815–1850*, London, 1973, p. 284. Dorothy Thompson (*The Chartists*, p. 269) has appropriately dubbed O'Brien 'the scourge of the middle classes in the early thirties'.

happiness in all countries'.[41] Subsequently, frequent reiterations resulted in ever stronger formulations:

the middle classes are the real tyrants of society. All that is mean, and grovelling, and selfish, and sordid, and rapacious, and harsh, and cold, and cruel, and usurious, belongs to this huxtering race ... To screw all they can out of poverty and weakness, and to seduce all they can out of powerful vice, is the grand business of their lives. Hence it is that they surpass the aristocracy in arrogance towards the poor, and the poor themselves, in obsequiousness towards the aristocracy. Oh! they are a dirty, mercenary race.[42]

Various components of the 'middle-class' rhetoric were enlisted and subverted in support of this onslaught from below. Thus, the key role of 'intelligence' in the 'middle-class idiom' should be kept in mind in reading the *Poor Man's Guardian*'s assertion that the 'working classes of the present day are far more intelligent than the middle classes of forty years ago – indeed we might say than the middle classes of the present day'. Similarly, the attempts to equate the 'middle class' with 'public opinion' provoked the periodical to protest that 'the middle class, which is decidedly the basest portion of society, has usurped almost the entire force of what is called *public opinion*'.[43] And with regard to the perennial concern of the 'middle class' to 'mov[e] heaven and earth to get rid of the assessed taxes', the *Poor Man's Guardian* commented acidly:

[41] Leading article, titled 'The March of Despotism: No Confidence to be Placed in the Middle Classes, as a Body ...': *Poor Man's Guardian* 94, 23 March 1833, vol. II, pp. 89–90. Compare the leading article in 161, 5 July 1834, vol. III, pp. 169–71: 'Progress of Despotism in America: The Middle Classes Shown to Be the Real Authors of Slavery in All Nations', which noted that 'it is curious to observe how the middle classes are enslaving every quarter of the world' (see below, p. 373); and 201, 11 April 1835, p. 491. And see G. Stedman Jones, 'Rethinking Chartism', in his *Languages of Class*, Cambridge, 1983, pp. 143–8; it is interesting to place Stedman Jones's discussion of the attitude of the *Poor Man's Guardian* towards the 'middle class' in the broader context of the uses of social vocabulary in the 1830s, a context in which this sudden shift to strong 'middle-class' language can be more fully understood.

[42] *Poor Man's Guardian* 115, 17 August 1833, vol. II, p. 262; the unusual use of 'race' here might have been a covert antisemitic slur (a suggestion I owe to Don Herzog). See similarly 126, 2 November 1833, p. 350; 144, 8 March 1834, vol. III, pp. 33–4; 156, 31 May 1834, pp. 131–2.

[43] Ibid., 101, 11 May 1833, vol. II, p. 145; 126, 2 November 1833, p. 350; and see 31, 14 January 1832, vol. I, p. 243, where intelligence was redefined as the genius of the producing classes.

since their accession to the franchises conferred by the Reform Bill, the middle classes have thought *only of themselves* ... the spirit in which they desire to exercise the franchise is so *exclusively selfish* as the aristocratic spirit which gave them a monopoly of it was arbitrary and unjust.[44]

The very grievance which had associated the 'middle-class idiom' of the 1790s most strongly with oppositional politics was now put forward as additional proof of 'middle-class' selfishness and complicity.

The prominence of the language of 'middle class' in the *Poor Man's Guardian* was tellingly illustrated in its paraphrasing of the pro-landed anti-reform writer James Bernard. Bernard published a book in which the category of 'middle-class' had not played any role. But in the hands of the *Poor Man's Guardian* Bernard's argument was recast into clear 'middle-class' language, as if his book had been a focused exposition of 'the demerits of a middle class'.[45] Previously, then, it had been the proponents of the 'middle class' who were inclined to recast the arguments of their rivals into 'middle-class' language. Now, the same alteration of social language was practiced no less effectively by the self-declared nemesis of that 'middle class'.

To be sure, the compelling dual framework characteristic of radical rhetoric did not simply disappear from the pages of the *Poor Man's Guardian*, as is apparent in the imputation of 'aristocratic spirit' to the 'middle class' in the passage above. Often, the newly acquired emphasis on the 'middle class' with its distinct and singular sins was coupled with attempts to superimpose it onto a basic dual social vision, attempts that resulted in obvious tensions. 'The history of mankind shows', the *Poor Man's Guardian* asserted on one occasion, 'that from the beginning of the world,

[44] Ibid., 96, 6 April 1833, vol. II, pp. 105–7; and see 88, 9 February 1833, p. 45 (letter from Henry Hunt); 100, 4 May 1833, p. 141 (letter from Vindex, titled 'The Middle Classes and the Assessed Taxes'). Compare also Feargus O'Connor in the *Northern Star* 2:82, 8 June 1839, p. 3.

[45] *Poor Man's Guardian* 168, 23 August 1834, vol. III, p. 226; the book under discussion was James E. Bernard, *Theory of the Constitution ... with an Enquiry how Far the Late Reform of Parliament Is, or Is not, Consistent with the Principles of the Constitution ...*, London, 1834. On the curious affinity between the social views of Bernard and the radicals see G. Claeys, 'A Utopian Tory Revolutionary at Cambridge: The Political Ideas and Schemes of James Bernard, 1834–1839', *Historical Journal* 25 (1982), pp. 583–603.

the rich of all countries have been in a permanent state of conspiracy to keep down the poor of all countries.' This stark duality, it went even further, could not be concealed by the niceties of social language: 'No matter by what names they may disguise their operations, the rich are everlastingly plundering, debasing, and brutalizing the poor.'[46] And yet, even while making this statement, the next page of the same article also reiterated the periodical's belief that 'of all the despotisms God ever permitted to scourge the world, the despotism of a middle class government is the worst'.[47] Ultimately, these different layers of radical social rhetoric were not easily reconciled; as Hetherington himself once discovered, when his attempt to marry the Owenite vision of productive and unproductive labour (with its reprehensible 'middlemen') with the post-1832 tripartite social scheme forced him to characterize all the 'middle class' – including, awkwardly, master-manufacturers – as 'dealers'.[48]

The hybridization of these two different conceptualizations of society in radical rhetoric at this juncture was visually exhibited in *A Map of Society Island*, a popular print published by Hetherington in 1831 (see figure 15). On the one hand, the pyramid-shaped map of society was most conspicuously divided into *two* by a

---

[46] *Poor Man's Guardian* 99, 27 April 1833, vol. II, p. 129. Gregory Claeys (in his *Citizens and Saints: Politics and Anti-Politics in Early British Socialism*, Cambridge, 1989, pp. 193–4) has tried to play down O'Brien's emphasis on the power of the new 'middle class', in order to safeguard the coherence of O'Brien's arguments – thus losing sight perhaps of the tension that cannot be explained away between his newly found 'middle-class' language and his Owenite distinction between productive and unproductive labour. For another case of such tensions see Iorwerth Prothero's discussion of William Benbow's social language in his 'William Benbow and the Concept of the "General Strike"', *Past and Present* 63 (1974), pp. 142–5.

[47] *Poor Man's Guardian* 99, 27 April 1833, vol. II, p. 130; and compare 156, 31 May 1834, vol. III, p. 132. Given these tensions, it is not surprising that the continual resort to the language of 'middle class', as before, did not necessarily imply a recognized and well-familiarized social referent. An uneasiness continued to prevail in the actual meaning of the term, used alternatively in reference to merchants, shopkeepers, £10 householders, or industrial employers; and often simply to denote a political regime rather than any specific social group. The uneasiness was once again betrayed in the frequent clause appended to the category of 'middle class', 'as they are called': see 49, 19 May 1832, vol. I, p. 393; 178, 1 November 1834, vol. III, p. 307; 201, 11 April 1835, p. 491.

[48] Quoted in G. Claeys, *Machinery, Money and the Millennium: From Moral Economy to Socialism, 1815–1860*, Princeton, 1987, pp. 137–8; and see there further examples of the novel introduction of 'middle-class' language into post-1832 Owenite accounts of exchange, including by Owen himself.

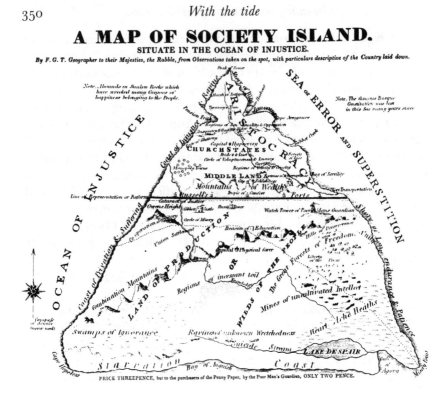

Figure 15. 'A Map of Society Island', 1831. *Source*: private collection.

thick black line that bounded the vast 'WILDS OF THE PEOPLE', alias the 'LAND OF PRODUCTION'; an obvious rendering into visual form of the older radical distinction between people and aristocracy together with the more recent distinction of radical political economists between productive and unproductive labour. On the other hand, the line dividing society in the middle turned out to be the recently demarcated 'Line of Representation or Reform', protected by 'Russell's Forts'; which made the 'MIDDLE LAND' at the centre of the image immediately recognizable as the 'middle-class' constituency about to be defined by the Reform Act. The accompanying text elaborated the superimposition of the dual on the tripartite:

The inhabitants [of 'MIDDLE LAND'] are crafty and mean, exceedingly cowardly, and very selfish ... lately they have entered into a lasting

treaty [with 'the regions above them'], called the *Reform Peace*, whereby
they mutually agree to refrain from attacking each other, and to combine
their efforts in totally subduing the unfortunate people of the Land of
Production.[49]

Again, the vituperation notwithstanding, this somewhat confused
conflation of different kinds of categorizations actually resulted
in a very familiar story.

Indeed, the most important point to make regarding the radical
uses of 'middle-class' language after the Reform Bill is the considerable common ground which they came to share with their
political rivals. At the very same time that the *Poor Man's Guardian*
and other like-minded voices were venting their rage against
the 'middle class', they were reconfirming precisely the same
understanding of post-1832 society and politics as that of the
'middle class's' staunchest proponents.[50] When 'Helot', for
example, publicly denounced the *Poor Man's Guardian*'s hostility
to the 'middle class', while the periodical tried in response to
'den[y] being the enemy of the middle classes *as such*', this was
an exchange framed within a vision of society shared by both
interlocutors (as well as their readers).[51] The following pages

[49] This print (inaccurately titled 'The Chart of Society') provoked a lengthy angry letter
to the editor of *The Globe and Traveller* (8924, 31 May 1831) by X. L., which was later
reprinted in X. L., *Letters on Parliamentary Reform, Dedicated to the Bishop of London*,
London, 1831, pp. 78–82. I am grateful to Gregory Claeys for his help in pursuing
and reproducing this print.

[50] Other periodicals in which Hetherington and/or O'Brien were involved, where similar
statements could be found, included the *'Destructive' and Poor Man's Conservative* (1833–
4) and *Hetherington's Twopenny Dispatch* (1834–6); and in the early 1840s, the *Northern
Star* and *McDouall's Chartist and Republican Journal*. See quotes and discussion in Thomp-
son, *The Making of the English Working Class*, pp. 821–3; H. Weisser, *British Working-Class
Movements and Europe 1815–1848*, Manchester, 1975, pp. 40–1, 64 (n. 107), 80–2; and J.
Epstein, *The Lion of Freedom: Feargus O'Connor and the Chartist Movement, 1832–1842*,
London, 1982, p. 275. Such formulations were to become staple rhetoric for the
Chartists (whose early members included both Hetherington and O'Brien). For an
early detailed example, see the disagreement between Daniel O'Connell and Feargus
O'Connor in 1839 as summarized by the latter in the *Northern Star* 2:82, 8 June 1839,
p. 3. For more vilifications of the 'middle class', encouraged by attempts to rejoin the
Chartists with the 'middle class' (such as the overtures of the Leeds Parliamentary
Reform Association, or Joseph Sturge's Complete Suffrage Union), see numerous quotes
in Epstein, *The Lion of Freedom*, chapter 7; Hollis, *Class and Conflict*, pp. 268–84; as
well as John Campbell, *An Examination of the Corn and Provision Laws, from Their First
Enactment to the Present Period*, Manchester, n.d. [1841/2?], rep. in *Chartist and Anti-Chartist
Pamphlets*, New York, 1986, p. 71 and passim.

[51] *'Helot's' Defence of Himself, O'Connell, & Catholic Emancipation: With a Word for Hume,
Cobbett, 'the Shopocracy,' and Middle Classes, against the Attacks of the Editor of 'The Poor
Man's Guardian'* . . ., London, 1834. 'Helot' replied to the *Poor Man's Guardian*'s denial:
'If continually terming them "the base middle classes," "the Thieves, the Plunderers

show how the *Poor Man's Guardian* and other radical voices were
likewise converging with Whigs and Tories in rewriting the history and politics of civilized societies in the same terms. Thus,
the contestation which had begun in the 1790s was now brought
to a close, at least for the time being: in the 1830s, just as in
the 1780s, conservatives, moderate reformers and radicals all
concurred again on a basic social framework, within which they
were offering conflicting evaluations of its constituents.

REWRITING HISTORY AND SOCIETY: THE MAKING OF THE 'MIDDLE-CLASS' NARRATIVE

We must leave to history to unfold the gradual rise of the trading and
manufacturing classes ... We need only ask the reader to form a
conception of the vastness of all that is implied in the words, growth
of a middle class; and then bid him reflect on the immense increase
of the numbers and property of that class throughout Great Britain,
France, Germany, and other countries, in every successive generation.
(John Stuart Mill, 1836)[52]

In the most advanced countries the classes are least distinguishable.
Below those members who, in European societies, are distinguished by
birth, there is class beneath class of capitalists, though it is usual to
comprehend them all, for convenience of speech, under the name of
the middle class. Thus society in Great Britain, France, and Germany
is commonly spoken of as consisting of three classes; while the divisions
of the middle class are, in fact, very numerous. (Harriet Martineau,
1838)[53]

It would not take much effort to expand the previous section
with more and more acknowledgments of the 'middle class' as
a principal node of power in the reformed polity. But the sudden
appeal of the category of 'middle class' was not limited only to
making sense of the conjunctural constellation of political forces

and Oppressers [sic] of the poor and working classes, the Mammon-worshippers, the
Slave-drivers, never acting honestly towards the people except from motives of expedi-
ency or necessity, the ruin of all empires, the infernal pests, the sordid shopocrats,"
and so forth, be not something of more than a gentle hint of enmity, I will allow he
is their most doating friend.' 'Helot', by contrast, was advocating organized cooperation
of 'the united working and middle classes' (pp. 8–9, 16).

[52] J. S. Mill, 'Civilization', *London and Westminster Review*, April 1836; rep. in *Collected Works*, vol. XVIII, pp. 121–2.
[53] Harriet Martineau, *How to Observe: Morals and Manners*, London, 1838, p. 190.

in the 1830s. It went further, transforming people's underlying understanding of their society, of their history, of their neighbours, of their world. The consequences were more far-reaching than, and only rarely anticipated by, the previous uses of this language. The 'middle class' became a quasi-magical component factored into descriptions and explanations of so many things, outside and beyond the immediate political debate.[54] The present section demonstrates one such development, in the rewriting of the history and phenomenology of civilized societies; the next chapter presents another, in what is perhaps the most tenacious of all attributes associated with the 'middle class' – the gendered demarcation of the public and the private.

Consider the two epigraphs juxtaposed above. On the one hand, we read John Stuart Mill's discussion of 'Civilization' (denoting not simply 'improvement' but a specific historical stage contrasted with barbarism), which – like progress – was straightforwardly equated with 'the growth of the middle class'; a process that characterized, indeed defined, all modern civilized societies. 'At no period could it be said that there was literally no middle class', Mill conceded; but in previous eras 'that class was extremely feeble, both in numbers and in power'. At present, by contrast (as he put it elsewhere), 'hardly anything now depends upon individuals, but all upon classes, and among classes mainly upon the middle class. That class is now the power in society, the arbiter of fortune and success.'[55] Moreover, Mill was convinced that not only the gradual rise of the 'middle class' in Britain, France and Germany, but also the significance of this history-shaping development, should be self-evident to every reader. It was the task of historians, he explained, to make it even more so, by providing the building blocks for this narrative – a task that many of them after 1832 did in fact undertake.

On the other hand, we encounter Harriet Martineau's publication two years later of what was in effect an introductory manual for social observation, in which the 'objective' truth of

[54] Compare Patrick Brantlinger's observation about 'a veritable "sea of faith" in and of the middle class, evident throughout the literature of the 1830s'; in his *The Spirit of Reform: British Literature and Politics, 1832–1867*, Cambridge, Mass., 1977, p. 19.
[55] Mill, 'Civilization', p. 121; essay on Tocqueville's *Democracy in America*, *Edinburgh Review*, October 1840, rep. in *Collected Works*, vol. xviii, p. 194.

such statements was proclaimed – *pace* John Stuart Mill – to be far from self-evident. Martineau did not deny that in 'barbarous countries . . . and in some few strongholds of feudalism' one can find a 'decided division of society into two classes', and that in such societies 'the Idea of Liberty is deficient or absent'. However, she believed that the more advanced a society became, the more refined and dense were its social gradations. Moreover, these gradations did not collapse into one: 'the small shopkeeper is not of the same class with the landowner, or wealthy banker, or professional man; while their views of life, their political principles, and their social aspirations, are as different as those of the peer and the mechanic.'[56] The category of 'middle class', therefore, which Martineau nowadays saw 'commonly' employed 'for convenience of speech' to characterize society in Britain, France and Germany (precisely Mill's chief examples), in fact defied and distorted the actual state of these societies. Whatever merits it may have had, Martineau was convinced – prefiguring the present argument – that this category did not simply mirror the social structure of civilized nations. Few observations could have left John Stuart Mill more puzzled.

Martineau, however, as she was well aware, was swimming against the current. Like Mill, many of her contemporaries were no less confident about the natural place of 'middle class' in social description and explanation. But at the same time it also remained true that this wide-spread conviction, universally applicable as it might have seemed, bore the distinct and sudden marks of recent political events. Take for example the writing of John Wade. In the first edition of the *Black Book* in 1820, we may recall, the only use Wade had for the 'middle class' was to condemn its 'culpable neutrality' (and hope to retrieve it from this mistaken path). The second edition of the *Black Book*, written in 1830 and published the following year, repeated Wade's opinion that 'reform may be delayed for a time by the apathy of

---

[56] Martineau, *How to Observe*, pp. 190–1. Indeed, in her *Society in America* (3 vols., London, 1837) she refrained from 'middle-class' language even when it was very likely ('There is no class of hereditary rich or poor. Few are very wealthy; few are poor', vol. I, p. 29); which contrasts with other 'middle-class'-based discussions of American society that were becoming frequent among English observers at that point, including John Stuart Mill: see below, pp. 373–5. A few years later, however, Martineau could be found employing the category of 'middle class' herself as relevant to the English context: see p. 407 n. 55.

the middling classes'; the only deviation from the words of 1820 was the substitution of 'backwardness' for their 'culpable neutrality' in the following sentence.[57] But how different was the next edition of 1832, prepared as the Reform Bill – by then virtually a *fait accompli* – was going through its third parliamentary reading! 'From the reign of king John, to that of Charles I.', Wade now wrote,

what most distinguished this interval was the growth of an entirely new order of vast power and influence who claimed for the first time a share in political government – namely, the MIDDLE CLASSES . . . These, hitherto unknown as an independent cast, had gradually and almost imperceptibly become influential enough to contest the prerogatives of the monarch in the legislature – make war upon him.

At that stage, however, although the 'middle classes' were strong enough to engage in a conflict, 'their day had not yet come. They conquered, but knew not how to preserve their conquest.' Political intelligence had not spread widely enough among the 'middle class' to allow it to construct successfully an alternative government, and consequently 'the power of the state fell back into the hands of its former possessors'. Having thus accounted for the English civil war, the Restoration, and the settlement of 1688 in terms of the relative strengths and weaknesses of the seventeenth-century 'middle class', Wade continued:

though the political power reverted to the King and Aristocracy, a vast influence was ever after exercised over public affairs by the middling classes; and we consider the Reform Bill of 1832 nothing more than an open and constitutional recognition of that authority in the body of the People, which, for the last century and a half, has never ceased to be indirectly, though often inefficiently, exercised over the national government.

These were the assertions of a man who only the previous year had castigated the 'middle classes' for obstructing reform by their apathy and backwardness! Wade's change of tune, suddenly assigning such a key role to a completely re-evaluated 'middle class', could hardly have been more striking, nor its timing more revealing. And it was surely not blunted by Wade's own admission that in actual fact the new franchise qualifications

---

[57] [John Wade], *The Black Book: Or, Corruption Unmasked!* . . ., London, 1820, p. 340. [Idem], *The Extraordinary Black Book* . . ., London, 1831, p. 347; and similarly p. 255.

were arbitrary and anything but uniform, including in numerous cases many of the working classes as well.[58]

Wade's abrupt conversion to 'middle-class' adulation led him to rewrite English history retrospectively, reinterpreting the key developments of the previous two centuries through a 'middle-class'-centred prism. The following year he reproduced these passages in his voluminous *History of the Middle and Working Classes*, probably the first work ever to have included the history of the 'middle class' in its title. Here Wade extended his historical gaze as far back as the thirteenth century, searching for signs 'indicating the rise of a middle class'; including, notably, the effects of the Reformation, through which 'the middling ranks insensibly advanced to wealth and independence'. Tellingly, Wade now also did not fail to mention in passing that he himself belonged to these 'middle classes of life' – a personal detail which he does not seem to have pointed out ever before.[59]

So here it was, the complete and unabridged narrative of the ever-rising 'middle class'. This narrative originated in the 1820s, when the politics of reform induced the representation of the 'middle class' as a new social constituency; it ripened during the debates on the Reform Bill, understandably focused on recent generations; and now it appeared in full bloom, going back to the origins of modern civilized society. Time and again, throughout the 1830s, we encounter writers who came to share Wade's revelation, that history became easier to grasp and to present when it was organized and explained in these terms. Prominent among them, of course, was the doyen of Whig history, Thomas Babington Macaulay.

In 1828, Macaulay had already stamped Oliver Cromwell with

---

[58] [John Wade], *The Extraordinary Black Book ... A New Edition, Greatly Enlarged and Corrected to the Present Time*, London, 1832, pp. 593, 605; see also p. 597. The apathy and backwardness passage was of course omitted from Wade's discussion of the 'middle class' in this edition. Signs of the change had in fact already been apparent in a last-minute appendix to the edition of 1831 (pp. 562–3), titled 'Parliamentary Reform under the New Ministry', in which Wade noted (inconsistently with the body of the work itself) the sympathy of the 'middle class' for limited parliamentary reform.

[59] [John Wade], *History of the Middle and Working Classes*, London, 1833, pp. 11, 45, 466. One should note the continuing interchangeability of 'middle class(es)', 'middle orders' and 'middling ranks' throughout the book, even at this stage and in such a context that universalized and objectified this category; as well as the continuing need to specify what this category, so central now to Wade's writing, actually meant (pp. 167, 177, 183, 456).

the badge of the 'middle class', having 'carried to the throne so large a portion of the best qualities of the middling orders'. In a pro-reform speech in 1831, Macaulay unfolded a historical theory of revolutions: revolutions, he told the House of Commons, occur when one part of the community expands, becomes stronger and demands a corresponding place in the system from which it had previously been excluded. Such had been the struggle between plebeians and patricians in Rome, and such was now the struggle of the 'middle class' against the aristocracy. But the 'middle class', Macaulay reassured his audience, was not too much of a novelty to be trusted: its sound loyalism to the crown, after all, had already been demonstrated in its opposition to the revolution against Charles I.[60] Over the next several years, Macaulay found the 'middle class' to have also been a major factor in the (responsible) opposition to Charles II during the Exclusion Crisis of 1678–9, as well as in mid-eighteenth-century politics. The real historical greatness of Pitt the elder, the Earl of Chatham, he told his readers in 1834, was in the fact

that he looked for support, not, like the Pelhams, to a strong Aristocratical connexion, not, like Bute, to the personal favour of the Sovereign, but to the middle class of Englishmen, – that he inspired that class with a firm confidence in his integrity and ability, – that, backed by them, he forced an unwilling court and an unwilling oligarchy to admit him to an ample share of power.

As John Clive has written (bringing to mind Pierre Rosanvallon's appraisal of Guizot), Macaulay 'was able to communicate the sense that the middle class was not only respectable, but, like the aristocracy, had its own glorious historical traditions and achievements to sustain it'.[61]

History, then, was being refashioned as the unfolding of the inevitable and unstoppable rise to power of the 'middle class', reaching its climax in the present. The rise of the 'middle class' became coterminous with the march of time. Ever since the time of the Normans, learned the readers of the *Westminster Review*,

---

[60] *Edinburgh Review* 48, September 1828, p. 145; see also 168. Thomas Macaulay, *A Speech Delivered in the House of Commons . . . on Lord John Russell's Motion for Leave to Bring in a Bill to Amend the Representation of the People in England And Wales*, London, 1831, pp. 14–15, 21–2, and passim.

[61] *Edinburgh Review*, 58, January 1834, p. 510; 61, July 1835, pp. 295, 300. J. Clive, *Macaulay: The Shaping of the Historian*, Cambridge, Mass., 1973, pp. 497–8.

'the gradual education of a few ... formed that new colony' in the heart of the common people, namely 'the middle class; and thus gradually, since we need not trace this progress, did England become what it is, in freedom, as in wealth and knowledge'. The medieval roots of this momentous development were emphasized somewhat repetitively by Archibald Alison in 1833: 'It was a singular combination of circumstances which rendered the middling ranks under the Norman princes so powerful ... which both created a middling class and secured its privileges.' Alison explained: whereas in Anglo-Saxon times 'no middle class was recognised in society', 'the Norman Conquest had laid the foundation of such a class, by dispossessing the numerous body of Saxon proprietors'; the consequence being that ever since, in contrast with other European nations, 'the [English] middling ranks, comparatively free from oppression, gradually grew in importance with the extension of their numbers, and the insensible increase of national opulence'. Lord Plunket provided a continuation of the story: 'Great and most important changes had taken place in England since the Revolution of 1688', he told the House of Lords; 'the rapid and astonishing influx of wealth had absolutely changed the whole state of the middle classes of society ... This class of persons had been raised in England into astonishing power, and they now came forward and demanded a reform with an irresistible pressure.'[62] Benjamin Disraeli, in *Sybil*, concurred: Lord Shelburne, in the late eighteenth century, 'was the first great minister who comprehended the rising importance of the middle class'; a realization that he passed on to his pupil William Pitt – who therefore insisted on 'curb[ing] the power of the patrician party by an infusion from the middle classes into the government of the country'.[63] For Macaulay it was Pitt the elder, for Disraeli Pitt the younger: whoever was one's political hero was now the hero of one's 'middle-class' story as well.

Or listen to the 1839 words of Montague Gore, a former liberal

---

[62] 'Library of Useful Knowledge': *Westminster Review* 7, April 1827, pp. 269–70. Archibald Alison, *History of Europe during the French Revolution*, Edinburgh, 1833, vol. 1, pp. 15, 22–5; also 17. *Hansard's Parliamentary Debates*, 3rd ser., 3, cols. 1043–4 (speech of 28 March 1831). For other examples in parliament, see the speeches of Francis Jeffrey, cols. 62–3; Lord John Russell, col. 309; or Colonel Torrens, 11, col. 516. And see above, pp. 307–8.

[63] Benjamin Disraeli, *Sybil: Or, the Two Nations*, London, 1913 (originally 1845), pp. 20–1.

MP who had turned staunchly conservative by the late 1830s (re-entering parliament as a conservative in 1841):

> If I were to refer to the past history of England, and to consider why this country has so pre-eminently flourished – why it has so long and so securely enjoyed the blessings of well regulated freedom ... I should be inclined to say, that to no one cause has this happy state of things been owing, more than to the existence of a *middle class* in society, which has moderated the passions, and formed a barrier against the excesses of aristocratic pride on the one hand, and democratic innovation on the other.

Gore's 'middle-class'-based narrative, too, ventured deep into the middle ages, inseparable from his understanding of the origins of liberty:

> At the period of the Norman Conquest the old Saxon principles were preserved among the middle orders; they formed at that period an intermediate and important body between the serfs, on the one hand, and the feudal barons on the other ... and it is to their fond regard for their ancient institutions, on the one hand, and their sturdy spirit of independence on the other, that we are indebted for the establishment of that well-regulated system of liberty, which has so long been the pride and boast of our island.[64]

In Gore's reconstruction of history, ever since the birth of the English nation, from William the Conqueror to the young Queen Victoria, from feudalism to Chartism, the key to liberty and stability was invariably held in the hands of the rising 'middle class'.

Pride of place among Tory writers was reserved, of course, for William Mackinnon and his inimitable obsession with the 'middle class'. In a 'Whiggish' tone pushed almost to the point of parody (which does cast some doubt on the usefulness, if not the political accuracy, of this term), Mackinnon constantly measured historical and political progress against the yardstick of 'middle-class' presence at each past epoch. The feudal middle ages in his view were despotic and dark because there 'scarcely was a middle class in existence'; and although that period did witness the Magna Carta, it was not really much of an achievement, since such a boon was of no use to a people without a 'middle class'.

---

[64] Montague Gore, *A Letter to the Middle Classes on the Present Disturbed State of the Country, Especially with Reference to the Chartist Meetings*, 3rd edn, London, 1839, pp. [3]–4.

(In passing, note that while Mackinnon, Alison and Gore were all now seeing the middle ages through a 'middle-class' lens, the actual picture which this lens conjured up for them was very different: the 'middle class', supposedly so meaningful to the historical account, was created *because* of the Norman conquest, *in spite* of the Norman conquest, or only centuries *after* the Norman conquest – depending on whose version of this history one chose to believe.) Then, to return to Mackinnon's reconstruction of the story, the peace under Henry VII was conducive to the growth of this much needed 'middle class', as was also Henry VIII's dissolution of the monasteries. Indeed, the Reformation – a key triumph of progress – was inevitably 'supported by the middle class of that day', but also 'assisted in a very powerful manner the progress of civilization, and, consequently, the [further] increase of the middle class'; as did also the benevolent reigns of Elizabeth and James I.[65] By contrast, Charles I's downfall resulted from his being 'totally ignorant . . . of any thing like a middle class' around him. Thus, long before Marx, Mackinnon had already offered a 'bourgeois interpretation' of the English revolution:

> the struggle between Charles I. and his parliament, was, in fact, the struggle between the king's prerogative, – that is, of a few courtiers and part of the lower class, against the middle class, such as it then was, together with that part of the upper class that united with them . . .
> The upper class was nearly divided; if it had been otherwise, the king could not have made so long a resistance as he did to the forces of parliament, as almost the whole of the middle class were against him.

Much like the French 'middle class' of 1789, however (a parallel that Mackinnon explicitly pointed out), the seventeenth-century 'middle class' was not yet strong enough to prevent the lower classes from carrying the English revolution to excesses; which was why the historical progress of England was only fully consummated now, two centuries later.[66]

---

[65] Compare Tocqueville's 1830s assertion that 'the stronghold of [English] Puritanism was in the middle classes' (*Democracy in America*, trans. Henry Reeve, London, 1835, vol. I, p. 31).

[66] [William A. Mackinnon], *On the Rise, Progress, and Present State of Public Opinion, in Great Britain, and Other Parts of the World*, London, 1828 (rep. Shannon, 1971), pp. 37–146, passim; quoted, pp. 40, 53, 55, 57, 59, 64–5. Interestingly, again, note how

Moreover, not only did Mackinnon produce an elaborate reworking of English history around the core theme of the 'middle class', he also carried this historical insight elsewhere and further back, into the ancient world. Roman society, with its patricians and plebeians, has always been represented as the *locus classicus* of a dual-framework society. But in the hands of William Mackinnon it was transformed into a society that had been mostly 'middle class'. After all, the Romans too (as well as the Greeks) were a model of civilization; and 'whenever civilization makes its appearance, a middle class in the community appears also, almost as a matter of course'.[67]

Of course, not everyone believed such blatant representations of the advent of the 'middle class' as the inexorable progress of liberty.[68] Yet even those who were less complacent about the political meaning of this narrative were also partaking in its construction. The *Poor Man's Guardian* may again serve as an example. 'Why were labourers in England better off six hundred years ago than they are now', asked the *Poor Man's Guardian*, 'and this notwithstanding that their facilities of increasing wealth are enormously multiplied?' The answer lay in the changing social structure: 'Simply because society was then less artificial than it is now. The aristocracy were few in number, and there was hardly a middle class at all.' For the *Poor Man's Guardian* too the increase of the 'middle class' turned out to have been a decisive factor in developments of the past several centuries, as well as in events closer in time. Ironically, one such event that the newspaper described as 'the work of this [middle] class' was the French war of the 1790s, with its horrific consequences: 'They got up and kept up that horrible war to prevent the working classes in England from imitating those of France.' The uses of 'middle-class' language thus went through a full reversal: from the 1790s' invocation of the 'middle class' primarily in *opposition*

Mackinnon's 'middle-class'-based interpretation of the English revolution was the exact opposite of that offered by Macaulay, as quoted above.

[67] Ibid., pp. 214–15. Indeed two decades later Mackinnon published an enlarged reworking of his ideas, now set explicitly as a universal historical narrative centred on the rise of the 'middle class', under the title *History of Civilisation* (2 vols., London, 1846). And compare Guizot's discovery of the Roman 'middle class': above, pp. 278–9.

[68] In addition to examples we have already encountered, see Macaulay's comments in the *Edinburgh Review* 58, October 1833, p. 244; and very similarly, John Allen's essay in 60, October 1834, p. 30.

to the war, to its 1830s' representation as the primary bearer of
responsibility for the very same war.[69]

Finally, let us look at a different kind of reworking of the
recent past, in the five-volume biography of William Wilberforce
published by his sons Robert Isaac and Samuel in 1838. Wilberforce, himself of mercantile origins, is often depicted as a quintessentially 'middle-class' figure, representing the Evangelical
wave – as expressed for instance in the struggle against slavery –
that was purportedly so intimately bound up with the emergence
of 'middle classness'.[70] And yet in fact, as we shall see further
in the next chapter, neither the Evangelicalism of the late eighteenth and early nineteenth centuries, nor Wilberforce as a key
figure in it, can be described in a meaningful way as straightforwardly 'middle class'. Wilberforce himself was quite slow and
ambiguous in embracing such an identity, to the extent that he
did so at all. At the same time that he expressed admiration for
landed gentlemen (the country gentry he regarded as 'the very
cement of society'), he did not refer often to the 'middle class';
and when he did, his 'middle class' turned out to be prone more
to corruption and immorality than to virtue. Whatever he was,
Wilberforce was no simple representative and advocate of the
'middle class', in particular not in the earlier parts of his career.[71]

In this light it is especially illuminating to read his portrayal
by his sons, written in the years immediately following his death
in 1833. Wilberforce's sons were as captivated by the explanatory
potential of the category of 'middle class' as anyone else at this
point. This became evident for instance in their description of
the Yorkshire Association of the 1780s as 'a union of all the
middle classes against the great barons of the county'; a conception which the Yorkshire country gentlemen themselves would

---

[69] *Poor Man's Guardian* 66, 15 September 1832, vol. I, p. 530; 214, 11 July 1835, vol. III,
p. 592. The same portrayal of the role of the 'middle class' in the French war was
suggested on the other side by Mackinnon, *On the Rise, Progress, and Present State of
Public Opinion*, pp. 134–7.

[70] For a recent example, see L. Davidoff and C. Hall, *Family Fortunes: Men and Women
of the English Middle Class 1780–1850*, London, 1987, p. 81. This representation is central
to C. Hall, 'The Early Formation of Victorian Domestic Ideology', in S. Burman
(ed.), *Fit Work for Women*, London, 1979, pp. 15–32.

[71] See below, p. 398. His opinion on the gentry is quoted in R. G. Thorne (ed.), *The
House of Commons 1790–1820*, London, 1986, vol. v, p. 558. In 1822 Wilberforce referred
to himself as 'born in the middle rank of life': Robert Isaac Wilberforce and Samuel
Wilberforce, *The Life of William Wilberforce*, 5 vols., London, 1838, vol. v, p. 147.

have found distinctly bizarre.[72] As it turns out, it was probably the two sons who likewise imposed a 'middle-class' interpretation on their father's life. Thus, when Wilberforce stood as a parliamentary candidate in Yorkshire in 1784, it does not appear that the issues brought up during the election campaign were formulated at all in 'middle-class' language. But from his sons' retrospect of the 1830s, his success in that campaign, as

a candidate who came forward upon ground which none had taken heretofore, was an intimation of that power, with which intelligence and property had now armed the middle ranks of society. As the man of the middle classes, he took his place in public life; as their representative, he was opposed alike to party influence and democratic licence; as their representative, he demanded and obtained the Abolition of the Slave Trade.[73]

The man, his constituency, his politics, his life-time crusade – all were now found to have been quintessentially 'middle class'. The rise of the 'middle class' – expressed in the confident language of the 1830s – became the master narrative through which Wilberforce's life, too, was being refashioned; and the manifest fact that in the 1780s nobody in Yorkshire had been concerned with the 'middle class' had absolutely nothing to do with it.

From these reconstructions of the past we can turn to reconstructions of society in the present, that were likewise dominated by the pervasive 'middle class'. Among many such social descriptions in the years immediately following 1832 one can mention Edward Bulwer-Lytton's *England and the English*, prompted by the Reform Bill and published in 1833, in which the social divide between aristocracy and 'middle class' was a central issue throughout;[74]

---

[72] Ibid., vol. I, p. 52.

[73] Ibid., vol. I, p. 64 (note again 'middle ranks' and 'middle classes'). In later expressing wonder about his success in these elections, Wilberforce himself referred only to 'my mercantile origin, my want of connexion or acquaintance with any of the nobility or gentry or Yorkshire' (p. 383); and only in 1812, upon his retirement from representing Yorkshire a generation later, did he mention once his 'influence with the middle ranks' there (vol. IV, p. 65).

[74] Bulwer-Lytton, *England and the English*: note in particular vol. I, pp. 26, 87; vol. II, pp. 31, 104. Bulwer-Lytton too found it necessary to specify whom he included in the category of 'middle class' (or 'middle order'), 'by which I mean chiefly shopkeepers and others engaged in trade' (vol. I, p. 176). The same social language was also central to Tocqueville's conversation with Bulwer-Lytton in August 1833: Alexis de Tocqueville, *Journeys to England and Ireland*, trans. G. Lawrence, ed. J. P. Mayer, New Haven, 1958, p. 56. See also G. K. Lewis, 'From Aristocracy to Middle Class:

or Edward Gibbon Wakefield's *England and America*, also published in 1833, in which the 'middle class' – famously dubbed by Wakefield 'the uneasy class' – was a key actor; or Peter Gaskell's 1836 investigation of the state of 'the manufacturing population', which was set against 'the progress of civilization' as 'displayed by the middle class of society'.[75] Or take another domain of public debate, that of education: it is surely significant that Thomas Arnold's first (and important) statement on 'The Education of the Middle Classes', a cause which became his Victorian hallmark, appeared in the *Sheffield Courant* in spring 1832, and began thus: 'We all are aware of the growing power of the middling classes of society, and we know that the Reform Bill will increase and consolidate it'; and therefore, 'the education of the middling classes *at this time*, is a question of the greatest national importance'.[76] Others used different means for this national task: the same years also witnessed a sudden outpouring of books of etiquette, directed specifically at the 'middle class'. Their writers apparently found it (in the words of one) 'highly desirable that the *agrémens* of society should be more generally diffused amongst the middle class' – on whom, according to the *Quarterly Review*, these works were indeed 'really exercising a widely-spread ... influence'.[77]

Bulwer-Lytton's *England and the English*', in his *Slavery, Imperialism, and Freedom: Studies in English Radical Thought*, New York, 1978, pp. 81–107. Finally, compare the anxiety about the 'lower[ing of] the aristocracy in the estimation of the middle classes' in the *Quarterly Review* 48, October 1832, p. 169 (Henry Taylor).

[75] Edward Gibbon Wakefield, *England and America: A Comparison of the Social and Political State of Both Nations*, New York, 1834 (originally 2 vols., London, 1833): see esp. pp. 60–2, 74, 98–102 (where English history since the eighteenth century was conceptualized around the 'middle class'). Peter Gaskell, *Artisans and Machinery: The Moral and Physical Condition of the Manufacturing Population* ..., London, 1836; quoted, p. 77.

[76] Reprinted in *The Miscellaneous Works of Thomas Arnold*, 2nd American edn, New York, 1846, p. 372 (my emphasis). On the importance of Arnold's 1832 statement in the subsequent debates on education, see D. I. Allsobrook, *Schools for the Shires: The Reform of Middle-Class Education in Mid-Victorian England*, Manchester, 1986, pp. 13–17; as Allsobrook points out, Arnold's conception of 'middle class' was anchored more in rural than in industrial England. Compare the 1839 'middle-class idiom' of John Gregory Jones, founder and secretary of the Liverpool Anglican 'middle-class' school, as quoted in ibid., p. 167; and also James Williamson, *On the Diffusion of Knowledge amongst the Middle Classes* ..., London, 1835, whose starting point was the 'process of intellectual growth, which has been taking place amongst the middle classes' (p. [1]; also p. 21 and passim). And see Francis Place's comments in 1836 on society's 'new form' in which the 'middle class' now became the fount of all knowledge and improvement (British Library, Add. Mss 27827, Place Papers, vol. 39, f. 235).

[77] *The Spirit of Etiquette*, London, 1837, p. ii; quoted in M. Curtin, 'A Question of Manners: Status and Gender in Etiquette and Courtesy', *Journal of Modern History* 57 (1985), p. 412 (and see pp. 411–13). *Quarterly Review* 59, October 1837, p. 396 (Abraham Hayward).

This distinguished list can go on and on. Consider political economy, a field with a distinct and self-sufficient vocabulary that heretofore had not been particularly prone to 'middle-class' language. But this was no longer true for *An Enquiry into the Principles of Population*, generally attributed to Thomas Rowe Edmonds, in which the 'middle class' turned out to be a major presence, pivotal throughout the whole argument. Edmonds argued that as society advanced it evolved into two social strata, the labouring classes and their employers – whom he called the 'middle class' (or 'middle rank', or 'middle order'). While he agreed with Malthus that at present there was a redundancy of population, he was much more optimistic about the possible outcome of the situation, the key to which was in the hands of the 'middle class'. Because the labourers were completely dependent upon their employers, it was 'upon the middle order of society, that the prosperity of the state and the comparative comfort of the labouring population depends'. Therefore, 'it is the want of a due proportion of the middle classes of society which causes the existing distress'. For Edmonds, then, England's social and economic problems boiled down to a deficiency in the number of the 'middle class', a deficiency which also deprived the lower orders of beneficial examples for emulation. The 'middle class' thus became the *deus ex machina* which would cure all social woes: perhaps not a major breakthrough in political economical thinking, but a perfect message for its date of publication – 1832.[78] Indeed, this particular timing appears all the more significant in light of Edmonds's previous venture into political economy, published only four years earlier, in which – despite an un-

---

[78] [Thomas Rowe Edmonds], *An Enquiry into the Principles of Population* ..., London, 1832, pp. 34–7. On this work see K. Smith, *The Malthusian Controversy*, New York, 1978 (originally 1951), pp. 198–202. Compare also the role of the 'middle class' in Archibald Alison, *The Principles of Population, and Their Connection with Human Happiness*, 2 vols., Edinburgh, 1840, passim (see vol. 1, p. 119: 'It is the establishment of a numerous and wealthy *middle class* . . . which preserves unbroken the chain of society, and renders the progress of wealth, fatal to the prosperity of despotic states [that are comprised only of rich and poor], instrumental only in increasing the industry, and improving the habits of those which are free.') Malthus himself, who had gradually come to incorporate a 'middle class' into his vision of society since the 1810s, also found it necessary in his revised edition of the *Principles of Political Economy* (published posthumously in 1836) to underscore further the importance of this 'middle class', now that (somewhat regrettably, in his view) it had come to dominate the political scene; rep. in *The Works of Thomas Robert Malthus*, eds. E. A. Wrigley and D. Souden, vols. v–vi, London, 1986 (vol. vi, pp. 280, 296, 303, for such additions to the original text of 1820).

remitting penchant for dividing society into various dyads and triads – the category of 'middle class' had played no role whatsoever.[79]

Like Mackinnon, Edmonds evaluated the prospects of different societies in terms of the development of their 'middle class', itself a yardstick for their social progress.[80] Indeed, once the 'middle class' became a paradigmatic lens through which to view civilized society, many observers naturally extended this new insight to other parts of the world. One obvious such extension, as before, was to France – both to analyses of its post-1830 circumstances and to a new wave of interpretations of the first French Revolution.

The French revolution of 1830, it has been suggested, did not immediately elicit as many 'middle-class' interpretations as might have been expected, perhaps because of their potentially embarrassing political ramifications. But in the years following the Reform Bill this reticence was no longer as evident. A particularly suggestive instance of conversion to a 'middle-class'-centred perspective on French affairs came from the pen of Henry Lytton Bulwer, the brother of Edward Bulwer-Lytton. In 1834 Bulwer published two volumes on France, titled *France, Social, Literary, Political*. Two years later he published a completely new version, under a new title: *The Monarchy of the Middle Classes: France, Social, Literary, Political*. Bulwer explained the change of title in the advertisement to the new book: 'The new title now added is given in consequence of the author having considered its former omission an error.' From one work to the next, within these

---

[79] T[homas] R[owe] Edmonds, *Practical Moral and Political Economy* ..., London, 1828; see the various divisions of society in pp. 42, 55, 107, and passim. And note the 'middling class' of wage earners on p. 115, obviously lacking the resonance which the language of 'middle class' will have acquired for Edmonds by 1832.

[80] One particular case in point was Ireland: in Edmonds's view, an important step towards the improvement of the condition of Ireland was 'totally to alter the sentiments of the Irish middle classes' (*An Enquiry into the Principles of Population*, p. 244). Indeed further research may find another consequence of the post–1832 conceptual upheaval, in the discovery of an Irish 'middle class', whose existence had previously been denied by various English observers (including Coleridge, p. 244 n. 36 above; *Leeds Mercury* 3284, 5 July 1828; or Canning's remark in 1799 as quoted in McCord, 'Some Difficulties of Parliamentary Reform', pp. 377–8). This suggestion might be supported for instance by the 1838 report of the Select Committee on Foundation Schools in Ireland, that was concerned with providing the Irish 'middle class' with 'that proper position in society to which they are entitled', and which would protect their society 'from the chaos of internal disorder'; quoted in Allsobrook, *Schools for the Shires*, p. 99.

couple of years, Bulwer discovered the importance of the 'middle classes' that he had 'omitted' previously. His new insight applied equally to France and to England: on the one hand quoting a French deputy who had stated that 'to the middle classes, then, to the middle classes alone belongs the government of France!'; and on the other, asserting gleefully that 'I look upon it as certain then, that in this country, we shall also see a monarchy of the middle classes, at no distant date.'[81] The same analogy also occurred to the editor of the *Poor Man's Guardian*: in France, as in England, 'all the sinews and strongholds of power are monopolized by the middle class', which accounted in his view for the 'baseness' of their government.[82]

This brings us once again – for the last time – to the continual project of reinterpreting the (first) French Revolution. In the 1830s, perhaps the most intriguing rewriting of the Revolution took place at the hands of conservative commentators, contrasting markedly with their earlier counterparts. For Montague Gore in 1839 the first French Revolution was the ultimate proof that the 'middle class' should not get involved in revolutionary activities (that is, Chartism): they ought to remember the fate of the French 'Nobles and privileged classes', who had supported the ideas that led to the Revolution only to find those ideas turned against themselves. On the other hand, Gore went on to suggest, a few 'resolute men' amongst the French 'middle class' at the time of the Revolution 'might have saved the throne and the monarchy'. So now it was

[81] Henry Lytton Bulwer, *The Monarchy of the Middle Classes: France, Social, Literary, Political, Second Series*, 2 vols., London, 1836, vol. I, advertisement, p. 7; vol. II, p. 81. In vol. I, pp. 4–7, Bulwer presented the familiar tale of the inevitable rise of the English 'middle class' from the early eighteenth century, linked to processes of social change; though he too, like other sobered observers, conceded that – unlike in France – in England, so far, 'their influence has been much exaggerated' (vol. II, p. 75). See also the section 'The Middle Class' in vol. II, pp. 74ff., characterizing it at length for different countries. In Bulwer's *France, Social, Literary, Political* (London, 1834), by contrast, which he had begun writing in 1830, he only mentioned briefly the post-1830 'government of the "bourgeoisie"' in France – without much emphasis or estimation. In the earlier book, moreover, Bulwer retained only the French terminology, even when looking comparatively at the English 'bourgeoisie' (vol. II, pp. 120, 127). The affinities between Bulwer's 1836 work and Edouard Alletz, *De la démocratie nouvelle, ou de mœurs et de la puissance des classes moyennes en France*, 2nd edn, 2 vols., Paris, 1838 (1st edn, 1837) are unmistakable, especially with the latter's section titled 'De la démocratie nouvelle, ou de la monarchie des classes moyennes en France' (vol. II, p. 289).

[82] *Poor Man's Guardian* 145, 15 March 1834, vol. III, p. 41; see likewise 74, 3 November 1832, vol. I, p. 593; 150, 19 April 1834, vol. III, p. 82; 161, 5 July 1834, pp. 170–1; 228, 17 October 1835, pp. 705–6. See also *Examiner* 1204, 27 February 1831, p. 136.

the conservative voice, echoing the British opposition liberals of the previous generation as well as the French liberals of the present one, that exonerated the 'middle class' from revolutionary tendencies. Archibald Alison made precisely the same point in his own anti-Chartist invective of that year: 'it was not by the conquest, but by the infatuation and weakness, of the middle classes, that the French Revolution was triumphant'.[83]

In his 1833 history of the French Revolution, by far the best-selling English book on the topic almost to the end of the nineteenth century, Alison had already elaborated his interpretation of the Revolution, attempting to accommodate it to the 'middle-class'-as-progress narrative (an effort successively enhanced in the subsequent editions of the next decade). By the eighteenth century, Alison wrote, 'the accumulated wealth of ages has rendered the [French] middle orders most powerful'. Inevitably, 'the natural progress of opulence, joined to the force of philosophical enquiry, spread an unruly spirit among the middling ranks', and they 'became conscious of their importance'. But then, once these circumstances set the Revolution in motion, 'with the acquisition of the power which belonged to the old noblesse, the middle classes have since succeeded to their licentiousness' – and in their self-betraying fall, they took the Revolution with them. However, Alison also stated – not too consistently – that the French Revolution 'was distinguished by violence, and stained with blood, because it originated chiefly with the labouring classes'.[84] One way or another, the inevitable rise of the 'middle class' explained the eruption of the Revolution, and its weakness explained its derailment.

And as for the *Poor Man's Guardian*, once again it did not dissent much from the Tory and liberal account; if anything, its own version was even more crystal-clear. The early stages of the

---

[83] Gore, *A Letter to the Middle Classes*, p. 13. *Blackwood's Edinburgh Magazine* 46, September 1839, pp. 289ff. (quoted, p. 301). The article invoked the authority of both Thiers and Alison (its anonymous author. . .), who had predicted that moderate reform limited to the 'middle class' would inevitably be followed by crises of a more radical nature.

[84] Alison, *History of Europe*, vol. I, pp. 58–9, 64, and passim; and the 1844 edn, pp. 137–8, 160, 253. On Alison's book and its popularity, see Ben-Israel, *English Historians on the French Revolution*, pp. 150–2; as Ben-Israel points out, in spite of Carlyle's dismissal of Alison as an 'Ultra-Tory, [who] therefore cannot understand the French Revolution', Alison's actual judgments were little different from any Whig's at this point. Compare also the opinion of William Mackinnon as discussed above, p. 292.

Revolution as the *Poor Man's Guardian* represented it had been entirely a 'middle-class' affair, which resulted in 'the middle-class Republic of 1791'. Subsequently the industrious orders had their own revolution, in which they 'compelled the middle classes to concede to those below them the rights which they had conquered for themselves from those above them'. Yet this 'famous democracy of 1793', whose hero was Robespierre, did not survive his death; 'the middle classes of France had, by force and fraud, despoiled the people' of this achievement. Instead, the people had to succumb to 'the directorial yoke which the middle classes wished to put upon them as a preliminary step to the re-establishment of the throne'.[85]

By now, in sum, the interpretations of the French Revolution, insofar as the role of the 'middle class' was concerned, had indeed moved a long way from their earliest pronouncements in the 1790s. Gone was Burke's unduly ambitious 'middle class' which had thrust itself aggressively and unnecessarily into the French social fabric, shattering its venerable equilibrium; gone was the sharp disagreement between liberals and conservatives on the role of the 'middle class' in the Revolution; gone was the radicals' inability to find in the French Revolution any 'middle class' at all. The moderate liberals of the 1790s may have lost then the political battle. But after forty years, it was their interpretation of the French Revolution, hedging between appreciation and embarrassment for the 'middle class's' part in it, which came closest to the common narrative sung by a chorus of conservatives, liberals and radicals in the 1830s.

In the case of France, of course, such 'middle-class'-based accounts dovetailed nicely with interpretations that were known to be prevalent among the French themselves. But this was surely not a prerequisite: British commentators were now discovering the relevance of a 'middle class' – whether in its presence or in its absence – to understanding a wide variety of other societies, that

---

[85] *Poor Man's Guardian* 77, 24 November 1832, vol. I, p. 617; 79, 8 December 1832, p. 637; 99, 27 April 1833, vol. II, p. 131; 109, 6 July 1833, p. 213; 235, 5 December 1835, vol. III, p. 760. The *Poor Man's Guardian*'s post-1832 'articulation of a new anti-bourgeois interpretation of the Revolution' has been noted in J. R. Dinwiddy, 'English Radicals and the French Revolution, 1800–1850', in F. Furet and M. Ozouf (eds.), *The Transformation of Political Culture 1789–1848*, Oxford, 1989, pp. 454–7. Similar images of the French Revolution, albeit in less detail, were repeated in Bulwer, *England and the English*, p. 325; and Wakefield, *England and America*, p. 100.

were not necessarily known to see themselves in this way. Take for instance the following succession of statements about Spain. Mackinnon was convinced that Spain had only a small and nascent 'middle class', which was politically weak – an opinion shared by Edmonds as well; the *Examiner*, on the other hand, applauded the potential of the Spanish 'middle classes' to lead a future constitutional revolution in their country; whereas the *Poor Man's Guardian* lamented the fact that the Spanish 'middle class' was already 'becoming triumphant'. As before, we can now proceed to explain the political (rather than social) underpinnings of these widely discrepant evaluations of the Spanish 'middle class';[86] but the more significant point here is that whatever gloss these observers were putting on the Spanish scene, they all did so in terms of the strength or weakness of the local 'middle class'.

Indeed we can use similar pronouncements during these years to travel far and wide: to Portugal, where (according to the *Poor Man's Guardian*) 'the middle class now bear the sway ... and bow every thing down in that country to their authority'; to Poland, whose 'middle classes' were criticized by the *Examiner* for their counter-revolutionary tendencies; to Venice, whose patrician oligarchy – so went the story in the *Edinburgh Review* – was perpetuated by oppressing the 'middle class'; or to India, whose future in Macaulay's view would be best guaranteed through the development of a 'middle class'. And once again the indefatigable William Mackinnon surpassed them all, in providing a veritable 'middle-class' world tour: from Genoa and Venice, which had

---

[86] Thus Mackinnon (*On the Rise, Progress, and Present State of Public Opinion*, pp. 247ff.) and Edmonds (*An Enquiry into the Principles of Population*, p. 37), for whom 'middle class' and liberty were directly correlated, were writing in 1828 and 1832, when Spain was still under the repressive regime of Ferdinand VII. The *Poor Man's Guardian*'s comments (228, 17 October 1835, vol. III, p. 706; also 212, 27 June 1835, pp. 576–7), however, were made a year after Ferdinand's successor, the regent Maria Cristina, granted under pressures from the liberal constitutionalists – those whom the *Examiner* (1208, 27 March 1831, p. 203) had depicted in 1831 as 'the best portion of the middle classes' – a very moderate constitution, to the dismay of the more progressive elements who undoubtedly commanded the *Guardian*'s sympathies. Similarly, earlier appraisals of the Spanish 'middle class' in the *Examiner* also followed political developments. In 1808 (16, 17 April 1808, p. 241) it proclaimed that in Spain 'a respectable middling class is not known'; but in celebrating the revolution of 1820, which forced Ferdinand to restore briefly the progressive constitution of 1812, the periodical ascribed it to the influence of 'the middle orders' (656, 23 July 1820, p. 473). Mackinnon, as might be expected, also ascribed these earlier constitutional efforts in Spain to the nascent 'middle class', and their failure to its weakness.

had an extensive 'middle class' in their former glorious past, but were now for the most part bereft of such a presence; through the Hanse Towns (strong 'middle class'), Germany (mixed verdict), the Dutch United Provinces (waned glory), Russia (lots of potential), the Swiss cantons (surprisingly strong), Turkey (none whatsoever), Mexico (considerable and on the rise), Brazil (far behind but not hopeless) and so on; and finally to Asia and Africa, summarily dismissed by Mackinnon as fanatical, despotic, and, of course, singularly deficient in any 'middle class'.[87] A universalized category indeed.

In short, then, an extensive array of British commentators seemed no longer able to describe the world or understand it without a 'middle class'. The powerful grip of this category over social imagination in the 1830s can be demonstrated further by one particularly revealing case, one that merits a brief pause – namely, the discussions of society in America.

What a comparison between the uses of 'middle-class' language in Britain and France has suggested in one way, a comparison between Britain and the United States may suggest in another. In the former case, we have seen that although Britain was surely in the lead in terms of social process and social formation, political circumstances had in fact placed France in the vanguard with regard to the confident view of society as characterized by the advent of a triumphant 'middle class'. The American case seems to be precisely the reverse. On the one hand, in terms of social structure, it was America that was surely in the lead. In the words of Jack Greene, following a long series of similar comments going back to Tocqueville, American society of the second half of the eighteenth century, by the sheer effects of its 'extraordinarily large number of families of independent middling status' (a larger proportion than in any other western society), had been 'a preponderantly middle class world'.[88] On the other

---

[87] *Poor Man's Guardian* 228, 17 October 1835, vol. III, p. 706. *Examiner* 1198, 16 January 1831, p. 40. *Edinburgh Review* 46, June 1827, esp. pp. 87, 100. Clive, *Macaulay*, p. 471. Mackinnon, *On the Rise, Progress, and Present State of Public Opinion*, pp. 207–320; see also his *History of Civilisation*, vol. II. And see the advice for the 'comparative historian' to assess different societies by their respective 'middle classes', in George Cornewall Lewis, *Remarks on the Use and Abuse of Some Political Terms*, London, 1832, pp. 145–7.

[88] J. P. Greene, *Pursuits of Happiness: The Social Development of Early Modern British Colonies and the Formation of American Culture*, Chapel Hill, 1988, p. 188 (and see further references there). The same point, basically, had already been made by Richard Price in his

hand, there seems to be very little American evidence from the late eighteenth and first half of the nineteenth centuries for the use of the category of 'middle class' either for self-identification or for identifying others. Various historians of the American 'middle class' in this period have studied it on an experiential level, assuming that what they describe was in fact an emerging 'middle-class' way of life rather than providing evidence that contemporaries perceived it as such.[89] According to Stuart Blumin, the most recent authority on the subject, 'the term "middle class" and nearly equivalent terms . . . appear far less in the [American] documentary record of the nineteenth century than might be supposed'.[90]

Some forty years ago, Louis Hartz had already suggested that the solution to this seeming paradox stems from the political circumstances: the lack of a political threat to this diffuse social group thwarted the possible inducement for an effective use of 'middle-class' language. American society, being a 'middle-class world' (in Greene's sociological terms), had perhaps no need for self-justification and legitimation by a 'middle-class idiom'.[91] To this may be added the presence of slaves in ante-bellum America,

---

Observations on the Importance of the American Revolution, and the Means of Making It a Benefit to the World, Boston, 1784 (same year as London edn), pp. 57–8.

[89] See the American studies cited in p. 379 n. 4.

[90] S. M. Blumin, 'The Hypothesis of Middle-Class Formation in Nineteenth-Century America: A Critique and Some Proposals', *American Historical Review* 90 (1985), p. 309. By mid nineteenth century this may have changed, when expressions of a 'middle-class idiom' similar to that in Britain, which had been 'rare in the 1830s', can be found: J. S. Gilkeson, *Middle-Class Providence, 1820–1940*, Princeton, 1986, (quoted, p. 55). G. J. Kornblith, 'The Self-Made Men: The Development of Middling Class Consciousness in New England', *The Massachusetts Review* 26 (1985), pp. 461–74. M. J. Burke, 'The Conundrum of Class: Public Discourse on the Social Order in America', unpublished Ph.D., University of Michigan, 1987. S. M. Blumin, *The Emergence of the Middle Class: Social Experience in the American City, 1760–1900*, Cambridge, 1989, pp. 1–2, 240–9, 288. More recently, Gordon Wood (*The Radicalism of the American Revolution*, New York, 1992, pp. 347–8) has asserted that already by the 1810s Americans were referring to themselves as a society dominated by the 'middling sort'. But Wood provides no support for this claim (the only *American* quote – as opposed to those from foreign observers – is that of Charles Ingersoll in 1810, which is in fact tellingly silent about any sort of 'middle class', referring only to patricians and plebeians, rich and poor, and the people); and it may be the case that Wood himself, in endorsing for the most part the claims of the 'middle-class idiom', has also rewritten the language of his subjects to display it.

[91] L. Hartz, *The Liberal Tradition in America*, New York, 1955, pp. 51–2. See also the recent discussion of the American 'political economy of aristocracy', developed by the

against the backdrop of which whites could preserve the illusion of equality among themselves and consequently a silence on differences of class. Once again, then, as the comparative perspective makes clear, the use of social language was not primarily determined by, nor did it simply reflect, an 'underlying' social formation.

The near-absence of 'middle-class' language in America highlights the significance of the fact that in the 1830s, as part of their reorganization of the world in 'middle-class' terms, British (and French) observers referred to American society time and again as dominated by a 'middle class' – thus predating the Americans themselves. 'There is, perhaps, no country in Europe', mused William Mackinnon, 'so favourable, from natural advantages, to the formation of a middle class of society, as the United States of America.' 'Who then are the real enemies of the American operatives, and of the American democracy?' demanded the *Poor Man's Guardian*; 'Why to be sure THE MIDDLE CLASSES. These are the real tyrants of America.' With fewer axes to grind, Henry Bulwer stated the basic insight which has been repeated by so many speakers ever since: 'In America there is no especial middle class; all the nation is composed of *our* middle class. This class were its original founders, and have been its constant settlers.'[92] From Alexis de Tocqueville to present-day historians, outsiders to early-nineteenth-century American society have repeatedly imposed upon it such a social scheme; a point forcefully driven home when the Frenchman (Tocqueville) actually ended up getting into an

revolutionary generation (for 'aristocracy' as a political rather than social category) and carried into the nineteenth century, which in spite of its antipathy to excessive wealth and to poverty seemed to lack any concept of a 'middle class': J. L. Huston, 'The American Revolutionaries, the Political Economy of Aristocracy, and the American Concept of the Distribution of Wealth, 1765–1900', *American Historical Review* 98 (1993), pp. 1079–105.

[92] Mackinnon, *On the Rise, Progress, and Present State of Public Opinion*, p. 303; and see pp. 300–6. For Mackinnon the main difference between the American and the English 'middle class' was that the former was in large part agricultural. *Poor Man's Guardian* 161, 5 July 1834, vol. III, pp. 169–71. See likewise 168, 23 August 1834, p. 227; 178, 1 November 1834, p. 307; 188, 10 January 1835, p. 386. Lytton Bulwer, *The Monarchy of the Middle Classes*, vol. II, p. 75. See similarly William Empson's observation about the origins of the immigration to America in 'that most valuable, but not most elegant portion of the English community, called the middle class': *Edinburgh Review* 55, July 1832, p. 500.

argument with the Englishman (Bulwer) over their respective comments about the exact nature of the 'middle class' in American society, a society to which both men and their social language were alien.[93]

Not that all foreign commentators necessarily shared this confident perception. Harriet Martineau, for one, while describing in effect the same American social structure lacking rich and poor, refrained from ascribing to it a 'middle class'. Matthew Bridges, who expressed in 1832 absolute confidence in the power of the 'middle class' in England, was much less confident when he tried to force this category upon the Americans, referring with manifest caution to 'what may not improperly be called (in a certain sense) the middle classes of the union'.[94] Traces of the process of extraction by which this language was transported from Britain to America were discernible in Bulwer's emphasis on the American nation consisting of '*our* middle class', as well as in the writing of John Stuart Mill. In reviewing Tocqueville, Mill stated:

in the constitution of modern society, the government of a numerous middle class is democracy. Nay, it not merely *is* democracy, but the only democracy of which there is yet any example; what is called universal suffrage in America arising from the fact that America is *all* middle class; the whole people being in a condition, both as to education and pecuniary means, corresponding to the middle class here.

While repeating (here and elsewhere) the 'middle-class nation' characterization of America, Mill too needed to explain that this was a heuristic observation, employing a familiar English category which he was extrapolating across the Atlantic Ocean: what the Americans perceived as universal suffrage was translatable to his

---

[93] Tocqueville argued that the analogy between the American and the French 'middle class' (but not the English) was stronger than Bulwer had allowed for: see Alexis de Tocqueville, *Œuvres complètes, tome VI: Correspondance anglaise*, ed. J. P. Mayer, Paris, 1954, vol I, pp. 320–1. For Tocqueville's own 'middle-class' language ('classes moyennes') with regard to America, see *Democracy in America*, vol. I, p. 31; and more strongly in his diaries, where he described America soon upon his arrival as a 'whole society [which] seems to have melted into a middle class', and later as invincible proof 'that the middle classes are capable of governing a state': quoted in G. W. Pierson, *Tocqueville and Beaumont in America*, New York, 1938, pp. 69–70, 548–9. See also p. 483, where – in an apparent exception to the predominant American silence (or perhaps as another example of a listener recasting the social language of his interlocutor into his own preferred formulations?) – Tocqueville actually quoted the mayor of Philadelphia as using assertive 'middle-class idiom'.

[94] Bridges, *An Address to the Electors of England*, p. 25. For Martineau, see above, n. 56.

readers in England in terms of what 'here' was the 'middle class'. Furthermore, he asked, did not 'the American people, both in their good qualities and in their defects, resemble anything so much as an exaggeration of our own middle class?' Mill indeed thought that Tocqueville had not stressed enough the 'middle-class' quality of American society: 'all the intellectual effects which M. de Tocqueville ascribes to Democracy, are [in fact] taking place under the Democracy of the middle class'. What Tocqueville should have pointed out, insisted Mill, was not 'the annihilation of the extremes' (typical only of America), but the more general phenomenon, common to both America and England – 'the growth of the middle class'.[95]

One is reminded here again of Mill's reverence for these words, 'growth of a middle class', which opened this section: what a powerful paradigm indeed this turned out to be in Britain of the 1830s, as a pervasive way of perceiving and rationalizing politics, society, and history (going further and further back in time), with regard to both Britain and elsewhere. Oddly, some historians have denied this development; notably J. G. A. Pocock, whose efforts to discredit the Marxist notion of a rising bourgeoisie have led him to dismiss the 'middle-class' language of the 1830s as the marginal pronouncements of 'an ideologue or two'.[96] In fact, it should by now be abundantly manifest that such pronouncements were no more marginal than they were ideologically bounded. Rather, they proved to be an extremely forceful and captivating torrent, engulfing everything in its way, and on whose waves one could find riders from all social stripes and political camps. By the 1830s, in sum, it was conspicuously true that a very large number of the British people came to see the 'middle class' as a statement of fact, contentious not in itself but only

---

[95] J. S. Mill on Tocqueville's *Democracy in America*, *Edinburgh Review* 72, October 1840; rep. in his *Collected Works*, vol. xviii, pp. 167, 193–6; also 200. Compare his essay 'State of Society in America', *London Review*, 2, January 1836, in ibid., p. 101: 'America is a republic peopled with a provincial middle class.' And see D. P. Crook, 'John Stuart Mill and America as a Middle-Class Democracy', in his *American Democracy in English Politics 1815–1830*, Oxford, 1965, pp. 176–86. Mill's formulation, on the equivalence of democracy and 'middle-class' rule, was strikingly similar to that of the French writer Edouard Alletz (1837): see above, n. 81.

[96] J. G. A. Pocock, *Virtue, Commerce, and History*, Cambridge, 1985, p. 208. See also Harold Perkin's surprising statement (in *The Structured Crowd: Essays in English Social History*, Brighton, 1981, p. 104) that 'the myth of middle-class rule [after 1832] had no foundation in contemporary middle-class opinion'.

in its evaluative implications, a purportedly objective and readily observable presence in the world around them. The invention of the Barthesian myth, of the reified and universalized 'middle class', together with the linear narrative of its inexorable historical rise, was completed.

CHAPTER II

1832 and the 'middle-class' conquest of the 'private sphere'

Our fashion may indeed be considered the aggregate of the opinions of our women ... The domestic class of women ... [is virtuous] in the very refraining from an attempt to influence public opinion.

(Edward Bulwer-Lytton, 1831)[1]

The middle classes interest themselves in grave matters: the aggregate of their sentiments is called OPINION. The great interest themselves in frivolities, and the aggregate of *their* sentiments is termed FASHION.

(Edward Bulwer-Lytton, 1833)[2]

Consider these two observations about fashion and opinion by the novelist Edward Bulwer-Lytton, penned two years apart. The affinities between them are manifest. So are the differences. The first was included in a comparison of 'the spirit of society' in England and France in 1831, a comparison that was dominated throughout by the fundamental dichotomy of 'public' and 'private', delineated as that between men and women. 'The proper sphere of woman', Bulwer-Lytton then stated further, 'is private life, and the proper limit to her virtues, the private affections'; in contrast with 'public opinion', that exclusive masculine realm that should remain free of 'feminine influence'.

But by 1833 Bulwer-Lytton's understanding of the antithesis between fashion and opinion had revealingly changed, replacing a polarity of gender with a polarity of class. He no longer designated 'fashion' as the aggregate of the opinions of women, but instead as the aggregate of the opinions of the upper classes;

---

[1] *Edinburgh Review* 52, January 1831, pp. 377–8.
[2] Edward George Bulwer-Lytton, *England and the English*, 2 vols., New York, 1833 (also published in London), vol. I, p. 87.

and 'public opinion' was no longer the domain of men, but instead the aggregate of the opinions of the 'middle class'. In the earlier text Bulwer-Lytton's approbation had been conferred upon women who remained in the private sphere and upon men who were well versed in public principles; in the second, it was reserved for the members of the 'middle class', who were now represented as agents operating *both* in private and in public. Bulwer-Lytton's 1833 'middle classes' were not only the familiar repository of responsible and informed opinion, but also that of 'sober and provident conduct . . . in their domestic relations';

> the middle classes [he wrote further], with us, have a greater veneration than others for religion; hence their disposition, often erroneous, to charity, in their situation of overseers and parochial officers; hence the desire (weak in the other classes), with them so strong, of keeping holy the Sabbath-day; hence their enthusiasm for diffusing religious knowledge among the negroes.[3]

'Middle classness', then, was by now associated with domestic virtue, with religiosity, with an evangelical impulse, with social control; that is to say, with a morality which prescribed both public and private (or familial) behaviour.

These two pronouncements, separated so suggestively by the Reform Act of 1832, point to another key manifestation of the explosion which it had triggered in the uses of 'middle-class' language. Now that this category (embedded in a narrative that became inseparable from the category itself) had come to assume such focal prominence in the articulation of experience and consciousness, conveying the confidence of objective, matter-of-factual inevitability, its uses were also expanded to the understanding of the familial or private sphere and its demarcation from the public one. Historians have repeatedly noted (without necessarily agreeing on details) that the period discussed in this book witnessed a significant reordering and redefinition of 'public' in antithesis to 'private', as a very particular construction of social reality, and moreover one with stringent prescriptive implications. Many historians – like many Victorians – have associated this fundamentally gendered development, entwined with a redefinition of 'femininity' in antithesis to 'masculinity', with the emergence of a 'middle class'. Indeed, in the influential work of Leonore

---

[3] Ibid., vol. I, pp. 44, 176–7.

Davidoff and Catherine Hall (and often elsewhere), domestic ideology (that legitimized this separation of spheres) as well as Evangelicalism (the religious movement that reinforced it) are found to have embodied the very quintessence of 'middle classness'.[4] But what was in fact the nature of the connection between these developments and a 'middle class'?

One possible answer is on the level of social practice. Here, however, recent work has cast considerable doubt on the social specificity and distinctiveness of domestic ideology, separation of spheres and Evangelicalism; that is to say, of those manifestations among men and women of what Davidoff and Hall have described as 'the commitment to an imperative moral code and the reworking of their domestic world into a proper setting for its practice'[5] – a commitment which in turn shaped their identities as men and women. Such impulses can readily be shown not only to have encompassed large segments of the landed classes and of the working population, but – more significantly – to have been no less central to the formation of the respective identities of these groups. Thus Peter Mandler and Linda Colley have both pointed to strong allegedly 'bourgeois' drives that were in fact key to the construction of a new identity for members of the landed elite of the late eighteenth and early nineteenth centuries, drives manifested in greater emphases on domestic morality, appearances of sobriety and earnestness, and serious religiosity. Evangelicalism too surely had a major impact upon the landed gentry.[6] At the other end of the social scale, Sonya Rose has

---

[4] L. Davidoff and C. Hall, *Family Fortunes: Men and Women of the English Middle Class, 1780–1850*, London, 1987. An earlier formulation can be found in C. Hall, 'The Early Formation of Victorian Domestic Ideology', in S. Burman (ed.), *Fit Work for Women*, London, 1979, pp. 15–32; reprinted, together with other pertinent essays, in C. Hall, *White, Male and Middle-Class: Explorations in Feminism and History*, New York, 1992. This argument has indeed become a cliché of historical writing about the 'middle class', a cliché which transcends the specificities of geographical or chronological boundaries. Thus there is for instance a surprising similarity between the arguments of Davidoff and Hall for England, and those that focus on evangelical religion and familial life as key to the development of the American 'middle class'; see notably M. P. Ryan, *Cradle of the Middle Class: The Family in Oneida County, New York, 1790–1865*, Cambridge, 1981. P. E. Johnson, *A Shopkeeper's Millennium: Society and Revivals in Rochester, New York, 1815–1837*, New York, 1978.

[5] Davidoff and Hall, *Family Fortunes*, p. 25. And see J. Newton, '*Family Fortunes*: "New History" and "New Historicism" ', *Radical History Review* 43 (1989), pp. 5–22.

[6] P. Mandler, *Aristocratic Government in the Age of Reform: Whigs and Liberals, 1830–1852*, Oxford, 1990. L. Colley, *Britons: Forging the Nation 1707–1837*, New Haven, 1992. See also P. Langford, *Public Life and the Propertied Englishman 1689–1798*, Oxford, 1991,

demonstrated persuasively the centrality of domesticity to the formation of a working-class identity in the nineteenth century, manifested in a pattern of values and behaviour that went back to eighteenth-century artisanal workshop culture.[7] And last but not least, doubts have also been raised about the appropriateness of the model of separate spheres in describing the actual life of women and men in the 'middle class' itself, as distinct from the prevalence of such a model in prescriptive writing.[8]

Second, and more germane to the present inquiry, is the level of meaning and language. The fact that a quintessential 'middle-class domesticity' was not unproblematically observable as social practice merely underscores a point that by now should be evident: namely, that given the contingent construction of the notions of 'middle class' and 'separate spheres' taken separately, the ostensible affinity between the two was also likely to be more of a particular representation of social experience than a straightforward 'objective' depiction of this experience. What needs to be revealed is the specific historical origins and logic

chapter 8; and for the landed elite sharing those purported 'middle-class' values, especially Evangelicalism, see P. Thane, 'Aristocracy and Middle Class in Victorian England: The Problem of "Gentrification" ', in A. M. Birke and L. Kettenacker (eds.), *Middle Classes, Aristocracy and Monarchy: Patterns of Change and Adaptation in the Age of Modern Nationalism*, Munich, 1989, pp. 95–8. Indeed one of the least satisfactory aspects of *Family Fortunes* is the strikingly stereotypical treatment of the landed classes, taking their most hostile and flat characterizations at face value, and thus allowing for exaggerated distinctions between them and a counter-stereotypical 'middle class'.

[7] S. O. Rose, *Limited Livelihoods: Gender and Class in Nineteenth-Century England*, Berkeley, 1992. Rose however remains undecided about the origin of this development, sometimes insisting on its origins in pre-industrial labouring culture (see pp. 141–2), while elsewhere leaving open the possibility of its trickling down from the ranks of the employers (p. 148; chapters 2–3). For an earlier argument along similar lines, which focuses on the independent logic and dynamic of the emergence of the domesticity ideal among the nineteenth-century working class, see W. Seccombe, 'Patriarchy Stabilized: The Construction of the Male Breadwinner Wage Norm in Nineteenth-Century Britain', *Social History* 11 (1986), pp. 53–76. Indeed, Catherine Hall herself has provided in another study ('The Tale of Samuel and Jemima: Gender and Working-Class Culture in Early-Nineteenth-Century England', in her *White, Male and Middle-Class*, pp. 124–50) an excellent example of the centrality of such gendered differentiation of the world for working-class people. Hall elegantly demonstrates how gendered constructions of the world – very similar to those which were allegedly specific to the 'middle class' – were in fact an integral part of working-class life; but then she insists on locating the origins of this working-class behaviour in quintessentially class-specific 'middle-class' values, thus undermining her own finding.

[8] A. Vickery, 'Golden Age to Separate Spheres? A Review of the Categories and Chronology of English Women's History', *Historical Journal* 36 (1993), esp. pp. 383–401. Note also the critique of a blanket notion of 'middle-class morality' in R. S. Neale, *Class and Ideology in the Nineteenth Century*, London, 1972, chapter 6.

of this coupling of 'middle class' with the domestic or familial sphere. As the passages from Bulwer-Lytton neatly suggest, the powerful purchase of this particular representation of social reality, just like the powerful purchase of the rising-'middle-class' historical narrative, should be seen within the broader context of the universalization of 'middle class' as the basis for conceptualizing society after 1832. The aftermath of the Reform Act witnessed not only the decisive proclamation of the 'middle class' as a powerfully rising social constituency at the core of the 'public'; it also witnessed a complementary proclamation of the 'middle class' as the epitome of hearth and home, at the core of the 'private'.

Indeed, it is the contrast between discussions of the 'middle class' and of the private/familial sphere before and after 1832 that is most revealing. In order to draw this contrast out, this chapter extends beyond the limits of political literature broadly conceived (the backbone of our discussion so far) to include a very different genre of writing, focusing on familial and domestic issues, which can be called domestic literature. Reviewing (albeit briefly) both genres, it will be suggested not only that within each one a clear change can be seen in the treatment of such issues before and after 1832; but also that in relation to each other, these two very different genres, in which 'middle class' (either restricted to men, or expanded to include women) and the familial sphere had for decades been discussed very differently, now suddenly came together, registering once again the powerful effects of the Reform Act in shaping people's representations of their society.

'MIDDLE CLASS' AND PUBLIC/PRIVATE, MASCULINE/ FEMININE BEFORE 1832

Before the 1830s there was nothing immediately self-evident about a connection between the 'middle class' and the domestic sphere. On the contrary, within the contemporary construction of the world as fundamentally divided along gendered lines into public and private (an antithesis which was extremely common in organizing and articulating people's experiences, regardless of its actual adequacy), the 'middle class' – as it was invoked in political language – was subsumed under this division and confined to one side of the boundary which it had erected, the public/masculine side. In the numerous discussions of 'middle-class' virtues that we have encountered, these virtues were for the most part recognizable as distinctly masculine; be it its vaunted independence – in the words of *The Oeconomist* of New-castle, its 'manly dignity of independence';[9] its intelligence – which meant, as we have seen, not mere intellect but more specifically political knowledge and judgment; or its being the class in which 'the strength of the Empire mainly rests'. Even when the private life or the invigorated religion of the 'middle class' were brought up, they were similarly gendered.[10] And when the 'middle class' was criticized, this too was done in masculine terms. Such was the case for instance for the Burkean writer of 1796 who accused the 'middle class' of undermining its social position through its ambition and wealth, both masculine attributes; not, as had been the standard argument in eighteenth-century critiques of commerce, through fashionable consumption and emulation of genteel society, mostly depicted as feminine.[11] So whereas the aristocracy was commonly undermined in the eyes of its critics by allegedly feminine traits, the 'middle class' was undermined in the eyes of *its* critics by allegedly masculine ones.

Of all the political moments before the 1830s when the language of 'middle class' might have been expected to cross over into domestic or familial issues, none was as suitable as during the famous agitation surrounding the trial of Queen Caroline in 1820; and therefore nowhere perhaps was the confinement of this language to the masculine political realm more striking. The trial was an attempt by George IV to divorce his wife, Caroline of Brunswick, from whom he had been separated soon after their

[9] *The Oeconomist* 9, September 1798, p. 238; and see also the strongly masculine paean to the 'middle class', contrasted with an effeminate aristocracy, in 1, January 1798, pp. 5–8. On 'independence' as masculine see Davidoff and Hall, *Family Fortunes*, p. 199; and compare Rose, *Limited Livelihoods*, p. 53. As Mrs John Sandford put it in the early 1830s: 'There is, indeed, something unfeminine in independence.' Mrs John Sandford, *Woman, in Her Social and Domestic Character*, Boston, 1838, from 2nd London edn (originally London, 1831), p. 14.

[10] See examples in pp. 177, 180. *The Declaration of the People of England to Their Sovereign Lord the King*, London, 1821, pp. 38–9; and note the masculine nature of 'middle-class' ambitions and temptations in this tract, as quoted in p. 219.

[11] *Two Letters, Addressed to His Grace the Duke of Bedford, and the People of England*, London, [1796?]; quoted above, p. 89.

marriage in 1795, but who decided upon the death of George III to return and assume the role of queen. Her husband brought an action against her in the House of Lords for divorce on grounds of adultery, and the ensuing proceedings (which commenced in August 1820) brought the alleged deeds and misdeeds of the Queen to an eager public. This was the only topic he had ever known, proclaimed William Hazlitt, that excited such 'a thorough popular feeling. It struck into the heart of the nation.' As William Cobbett added, it 'let loose for a time every tongue and pen in England'.[12]

The trial became a *cause célèbre* for the critics of Old Corruption, and no less so for the critics of aristocratic morality, in particular the sexual double standard it was thought to embody. Caroline was represented (albeit rather incongruously) as the virtuous heroine, the symbol of dependent womanhood, the wronged woman. Here, then, was an effective lever for criticizing aristocratic sexual practices and matrimonial behaviour in the name of domestic morality and propriety; as one pamphleteer put it bluntly, 'half our nobility are recorded adulterers, or victims of adultery'.[13] But, contrary to what the historiographical emphasis on 'middle-class domesticity' might have led us to believe, these aristocratic mores were *not* criticized in the name of the 'middle class'.[14] One can easily imagine how such anti-aristocratic attacks

---

[12] Both quoted in the best study of this episode, T. W. Laqueur, 'The Queen Caroline Affair: Politics as Art in the Reign of George IV', *Journal of Modern History* 54 (1982), pp. 417–66. Charles Greville similarly noted: 'Since I have been in the world I never remember any question which so exclusively occupied everybody's attention, and so completely absorbed men's thoughts and engrossed conversation': *The Greville Memoirs 1814–1860*, eds. L. Strachey and R. Fulford, London, 1938, vol. 1, pp. 105–6; see also p. 99. For other recent discussions of this affair, see I. J. Prothero, *Artisans and Politics in Early Nineteenth-Century London: John Gast and His Times*, Folkestone, 1979, chapter 7. A. Clark, 'Queen Caroline and the Sexual Politics of Popular Culture in London, 1820', *Representations* 31 (1990), pp. 47–68. T. L. Hunt, 'Morality and Monarchy in the Queen Caroline Affair', *Albion* 23 (1991), pp. 697–722.

[13] John Macrainbow (pseud.), *A Volley at the Peers both Spiritual and Temporal, or, a Veto upon the Votes of Some of Them: Facts Respecting Baron Bergami . . .*, London, [1820], p. 11.

[14] In the framework of the argument put forth by Davidoff and Hall (*Family Fortunes*, pp. 150–5), the Queen Caroline affair was the culmination of the emerging 'middle-class' domesticity, which by this stage had become sufficiently assertive to have turned into a direct political challenge. 'The reaction to the whole episode', they write, 'marks one of the first *public* moments at which one view of marriage and of sexuality was decisively rejected in favour of another.' Caroline in fact came to stand vicariously for her daughter Charlotte, a true symbol of happy domestic life, who had died three years earlier. Charlotte, Davidoff and Hall suggest, 'would have been a monarch such as the middling classes sought, sharing their values, enjoying their pastimes'. Having

could have fruitfully incorporated images of 'middle-class' domestic happiness and matrimonial bliss, of 'middle-class' men as
virtuous caring husbands and 'middle-class' women as exemplary
demure wives, all paraded as a counter-model to the dissolute
life of the upper classes. Yet overwhelmingly this does not seem
to have been the case; and this point holds good – as we shall
see in a moment – even in those instances when the 'middle
class' *was* invoked explicitly by the Queen's supporters.

Rather, bringing to a climax what we have seen as a dominant
trend of the late 1810s, the Queen's cause – which in fact
mobilized an unusually broad cross-class alliance – was represented time and again as that of 'public opinion' (see figure
6). The pages of the *Examiner*, for example, like innumerable
other interventions in this debate, were dense with comments on
the 'Tribunal of Public Opinion' which must determine the
outcome of the affair; and when it was over, with celebrations
of 'what public opinion, without physical force, can effect against
established corruption'. Crucially, as these quotations show by
the allusions to a judicial tribunal and to physical force, this
'public opinion' was constructed as altogether *male*. It represented
public (political) 'intelligence, virtue, and integrity', and as such
was antithetical to 'any set of privileged men who can suppose
they possess a monopoly of national wisdom'.[15] Defined through
the gendered differentiation of 'public' and 'private', 'public opinion' combined on the one hand a particular conception of
politics as the exclusive domain of politically informed – 'intelligent' – men and as the embodiment of their sound judgment;
and on the other hand, a particular conception of masculinity,

---

lost Charlotte, it was Caroline who became the incarnation of the struggle between
these 'two worlds', that of the profligate aristocracy and that of the domestic 'middle
class'.
15 *Examiner* 654, 9 July 1820, pp. 433–4; 661, 27 August 1820, p. 555; 673, 19 November
1820, p. 741. Shortly thereafter the *Examiner* described this affair as 'one of the strongest
spontaneous expressions of public opinion that was ever evinced in any age or country':
683, 4 February 1821, p. 66 (repeated 685, 18 February 1821, p. 105). For examples
of the ubiquitous appeals to 'public opinion' during this agitation see chapter 6, note
10, as well as *A Warning to Noble Lords previous to the Trial of Queen Caroline. By a Loyal
Subject*, London, [1820?], p. 9 (where 'public opinion' was defined as 'the opinion of
men'). Henry Bathurst, *A Sermon, Intended to Have Been Preached before . . . the Queen, on
the Occasion of her Public Thanksgiving at St Paul's Cathedral . . . 29th of November, 1820:
With an Introductory Letter to the Bishop of Llandaff*, London, 1820, pp. 10–12. *A Full
Report of the Middlesex County Meeting, Held at Hackney, on Tuesday, August 8, 1820, To
Take into Consideration the Propriety of Presenting an Address to the Queen . . . Speeches of Sir
Francis Burdett . . .*, London, [1820], p. 15 (Hobhouse's speech).

revealed through and embodied in men's public/political behaviour. Both these aspects of 'public opinion' were strongly evoked by the Queen's misfortunes: if Caroline was the wronged woman, then – in Davidoff and Hall's words – it was felt that 'the "manly" and the "courageous" must rise up and protect her'. 'Public opinion' was the collective embodiment of this manliness. As one of many pro-Caroline pamphleteers put it, 'I would tremble for the fate of every woman in this country, if I did not see arrayed against this foul persecution, all the manly virtues of the land.' These manly virtues found expression in the 'public opinion [that] pronounced its verdict on the whole proceeding'.[16]

So 'public opinion' was put forward as the main protagonist against aristocratic and ministerial corruption in the Caroline affair; and it was this understanding of the political situation that determined and contained the uses to which the language of 'middle class' was put within it. It was only through its role within this manly 'public opinion', pertaining exclusively to the public political sphere, that the 'middle class' was found to be relevant to the Queen's cause. In this, of course, this episode was no different from the other political conflicts of the late 1810s that preceded it, in which the partisan alignment of the 'middle class', crucial to proclaiming the putative verdict of 'public opinion', had been a recurrently contested issue.

Thus Thomas Creevey, for example, believed that all 'middle orders' supported the Queen. 'The people all favour the Queen, including the respectable middle ranks', concurred Lady Palmerston. J. R. McCulloch was apprehensive lest mob violence in support of the Queen might distance 'the greater part of the middle classes who are now united with them'. Thomas Malthus, on the contrary, regretted the extent to which the affair 'has tended so much to increase the separation of the higher and the middle classes'.[17] The *Examiner* (in which the apogee of reverence to the role of 'public opinion' during these months coincided with a

---

[16] Davidoff and Hall, *Family Fortunes*, p. 151. *The King's Treatment of the Queen Shortly Stated to the People of England*, 2nd edn, London, 1820, pp. 21, 31; and passim. Compare the words of Sir Francis Burdett, that the Queen's cause was 'calculated . . . to rouse the energies of every manly mind in support of the sex oppressed, in vindication of an injured woman': *A Full Report of the Middlesex County Meeting*, p. 10.

[17] *The Works and Correspondence of David Ricardo*, ed. Piero Sraffa, Cambridge, 1952, vol. VIII, p. 314: McCulloch to Ricardo, 28 November 1820; p. 308, Malthus to Ricardo, 27 November 1820. For Creevey and Lady Palmerston see Laqueur, 'The Queen Caroline Affair', p. 427.

conspicuous lull in its 'middle-class' language relative to its prevalence both before and after) deviated from this overall silence
twice, in both cases to tie the 'middle class' with this 'public
opinion'. Thus on one occasion it noted the 'subscriptions among
the middling ranks' in favour of the Queen; and on another, the
support she had received from all social classes, including 'the
middle class [who] have indeed got at least the privilege of judging
for themselves which was so long denied to them by priests and
nobles'.[18] Lord Lyttelton made the gendered aspect of these utterances more explicit when he expressed his belief that the 'middle
classes' supported the Queen 'almost to a man'. Finally, listen to
the Queen herself: in response to one address of support she
lamented that the higher ranks, 'where most independence ought
to be displayed, and most virtue to be seen . . . [have] become
the most unsound part of the constitution'.

> Hence [continued the Queen,] the middle and subordinate ranks have
> little to expect from those above them; and they have, therefore, no
> other hope left of checking the progress of corruption, and of preventing
> the total destruction of liberty, than by a firm and energetic union
> among themselves.[19]

The Queen too invoked the 'middle class' not in the context of
the peculiarities of her own story, nor was it its domestic virtue
which she contrasted with the deficient virtue of the higher
orders. Instead, she introduced the 'middle class' into the familiar
constitutional critique of government, based on the venerable
antithesis of liberty and corruption: the basic materials of public
political language.

In sum, then, it was as part of (male) 'public opinion', as a

---

[18] *Examiner* 674, 26 November 1820, p. 763; 676, 10 December 1820, p. 785. Regarding
the recurrence of 'middle-class' language in the *Examiner*, a very crude enumeration
reveals that during the nine months between the massacre at St Peter's Fields in
Manchester and the beginning of the Caroline affair (September 1819–June 1820), the
language of 'middle class' was employed meaningfully in the *Examiner* at least eleven
times, introduced into discussions of the hottest political issues of the day as well as
of less contested topics. During the next seven months (July 1820–January 1821),
dominated by the debates on the Queen's trial, only three such instances can be
found; which again contrasts with eight further such instances in the following three
months (February–April 1821), once the Caroline agitation had subsided.

[19] Lyttelton to Charles Bagot, 9 August 1820; quoted in Lewis Melville, *An Injured Queen:
Caroline of Brunswick*, London, 1912, vol. II, p. 472. *Selections from the Queen's Answers to
Various Addresses Presented to Her . . .*, 4th edn, London, 1821, p. 46; also quoted in *The
Anti-Jacobin Review and Magazine* 59, February 1821, p. 562.

political audience and a partisan public, that the participation of the 'middle class' in this popular agitation was invoked and asserted. But none of these speakers noted a particular link between the *contents* of the issue at hand and the participation of the 'middle class'. They did not find any particular 'middle-class' essence in this political struggle, to distinguish it from previous political confrontations – notably those surrounding the massacre of Peterloo – in which 'public opinion' (and through it the 'middle class') had recently been involved. Indeed, on the part of the ministerialist camp, the support of the 'middle class' could be claimed no less confidently to have been arrayed *against* the Queen: as was the case for the correspondent of the *Anti-Jacobin Review* who contrasted the 'abandoned rabble' on the side of the Queen with the 'quiet good sense' of 'the majority of Englishmen in the middle ranks of life', rallied – so he asserted – against her. And in ironic symmetry, one can similarly find popular radical voices, celebrating 'public opinion' as an exclusively popular entity, whose understanding of the support for the Queen likewise excluded from it – in the words of the *Black Dwarf* – 'both the *higher* and the *middling classes*'.[20] Thus, while the trial of Queen Caroline touched upon issues of private *and* public, bringing to the political purview issues of domestic life, matrimonial behaviour and sexual mores, and while all of these did have a class angle in that they were exploited in formulating anti-aristocratic criticisms, nevertheless the notion of 'middle class' was confined only to discussions of the public – that is, of the behaviour of males in the political sphere. The 'middle class' was found relevant only to the composition of 'public opinion'; it was *not* found relevant to the discussions of the domestic issues at hand, and in particular was not a source for an alternative model of private/familial behaviour.[21]

---

[20] *Anti-Jacobin Review and Magazine* 58, July 1820, p. 486 (signed R. de B.). *Black Dwarf* 6:15, 11 April 1821, p. 509.

[21] I have found one apparent exception to these observations, in an address to the Queen from 'married ladies' (after all, the fact that 'public opinion' was represented as masculine should not obscure the fact that the intervening public at this juncture was far from exclusively male). However, this address (rep. in the *Examiner* 660, 20 August 1820, p. 543) was a self-conscious transgression of the boundaries between the domestic and the public; and it is only in the context of such an avowed transgression that we find the language of 'middle class' crossing boundaries as well, carried – by women – from the public political realm into their own suddenly politicized domestic experiences (and even then, not in the context of the Queen's cause, but of their own apology). For more detail, see D. Wahrman, ' "Middle-Class" Domesticity Goes Public: Gender,

For another illustration of this restriction of 'middle class' to the masculine/public realm, let us look again at James Mill. His *Essay on Government*, we may recall, written the same year as the trial of Queen Caroline, was an argument in favour of universal male suffrage, tempered by an emphasis on the virtues of the 'middle ranks' whose beneficial influence would keep such a political system under proper control. The combination of Mill's explicit rejection of the enfranchisement of women on the grounds of their dependence, and of his song of praise for the 'intelligent and virtuous' 'middle rank' as a crucial political influence, as well as a pillar of science, arts and legislation, underscored and reinforced his exclusively masculine representation of their virtues and talents. Moreover, writing under the recent impact of Peterloo, Mill also observed that manufacturing districts with 'a very great deficiency of a middle rank' may occasionally be disturbed by 'a mob, more than half composed, in the greater number of instances, of *boys and women*'; implying in this way that the ample presence of a 'middle class' was what was required to safeguard the proper *manly* nature of political behaviour.[22]

Shortly thereafter, in his *Elements of Political Economy*, Mill reiterated that 'the men of middling fortunes' were those 'to whom society is generally indebted for its greatest improvements', and who are consequently the most desirable social group. They 'are the men, who, having their time at their own disposal, freed from the necessity of manual labour, subject to no man's authority, and engaged in the most delightful occupations, obtain, as a class, the greatest sum of human enjoyment'. Not only did Mill speak specifically of 'middle-class' *men*; he also located the vaunted happiness associated with the 'middle class' not in their homes, but in advantages which in his construction were distinctly masculine. The freedom from the necessity of manual labour was a sign of class status among *men*; women's work (hardly 'occupations') was conceptualized in different terms. And regarding the independence from other men's authority, this of course was precisely the position which Mill had denied for women in his *Essay*, therefore dismissing their right to vote. The

Class, and Politics from Queen Caroline to Queen Victoria', *Journal of British Studies* 32 (1993), pp. 408–9.

[22] James Mill, *An Essay on Government*, ed. E. Barker, Cambridge, 1937, pp. 71–3 (my emphasis); and for the explicit exclusion of women, p. 45.

same gendering of the 'middle class's' contribution to society continued:

it is by this class of men that knowledge is cultivated and enlarged; it is also by this class that it is diffused; it is this class of men whose children receive the best education, and are prepared for all the higher and more delicate functions of society, as legislators, judges, administrators, teachers, inventors in all the arts, and superintendents in all the more important works.[23]

For James Mill, then, the 'middle class' was represented by men, male participants in various forms of public life – management of labour, politics, legislation and administration of justice. The virtues of their domestic life were introduced only implicitly, hidden in the reference to the superior education of their (male) children. These observations gain further significance when juxtaposed with Mill's *Analysis of the Phenomena of the Human Mind* (1829). Dealing there with issues of friendship, sentiments and the family, Mill wrote: 'The circumstances of Families, in the two opposite states, of great poverty, and great opulence, are unfavourable to the formation of those associations of which the parental affection consists.'[24] The basic argument of this passage, explaining the advantageous consequences of a middle station, was obviously reminiscent of the previous ones quoted above. Yet in a context which located the singular benefits of this social position not in public or political life but rather in familial happiness and parental affection, Mill had it all reversed: here familial life received his explicit attention, and it was 'middle-class' identity which was introduced only implicitly, hidden – albeit rather thinly veiled – and not mentioned by name.

When James Mill's *Essay on Government* was published in pamphlet form in 1825, one of the most vehement reactions it elicited, provoked by its exclusion of women from political rights, was that published under the name of William Thompson. Thompson

---

[23] *Elements of Political Economy*, 3rd edn, revised and corrected, London, 1826 (1st edn, 1821), in James Mill, *Selected Economic Writings*, ed. D. Winch, Chicago, 1966, pp. 241–2.

[24] J. Mill, *Analysis of the Phenomena of the Human Mind*, London, 1829; new edn, ed. J. S. Mill, London, 1869, vol. II, p. 222. Compare also Mill's very similar discussion of the leisured class above manual labour in the article on education for the supplement of the *Encyclopaedia Britannica*. Although it incorporated yet again his basic insight about the most beneficial structure of society, in the context of education – as in the context of family affections – Mill formulated it without 'middle-class' language: W. H. Burston (ed.), *James Mill on Education*, Cambridge, 1969, pp. 41–119.

was an Irishman of a rich mercantile and landowning family
(one of his books he signed 'One of the Idle Classes'), who
turned socialist and feminist and wrote prolifically in the 1820s,
in particular in favour of cooperative enterprises.[25] His two most
important works were the response to Mill, titled *Appeal of One
Half the Human Race, Women, against the Pretensions of the Other Half,
Men, to Retain them in Political, and Thence in Civil and Domestic
Slavery* (1825), and *An Inquiry into the Principles of the Distribution
of Wealth Most Conducive to Human Happiness*, published the previous
year. In the context of the present argument, a comparison of
the respective images of society which informed both works is
quite telling.

A main goal of Thompson's earlier book, part of the aforementioned wave of popular interest in political economy during the
1820s (though possibly more verbose than other works in this
genre), was to uncover 'the natural laws of distribution [of
property]'. Under such laws excessive poverty and excessive
wealth would disappear, and with them 'the peculiar vices of
luxury and want'.

The vices of the very poor and the vices of the very rich, [continued
Thompson,] mutually productive of each other . . . are the great moral
sources of human misery. The middling class, those who are above
want and not exposed to luxury, are comparatively, and many of them
absolutely, moral, commanding their passions, and endeavouring to
diffuse happiness around them.

Furthermore, whatever caveats could be found for this statement,
they were surely not the fault of this 'middle class':

If the middling classes are not, in most communities, as perfect as the
theory of their situation would make them, the reason is, that they live
in the midst of, and of course exposed to, the contaminating atmosphere
and the touch of the vices of both poor and rich.

Nevertheless, Thompson explained, 'they are justly spoken of as
the class that supplies the materials for whatever of commanding

[25] On William Thompson and his writings see R. K. P. Pankhurst, *William Thompson
(1775–1833): Britain's Pioneer Socialist, Feminist, and Co-operator*, London, 1954. N. W.
Thompson, *The People's Science: The Popular Political Economy of Exploitation and Crisis
1816–1834*, Cambridge, 1984. W. Stafford, *Socialism, Radicalism, and Nostalgia: Social
Criticism in Britain, 1775–1830*, Cambridge, 1987, chapter 11. G. Claeys, *Machinery, Money
and the Millennium: From Moral Economy to Socialism, 1815–1860*, Princeton, 1987, chapter 4.

intellect, attractive virtue, and persevering activity, society can boast'. Indeed, Thompson argued – in a similar vein to Mill's *Essay* as well as many others in the early 1820s – that since the poor lacked knowledge, and the rich lacked sympathy, it would be best to place legislation in the hands of those occupying 'the large intermediate space between the two'.[26] In an ideal society with a befitting distribution of property all would become, in effect, 'middle class'.

But the social vision that Thompson introduced here into discussions of distribution of property and of participation in politics, which hinged upon the 'middle class' and its virtues relevant to these spheres, contrasted sharply with the language of the *Appeal of One Half the Human Race* of the following year. Importantly, this book was not purely his male voice: as Thompson made clear, it represented the joint outcome of his interaction with the feminist Saint-Simonian Anna Wheeler, with whom he had had a close relationship. 'To separate your thoughts from mine', Thompson wrote in the introductory letter addressed to Wheeler, 'were now to me impossible, so amalgamated are they with my own.' In this book, he stated, 'I have endeavoured to arrange the expression of those feelings, sentiments, and reasonings, which have emanated from your mind.'[27]

The concerns of the *Appeal of One Half the Human Race*, commonly seen as the most important feminist tract since Mary Wollstonecraft's *Vindication of the Rights of Woman*, were different from those of Thompson's *Inquiry into the Principles of the Distribution of Wealth*. This book belonged to no similarly well-trodden genre. In the *Appeal* the very definitions of property and politics – the very terms which constituted the common basis of public political debate – were opened to question, in relation to the distribution of power between the sexes. In response to Mill's brief dismissal of women's right to vote on the grounds that their interests were represented by their fathers or husbands, Thompson launched a

---

[26] [William Thompson], *An Inquiry into the Principles of the Distribution of Wealth Most Conducive to Human Happiness* ..., London, 1824, pp. 173, 184, 208–9, 216–17, 259–60.

[27] William Thompson, *Appeal of One Half the Human Race, Women, against the Pretensions of the Other Half, Men, to Retain Them in Political, and Thence in Civil and Domestic Slavery*, [London?], 1825 (rep. edn, London, 1983), pp. [xxi]–xxii. See B. Taylor, *Eve and the New Jerusalem: Socialism and Feminism in the Nineteenth Century*, New York, 1983, pp. 22–4. On the influence of this book see also T. Ball, 'Utilitarianism, Feminism and the Franchise: James Mill and His Critics', *History of Political Thought* 1 (1980), pp. 110–12.

comprehensive onslaught on men's subjugation of women, founded on the exclusion of women from everything intellectual and political. While 'business, professions, political concerns, local affairs, the whole field of sciences and arts, are open to the united and mutually sympathizing efforts of the males', he wrote, women were excluded; and 'by shutting them out from all means of intellectual culture, and from the view of and participation in the real incidents of active life', they were 'confined, like other domestic animals, to the house and its little details'. This deplorable separation of spheres, Thompson emphasized, was certainly not class specific:

While the wife is imprisoned at home (*the wife of the richest as well as of the poorest man in the country*, if he so think fit to direct), counting or swallowing her sorrows, or playing with bird, kitten, needle, or novel, the husband is enjoying abroad the manly pleasures of conviviality.

With incisive acuity Thompson dissected the male construction of the political, a process of which Mill's *Essay* was but one manifestation. He exposed the ways in which notions of 'intelligence' and 'independence' were appropriated and monopolized by men, and enlisted for the oppression of women. Thompson's wrath was directed with particular ferocity at that venerated political idol of late, 'public opinion': far from embodying universal judgment, he pointed out, it was a 'male-created and male-supported public opinion', the 'fruit of the selfish conspiracy of men', and thus 'the public opinion of the oppressors, of the males of the human race in their own favor'.[28]

In its critical exposure of the very assumptions and power relationships underlying the construction of the political, the book of 1825 – encompassing the thoughts of both William Thompson and Anna Wheeler – followed quite different game-rules from Thompson's contribution to political economy of the previous year, which in its questions and modes of argumentation had conformed to the established forms of political writing. This change entailed clear consequences for the respective depictions of society in both works. Whereas in the earlier work the 'middle class' had formed an important constituent of Thompson's understanding of politics and of public life, now

---

[28] Thompson, *Appeal of One Half the Human Race*, pp. 35, 39, 53, 61, 68–9, 77 (my emphasis).

he basically shunned it, just as he now shunned 'public opinion' – which in the *Inquiry* he had still considered as a generally beneficial influence. The 'middle class' was now exposed as part of that political language bolstering the oppressive system which the *Appeal* wished to dismantle. The system of Mill, and others 'of the school of those reformers called political economists', Thompson wrote in the *Appeal*, 'is still founded on exclusions'; 'their little theories' were 'aiming at the utmost at increasing the number of *what they style the happy middling orders*, but leaving the great bulk of human beings to eternal ignorance and toil, requited by the mere means of prolonging from day to day an unhealthy and precarious existence'.[29] The 'middle class', postulated as an observable social fact in his earlier work, now lost its objective, matter-of-factual existence and was exposed as a particular construction of such theorists, as a contested term which served a specific political agenda. And the purported happiness of this 'middle class', which Thompson himself had confidently hailed the previous year, was now found to have been in fact a wilful representation concealing the selfish subjugation of others. When Thompson rejected the demarcation of masculine versus feminine and of public versus private underpinning the construction of politics (including that in his own earlier work), he also rejected the language of 'middle class' which was directly implicated in this masculinization of the political sphere.[30] Ironically, it may be added, in this Thompson and his adversary Mill were much alike: for both, 'middle

---

[29] Ibid., p. xxx (my emphasis).

[30] Indeed, in a context like this which emphasized feminine and familial perspectives, Thompson (ibid., pp. 45–7) actually provided a detailed alternative conceptualization of society, one which was not based on class: it can be described as a schema of concentric circles of human affinity. The most external circle was 'an identity of interest between all human beings of all nations'. Next was 'an identity of interest, less confined and less difficult to ordinary comprehension, between all the members . . . male and female, of the same political community'. The circles of affinity became smaller and tighter: 'There is a still stronger and plainer identity of interest between those of the same province or town, from circumstances increasing in number as the circle lessens, affecting the well-being of each individual within such circle. A still stronger and more palpable identity of interest prevails between the members of the same family', and finally this series of interests converged on 'every *individual* of every family'. Thus Thompson's alternative vision of society was completed: a series of concentric circles converging on the individual – a scheme in which the language of 'middle class' had no place, but which did accommodate both the family as a key social unit and women as independent and equal members of the community.

classness' was a relevant category for masculine agency in politics and in political economy. But both, when they wished to expand agency beyond that which was exclusively male, while exceeding the boundaries of established political writing (as Thompson did truculently in the *Appeal*, and Mill more peacefully in the *Analysis of the Phenomena of the Human Mind*), also chose to sidestep 'middle-class'-based conceptualizations of society.

Finally, nowhere was the dissociation between the language of 'middle class' and the familial domain more clear than in the paeans to the virtues of the 'middle class' that were trumpeted daily in the debates over the Reform Bill itself. It was not because of the domestic, familial, matrimonial and private virtues of the 'middle class' that an extension of the franchise was demanded on their behalf. Instead they were repeatedly put forward as, in the words of the Benthamite MP Charles Buller, 'the possessors of the wealth and intelligence of the country, [and] the natural leaders of the physical force of the community' – all of which represented restrictively male, public attributes.[31] It is also revealing that when Macaulay – a major advocate of votes for the 'middle class' as carrier of political opinion – wrote in summer 1831 about the appreciation of the English people for 'the importance of domestic ties' and 'domestic happiness', and their resulting reactions to moral transgressions, he referred only to reactions displayed either 'by the higher orders' or 'by the lower'. Even now, in the midst of the intense political debates on the nature of the 'middle class' during the agitation for the Reform Bill, Macaulay did not find use for the category of 'middle class' in discussing domestic virtues.[32] It was this con-

---

[31] Charles Buller, *On the Necessity of a Radical Reform*, London, 1831, p. 19.

[32] *Edinburgh Review* 53, June 1831, pp. 547–8. Compare also the 'Country Gentleman' who supported the enfranchisement of the 'middle class' as paragons of intelligence, aptitude for business and competent political judgment – obviously, in this context, masculine traits (see above, p. 319). Earlier in the same pamphlet, however, when he censured the upper classes for 'wasteful extravagance and ostentation in all their *domestic* establishments' and for being 'utterly unacquainted with any of the details of economy that ought to regulate *private life*', the 'Country Gentleman', while pronouncing what historians often perceive as a quintessentially 'middle-class' critique (a fact interesting in its own right), failed to make any reference whatsoever to the 'middle class'. (*Alarming State of the Nation Considered: The Evil Traced to Its Source, and Remedies Pointed out. By a Country Gentleman*, London, 1830, pp. 45–6, 64–5; my emphases.)

sistent dissociation of the 'middle class' and the familial or domestic realm that was about to change, very soon thereafter, quite radically.

Before examining the impending change more closely, however, let us expand the horizons of our survey. The discussion so far has concentrated on writings that formed part of the public political process and conformed to the customary forms of political communication, and that were moreover produced overwhelmingly by men to address predominantly male audiences. Now this literature obviously did not lack opportunities to refer to familial and domestic issues. But nevertheless, issues such as domesticity and familial behaviour cannot be discussed without looking at that very different genre of writing which I have called domestic literature, devoted to these issues, and written in considerable part by women and for women. Overall, the incidence of 'middle-class' language in domestic literature was significantly lower than in political literature, and its pace of change less abrupt. Moreover, the following examples will suggest that before 1832 the uses of a 'middle-class'-based conceptualization of society in this domestic literature were quite different from those in the political one, adding a further dimension to the basic argument about the conditionality of the perceived existence of a 'middle class'. Having a dynamic of its own, the story of the language of 'middle class' in this literature for the most part did not need to and did not conform to the chronology of its evolution within political language, a chronology determined by political events; so that when these two parallel yet independent developments did meet, in the 1830s, their fusion was in itself a significant turn of events.

A good place to start is with one of the most influential writers on domesticity in the early nineteenth century, Hannah More. Born into the gentry (a fact in itself not uninteresting, considering the purported quintessential 'middle classness' of such a worldview), More became a major Evangelical writer of religious, moral and political works. In her *Strictures on the Modern System of Female Education* of 1799, even as she was exhorting women to support the country through the turbulent crises of the 1790s, she still admonished against any involvement of women in warfare or politics.[33] She saw her writing as operating, indeed, within a very separate sphere: addressing women – primarily upper-class women – with regard to their domestic duties and domestic behaviour. And within such a context, in a realm of discussion that had little overlap with most sources we have seen so far, the behaviour of the 'middle class' – of the *women* of the 'middle class' – was indeed an explicit topic of discussion.

Criticizing upper-class women's education for its exclusive emphasis on rendering them 'accomplished', More wrote: 'This frenzy of accomplishments, unhappily, is no longer restricted within the usual limits of rank and fortune; the middle orders have caught the contagion, and it rages downward with increasing and destructive violence.' Consequently, she warned,

this very valuable part of society is declining in usefulness . . . till this rapid revolution of the manners of the middle class has so far altered the character of the age, as to be in danger of rendering obsolete the heretofore common saying, 'that most worth and virtue are to be found in the middle station.'

More conceived of the 'middle class' as a key rung in the social ladder through which vices trickled down from the apex of society to its base: vices, not virtues. In prescriptive terms she was not unaware of the praises attributed to 'the middle station'. But what she saw around her was precisely the reverse: 'this class of females', she observed in even stronger words, 'in what relates both to religious knowledge and to practical industry, falls short both of the very high and the very low'.[34] For More the 'middle class' was relevant to domestic issues – in fact, its only distinct incarnation was 'middle-class' women; and far from being the epitome of worth, they were in danger of arriving last in the parade of the virtuous.

[33] Hannah More, *Strictures on the Modern System of Female Education: With a View of the Principles and Conduct Prevalent among Women of Rank and Fortune* (originally 1799); in *The Works of Hannah More*, 7 vols., New York, 1835, vol. VI, p. 13.

[34] Ibid., pp. 38–9. This vision of immorality trickling down from upper-class to 'middle-class' women was shared, on the other side of the political spectrum, by the rational Dissenter Mary Hays, in her (anonymous) *Appeal to the Men of Great Britain in Behalf of Women*, London, 1798, p. 81. And compare also the conservative Laetitia Matilda Hawkins, in her (likewise anonymous) *Letters on the Female Mind, Its Powers and Pursuits . . .*, London, 1793, pp. 65–6; 'What is called the middle station of life' – a station to which she claimed to belong (p. 4) – 'is, undoubtedly, the most conducive to comfort; but I doubt whether, in the scale of merit, those who compose it stand as high as the lower classes of the community.'

From More's vision of the 'middle class' we can move to that of another woman of similar Evangelical opinions, the novelist and moralist Jane West. In the early 1800s West wrote two multi-volume works of moral and religious advice, one addressed to young men, the other to young women. Both, she explained in their introductions, were intended to rectify the deficiency of existing moralistic literature, in which 'the *extremes* of society were chiefly attended to', but in which, as a consequence, 'that numerous and important body the middle classes of society, whose duties are more complicated, and consequently most difficult, [was] being generally overlooked'.[35] Like More, for this proponent of Evangelicalism and domesticity a major concern was 'the levity and dissipation of the middle ranks [which] are the singular and alarming characteristics of the present times'. This, she explained, was a recent development:

the middle classes, where temperance, diligence, and propriety used to reside, the favourite abode of rectitude, good sense, and sound piety, have undergone a change within the last fifty years which must startle every considerate mind; so far as it relates to women ... it presents a topic demanding our close attention.

Elsewhere West noted nostalgically the older ways of the 'middle class', which in previous times had been noted for its 'political importance ... general information, sound sense, and unsophisticated manners'; and no less for 'the blameless occupations, domestic tenderness, modesty, simplicity, and unaffected gentleness, that distinguished their wedded partners' – that is, the 'middle-class' women. In particular, until recently the 'middle ranks of society' had been 'most regular in the observance of religious duties'; though she expressed 'a fear, that the distinction which was so honorable to the middle ranks of life will soon disappear'.[36] For West, too, the prescriptive ideal of 'middle-class' virtues included explicitly both public political virtues (for men) and private domestic ones (for both men and women); and for her,

[35] Mrs [Jane] West, *Letters to a Young Lady, in Which the Duties and Character of Women are Considered, Chiefly with a Reference to Prevailing Opinions*, 3 vols., London, 1806, vol. I, p. vii; and *Letters Addressed to a Young Man, on His First Entrance into Life, and Adapted to the Peculiar Circumstances of the Present Times*, 3 vols., Charlestown, 1803 (originally London, 1801), vol. I, p. viii.
[36] West, *Letters to a Young Lady*, vol. I, pp. 138–41, 193–4. See also her *Letters Addressed to a Young Man*, vol. I, pp. 73–4.

too, this ideal was in imminent danger of irreversible corruption.

Indeed, despite Jane West's charge about the oversight of other moralists, such concerns were becoming clichés of this genre of Evangelical writing. The moral dangers of the present times, wrote the domestic ideologue Ann Martin Taylor, were 'peculiarly injurious to those [women] of the middle ranks', who she therefore singled out as the targets of her domestic advice. 'To young people in the middle classes of society,' echoed her daughter Jane Taylor, 'the acquirements called accomplishments, are generally worse than useless.'[37] The natural modesty of the female sex, asserted the theologian and moralist George Walker, might be looked for 'in the higher and lower classes, who, from very opposite causes, are rendered equally independent and free'; but it was 'the dames of middle rank' – in this context, suddenly discovered to be the *least* independent and free – that were most 'reluctant ... to quit the fashionable manners'. And there was of course the most prominent Evangelical of all, William Wilberforce, who prefigured the same argument a few years earlier in an examination of religious principles among 'the higher and middle classes': 'the middling classes are daily growing in wealth and consequence', Wilberforce observed; but 'with the comforts and refinements, the vices also of the higher orders are continually descending', thus 'diffusing throughout the middle ranks those relaxed morals and dissipated manners, which were formerly confined to the higher classes of society'.[38] Arthur Young agreed with Wilberforce on this point;

---

[37] [Ann Martin] Taylor, *Practical Hints to Young Females, on the Duties of a Wife, a Mother and a Mistress of a Family*, 3rd edn, London, 1815 (same year as 1st edn), pp. [iii]–v, 2–3. Jane Taylor, *The Contributions of Q. Q. to a Periodical Work: With Some Pieces Never before Published*, from 5th London edn, Boston, 1831 (consisting of contributions to the *Youth's Magazine* between 1816 and 1822), vol. I, p. 192 (also 233). Compare also [John Corry], *A Satirical View of London at the Commencement of the Nineteenth Century, by an Observer*, London, 1801, p. 106. On the Taylors see Davidoff and Hall, *Family Fortunes*, pp. 172–7 and passim.

[38] George Walker, *Essays on Various Subjects ... to Which is Prefixed a Life of the Author*, 2 vols., London, 1809, vol. II, p. 249. William Wilberforce, *A Practical View of the Prevailing Religious System of Professed Christians, in the Higher and Middle Classes in This Country, Contrasted with Real Christianity*, 5th edn, London, 1797 (same year as 1st edn), pp. 237, 240; see also pp. 111–12. Contrast these words with those that Wilberforce employed in parliament, in a *political* context, in which the 'middle class' turned out to be once again the familiar well-informed and responsible carriers of 'public opinion', and, of course, men: *Parliamentary History of England* 36, col. 996 (speech of 24 November 1802).

and Thomas Gisborne expressed similar concerns in another work that also discussed specifically 'the higher and middle classes'.[39]

To sum up, then, in domestic literature before 1832 the understanding of 'middle class' – with regard to its gender, and to its relationship to the familial or domestic sphere – appears to have been rather different from that in political language. Whereas in pre-1832 political language the 'middle class' was dissociated from the domestic or the familial sphere and confined to the masculine public realm, this coupling did appear in the domestic literature; and whereas the politically invoked 'middle class' was so often portrayed as the repository of moral *virtue*, in the Evangelical-influenced discussions of familial and domestic issues they were mostly represented as peculiarly prone to moral *corruption*. (Of course, these two genres of writing, while very different, were not hermetically sealed from each other; and the distance between them makes the crossing of boundaries and points of contact all the more interesting. However their discussion would take us too far afield.[40]) That the domestic literature, albeit in its own slow-paced and low-keyed way, differed in its uses of 'middle-class' language from the political one should not surprise us; after all, there was nothing essential about the *presence* of a link between the familial/feminine domain and the 'middle class' in this genre of domestic writing, any more than there was something essential about the *absence* of such a link in pre-1832 political writing. Just as we have seen representations of society within political language differentiated along political partisan lines, so could social language also be differentiated between different genres of writing engaging in different debates. In neither case, of course, was any side of

[39] Arthur Young, *An Enquiry into the State of the Public Mind amongst the Lower Classes: And on the Means of Turning It to the Welfare of the State. In a Letter to William Wilberforce, Esq. MP*, London, 1798, p. 33. Thomas Gisborne, *An Enquiry into the Duties of Men in the Higher and Middle Classes of Society in Great Britain, Resulting from Their Respective Stations, Professions and Employments*, London, 1794. Gisborne was particularly concerned with the potential immorality inherent in the mercantile world, devoting to it considerably more attention than to the moral risks of any other occupation.

[40] A case in point, for instance, is Mary Wollstonecraft, whose writing – which defiantly transgressed the boundaries of these debates – included seemingly inconsistent statements about 'middle classness' as a state that could or could not be attained by women. For this and other examples, see Wahrman, ' "Middle-Class" Domesticity Goes Public'.

the argument, as it were, more faithful to social reality than
the other: once again, they were all part of the range of diverging
constructions possible in that space between social experience
and its representation. But having seen these divergent representations in the decades preceding the Reform Act, it is time to
examine how they transformed and converged in its aftermath,
thus propelling forward that particular construction of 'middle-
class domesticity' (or 'middle-class values') which has coloured
so much of the thinking about the 'middle class' ever since.

'MIDDLE-CLASS' DOMESTICITY GOES PUBLIC

Whereas 'middle-class' domesticity played little part in leading
up to the Reform Act, the expansion of 'middle-class' virtues to
encompass domestic life was one of its important consequences
in both political *and* domestic writing. To begin with the former,
this abrupt transformation has already been attested to by the
two passages of Edward Bulwer-Lytton that opened this chapter,
in which a primacy of gender distinctions between public and
private in 1831 was overshadowed in 1833 by the category 'middle
class' engulfing both public and private.

Another suggestive contrast may be made between two analogous statements of father and son in Leeds, Edward Baines
Sr – the Dissenting liberal tradesman, printer and editor from
1801 of the *Leeds Mercury* – and Edward Baines Jr, who in the
1820s succeeded his father at the *Mercury* and later became known
as the chronicler of the cotton manufactures. 'Never, in any
country beneath the sun,' declared Baines the elder in 1820, 'was
an order of men more estimable and valuable, more praised and
praiseworthy, than the middle class of society in England'; their
moral character manifest itself in 'their truly loyal and constitutional principles, their extensive information, and their correct
knowledge of the interests of trade.'[41] But when his son closely
echoed this tribute twenty years later, his precise words also
registered significant changes:

we do not believe there is in the world a community so virtuous, so
religious and so sober minded as the middle classes of England ...
few do not regularly attend a place of public worship ... for a safe,

---

[41] *Leeds Mercury* 53:2847, 1 January 1820, editorial.

intelligent and independent constituency, the substance and staple must be found in the middle class.[42]

For Baines Jr, a decade after the Reform Act, the 'middle class' was no longer 'an order of men' but 'a community'. And while he stressed its virtues, ultimately, in order to buttress its claim – that is, its men's claim – for the franchise, he now began the enumeration of these virtues with an emphasis on its (familial) religious behaviour and on its sobriety, only then leading to what previously had been the core of the 'middle class's' claim to fame – intelligence and independence.

It is edifying to follow Baines the younger for another decade, to his publication of his father's biography. Reminiscent of the way that Wilberforce's sons rewrote their father's life, Baines Jr began the reconstruction of his own father's life precisely with what he perceived to have been an essential link between the latter's 'middle classness' and purported 'middle-class values', a link which his father himself might not have found as natural and inevitable. Biographies of statesmen, warriors and men of genius (that is, of exclusively public men), Baines Jr suggested in the preamble to the book, were of limited 'practical usefulness' for the 'middle class'. Instead, a biography of a man like his father – a different kind of man – 'may be held up as a model to our active and intelligent middle classes'. (Arguably, it may be noted, the purview of 'intelligence' had by now itself been expanded beyond a concentration on the political.) He went on to present Baines Sr – posthumously – as the paragon of (mid Victorian) 'middle-class values', both public *and* private: his father, he wrote, had been an 'example of energy, prudence, and integrity in business, of earnest patriotism in a political career, of benevolent zeal for all social improvement, of the qualities that adorn society and sweeten domestic life'.[43]

Another father-and-son contrast can be gleaned from the writings of the two Mills, James and John Stuart. The father, we have seen, used the language of 'middle class' for men in political

---

[42] Edward Baines, *Household Suffrage and Equal Electoral Districts ... Letters to Hamar Stansfield, Esq.*, Leeds, 1841; quoted in R. J. Morris, *Class, Sect and Party: The Making of the British Middle Class, Leeds 1820–1850*, Manchester, 1990, p. 10.

[43] Edward Baines [Jr], *The Life of Edward Baines, Late MP for the Borough of Leeds*, London, 1851, p. [5]. See also D. Fraser, 'Edward Baines', in P. Hollis (ed.), *Pressure from Without in Early Victorian England*, London, 1974, p. 184.

settings, but did not use it in the context of familial settings and parental affection. Compare the following passage by his son, John Stuart Mill, four years after the Reform Act: 'The virtues of a middle class are those which conduce to getting rich – integrity, economy, and enterprise – along with family affections, inoffensive conduct between man and man, and a disposition to assist one another, whenever no commercial rivalry intervenes.'[44] The virtues of the 'middle class' for Mill the younger were manifested in the life it led, not in its political behaviour. The masculine attributes here had less to do with politics and more with business. And, in contrast with his father, John Stuart Mill also directly linked 'middle classness' to 'family affections'.

Many other such voices, introducing the category of 'middle class' into discussions of familial, domestic and feminine life after 1832, can readily be adduced. Thus, in Thomas Rowe Edmonds's optimistic scenario for a 'middle-class'-led resolution of England's social problems, published in 1832, it was imperative to teach the labouring classes 'the same habit of restraint in marriage as is practised in the middle classes of society', as well as 'their own prudence and increased frugality'; indeed, the whole purpose of social legislation was 'to assimilate the habits of the poor to those of the middle classes'.[45] And when William Empson referred in 1833 to 'that fortunate and happy middle class, which is the most favourable position for the virtues', he meant not their previously acclaimed political virtues, but instead, as he explicated further, a particular praise (prefiguring John Stuart Mill's language) 'especially for the most delightful part of them, – family affection'. The same year also saw Edward Gibbon Wakefield produce a 'faithful sketch from domestic life among the English middle class', referring – like Edmonds – specifically to the Malthusian virtues of their marital relationships: 'Among the middle class, among all classes except the highest and the lowest, "moral restraint" is a confirmed habit.' Foreshadowing later criticisms of Victorian 'middle-class' hypocrisy, Wakefield also

[44] John Stuart Mill in the *London Review* 2, January 1836; rep. in his *Essays on Politics and Society*, in *Collected Works*, vol. xviii, Toronto, 1977, p. 101.

[45] [Thomas Rowe Edmonds], *An Enquiry into the Principles of Population* . . ., London, 1832, pp. 49–50, 125, and passim. Compare also the antithetical juxtaposition of lower-class and 'middle-class' domestic behaviour and manners in Peter Gaskell, *Artisans and Machinery: The Moral and Physical Condition of the Manufacturing Population* . . ., London, 1836.

pointed out that this was 'the cause of that exuberant prostitution' in England; and that 'another effect of "moral restraint" among the middle class is, that a great proportion of the females in that class are doomed to celibacy'.[46] Or take Henry Brougham: before the Reform Bill, Brougham repeatedly noted the 'middle class' for what he described in one essay of 1829 as its 'plain [political] good sense, *manly* sentiment, and virtuous conduct'. By contrast, moreover, the same essay continued with an analogy between the assailed virtues of the aristocracy and the assailed virtues of *women*. But whereas in 1829 Brougham had thus associated the aristocracy with femininity and the 'middle class' with masculinity, by 1835 – writing under the guise of Isaac Tomkins – he consciously paid as much attention to the social prospects of 'middle-class' women, *vis à vis* the aristocracy, as he did to those of 'middle-class' men.[47]

Of course, the expansion of the language of 'middle class' into the prescriptive depictions of the familial sphere dictated certain virtues for both men and women, complementing each other according to their assigned roles. The vision of the happy hearth and home shaped not only women's lives, but also imposed requirements on men both at home and at work, where they were expected to provide their families with a secure living. In the words of Sonya Rose, male breadwinning and female domesticity were 'twin ideals'.[48] Consequently, as we have seen in John Stuart Mill's enumeration of the qualities of the 'middle class', the focus of the prescriptions for 'middle-class' men's *public* virtues expanded, to include not only the political arena but also the workplace and the marketplace. Thus Archibald Alison wondered

---

[46] *Edinburgh Review* 57, July 1833, p. 479. Edward Gibbon Wakefield, *England and America: A Comparison of the Social and Political State of Both Nations*, New York, 1834 (originally 2 vols., London, 1833), p. 73. The Malthusian marriage habits of the 'middle class' were likewise noted in Archibald Alison, *The Principles of Population, and Their Connection with Human Happiness*, 2 vols., Edinburgh, 1840, vol. I, pp. 111–15. Indeed they were also noted in Robert Southey's *Sir Thomas More: Or, Colloquies on the Progress and Prospects of Society*, 2 vols., London, 1829: at that earlier stage, however, Southey pointed to these late-marriage habits of the 'middle class' as having *deleterious* effects on morals and, most ironically in view of future clichés, as *undermining* women's attainment of 'domestic happiness' (pp. 141, 295–6).

[47] *Edinburgh Review* 49, March 1829, pp. 49–50 (my emphasis). Isaac Tomkins (that is Henry Brougham), *Thoughts upon the Aristocracy of England*, 5th edn, London, 1835: esp. the symmetrical discussion of the 'middle-class' brother-and-sister in pp. 9–12.

[48] Rose, *Limited Livelihoods*, p. 145 and passim. See also Seccombe, 'Patriarchy Stabilized'.

in the *Blackwood's Edinburgh Magazine* in 1839 'how is it that the middle classes so generally enjoy competence and comfort'; to which he replied, 'simply because they practise order, regularity, and economy in their dwellings; because they put a bridle on their licentious appetites; because they restrain present desire, from a sense of future benefit; because they sacrifice sensual and selfish gratification on the altar of domestic duty.' If only 'the working-classes would acquire such habits' (whose manifestations would include, for instance, such prudent measures as life insurances and saving banks), Alison suggested wishfully, all political problems would cease. And again: 'there unquestionably exists among the middle classes more prudence, foresight, and economy; more patient industry and unobtrusive virtue; more strenuous exertion, and heroic self-denial, than in any other class in the community'. Robert Peel likewise praised the 'middle class' in 1835 for the 'qualities of diligence, of the love of order, of industry, of integrity in commercial dealings'.[49] The invention of 'middle-class values' had been completed: representations of 'middle-class' domestic behaviour were now inextricably intertwined with representations of their public behaviour. And insofar as the latter was concerned, the emphasis in discussing 'middle-class' men and manliness was no longer only on their manly intelligence and independence in support of public political causes, but also on their (no less) manly sobriety and industriousness in support of their dependent families.[50]

So much for the transformations induced by the Reform Act in the discussion of such issues within political language; but what were its consequences for what we have called domestic literature, if any? Consider the following assertions: 'It is, therefore, to the

[49] *Blackwood's Edinburgh Magazine* 46, September 1839, pp. 295, 300. Robert Peel, *Speech of Sir Robert Peel, Bart. Delivered at Merchant Tailors' Hall, 11th May, 1835*, 8th edn, London, 1835, p. 9. For another example that year, see *Three Letters to the People. By One of the Middling Classes*, London, [1835], pp. 125–6.

[50] Of course, the argument is not that such assertions of 'middle-class values' were new and unprecedented. Obviously they could be found before, as when John Wilkes's mother had already tried many decades earlier to dissuade her son from a compromising liaison by arguing that 'the Midling Class of People (thank Heaven) revere Virtue, and see Vice countenanced by a Magistrate with *double* abhorrence' (Sarah Wilkes to John Wilkes, 23 October 1771; Clements Library, Wilkes Mss. I am grateful to John Sainsbury for this reference). Once again, what is significant here is not the novelty of the idea, but the novelty in the resonance and scope of its uses.

middle class almost exclusively that we must look for good society'; 'In these days, the middle class is more enlarged and powerful.' Written in 1836, these pronouncements were hardly unusual. Only that in this case they were not part of a political, historical or sociological treatise; theirs was a less likely venue, which bore the title *Exercises for Ladies: Calculated to Preserve and Improve Beauty.*[51] 'In this class,' the author explained further, 'society is often full of charm ... the wish to please inspires those affectionate manners, those obliging expressions, and those sustained attentions, which alone render social unions pleasant and desirable.' Nor was this fusion of political, social and sentimental appraisal of the 'middle class', in such a context, unique. Indeed it now quickly became staple in such writings too, celebrating 'middle-class' life – private and public – in ever-strengthening terms.

Take for example Mrs Sarah Stickney Ellis, who has been described as 'probably the best known ideologue of domesticity'. In her *Women of England* of 1839 Ellis explained that the national character of English women cannot be gleaned from aristocratic women, who are too influenced by foreign manners, nor from lower-class women, whose predicaments homogenize their needs and experiences with lower-class women of other nations. Rather, its repository is the 'middle class', a category whose striking profusion throughout Ellis's book was itself a sign of the times, unprecedented in similar works. 'The middle class', she asserted, 'must include so vast a portion of the intelligence and moral power of the country at large, that it may not improperly be designated the pillar of our nation's strength.'[52] And now that 'middle-class' men received their due, in terms so familiar, she could turn her attention to the women: 'in the situation of the middle class of women in England', Mrs Ellis wrote, 'are combined advantages in the formation of character, to which they owe much of their distinction, and their country much of her

---

[51] Donald Walker, *Exercises for Ladies: Calculated to Preserve and Improve Beauty, and to Prevent and Correct Personal Defects, Inseparable from Constraining or Careless Habits: Founded on Physiological Principles*, London, 1836, p. 186.

[52] Mrs [Sarah Stickney] Ellis, *The Women of England, Their Social Duties, and Domestic Habits*, 6th edn, London, n.d. (1850?; 1st edn, 1839), pp. 13–14. Davidoff and Hall, *Family Fortunes*, pp. 182–5; it is hardly a coincidence that Ellis's is the only contemporary discussion of the 'middle class' which Davidoff and Hall chose to quote throughout their book.

moral worth'. 'Middle-class' women were characterized by 'the highest tone of moral feeling', as well as by devotion to 'domestic duties'. The latter 'is an appropriate sphere for women to move in, from which those of the middle class in England seldom deviate very widely'. And even better, Mrs Ellis asserted further,

> Amongst families in the middle class of society in this country, those who live without regard to religion are exceptions to the general rule; while the great proportion of individuals thus circumstanced ... are materially affected in their lives and conduct by the operation of christian principles upon their own minds.[53]

So here we have it, the whole construction of the famous 'middle-class values', focused on domesticity and religion; and presented as confident matter-of-factual observations. Gone were the doubts and apprehensions which repeatedly plagued the earlier Evangelical writings on this 'middle class' and its proclivity for moral degeneracy. Indeed quite the contrary: as another woman writing about women the following year asserted at some length, the 'middle class' (she now believed) was *less* susceptible to corruption than either the higher or the lower orders, being led by its peculiar employments to superior morality and judgment in business and in private life, as well as in politics. Indeed her discussion of 'middle-class' men became indistinguishable from that of the encomiastic male political writers: 'we hear commonly of the passions of the multitude, of the vices and follies of the aristocracy, but of the *opinions* of the middle class, and these are really what sways them the most.'[54] Virtually the words of Edward Bulwer-Lytton.

---

[53] Ellis, *The Women of England*, pp. 21, 28, 36–7, 72–3; and passim. Ellis also used the term 'middle rank': see p. 213. Compare also her relentless panegyrics to the 'middle class' for their intelligence, influence and heritage of liberty, as well as for their 'fire-side pleasures' and 'domestic joy', in her *The Wives of England, Their Relative Duties, Domestic Influence, and Social Obligations*, New York (also London), 1843, pp. 156–7, 161–2. As with other aspects of the representation of the 'middle class' in the 1830s, it may be added, the Edinburgh reviewers had already prefigured some of these developments in the mid-1820s: see *Edinburgh Review* 41, January 1825, pp. 309–11 (Jeffrey); 44, September 1826, p. 440 (Mackintosh).

[54] *Woman's Rights and Duties Considered with Relation to Their Influence on Society and on Her Own Condition. By a Woman*, 2 vols., London, 1840, vol. II, pp. 59, 106–7, 131–3. See also William Cobbett's *Advice to Young Men, and (Incidentally) to Young Women, in the Middle and Higher Ranks of Life*, London, 1829: in this domestic manual addressed 'to persons in the middle ranks of life', Cobbett asserted that 'a *knowledge of domestic affairs* is so necessary in every wife', whereas *men's* happiness 'is to be found only in *independence*' (rep. edn, Oxford, 1906, pp. 10, 114).

Within a short while the status of this 'middle-class' domesticity as objective, observable, incontestable fact rapidly came to be taken for granted, and consequently formed a natural point of departure for those seeking change. 'The majority of the middle classes', summed it up a daughter of a Glasgow merchant writing against the separation of spheres in 1843, 'think that woman's duties are comprised in good humour and attention to her husband, keeping her children neat and clean, and attending to domestic arrangements.' And a decade later, a powerful critique of the domestic confinement of women pinned the evil in its very first sentence on 'some of the middle ranks'. Continuing in a similar vein for more than four hundred pages, it condemned those domestic habits that were 'characteristic of the lot that falls to women in the middle ranks', as distinct from those of the upper and lower classes; assertions that were joined with no less confident pronouncements of the 'middle class' as having been 'the latest formed in the social framework' and having acquired recently 'the greatest political weight'. By now, it was obvious, alongside the rising 'middle-class' historical narrative, the perception of a rigid gendered separation of spheres as a peculiar 'middle-class domesticity' had also become a universal commonplace.[55]

In her *Gender and the Politics of History*, Joan Scott has stated that 'the concept of class in the nineteenth century relied on gender for its articulation'.[56] Of course, one can no less plausibly add that the construction of gender differentiations likewise relied on class for its articulation. But, as this chapter has suggested, there was more than one way in which these axes of representation could in fact rely upon each other at different historical moments.

---

[55] Marion Reid, *A Plea for Woman*, Edinburgh, 1843; rep. edn, Edinburgh, 1988, p. 11 (modern pagination). John Luguid Milne, *Industrial Employment of Women in the Middle and Lower Ranks*, rev. edn, London, 1870 (originally London, 1857), pp. 1–2, 20–4, 139. Milne's argument, about 'that curse of modern middle-class existence' that made women their victim, was picked up and elaborated the following year in *The English Woman's Journal* 1, June 1858, pp. 222–5. Interestingly, it was Harriet Martineau (in her *Household Education*, London, 1849) who once again saw through the contingency of this construction and expressed doubts about its actual veracity: in her view, the delayed marriages 'among the middle classes of our country' at present worked *against* the confinement of women to domestic caretaking, that formerly (but no longer) had been the destiny of every woman (Boston edn, 1880, p. 275).

[56] J. Scott, 'Gender: A Useful Category of Historical Analysis', in her *Gender and the Politics of History*, New York, 1988, p. 48.

During most of the period discussed in this book, the political construction of 'middle classness' was apparently subsumed under and contained by the boundaries imposed upon the world by the articulation of a particular gendered differentiation of 'public' and 'private', 'masculine' and 'feminine'. After 1832, by contrast, the conceptual hierarchy was reversed: now 'middle classness' came to be identified with the very principle of this gendered differentiation, and thus to precede it. Ironically, it took a major political event to liberate the vision of a beneficial 'middle class' from its confinement to the masculine public/political realm, elevating it to the point that 'middle-class' identity came to encompass both 'public' and 'private', 'masculinity' and 'femininity'. And it was then that the political invocations of the 'middle class' converged with what might be called for symmetry its domestic invocation, a much less loaded construction that previously had been quite distinct from that in politics.

In sum, the expansion of the jurisdiction of 'middle class' in political language to include the private and the feminine as well as the public and the masculine; the infusion of the rising 'middle-class' progress narrative into domestic literature; and the consequent bridging of the distance between the uses of 'middle class' in these very disparate genres of writing – these were all new beginnings of the 1830s, which represented distinct breaks with the practices of the earlier decades. Taken together, they attest once again to the powerful effects of the developments of that particular moment – developments which unfolded in the political arena – in inscribing the category of 'middle class' so broadly onto the most fundamental ways in which social experiences were organized and constructed. These observations caution us once again as to the very specific historical origins of notions that have been bequeathed to us as naturalized and universal. Like the careful scepticism that should accompany 'middle class' as a straightforward sociological concept or historical narrative, so the picture of the 'middle class' as the epitome of hearth and home should be viewed not as a straightforward snapshot of essential social practice, but rather as a charged and contingent historical invention. We should not accept 'middle-class values' uncritically as objectively and essentially 'middle class', any more than we accept them uncritically as objective and essential 'values'.

Epilogue

What ever happened later? It should be clear that although the 1830s represent a moment of closure for the story told here, a moment when a powerful consensus had left relatively little room for contention in the space between social reality and its possible representations, this was not a situation the dynamics and meaning of which necessarily remained stable over longer stretches of time. 'The rise of the middle class' narrative implied that the 'middle class' was there to stay; the heyday of the category of 'middle class' as key to social conceptualization was by its very nature less immutable.

At first, indeed, the language of 'middle class' might have seemed to go from strength to strength. Thus, it became centrally implicated in the major political conflict of the following decade – the agitation for the repeal of the corn laws, which finally succeeded in 1846. Following decades in which the issue of the corn laws had been discussed in specific sectional terms that were well suited for the very specific interests involved, the final crescendo of anti-corn law agitation in the early 1840s saw the introduction of the language of 'middle class' with increasing effectiveness: Richard Cobden used it in 1841, John Bright in 1842, Joseph Parkes in 1843.[1] It was Cobden's oft-cited judgment

---

[1] See quotes in N. McCord, *The Anti-Corn Law League 1838–1846*, 2nd edn., London, 1968, pp. 115, 117, 127, 136. The earliest instance of direct anti-corn law 'middle-class' language of which I am aware was R[obert] Torrens, *Three Letters to the Marquis of Chandos, on the Effects of the Corn Laws*, London, 1839, p. 30. In some cases, the identification of the repealers as 'middle class' might have been prompted by their *opponents*: the only 'middle-class' language in the 365 questions and answers included in T. Perronet Thompson's *Corn-Law Fallacies, with the Answers (Reprinted from The Sun Newspaper)*, London, 1839, for example, were three hostile citations from the *Conservative Journal and Church of England Gazette* of late 1838, demanding to know whether the repeal of the corn laws, while harming the proprietors of land, would be 'of any advantage to the middle classes of society' (pp. 22, 29). Likewise, the Chartist *London*

that the Anti-Corn Law League had been 'a middle-class set of agitators' who had operated 'by those means by which the middle class usually carries on its movements'. The government was now executed 'through the *bonâ fide* representatives of the middle class', Cobden told Peel; 'The Reform Bill decreed it; the passing of the Corn Bill has realized it.'[2]

But then, rather suddenly, the language of 'middle class' appears to have receded far into the background of British politics. In part, this might have been brought about by the very success of the campaign against the corn laws, which catalysed the identification of the 'middle class' with the manufacturing interest, that is to say with the industrialists. Together with (what was left of) its inclusive vagueness, the language of 'middle class' lost perhaps some of its appeal and political potential. But be that as it may, it seems true, as Gareth Stedman Jones notes, that references to, let alone celebrations of, the 'middle class' faded out from some point in the 1840s onwards. 'Middle-class idiom' did not become the hallmark of a new industrializing society nor of an ascendant liberalism. A change had occurred, which is nicely suggested by Macaulay's *History of England* (1848–59): unlike his own speeches and writings of the 1820s and 1830s, Macaulay now assigned the 'middle class' no significant role in his historical narrative, not even in such contexts as parliamentary reform, the growth of towns, and financial and commercial crises.[3]

It is hard to assess the meaning of such changes without more

---

Democrat of 13 April 1839 identified the repeal as a 'middle-class' cause: cited in McCord, *The Anti-Corn Law League*, p. 56.

[2] J. Morley, *The Life of Richard Cobden*, London, 1881, vol. I, pp. 249, 395; quoted in A. Briggs, 'Middle-Class Consciousness in English Politics, 1780–1846', *Past and Present* 9 (1956), pp. 65, 71. Briggs finds in these quotes support for his own story of the emergence of 'middle-class consciousness', which in its basic lines is hardly distinguishable from Cobden's. Other historians, however, have doubted whether the repeal of the corn laws was indeed a triumph of a 'middle class': see G. Kitson Clark, 'The Repeal of the Corn Laws and the Politics of the Forties', *Economic History Review* 2nd ser., 4 (1951) pp. 1–13, arguing that it was more an aristocratic change of heart than a 'middle-class' triumph; also W. O. Aydelotte, 'The Country Gentleman and the Repeal of the Corn Laws', *English Historical Review* 82 (1967), pp. 47–60.

[3] Thomas Babington Macaulay, *The History of England from the Accession of James the Second*, ed. C. H. Firth, London, 1914, vol. I, pp. 323ff.; vol. v, pp. 2287–92; vol. vi, chapter 22. G. Stedman Jones, 'The Rise and Fall of "Class Struggle": "Middle Class" and "Bourgeoisie", 1789–1850', in his projected *Visions of Prometheus*. I am grateful to Professor Stedman Jones for allowing me to cite his forthcoming chapter.

detailed knowledge of the stakes involved in differing conceptualizations of society at this juncture – stakes that by now might
well have been rather different from those during the period
discussed in this book. Indeed, by the debates on the second
Reform Bill in the second half of the 1860s, when the language
of 'middle class', unsurprisingly, picked up again, many key
speakers – take for instance Gladstone, Bagehot or Matthew
Arnold – were quick to repudiate publicly any 'middle-class
idiom'.[4] The political circumstances, alliances and agendas were
different; people's perceptions of social reality were different; and
the implications and consequences of different ways of conceptualizing society, as they had been negotiated and contested in
the decades following the 1830s, were different. But whatever
picture will emerge in future studies for the uses of 'middle class'
and other social categories during the high Victorian era and
subsequently, it is already clear that the story of the language
of 'middle class' once again defies the urge to understand it as
some form of linear progression, inexorably riding forth on the
crest of social change.

But whereas the legacy of the climactic 1830s for the future
political uses of 'middle-class' language was uncertain, the legacy
of these years for the future historical uses of the 'middle-class'
narrative was ultimately less so. A key vehicle here was of course
the writings of Karl Marx and Friedrich Engels. Their conceptual
framework, derived – as Stedman Jones points out – primarily
from recent developments in conceptualizing society and politics
in France, did not seem incongruous in the British linguistic (if
not necessarily the political) context as well, once they had
crossed the Channel. Thus Engels asserted upon his first visit to

---

[4] When Gladstone announced to parliament his conversion to the cause of further reform
in 1864, he said: 'I, for one, cannot admit that there is that special virtue in the
nature of the middle class which ought to lead to our drawing a marked distinction
. . . between them and a select portion of the working classes'; quoted in P. Stansky,
Gladstone: A Progress in Politics, New York, 1979, p. 100. Walter Bagehot (*The English
Constitution*, ed. R. H. S. Crossman, Ithaca, 1963, p. 247) affirmed in 1867 that 'the
middle classes . . . are in the present day the despotic power in England'. And as for
Matthew Arnold, his famous denunciations of the 'middle class' as vulgar and philistine,
and of their 'incomparable self-satisfaction' (*Culture and Anarchy*, London, 1869, pp.
75–81 and passim), apparently first appeared with extraordinary force in his essay of
1866 'My Countrymen': R. H. Super (ed.), *Matthew Arnold: Culture and Anarchy with
Friendship's Garland and Some Literary Essays*, Ann Arbor, 1980, pp. 3–31.

England in 1844 that 'to the extent that the influence of the actual middle class [in England] is on the whole much greater than that of the aristocracy, to that extent the middle class does indeed rule'; and Marx, when he arrived in London in 1850, noted the 'new, more colossal bourgeoisie' whose omnipotence was consolidated by 'the Reform Bill put[ting] direct political power into its hands'.[5] But Marx and Engels then transcended the historical specificities of the particular linguistic contexts that had set the scene for their evolving vocabulary, and moulded it into a universal theory of history with a distinctive 'middle-class' (or 'bourgeois') stage between aristocratic feudalism and working-class socialism. There are 'great social and economical laws', Marx wrote, 'which must eventually insure' that 'the same industrial wave which has borne the middle class up against the aristocracy' will likewise be 'bearing the working classes up against the middle classes'.[6] And then of course there were the famous generalizations of the *Communist Manifesto*. Even within Britain itself, however, as Perry Anderson has observed, the attempt to give the 'middle-class' narrative the status of historical truth, indeed of a universally valid historical law, sat uneasily with Marx and Engels's discerning observations about the very different realities of social power around them. Thus Engels in 1844 also pointed to the immense power of the aristocracy; and Marx, a decade later, concluded sneeringly that English feudalism 'will not perish beneath the scarcely perceptible dissolving processes of the middle class'.[7]

[5] F. Engels, 'The Condition of England II: The English Constitution', in K. Marx and F. Engels, *Collected Works*, London, 1975, vol. III, pp. 497–8. Steven Marcus has noted in Engels's writing on Manchester in 1844 a 'tendency to mythologize the middle classes as a whole': S. Marcus, *Engels, Manchester, and the Working Class*, New York, 1985, p. 232. K. Marx's review of Guizot, written February 1850; cited in P. Anderson, *English Questions*, London, 1992, pp. 122–3. Three years later Marx criticized William Cobbett for having failed to understand 'the causes; the new social agencies' behind what Cobbett had perceived as the decline of the English people, namely – explained Marx – the 'ascendancy of the middle class'; Cobbett simply 'did not see the modern bourgeoisie'. (Letter to *New York Daily Tribune*, 22 July 1853; in *Collected Works*, London, 1979, vol. XII, p. 189.) And compare also Marx's understanding of the Reform Bill as quoted in p. 331 n. 9.
[6] K. Marx, 'The English Middle Class', *New York Daily Tribune*, 1 August 1854; in *Collected Works*, London, 1980, vol. XIII, p. 665. On the insensitivity of the Marxist theoretization to the particular historical contexts in which its language had evolved see Stedman Jones, 'The Rise and Fall of "Class Struggle"'.
[7] Marx, 'The English Middle Class'. See Anderson, *English Questions*, pp. 123–5. The distance between Engels's 1844 observations in England (seen as a special historical

In retrospect, it is more than a trifle ironic that the historical analysis of Marx and Engels, at the same time that it announced the imminent termination of the rule of the 'middle class', by virtue of this very announcement helped to perpetuate the 'middle-class' storyline. Indeed, the 'middle-class'-centred interpretation of history has been one point of remarkable congruence between Marxist/socialist and liberal histories.[8] Both historiographical traditions attach crucial importance to social processes of industrialization and/or modernization; both present the formation of a 'middle class' as a key component of this social process; both ascribe much importance to the agency of the typical (or stereotypical) individualist 'bourgeois' entrepreneur; both read politics as the outcome of social change; both therefore wish to identify the signs of 'middle-class' rule (be it an unfortunate yet necessary intermediate stage to a better world, or the epitome of social progress and liberal democracy); and thus, ultimately, both of these powerful traditions – which together encompass the lion's share of English history writing – have continually reinforced the stronghold of the 'middle-class' narrative over modern history.

Marx and Engels notwithstanding, 'middle-class'-based historical accounts do not seem to have been common in mid Victorian England, but to have arrived later. 'The great middle-class', declared the novelist and historian Walter Besant in a book of retrospect at Queen Victoria's Jubilee, 'supposed, before the advent of Mr Matthew Arnold, to possess all the virtues; to be the backbone, stay, and prop of the country – must have a chapter to itself.' And indeed it did: commencing in the 1880s and peaking in the first two decades of the twentieth century, the revival of such historical accounts was in tune with a more

case) and his later theoretizations with Marx (in which England was considered as a model test case), a distance that entailed a specific reevaluation of the German 'middle class' to fit this general theory, is pointed out in G. Stedman Jones, 'Engels and the History of Marxism', in *The History of Marxism, Volume One: Marxism in Marx's Day*, ed. E. J. Hobsbawm, Bloomington, 1982, esp. pp. 315–16.

[8] Take as another example Marx and Cobden: although Marx saw Cobden as a typical member of the exploitative and selfish 'middle class', when he identified both the Reform Bill of 1832 and the repeal of the corn laws in 1846 as 'movements of the Bourgeoisie', his interpretation was hardly distinguishable from that which Cobden himself had asserted so proudly. (K. Marx, 'The Elections in England: Tories and Whigs', *New York Daily Tribune*, 21 August 1852; in *Collected Works*, vol. XI, p. 330. For Marx on Cobden, see for example his 'The English Middle Class', p. 663.)

general wave of interest in economic history, especially in the 'industrial revolution' and its social consequences.[9] This was also a period of an evident decline of land, to which the rise of a 'middle class' was a plausible corollary. The change is revealed for instance in the different editions of John Richard Green's highly Whiggish and immensely popular *Short History of the English People*. Green's account of the nineteenth century in the first edition of 1874 did not include the 'middle class' at all; and it remained to his wife, the radical historian Alice Green, in her revised edition of 1916, to include 'the industrial revolution' which 'created a society unknown before – a middle class of prodigious wealth and activity, and a vast working class on the borders of starvation'.[10]

Alice Green's indictment was central to an important group of writers during these years, the Fabian socialist historians. In order to explain the condition of the losers of the 'industrial revolution' – in their view, the majority of the people – they needed also its winners, the 'middle class'; and in order to have a proper working-class labour party, they needed to assert the previous existence of a 'middle-class' liberal party. The rudiments were laid in Sidney Webb's essay on the historical basis of socialism that opened the important collection of *Fabian Essays in Socialism* published in 1889. Webb described how 'the rise of towns by the growth of trade gradually created new centers of independence and new classes', processes which eventually bore their political fruit in 'the great Reform Bill of 1832, by which the reign of the middle class superseded aristocratic rule', but – crucially – left the people out; a straightforward story that remained basically unchanged all the way down to the writing of the Fabian historian G. D. H. Cole a generation later.[11] Such

[9] See D. Cannadine, 'The Present and the Past in the English Industrial Revolution 1880–1980', *Past and Present* 103 (1984), pp. 133–9. W. Besant, *Fifty Years Ago*, New York, 1888, chapter 6: 'With the Middle-Class', p. 85.

[10] J. R. Green, *A Short History of the English People*, London, 1874, epilogue; and new edition, 'revised and enlarged, with epilogue by Alice Stopford Green', London, 1916, p. 838. R. J. Morris, *Class, Sect and Party: The Making of the British Middle Class, Leeds 1820–1850*, Manchester, 1990, p. 2, has quoted this passage, erroneously taking it to express the opinion of J. R. Green himself.

[11] S. Webb, 'The Basis of Socialism: Historic', in G. B. Shaw (ed.), *Fabian Essays on Socialism*, American edn, New York, 1891, pp. 12, 14. The Fabians saw their own mission as one of atonement for the 'middle class', emanating from what Beatrice Webb described as their 'consciousness of sin [which] was a collective or class consciousness'; in the words of Arnold Toynbee in 1883 which she quoted with approval,

socialist interpretations of history moreover coincided, as Perry Anderson has noted, with an unprecedented flourishing of Marxist interest in the notion of 'bourgeois revolution' during the golden age of classical Marxism before and during the first world war, particularly in the Russian revolutionary movement.[12]

The early decades of the twentieth century also witnessed the publication of some of the classics of liberal writing. The impulses behind the Edwardian 'New Liberalism', it may be noted, were not altogether alien to those driving the Fabian socialists; while among less progressive circles the rise of labour aroused yet again feelings of threat for the 'middle class'.[13] Take for example Albert Venn Dicey's *Lectures on the Relation between Law and Public Opinion* (lectured 1898, published 1905), a major retrospective statement of nineteenth-century liberalism, which represented the Reform Bill of 1832 – once again – as a measure whose 'aim was to diminish the power of the gentry, and to transfer predominant authority to the middle classes', an aim which in Dicey's view it had entirely achieved. Walter Lyon Blease's 1913 history of English liberalism included a chapter on the aftermath of 1832 titled, predictably enough, 'The Middle Class Supremacy'. And then of course there was the Whiggish George Macaulay Trevelyan, great-nephew of T. B. Macaulay, whose celebrations of

---

'We – the middle classes, I mean, not merely the very rich – we have neglected you; ... we have sinned against you grievously ... but if you will forgive us ... we will devote our lives to your service.' B. Webb, *My Apprenticeship*, ed. N. MacKenzie, Cambridge, 1979 (originally 1926), pp. 180–3. Compare also H. M. Hyndman, leader of the Social Democratic Federation, whose *Historical Basis of Socialism in England*, London, 1883, avowedly influenced by Marx, included a chapter titled 'The Rise of the Middle Class'. For G. D. H. Cole, see his *A Short History of the British Working Class Movement, 1789–1927*, London, 1952 (originally 1925, 1927), pp. 64, 143, 145, 150–1; and G. D. H. Cole and R. Postgate, *The British Common People 1746–1946*, New York, 1939 (originally 1938), pp. 226–7.

[12] See Anderson, *English Questions*, pp. 107–8; this notion was in fact not very common in Marx's own writings.

[13] See P. F. Clarke, *Lancashire and the New Liberalism*, Cambridge, 1971. The first decade of the twentieth century saw much resentment among a self-proclaimed 'middle class', and much concern over its alienation from the working class. Manifestations of these concerns included the right-wing Middle Class Defence Organisation, which claimed seventy committees by July 1906; and George Sims's articles in the nominally liberal *The Tribune*, titled 'The Bitter Cry of the Middle Classes' (July 1907), that provoked a flood of letters expressing the grievances of the 'middle class' (often, familiarly, regarding unfair taxation). See H. V. Emy, *Liberals Radicals and Social Politics 1892–1914*, Cambridge, 1973, pp. 171–3.

the 'middle class' vied with those of his forebear: for him, simply, the Reform Act 'peacefully hand[ed] over the power of the aristocracy to the middle class'.[14] Moreover, Tory historians, no less critical of the individualistic and selfish 'middle class' than the socialists, could also make use of this framework: as was the case for O. F. Christie, who nostalgically lamented the 'Revolution of 1832' by which 'the middle class enter[ed] into power'.[15]

Around the turn of the century, as interest in social (as distinct from political) history increased, and as social sciences shifted to empirical present-minded studies, the confidence in the category of 'middle class' continued to mount. The six-volume *Social England: A Record of the Progress of the People*, published in 1904, duly included a chapter with that clichéd title, 'The Rule of the Middle Class'; and in 1907 A. F. Pollard – in Jack Hexter's view, a representative of 'the best thought of fifty years ago' – proclaimed 'the advent of the middle classes' as one of two key developments in the rise of modernity over the ruins of the middle ages (the other being the emergence of the national state).[16] In 1917 R. H. Gretton published *The English Middle Class*, the first work to have taken the 'middle class' as its whole subject. Gretton attempted a 'scientific' approach to the history

[14] A. V. Dicey, *Lectures on the Relation between Law and Public Opinion in England during the Nineteenth Century*, rep. edn, New Brunswick, 1981, pp. 185–6. W. L. Blease, *A Short History of English Liberalism*, London, 1913, pp. 168ff.; and see p. 73, where the 'middle class' is presented as the consequence of 'the Industrial Revolution'. G. M. Trevelyan, *Lord Grey of the Reform Bill*, London, 1920, p. 245. One might add Elie Halévy, the French liberal historian, who also depicted 1832 as a class victory of 'the vast middle class electorate'; which left him with the puzzling enigma, why did this 'middle-class' electorate return a parliament of aristocrats and country gentlemen: E. Halévy, *A History of the English People in the Nineteenth Century III: The Triumph of Reform 1830–1841*, London, 1950 (1st French edn, 1923), pp. 62–4.

[15] O. F. Christie, *The Transition from Aristocracy 1832–1867*, London, 1928, table of contents. Christie too included a chapter titled 'The Middle Class'. See similarly G. C. Brodrick, *The Political History of England: The History of England from Addington's Administration to the Close of William IV.'s Reign 1801–1837*, completed and revised by J. K. Fotheringham, London, 1906, pp. 307–8.

[16] H. D. Traill and J. S. Mann (eds.), *Social England: A Record of the Progress of the People*, 1904; rep. edn., Westport, Conn., 1969, vol. VI, chapter 23. A. F. Pollard, *Factors in Modern History*, 3rd edn, London, 1932 (originally 1907), pp. 32–51 (quoted, pp. 42, 44); and compare idem, *The History of England: A Study in Political Evolution*, London, 1912, pp. 96, 178–80. J. H. Hexter, 'Factors in Modern History', in his *Reappraisals in History*, Chicago, 1961, p. 27. See also W. Cunningham, *The Growth of English Industry and Commerce in Modern Times*, Cambridge, 1892, p. 10.

of 'the rise of the middle class', again going back to the late middle ages, and peaking in the eighteenth century, when it had 'entirely coloured the national outlook'.[17] Concurrently, another indication of the increasing confidence in this matter-of-factual historical narrative was its deep permeation into textbooks, in even more schematized and less problematized formulations.[18]

The second generation of studies of the industrial revolution, as David Cannadine has shown, which peaked during the period of pessimism and anxiety about economic growth between the mid-1920s and the mid-1950s, stressed gradual and cyclical views of economic change. In such a historiographical climate, the 'middle class' was more often incorporated into much longer (and not necessarily as linear) narratives. For E. Lipson, a major pillar of gradualistic revisionism, the 'middle class' had been born in the towns of the middle ages, and had first displayed its economic power during its assault on the monarchy in the century before the civil war – though only 1832 secured its

---

[17] R. H. Gretton, *The English Middle Class*, London, 1917; quoted, p. 158. See also idem, *A Modern History of the English People*, 2nd edn, London, 1914, vol. I, pp. 17, 61. Compare the depictions of the Victorian 'middle-class supremacy' in E. Wingfield-Stratford, *The History of English Patriotism*, London, 1913, vol. II, pp. 265–99 ('The Middle Class Ascendancy'); idem, *The History of British Civilization*, London, 1928, pp. 243, 284, 930, and 968ff.: 'The Age of Middle Class Liberalism'. And see the discovery of H. R. G. Greaves (of the London School of Economics) that the key to the efficient working of the British constitution was the 'middle class', the victor of 1832, which 'provides a complete co-ordination between the political and the social structure'; in his *The English Constitution*, New York, 1941 (originally London, 1938), pp. 20, 121, 281–2, 292.

[18] Random early examples include: Rev. J. Franck Bright, [Master of University College, Oxford] *A History of England: Period III. Constitutional Monarchy: William and Mary to William IV. 1689–1837*, New York, 1885 (originally London, 1875–7), p. 1432 ('The aristocratic classes, which had hitherto had the monopoly of power, were forced [in 1832] to admit to an equality with themselves the middle class, which the progress of society, and the wonderful advance of material improvement during the last half century, had raised to a position so important that its claims could no longer be withstood'). C. A. Fyffe, *A History of Modern Europe 1792–1878*, popular edn, New York, 1895 (originally 1886), pp. 643–5. C. Ransome, *An Advanced History of England From the Earliest Times to the Present Day*, London, 1895, p. 944. W. H. S. Aubrey, *The Rise and Growth of the English Nation with Special Reference to Epochs and Crises: A History of and for the People*, New York, 1901 (originally London, 1895), vol. I, pp. 165, 267; vol. II, p. 33 (the index of this book actually has an entry 'middle class, rise of'). A. Hassall, *A Class Book of English History for the Use of Middle Forms of Schools . . .*, 6th edn, rev., London, 1912 (originally 1901), p. 535. F. W. Tickner, *A Social and Industrial History of England*, London, 1915, passim. And see the numerous examples in V. E. Chancellor, *History for Their Masters: Opinion in the English History Textbook 1800–1914*, New York, 1970, pp. 30–2.

supremacy. Frederic Milner's significantly titled *Economic Evolution in England* placed the power of the 'middle class' even earlier.[19] And in R. H. Tawney's long-term analysis of the religious foundations of capitalist society, the heyday of the rising 'middle class' was the sixteenth and seventeenth centuries, when it had been the natural locus of puritanism; a distinctiveness which in fact it lost thereafter, as it became integrated into a joined plutocracy with the landed classes. Unsurprisingly, these were also the decades that produced Louis Wright's renowned *Middle-Class Culture in Elizabethan England*.[20]

Thus we arrive at history writing after the Second World War. Powerful trends now joined in the further reinforcement of the 'middle-class' storyline: the confident and celebratory body of writing on the industrial revolution – W. W. Rostow's 'take-off' – which took its cue from the post-war economic boom; the influence of the French *Annalistes*, who saw politics and consciousness as derivative from socio-economic *conjunctures*; the sway of Marxist interpretations of the English civil war and the French Revolution as 'bourgeois revolutions', in the hands of such masters as Christopher Hill and Georges Lefebvre; and, from the 1960s, the emergence of a powerful school of labour historians for whom the 'middle class' was a necessary backcloth for the development of the working class. The influence of the latter, indeed, has been not only in reaffirming the 'middle-class' narrative, but also in impeding its more profound investigation, as an issue outside the circumference of their empathies and historical sensitivities. In E. P. Thompson's *The Making of the English Working Class*, for instance, the inimitably sensitive treatment of the working class is coupled with unprob-

---

[19] E. Lipson, *The Growth of English Society: A Short Economic History*, London, 1949, pp. 22, 174–6, 258–9, 318. These passages were mostly included in his earlier *The Economic History of England*, London, 1961 (originally 1931): see vol. I, pp. 177, 455; vol. II, pp. cxx–cxxv, cxxxvii, cxl. F. Milner, *Economic Evolution in England*, London, 1931, pp. 63, 75, 165, 291. Another influential account was Paul Mantoux's *The Industrial Revolution in the Eighteenth Century* (French edn, 1906, English translation, 1928); rep. edn, Chicago, 1983, esp. pp. 95, 134, 158, 373. And see Cannadine, 'The Present and the Past in the English Industrial Revolution', pp. 139–49.

[20] R. H. Tawney, *Religion and the Rise of Capitalism: A Historical Study (Holland Memorial Lectures, 1922)*, New York, 1926, pp. 87, 94, 111–12, 177, 207–8, 211, 266. See also idem, 'Harrington's Interpretation of His Age' (originally 1941), in J. M. Winter (ed.), *History and Society: Essays by R. H. Tawney*, London, 1978, pp. 73–4. L. B. Wright, *Middle-Class Culture in Elizabethan England*, Chapel Hill, 1935.

lematized implied assumptions about the 'middle class', summed up in the curt assertion that 'the years between the French Revolution and the Reform Bill had seen the formation of a middle-class "class consciousness"'. Or take Dorothy Thompson's meticulous study of Chartism, which at the same time proclaims summarily that 'the middle classes had been an articulate presence in British political life since the seventeenth century'.[21] So the more detailed analysis of the 'middle class' was left to Whiggish social historians such as Asa Briggs and Harold Perkin, whose very premises insured that the foundations of the 'middle-class' narrative were never taken to task.[22]

By and large, therefore, in spite of occasional sceptics,[23] and in spite of mounting difficulties (amplified, as we have seen, by the recent reversion of the economic-historical pendulum to long-term gradualism in the understanding of industrialization and social change), the 'middle-class' paradigm as it evolved

[21] E. P. Thompson, *The Making of the English Working Class*, London, 1963, p. 820. See similarly his 'Eighteenth-Century English Society: Class Struggle without Class?', *Social History* 3 (1978), p. 143, for the unquestioned emergence of the 'middle class' as a *deus ex-machina* (literally) in the 1780s. Thompson has commented on this issue in his *Customs in Common*, London, 1991, pp. 87–90. D. Thompson, *The Chartists: Popular Politics in the Industrial Revolution*, New York, 1984, p. 252. It may be noted, moreover, that Dorothy Thompson's statement is not easily reconcilable with that of Edward Thompson's. Compare also the unproblematic identification and portraiture of the 'middle class' in E. Hobsbawm, *Industry and Empire: An Economic History of Britain since 1750*, London, 1968, pp. 3, 65; idem, *The Age of Capital 1848–1875*, New York, 1975, chapter 13. And in G. Stedman Jones's *Languages of Class*, Cambridge, 1983, revealingly, the index has no entry for 'middle class', but only for 'radical conception of the middle classes'.

[22] See A. Briggs's declaration in his *Age of Improvement 1783–1867* (New York, 1959, p. 3) that the first seventy years of the nineteenth century 'had been dominated by the rise of the middle classes. The middle classes had been the carriers not only of Free Trade but of the very idea of improvement itself.' Also idem, 'Middle-Class Consciousness in English Politics, 1780–1846'. H. Perkin, *The Origins of Modern English Society 1780–1880*, London, 1969.

[23] The power of the 'bourgeois paradigm', that associates historical change with 'a triumphant bourgeoisie, the bearer of knowledge, innovation and progress', in 'determin[ing] the framework of nearly all historical debates', has been critically noted in E. M. Wood, *The Pristine Culture of Capitalism: A Historical Essay on Old Regimes and Modern States*, London, 1991 (quoted, pp. 2–3). And compare G. Kitson Clark's bemused complaint in 1951, that 'to-day ... the strange desire of modern historians [is] to describe everything in mid-nineteenth century England as betokening the "triumph of the middle class"' ('The Repeal of the Corn Laws', p. 3). And see the reservations in his *The Making of Victorian England*, Bristol, 1985 (originally 1962), pp. 118–19; but note p. 123, where the 'middle-class' storyline seems to have scored yet another victory. For another expression of uneasiness, which stresses the attractiveness of this category to different post-factum commentators, see I. Wallerstein, 'The Bourgeois(ie) as Concept and Reality', *New Left Review* 167 (1988), pp. 91–106.

from the early nineteenth century has maintained its unquestioned sway over the writing of British history; which brings us back a full cycle to the historiographical impasse that had provoked this study to begin with.

Index